AA

The Complete

ATLAS OF BRITAIN

1991

13th edition September 1990
12th edition October 1989
11th edition October 1988
10th edition October 1987
9th edition October 1986
Reprinted March 1987
8th edition October 1985
7th edition October 1984
Reprinted May 1985
6th edition March 1984
5th edition January 1983
4th edition October 1981
3rd edition January 1981
2nd edition January 1980
1st edition April 1979

Published by The Automobile Association, Fanum House, Basingstoke,
Hampshire RG21 2EA. ISBN 07495 00409

Printed by Graficromo S A, Spain

The contents of this book are believed correct at the time of printing.
Nevertheless, the publisher can accept no responsibility for errors or
omissions, or for changes in the details given.

Mapping produced by the Cartographic Department of The Automobile
Association. This atlas has been compiled and produced from the Automaps
database utilising electronic and computer technology.

Information on National Parks provided by the Countryside Commission for
England & Wales.

Information on National Scenic Areas – Scotland provided by the Countryside
Commission
for Scotland.

Information on Forest Parks provided by the Forestry Commission.

Blue Flag beaches are those designated by the European Blue Flag Campaign
and sponsored by the Commission of the European Communities. The ones
indicated in this atlas are the beaches which, in 1989, met certain
environmental criteria.

The RSPB sites shown are a selection chosen by the Royal Society for the
Protection of Birds.

Picnic sites are those inspected by the AA and are located on or near
A and B roads.

Every effort has been made to ensure that the contents of our new database
are correct. However, if there are any errors or omissions, please write to the
Cartographic Editor, Publishing Division, The Automobile Association, Fanum
House, Basingstoke, Hampshire RG21 2EA.

A CIP catalogue record for this book is available from the British Library.

Contents

Using this atlas

Whether you wish to trace the route of the M4 from London to South Wales, find the most direct route from Ipswich to Liverpool, pick your way round Coventry, or need to solve any other journey planning problem the Complete Atlas of Britain is an essential guide.

ROUTE PLANNING
Specially designed route planning maps, showing a basic road network of motorways, primary routes and most A roads, help you plan long distance journeys quickly and easily.

ATLAS
Clear, easy-to-read mapping helps you to plan more detailed journeys, and provides a wealth of information for the motorist. All motorways, primary, A and B roads and unclassified roads are shown. The atlas also identifies those roads outside urban areas which are under construction. Additional features include rivers, lakes and reservoirs, railway lines, interesting places to visit, picnic sites and Tourist Information Centres, and to assist you in estimating journey length, distances are shown in miles between blue marker symbols.

Motorway   A road   Primary routes

Motorways and junctions   Primary route   Railway   Reservoir or large water feature   Named place of interest   Road under construction   Urban area   Other A road   Village or hamlet

Tourist Information Centre   B road   Mileage   River   Unclassified road

FERRY AND RAIL ROUTES
Coastal stretches of mapping provide basic off-shore information including ferry routes within Great Britain and to the Continent, to assist you in planning journeys overseas. Throughout the atlas, railway lines with stations and level crossings are shown, to assist with general navigation or rail travel requirements.

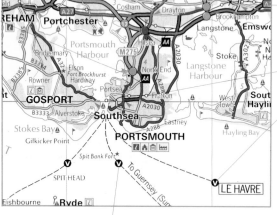

AA Port Shop   Level crossing   Railway station   Continental ferry routes   Local ferry route

TOURISM AND LEISURE
Red pictorial symbols and red type, highlight numerous places of interest, catering for every taste. Red symbols within yellow boxes show tourist attractions in towns. Use them to plan days out or places to visit on holiday. Remember to check opening times before you visit to avoid disappointment.

Tourist attraction within urban area   National trails marked   Place of interest located and named

AA viewpoint   Tourist Information Centre

MOTORWAYS
The principal motorway maps, arranged in easy-to-follow strip form, highlight junctions, exit signs, service areas, and access on and off the motorway.

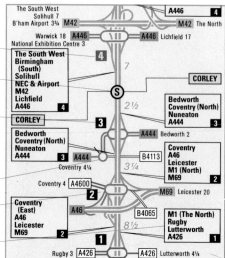

Restricted junction   Motorway service area   Numbered junction (unrestricted access)   Access roads on and off the motorway   Junction layout   Signposts as seen from the motorway

PORTS AND AIRPORTS

Maps show the major Channel and east coast ports, plus detailed maps of the main airports in Britain, giving approach roads as well as car parking facilities, and information about garages, hotels and public transport services. The map on page 119 locates *all* British ports and airports.

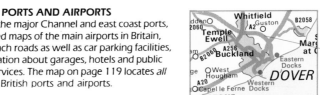

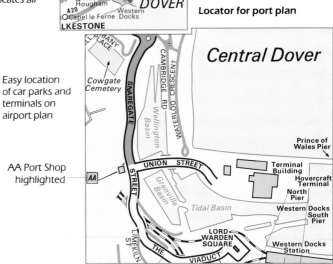

District map showing main road links

Road number for major approach roads

Locator for port plan

Central Dover

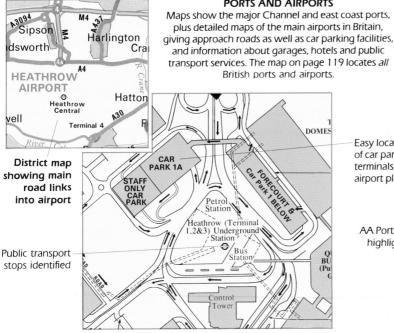

District map showing main road links into airport

Public transport stops identified

Easy location of car parks and terminals on airport plan

AA Port Shop highlighted

Local approach road named

Ship piers, ferry and hovercraft terminals and railway station clearly shown

TOWN PLANS

Up-to-date, fully-indexed town plans show AA recommended roads and other practical information such as one way streets, car parks and restricted roads, making navigation much easier. Area plans show major road networks into and out of the region.

Area map showing main road links and neighbouring towns

AA recommended throughroutes clearly identified

Town parking facilities

Locator for town plan

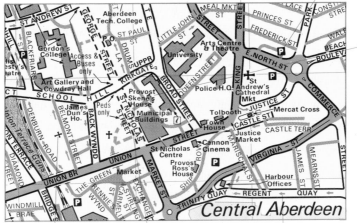

Central Aberdeen

Major buildings and places of interest highlighted and named

Street index with every plan

Aberdeen

Abbotsford Lane	C2-D2
Academy Street	C4-D4
Advocates Road	E8
Affleck Street	D3
Albert Quay	E3-F3
Albert Place	A5-A6
Albert Street	A4-A5
Albert Terrace	A4-A5
Albury Place	B2-C2
Albury Road	B2-C2-C3
Albyn Grove	A4

Churches located

Pedestrian areas located

One way streets shown

LONDON

Easy-to-read, fully-indexed street maps of Inner London, provide a simple guide to finding your way around the city.

One way systems clearly shown

Underground railway stations located and named

Major places of tourist interest shown

Open spaces and parks highlighted

Garage parking identified

AA recommended routes for easier navigation

Alphabetical street index

Tudor St EC4	184..	M
Tufton St SW1	188..	H
Turk's Row SW3	187..	K
Turnmill St EC1	184..	F
Turpentine Ln SW1	187..	L
Turquand St SE17	200..	G
Tyers St SE11	188..	M
Tyer's Ter SE11	188..	M
Tysoe St EC1	184..	B
Udall St SW1	188..	G
Ufford St SE1	189..	E
Ulster Pl NW1	182..	F
Union St SE1	189..	B

Signs and symbols

To assist you in journey planning and making the most of the comprehensive information contained in this atlas, it helps if you understand the signs on the roads and the symbols used on the maps. The principal benefit of the Department of Transport road signs is that the primary road signs (green) indicate the most *straightforward* route between one town and another. They do not necessarily indicate the most *direct* route, but it should be remembered that direct routes may not be the quickest, or the easiest to follow.

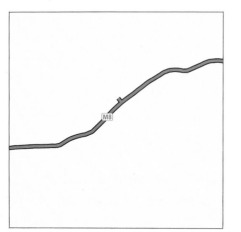

MOTORWAYS

On the map – all motorways are blue. Motorway signposts have white lettering on a blue background. Advance direction signs approaching an interchange generally include the junction number in a black box. On the map, the junction number appears in white on a solid *blue* circle.

A white number on a solid *red* circle indicates restricted access on or off the motorway at that point.

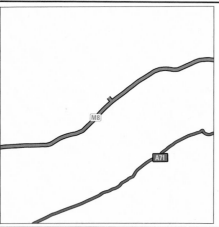

PRIMARY ROUTES

On the map – all the primary routes are green. The signposts on primary roads are also green, with white lettering and yellow numbers. Apart from the motorways, primary routes are the most important traffic routes in both urban and rural areas. They form a network of throughroutes connecting 'primary towns', which are generally places of traffic importance. Primary routes are usually along A roads.

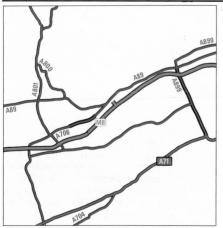

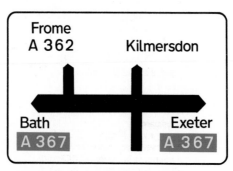

A ROADS

On the map – all A roads are shown in red, unless part of the primary network when they are green. The signposts along these roads have black lettering on a white background. At a junction with a primary route, the primary road number appears yellow in a green box.

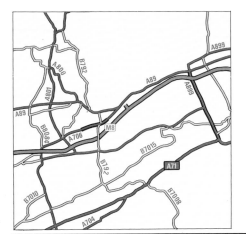

B ROADS

On the map – all B roads not in the primary network are represented in yellow. The signs on B roads are black lettering on a white background, the same as for A roads.

UNCLASSIFIED ROADS

On the map – all unclassified (unnumbered) roads are white. New signposts along unclassified roads are usually of the 'local direction' type. These have black lettering on a white background with a blue border. Many minor roads still have pre-World War II 'finger' post signs.

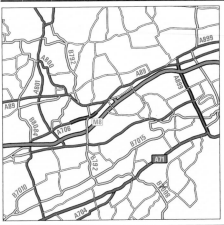

PLACE NAMES

Throughout the atlas, the size of lettering and its style is an indication of the size and importance of a place or location. This is generally related to population. All places with over 3,000 inhabitants are shown, plus there is a selection of smaller locations which are useful navigation points or possible destinations in some of the more isolated rural areas.

The section of map below highlights the various population categories and explains the difference in the size and style of lettering. The name London is a special category as it has a population in excess of 8 million.

Stourbridge
Places with this style and size of lettering include major towns and cities with populations between 50,000 and 200,000.

Birmingham
Places using this style and size of lettering indicate cities and very large towns with populations between 200,000 and 500,000.

King's Norton
This style and size of lettering is used to show suburban locations within large urban areas. Their population size is included within the 200,000 and 500,000 category.

Chaddesley Corbett
This style and size of lettering is used to show villages and hamlets with less than 3,000 inhabitants. In isolated rural areas in the north a selection of crossroads and farms are shown in slightly smaller lettering—Auchnotteroch

Bromsgrove
Metropolitan Districts, larger market and developing towns with populations between 10,000 and 50,000 are indicated by this size and style of lettering.

Alvechurch
Locations shown in this style and size of lettering are generally small market towns or developing communities situated on the fringes of large urban areas. Their populations vary between 3,000 and 10,000 inhabitants.

Journey planning

Whether you are planning a journey for business or for pleasure, the Complete Atlas will make it much easier. A little preparation can save valuable time.

Alertness
If you are planning a long journey, or just going out for the day, it is essential you set out feeling alert and confident. Tired, frustrated drivers are a potential danger to themselves, to their passengers and to other road users. You will feel more capable of dealing with unexpected situations, and have a more comfortable journey if you plan ahead.

CHECK LIST
On long journeys, in particular, it pays to make a check list of thing to do, even down to cancelling the milk and papers, taking the dog to the kennels, making sandwiches and a thermos, checking the roof rack and locking the door. We all forget something at some time or other! Have you never set off without having to stop just a few miles from home to wonder if you had remembered to turn the gas off?

PREPARATION
How to get there
The special route planning maps will help you to plan a basic route, and the atlas will enable you to make a more detailed one. (Taking a note of road numbers, towns and directions is useful, as this reduces the need to consult the atlas on the way.)

Distance and time
One of the fundamental considerations to be taken into account when planning any journey is how far it is. The mileage chart on the inside back cover will help you estimate the distance and this in turn can help you calculate your journey time. On the atlas, distances between places are indicated as blue numbers between blue arrowheads eg. ◀ 12 ▶ Do not forget to allow extra time for peak hours and holiday weekends.

Motorways
Despite ever-increasing traffic, motorways are still the quickest and most efficient means of travelling across the country. The map on page 108 gives an overall picture of the system, while pages 109 to 118 show the principal motorways.

A Roads
London is the hub for the spokes of roads numbered A1 to A6, and Edinburgh is the hub for the A7, A8 and A9.

Starting with the A1 running north from London, the roads radiate clockwise: the A2 runs generally east, the A3 south-west etc. This system has made the numbering of other roads very simple. Generally, the lower the subsequent number, the closer the road's starting point to London – similarly to Edinburgh.

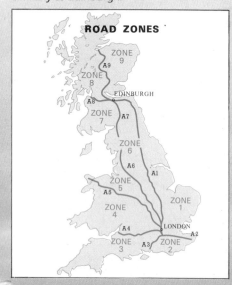

DELAYS AND HOLD-UPS
Radio
Frequent radio bulletins are issued by the BBC and Independent Local radio stations on road conditions, possible hold-ups etc, and these can be of great assistance. By tuning in to the local stations as you pass through the area, you can avoid delays, and prepare yourself to make changes to your route. However, local radio does not yet cover the entire country. For radio frequencies consult the map on the inside back cover.

AA Roadwatch
However, if you require this information *before* setting out, you can call AA Roadwatch. This service provides information (updated every 15 minutes) on major roadworks and weather conditions for the whole country, and can be used as part of your basic journey planning. (See inside front cover.)

Getting the most out of the maps
The mapping contains a wide range of practical information for the motorist. Not only does it show the existing road network, but it also shows new roads which are due to be opened shortly or within approximately the next 12 months. It even indicates where A and B roads are very narrow in the Scottish Highlands. Passing bays are usually provided on these roads at regular intervals.

In addition you can use the atlas to plan trips and days out. Look for the special red tourist symbols and red names. The attractions highlighted in this way range from the cultural and historic – abbeys, museums, stately homes, to the sporting – cricket, golf, gliding, horseracing, and include Tourist Information Centres and AA viewpoints.

You can find any place listed in the index by using the National Grid, which is explained in simple terms below.

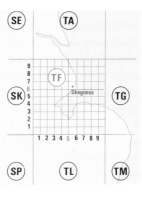

FINDING YOUR PLACE
One of the unique features of AA mapping is the use of the National Grid system.

It covers Britain with an imaginary network of squares, using blue horizontal lines called northings and vertical lines called eastings.

On the atlas pages these lines are numbered along the bottom and up the left hand side.

Each entry in the index is followed by a page number, two letters denoting an area on the map and a 4-figure grid reference. You will not need to use the two letters for simple navigation, but they come in useful if you want to use your map in relation to the rest of the country and other map series.

For quick reference, the 4 figures of the grid reference in the index are arranged so that the 1st and 3rd are larger in size than the 2nd and 4th.

The 1st figure shows which number along the bottom to locate, and the 3rd figure, which number up the left hand side. These will indicate the square in which you will find the place name. However, to pinpoint a place more accurately, you use the 2nd and 4th numbers also. The 2nd will tell you how many imaginary tenths along the bottom line to go from the 1st number, and the 4th will tell you how many tenths up the line to go from the 3rd number.

Where these two lines intersect, you will locate your place. Eg Skegness 51 TF **56**63. Skegness is located on page 51, within grid square TF. Its exact location is **56**63.

If you find you get the numbers confused, it might help if you can imagine entering a house, walking in the door and along a corridor first, and then going up the stairs, then you will remember how to get them in the correct order.

Phone before you go

Ring our famous ROADWATCH service for the latest reports on traffic hold-ups and roadworks, and our WEATHERWATCH service for the latest weather reports.

DIAL 0836-401

plus the 3 digits for the appropriate area (see maps below).

NATIONAL TRAFFIC, ROADWORKS AND WEATHER

Wherever you're driving call the AA's ROADWATCH service for the latest traffic reports.

For a report on the National Motorway Network dial **0836-401 110**

ROADWATCH

LONDON AND SOUTH-EAST TRAFFIC, ROADWORKS AND WEATHER

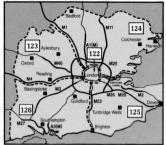

If you're driving in the London and South-eastern areas phone before you go - and save yourself time and frustration.

For a report on the M25 ORBITAL dial **0836-401 127**

For London Special Events (certain weekends only) dial **0836-401 128**

NATIONAL WEATHER FORECASTS

Call the AA's WEATHERWATCH service for the latest weather report followed by a 2-day forecast.

For the National Weather Forecast dial **0836-401 130**

WEATHERWATCH

AA WEATHERWATCH forecasts are compiled by The Weather Department Ltd. Calls are charged at 25p per minute cheap rate, 38p per minute at all other times.

The Complete Atlas of Britain combines superb mapping with accurate and practical route-finding information which are designed to help you complete a journey as quickly and easily as possible.

Planning your route
The route planning maps on the following pages are an invaluable guide when deciding on a *general route*.

These maps show the principal routes throughout the country and you can use them to plan a *basic route*.

Look for the name of your destination in the index section at the back of the book. The entry is followed by an atlas page number and a National Grid reference.

Turn to the atlas page indicated and use the grid reference to pinpoint the place (see page 9 for an explanation of how to use the reference).

When you have located it, find the nearest place to it shown on the route-planner maps.

In the same way, by locating the nearest place to your start point, you can plot the route between the two.

A more detailed route can be worked out from studying the main atlas.

Remember to take a note of road numbers and directions, then you will not need to stop to use the atlas while on the journey.

Frequent bulletins are issued both by national and local radio stations and AA Roadwatch on road conditions, local hold-ups, weather etc. You will find these regional radio frequencies on the relevant pages of the routeplanning maps, and AA Roadwatch numbers on this page. The radio stations are in **bold type** and are followed by the FM frequency (MH_z), then the MW frequency (KH_z), eg **RADIO SCOTLAND** 92.5-94.7 810.
In some cases, there is only one frequency.

BBC
Radio Scotland
92.5-94.7 810 North West Scotland 97.7-99.3 810

IBA
Moray Firth Radio
Inverness 97.4 1107/271
Northsound Radio
Aberdeen 96.9 1035/290
Radio Clyde
Glasgow 102.5 1152
Radio Forth
Edinburgh 97.3 1548
Radio Tay
Dundee 102.8 1161 Perth 96.4 1548

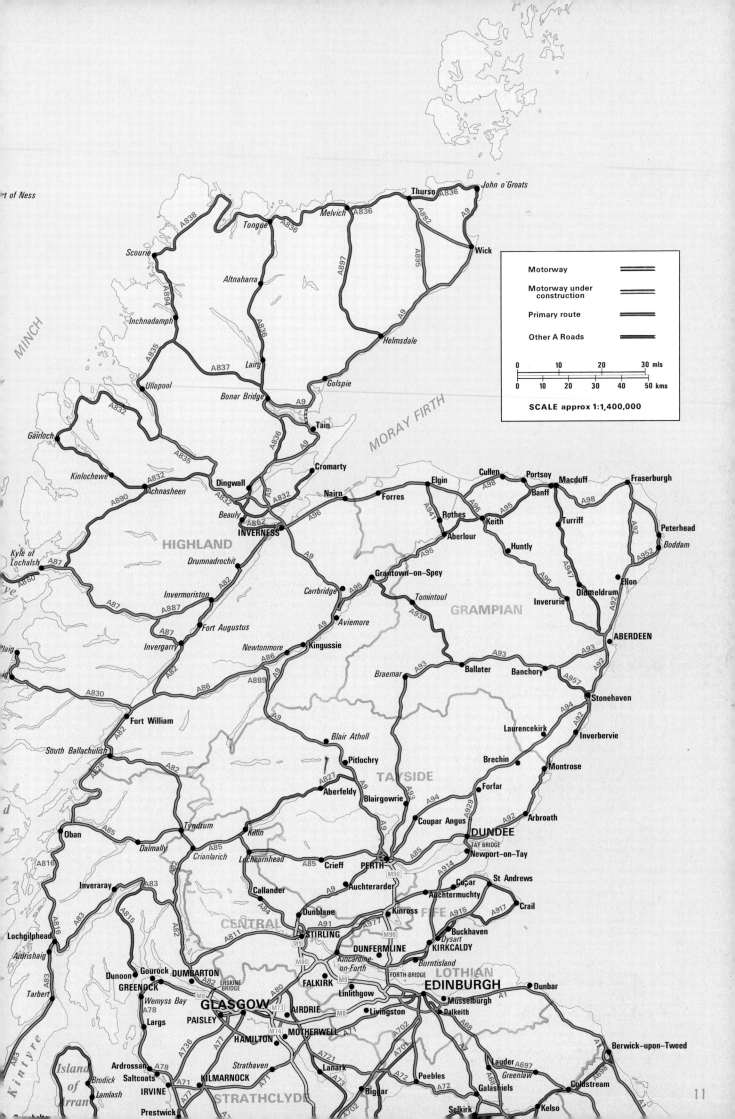

SCALE approx 1:1,400,000

11

BBC
Greater Manchester Radio
95.1 1458
Radio Cleveland
95.0 1548
Radio Cumbria
North Cumbria 95.6 756
Whitehaven 95.6 1458
Radio Cumbria (Furness)
South Cumbria 96.1 837
Kendal 95.2 837
Windermere 104.2 837
Radio Derby
104.5 1116 Derby 94.2 1116
Bakewell & Matlock 95.3
Buxton 96
Radio Humberside
95.9 1485
Radio Lancashire
95.5 855 Lancaster 104.5 1557
South Lancashire 103.9 855
Radio Leeds
92.4 774 Leeds 103.9 Ilkley/
Otley 95.3 774
Radio Lincolnshire
94.9 1368
Radio Merseyside
95.8 1485
Radio Newcastle
N.E. Northumberland 96.0
1458 Newcastle & Durham
104.4 1458
Radio Nottingham
103.8 1521 Central Notts. 95.5
1584
Radio Sheffield
104.1 1035 Sheffield 88.6 1035
Radio Shropshire
96.0 1584 Ludlow 95.0
1584
Radio Stoke
94.6 1503
Radio Wales
882 Radio Cymru
(Welsh Language Service)
92.5–94.5
Radio York
103.7 666 Scarborough 95.5
1260 Central N. Yorks 104.3
666

IBA
Bradford City Radio
103.2
KFM
Stockport 104.9
Marcher Sound
Wrexham & Deeside 103.4
1260
Metro Radio
Tyne & Wear 97.1 1152
Newcastle 103 1152
Pennine Radio
Bradford 97.5 1278
Huddersfield/Halifax 102.5
1530
Piccadilly Radio
103 1152
Radio Aire
Leeds 96.3 828
Radio Borders
Berwick 97.5 Eyemouth 103.4
Peebles 96.8 Selkirk 96.8
Radio City
Liverpool 96.7 1548
Radio Hallam
Sheffield 97.4 1548 Rotherham
96.1 1548 Doncaster 103.4
990 Barnsley 102.9 1305
Radio Trent
Nottingham 96.2 999
Derby 102.8 945
Red Rose Radio
Blackpool & Preston 97.4 999
Signal Radio
Stoke-on-Trent 102.6 1170
N. Staffs 96.4 1170
Stafford 96.9 1170
Sunset Radio
Manchester 102.0
TFM Radio Teesside
96.6 1170
Viking Radio
Humberside 96.9 1161
West Sound
Ayr 96.7 1035 Girvan 97.5
1035

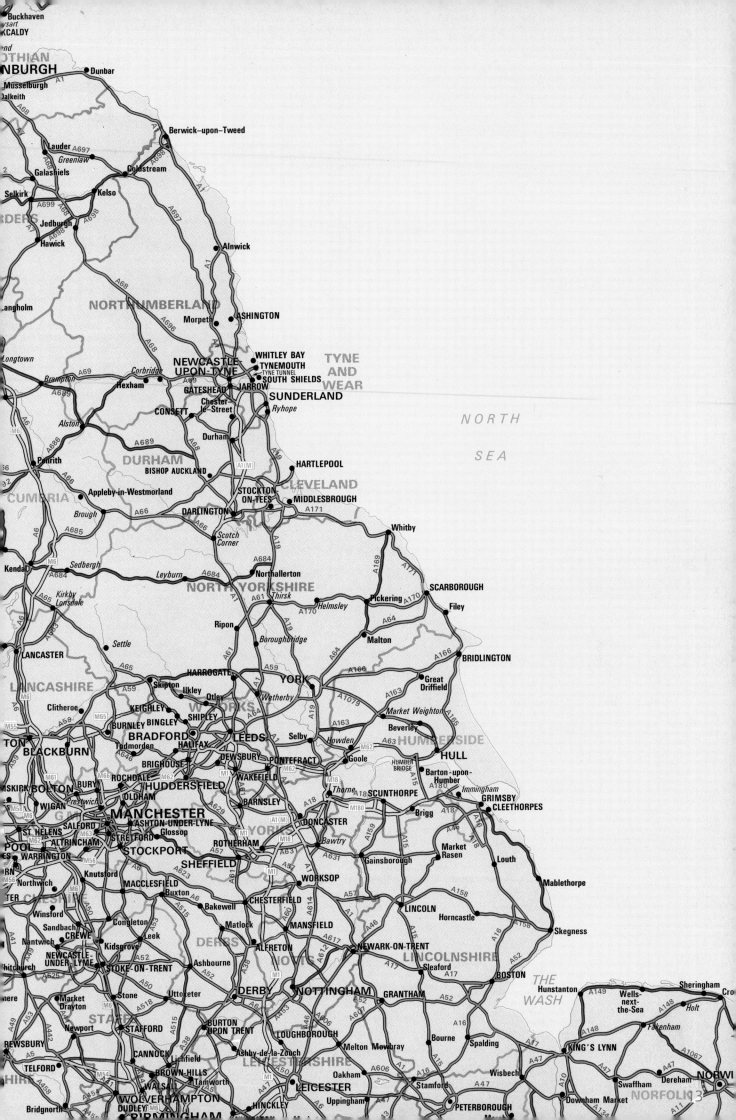

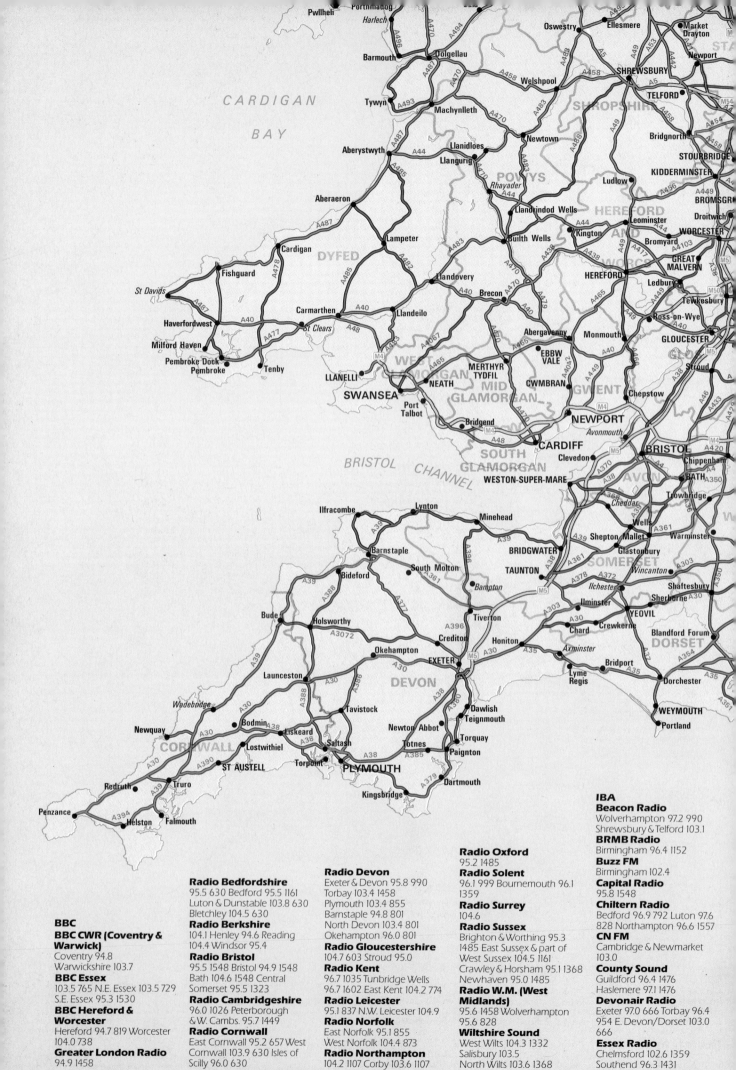

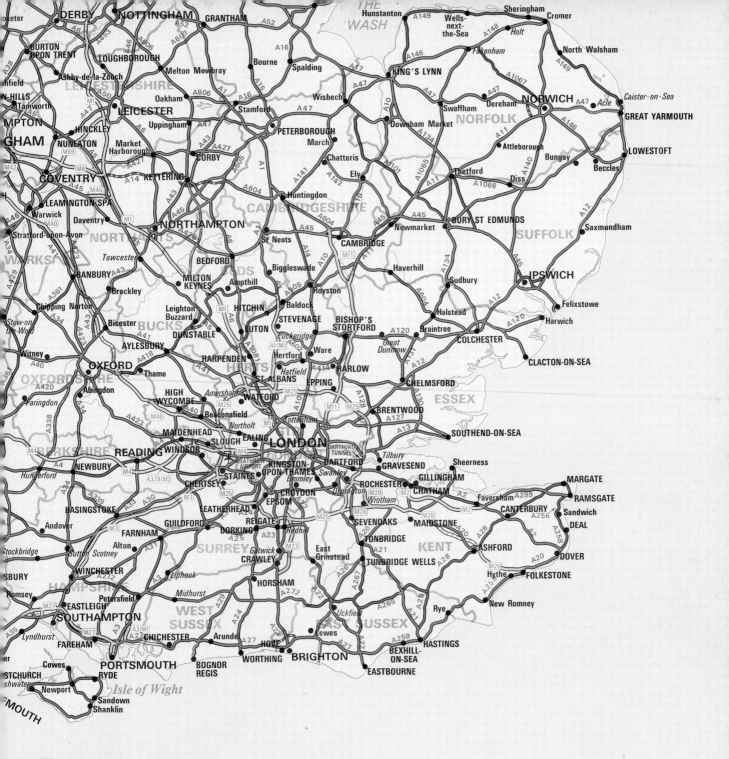

Fox FM
Oxford 102.6 Banbury 97.4

Greater London AIR (Airport Information)
Heathrow/Gatwick Airports 1584

GWR
Avon & N. Som. 96.3 1260
Bath 103.0 1260 Swindon 97.2
1161 W. Wilts 102.2 936
Marlborough 96.5

Hereward Radio
Peterborough 102.7 1332

Horizon Radio
Milton Keynes 103.3

Invicta Radio
Kent 103.1 1242 Canterbury
102.8 603 Thanet 95.9 603
Dover/Folkestone 97.0 603
Ashford 96.1 603

LBC
97.3 1152

Leicester Sound
Leicester 103.2 1260

London Jazz Radio
102.2

Mercia Sound
Coventry 97.0 1359
Leamington Spa 102.9 1359

Ocean Sound
Southampton, S.W. Hants &
I.O.W. 103.2 1557 Winchester
96.7 Portsmouth, S.E. Hants &
Chichester 97.5 1170

Orchard FM
Yeovil/Taunton 102.6

Plymouth Sound
Plymouth 97.0 1152. Tavistock
96.6 1152

Radio 210
Thames Valley 97.0 1431
Basingstoke, Andover 102.9
1431

Radio Broadland
Gt. Yarmouth & Norwich 102.4
1152

Radio Harmony
Coventry 102.6

Radio Mercury
Crawley/Reigate 102.7 1521
Horsham 97.5 1521

Radio Orwell
Ipswich 97.1 1170

Radio Wyvern
Hereford 97.6 954
Worcester 102.8 1530

Red Dragon Radio
Cardiff 103.2 1359
Newport 97.4 1305

Saxon Radio
Bury St. Edmunds 96.4 1251

Severn Sound
Cheltenham and Gloucester
102.4 774. Stroud 103.0 774

Southern Sound
Brighton 103.5 1323
Eastbourne 102.4 1323
Hastings 97.5 1323
Newhaven 96.9 1323

Swansea Sound
96.4 1170

2CR (Two Counties Radio)
Bournemouth 97.2 828.

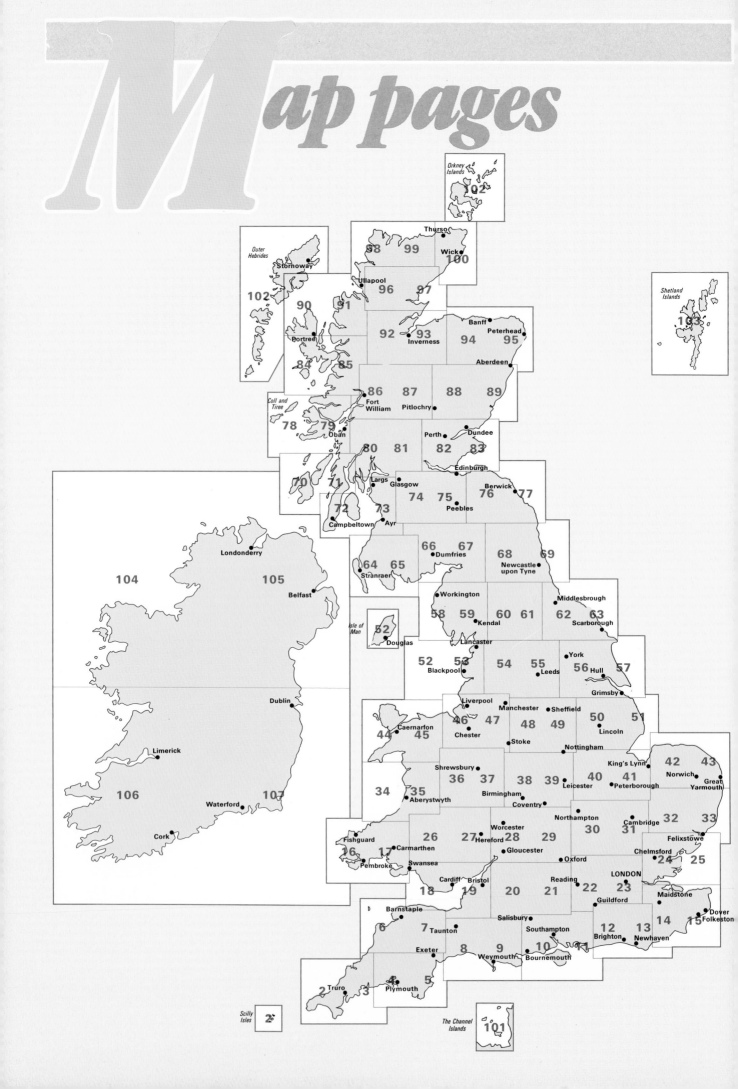

Map symbols

MOTORING INFORMATION		TOURIST INFORMATION	
Motorway with number	Vehicle ferry – Great Britain	Tourist Information Centre	Hill fort
Motorway junction with and without number	Vehicle ferry – Continental	Tourist Information Centre (summer only)	Roman antiquity
Motorway junction with limited access	Hovercraft ferry	Abbey, cathedral or priory	Prehistoric monument
Motorway service area	Airport	Ruined abbey, cathedral or priory	Battle site with year
Motorway and junction under construction	Heliport	Castle	Preserved railway/ steam centre
Primary route single/dual carriageway	Railway line/in tunnel	Historic house	Cave
Primary route service area	Railway station and level crossing	Museum or art gallery	Windmill
Other A road single/dual carriageway	AA Shop – full services	Industrial interest	Golf course
B road single/dual carriageway	AA Roadside Shop – limited services	Garden	County cricket ground
Unclassified road single/dual carriageway	AA Port Shop – open as season demands	Arboretum	Rugby Union national ground
Road under construction	AA telephone	Country park	International athletics stadium
Narrow primary, other A or B road with passing places (Scotland)	BT telephone in isolated places	Agricultural showground	Horse racing
Road tunnel	Urban area/village	Theme park	Show jumping/equestrian circuit
Steep gradient (arrows point downhill)	Spot height in metres	Zoo	Motor racing circuit
Road toll	River, canal, lake	Wildlife collection – mammals	Coastal launching site
Distance in miles between symbols	Sandy beach	Wildlife collection – birds	Ski slope – natural
	County boundary	Aquarium	Ski slope – artificial
	National boundary	Nature reserve	Other places of interest
	Page overlap and number	RSPB site	Boxed symbols indicate attractions within urban areas
		Nature trail	National Park (England & Wales)
		Forest drive	National Scenic Area (Scotland)
		National trail	Forest Park
		AA viewpoint	Heritage Coast
		Picnic site	Blue flag beach

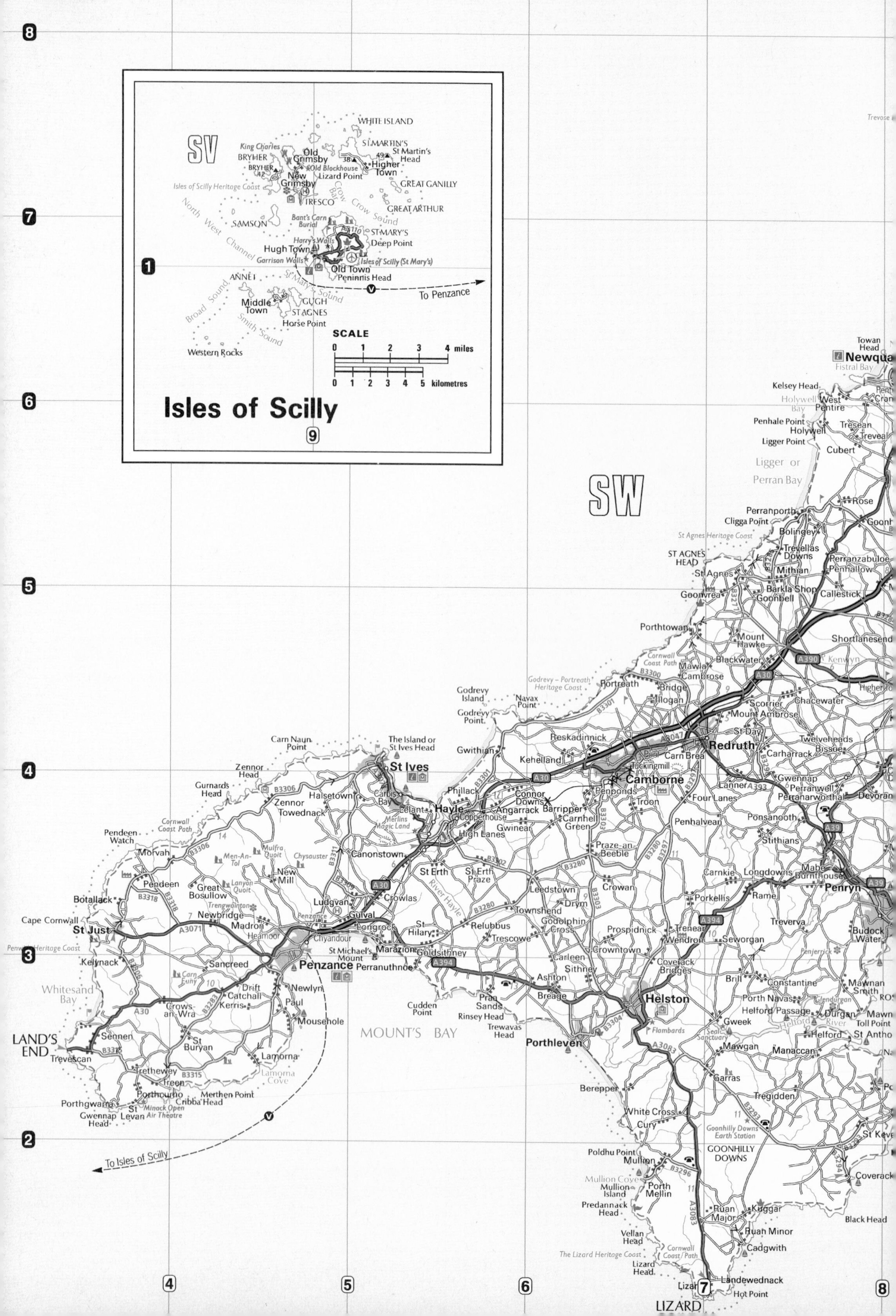

8

7

6

5

4

3

2

Isles of Scilly

SV

WHITE ISLAND

ST MARTIN'S
St Martin's Head
Higher Town
King Charles
BRYHER
Old Grimsby
Old Blockhouse
Lizard Point
New Grimsby
GREAT GANILLY
Isles of Scilly Heritage Coast
TRESCO
GREAT ARTHUR
North West Channel
SAMSON
Bant's Carn Burial
Crow Crow Sound
ST MARY'S
Deep Point
Harry's Walls
Hugh Town
Isles of Scilly (St Mary's)
Garrison Walls
Old Town
ANNET
Peninnis Head
St Mary's Sound
To Penzance
Broad Sound
Middle Town
GUGH
ST AGNES
Horse Point
Smith Sound
Western Rocks

SCALE

0   1   2   3   4 miles

0 1 2 3 4 5 kilometres

9

SW

Towan Head
Newquay
Fistral Bay
Kelsey Head
Holywell Bay
Penhale Point
West Pentire
Holywell
Ligger Point
Tresean
Treveal
Cubert
Ligger or Perran Bay
St Agnes Heritage Coast
Perranporth
Cligga Point
Rose
Goon
Bolingey
Trevellas Downs
Perranzabuloe
Penhallow
ST AGNES HEAD
St Agnes
Mithian
Barkla Shop
Callestick
Goonvrea
GoonBell
Porthtowan
Mount Hawke
Shortlanesend
Cornwall Coast Path
Mawla
Blackwater
A390
Kenwyn
Godrevy-Portreath Heritage Coast
Portreath
Bridge
Cambrose
Illogan
Scorrier
Chacewater
Higher
Godrevy Island
Navax Point
Carn Brea
Mount Ambrose
St Day
Redruth
Twelveheads
Godrevy Point
Reskadinnick
Tuckingmill
Carharrack
Bissoe
Gwithian
Kehelland
Camborne
Gwennap
Perranwell
Devoran
Phillack
Connor Downs
Lanner
Perranarworthal
Carn Naun Point
The Island or St Ives Head
Hayle
Angarrack
Barripper
Carnhell Green
Four Lanes
Ponsanooth
Zennor Head
St Ives
Copperhouse
Gwinear
Penhalvean
Stithians
Gurnards Head
Carbis Bay
Troon
A39
Zennor
Halsetown
Lelant
High Lanes
Praze-an-Beeble
Carnkie
Longdowns
Mabe Burnthouse
Towednack
Merlins Magic Land
B3280
Drym
Crowan
Porkellis
Rame
Penryn
Pendeen Watch
Canonstown
Leedstown
A35
Morvah
Men-an-Tol
St Erth
St Erth Praze
Townshend
Godolphin Cross
Prospidnick
Carnkie
Treneal
Treverva
Mulfra Quoit
Chysauster
Crowlas
Relubbus
Carleen
Wendron
Seworgan
Budock Water
Pendeen
Great Bosullow
Lanyon Quoit
New Mill
Ludgvan
Trescowe
Sithney
Coverack Bridges
Botallack
Trengwainton
A30
Gulval
St Hilary
Crowntown
Brill
Constantine
Mawnan Smith
Cape Cornwall
St Just
A3071
Madron
Longrock
Marazion
Goldsithney
Ashton
Breage
Helston
Porth Navas
Durgan
Mawnan
Penwith Heritage Coast
Heamoor
Chyandour
Perranuthnoe
A394
Gweek
Helford
Toll Point
Kelynack
Sancreed
Penzance
Prah Sands
A3083
Mawgan
St Antho
Carn Euny
Drift
Newlyn
Cudden Point
Rinsey Head
Seal Sanctuary
Helford River
Manaccan
Whitesand Bay
Crows-an-Wra
Catchall
Kerris
Paul
Trewavas Head
Porthleven
Flambards
Garras
Tregidden
Sennen
St Buryan
Mousehole
MOUNT'S BAY
Berepper
Garras
LAND'S END
Trevescan
Lamorna
Trethewey
Treen
Lamorna Cove
White Cross
Cury
Goonhilly Downs Earth Station
St Kev
Porthgwarra
Merthen Point
Cribba Head
GOONHILLY DOWNS
Coverack
Gwennap Head
Porthcurno
Minack Open Air Theatre
To Isles of Scilly
Poldhu Point
Mullion
Mullion Cove
Mullion Island
Porth Mellin
B3296
Predannack Head
Ruan Major
Kuggar
Black Head
Vellan Head
Ruan Minor
Cadgwith
Cornwall Coast Path
The Lizard Heritage Coast
Lizard Head
Landewednack
Lizard
Hot Point
LIZARD

4   5   6   7   8

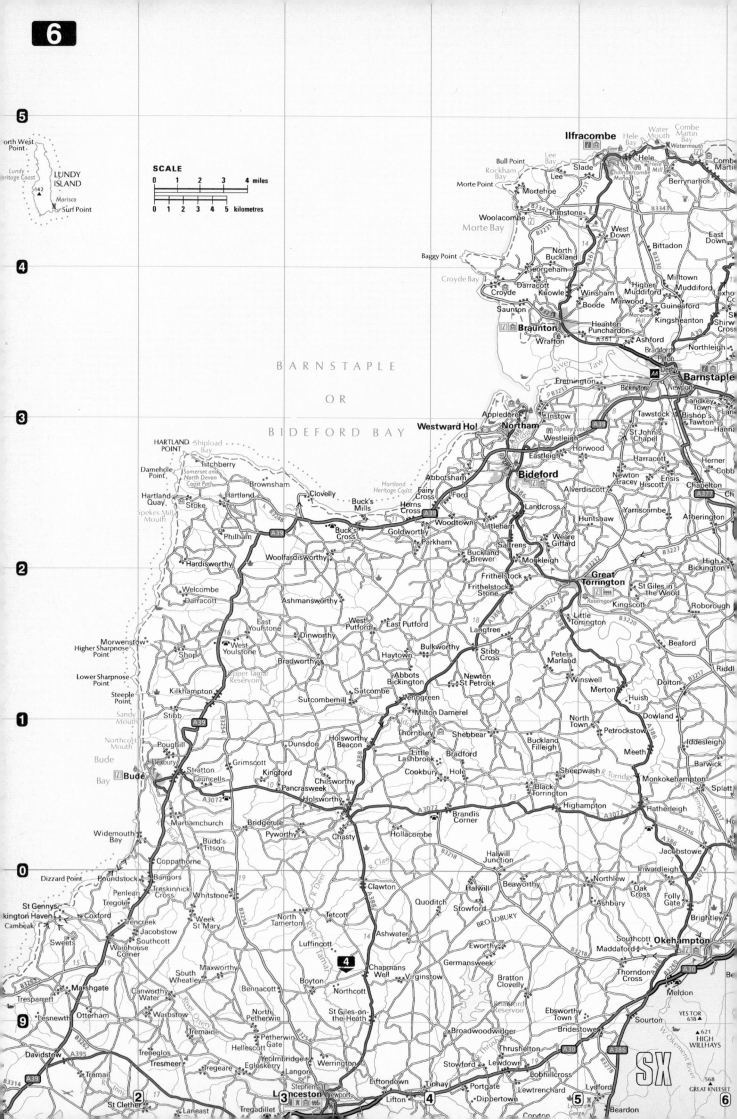

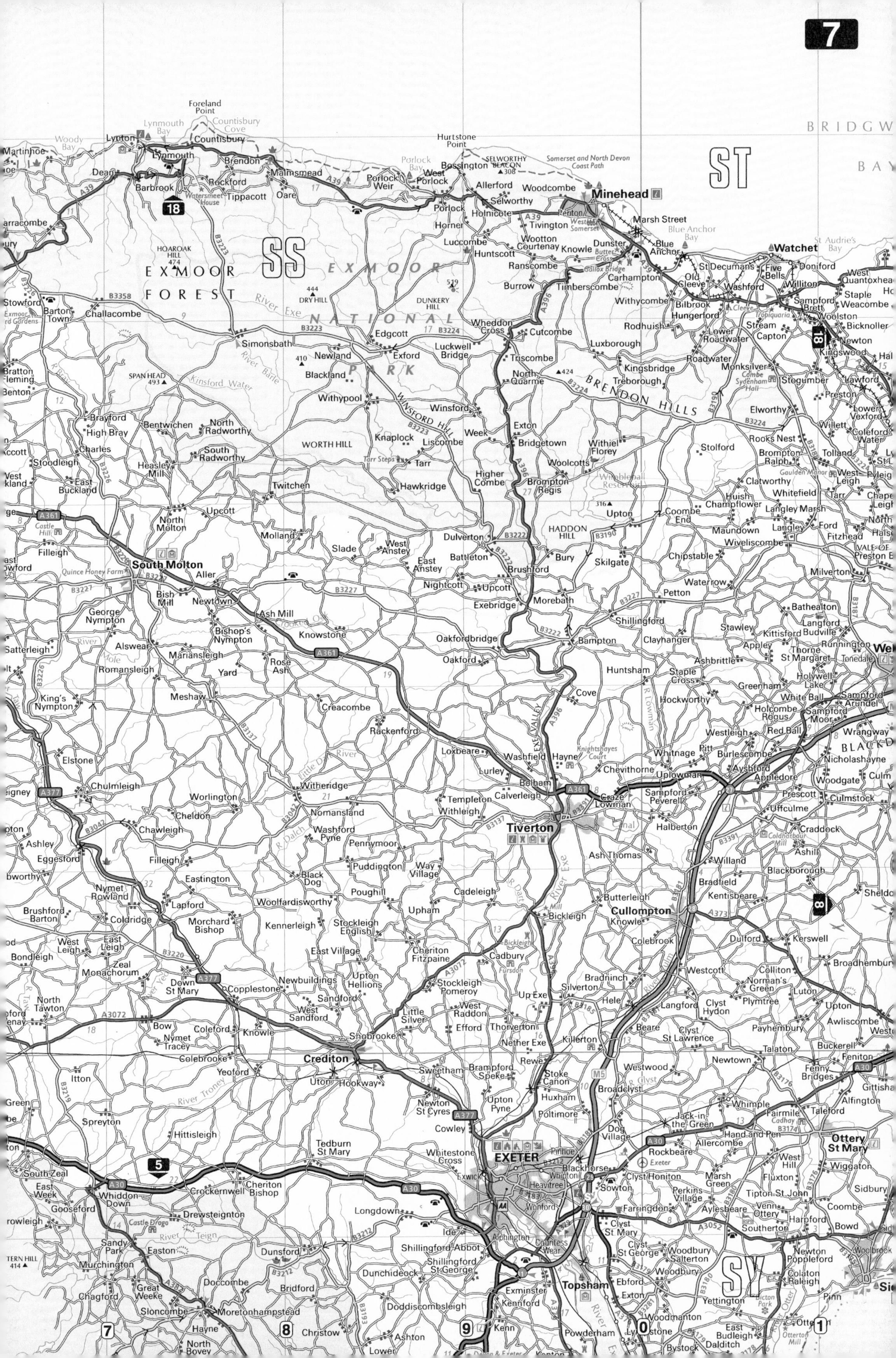

EXMOOR FOREST

EXMOOR NATIONAL PARK

BRENDON HILLS

BLACKD

BRIDGW
ST
BAY

SS

SY

Lynton · Lynmouth · Countisbury · Foreland Point · Countisbury Cove · Lynmouth Bay · Woody Bay · Martinhoe · Dean · Barbrook · Barracombe · Brendon · Rockford · Tippacott · Oare · Malmsmead · Watersmeet House · Porlock Weir · Porlock · Porlock Bay · Bossington · Allerford · Selworthy · Holnicote · Woodcombe · SELWORTHY BEACON · Hurtstone Point · Minehead · Periton · West Somerset · Marsh Street · Blue Anchor Bay · Blue Anchor · Dunster · Butter Cross · Gallox Bridge · Carhampton · Old Cleeve · Watchet · St Decumans · Five Bells · Washford · Williton · Doniford · West Quantoxhead · Staple · Weacombe · Woolston · Bicknoller · Newton · Kingswood

HOAROAK HILL 474 · Challacombe · Stowford · Barton Town · Exmoor Gardens · River Exe · DRY HILL 444 · DUNKERY HILL 519 · Wheddon Cross · Cutcombe · Luxborough · Withycombe · Rodhuish · Lower Roadwater · Bilbrook · Hungerford · Stream · Capton · Tropiquaria · Roadwater · Monksilver · Combe Sydenham Hall · Stogumber · Preston · Lower Vexford · Lawford · Hal

Bratton Fleming · Benton · SPAN HEAD 493 · Kinsford Water · Simonsbath · Newland · Exford · Edgcott · Blackland · Luckwell Bridge · Triscombe · North Quarme · ▲424 · Kingsbridge · Treborough · BRENDON HILLS · Elworthy · Willett · Coleford · Water · Tolland · Chapel Leigh

Brayford · High Bray · Bentwichen · North Radworthy · South Radworthy · Heasley Mill · Charles · East Buckland · Twitchen · WORTH HILL · Knaplock · Tarr · Tarr Steps · Hawkridge · Withypool · Winsford · WINSFORD HILL · Week · Liscombe · Higher Combe · Exton · Bridgetown · Withiel Florey · Woolcotts · Brompton Regis · Wimbleball Reservoir · 316▲ · Upton · Coombe End · Rooks Nest · Brompton Ralph · Gauldon Manor · Huish Champflower · Clatworthy · Whitefield · Langley Marsh · Langley · Ford · Fitzhead · VALE OF PRESTON Pk

North Molton · Upcott · Molland · Slade · West Anstey · East Anstey · Dulverton · Battleton · Brushford · Bury · Skilgate · HADDON HILL · Chipstable · Waterrow · Petton · Stawley · Batheally · Milverton · Langford Budville · Runnington · Tonedale · Well

South Molton · Castle Hill · Filleigh · Quince Honey Farm · Aller · Bish Mill · Newtown · Bishop's Nympton · Ash Mill · Knowstone · Nightcott · Upcott · Exebridge · Morebath · Shillingford · Bampton · Clayhanger · Ashbrittle · Appley · Kittisford · Greenham · Thorne St Margaret · Holywell Lake · White Ball · Sampford Arundel · Wellington

George Nympton · Alswear · Mariansleigh · Yard · Rose Ash · Oakfordbridge · Oakford · Huntsham · Cove · Staple Cross · Hockworthy · Westleigh · Holcombe Rogus · Red Ball · Sampford Moor · Wrangway

King's Nympton · Romansleigh · Meshaw · Creacombe · Rackenford · Loxbeare · Washfield · Hayne · Lurley · Calverleigh · Chevithorne · Uplowman · Whitnage · Pitt · Burlescombe · BLACKD · Nicholashayne · Woodgate · Culm

Elstone · Chulmleigh · Worlington · Cheldon · Chawleigh · Witheridge · Nomansland · Templeton · Withleigh · Bolham · Knightshayes Court · Craze Lowman · Sampford Peverell · Appledore · Prescott · Ashbrittle · Ufculme · Culmstock · Craddock · Coldharbour Mill · Ashill

Ashley · Eggesford · Brushford Barton · Coldridge · West Leigh · East Leigh · Nymet Rowland · Lapford · Morchard Bishop · Kennerleigh · Stockleigh English · East Village · Washford Pyne · Pennymoor · Black Dog · Puddington · Way Village · Poughill · Cadeleigh · Upham · Bickleigh · Butterleigh · Willand · Bradfield · Kentisbeare · Blackborough · Sheldon · Tiverton · Ash Thomas · Cullompton · Knowle · Colebrook · Dulford · Kerswell · Broadhembury

North Tawton · Bondleigh · Zeal Monachorum · Down St Mary · Copplestone · Newbuildings · Sandford · Upton Hellions · Cheriton Fitzpaine · Cadbury · Stockleigh Pomeroy · Fürsdon · Silverton · Bradninch · Hele · Langford · Westcott · Colliton · Norman's Green · Plymtree · Luton · Upton · Awliscombe · West

Bow · Nymet Tracey · Coleford · Knowle · West Sandford · Little Silver · West Raddon · Thorverton · Up Exe · Nether Exe · Efford · Rewe · Killerton · Beare · Clyst St Lawrence · Talaton · Buckerell · Feniton

Crediton · Shobrooke · Golebrooke · Yeoford · Uton · Hookway · Brampford Speke · Stoke Canon · Huxham · Westwood · Stoke · Newton · Fenny Bridges · Gittisham · Alfington · A30 · Ottery St Mary

Itton · Spreyton · Hittisleigh · Tedburn St Mary · Sweetham · Newton St Cyres · Cowley · Poltimore · Broadclyst · Dog Village · Jack-in-the-Green · Cadhay · Hand-and-Pen · Allercombe · Taleford · Wiggaton

South Zeal · East Week · Gooseford · Whiddon Down · Crockernwell · Cheriton Bishop · Longdown · Whitestone Cross · Ide · Upton Pyne · EXETER · Heavitree · Wonford · Rockbeare · Blackhorse · Clyst Honiton · Sowton · Marsh Green · Fluxton · West Hill · Tipton St John · Sidbury · Coombe

TERN HILL 414 · Sandy Park · Castle Drogo · Murchington · Easton · Drewsteignton · Dunsford · Shillingford Abbot · Shillingford St George · Ide · Kennford · Exwick · Alphington · Exminster · Countess Wear · Clyst St Mary · Clyst St George · Woodbury Salterton · Woodbury · Harpford · Bowd · Southerton · Venn Ottery · Aylesbeare · Perkins Village · Farringdon · Clyst George

Chagford · Great Weeke · Sloncombe · Hayne · Moretonhampstead · North Bovey · Christow · Ashton · Lower · Doccombe · Bridford · Doddiscombsleigh · Dunchideock · Topsham · Exminster · Powderham · Kenn · Woodmanton · Lympstone · Woodbury · East Budleigh · Dalditch · Otterton · Bystock · Bicton Park · Colaton Raleigh · Newton Poppleford · Woolbrook · Sid

Barton Town · B3358 · B3223 · B3224 · B3222 · B3227 · B3226 · A361 · A377 · A3072 · A30 · A396 · A39 · M5

18 · 5 · 8 · 7 · 9 · 0 · 1

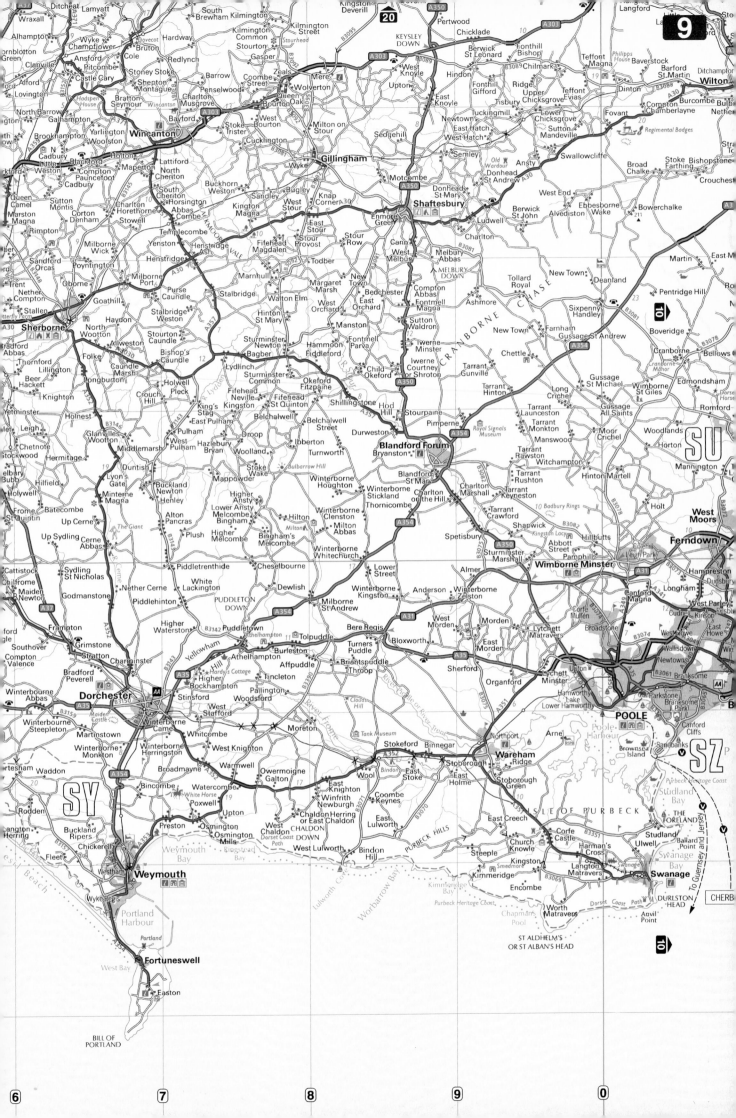

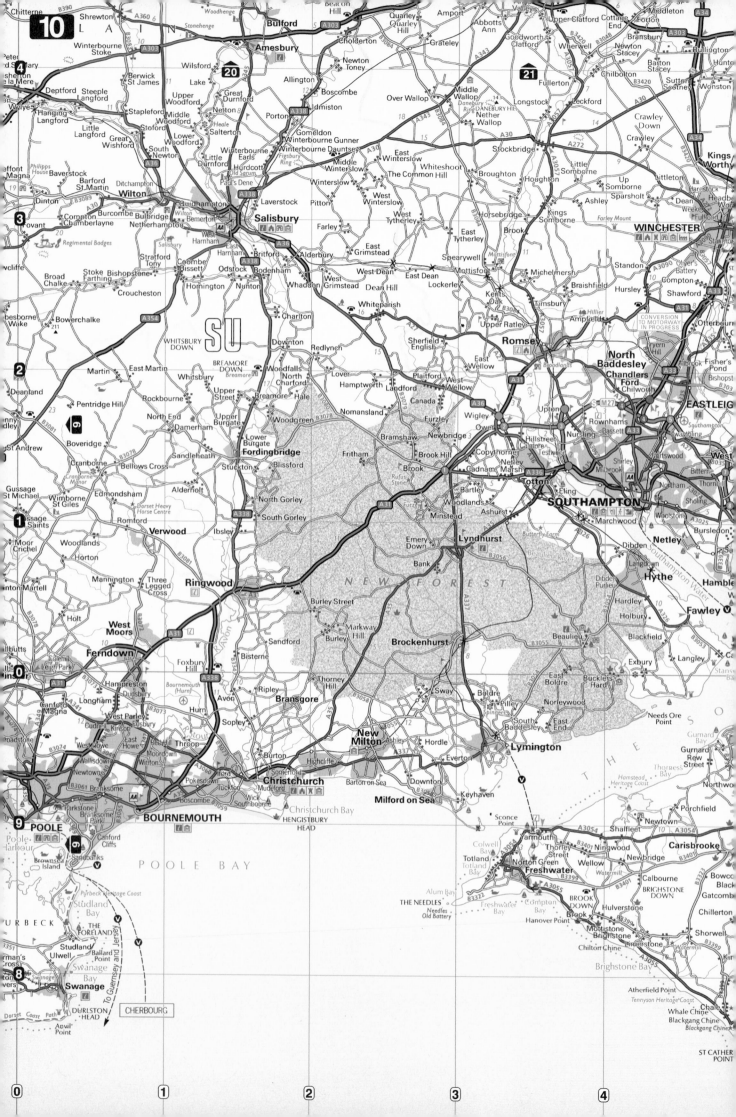

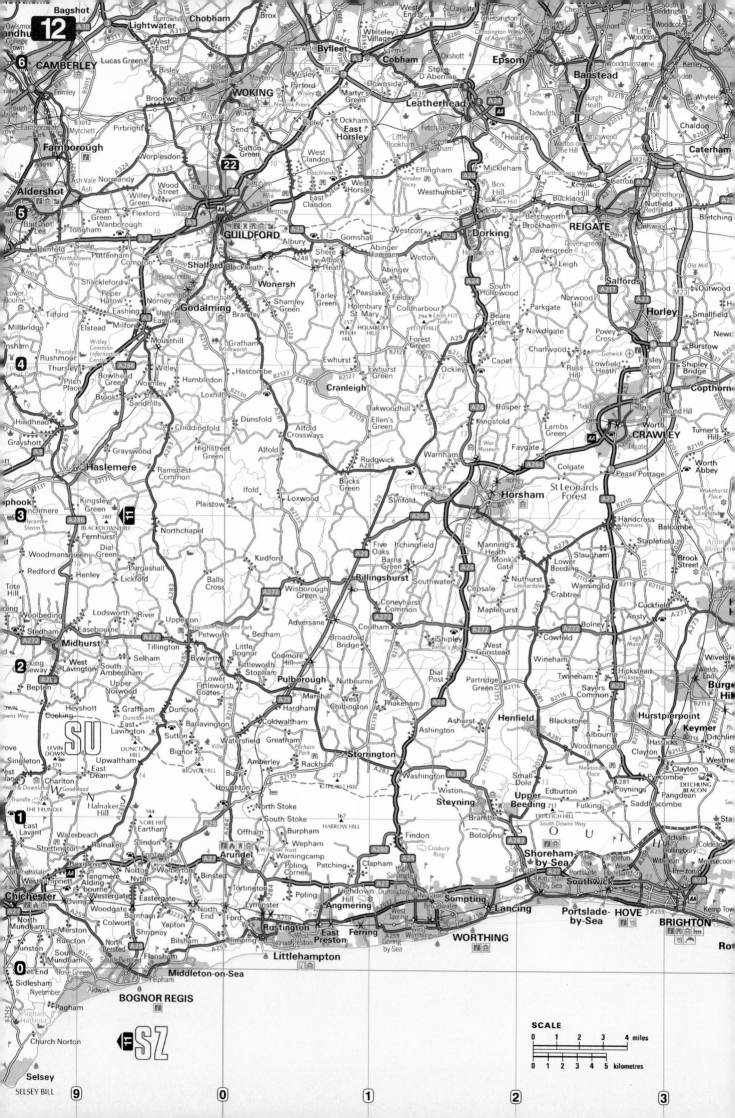

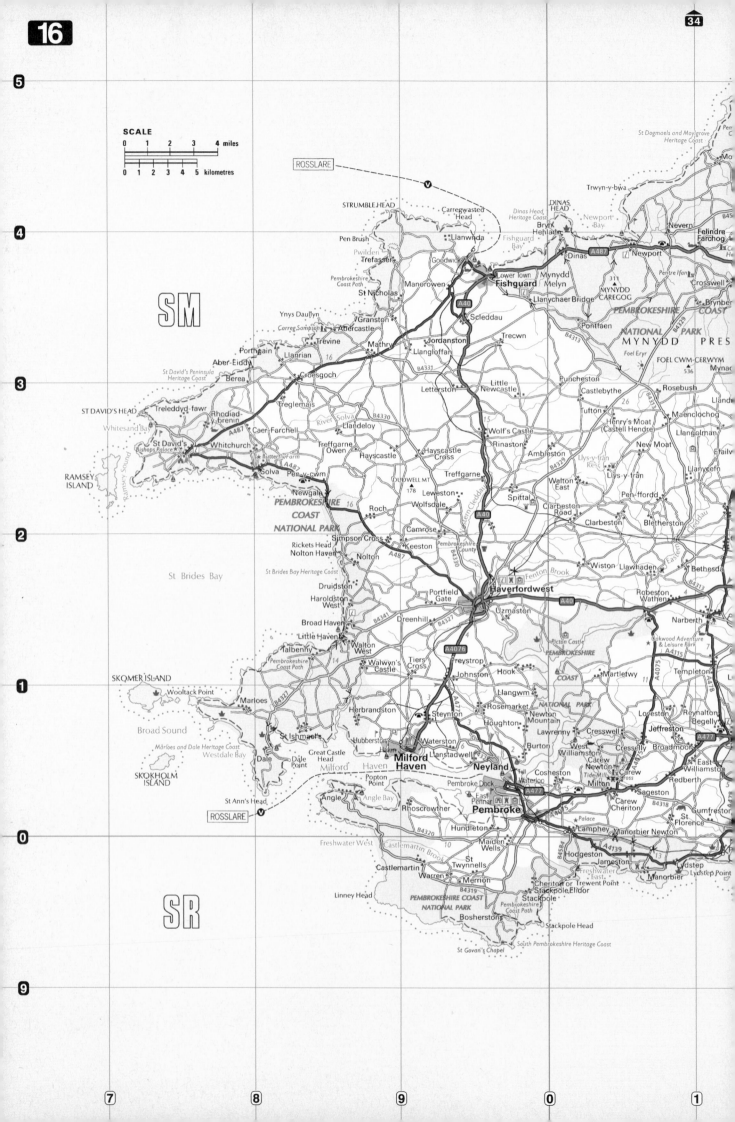

SCALE

0 1 2 3 4 miles

0 1 2 3 4 5 kilometres

ROSSLARE

SM

SR

St Dogmaels and Moylgrove
Heritage Coast

Mo

Trwyn-y-bwa

B45

Nevern

Felindre
Farchog

STRUMBLE HEAD

Carregwasted
Head

Dinas Head
Heritage Coast

DINAS
HEAD

Newport
Bay

Bryn
Henllan

DINAS

A487

Newport

Crosswell

Pen Brush

Llanwnda

Goodwick

Lower Town

Pembrokeshire
Coast Path

Trefasser

Manorowen

St Nicholas

Mynydd
Melyn

Pentre Ifan

Brynber

Llanychaer Bridge

MYNYDD
CAREGOG

311

Fishguard

Fishguard
Bay

A40

Scleddau

Llanchaer

PEMBROKESHIRE COAST

Foel Eryr

NATIONAL PARK

MYNYDD PRES

Ynys Daullyn

Granston

Abercastle

Jordanston

Llangloffan

Trecwn

Pontfaen

FOEL CWM-CERWYM

536

Mynac

Carreg Sampson

Mathry

B4313

Porthgain

Trevine

Aber-Eiddy

Llanrian

16

St David's Peninsula
Heritage Coast

Berea

Croesgoch

Treglemais

B4331

Letterston

Little
Newcastle

Puncheston

Castlebythe

Rosebush

Lland

B4313

26

ST DAVID'S HEAD

Treleddyd-fawr

Rhodiad-
y-brenin

River Solva

B4330

Wolf's Castle

Tufton

Henry's Moat
(Castell Hendre)

Maenclochog

Whitesand Bay

A487

Caer Farchell

Llandeloy

15

Rinaston

Llangolman

Efaily

RAMSEY
ISLAND

St David's

Bishops Palace

Whitchurch

Butterfly Farm

Treffgarne
Owen

Hayscastle

Hayscastle
Cross

Treffgarne

Ambleston

New Moat

Llanycefn

Solva

Pen-y-cwm

DUDWELL MT
178

Leweston

B4329

Llys-y-fran
Rest

Llys-y-fran

Pen-fford

Newgale

Wolfsdale

Spittal

Walton
East

PEMBROKESHIRE
COAST
NATIONAL PARK

16

Roch

Camrose

Clarbeston
Road

Clarbeston

Bletherston

Bethesda

Rickets Head

Nolton Haven

Simpson Cross

Keeston

A487

Pembrokeshire
County

B4330

Fenton Brook

Wiston

Llawhaden

B4313

Nolton

St Brides Bay

St Brides Bay Heritage Coast

Druidston

Haroldston
West

Portfield
Gate

Haverfordwest

A40

Robeston
Wathen

4

Narberth

Broad Haven

B4341

Dreenhill

B4327

Uzmaston

SKOMER ISLAND

Little Haven

Walton
West

B4327

Walwyn's
Castle

Tiers
Cross

A4076

Freystrop

Johnston

Hook

Oakwood Adventure
& Leisure Park

A4115

Wooltack Point

Marloes

Talbenny

Pembrokeshire
Coast Path

14

Llangwm

PEMBROKESHIRE

Martletwy

Loveston

A4075

Templeton

A478

Broad Sound

Herbrandston

Rosemarket

COAST

11

Reynalton

Begelly

Mârloes and Dale Heritage Coast

St Ishmael's

Steynton

Houghton

Newton
Mountain

NATIONAL PARK

Cresswell

Jeffreston

A477

Westdale Bay

Hubberston

Waterston

3

Lawrenny

West
Williamston

Broadmoor

SKOKHOLM
ISLAND

Dale

Dale
Point

Great Castle
Head

Milford Haven

Milford
Haven

Llanstadwell

Neyland

Burton

Carew
Newton

Cresselly

Carew

East
Williamston

St Ann's Head

Popton
Point

Coshestön

Tide Mill

Milton

Redberth

Sageston

Gumfrestor

ROSSLARE

Angle

Angle Bay

Pembroke Dock

2

East
Pennar

Waterloo

A477

Carew
Cheriton

B4318

St
Florence

Rhoscrowther

Pembroke

Palace

5

Freshwater West

Castlemartin Brook

Hundleton

Lamphey

Manorbier Newton

Maiden
Wells

A4139

13

B4320

10

St
Twynnells

Hodgeston

Jameston

Lydstep

Castlemartin

Warren

Merrion

Freshwater
East

Manorbier

Lydstep Point

Linney Head

B4319

Cheriton or Trewent Point

Stackpole Elidor

PEMBROKESHIRE COAST
NATIONAL PARK

Stackpole

Pembrokeshire
Coast Path

Bosherston

Stackpole Head

South Pembrokeshire Heritage Coast

St Govan's Chapel

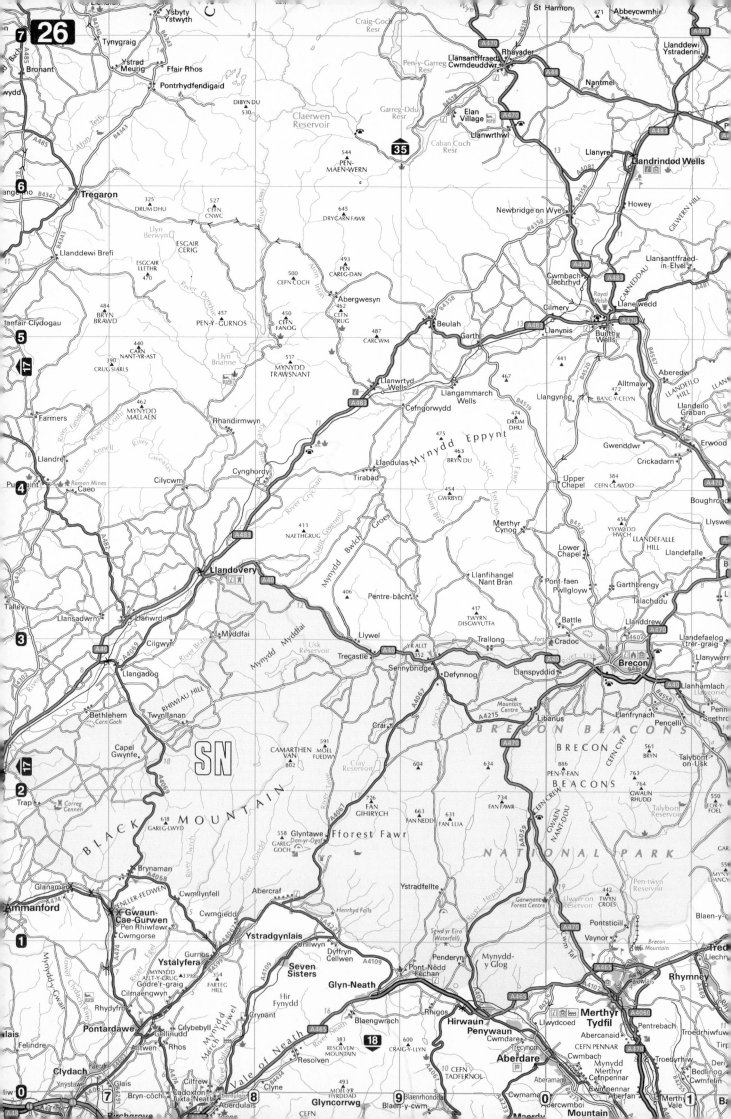

34

44

Aberdaron Llanfaelrhys rth Neigwl
Bwlchtocyn
St Tudwal's
Island East
St Tudwal's
Island West
Porth
Ceiriad
Porth
Ysgo
Aberdaron
Bay

Shell Island Maes Art
Tourist Vill

Dyffry
Ardudv
Llanddwy

St Mary's
BARDSEY
ISLAND
sey Sound

2

Barm
Ba

SCALE
0   1   2   3   4 miles

0 1 2 3 4 5 kilometres

F

1

SH

Aber
Dysynni

Tywyn

0

C A R D I G A N

B A Y

9

Clarach B

☆☒♨♿★ Aberystwyth

8

Aberystwyth and Distri

Blaenplwyf

SN

A487

Ceredigion·
Heritage Coast   Llanddei
16

Llanrhystud

7

Llansantffraid
Llanon

Nebo

Jo

Aberarth
A487
Aberaeron
B4577

Cilcennin

A482

6

New Quay
Maen-y-groes
Ceredigion
Heritage Coast
Nanternis
Ynys-Lochtyn
Llwyndafydd

Llanina
Gilfachrheda
Llwyncelyn
Oakford

Cross
Inn
Llanarth
A487
Caerwedros

Dihewyd
B4342
Llan og
Pontgarreg
Ceredigion

Mydroilyn

Trefilan
Ystrad
Aeron
Talsarn

Temple Bar

1   **16**   **2**   **3**   **4**   **17**   **5**

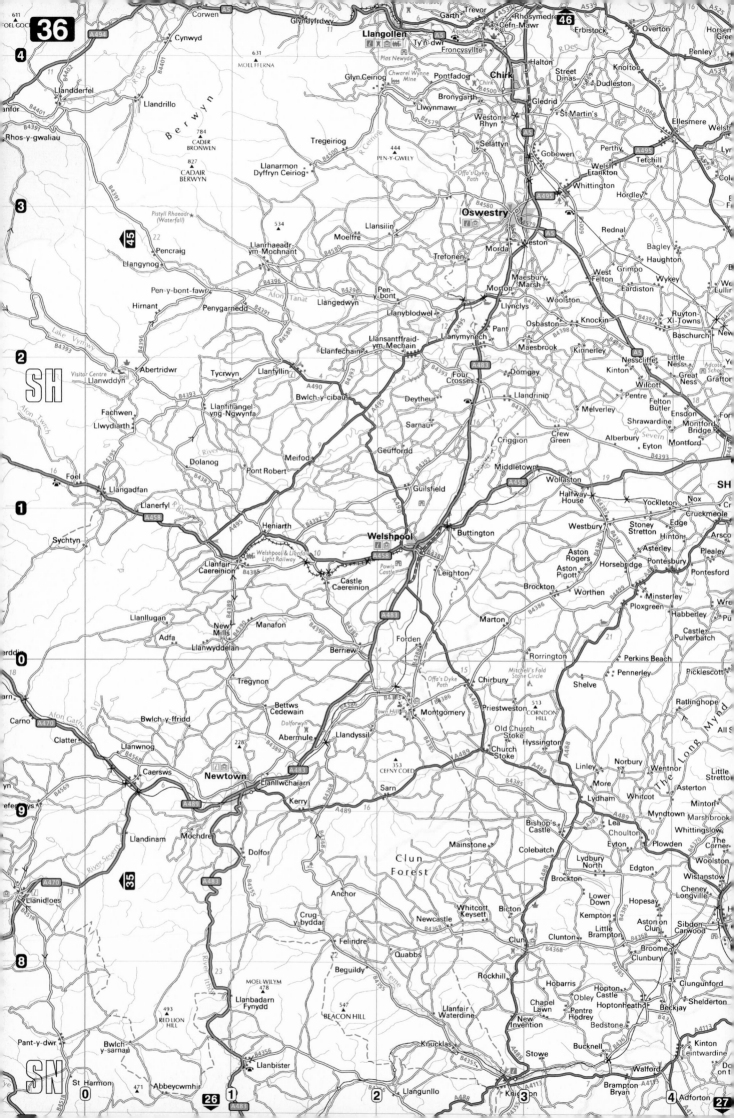

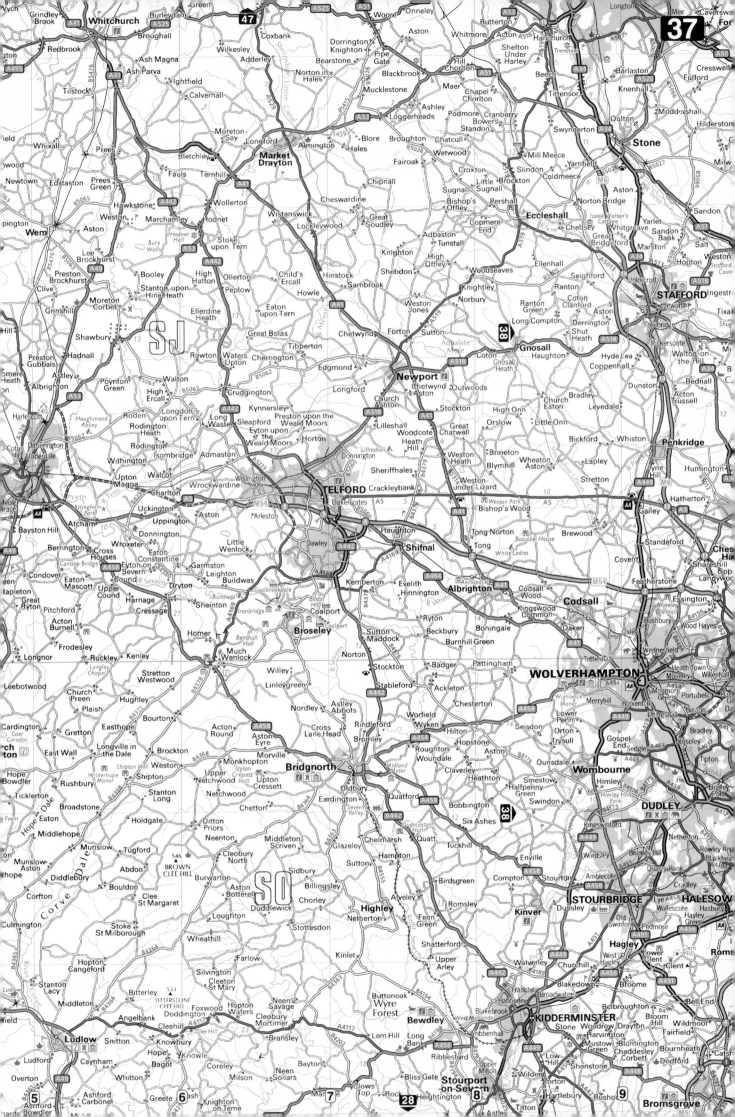

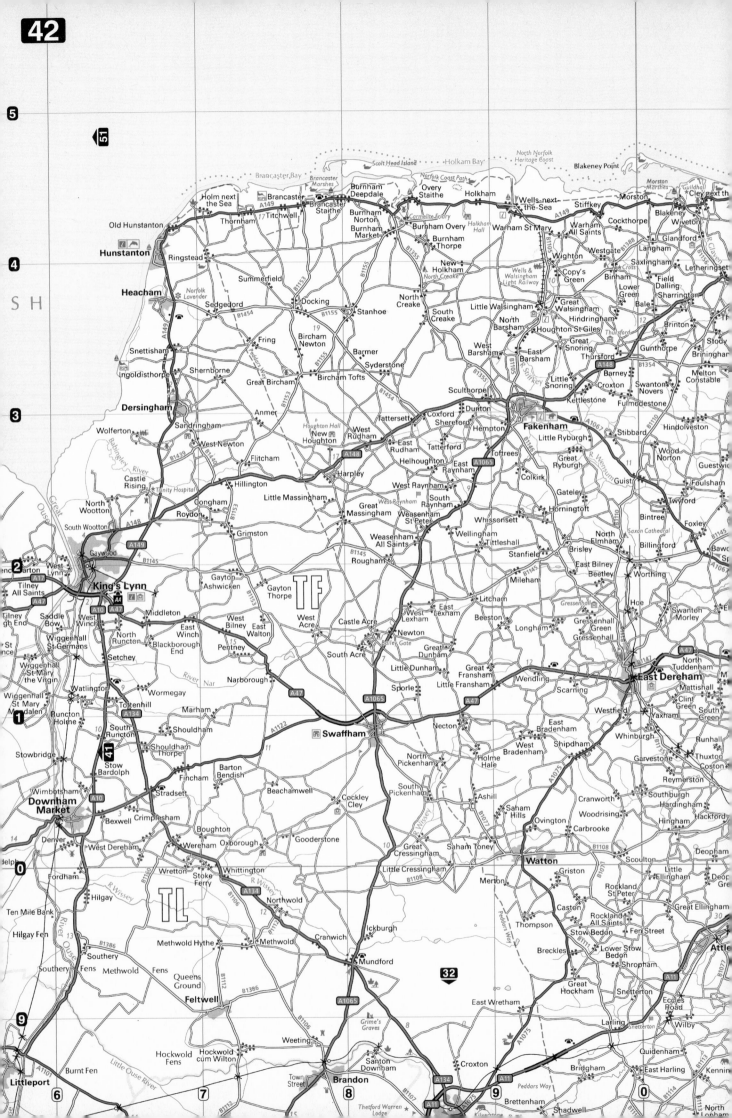

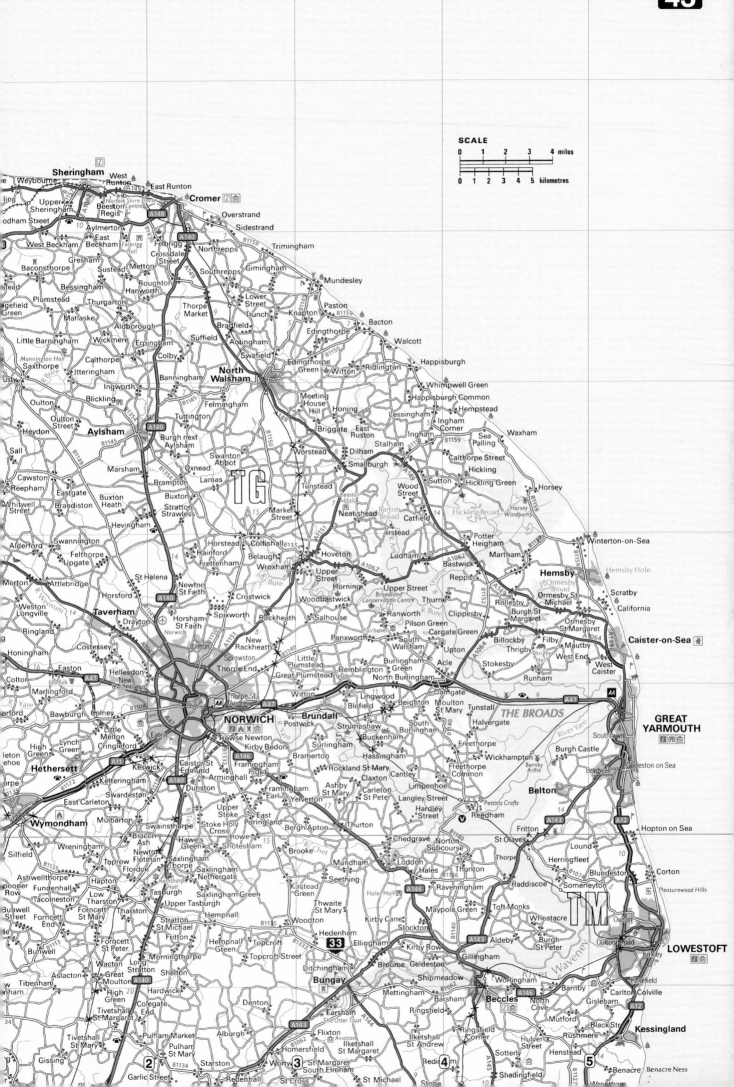

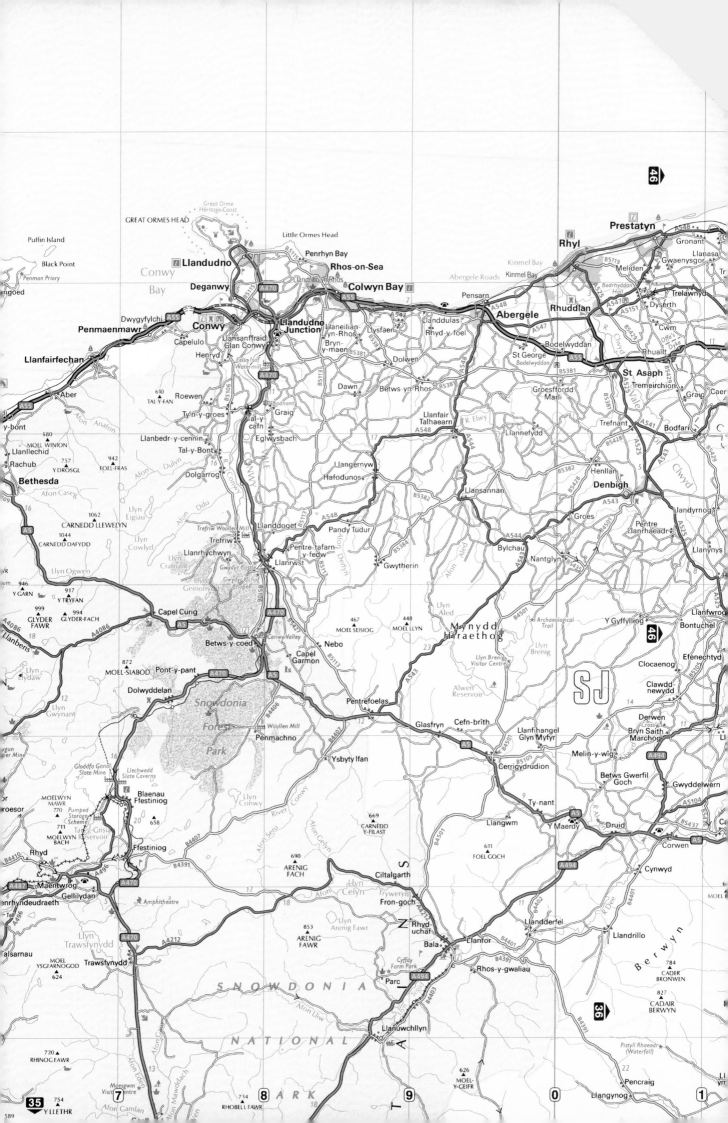

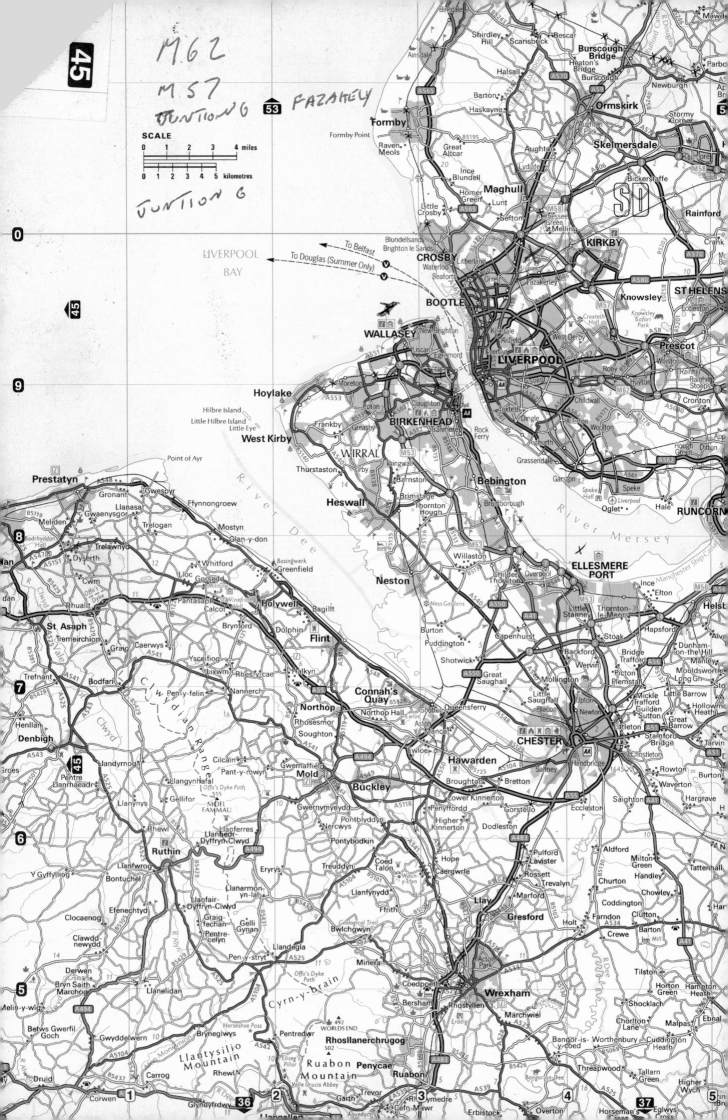

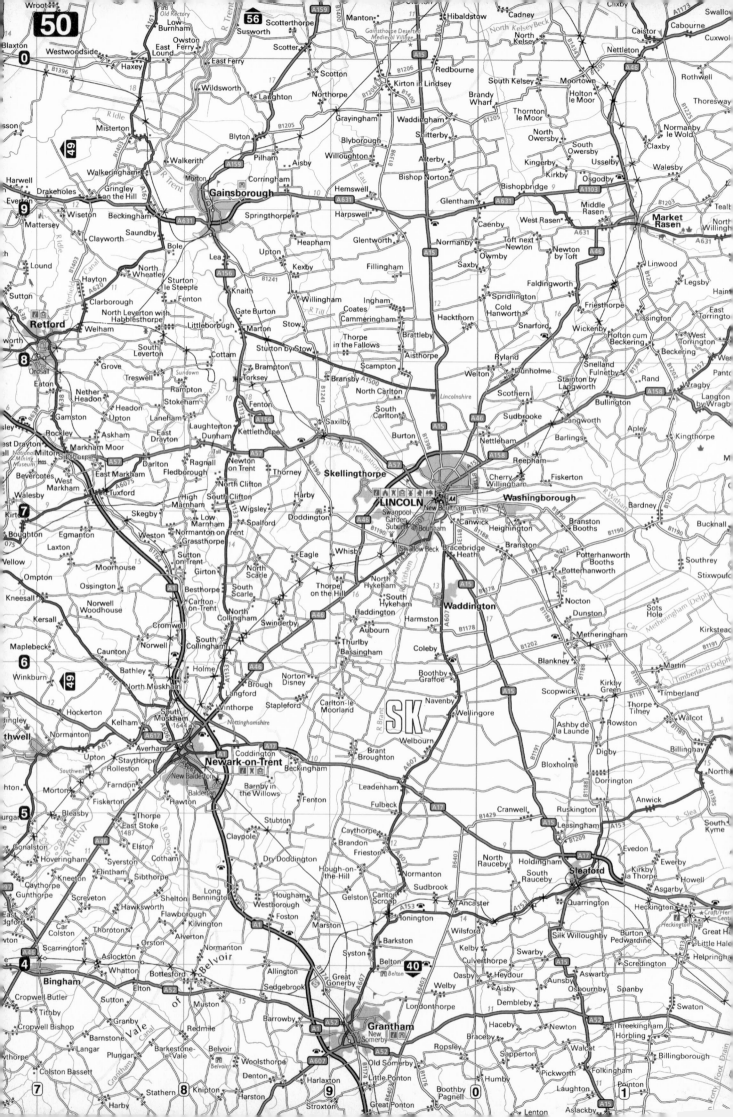

Isle of Man

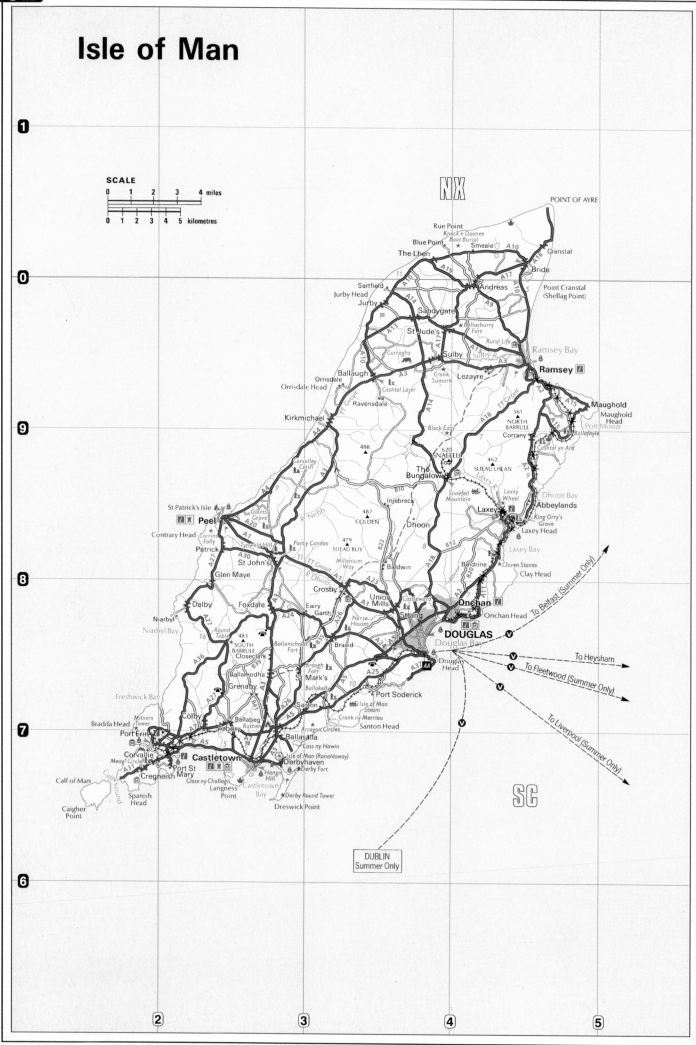

SCALE

0 1 2 3 4 miles

0 1 2 3 4 5 kilometres

NX

POINT OF AYRE

Rue Point
Knock e Doonee
Boat Burial
Blue Point
Smeale A10
The Lhen
Cranstal
A16
Bride
Point Cranstal
(Shellag Point)
Sartfield
A19
A17
Jurby Head
Andreas
A10
Jurby
A14
Sandygate
A9
St Jude's
Ballachurry
Fort
Rural Life
Curraghs
Sulby
A13
Sulby R.
Ramsey Bay
Ballaugh
A3
Lezayre
A2
Ramsey
Orrisdale
Cronk
Sumark
Orrisdale Head
Cashtal Lajer
A14
A18
561
NORTH
BARRULE
Maughold
Maughold
Head
Kirkmichael
Block Eary
Corrany
Port Mooar
A4
620
SNAEFELL
Cashtal yn Ard
Ballafayle
A15
488
Corvalley
Caich
462
SLIEAU LHEAN
A3
The
Bungalow
Dhoon Bay
St Patrick's Isle
Giants
Grave
Injebreck
B10
Snaefell
Mountain
Laxey
Wheel
Abbeylands
Peel
R. Nebb
Laxey
King Orry's
Grave
Contrary Head
Corrins
Folly
487
COLDEN
Dhoon
Laxey Head
Patrick
Tynwald Hill
Port y Candas
479
SLIEAU RUY
B22
Laxey Bay
A20
A30
St John's
TT Circuit
Millenium
Way
Baldwin
B12
Glen Maye
R. Dhoo
A23
A18
Baldrine
Clay Head
Dalby
Foxdale
Crosby
Cloven Stones
Niarbyl
A24
Eairy
Garth
A26
Union
Mills
Castleward
Onchan
A2
Niarbyl Bay
Round
Table
483
SOUTH
BARRULE
Norse
Houses
Strang
Onchan Head
To Belfast (Summer Only)
16
Closeclark
Ballanicholas
Fort
Braaid
A21
DOUGLAS
Douglas Bay
A36
Broogh
Fort
A25
AA
To Heysham
Ballamodha
St Mark's
Douglas
Head
To Fleetwood (Summer Only)
Grenaby
A5
Ballakelly
10
Freshwick Bay
Santon
Port Soderick
To Liverpool (Summer Only)
Colby
Isle of Man
Steam
Bradda Head
Milners
Tower
Ballabeg
Rushen
Arbory
Cronk ny Merriu
Santon Head
A5
Port Erin
A7
Cass ny Hawin
Corvalle
Meayl Circle
A31
Ballasalla
Arragon Circles
Isle of Man (Ronaldsway)
Cregneish
Port St
Mary
Castletown
Derbyhaven
Derby Fort
Calf of Man
A31
Close ny Chollagh
Hango
Hill
Castletown
Bay
Derby Round Tower
Spanish
Head
Langness
Point
Dreswick Point
Caigher
Point
SC

DUBLIN
Summer Only

Wold
ewton
Burton
Fleming
Grindale
Thwing
Boynton
B1253
Rudston
Monolith
Bessingby
Haisthorpe
Carnaby
Kilham
Burton
Agnes
Thornholme
Norman
Manor House
Carnaby
A165
Hilderthorpe
Bridlington

Speeton
Buckton
B1229
Bempton
Thornwick Bay
Flamborough Head
Heritage Coast
Selwicks Bay
FLAMBOROUGH
HEAD
Flamborough
Sewerby

BRIDLINGTON
BAY

SCALE
0   1   2   3   4 miles
0 1 2 3 4 5 kilometres

arva
Lowthorpe
Nafferton
Harpham
B1249
Wansford
kerne
Great
Kelk
Gembling
Lisset
Foston
on the
Wolds
Beeford
B1249
Brigham
North
Frodingham
A165

Fraisthorpe

Gransmoor
Barmston
Ulrome
B1242
B1242
Skipsea

Dunnington
Atwick
Bewholme
Nunkeeling
Brandesburton
Hornsea
Hornsea
Mere
B1242

Aike
m
everley
Leven
Catwick
B1244
Routh
Long
Riston
B1243
Rise
Arnold
Tickton
North Skirlaugh
Woodmansey
A165
Wawne
Thearne
Swine
Dunswell
Coniston
13
Ganstead
Wyton
B1238
Bilton
B1237
Sutton
on Hull
Newland
A1165
Stoneferry
B1233
A165
ast
lla
AA
KINGSTON UPON HULL
A63
6
Marfleet
A1033

Seaton
Sigglesthorne
Hornsea
Pottery
Little
Hatfield
Goxhill
Rolston
Mappleton
Mappleton Sands

Great Hatfield
Great Cowden
Withernwick
New
Ellerby
Marton
West
Newton
Aldbrough
17
Old
Ellerby
South Skirlaugh
Flinton
Burton Constable
Hall
Garton
Humbleton
Hilston
Sproatley
Lelley
Owstwick
Elstronwick
Tunstall
Preston
Burton
Pidsea
Roos
Rimswell
Owthorne
Withernsea
Hedon
Burstwick
Halsham
Hollym
Paull
Thorngumbald
Keyingham
Winestead
4
A1033
Ottringham
A1033
Holmpton

TA

New
Holland
arrow
aven
Goxhill
East
Halton
Thornton
Abbey
Thornton
Curtis
North
Killingholme
South
Killingholme
Immingham
Dock
upon-
ber
A1077
13
B1206
14
Wootton
Ulceby
Skitter
A160
A1173
Ulceby
B1211
Immingham
Habrough
15
A180
Croxton
Kirmington
Brocklesby
B1211
B1210
A180
Stallingborough
Melton
Ross
A18
Barnetby
le Wold
Great
Limber
12
Healing
Keelby
Humberside
B1210
Great
Coates
Riby
GRIMSBY
West
Marsh
Aylesby
A180
Old
Clee
Bigby
84
erby
Searby
Owmby
Grasby
9
Clixby
A1173
Swallow
Cabourne
Bradley
Laceby
Nunsthorpe
Scartho
A46
Irby upon Humber
Barnoldby le Beck
A16
New Waltham
Waltham
Holton le Clay
A1098
Cleetorpes
Thrunscoe
Humberston
A1031

RIVER HUMBER

Patrington
B1445
Welwick
Weeton
Skeffling
Easington
Kilnsea
Spurn Head Heritage Coast
SPURN HEAD

V
ROTTERDAM (EUROPOORT)
ZEEBRUGGE

50
1
2
3
51
4
5
Caistor
Beelsby
Brigsby
Ashby
Cuxwold

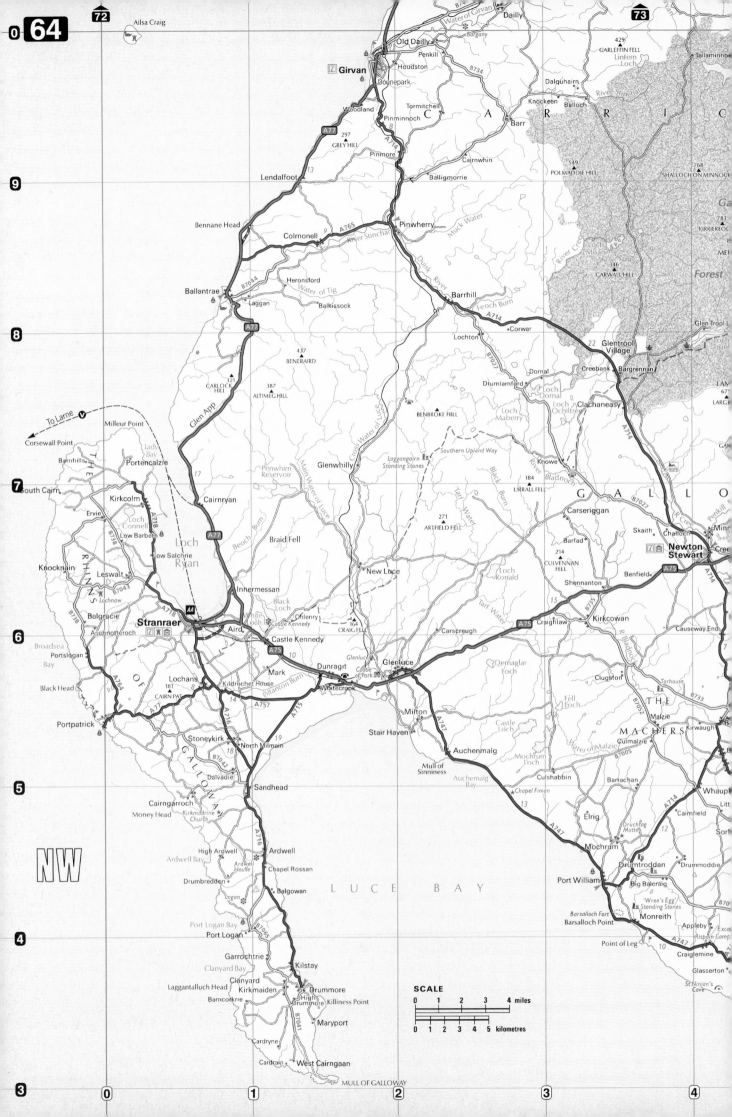

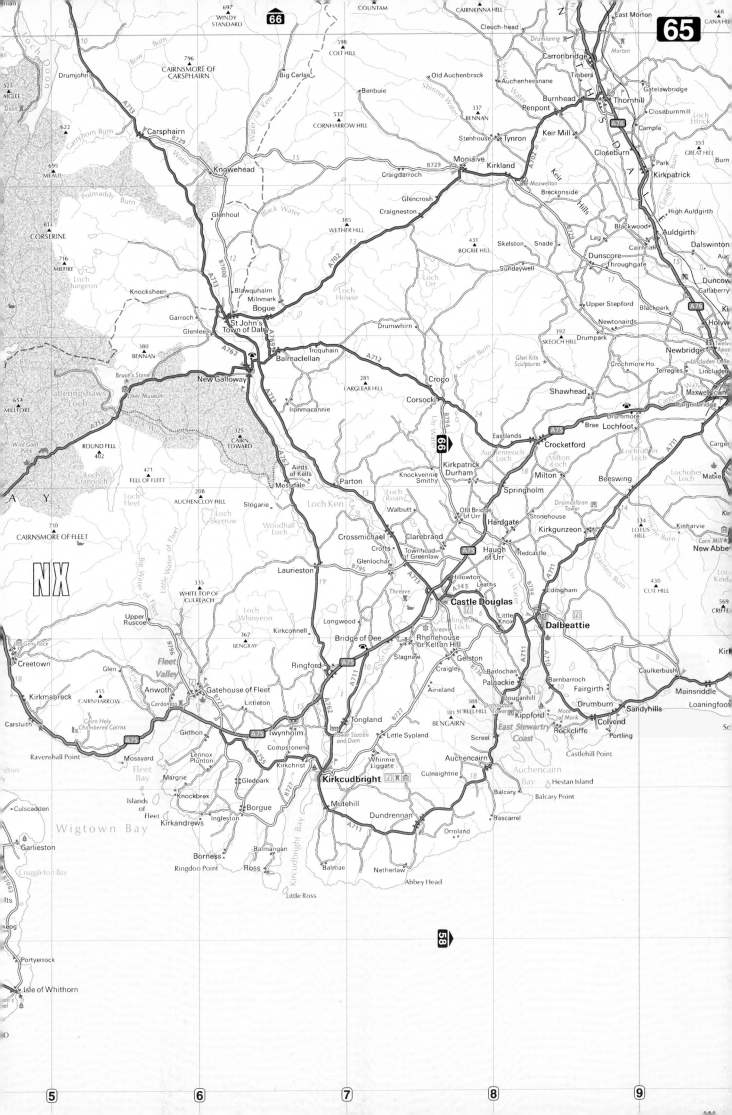

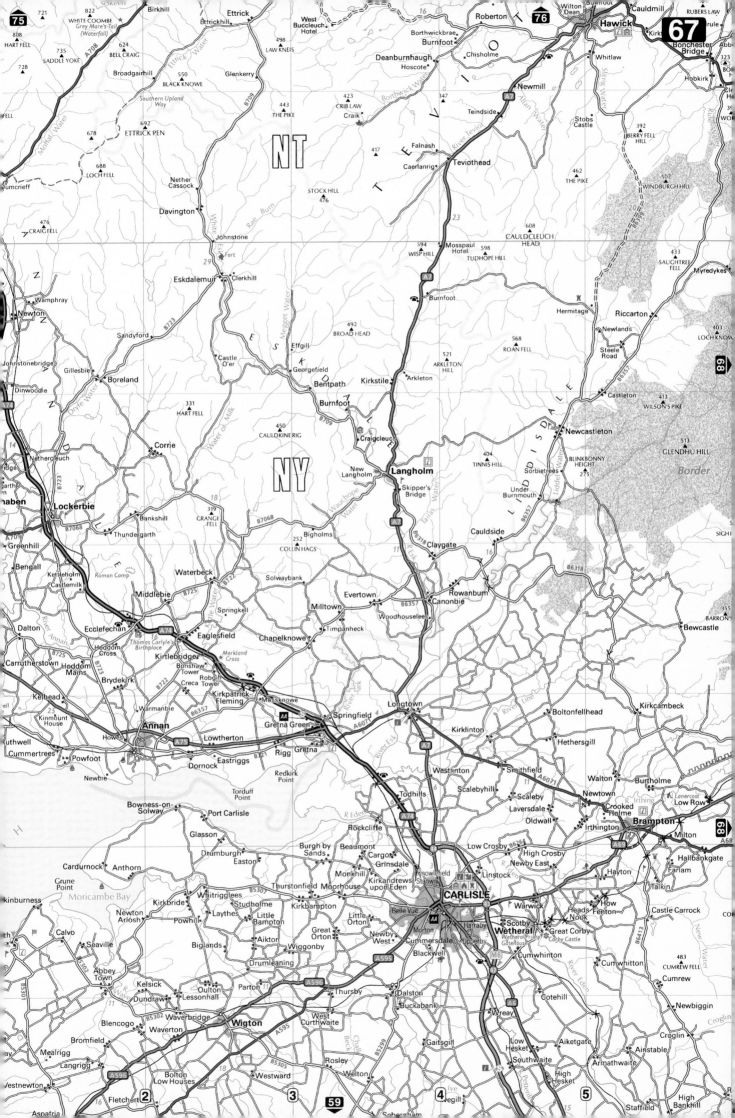

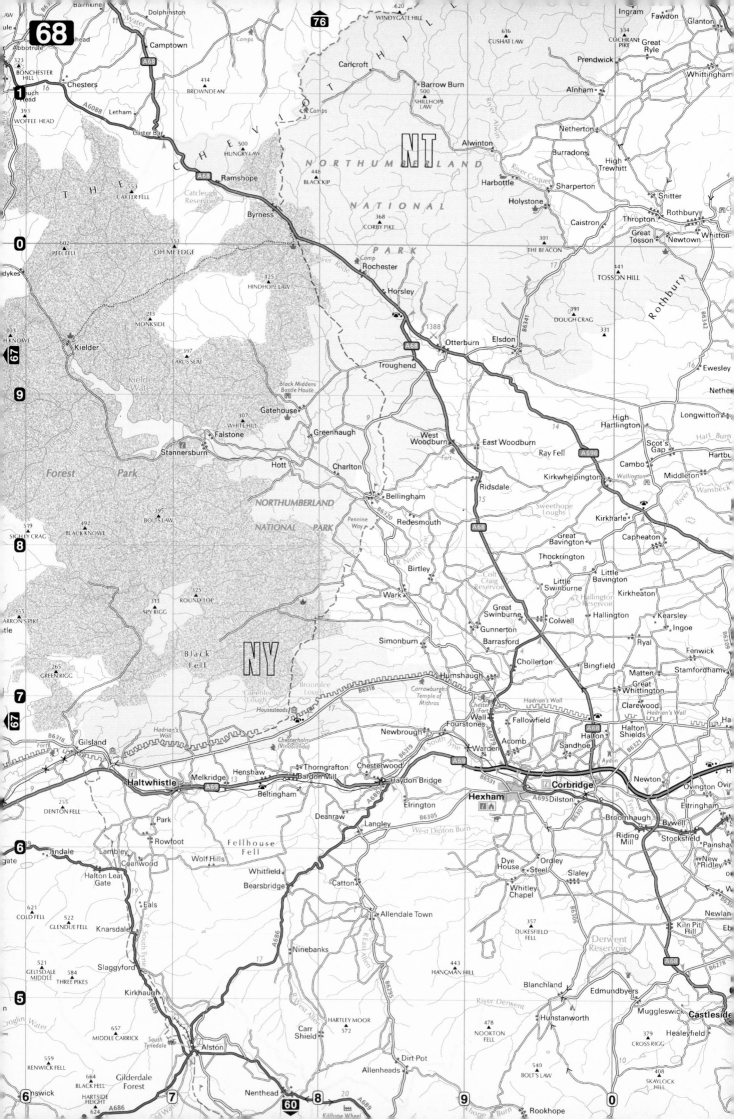

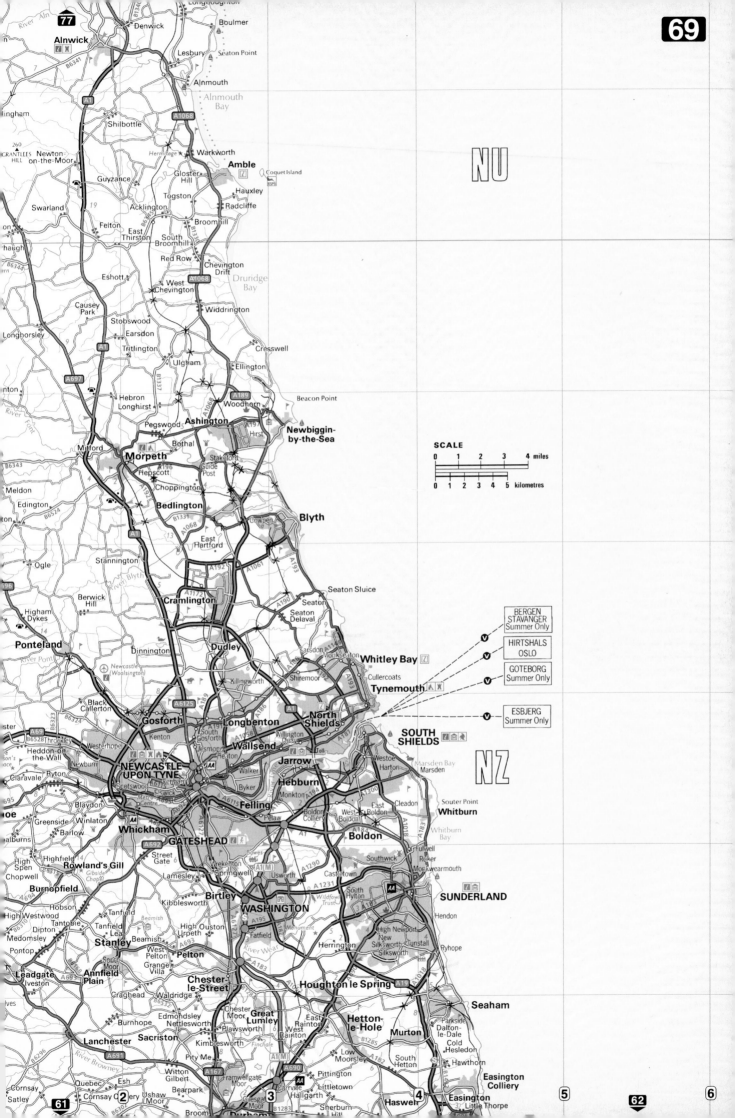

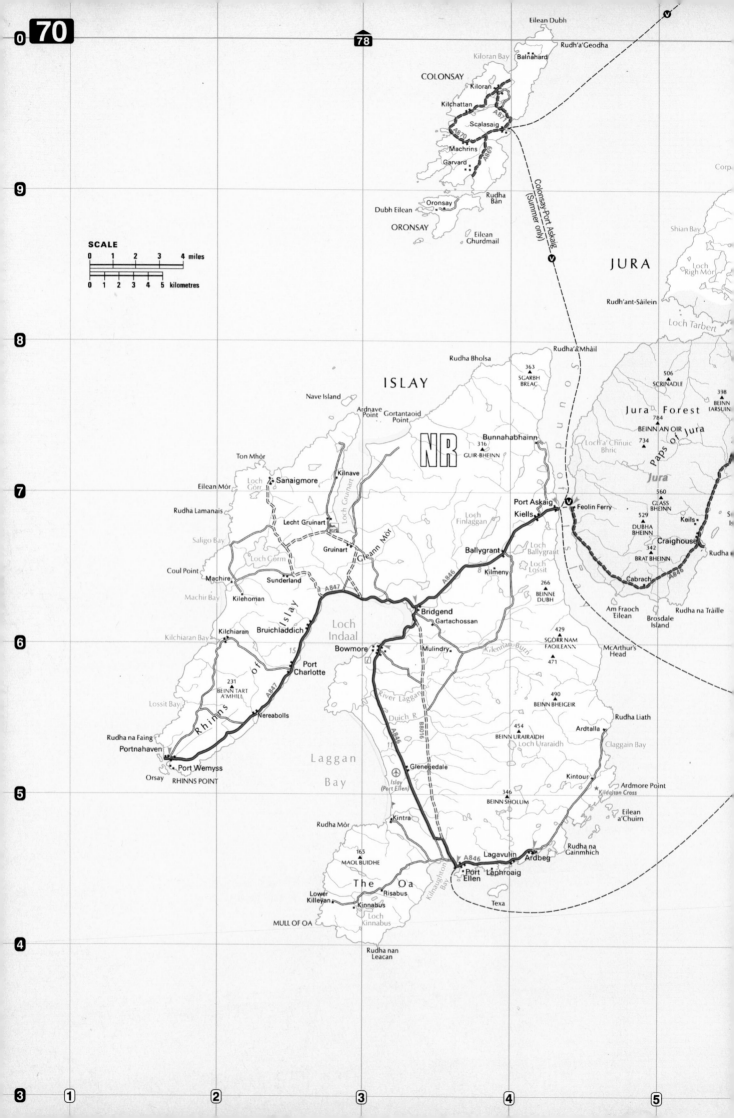

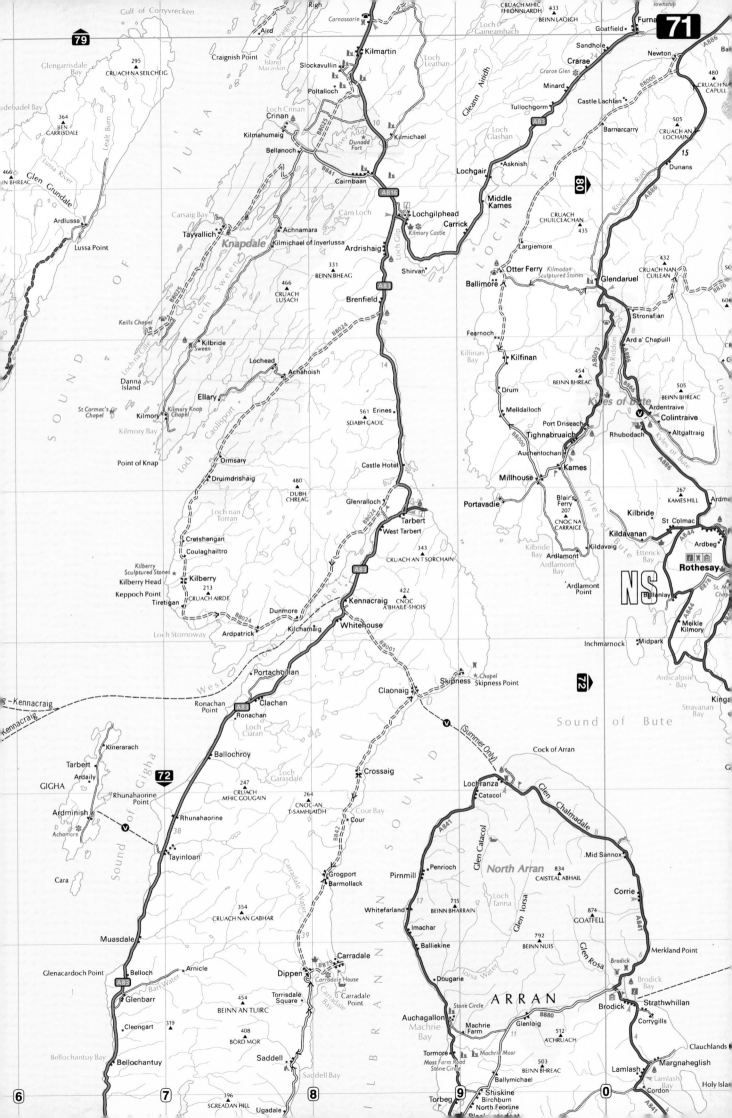

Gulf of Corryvrecken

Righ

CRUACH MHIC
FHIONNLARDH

33

BEINN LAOIGH

Goatfield

Furna

Carnassarie

Glengarrisdale
Bay

295

CRUACH NA SEILCHEIG

Aird

Craignish Point

Kilmartin

Crarae Glen

Sandhole

Crarae

Newton

A886

Island
Macaskin

Slockavullin

Loch
Leathan

Minard

B8000

480

CRUACH NA
CAPULL

debadel Bay

364
BEN
CARRISDALE

Poltalloch

Loch Crinan

Tullochgorm

Castle Lachlan

505

Crinan

A83

Barnarcarry

CRUACH AN
LOCHAIN

Lussa River

Kilmahumaig

River Add

Kilmichael

10

Dunadd
Fort

Asknish

15

Dunans

Glen Grundale

IN BHREAC

Bellanoch

B8025

Lochgair

Ardlussa

Cairnbaan

Loch
Glashan

A886

Lussa Point

A816

Loch Gilp

Lochgilphead

Middle
Kames

80

Carsaig Bay

Tayvallich

Knapdale

Achnamara

Kilmichael of Inverlussa

Ardrishaig

Kilmory Castle

Carrick

CRUACH
CHUILCEACHAN
435

River

Loch Sween

B8025

331

BEINN BHEAG

Shirvan

Largiemore

432

CRUACH NAN
CUILEAN

466
CRUACH
LUSACH

Brenfield

A83

Otter Ferry

Kilmodan
Sculptured Stones

Glendaruel

Keills Chapel

Ballimore

60

Kilbride
Sween

Lochead

Fearnoch

Stronafian

Danna
Island

Achahoish

B8024

14

Kilfinan
Bay

Kilfinan

454

Ard a' Chapuill

B8003

Loch Riddon

B836

St Cormac's
Chapel

Ellary

Loch Caolisport

Kilmory
Knap
Chapel

561

Erines

SLIABH GAOIL

Drum

BEINN BHREAC

505

BEINN BHREAC

Kyles of Bute

Kilmory

Melldalloch

Ardentraive

V

Colintraive

Kilmory Bay

Castle Hotel

Port Driseach

Rhubodach

Altgaltraig

Point of Knap

Ormsary

Druimdrishaig

480
DUBH
CHREAG

Glenralloch

B8024

Tighnabruaich

Auchenlochan

267
KAMES HILL

Ardma

Loch nan
Torran

Tarbert

West Tarbert

Kames

Kilbride

St Colmac

A844

Cretshengan

Coulaghailtro

343

CRUACH AN T SORCHAIN

Millhouse

Kildavanan

Ardbeg

Kilberry
Sculptured Stones

Portavadie

Blair's
Ferry

Kilbride
Bay

X

Rothesay

NS

Kilberry
Head

Kilberry

422
CNOC
A'BHAILE-SHOIS

207

CNOC NA
CARRAIGE

Ballanlay

213
CRUACH AIRDE

Kennacraig

Ardlamont

Kildavaig

Etterick
Bay

St Mo
Chap

Keppoch Point

Tiretigan

B8024

Dunmore

Whitehouse

Ardlamont
Bay

Meikle
Kilmory

Loch Stornoway

Ardpatrick

Kilchamaig

B8001

Ardlamont
Point

Inchmarnock

Midpark

Ardscalpsie
Bay

Portachoillan

Chapel
Skipness Point

72

Kinga

Kennacraig

Clachan

Ronachan
Point

Skipness

Claonaig

Sound of Bute

Stravanan
Bay

Kennacraig

Ronachan

Loch
Ciaran

(Summer Only)

V

Cock of Arran

Kinerarach

Ballochroy

72

Lochranza

Glen Chalmadale

8

Tarbert

Ardaily

GIGHA

247
CRUACH
MHIC GOUGAIN

Loch
Garasdale

264
CNOC-AN
T-SAMHLAIDH

Catacol

Rhunahaorine
Point

Cour Bay

Glen Catacol

North Arran

Ardminish

V

Rhunahaorine

Cour

834

CAISTEAL ABHAIL

Mid Sannox

Achamore

38

Penrioch

Glen Iorsa

Corrie

Cara

Tayinloan

Grogport

Pirnmill

715

BEINN BHARRAIN

874

GOATFELL

Barmollack

Loch
Tanna

Muasdale

354
CRUACH NAN GABHAR

39

Whitefarland

792

BEINN NUIS

Merkland Point

Imachar

Brodick

Glenacardoch Point

Belloch

Arnicle

Carradale

Balliekine

Brodick
Bay

A83

B879

Glenbarr

Dippen

Carradale House

Dougarie

Glenloig

512
ACHRUACH

Corrygills

Cleongart

319

454

Torrisdale
Square

Carradale
Point

A R R A N

B880

Strathwhillan

Bellochantuy Bay

Bellochantuy

Saddell

396
SGREADAN HILL

BEINN AN TUIRC

408
BÖRD MOR

Auchagallon
Machrie
Bay

Machrie
Farm

11

Stone Circle

Clauchlands

Tormore

Moss Farm Road
Stone Circle

503
BEINN BHREAC

Lamlash

Margnaheglish

Saddell Bay

Ugadale

Torbeg

Shiskine
Birchburn

Machrie Moor

Ballymichael

North Feorline

Cordon

Lamlash
Bay

Holy Island

Black

6

7

8

9

0

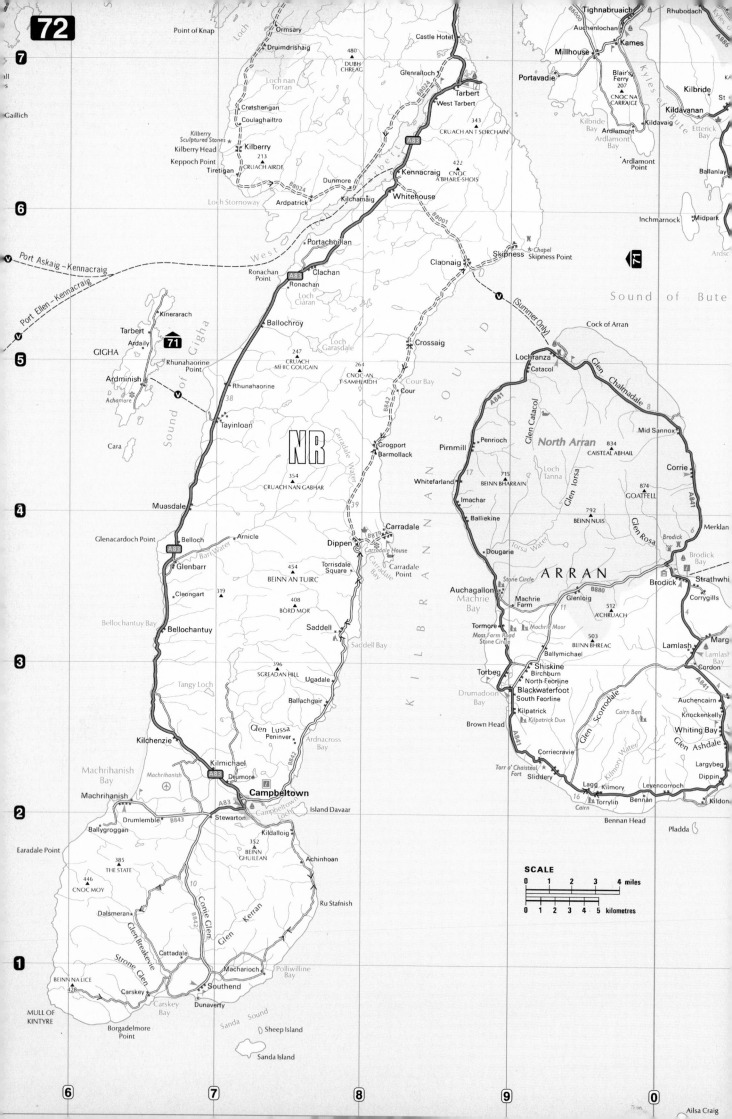

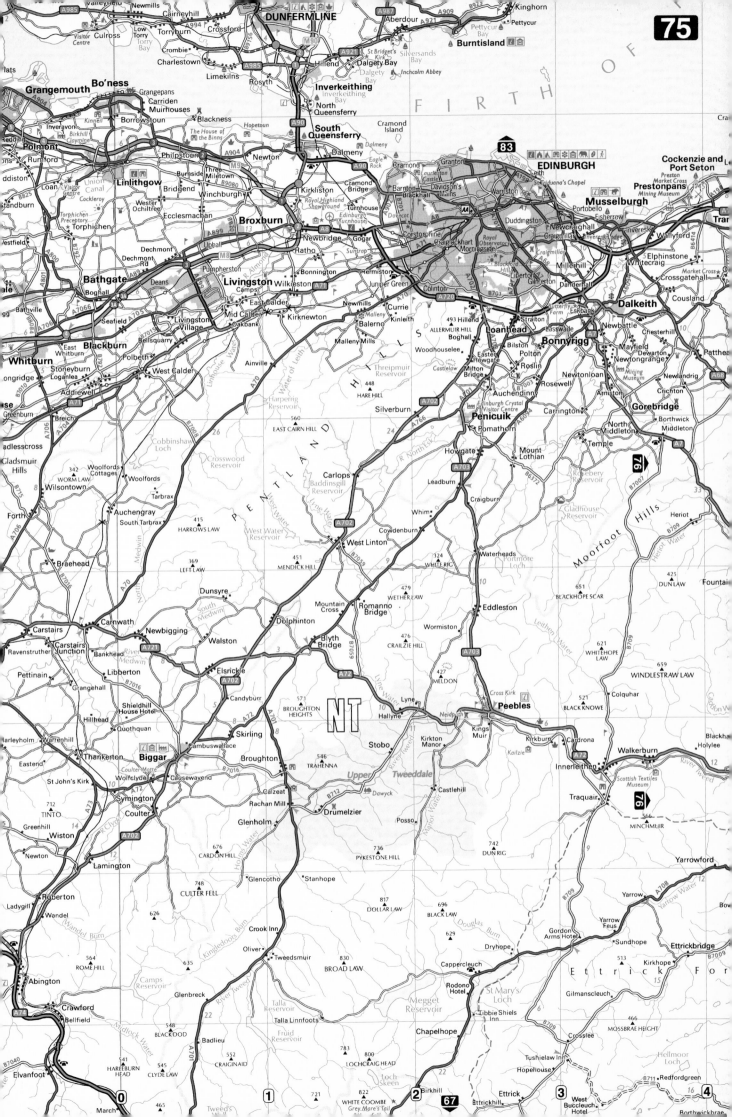

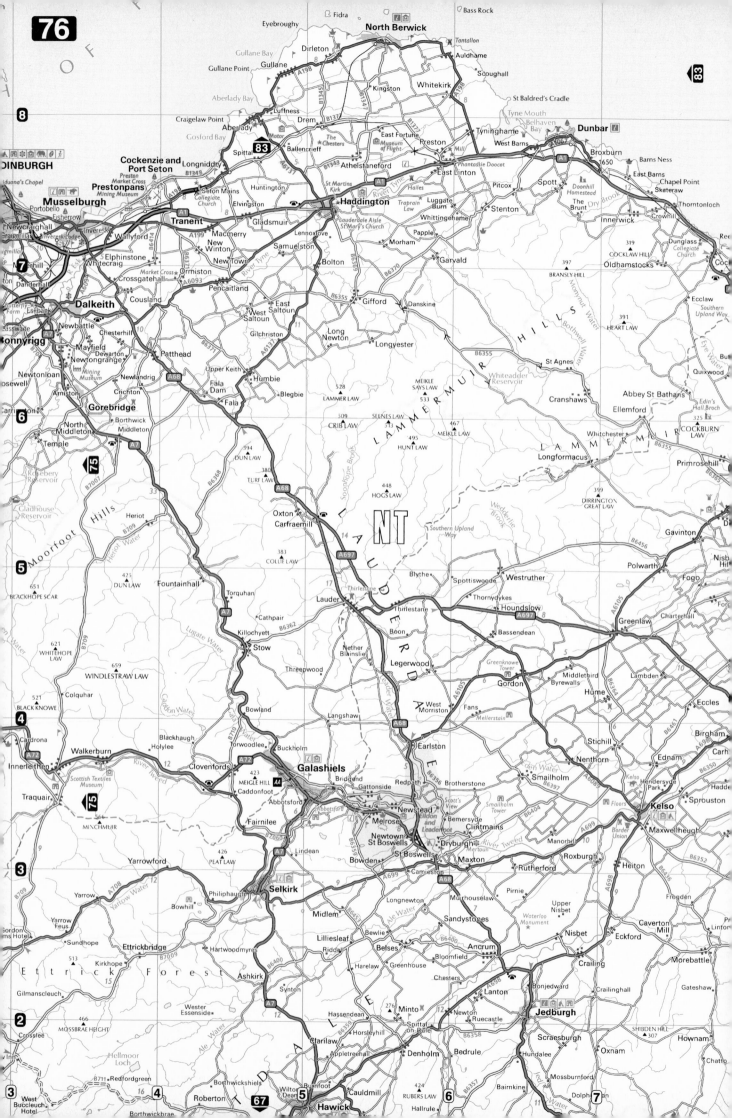

SCALE

0 1 2 3 4 miles

0 1 2 3 4 5 kilometres

Fast Castle Head

ST ABB'S HEAD

196
BROWN RIG
1107

St Abbs

Coldingham Bay

Coldingham

21 Houndwood 22 Eyemouth

Heugh Head Cairncross

B6438 Reston A1 Burnmouth

Y HILL Ayton
Auchencrow

B6437 Lamberton

East Blanerne Chirnside Marshall Meadows Bay

Edington

Foulden North Northumberland
Heritage Coast

Chirnsidebridge A1
Whiteadder

Broadhaugh Water A6105

Allanton Hutton Tithe Barn
1333

Blackadder
Water

Blackadder B6460 Paxton Barracks
Town Ramparts

B6461
Sunwick

Whitsome Hilton Fishwick Berwick-upon-Tweed

Swinton 13 Tweedmouth

East Ord Spittal

Upsettlington A698 Horncliffe

Ladykirk Horndean Huds Head

Ladykirk Murton
Ho.

B6437 Scremerston

Norham Thornton

Ladykirk B6470 Cheswick

NU

CAUSEWAY
FLOODED
AT HIGH TIDE

HOLY ISLAND

Swinton Ancroft A1 Haggerston Holy
Island

imprim Lindisfarne

River Tweed B6525 Beal Lindisfarne
Priory

Duddo Castle Point

Lennel Bowsden Guile Point

Cornhill-on- Etal East Fenwick
Tweed Kyloe North Northumberland
Heritage Coast
Crookham Lowick

Heatherslaw Buckton FARNE
Mill ISLANDS

Branxton The Lady Inner
1513 Waterford Hall Sound

Ford St Cuthbert's Budle Staple
Cave Bay Sound

Howtel Fenton Belford Bamburgh
Town B1342

B6396 Milfield B1341 B1340

B6352 Thornington Nesbit B6349

Lanton Doddington Lucker

R Glen Seahouses

Coupland B6525 North
Kirknewton Yeavering Sunderland

Hethpool Akeld B6348 Beadnell

A697 Warenford Swinhoe

Wooler Chatton Newstead Chathill

Beadnell Bay

NORTHUMBERLAND Newtown Ros Castle Tughall
Ellingham Preston
525 Chillingham High Newton
PRESTON HILL by-the-Sea

NATIONAL PARK North Brunton
Charlton
267 Christon
CATERAN HILL Falloden Bank Embleton

816 Ilderton Old Bewick Ditchburn South Embleton
Charlton Bay
THE CHEVIOT New Rock
Bewick Dunstanburgh

564 Eglingham Dunstan Craster

A697 Rennington Stamford Howick
Howick
Hall

567 Beanley
DUNMOOR HILL

Hartside Cullernose Point
620 Branton Howick
WINDYGATE HILL Ingram Fawdon Powburn Longhoughton
Sourhope Glanton River Aln Denwick Boulmer

Pennine Way

8 9 0 1 69 2 3

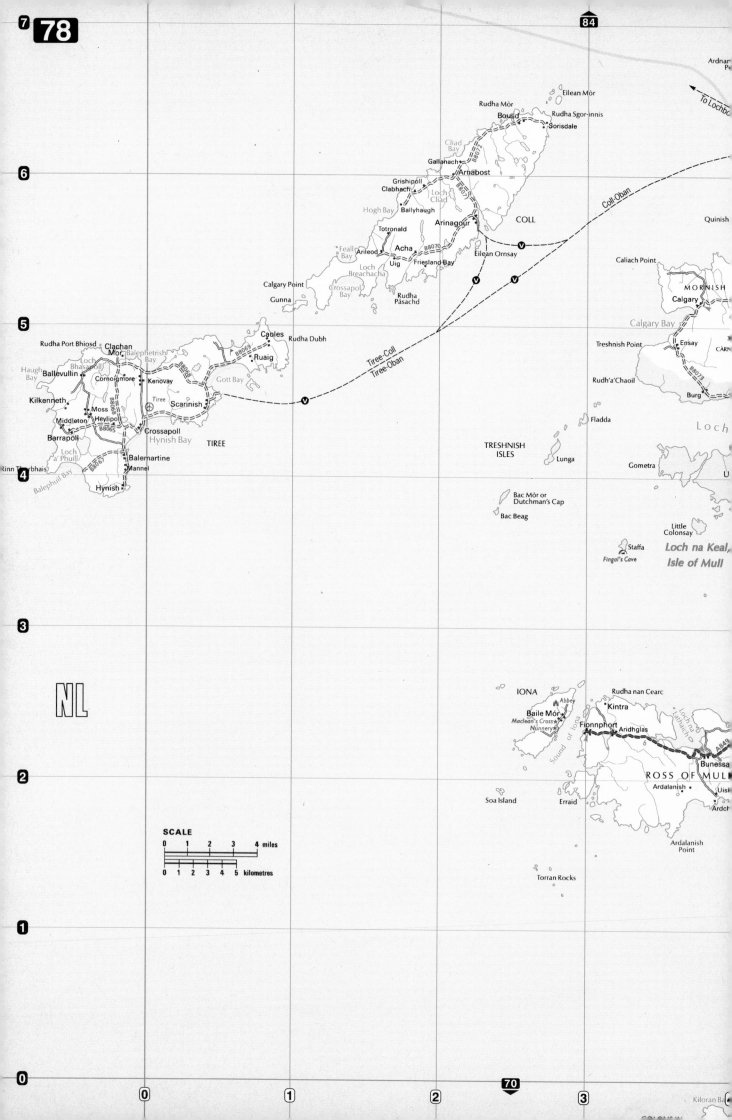

Ardnar
Pe

To Lochbo

Eilean Mòr
Rudha Mòr
Bousd
Rudha Sgor-innis
Sorisdale
Gallanach
Cliad
Bay
Arnabost
Grishipoll
Clabhach
Loch
Cliad
Ballyhaugh
COLL
Hogh Bay
Totronald
Arinagour
Coll-Oban
Quinish
Feall
Bay
Arileod
Acha
B8070
Uig
Friesland Bay
Eilean Ornsay
V
Caliach Point
Calgary Point
Loch
Breachacha
Gunna
Crossapol
Bay
Rudha
Pàsachd
V
MORNISH
Calgary
V
Calgary Bay
Caoles
Rudha Dubh
Treshnish Point
Ensay
CÀRN
Rudha Port Bhiosd
Clachan
Mòr
Balephetrish
Bay
B8069
Ruaig
Tiree-Coll
Tiree-Oban
Rudh'a'Chaoil
Haugh
Bay
Loch
Bhasapoll
Cornaigmore
Kenovay
Gott Bay
Ballevullin
B8068
V
Burg
Kilkenneth
B8066
Moss
Tiree
Scarinish
Loch
Middleton
Heylipoll
Fladda
Barrapoll
B8065
Crossapoll
Hynish Bay
TIREE
TRESHNISH
ISLES
Loch
Rinn Thorbhais
Loch
a' Phuill
Balemartine
B8067
Mannel
Lunga
Gometra
U
Balephuil Bay
Hynish
Bac Mòr or
Dutchman's Cap
Bac Beag
Little
Colonsay

NL

Loch na Keal,
Isle of Mull

Staffa
Fingal's Cave

IONA
Rudha nan Cearc
Abbey
Kintra
Baile Mòr
Maclean's Cross
Nunnery
Fionnphort
Aridhglas
Loch na
Lathaich
A849
Bunessa
ROSS OF MUL
Ardalanish
Uisl
Soa Island
Erraid
Ardc
Ardalanish
Point

Torran Rocks

Kiloran Ba

SCALE

0   1   2   3   4 miles

0 1 2 3 4 5 kilometres

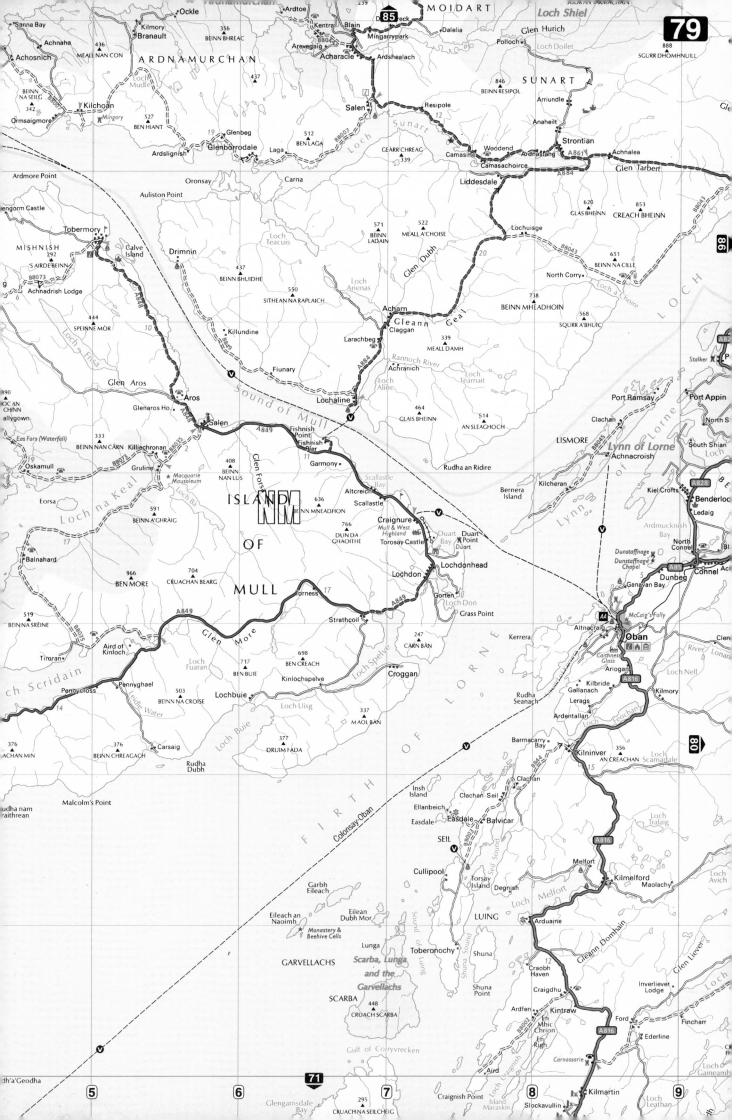

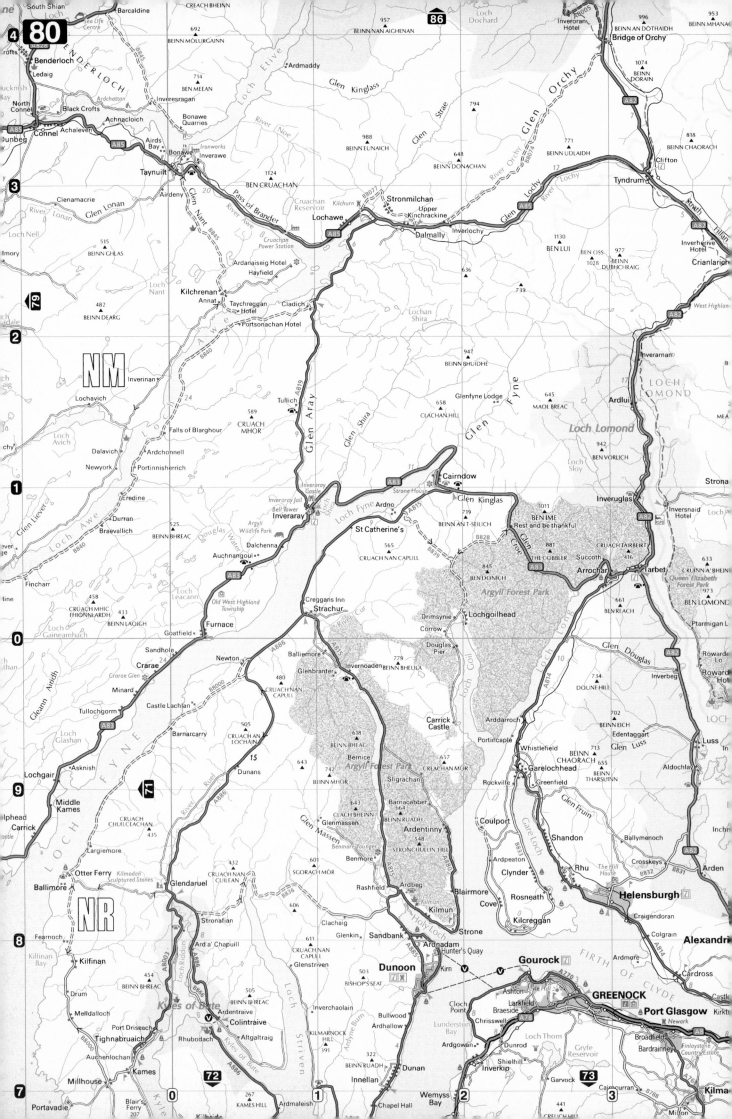

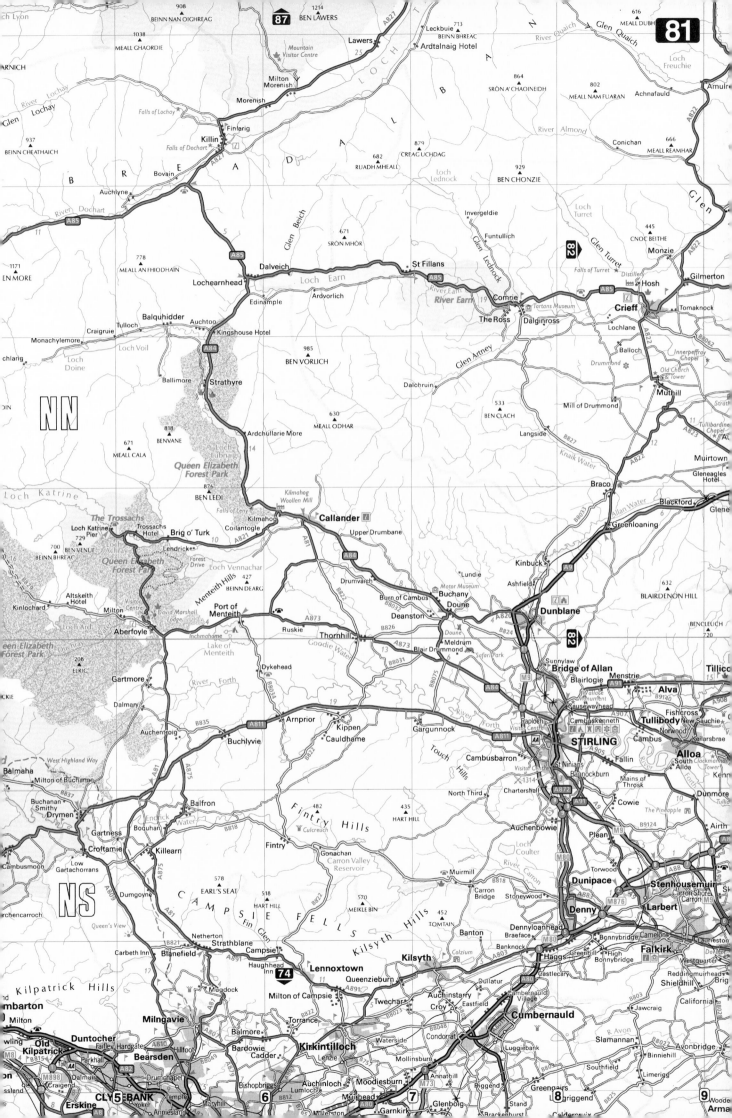

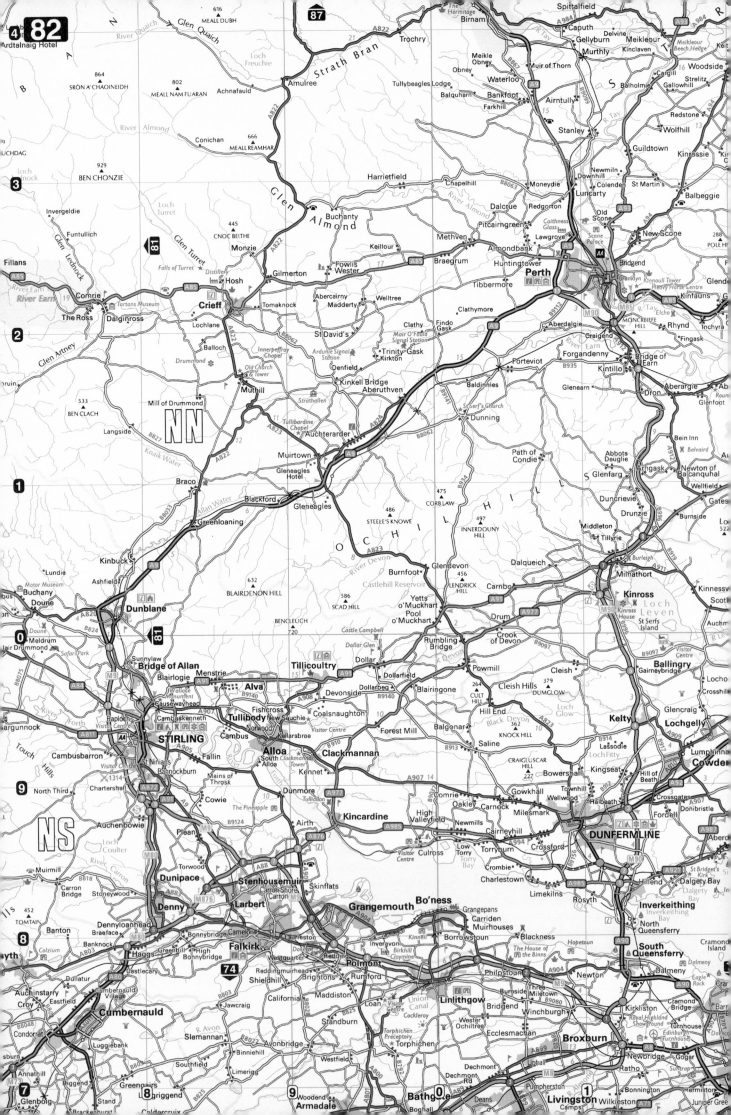

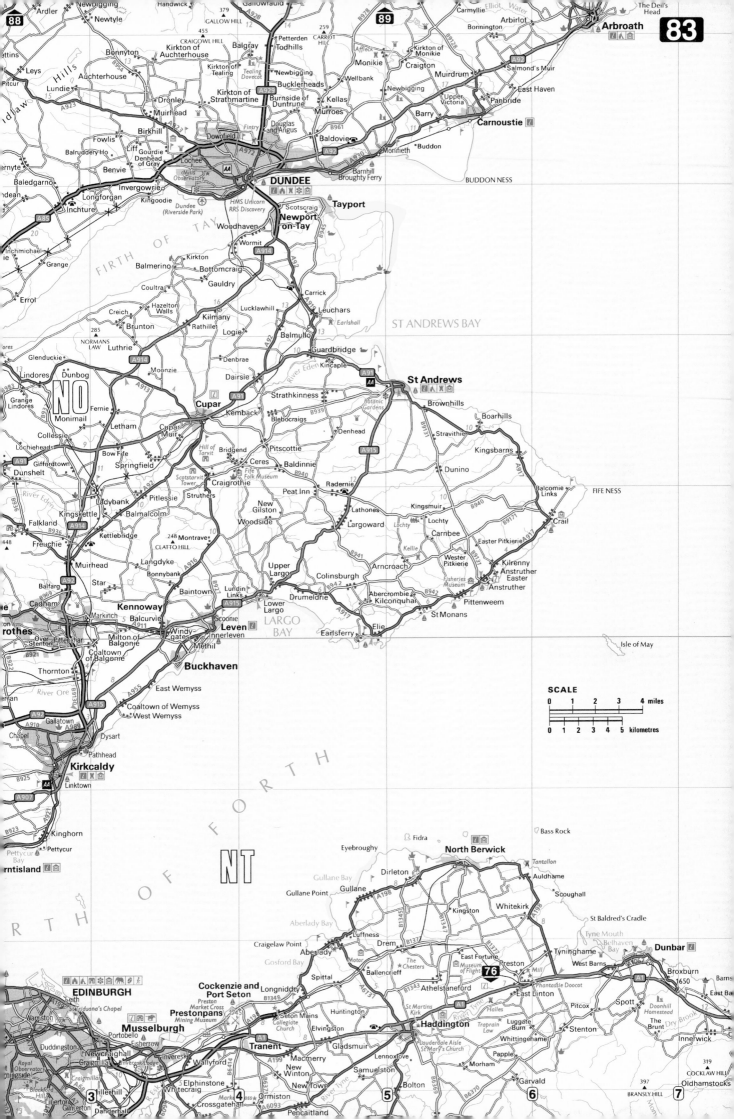

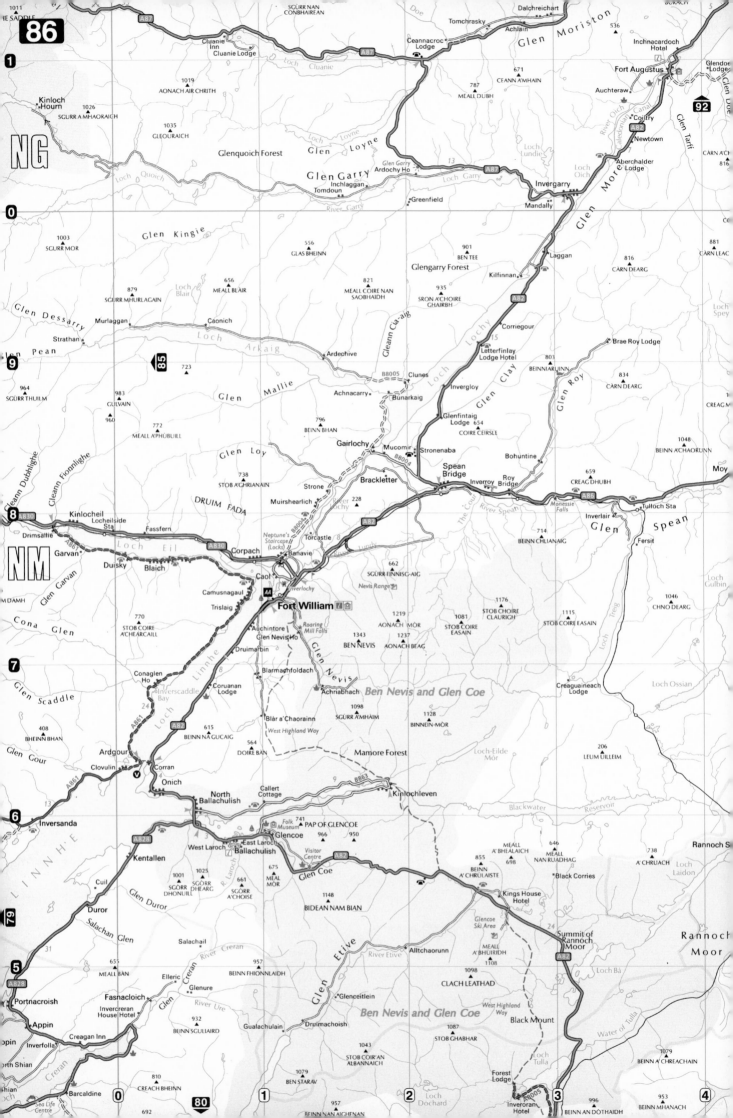

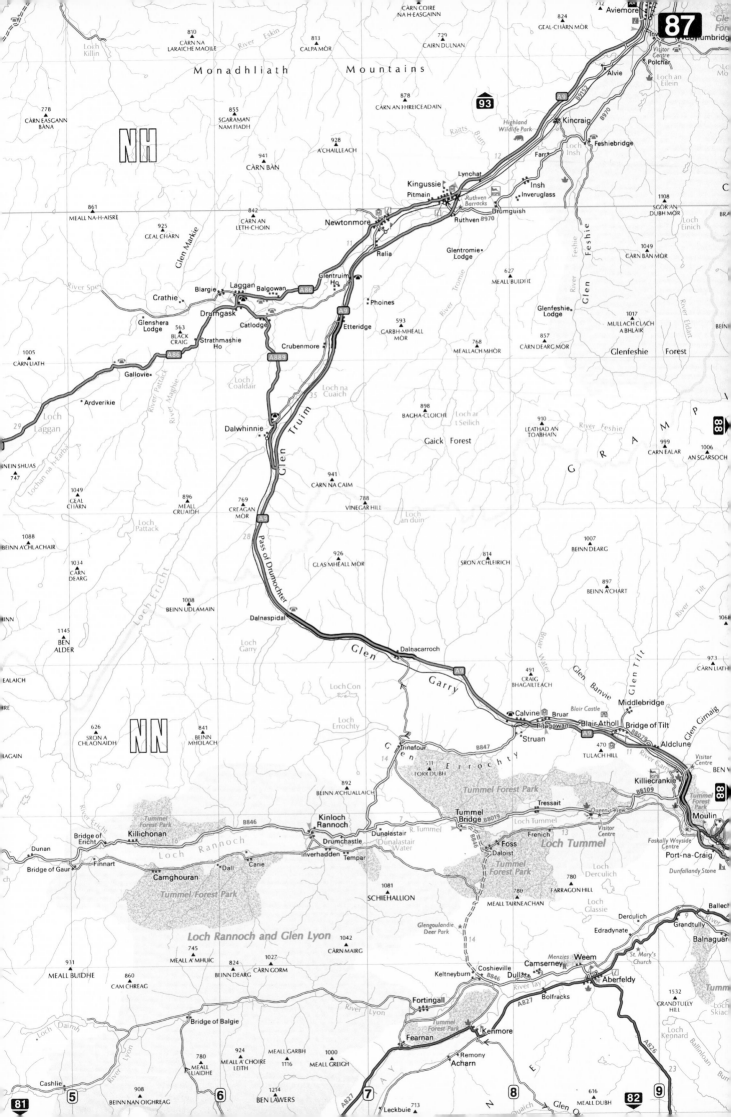

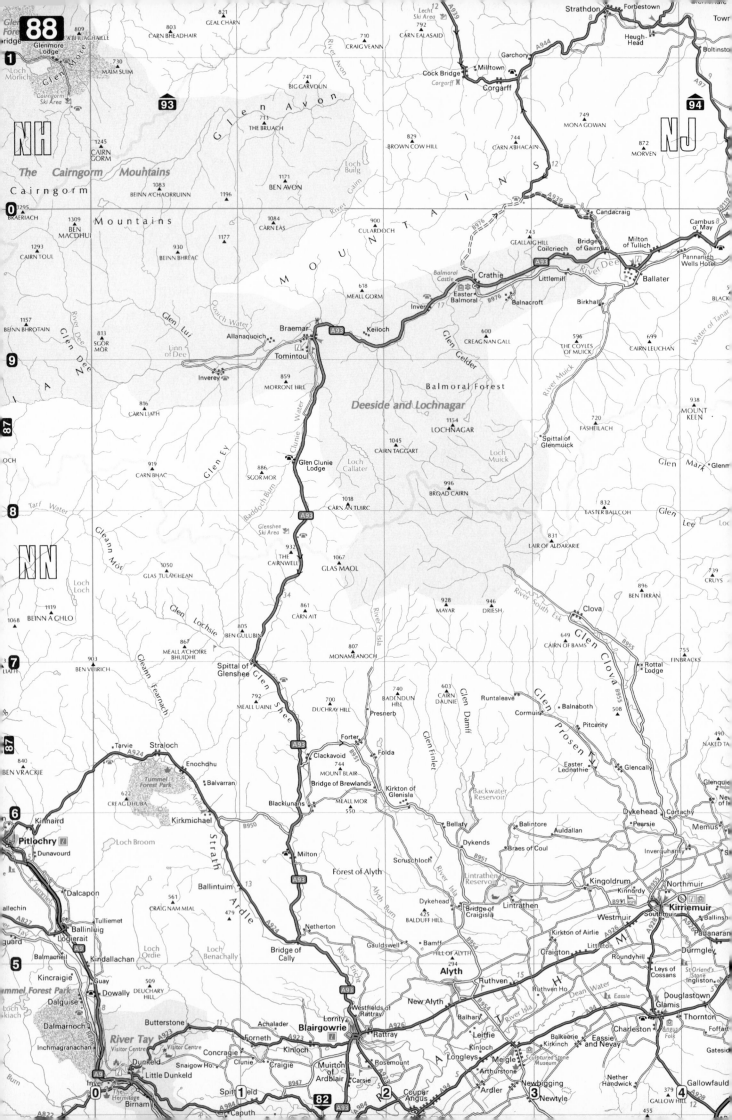

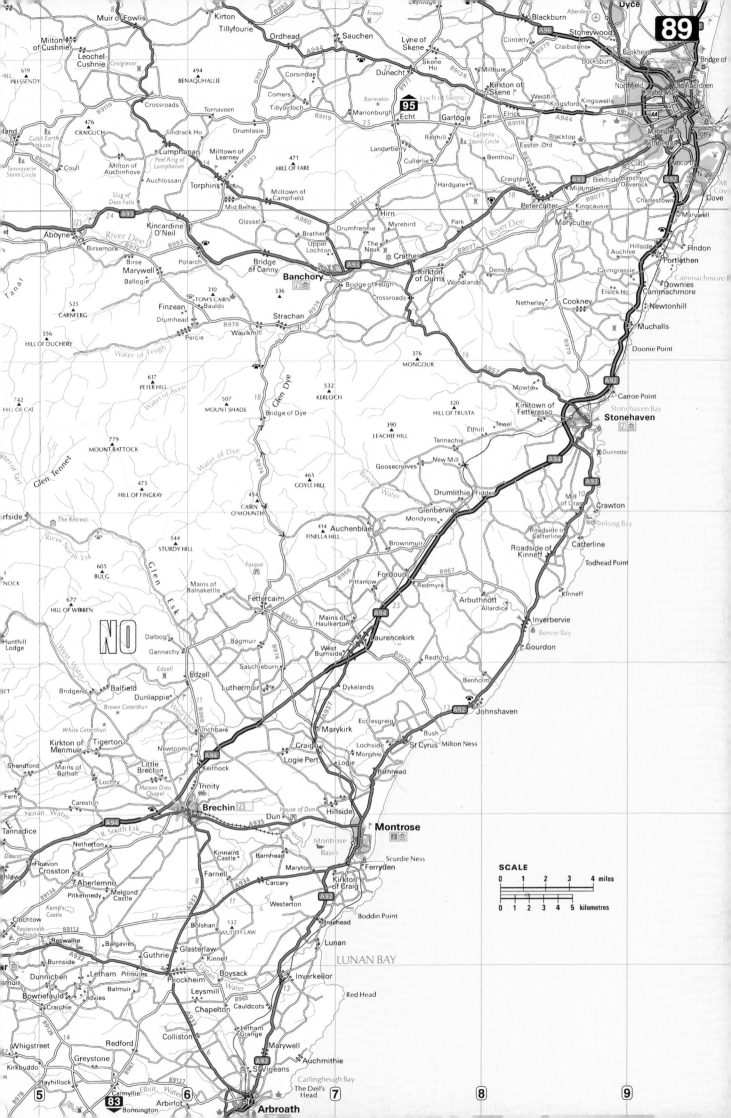

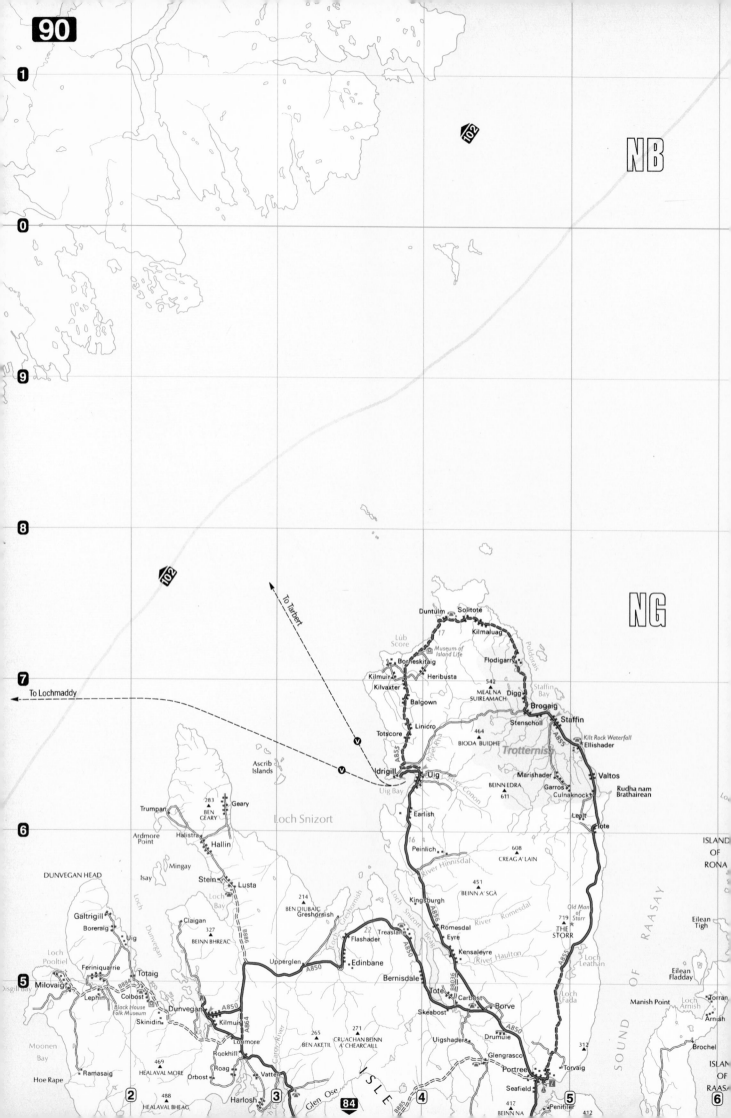

NB

NG

To Tarbert

To Lochmaddy

Duntulm Solitote
Kilmaluag
Lùb
Score   Museum of
Island Life   Flodigarry
Borneskitaig
Kilmuir Heribusta
Kilvaxter 542
Balgown   MEAL NA   Digg
SUIREAMACH   Brogaig
Linicro   Stenscholl Staffin
Totscore 464   Kilt Rock Waterfall
BIODA BUIDHE   Ellishader
Trotternish
Idrigill   Marishader   Valtos
Uig   BEINN EDRA   Garros
611   Culnaknock   Rudha nam
Brathairean
Ascrib
Islands   Earlish   Lealt
Uig Bay   Tote
283   Geary
Trumpan   BEN   16   ISLAND
GEARY   Peinlich   608   OF
Loch Snizort   CREAG A'LAIN   RONA
Ardmore   Halistra
Point   Hallin   451
Mingay   BEINN A'SGA
DUNVEGAN HEAD   Isay   719 Old Man
Stein Lusta   Kingsburgh   of Storr
214   Romesdal   THE STORR
Galtrigill   BEN DIUBAIG   Eyre
Boreraig   Greshornish   22 Treaslane   Kensaleyre
Uig   Claigan   327   Flashader   Eilean
BEINN BHREAC   Upperglen   Edinbane   Tigh
Loch
Pooltiel   Feriniquarrie   Bernisdale   Eilean
Milovaig   Totaig   Tote   Fladday
Colbost   Skeabost   Borve   Manish Point Loch
Lephin   Black House   Carbost   Arnish
Folk Museum   Dunvegan   Drumie   Torran
Skinidin   Kilmuir   271 Uigshader   312   Brochel
Moonen   Longmore   265 CRU'ACHAN BEINN   Glengrasco   ISLAND
Bay   Rockhill   BEN AKETIL A'CHEARCAILL   Portree Torvaig   OF
Ramasaig   469   Roag Vatten   RAASAY
Hoe Rape   HEALAVAL MORE Orbost   Seafield
488   Penifiler
HEALAVAL BHEAG   Harlosh   417
BEINN NA

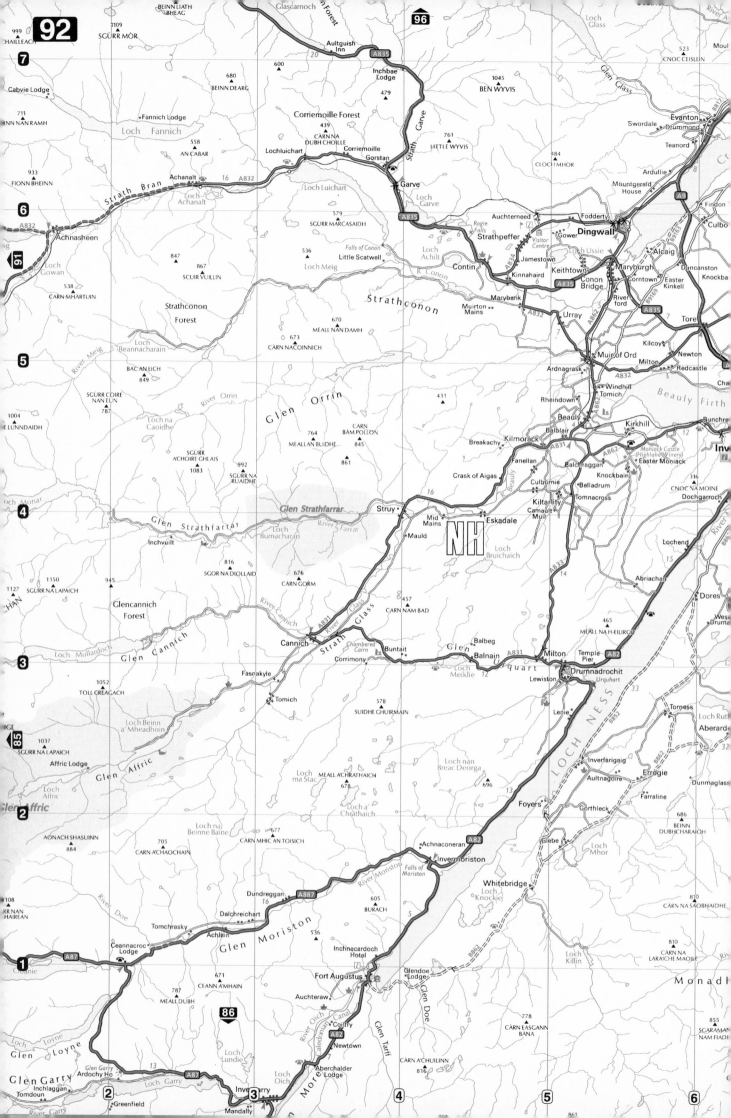

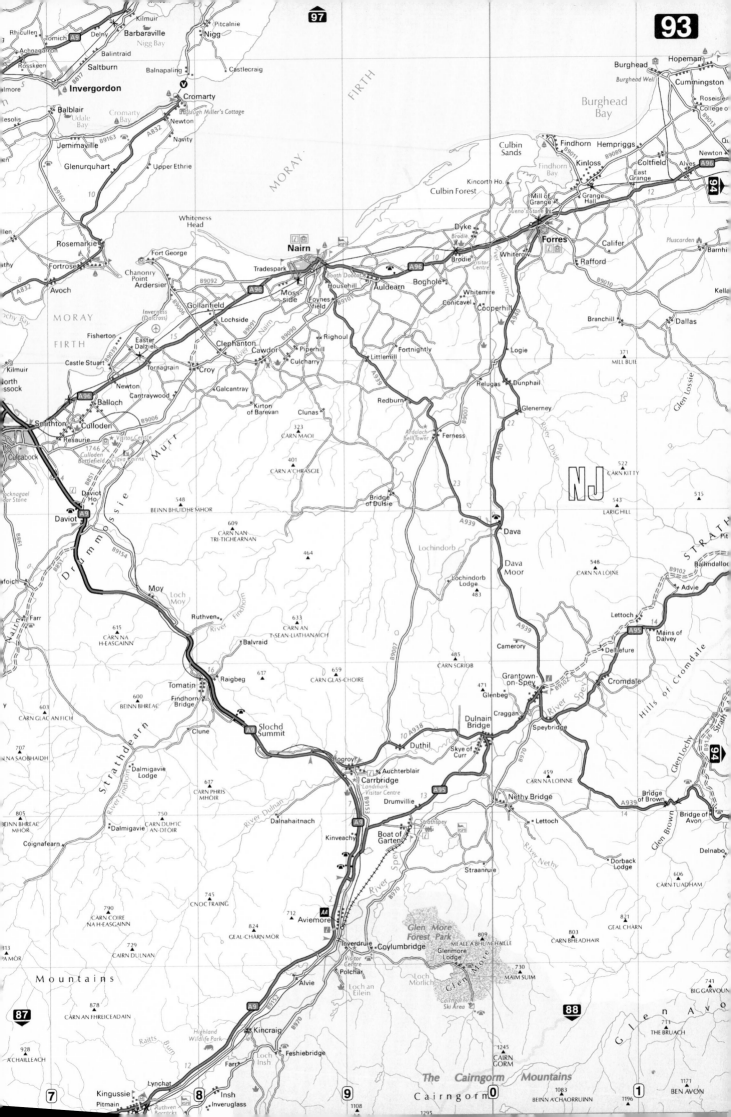

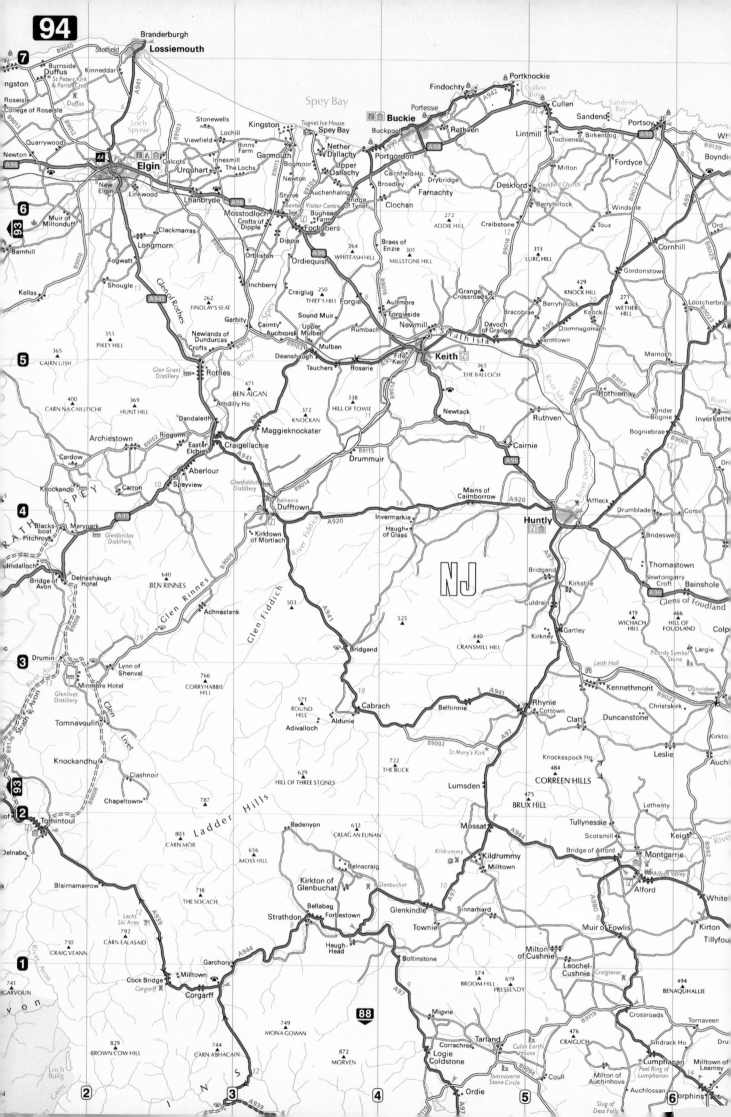

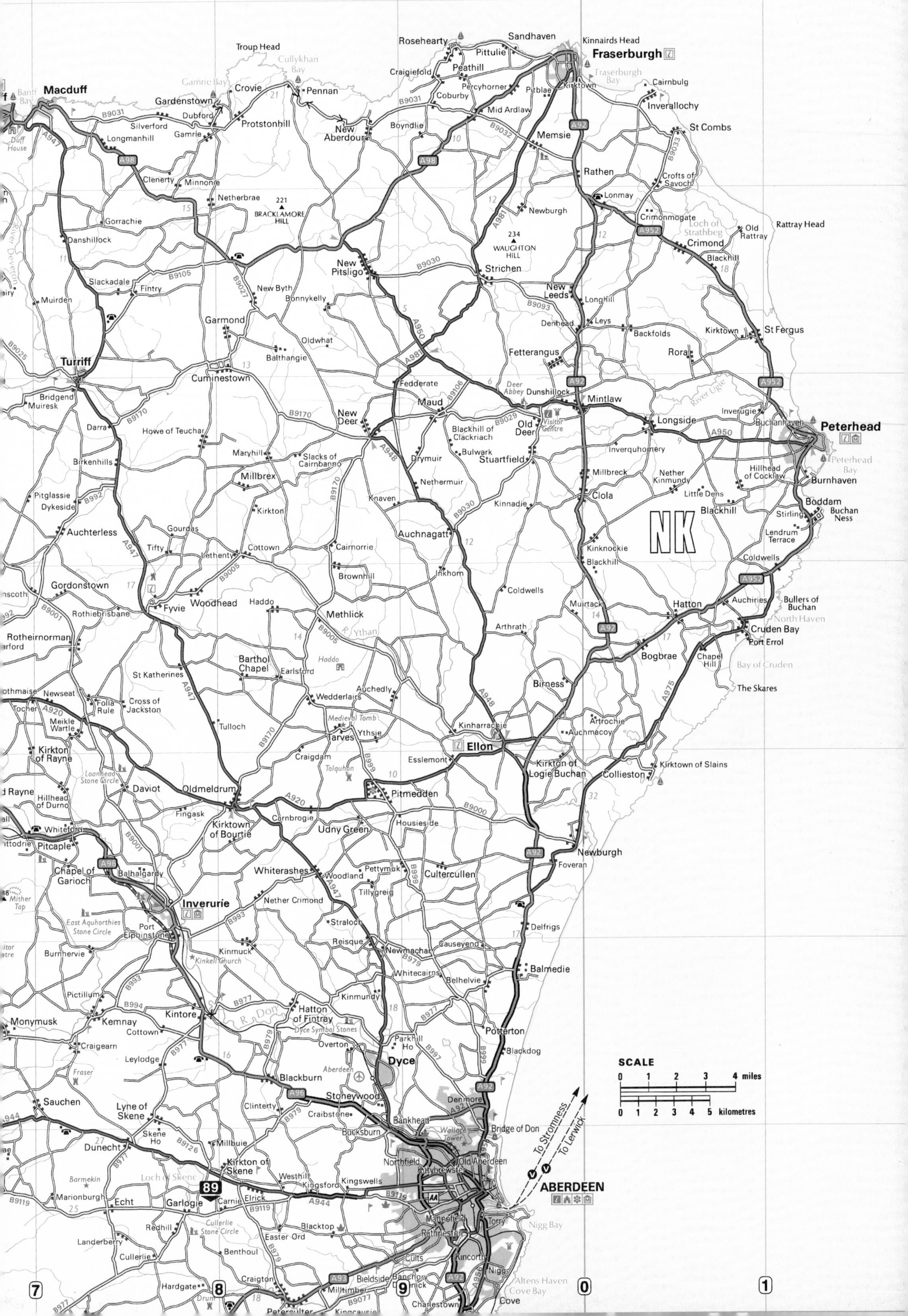

Troup Head
Rosehearty
Sandhaven
Kinnairds Head
Fraserburgh
Pittulie
Peathill
Craigiefold
Percyhorner
Pitblae
Kirktown
Fraserburgh Bay
Cairnbulg
Crovie
Pennan
Coburby
Mid Ardlaw
Inverallochy
Macduff
Gardenstown
Dubford
Protstonhill
New Aberdour
Boyndie
Memsie
St Combs
Banff Bay
Silverford
Longmanhill
Gamrie
Clenerty
Minnonie
Netherbrae
Rathen
Crofts of Savoch
Duff House
Newburgh
Lonmay
Crimonmogate
Loch of Strathbeg
Old Rattray
Rattray Head
Gorrachie
Danshillock
BRACKLAMORE HILL
Strichen
Crimond
Blackhill
Muirden
Slackadale
Fintry
New Pitsligo
New Byth
WAUGHTON HILL
New Leeds
Longhill
Kirktown
St Fergus
Garmond
Bonnykelly
Longhill
Leys
Backfolds
Rora
Turriff
Oldwhat
Balthangie
Feddas
Maud
Deer Abbey
Dunshillock
Mintlaw
Inverugie
Buchanhaven
Peterhead
Cuminestown
Fedderate
Old Deer
Visitor Centre
Longside
Bridgend Muiresk
Darra
New Deer
Blackhill of Clackriach
Bulwark
Stuartfield
Inverquhomery
Nether Kinmundy
Peterhead Bay
Birkenhills
Maryhill
Slacks of Cairnbanno
Nethermuir
Drymuir
Millbreck
Clola
Little Dens
Blackhill
Burnhaven
Pitglassie
Dykeside
Millbrex
Knaven
Kinnadie
Kinknockie
Blackhill
Boddam
Buchan Ness
Auchterless
Gourdas
Kirkton
Cairnorrie
Auchnagatt
Coldwells
Stirling
Lendrum Terrace
Tifty
Lethenty
Cottown
Brownhill
Inkhorn
Coldwells
Muirtack
Coldwells
Auchiries
Bullers of Buchan
Gordonstown
Fyvie
Woodhead
Haddo
Methlick
Arthrath
Hatton
North Haven
Rothiebrisbane
R Ythan
Arthrath
Birness
Bogbrae
Chapel Hill
Cruden Bay
Port Errol
Rotheirnorman
Bartol Chapel
Earlsford
Haddo
Auchedly
Wedderlairs
Birness
Bay of Cruden
The Skares
Newseat
Tocher
Tolla Rule
Cross of Jackston
Tulloch
Medieval Tomb
Kinharrachie
Artrochie
Auchmacoy
Meikle Wartle
Tarves
Ythsie
Ellon
Kirkton of Logie Buchan
Collieston
Kirkton of Rayne
Craigdam
Tolquhon
Esslemont
Kirktown of Slains
Daviot
Oldmeldrum
Carnbrogie
Pitmedden
Housieside
Newburgh
Rayne
Loanhead Stone Circle
Kirkton of Bourtie
Udny Green
Foveran
Hillhead of Durno
Fingask
Whiteford
Pitcaple
Balhalgardy
Whiterashes
Pettymuk
Woodland
Tillygreig
Cultercullen
Chapel of Garioch
Inverurie
Nether Crimond
Delfrigs
Mither Tap
Straloch
East Aquhorthies Stone Circle
Port Elphinstone
Reisque
Newmachar
Causeyend
Burnhervie
Kinmuck
Whitecairns
Balmedie
Pictillum
Kinkell Church
Kinmundy
Belhelvie
Monymusk
Kemnay
Cottown
Kintore
Hatton of Fintray
R Don
Dyce Symbol Stones
Potterton
Craigearn
Leylodge
Overton
Parkhill Ho
Blackdog
Fraser
Blackburn
Dyce
Sauchen
Lyne of Skene
Clinterty
Craibstone
Stoneywood
Denmore
Bridge of Don
To Stromness
To Lerwick
Kirkton of Skene
Westhill
Kingsford
Kingswells
Bankhead
Bucksburn
Wallace Tower
Skene Ho
Millbuie
Northfield
Old Aberdeen
Kittybrewster
Aberdeen
Dunecht
Kirkton of Skene
Echt
Garlogie
Carnie
Elrick
Cullerlie Stone Circle
Blacktop
Easter Ord
Cults
Kincorth
Nigg Bay
Redhill
Cullerlie
Benthoul
Craigton
Peterculter
Bieldside
Banchory
Milltimber
Charlestown
Cove
Altens Haven
Cove Bay

SCALE
0 1 2 3 4 miles
0 1 2 3 4 5 kilometres

NK

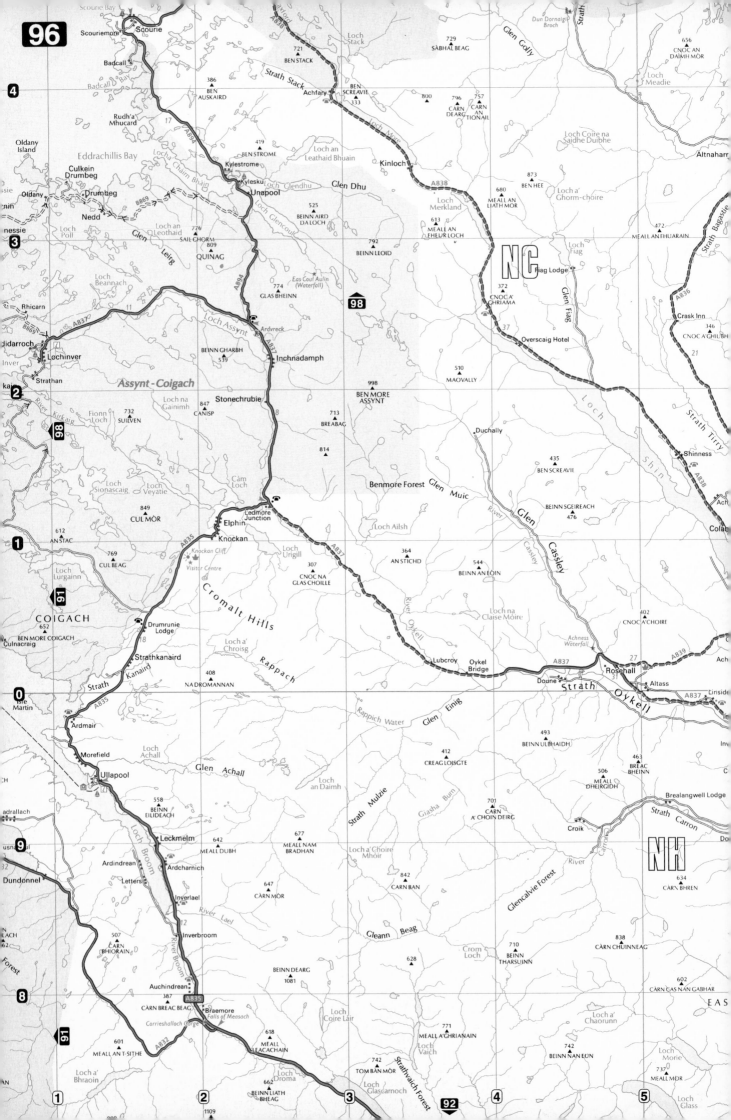

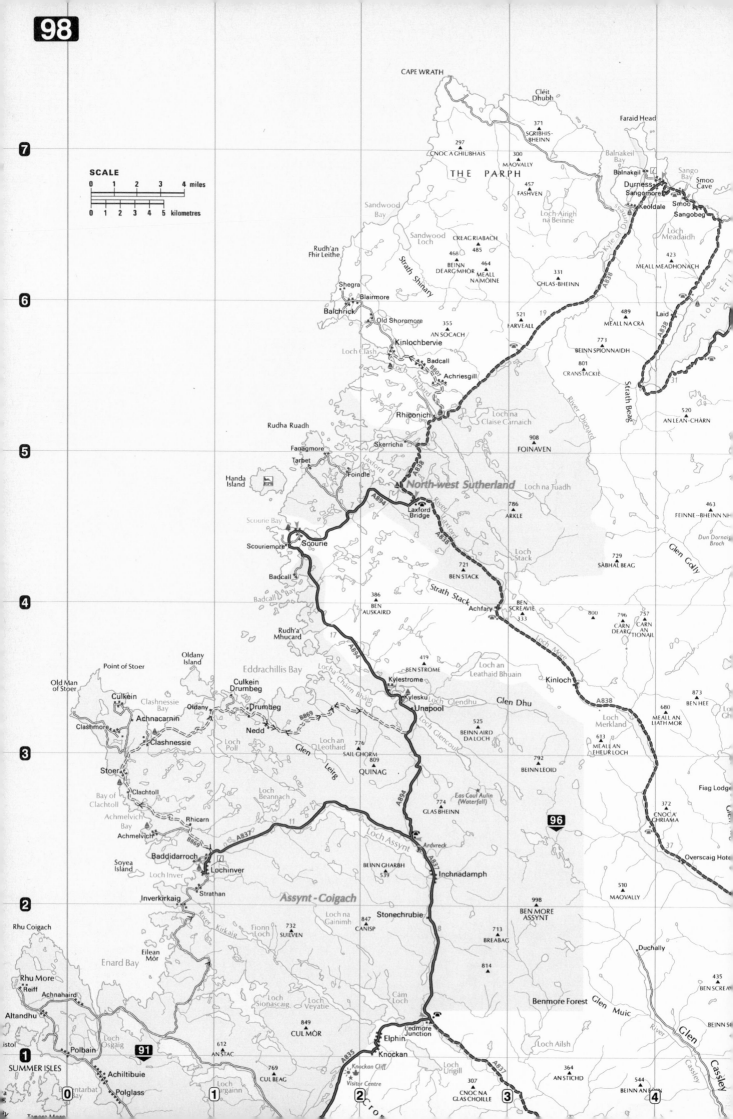

SCALE

0 1 2 3 4 miles

0 1 2 3 4 5 kilometres

CAPE WRATH

Cléit Dhubh

Faraid Head

371 SGRIBHIS-BHEINN

297

Balnakeil Bay

CNOC A GHIUBHAIS

300 MAOVALLY

THE PARPH

Balnakeil

Sango Bay

Durness

Smoo Cave

457 FASHVEN

Sangomore

Smoo

Keoldale

Sangobeg

Sandwood Bay

Loch Airigh na Beinne

Loch Meadaidh

Sandwood Loch

CREAG RIABACH

485

423 MEALL MEADHONACH

Rudh'an Fhir Leithe

468 BEINN DEARG MHOR

464 MEALL NAMÓINE

331 CHLAS-BHEINN

Strath Shinary

Shegra

489 MEALL NA CRÀ

Laid

Blairmore

Balchrick

521 FARVEALL

19

Old Shoremore

773 BEINN SPIONNAIDH

520 AN LEAN-CHÀRN

355 AN SOCACH

Kinlochbervie

801 CRANSTACKIE

Strath Beag

Badcall

Achriesgill

Loch Inchard

Rhiconich

Rudha Ruadh

Loch na Claise Carnaich

908 FOINAVEN

Skerricha

Fanagmore

Tarbet

Foindle

North-west Sutherland

Loch na Tuadh

463 FEINNE--BHEINN NH

Handa Island

Laxford Bridge

786 ARKLE

Dun Dornaig Broch

Scourie Bay

721 BEN STACK

729 SABHAL BEAG

Glen Golly

Scouriemore

Scourie

Loch Stack

Badcall

Strath Stack

386 BEN AUSKAIRD

BEN SCREAVIE

Achfary

333

800

796 CARN DEARG

757 CARN AN TIONAIL

Rudh'a' Mhucard

17

Loch More

Oldany Island

Point of Stoer

Eddrachillis Bay

419 BEN STROME

Loch an Leathaid Bhuain

Kinloch

A838

873 BEN HEE

Old Man of Stoer

Culkein Drumbeg

Locha Chàirn Bhàin

Kylestrome

Kylesku

Unapool

Glen Dhu

680 MEALL AN LIATH MOR

Culkein

Clashnessie Bay

Oldany

Drumbeg

B869

Loch Glendhu

Glen Dhu

Loch Merkland

613 MEALL AN FHEUR LOCH

Achnacarnin

Nedd

525 BEINN AIRD DA LOCH

Clashmore

Clashnessie

Loch Poll

Glen Leirg

776 SAIL GHORM

809 QUINAG

792 BEINN LEOID

372 CNOC A' GHRIAMA

Fiag Lodge

Stoer

Bay of Clachtoll

Clachtoll

Loch Beannach

774 GLAS BHEINN

Eas Coul Aulin (Waterfall)

37

Overscaig Hote

Achmelvich Bay

Rhicarn

11

Achmelvich

B869

A837

A894

BEINN GHARBH 539

Ardvreck

Inchnadamph

Baddidarroch

Lochinver

Soyea Island

Loch Inver

Strathan

998 BEN MORE ASSYNT

510 MAOVALLY

Duchally

Inverkirkaig

Assynt-Coigach

Stonechrubie

713 BREABAG

435 BEN SCREA

Rhu Coigach

River Kirkaig

Fionn Loch

732 SUILVEN

Loch na Gainimh

847 CANISP

814

Benmore Forest

Glen Muic

BEINN S

Enard Bay

Eilean Mòr

Càm Loch

Rhu More

Reiff

Loch Sionascaig

Loch Veyatie

849 CUL MÒR

Ledmore Junction

Loch Ailsh

Glen

Achnahaird

Elphin

A835

River Cassley

istol

Altandhu

612 AN STAC

Knockan

364 AN STICHD

544 BEINN AN EOIN

Polbain

91

769 CUL BEAG

Knockan Cliff

Loch Urigill

307 CNOC NA GLAS CHOILLE

SUMMER ISLES

Visitor Centre

Achiltibuie

Polglass

96

1 **2** **3** **4**

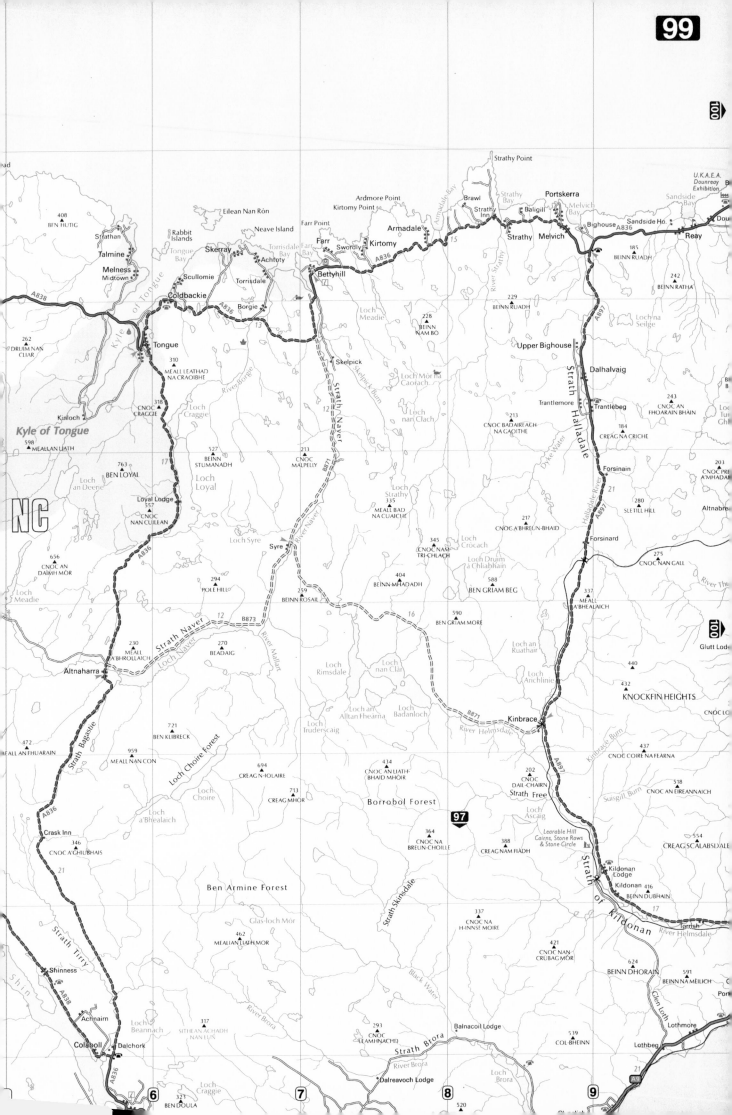

NC

U.K.A.E.A.
Dounreay
Exhibition

Strathy Point

Ardmore Point
Kirtomy Point   Brawl   Strathy   Portskerra
                       Strathy   Bay   Baligill   Melvich
Eilean Nan Ròn   Strathy   Bighouse   Sandside Hó.
                    Farr Point   Inn   A836   Sandside
408   Rabbit   Neave Island   Farr   Armadale   Bay
BEN HUTIG Islands   Torrisdale Farr   15   Strathy   Melvich   Reay   Dou
Strathan   Tongue   Bay   Bay Swordly Kirtomy   Strathy
Talmine   Skerray   A836   185
                   Achtoty   Bettyhill   BEINN RUADH
Melness   Scullomie Torrisdale   242
Midtown   229   BEINN RATHA
Coldbackie   Loch   228   BEINN RUADH
A838   Borgie   Meadie   BEINN
A836   13   NAM BÒ   Upper Bighouse   Loch na
262   Seilge
DRUIM NAN   Tongue   Loch Mór na
CLIAR   Skelpick   Caorach   Trantlemore   Dalhalvaig   B
310   Trantlebeg
MEALL LEATHAD   12   Loch   243   Loc
NA CRAOIBHE   nan Clach   213   CNOC AN Tu
318   Loch   Loch   CNOC BADAIREACH 184 FHOARAIN BHÀIN Gh
CNOC   Craggie   Strathy 335   NA GAOITHE   CREAG NA CRICHE
Kinloch   CRAGGIE   MEALL BAD   203
                                                           NA CUAICHE   Forsinain   CNOC PRI
Kyle of Tongue 598   527   213   21   A'MHADA
MEALLAN LIATH   BEINN   CNOC   280
                               STUMANADH MALPELLY   217   SLE TILL HILL   Altnabre
763   345 Loch   CNOC A'BHREUN-BHAID
BEN LOYAL   Loch   CNOC Cròcach
              Loyal   Loch Syre   NAM
Loch   557   TRI-CHLACH Loch Druim   Forsinard
an Deere   Loyal Lodge   Syre   a Chliabhain   275
           CNOC   404   CNOC NAN GALL
           NAN CUILEAN   BEINN MHADADH BEN GRIAM BEG   337
656   294   259   MEALL   River Th
CNOC AN   POLE HILL   BEINN ROSAIL   590   A'BHEALAICH
DAIMH MÒR   12   BEN GRIAM MORE
Loch   B873   16   100
Meadie   River Mallart   Loch an
           230   270   Ruathair   Glutt Lod
           MEALL   BEADAIG   Loch   Loch
           A'BHROLLAICH   nan Clar   Loch   Arichlinie   440
Altnaharra   Loch   Loch   Badanloch   432
                                          Rimsdale an   KNOCKFIN HEIGHTS
                          721   Alltan Fhearna   B871   CNOC LO
472   BEN KLIBRECK Loch   Kinbrace
MEALL AN FHUARAIN   959   Loch   Truderscaig   River Helmsdale   437
                       MEALL NAN CON Choire   CNOC COIRE NA FEARNA
           Strath   Forest   202
           Bagastie   694   434   CNOC DAIL-CHAIRN   518
                                CREAG N-IOLAIRE CNOC AN LIATH-   Strath Free   CNOC AN EIREANNAICH
                                 713   BHAID MHÓR   Loch
Crask Inn   CREAG MHOR   Borrobol Forest Ascaig   554
346   CREAG SCALABSDALE
CNOC A'GHIUBHAIS   97   Learable Hill
                                                                    Cairns, Stone Rows
21   364   & Stone Circle   Kildonan
                                CNOC NA   Lodge
                                BREUN-CHOILLE   388   Kildonan 416
              Ben Armine Forest   CREAG NAM FIADH   BEINN DUBHAIN
                                                                                      17
Strath Tirry   Glas-loch Mór   462   Strath
                               MEALLAN LIATH MOR   337   of
Shinness   CNOC NA   Kildonan River Helmsdale
                                                H-INNSE MOIRE   Torrish
Shin   A838   421
Achnairn   CNOC NAN   624
                   317   CRUBAG MOR   BEINN DHORAIN 591
Colaboll Dalchork SITHEAN ACHADH   BEINN NA MEILICH Por
              Loch NAN EUN   River Brora   293   Balnacoil Lodge   539
              Beannach   CNOC   COL-BHEINN   Lothmore
Loch   LEAMHNACHD   Glen Loth
Craggie   River Brora   Strath Brora   Lothbeg
323   Dalreavoch Lodge   Loch   21
BEN DOULA 6   520   7   8 Brora   9

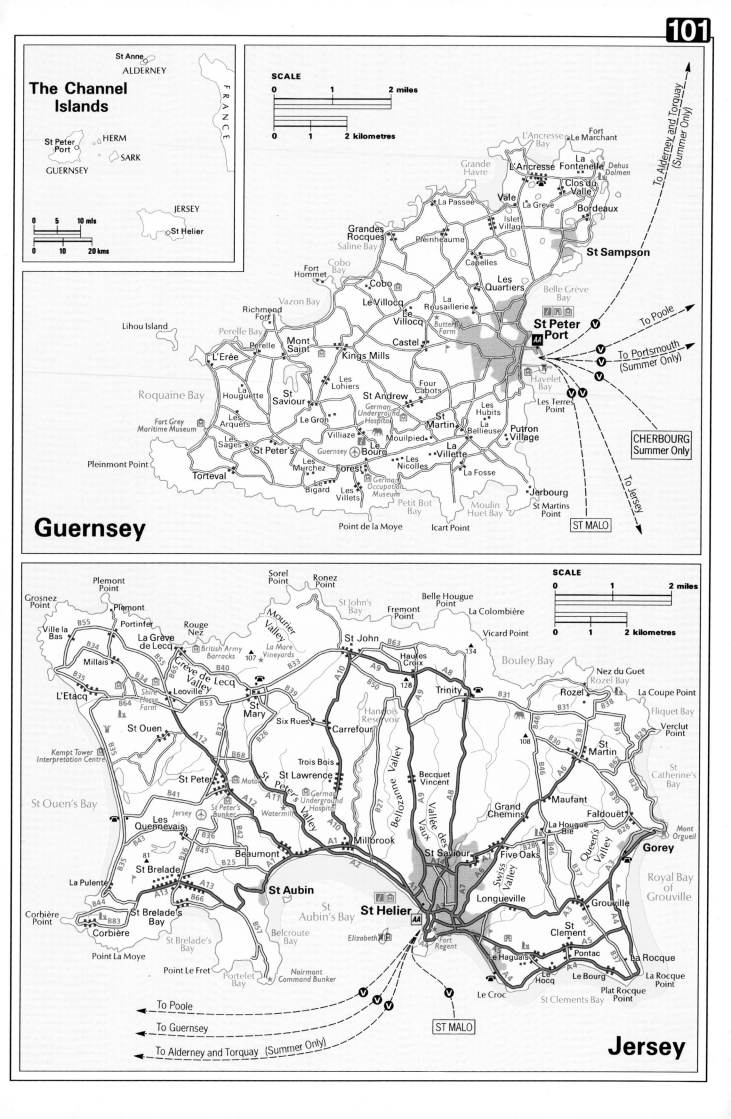

The Channel Islands

St Anne
ALDERNEY

St Peter Port
HERM
SARK
GUERNSEY

JERSEY
St Helier

0   5   10 mls
0   10   20 kms

Guernsey

SCALE
0   1   2 miles
0   1   2 kilometres

To Alderney and Torquay (Summer Only)

L'Ancresse Bay
Fort Le Marchant
La Fontenelle
Dehus Dolmen
Clos du Valle
Grande Havre
L'Ancresse
Vale
La Grève
Bordeaux
La Passee
Islet Village
St Sampson
Grandes Rocques
Pleinheaume
Capelles
Les Quartiers
Saline Bay
Belle Grève Bay
Fort Hommet
Cobo Bay
Cobo
La Rousaillerie
St Peter Port
Vazon Bay
Le Villocq
Le Villocq
Castel
Butterfly Farm
AA
Richmond Fort
Mont Saint
Kings Mills
Havelet Bay
Perelle
Lihou Island
Perelle Bay
L'Erée
Les Lohiers
Four Cabots
Les Terres Point
La Houguette
St Saviour
St Andrew
German Underground Hospital
Les Hubits
To Poole
Roquaine Bay
Le Gron
St Martin
La Bellieuse
To Portsmouth (Summer Only)
Les Arquêts
German Occupation Museum
Villiaze
Moulipied
La Villette
Putron Village
Fort Grey Maritime Museum
Les Sages
St Peter's
Le Bourg
Guernsey
Les Murchez
Forest
Les Nicolles
La Fosse
CHERBOURG Summer Only
Pleinmont Point
Le Bigard
Les Villets
Jerbourg
St Martins Point
To Jersey
Torteval
Petit Bot Bay
Moulin Huet Bay
Point de la Moye
Icart Point
ST MALO

Jersey

SCALE
0   1   2 miles
0   1   2 kilometres

Grosnez Point
Plemont Point
Plemont
Sorel Point
Ronez Point
Belle Hougue Point
Ville la Bas
B55
Portinfer
Mourier Valley
St John's Bay
Fremont Point
La Colombière
Vicard Point
La Grève de Lecq
Rouge Nez
La Mare Vineyards
St John
B63
Bouley Bay
Millais
B34
British Army Barracks
107
B33
Hautes Croix
Nez du Guet
Rozel Bay
B35
Grève de Lecq Valley
Leoville
B40
B39
B50
128
Trinity
B31
Rozel
La Coupe Point
L'Etacq
Shire Horse Farm
B53
St Mary
Six Rues
Hanois Reservoir
B31
Fliquet Bay
B64
B32
B26
Carrefour
108
B46
St Martin
B38
Verclut Point
St Ouen
A12
Trois Bois
B30
B38
Kempt Tower Interpretation Centre
B68
St Lawrence
Bellozanne Valley
Becquet Vincent
Maufant
B46
St Catherine's Bay
B35
St Peter
Motor Museum
German Underground Hospital
Vallée des Vaux
Grand Chemins
La Hougue Bie
Faldouët
St Ouen's Bay
A12
B41
Jersey Airport
St Peter's Bunker
Watermill
A11
A10
Five Oaks
B46
Queen's Valley
B28
Les Quennevais
A1
Millbrook
A9
Swiss Valley
Mont Orgueil
B43
B36
Beaumont
St Saviour
A8
A3
Gorey
B25
A2
A7
Longueville
Grouville
Royal Bay of Grouville
St Brelade
81
B36
B43
St Aubin
St Helier
AA
Grand Chemins
A3
A4
La Pulente
B44
St Aubin's Bay
St Clement
A5
B66
Elizabeth Castle
Fort Regent
Pontac
La Rocque
Corbière Point
B83
St Brelade's Bay
B51
Belcroute Bay
A1
Le Haguais
B37
Corbière
St Brelade's Bay
A44
Le Bourg
La Rocque Point
Point La Moye
Noirmont Command Bunker
Le Hocq
Plat Rocque Point
Point Le Fret
Portelet Bay
Le Croc
St Clements Bay
To Poole
To Guernsey
ST MALO
To Alderney and Torquay (Summer Only)

FRANCE

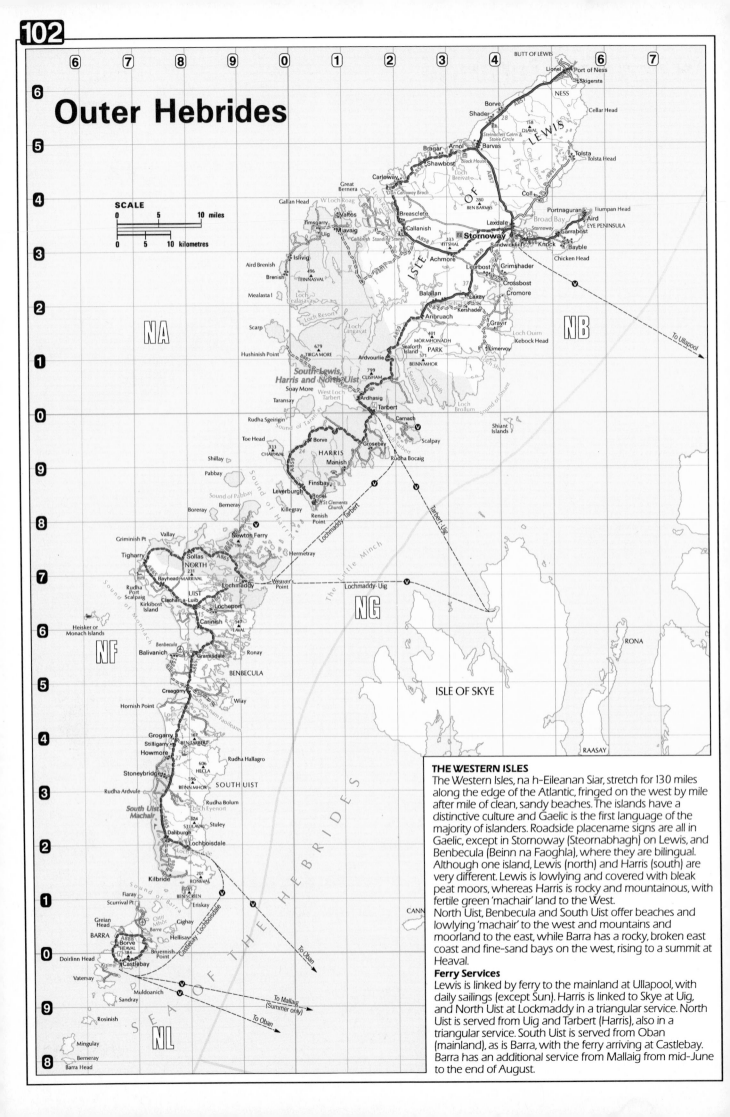

Outer Hebrides

THE WESTERN ISLES

The Western Isles, na h-Eileanan Siar, stretch for 130 miles along the edge of the Atlantic, fringed on the west by mile after mile of clean, sandy beaches. The islands have a distinctive culture and Gaelic is the first language of the majority of islanders. Roadside placename signs are all in Gaelic, except in Stornoway (Steornabhagh) on Lewis, and Benbecula (Beinn na Faoghla), where they are bilingual. Although one island, Lewis (north) and Harris (south) are very different. Lewis is lowlying and covered with bleak peat moors, whereas Harris is rocky and mountainous, with fertile green 'machair' land to the West.

North Uist, Benbecula and South Uist offer beaches and lowlying 'machair' to the west and mountains and moorland to the east, while Barra has a rocky, broken east coast and fine-sand bays on the west, rising to a summit at Heaval.

Ferry Services

Lewis is linked by ferry to the mainland at Ullapool, with daily sailings (except Sun). Harris is linked to Skye at Uig, and North Uist at Lockmaddy in a triangular service. North Uist is served from Uig and Tarbert (Harris), also in a triangular service. South Uist is served from Oban (mainland), as is Barra, with the ferry arriving at Castlebay. Barra has an additional service from Mallaig from mid-June to the end of August.

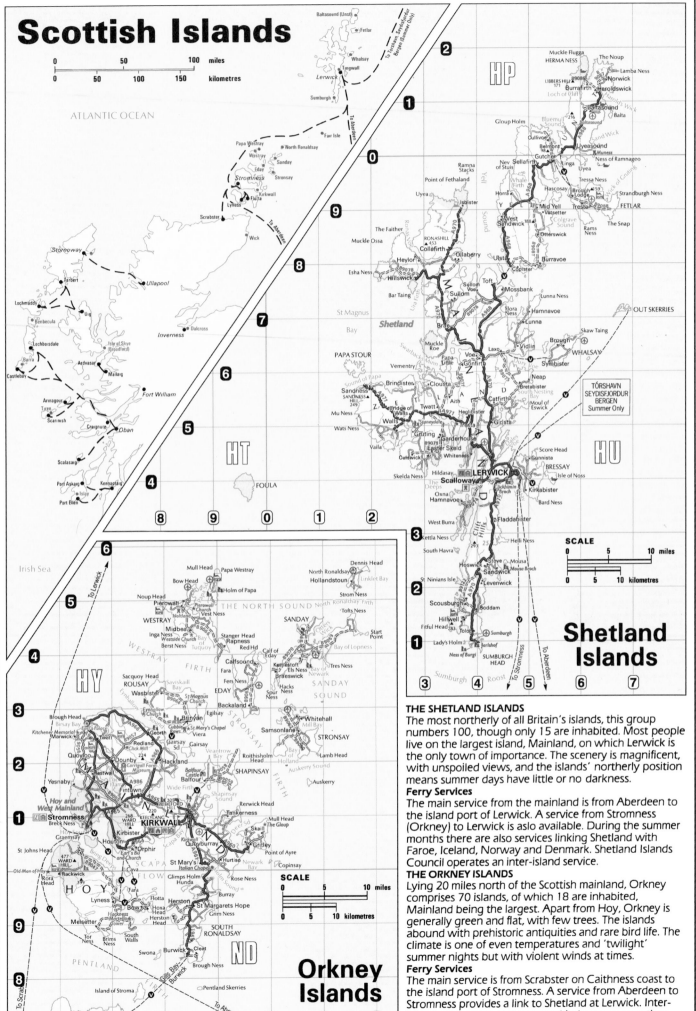

Scottish Islands

Shetland Islands

Orkney Islands

THE SHETLAND ISLANDS
The most northerly of all Britain's islands, this group numbers 100, though only 15 are inhabited. Most people live on the largest island, Mainland, on which Lerwick is the only town of importance. The scenery is magnificent, with unspoiled views, and the islands' northerly position means summer days have little or no darkness.

Ferry Services
The main service from the mainland is from Aberdeen to the island port of Lerwick. A service from Stromness (Orkney) to Lerwick is aslo available. During the summer months there are also services linking Shetland with Faroe, Iceland, Norway and Denmark. Shetland Islands Council operates an inter-island service.

THE ORKNEY ISLANDS
Lying 20 miles north of the Scottish mainland, Orkney comprises 70 islands, of which 18 are inhabited, Mainland being the largest. Apart from Hoy, Orkney is generally green and flat, with few trees. The islands abound with prehistoric antiquities and rare bird life. The climate is one of even temperatures and 'twilight' summer nights but with violent winds at times.

Ferry Services
The main service is from Scrabster on Caithness coast to the island port of Stromness. A service from Aberdeen to Stromness provides a link to Shetland at Lerwick. Inter-island services are also operated (advance reservations necessary).

Ireland

Abbeydorney G2
Abbeyfeale G2
Abbeyleix G4
Adamstown G4
Adare G2
Adrigole H2
Ahascragh F3
Aghoghill D5
Aillhies H1
Anascaul H1
Annalong E5
Annestown H4
Antrim D5
Ardagh G2
Ardara D3
Ardcath F5
Ardee E4
Ardfert G2
Ardfinnan G3
Ardglass E5
Ardgroom H1
Arklow G5
Armagh D4
Armoy C5
Arthurstown H4
Arvagh E4
Ashbourne F4
Ashford F5
Askeaton G2
Athboy E4
Athea G2
Athenry F3
Athleague F3
Athlone F3
Athy F4
Augher D4
Aughnacloy D4
Aughrim G5
Avoca G5

Bailieborough E4
Balbriggan F5
Balla E2
Ballacolla G4
Ballaghaderreen E3
Ballina G3
Ballina E2
Ballinafad E3
Ballinagh E4
Ballinakill G4
Ballinalee E3
Ballinamallard D4
Ballinamore F3
Ballinascarty H2
Ballinasloe F3
Ballindine E2
Ballineen H2
Ballingarry G3
Ballingarry G2
Ballingeary H2
(Beal Atha an Ghaorfthaidh)
Ballinhassig H3
Ballinlough E3
Ballinrobe E2
Ballinspittle H2
Ballintober E3
Ballintra D3
Ballivor F4
Ballon G4
Ballybaun F3
Ballybay E4
Ballybofey D3
Ballybunion G2
Ballycanew G5
Ballycarry D5
Ballycastle D2
Ballycastle C5
Ballyclare D5
Ballyconnely F1
Ballycotton H3
Ballycumber F3
Ballydehob J2
Ballydesmond H2
Ballyduff H3
Ballyduff G2
Ballyfarnan E3
Ballygalley D5
Ballygar F3
Ballygawley D4
Ballygowan D5
Ballyhaise E4
Ballyhale H3
Ballyhaunis E3
Ballyhean E2
Ballyheige G1
Ballyjamesduff E4
Ballykeeran F3
Ballylanders G3
Ballylongford G2
Ballylooby G3
Ballylynan G4
Ballymahon F3
Ballymakeery H2
Ballymaloe H3
Ballymena D5
Ballymoe E3
Ballymoney C4
Ballymore F3
Ballymore Eustace F4
Ballymote E3
Ballynahinch D5
Ballynure D5

Ballyragget G4
Ballyroan G4
Ballyronan D4
Ballysadare E3
Ballyshannon D3
Ballyvaughan F2
Ballywalter D5
Balrothery F5
Baltimore J2
Baltinglass G4
Banagher F3
Banbridge D5
Bandon H2
Bangor D5
Bangor Erris E2
Bansha G3
Banteer H2
Bantry H2
Barryporeen H3
Beaufort H2
Belcoo D3
Belfast D5
Belgooly H3
Bellaghy D4
Belleek D3
Belmullet E2
(Beal an Mhuirhead)
Belturbet E4
Benburb D4
Bennettsbridge G4
Beragh D4
Birr F3
Blacklion D3
Blackwater G5
Blarney H3
Blessington F4
Boherbue H2
Borris G4
Borris-in-Ossory G3
Borrisokane F3
Borrisoleigh G3
Boyle E3
Bracknagh F4
Bray F5
Bridgetown H4
Brittas F4
Broadford G3
Broadford G2
Broughshane D5
Bruff G3
Bruree G3
Bunclody G4
Buncrana C4
Bundoran D3
Bunnahowen D2
Bunnyconnellan E2
Bushmills C4
Butler's Bridge E4
Buttevant H2

Cadamstown F3
Caherconlish G3
Caherdaniel H1
Cahir G3
Cahirciveen H1
Caledon D4
Callan G4
Caltra F3
Camolin G4
Camp G1
Cappagh White G3
Cappamore G3
Cappoquin H3
Carlanstown E4
Calingford E5
Carlow G4
Camdonagh C4
Carnew G4
Carnlough C5
Carracastle E3
Carrick D3
(An Charraig)
Carrickfergus D5
Carrickmacross E4
Carrickmore D4
Carrick-on-Shannon E3
Carrick -on-Suir G4
Carrigahorig F3
Carrigaline H3
Carrigallen E3
Carriganimmy H2
Carrigans C4
Carrigtohill H3
Carrowkeel C4
Carryduff D5
Cashel G3
Castlebar E2
Castlebellingham E5
Castleblayney E4
Castlebridge G4
Castlecomer G4
Castle Cove H1
Castlederg D4
Castledermot G4
Castleisland G2
Castlemaine H2
Castlemartyr H3
Castleplunkett E3
Castlepollard E4
Castlerea E3
Castlerock C4
Castleshane E4
Castletown H4
Castletownbere H1

Castletownroche H3
Castletownshend J2
Castlewellan E5
Causeway G2
Cavan E4
Ceanannus Mor (Kells) E4
Celbridge F4
Charlestown E3
Clady D4
Clane F4
Clara F3
Clarecastle G2
Claremorris E2
Clarinbridge F2
Clashmore H3
Claudy C4
Cliffony D3
Clogan F3
Clogh G4
Clogheen H3
Clogher D4
Clohamon G4
Clonakilty H2
Clonard F4
Clonaslee F4
Clonbulloge F4
Clonbur (An Fhairche) E2
Clondalkin F4
Clones E4
Clonmany C4
Clonmel G3
Clonmellon E4
Clonmore G3
Clonony F3
Clonoulty G3
Clonroche G4
Clontibret E4
Cloonbannin H2
Cloondara E3
Cloonkeen H2
Cloonlara G3
Clough D5
Cloughjordan F3
Cloyne H3
Coagh D4
Coalisland D4
Cobh H3
Coleraine C4
Collinstown E4
Collon G4
Collooney E3
Comber D5
Conna H3
Cookstown D4
Coole E4
Cooraclare G2
Cootehill E4
Cork H3
Cork Airport H3
Cornamona F2
Corofin F2
Courtmacsherry H2
Courtown Harbour G5
Craigavon D5
Craughwell F3
Creggs F3
Cresslough C3
Croagh G2
Crolly (Croithli) C3
Crookedwood E4
Crookhaven J1
Crookstown H2
Croom G2
Crossakeel E4
Cross Barry H2
Crosshaven H3
Crossmaglen E4
Crossmolina E2
Crumlin D5
Crusheen F2
Culdaff C4
(An Charraig)
Culleybackey D5
Curracloe G4
Curraghboy F3
Curry H3

Daingean F4
Delvin E4
Derrygonnelly D3
Derrylin E4
Dervock C4
Dingle (An Daingean) H1
Doagh D5
Donaghadee D5
Donaghmore E4
Donegal D3
Doneraile H3
Doonbeg G2
Douglad H3
Downpatrick D5
Dowra E3
Draperstown D4
Drimoleague H2
Dripsey H2
Drogheda E5
Droichead Nua F4
(Newbridge)
Dromahair D3
Dromcolliher H2
Dromore D4

Dromore D4
Dromore West D2
Drum E4
Drumconrath E4
Drumkeeran E3
Drumlish E3
Drumod E3
Drumquin D4
Drumshanbo E3
Drumsna E3
Duagh G2
Dublin F5
Duleek E4
Dunboyne F4
Duncormick H4
Dundalk E5
Dunderrow H2
Dundrum E5
Dunfanaghy C3
Dungannon D4
Dungarvan H3
Dungarvan G4
Dungiven C4
Dungloe C3
Dungourney H3
Dunkineely D3
Dun Laoghaire F5
Dunlavin F4
Dunleer E4
Dunloy C5
Dunmanway H2
Dunmore E3
Dunmore East H4
Dunmurry D5
Dunshauglin F4
Durrow G4
Durrus H2

Eaky D2
Edenderry F4
Edgeworthstown E3
Eglinton C4
Elphin E3
Emyvale D4
Enfield F4
Ennis G2
Enniscorthy G4
Enniscrone D2
Enniskean H2
Enniskillen D4
Ennistymon F2
Eyrecourt F3

Farnaght E3
Farranfore H2
Feakle F3
Fenagh E3
Fermoy H3
Ferns G4
Fethard H4
Fethard G4
Finnea E4
Fintona D4
Fivemiletown D4
Fontstown F4
Foulksmills G4
Foxford E2
Foynes G2
Freemount G2
Frenchpark E3
Freshford G4
Fuerty E3

Galbally G3
Galway F2
Garrison D3
Garvagh C4
Geashill F4
Gilford D5
Glandore J2
Glanmire H3
Glanworth H3
Glaslough D4
Glassan F3
Glenamaddy E3
Glenarm D5
Glenavy D5
Glenbeigh H1
Glencolumbkille D3
(Gleann Cholm Cille)
Glendalough F5
Glenealy G5
Glenfarne D3
Glengarriff H2
Glenmore G4
Glenties D3
Glenville H3
Glin G2
Glinsk F2
(Glinsce)
Golden G3
Goleen J1
Goresbridge G4
Gorey G5

Gort F2
Gortin D4
Gowran G4
Graiguenamanagh G4
Graliagh G3
Granard E4
Grange D3
Greencastle E5
Greyabbey D5
Greystones F5
Gulladuff D4

Hacketstown G4
Headford F2
Herbertstown G3
Hillsborough D5
Hilltown E5
Hospital G3
Holycross G3
Holywood D5
Howth F5

Inch H1
Inchigeelagh H2
Inishannon H2

Johnstown G3

Kanturk H2
Keadue E3
Keady E4
Keel E1
Keenagh E3
Kells D5
Kenmare H2
Kesh D3
Kilbeggan F4
Kilberry E4
Kilbrittain H2
Kilcar D3
(Cill Charthaigh)
Kilcock F4
Kilcolgan F2
Kilconnell F3
Kilconnell F3
Kilcoole F5
Kilcormac F3
Kilcullen F4
Kilcurry F4
Kildare F4
Kildavin G4
Kildorrery H3
Kildress D4
Kilfenora F2
Kilfinnane G3
Kilgarvan H2
Kilkee G2
Kilkeel E5
Kilkelly E3
Kilkenny G4
Kilkieran F2
(Cill Ciarain)
Kilkinlea G2
Kill H4
Killadysert G2
Killala D2
Killaloe D2
Killarney H2
Killashandra E4
Killashee G3
Killeagh H3
Killeigh F4
Killenaule G3
Killimer G2
Killimor F3
Killiney F5
Killinick H4
Killorglin H1
Killough E5
Killucan F4
Killybegs D3
Killyleagh D5
Kilmacanoge F5
Kilmacrenan C3
Kilmacthomas H4
Kilmaganny G4
Kilmaine E2
Kilmallock G3
Kilmanagh G4
Kilmanahan G3
Kilmeaden H4
Kilmeage F4
Kilmeedy G2
Kilmichael H2
Kilmore Quay H4
Kilnaleck E4
Kilrea C4
Kilrush G2
Kilsheelan G3
Kiltealy G4
Kiltegan G4
Kiltimagh E2
Kiltoom F3
Kingscourt E4

Kinlough D3
Kinnegad F4
Kinnitty F3
Kinsale H3
Kinvarra F2
Kircubbin D5
Knock G2
Knockcroghery E3
Knocklofty G3
Knockmahon H4
Knocktopher G4

Lahinch G2
Lanesborough E3
Laragh F5
Lauragh H1
Laurencetown F3
Leap G2
Leenene E2
Leighlinbridge G4
Leitrim E3
Leixlip F4
Lémybrien H3
Letterfrack E2
Letterkenny C3
Lifford D4
Limavady C4
Limerick G3
Lisbellaw D4
Lisburn D5
Liscarroll G2
Lisdoonvarna F2
Lismore H3
Lisnaskea D4
Lisryan E4
Listowel G2
Loghill G2
Londonderry C4
Longford E3
Loughbrickland D5
Loughgall D4
Loughglinn E3
Loughrea F3
Louisburgh E2
Lucan F4
Lurgan D5
Lusk F5

Macroom H2
Maghera E5
Maghera D4
Magherafelt D4
Maguiresbridge D4
Malahide F5
Malin C4
Malin More D3
Mallow H2
Manorhamilton D3
Markethill D4
Maynooth F4
Maze D5
Middletown D4
Midleton H3
Milford C4
Millstreet H2
Milltown H2
Milltown Malbay G2
Mitchelstown H3
Moate F3
Mohill E3
Molls Gap H2
Monaghan E4
Monasterevin F4
Moneygall G3
Moneymore D4
Monivea F3
Mooncoin H4
Moorfields D5
Mount Bellew F3
Mount Charles D3
Mountmellick F4
Mountrath F4
Mountshannon F3
Mourne Abbey H3
Moville C4
Moy D4
Moylett E4
Moynalty E4
Moyvore F3
Muckross H2
Muff C4
Muine Bheag G4
Mullabohy H4
Mullagh F4
Mullinavat G4
Mullingar F4
Myshall G4

Naas F4
Nad H2
Naul F5
Navan E4
Neale E2
Nenagh G3

Newbliss E4
Newcastle E5
Newcastle West G2
Newinn G3
Newmarket F2
Newmarket-on-Fergus G2
Newport E3
Newport E2
New Ross G4
Newry E5
Newtown G4
Newtownabbey D5
Newtownards D5
Newtown Butler E4
Newtown Forbes E3
Newtownhamilton E4
Newtown Mount Kennedy F5
Newtownstewart D4
Nobber E4

Oilgate G4
Oldcastle E4
Omagh D4
Omeath E5
Oola G3
Oranmore F2
Oughterard F2
Ovens H2

Pallasgreen G3
Parknasilla H1
Partry E2
Passage East H4
Passage West H3
Patrickswell G3
Paulstown G4
Pettigo D3
Plumbridge D4
Pomeroy D4
Portadown D4
Portaferry D5
Portarlington F4
Portavogie D5
Portglenone D5
Port Laoise F4
Portmarnock F5
Portrane F5
Portroe G3
Portrush C4
Portstewart C4
Portumna F3
Poyntzpass D5

Raharney F4
Randalstown D5
Rasharkin C4
Rathangen F4
Rathcoole F4
Rathcormack H3
Rathdowney G3
Rathdrum G5
Rathfriland E5
Rathkeale G2
Rath Luric G2
(Charleville)
Rathmelton C4
Rathmolyon F4
Rathmore H2
Rathmullan C4
Rathnew F5
Rathowen E4
Rathvilly G4
Ratoath F4
Ray C4
Ring H3
(An Rinn)
Ringaskiddy H3
Riverstown F3
Rockcorry E4
Roosky E3
Rosapenna C3
Rosebercon G4
Roscommon E3
Roscrea F3
Ross Carbery J2
Rosscor D3
Rosses Point D3
Rosslare Harbour H4
Rosslea E4
Rostrevor E5
Roundstone F2
Roundwood F5
Rush F5

St Johnstown C4
Saintfield D5
Sallins F4
Scarriff G3
Scartaglen H2
Scarva D5
Schull J2
Scramoge E3
Scribbagh D3
Seskinore D4
Shanagolden G2
Shannon Airport G2
Shannonbridge F3
Shercock E4
Shillelagh G4
Shinrone F3
Shrule F2
Silvermines G3
Sixmilebridge G2
Skerries F5
Skibbereen J2
Slane E4
Sligo D3
Smithborough E4
Sneem H1
Spiddal F2
(An Spideal)
Sporthouse Cross Roads H4
Stewartstown D4
Stonyford G4
Strabane D4
Stradbally F4
Stradone E4
Strandhill D3
Strangford D5
Stranorlar D3
Stratford F4
Strokestown E3
Summerhill F4
Swanlinbar E3
Swatragh D4
Swinford E3
Swords F5

Taghmon G4
Tagoat H4
Tahilla H1
Tallaght F5
Tallow H3
Tallowbridge H3
Tandragee D5
Tang F3
Tarbert G2
Templemore G3
Templepatrick D5
Templetouhy G3
Termonfeckin E5
Thomas Street F3
Thomastown G4
Thurles G3

Timahoe G4
Timoleague H2
Tinahely G4
Tipperary G3
Tobercurry E3
Tobermore D4
Togher F3
Toomyvara G3
Toormore J1
Tralee G2
Tramore H4
Trim F4
Tuam F2
Tuamgraney G3
Tulla G2
Tullamore F4
Tullow G4
Tulsk E3
Turlough E2
Tyholland D4
Tyrrellspass F4

Urlingford G3

Virginia E4

Waddington D4
Warrenpoint E5
Waterford H4
Watergrasshill H3
Waterville H1
Westport E2
Wexford G4
Whitegate H3
Whitehead D5
Wicklow G5
Woodenbridge G4
Woodford F3

Youghal H3

C

D

E

Aran Island

Gwe

Rossan Point
Glencolumbkille (Gleann Chol Cille)
Malin More
Glencolumbkille Folk Museum
1972
Carrick (An Cr)
SLIEVE LEAGUE
Kilcar (Cill Charthaigh)

St John's P

Inishmurray

Donegal

Grange
Lissadell House
Rosses Point
Sligo Bay

Erris Head
Broad Haven
Downpatrick Head
Ballycastle
Killala
Easky
Dromore West
Strandhill

Belmullet (Béal an Mhuirhead)
Burnahowen
Carrowmore Lough
Killala Bay
Enniscrone

Inishkea
Bangor Erris
Bunnyconnellan

Duvillaun More
Blacksod Bay
Crossmolina
Ballina

Achill Head
SLIEVE MORE
Keel
2204
2369
NEPHIN 2646
Connaught Regional Airport
Tobercurry
Curry
Colooney

Achill Island
Lough Feeagh
Foxford
Charlestown
Carracastle

Newport
Lough Conn
Lough Cullin
Clew Bay
Swinford
Turlough
Kilkelly
Kiltimagh
Ballaghad

Clare
Westport
Castlebar
Ballyhean
Ballyhean
Frenchpark

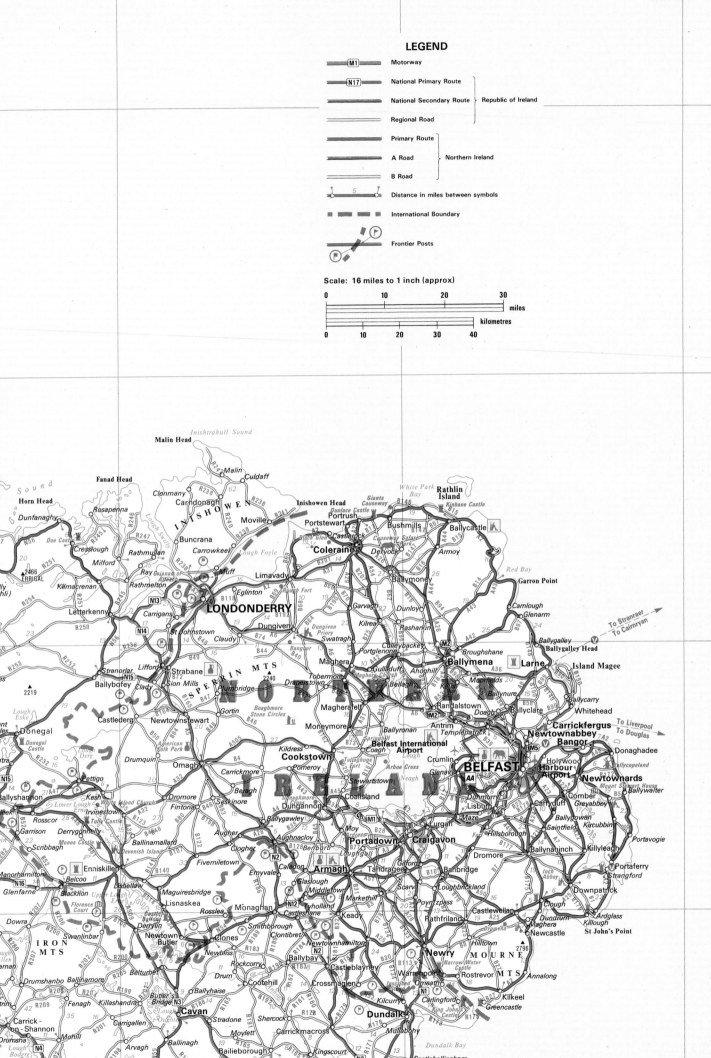

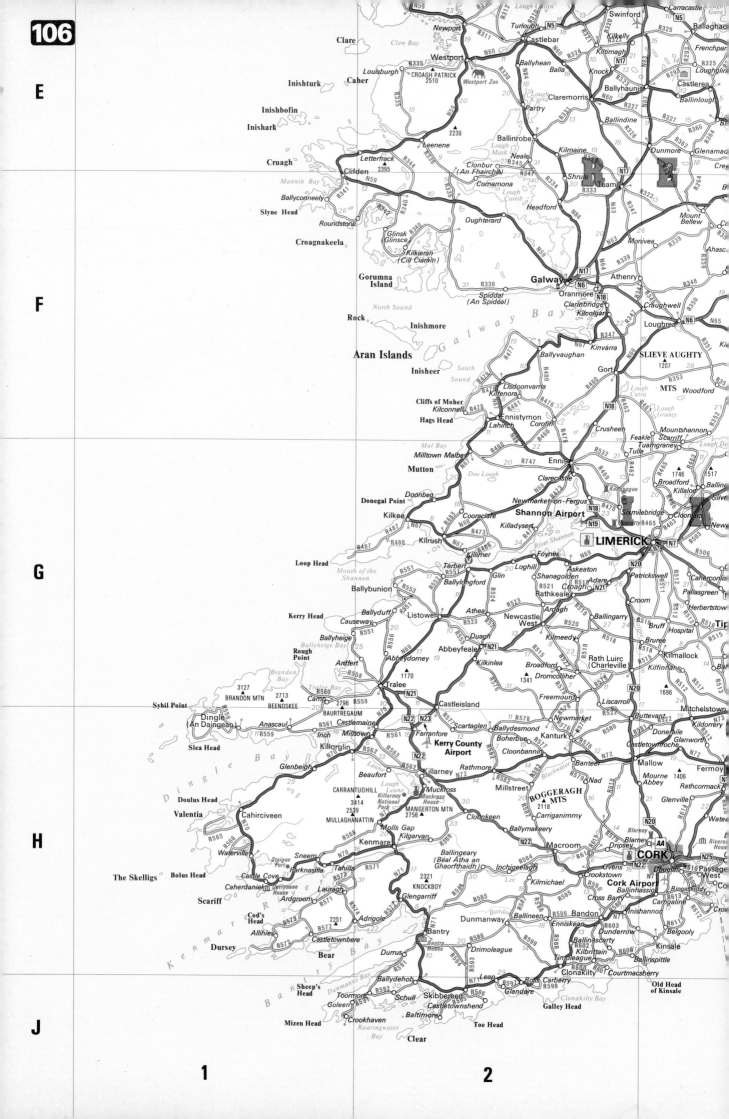

Motorways

Listed below are the motorways which appear on the following pages.

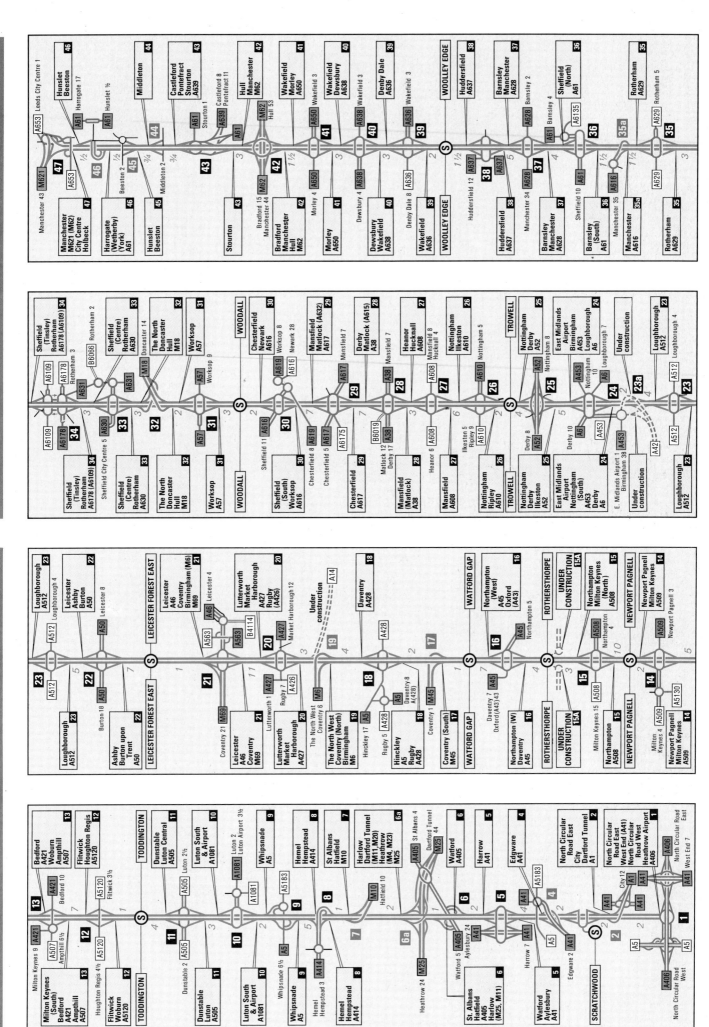

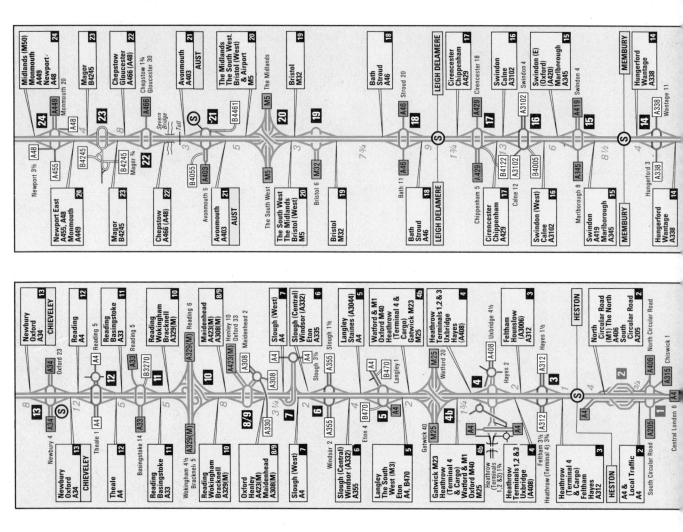

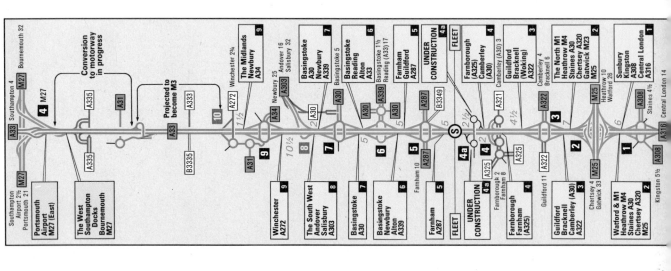

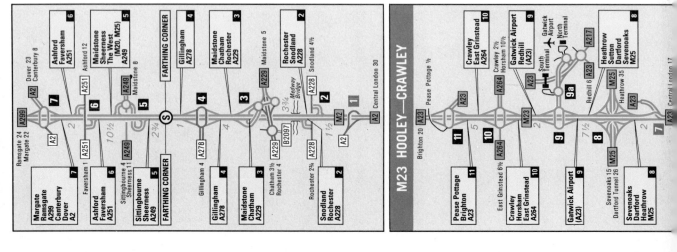

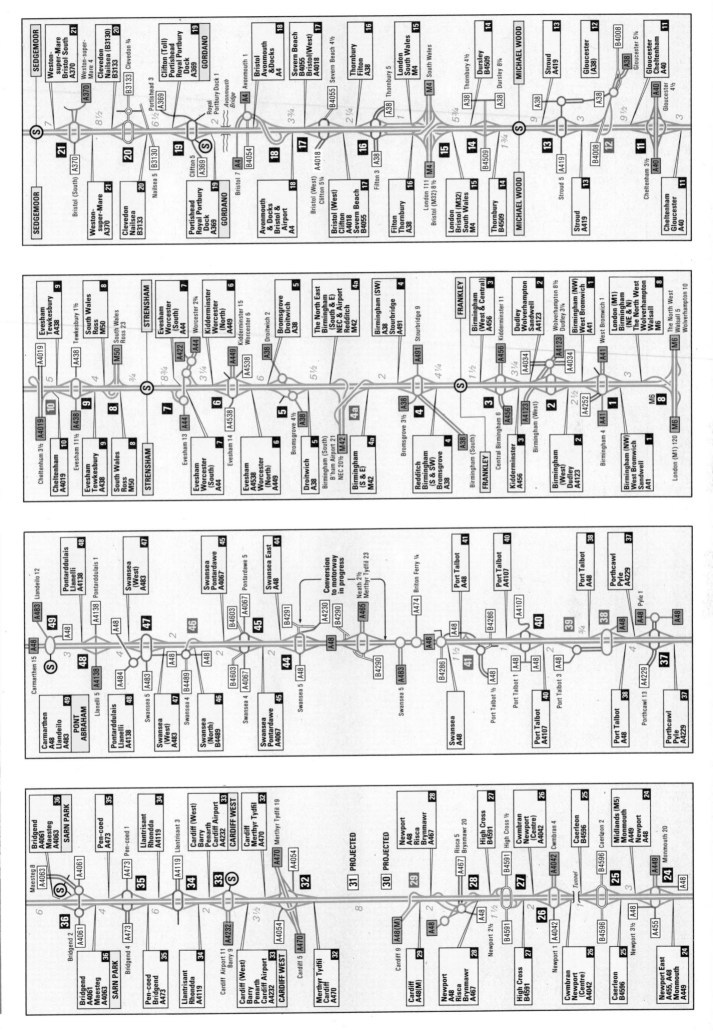

111

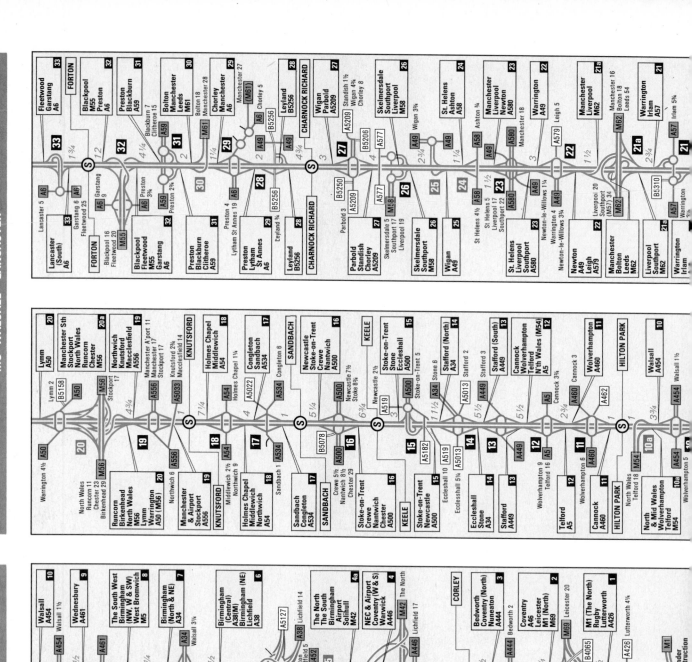

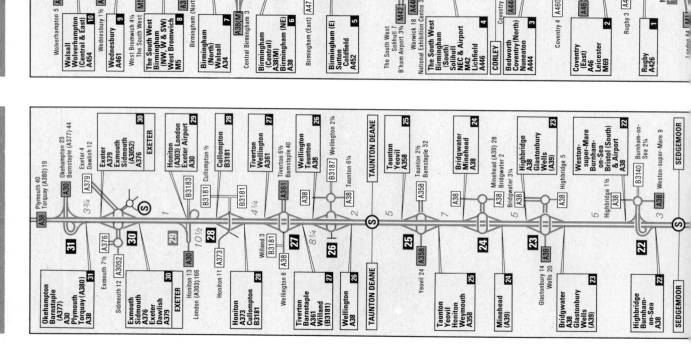

M8 Glasgow Airport – Glasgow Cross (Junctions 28–15)

Northbound panels:
- 28 Glasgow Airport
- 27 Renfrew Paisley A741
- 26 Renfrew (A8) Hillington A736
- 25 Clyde Tunnel A739
- 24 Kilmarnock Govan (A77)
- 21 City Centre (S) East Kilbride (A730)
- 19 Clydebank SEC A814
- 18 Anderston Charing Cross City Centre
- 17 Dumbarton A82
- 15 Kirkintilloch Glasgow Cross A803

Southbound panels:
- 28 Glasgow Airport
- 27 Renfrew Paisley A741
- 26 Renfrew (A8) Hillington A736
- 25 Clyde Tunnel A739
- 24 Irvine (A736)
- 23 Govan B768
- 22 Kilmarnock Prestwick Airport M77
- 20 East Kilbride City Centre (South) (A730)
- 19 Clydebank SEC Anderston Partick A814
- 18 Charing Cross
- 17 Dumbarton Kelvinside A82
- 16 City Centre Aberfoyle (A81) Cowcaddens A804
- 15 Kirkintilloch Glasgow Cross A803

M8 Fruit Market – Forth Road Bridge (Junctions 14–2)

Top panels:
- 14 Fruit Market
- 13 Carntyne
- 12 Stirling A80
- 11 Garthamlock Queenslie
- 10 Easterhouse Barlanark
- 9 Easterhouse Baillieston
- 8 Carlisle M73 (M74) Coatbridge A89 Edinburgh A8
- 5 Shotts Harthill (B7066) B7057
- HARTHILL
- 4 Bathgate Whitburn Falkirk A801
- 3a Livingston (A779)
- 3 Broxburn A89 Stirling Forth Road Br. M9 Edinburgh & Airport A8
- 2 Forth Road Br.

Bottom panels:
- 13 Fruit Market Dennistoun
- 12 Stirling Riddrie A80
- 11 Stepps Queenslie
- 10 Easterhouse Barlanark
- 8 M73
- 6 Airdrie Lanark Motherwell (A723) A73
- 5 Shotts Harthill (B7066) B7057
- HARTHILL
- 4 Bathgate Whitburn Falkirk A801
- 3a Bathgate Livingston W. (A779)
- 3 Livingston A899
- 2 Edinburgh A8

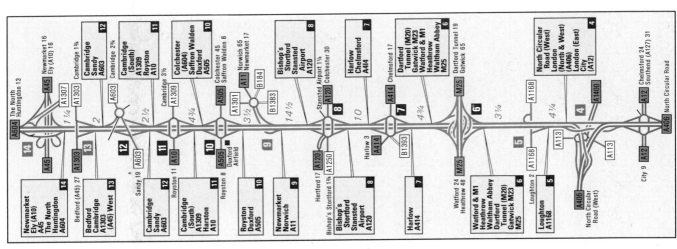

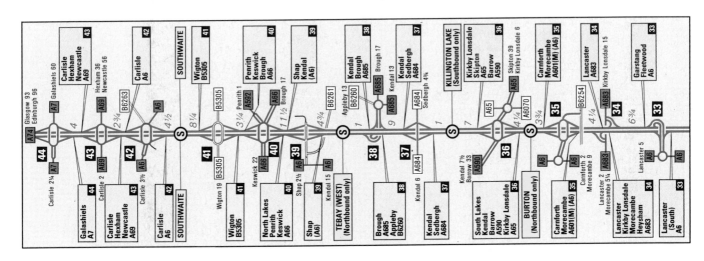

M27 CADNAM—PORTSMOUTH

M20 SWANLEY—FOLKESTONE

M74 GLASGOW—DOUGLAS (A70)

M73 EAST OF GLASGOW

M8 GLASGOW AIRPORT—BISHOPTON

M9 EDINBURGH—DUNBLANE

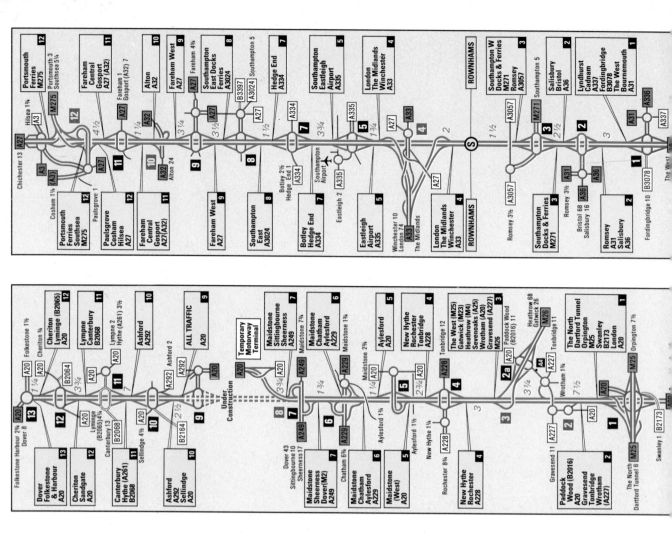

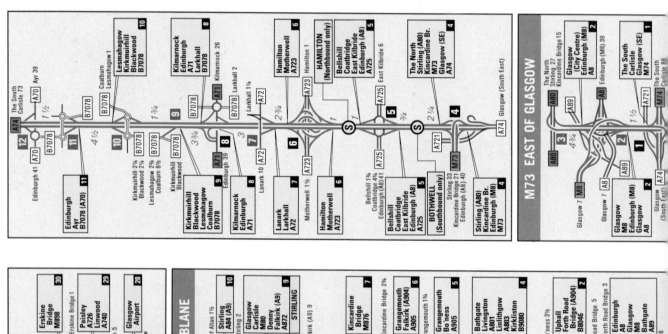

114

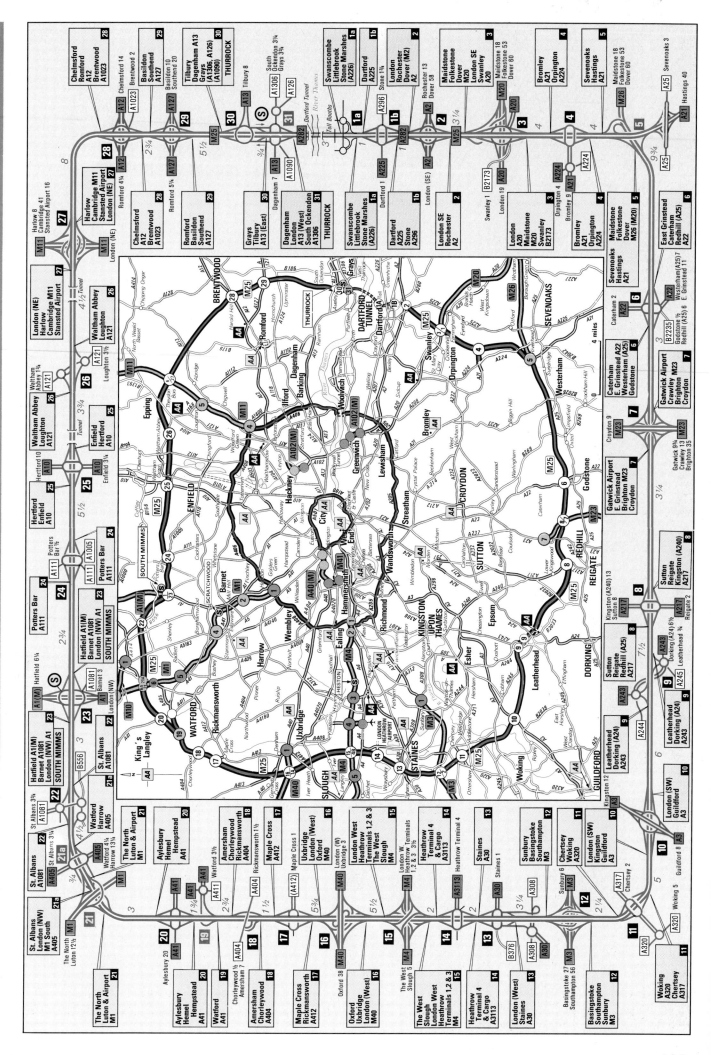

M54 TELFORD MOTORWAY

M56 NORTH CHESHIRE MOTORWAY

M61 GRT. MANCHESTER—CHORLEY

M42 BROMSGROVE—MEASHAM

M40 LONDON—WARWICK

M40 WARWICK—BIRMINGHAM (M42)

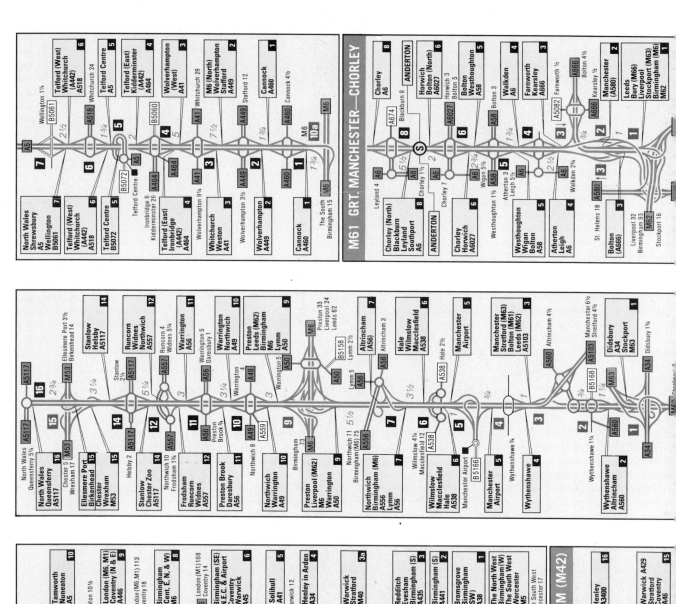

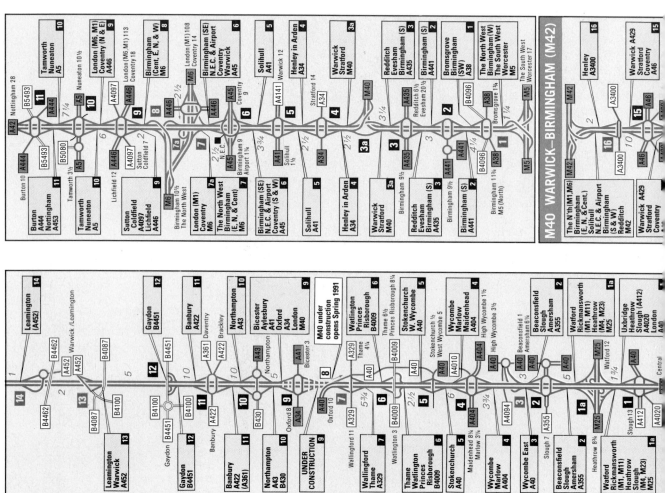

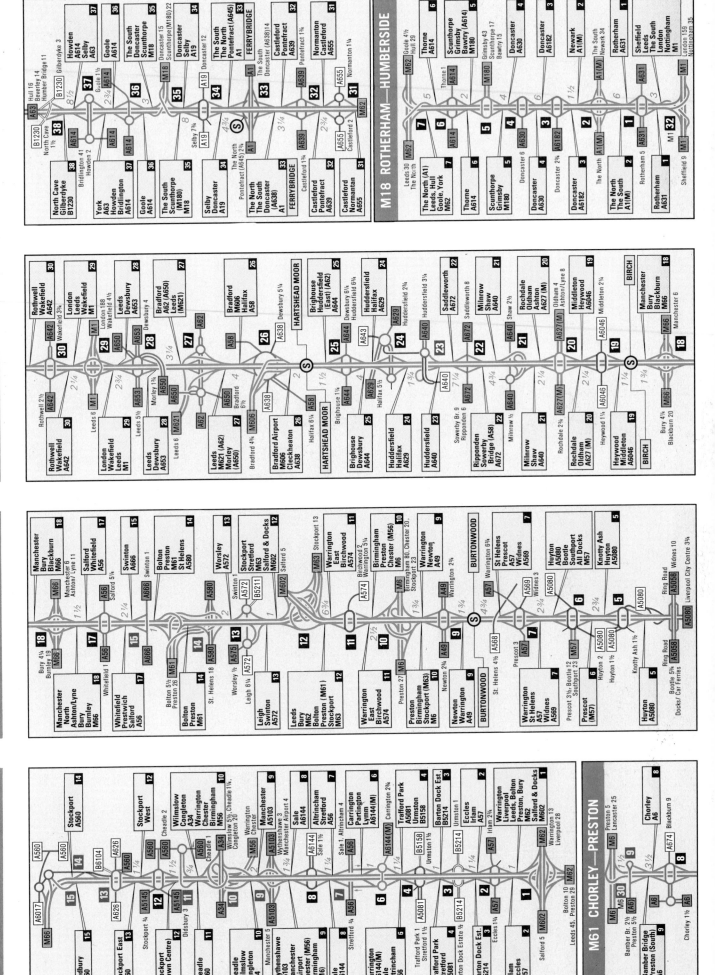

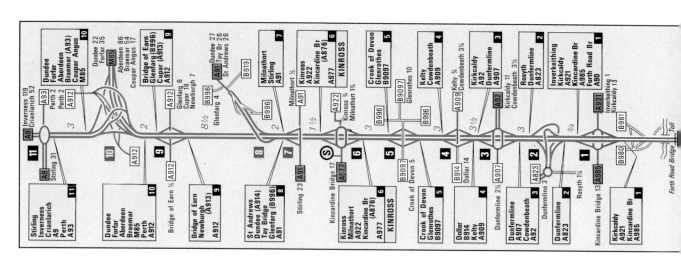

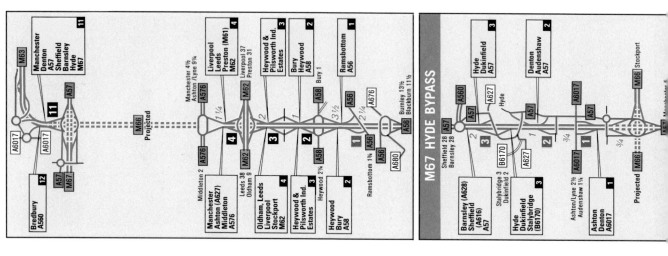

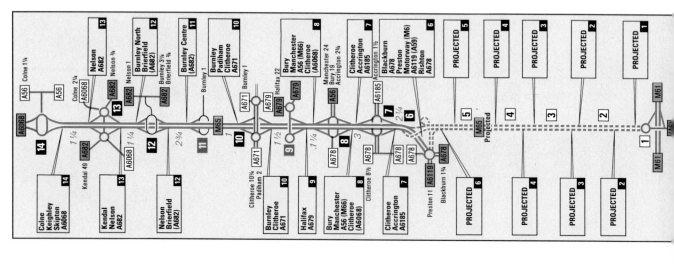

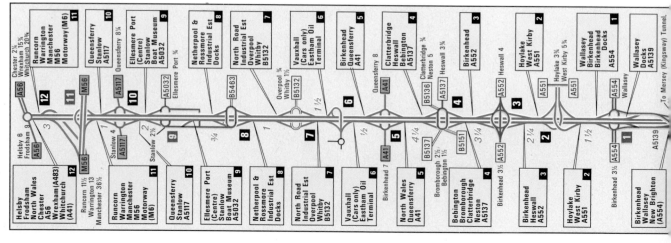

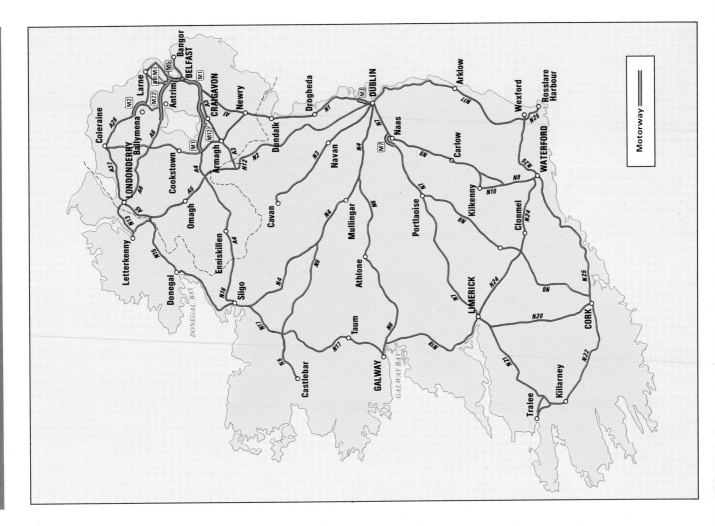

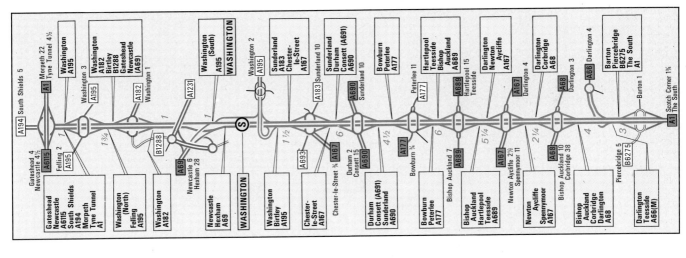

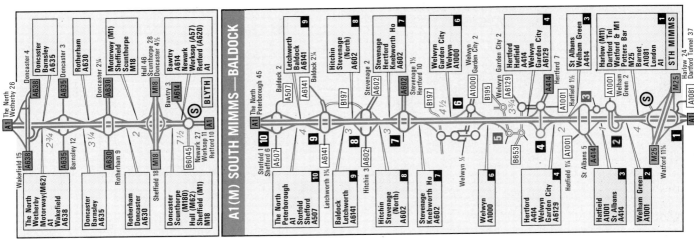

119

Ports and airports

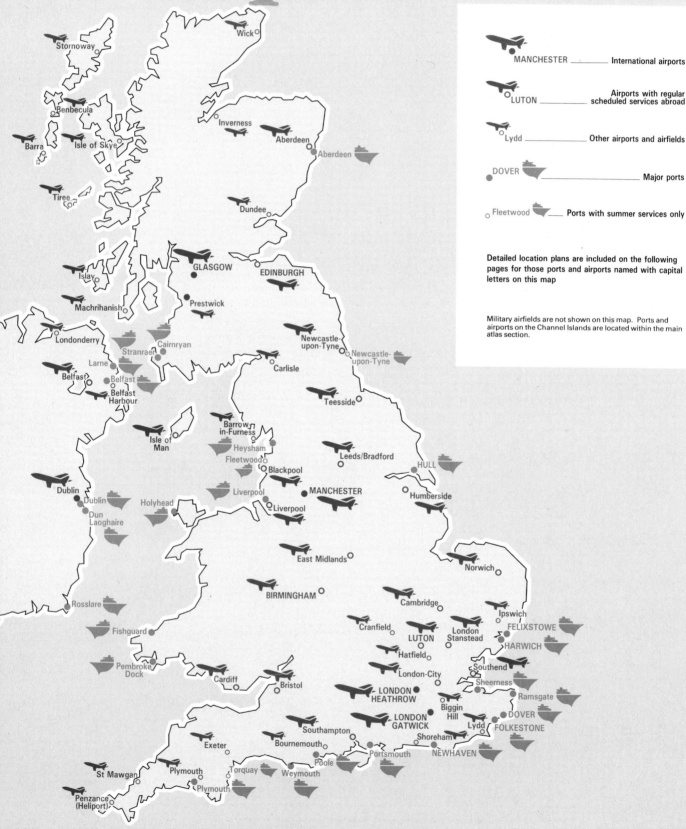

MANCHESTER _____ International airports

LUTON _____ Airports with regular scheduled services abroad

Lydd _____ Other airports and airfields

DOVER _____ Major ports

Fleetwood _____ Ports with summer services only

Detailed location plans are included on the following pages for those ports and airports named with capital letters on this map

Military airfields are not shown on this map. Ports and airports on the Channel Islands are located within the main atlas section.

Wick
Stornoway
Benbecula
Barra   Isle of Skye
Tiree
Inverness
Aberdeen
Aberdeen
Dundee
GLASGOW   EDINBURGH
Islay
Prestwick
Machrihanish
Newcastle-upon-Tyne
Londonderry   Cairnryan   Newcastle-upon-Tyne
Larne   Stranraer
Belfast   Carlisle
Belfast
Belfast Harbour   Teesside
Isle of Man   Barrow-in-Furness
Heysham   Leeds/Bradford
Fleetwood
Dublin   Blackpool   HULL
Dublin   Liverpool   MANCHESTER
Dun Laoghaire   Holyhead   Liverpool   Humberside
East Midlands
Rosslare   Norwich
BIRMINGHAM   Cambridge
Fishguard   Cranfield   Ipswich   FELIXSTOWE
LUTON   London Stanstead   HARWICH
Pembroke Dock   Hatfield   Southend
Cardiff   Bristol   London-City   Sheerness
LONDON HEATHROW   Ramsgate
Biggin Hill   DOVER
LONDON GATWICK   Lydd   FOLKESTONE
Southampton   Shoreham
Exeter   Bournemouth   NEWHAVEN
Poole   Portsmouth
St Mawgan   Plymouth   Torquay   Weymouth
Plymouth
Penzance (Heliport)

120

HEATHROW AIRPORT Tel 081-759 4321 (Airport Information)

Heathrow one of the world's busiest international airports, lies sixteen miles west of London. The airport is situated on the Piccadilly Underground line at Heathrow Central station. It is also served by local bus and long distance coach services. For short term parking multi-storey car parks are sited at each of the passenger terminals Tel: 081-745 7160 (terminals 1,2,3) 081-759 4931 (terminal 4). Charges for the long term car parks on the northern perimeter road are designed to encourage their use for a stay in excess of four hours. A free coach takes passengers to and from the terminals. Commercial garages offering long-term parking facilities within easy reach of the airport include: Quo-Vadis Airport Parking Tel: 081-759 2778; Airways Cranford Parking Tel: 081-759 9661; Flyaway Car Storage Tel: 081-759 1567 or 2020; and National Car Parks Tel: 081-759 9878. Car Hire: Avis Rent-A-Car Tel: 081-897 2621; Budget Rent-A-Car Tel: 081-759 2216; Godfrey Davis Europcar Tel: 081-897 0811/5; Guy Salmon Tel: 081-897 0541; Hertz Rent-A-Car Tel: 081-897 3347; Kenning Car Hire Tel: 081-759 9701 and EuroDollar Rent-A-Car Tel: 081-897-3232. The 4-star hotels in the area are The Excelsior Tel: 081-759 6611; the Heathrow Penta Tel: 081-897 6363; the Holiday Inn Tel: (0895) 445555. The 3-star hotels are the Berkeley Arms Tel: 081-897 2121; the Ariel Tel: 081-759 2552; the Post House Tel: 081-759 2323; and the Skyway Tel: 081-759 6311.

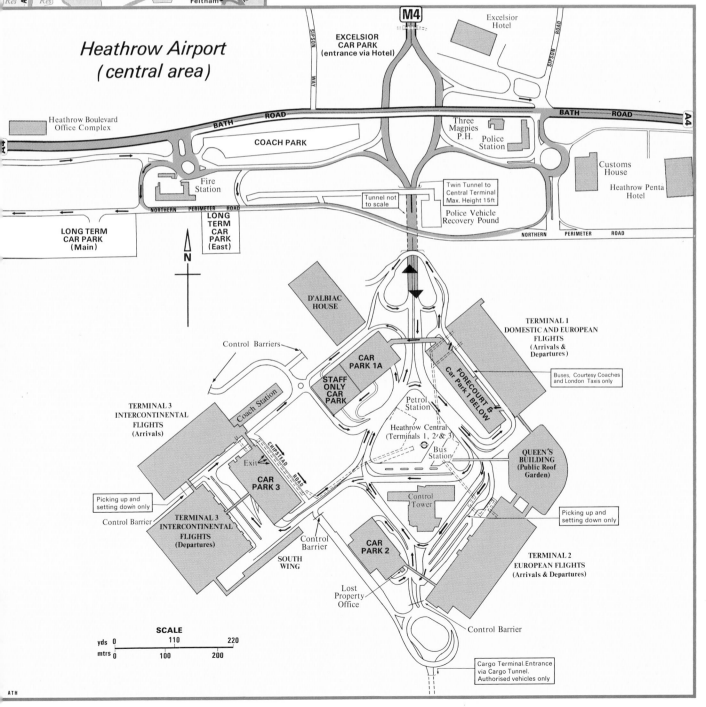

Heathrow Airport (central area)

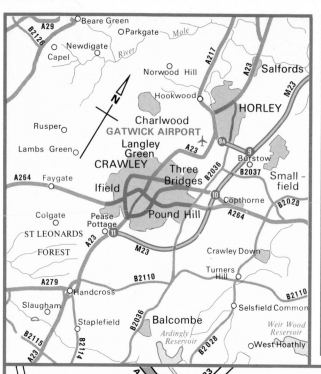

GATWICK AIRPORT Tel: (0293) 28822 or 081-668 4211.
London's second airport is served by regular bus and coach services.
There is a fast 15-minute rail service linking London (Victoria) with
Gatwick 24 hours a day. Parking: ample multi-storey and open-air
car parking is available. For latest prices tel: Gatwick (0293) 789812
South Terminal, and Gatwick (0293) 502747 for North Terminal.

MANCHESTER AIRPORT Tel: 061-489 3000. Situated nine miles
south of the city. Manchester Airport provides regular scheduled
services for many of the leading airlines. A spacious concourse,
restaurants and parking facilities are available for passengers. For
parking enquiries Tel: 061-489 3723 or 061-489 3000 ext 4635 or
2021.

LUTON AIRPORT Tel:(0582)405100. Used mainly for package
holiday tour operators, the airport has ample open-air car parking.
Covered garage space is available from Central Car Storage Tel:
(0582) 26189 or (0582)20957 for a booking form. Allow five
weeks.

BIRMINGHAM AIRPORT Tel: 021-767 5511. A three-storey
terminal building gives access from the first floor to the Maglev
transit system which offers a 90 second shuttle service to
Birmingham International Railway Station. Multi-storey parking for
800 cars and surface parking is available for 4,400 cars. Tel:
021-767 7861.

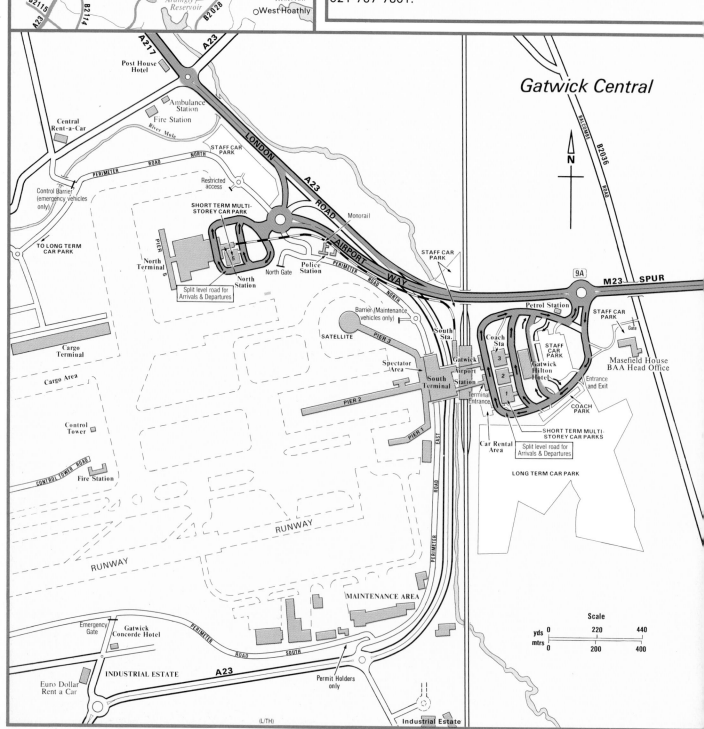

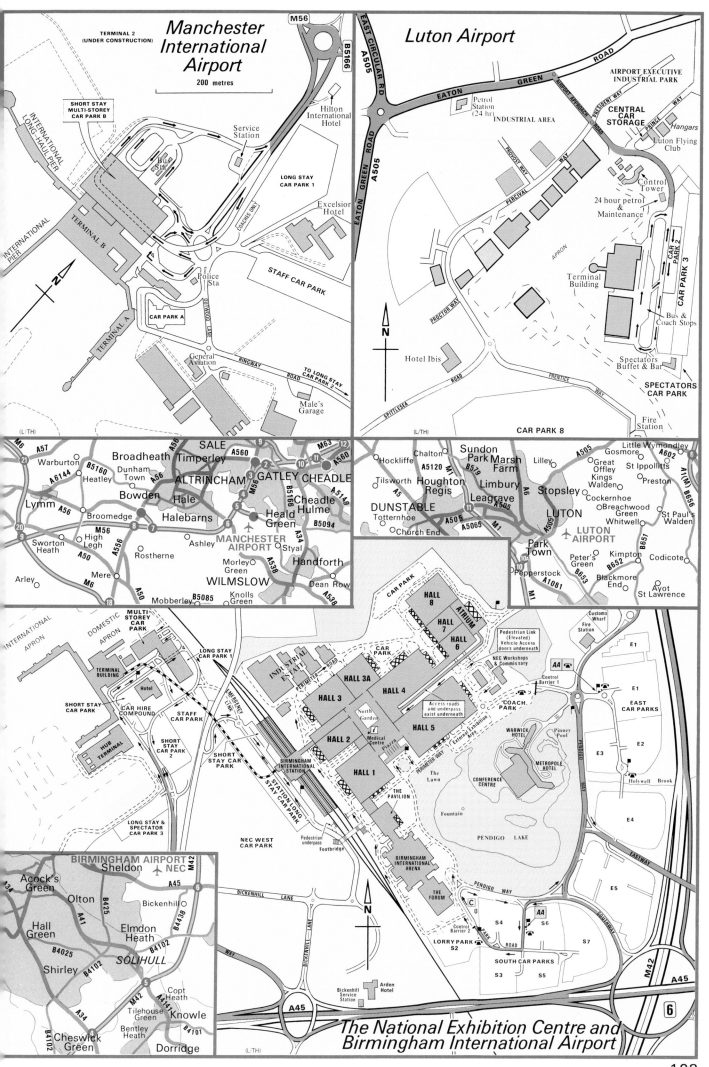

Manchester International Airport

TERMINAL 2 (UNDER CONSTRUCTION)

200 metres

SHORT STAY MULTI-STOREY CAR PARK B

M56

B5166

Hilton International Hotel

Service Station

Bus Sta

LONG STAY CAR PARK 1

Excelsior Hotel

TERMINAL B

INTERNATIONAL LONG-HAUL PIER

COACHES ONLY

STAFF CAR PARK

INTERNATIONAL PIER

N

Police Sta

OUTWOOD LANE

CAR PARK A

TERMINAL A

General Aviation

RINGWAY ROAD

TO LONG STAY CAR PARK 2

Male's Garage

(L/TH)

Luton Airport

EAST CIRCULAR RD

A505

B5166

EATON GREEN ROAD

AIRPORT EXECUTIVE INDUSTRIAL PARK

PRESIDENT WAY

PRINCE WAY

Petrol Station (24 hr)

INDUSTRIAL AREA

CENTRAL CAR STORAGE

Hangars

Luton Flying Club

EATON GREEN ROAD

A505

PERCIVAL WAY

PROVOST WAY

APRON

Control Tower

24 hour petrol & Maintenance

CAR PARK 2

CAR PARK 3

PROCTOR WAY

N

Terminal Building

Bus & Coach Stops

Hotel Ibis

SPITTLESEA ROAD

PRENTICE WAY

Spectators Buffet & Bar

SPECTATORS CAR PARK

CAR PARK 8

Fire Station

(L/TH)

M6
A57
21
Warburton
B5160
Heatley
A6144
Dunham Town
A56
SALE
Broadheath Timperley
A560
ALTRINCHAM
GATLEY CHEADLE
M63
12
9
2
11
10
A56
A560
Bowden
Hale
M56
A5149
Cheadle Hulme
Lymm
A56
Halebarns
Heald Green
B5094
20
8
7
Broomedge
Cheadle Hulme
9
Sworton Heath
High Legh
A556
Rostherne
Ashley
MANCHESTER AIRPORT
Styal
A34
Arley
Mere
A50
M6
Morley Green
A538
Handforth
18
Mobberley
B5085
Knolls Green
WILMSLOW
Dean Row
A538
WILMSLOW

Hockliffe
Chalton
Sundon Park
Marsh Farm
Lilley
A505
Little Wymondley
Gosmore
A602
Tilsworth
A5120
M1
B579
Houghton Regis
Limbury
Great Offley
Kings Walden
St Ippollitts
Preston
A5
Leagrave
A6
Stopsley
Cockernhoe
B656
A1(M)
DUNSTABLE
Totternhoe
11
A505
A505
LUTON
Breachwood Green
St Paul's Walden
Church End
A5065
M1
LUTON AIRPORT
Whitwell
B651
Park Town
Peter's Green
Kimpton
Codicote
10A
Pepperstock
B652
B653
Blackmore End
10
A1081
M1
Ayot St Lawrence

Birmingham International Airport / The National Exhibition Centre

INTERNATIONAL APRON
DOMESTIC APRON
MULTI-STOREY CAR PARK
LONG STAY CAR PARK 1
TERMINAL BUILDING
Hotel
SHORT STAY CAR PARK
CAR HIRE COMPOUND
STAFF CAR PARK
HUB TERMINAL
SHORT STAY CAR PARK 2
SHORT STAY CAR PARK
EMERGENCY LINK
LONG STAY & SPECTATOR CAR PARK 3
BIRMINGHAM INTERNATIONAL STATION
STATION LONG STAY CAR PARK
NEC WEST CAR PARK
Pedestrian underpass
Footbridge

CAR PARK
HALL 8
ATRIUM
HALL 7
HALL 6
PERIMETER ROAD
CAR PARK
Pedestrian Link (Elevated) Vehicle Access doors underneath
NEC WORKSHOPS & Commissary
Customs Wharf
Fire Station
E1
AA
Control Barrier 1
EAST CAR PARKS
HALL 3A
HALL 4
Access roads and underpass exist underneath
COACH PARK
PINDIGO WAY
E1
HALL 3
North Garden
HALL 5
WARWICK HOTEL
Pinney Pool
E3
E2
HALL 2
Piazza
Medical Centre
External Exhibition Area
PERIMETER WAY
METROPOLE HOTEL
Holywell Brook
HALL 1
THE PAVILION
The Lawn
CONFERENCE CENTRE
Fountain
PENDIGO LAKE
E4
BIRMINGHAM INTERNATIONAL ARENA
PENDIGO WAY
EASTWAY
E5
THE FORUM
C
AA
Control Barrier 2
S4
S6
SOUTHWAY
M42
LORRY PARK S2
ROAD
S7
A45
S3
S5
SOUTH CAR PARKS

BIRMINGHAM AIRPORT NEC
M42
Acock's Green
A34
Sheldon
A45
6
Olton
B425
Bickenhill
B4438
Hall Green
A41
B4102
Elmdon Heath
A4025
SOLIHULL
B4102
Shirley
B4102
5
Copt Heath
M42
Tilehouse Green
A4141
Knowle
B4102
Bentley Heath
B4101
Cheswick Green
Dorridge

BICKENHILL LANE

WAY

N

A45

Arden Hotel

Bickenhill Service Station

(L/TH)

6

A45

M42

The National Exhibition Centre and Birmingham International Airport

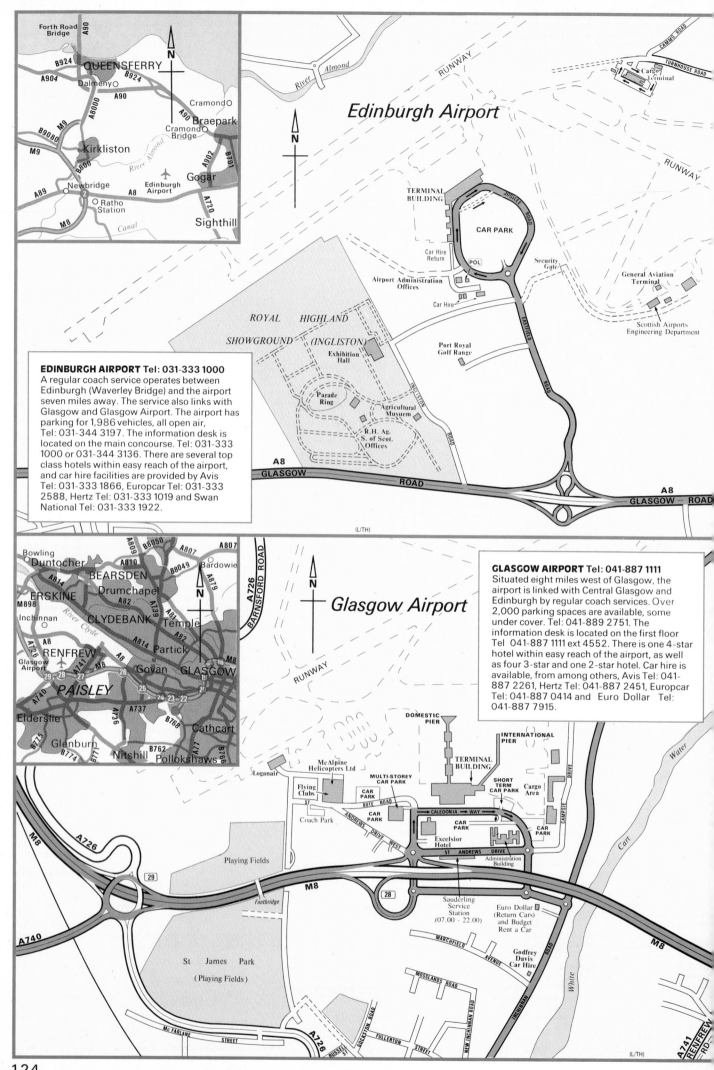

Edinburgh Airport

EDINBURGH AIRPORT Tel: 031-333 1000
A regular coach service operates between Edinburgh (Waverley Bridge) and the airport seven miles away. The service also links with Glasgow and Glasgow Airport. The airport has parking for 1,986 vehicles, all open air, Tel: 031-344 3197. The information desk is located on the main concourse. Tel: 031-333 1000 or 031-344 3136. There are several top class hotels within easy reach of the airport, and car hire facilities are provided by Avis Tel: 031-333 1866, Europcar Tel: 031-333 2588, Hertz Tel: 031-333 1019 and Swan National Tel: 031-333 1922.

Glasgow Airport

GLASGOW AIRPORT Tel: 041-887 1111
Situated eight miles west of Glasgow, the airport is linked with Central Glasgow and Edinburgh by regular coach services. Over 2,000 parking spaces are available, some under cover. Tel: 041-889 2751. The information desk is located on the first floor Tel 041-887 1111 ext 4552. There is one 4-star hotel within easy reach of the airport, as well as four 3-star and one 2-star hotel. Car hire is available, from among others, Avis Tel: 041-887 2261, Hertz Tel: 041-887 2451, Europcar Tel: 041-887 0414 and Euro Dollar Tel: 041-887 7915.

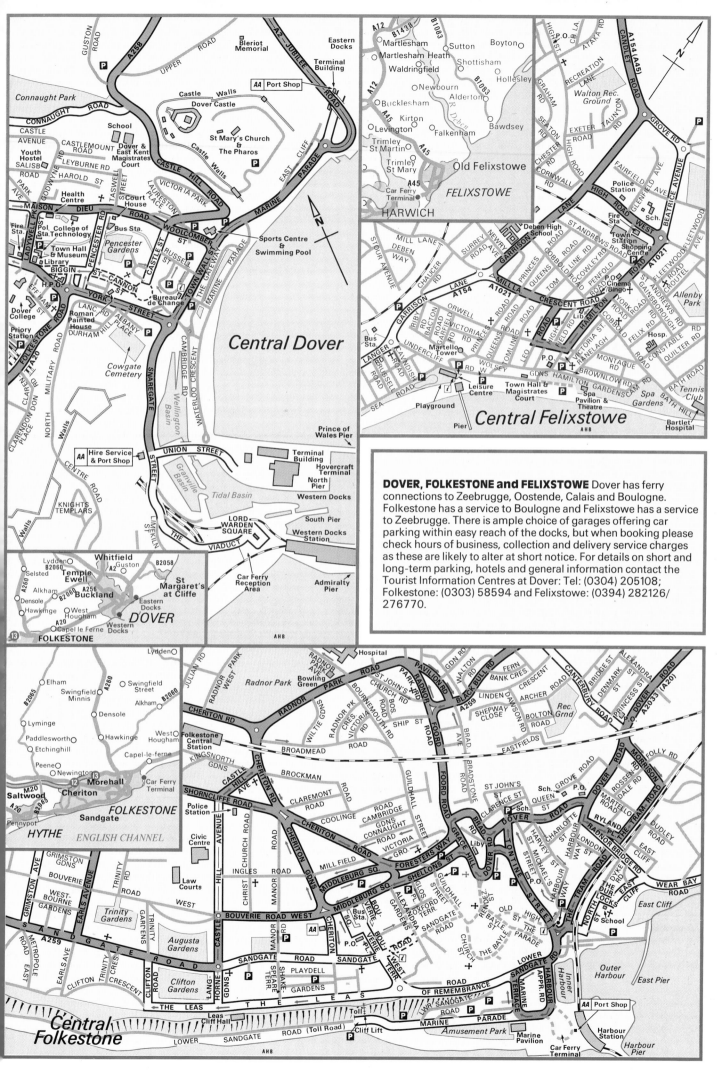

DOVER, FOLKESTONE and FELIXSTOWE Dover has ferry
connections to Zeebrugge, Oostende, Calais and Boulogne.
Folkestone has a service to Boulogne and Felixstowe has a service
to Zeebrugge. There is ample choice of garages offering car
parking within easy reach of the docks, but when booking please
check hours of business, collection and delivery service charges
as these are likely to alter at short notice. For details on short and
long-term parking, hotels and general information contact the
Tourist Information Centres at Dover: Tel: (0304) 205108;
Folkestone: (0303) 58594 and Felixstowe: (0394) 282126/
276770.

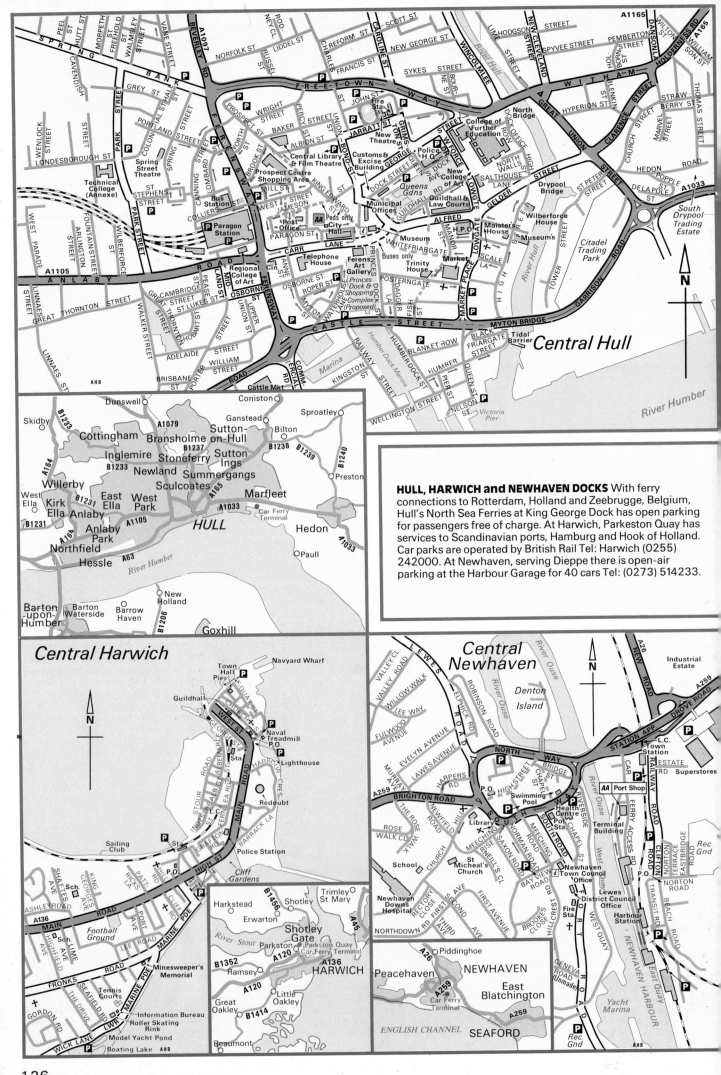

Town plans

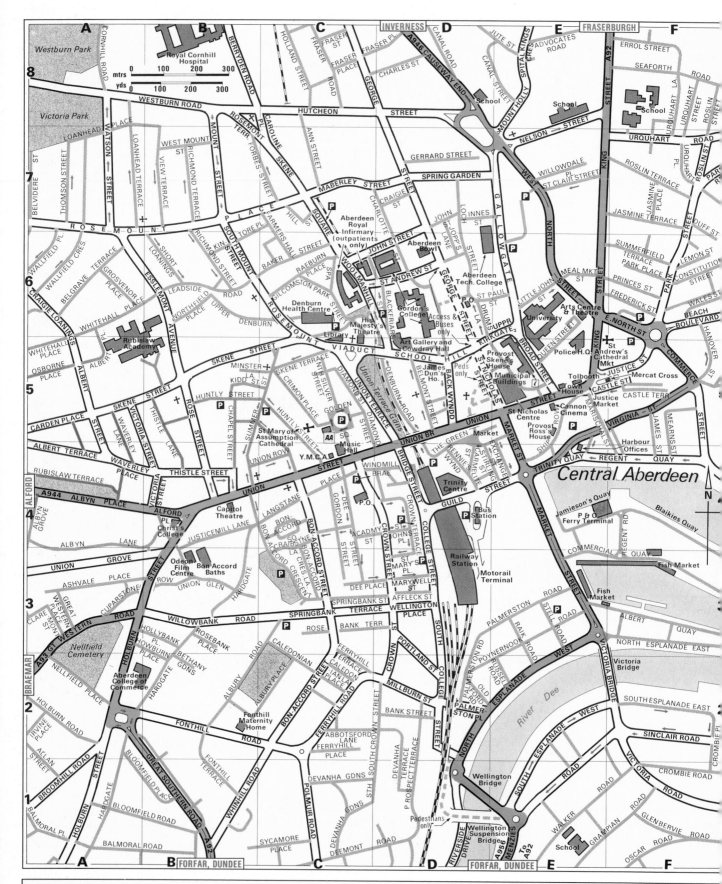

Aberdeen

Granite gives Aberdeen its especial character; but this is not to say that the city is a grim or a grey place, the granites used are of many hues – white, blue, pink and grey. Although the most imposing buildings date from the 19th century, granite has been used to dramatic effect since at least as early as the 15th century. From that time dates St Machar's Cathedral, originally founded in AD580,

but rebuilt several times, especially after a devasting fire started on the orders of Edward III of England in 1336. St Machar's is in Old Aberdeen, traditionally the ecclesiastical and educational hub of the city, while 'New' Aberdeen (actually no newer) has always been the commercial centre. Even that definition is deceptive, for although Old Aberdeen has King's College, founded in 1494, New Aberdeen has Marischal College, founded almost exactly a century later (but rebuilt in 1844)

and every bit as distinguished as a seat of learning. Both establishments functioned as independent universities until they were merged in 1860 to form Aberdeen University. The North Sea oil boom has brought many changes to the city, some of which threatened its character. But even though high-rise buildings are now common, the stately façades, towers and pillars of granite still reign supreme and Union Street remains one of the best thoroughfares in Britain.

128

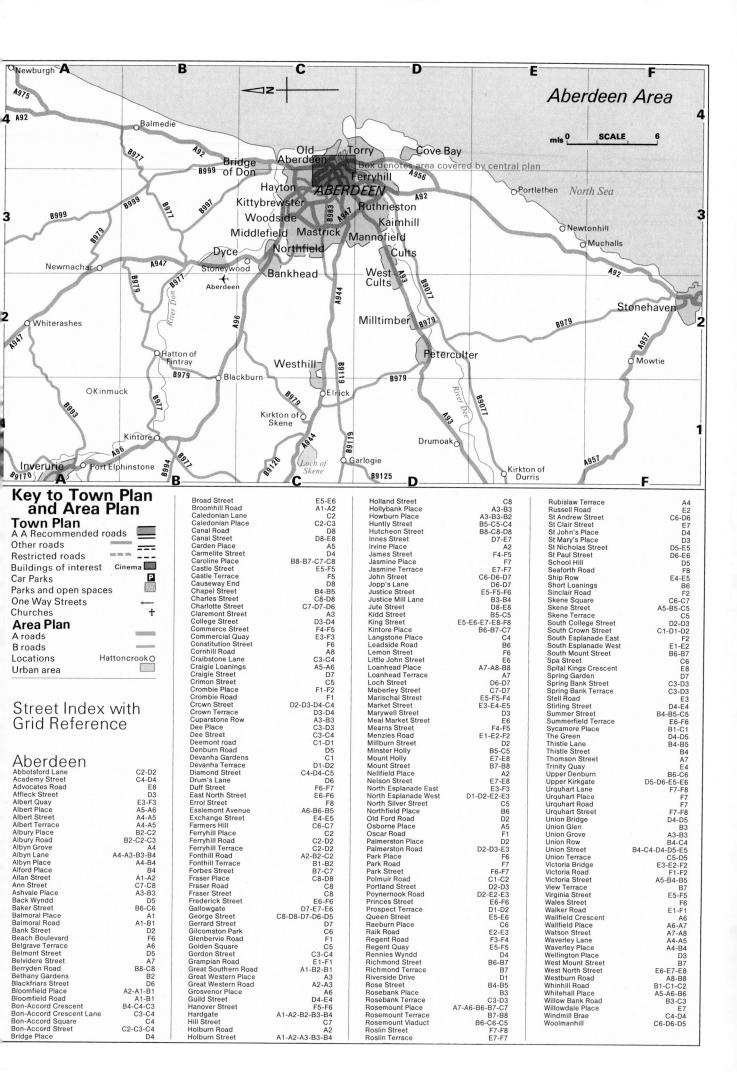

Aberdeen Area

mls 0 SCALE 6

North Sea

Box denotes area covered by central plan

Key to Town Plan and Area Plan

Town Plan

A A Recommended roads
Other roads
Restricted roads
Buildings of interest   Cinema
Car Parks   P
Parks and open spaces
One Way Streets
Churches   †

Area Plan

A roads
B roads
Locations   Hattoncrook ○
Urban area

Street Index with Grid Reference

Aberdeen

Abbotsford Lane	C2-D2
Academy Street	C4-D4
Advocates Road	E8
Affleck Street	D3
Albert Quay	E3-F3
Albert Place	A5-A6
Albert Street	A4-A5
Albert Terrace	A4-A5
Albury Place	B2-C2
Albury Road	B2-C2-C3
Albyn Grove	A4
Albyn Lane	A4-A3-B3-B4
Albyn Place	A4-B4
Alford Place	B4
Allan Street	A1-A2
Ann Street	C7-C8
Ashvale Place	A3-B3
Back Wynd	D5
Baker Street	B6-C6
Balmoral Place	A1
Balmoral Road	A1-B1
Bank Street	D2
Beach Boulevard	F6
Belgrave Terrace	A6
Belmont Street	D5
Belvidere Street	A7
Berryden Road	B8-C8
Bethany Gardens	B2
Blackfriars Street	D6
Bloomfield Place	A2-A1-B1
Bloomfield Road	A1-B1
Bon-Accord Crescent	B4-C4-C3
Bon-Accord Crescent Lane	C3-C4
Bon-Accord Square	C4
Bon-Accord Street	C2-C3-C4
Bridge Place	D4

Broad Street	E5-E6
Broomhill Road	A1-A2
Caledonian Lane	C2
Caledonian Place	C2-C3
Canal Road	D8
Canal Street	D8-E8
Carden Place	A5
Carmelite Street	D4
Caroline Place	B8-B7-C7-C8
Castle Street	E5-F5
Castle Terrace	F5
Causeway End	D8
Chapel Street	B4-B5
Charles Street	C8-D8
Charlotte Street	C7-D7-D6
Claremont Street	A3
College Street	D3-D4
Commerce Street	F4-F5
Commercial Quay	E3-F3
Constitution Street	F6
Cornhill Road	A8
Craibstone Lane	C3-C4
Craigie Loanings	A5-A6
Craigie Street	D7
Crimon Street	C5
Crombie Place	F1-F2
Crombie Road	F1
Crown Street	D2-D3-D4-C4
Crown Terrace	D3-D4
Cuparstone Row	A3-B3
Dee Place	C3-D3
Dee Street	C3-C4
Deemont road	C1-D1
Denburn Road	D5
Devanha Gardens	C1
Devanha Terrace	D1-D2
Diamond Street	C4-D4-C5
Drum's Lane	D6
Duff Street	F6-F7
East North Street	E6-F6
Errol Street	F8
Esslemont Avenue	A6-B6-B5
Exchange Street	E4-E5
Farmers Hill	C6-C7
Ferryhill Place	C2
Ferryhill Road	C2-D2
Ferryhill Terrace	C2-D2
Fonthill Road	A2-B2-C2
Fonthill Terrace	B1-B2
Forbes Street	B7-C7
Fraser Place	C8-D8
Fraser Road	C8
Fraser Street	C8
Frederick Street	E6-F6
Gallowgate	D7-E7-E6
George Street	C8-D8-D7-D6-D5
Gerrard Street	D7
Gilcomston Park	C6
Glenbervie Road	F1
Golden Square	C5
Gordon Street	C3-C4
Grampian Road	E1-F1
Great Southern Road	A1-B2-B1
Great Western Place	A3
Great Western Road	A2-A3
Grosvenor Place	A6
Guild Street	D4-E4
Hanover Street	F5-F6
Hardgate	A1-A2-B2-B3-B4
Hill Street	C7
Holburn Road	A2
Holburn Street	A1-A2-A3-B3-B4

Holland Street	C8
Hollybank Place	A3-B3
Howburn Place	A3-B3-B2
Huntly Street	B5-C5-C4
Hutcheon Street	B8-C8-D8
Innes Street	D7-E7
Irvine Place	A2
James Street	F4-F5
Jasmine Place	F7
Jasmine Terrace	E7-F7
John Street	C6-D6-D7
Jopp's Lane	D6-D7
Justice Street	E5-F5-F6
Justice Mill Lane	B3-B4
Jute Street	D8-E8
Kidd Street	B5-C5
King Street	E5-E6-E7-E8-F8
Kintore Place	B6-B7-C7
Langstone Place	C4
Leadside Road	B6
Lemon Street	F6
Little John Street	E6
Loanhead Place	A7-A8-B8
Loanhead Terrace	A7
Loch Street	D6-D7
Maberley Street	C7-D7
Marischal Street	E5-F5-F4
Market Street	E3-E4-E5
Marywell Street	D3
Mearns Street	F4-F5
Meal Market Street	E6
Menzies Road	E1-E2-F2
Millburn Street	D2
Minster Holly	B5-C5
Mount Holly	E7-E8
Mount Street	B7-B8
Nellfield Place	A2
Nelson Street	E7-E8
North Esplanade East	E3-F3
North Esplanade West	D1-D2-E2-E3
North Silver Street	C5
Northfield Place	B6
Old Ford Road	D2
Osborne Place	A5
Oscar Road	F1
Palmerston Place	D2
Palmerston Road	D2-D3-E3
Park Place	F6
Park Road	F7
Park Street	F6-F7
Polmuir Road	C1-C2
Portland Street	D2-D3
Poynernook Road	D2-E2-E3
Princes Street	E6-F6
Prospect Terrace	D1-D2
Queen Street	E5-E6
Raeburn Place	C6
Raik Road	E2-E3
Regent Road	F3-F4
Regent Quay	E5-F5
Rennies Wynd	D4
Richmond Street	B6-B7
Richmond Terrace	B7
Riverside Drive	A8-B8
Rose Street	B4-B5
Rosebank Place	B3
Rosebank Terrace	C3-D3
Rosemount Place	A7-A6-B6-B7-C7
Rosemount Terrace	B7-B8
Rosemount Viaduct	B6-C6-C5
Roslin Street	F7-F8
Roslin Terrace	E7-F7

Rubislaw Terrace	A4
Russell Road	E2
St Andrew Street	C6-D6
St Clair Street	E7
St John's Place	D4
St Mary's Place	D3
St Nicholas Street	D5-E5
St Paul Street	D6-E6
School Hill	D5
Seaforth Road	F8
Ship Row	E4-E5
Short Loanings	B6
Sinclair Road	F2
Skene Square	C6-C7
Skene Street	A5-B5-C5
Skene Terrace	C5
South College Street	D2-D3
South Crown Street	C1-D1-D2
South Esplanade East	F2
South Esplanade West	E1-E2
South Mount Street	B6-B7
Spa Street	C6
Spital Kings Crescent	E8
Spring Garden	D7
Spring Bank Street	C3-D3
Spring Bank Terrace	C3-D3
Stell Road	E3
Stirling Street	D4-E4
Summer Street	B4-B5-C5
Summerfield Terrace	E6-F6
Sycamore Place	B1-C1
The Green	D4-D5
Thistle Lane	B4-B5
Thistle Street	B4
Thomson Street	A7
Trinity Quay	E4
Upper Denburn	B6-C6
Upper Kirkgate	D5-D6-E5-E6
Urquhart Lane	F7-F8
Urquhart Place	F7
Urquhart Road	F7
Urquhart Street	F7-F8
Union Bridge	D4-D5
Union Glen	B3
Union Grove	A3-B3
Union Row	B4-C4
Union Street	B4-C4-D4-D5-E5
Union Terrace	C5-D5
Victoria Bridge	E3-E2-F2
Victoria Road	F1-F2
Victoria Street	A5-B4-B5
View Terrace	B7
Virginia Street	E5-F5
Wales Street	F6
Walker Road	E1-F1
Wallfield Crescent	A6
Wallfield Place	A6-A7
Watson Street	A7-A8
Waverley Lane	A4-A5
Waverley Place	A4-B4
Wellington Place	D3
West Mount Street	B7
West North Street	E6-E7-E8
Westburn Road	A8-B8
Whinhill Road	B1-C1-C2
Whitehall Place	A5-A6-B6
Willow Bank Road	B3-C3
Willowdale Place	E7
Windmill Brae	C4-D4
Woolmanhill	C6-D6-D5

129

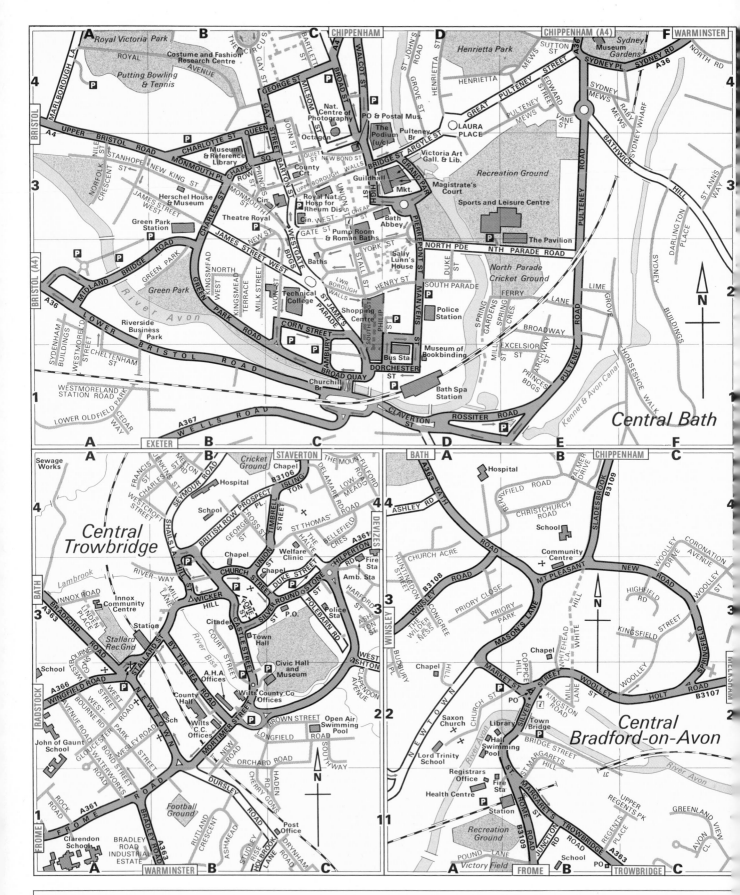

Bath

This unique city combines Britain's most impressive collection of Roman relics with the country's finest Georgian townscape. Its attraction to Romans and fashionable 18th-century society alike was its mineral springs, which are still seen by thousands of tourists who visit the Roman Baths every year. They are now the centre-piece of a Roman museum, where exhibits give a vivid impression of life 2000 years ago. The adjacent Pump Room to which the waters were piped for drinking was a focal point of social life in 18th-and 19th-century Bath.

The Georgian age of elegance also saw the building of Bath's perfectly proportioned streets, terraces and crescents. The finest examples are Queen Square, the Circus, and Royal Crescent, all built of golden local stone. Overlooking the Avon from the west is the great tower of Bath Abbey - sometimes called the "Lantern of the West"

because of its large and numerous windows.

Bath has much to delight the museum-lover. The Holburne Museum in Great Pulteney Street houses collections of silver, porcelain, paintings, furniture and glass of all periods.

The Assembly Rooms in Bennett Street, very much a part of the social scene in Georgian Bath, are now the home of the Museum of Costume with displays illustrating fashion through the ages.

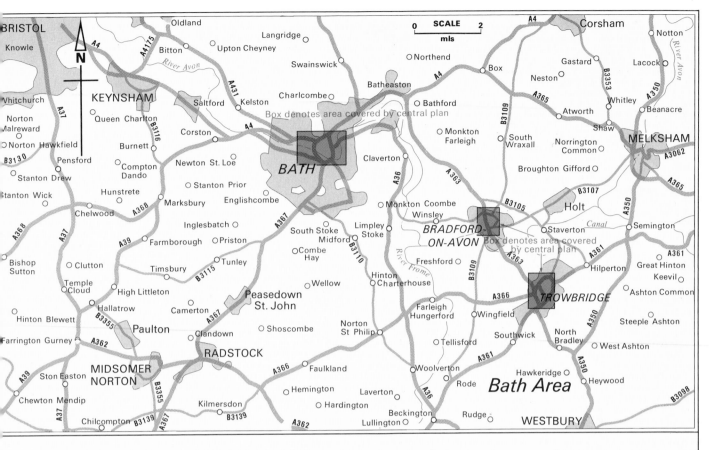

Bath Area

Key to Town Plan and Area Plan

Town Plan

A A Recommended roads
Other roads
Restricted roads
Buildings of interest — Library
Car Parks — P
Parks and open spaces
Churches — †

Area Plan

A roads
B roads
Locations — Box ○
Urban Area

Street Index with Grid Reference

Central Bath

Ambury	C1-C2
Archway Street	E1-E2
Argyle Street	D3-D4
Avon Street	C4
Bartlett Street	C3
Barton Street	C3
Bathwick Hill	E3-F3
Bridge Street	C3-D3
Broadway	E2
Broad Street	C3-C4
Broad Quay	C1
Chapel Row	D3
Charles Street	B2-B3
Charlotte Street	B3-B4
Cheap Street	C3
Cheltenham Street	A1
Claverton Street	C1-D1
Corn Street	C2
Darlington Place	F2-F3
Dorchester Street	C1-D1
Duke Street	D2
Edward Street	E4
Excelsior Street	E1
Ferry Lane	D2-E2
Gay Street	B4-C4-C3

George Street	B4-C4
Grand Parade	D3
Great Pulteney Street	D4-E4
Green Park	A2-B2
Green Park Road	B1-B2-C2-C1
Grove Street	D3-D4
Henrietta Mews	D4-E4
Henrietta Street	D4
Henry Street	C2-D2
High Street	C3
Horseshoe Walk	F1
James Street West	A3-B3-B2-C2
John Street	C3-C4
Kingsmead North	B2
Kingsmead Terrace	B2
Kingsmead West	B2
Laura Place	D3-D4
Lime Grove	E2-F2-F1
Lower Bristol Road	A2-A1-B1-C1
Lower Borough Walls	C2
Lower Oldfield Park	A1
Manvers Street	D1-D2
Marlborough Lane	A4
Midland Bridge Road	A2-B2-B3
Milk Street	B2
Mill Street	D1
Milsom Street	C3-C4
Monmouth Place	B3
Monmouth Street	B3-C3
New Street	B2-B3-C3
New Bond Street	C3
New King Street	A3-B3
Nile Street	A3
Norfolk Crescent	A3
North Parade	D2
North Parade Road	D2-E2
North Road	F4
Philip Street	C1-C2-D2
Pierrepont Street	E1
Princes Buildings	E1
Princes Street	B3
Pulteney Mews	E4
Pulteney Road	E1-E2-E3-E4
Queen Square	B3-B4-C4-C3
Quiet Street	C3
Raby Mews	E4-F4
Rossiter Road	D1-E1
Royal Avenue	A4-B4
St Ann's Way	F3
St Jame's Parade	C2
St John's Road	D4r
Southgate	C1-C2
South Parade	D2
Spring Crescent	E2
Spring Gardens	D2
Stall Street	C2-C3
Stanhope Street	A3
Sutton Street	E4
Sydenham Buildings	A1-A2
Sydney Buildings	F1-F2-F3
Sydney Mews	E4-F4
Sydney Place	E4-F4
Sydney Road	F4
Sydney Wharf	F3-F4
The Circus	B4
Union Street	C3
Upper Borough Walls	C3
Upper Bristol Road	A4-A3-B3

Vane Street	E4
Walcot Street	C3-C4
Wells Road	A1-B1-C1
Westgate Buildings	C2-C3
Westgate Street	C3
Westmoreland Station Road	A1
Westmoreland Street	A1
York Street	C2-D2-D3

Trowbridge

Ashmead	D1
Ashton Street	C3
Avenue Road	A2
Bellefield Crescent	C4
Bond Street	A1-A2
Bradford Road	A2-A3
Bradley Road	A1-B1
British Row	B4
Brown Street	B2-C2
Bythesea Road	B2-B3
Castle Street	B2-B3
Charles Street	A4-B4
Cherry Gardens	B1-C1
Church Street	B3-C3
Clapendon Avenue	C2
Court Street	B2-B3
Cross Street	B4-C4
Delamare Road	C4
Dynham Road	C1
Duke Street	C3-C4
Dursley Road	B1-C1
Fore Street	B3
Francis Street	A4-B4
Frome Road	A1-B1
Fulford Road	C4
George Street	B4
Gloucester Road	A2
Haden Road	C1
Harford Street	C3
Hill Street	B3
Hilperton Road	C3-C4
Holbrook Lane	B1-C1
Innox Road	A3
Islington	C4
Jenkins Street	A4-B4
Linden Place	A3
Longfield Road	B2-C2
Lowmead	C4
Melton Road	B4
Mill Lane	B3
Mortimer Street	B2
New Road	B1-B2
Newtown	A2-B2
Orchard Road	B1-B2-C2-C1
Park Street	A2-A1-B1
Polebarn Road	C3
Prospect Place	D4-C4
River Way	A3-B3
Rock Road	A1
Roundstone Street	C3
Rutland Crescent	B1
St Thomas' Road	C4
Seymour Road	B4
Shails Lane	B3-B4
Silver Street	B3-C3

Southway	C2
Stallard Street	A2-A3-B3
Studley Rise	B1
The Hayle	C4
The Mount	C4
Timbrell Street	C4
Union Street	B3-B4-C4-C3
Waterworks Road	A1-A2
Wesley Road	A2-B2
West Street	A2
West Ashton	C2-C3
Westbourne Gardens	A2-A3
Westbourne Road	A2
Westcroft Street	A4-B4
Wicker Hill	B3
Wingfield Road	A2

Bradford-upon-Avon

Ashley Road	A4
Avon Close	C1
Bath Road	A3-A4-B4-B3
Berryfield Road	A4-B4
Bridge Street	B2
Christchurch Road	B4
Christchurch Road	B4
Church Acre	A4
Church Street	A2-B2
Conigre Hill	A2-A3
Coppice Hill	B2-B3
Coronation Avenue	C3-C4
Greenland View	C1
Highfield Road	C3
Holt Road	B2-C2
Huntingdon Street	A3
Kingston Road	B2
Junction Road	B1
Market Street	A2-B2
Masons Lane	A3-B3
Mill Lane	B2
Mount Pleasant	B3
Newtown	A1-A2-A3
New Road	B3-C3
Palmer Drive	B4
Pound Lane	A1-B1
Priory Close	A3-B3
Priory Park	A3-B3
Regents Place	B1-C1
Rome Road	B1
St Margaret's Place	B1-B2
St Margaret's Street	B1-C2
Silver Street	B2
Sladesbrook	B3-B4
Springfield	C2-C3
The Wilderness	A3
Trowbridge Road	B1
Upper Regents Park	B1-C1
White Hill	B2-B3
Whitehead Lane	B2-B3
Winsley Road	A3-A4
Woolley Drive	C3-C4
Woolley Street	C2-C3

HTT

131

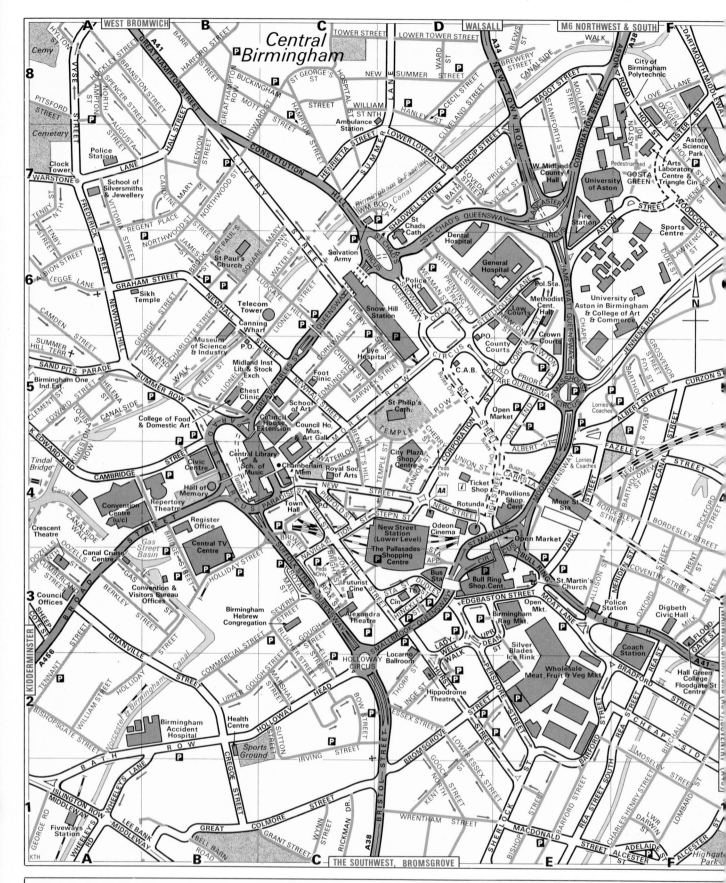

Birmingham

It is very difficult to visualise Birmingham as it was before it began the growth which eventually made it the second-largest city in England. When the Romans were in Britain it was little more than a staging post on Icknield Street. Throughout medieval times it was a sleepy agricultural centre in the middle of a heavily-forested region. Timbered houses clustered together round a green that was

eventually to be called the Bull Ring. But by the 16th century, although still a tiny and unimportant village by today's standards, it had begun to gain a reputation as a manufacturing centre. Tens of thousands of sword blades were made here during the Civil War. Throughout the 18th century more and more land was built on. In 1770 the Birmingham Canal was completed, making trade very much easier and increasing the town's development dramatically. All of that pales into near

insignificance compared with what happened in the 19th century. Birmingham was not represented in Parliament until 1832 and had no town council until 1838. Yet by 1889 it had already been made a city, and after only another 20 years it had become the second largest city in England. Many of Birmingham's most imposing public buildings date from the 19th century, when the city was growing so rapidly. Surprisingly, the city has more miles of waterway than Venice.

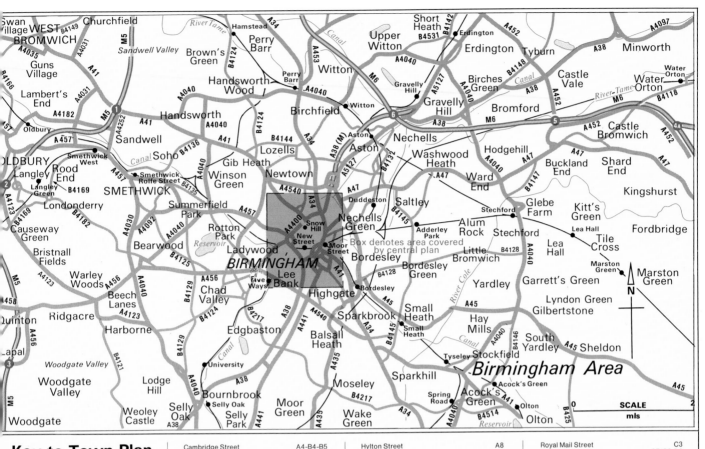

Key to Town Plan and Area Plan

Town Plan

AA Recommended roads
Restricted roads
Other roads
Buildings of interest — Station
One Way Streets
Car Parks — P
Parks and open spaces
Churches — +

Area Plan

A roads
B roads
Locations — Meer End O
Urban area

Street Index with Grid Reference

Birmingham

Adelaide Street	F1
Albert Street	E4-E5-F5
Albion Street	A6
Alcester Street	F1
Allison Street	E3
Aston Road	F8-E8-F8-F7
Aston Street	E6-E7-F7
Augusta Street	A7-A8
Bagot Street	E8
Barford Street	E1-E2-F2
Barr Street	B8
Bartholomew Street	F4-F5
Barwick Street	C5-D5
Bath Row	A1-A2-B2
Bath Street	D7
Beak Street	C3
Bell Barn Road	B1
Bennett's Hill	C4-C5
Berkley Street	A3-B3
Birchall Street	F1-F2
Bishop Street	E1
Bishopsgate Street	A2
Blews Street	E8
Blucher Street	C2-C3
Bordesley Street	E4-F4-F3
Bow Street	C2
Bradford Street	E3-E2-F2
Branston Street	A8-B8-B7
Brewery Street	E8
Bridge Street	B3-B4
Bristol Street	C1-D1-D2-C2
Broad Street	A2-A3-A4-B4
Bromsgrove Street	D1-D2-E2
Brook Street	B6
Brunel Street	C3-C4
Buckingham Street	B8-C8
Bull Ring	E3
Bull Street	D5-E5-E4

Cambridge Street	A4-B4-B5
Camden Street	A5-A6
Cannon Street	D4
Caroline Street	B6-B7
Carrs Lane	E4
Cecil Street	D8
Chapel Street	E5-E6
Charles Henry Street	F1
Charlotte Street	B5-B6
Cheapside	F1-F2
Cherry Street	D4-D5
Church Street	C6-C5-D5
Clement Street	A5
Cleveland Street	D7-D8-E8
Colmore Circus	D5-D6
Colmore Row	C4-C5-D5
Commercial Street	B2-B3-C3
Constitution Hill	B7-C7
Cornwall Street	C5-C6
Corporation Street	D4-D5-E5-E6-E7-E8-F8
Coventry Street	E3-F3
Cregoe Street	B1-B2
Cumberland Street	A3
Curzon Street	F5
Dale End	E4-E5
Dartmouth Middleway	F7-F8
Digbeth	E3-F3
Dudley Street	D3
Duke Street	F6
Edgbaston Street	D3-E3
Edmund Street	C5-D5
Edward Street	A5
Ellis Street	C2-C3
Essex Street	D2
Fazeley Street	E5-E4-F4
Fleet Street	B5
Floodgate Street	F3
Fox Street	F5
Frederick Street	A6-A7
Gas Street	A3-B3
George Road	A1
George Street	A5-B5-B6
Gooch Street North	D1-D2
Gosta Green	F7
Gough Street	C3
Graham Street	A6-B6
Grant Street	C1
Granville Street	A3-A2-B2
Great Charles St Queensway	B5-C5-C6
Great Colmore Street	B1-C1-D1
Great Hampton Row	B8
Great Hampton Street	A8-B8
Grosvenor Street	F5-F6
Hall Street	B7-B8
Hampton Street	C7-C8
Harford Street	B8
Hanley Street	D7-D8
Helena Street	A5
Heneage Street	F7
Henrietta Street	C7-D7
High Street	D4-E4
Hill Street	C4-C3-D3
Hinckley Street	D3
Hockley Street	A8-B8
Holland Street	B5
Holliday Street	A2-B2-B3-C3-C4
Holloway Circus	C2-C3-D3-D2
Holloway Head	B2-C2
Holt Street	F7-F8
Hospital Street	C7-C8
Howard Street	B7-C7-C8
Hurst Street	D3-D2-E2-E1

Hylton Street	A8
Inge Street	D2
Irving Street	C2-D2
Islington Row Middleway	A1
James Street	B6
James Watt Queensway	E5-E6
Jennens Road	E5-F5-F6
John Bright Street	C3-C4
Kent Street	D1-D2
Kenyon Street	B7
King Edward's Road	A4-A5
Kingston Row	A4
Ladywell Walk	D2-D3
Lancaster Circus	E6-E7
Lawrence Street	F6-F7
Lee Bank Middleway	A1-B1
Legge Lane	A6
Lionel Street	B5-C5-C6
Lister Street	F7-F8
Livery Street	B7-C7-C6-D6-D5
Lombard Street	F1-F2
Louisa Street	A5
Love Lane	F8
Loveday Street	D7
Lower Darwin Street	F1
Lower Essex Street	D2-D1-E1
Lower Loveday Street	D7
Lower Tower Street	D8
Ludgate Hill	B6-C6
Macdonald Street	E1-F1
Marshall Street	C2
Mary Street	B7
Mary Ann Street	C6-C7
Masshouse Circus	E5
Meriden Street	E3-F3
Milk Street	F3
Moat Lane	E3
Molland Street	E8
Moor Street Queensway	E4-E5
Moseley Street	E2-F2-F1
Mott Street	B8-C8-C7
Navigation Street	C3-C4
New Street	C4-D4
New Bartholomew Street	F4
New Canal Street	F4-F5
Newhall Hill	A5-A6
Newhall Street	B6-B5-C5
New Summer Street	C8-C8
Newton Street	E5
New Town Row	D8-E8-E7
Northampton Street	A8
Northwood Street	B6-B7
Old Square	D5-E5
Oozells Street	A3-A4
Oozells Street North	A3-A4
Oxford Street	F3-F4
Oxygen Street	F7-F8
Paradise Circus	B4-B5
Paradise Street	C4
Park Street	E3-E4
Pershore Street	D3-D2-E2
Pickford Street	F4
Pinfold Street	C4
Pitsford Street	A8
Price Street	D7-E7
Princip Street	D7-E7-E8
Printing House Street	D6
Priory Queensway	E5
Rea Street	E2-F2-F3
Rea Street South	E1-F1-F2
Regent Place	A7-B7
Rickman Drive	C1

Royal Mail Street	C3
St Chad's Circus	C7-C6-D6
St Chad's Queensway	D6-D7-E7
St George's Street	C8
St Martin's Circus	D3-D4-E4-E3
St Paul's Square	B7-B6-C6
Sand Pits Parade	A5
Severn Street	C3
Shadwell Street	D6-D7
Sheepcote Street	A3
Sherlock Street	D1-E1-E2
Smallbrook Queensway	C3-D3
Snow Hill Queensway	D6
Spencer Street	A8-A7-B7
Staniforth Street	E7-E8
Station Approach	D3
Station Street	D3
Steelhouse Lane	D6-E6
Stephenson Street	C4-D4
Suffolk Street Queensway	B4-C4-C3
Summer Hill Terrace	A5
Summer Row	A5-B5
Summer Lane	C7-D7-D8
Sutton Street	C2
Temple Row	C5-D5
Temple Street	D4-D5
Tenby Street	A6-A7
Tenby Street North	A7
Tennant Street	A2-A3
Thorp Street	D2-D3
Tower Street	C8-D8
Trent Street	F3-F4
Union Street	D4
Upper Dean Street	D3-E3
Upper Gough Street	B2-C2-C3
Vesey Street	D7-E7
Vittoria Street	A6-A7
Vyse Street	A7-A8
Ward Street	D8
Warstone Lane	A7-B7
Water Street	C6
Waterloo Street	C4-C5-D5
Weaman Street	D6
Wheeley's Lane	A1-B1-B2
Wheeley's Road	A1
Whittall Street	D6-E6
William Booth Lane	C7-D7
William Street	A2
William Street North	C8-D8
Woodcock Street	F6-F7
Wrentham Street	D1-E1
Wynn Street	C1

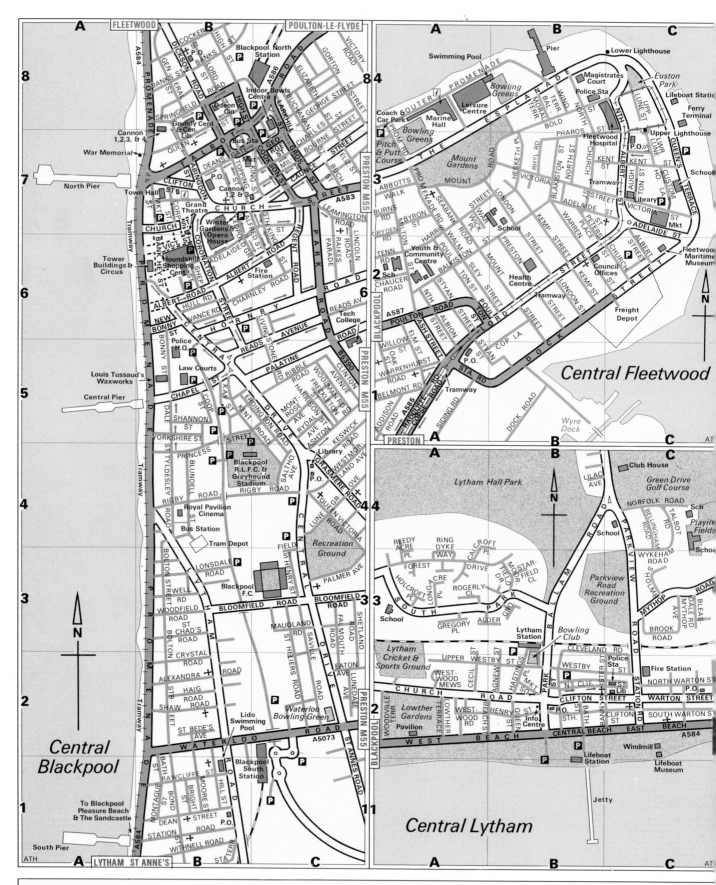

Blackpool

No seaside resort is regarded with greater affection than Blackpool. It is still the place where millions of North Country folk spend their holidays; its famous illuminations draw visitors from all over the world. It provides every conceivable kind of traditional holiday entertainment, and in greater abundance than any other seaside resort in Britain. The famous tower – built in the 1890s as a replica of the Eiffel Tower – the three piers, seven miles of promenade, five miles of illuminations, countless guesthouses, huge numbers of pubs, shops, restaurants and cafes play host to eight million visitors a year.

At the base of the tower is a huge entertainment complex that includes a ballroom, a circus and an aquarium. Other 19th-century landmarks are North Pier and Central Pier, the great Winter Gardens and Opera House and the famous trams that still run along the promenade – the only electric trams still operating in Britain. The most glittering part of modern Blackpool is the famous Golden Mile, packed with amusements, novelty shops and snack stalls. Every autumn it becomes part of the country's most extravagant light show – the illuminations – when the promenade is ablaze with neon representations of anything and everything from moon rockets to the Muppets. Autumn is also the time when Blackpool is a traditional venue for political party conferences.

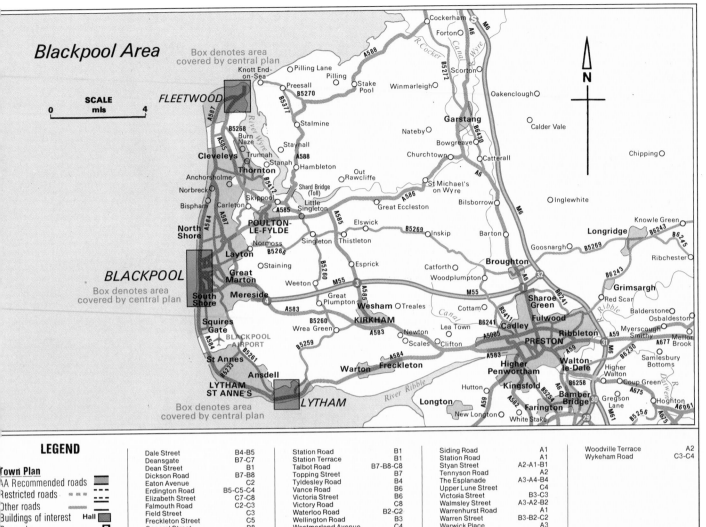

Blackpool Area

Box denotes area covered by central plan

SCALE
mls
0 — 4

N

FLEETWOOD

BLACKPOOL

Box denotes area covered by central plan

Box denotes area covered by central plan

LYTHAM

LYTHAM ST ANNE'S

LEGEND

Town Plan
- AA Recommended roads
- Restricted roads
- Other roads
- Buildings of interest — Hall
- Car parks — P
- Parks and open spaces

Area Plan
- A roads
- B roads
- Locations — Trunnah ○
- Urban area

Street Index with Grid Reference

Blackpool

Abingdon Street	B7
Adelaide Street	B6-B7-C7
Albert Road	B6-C6
Alexandra Road	B2
Alfred Street	B7-C7-C6
Ashton Road	C4-C5
Bank Hey Street	B6-B7
Banks Street	B8
Bath Street	B1-B2
Bloomfield Road	B3-C3
Blundell Street	B4
Bolton Street	B2-B3-B4
Bond Street	B1-B2
Bonny Street	B5-B6
Bright Street	B1
Buchanan Street	C7-C8
Caunce Street	C7-C8
Central Drive	B6-B5-C5-C4-C3-C2
Chapel Street	B5
Charles Street	C7-C8
Charnley Road	B6-C6
Church Street	B7-C7
Clifton Street	B7
Clinton Avenue	C5
Cocker Street	B8
Cookson Street	B8-B7-C7
Coop Street	B5
Coronation Street	B5-B6-B7
Corporation Street	B7
Crystal Road	B2

Dale Street	B4-B5
Deansgate	B7-C7
Dean Street	B1
Dickson Road	B7-B8
Eaton Avenue	C2
Erdington Road	B5-C5-C4
Elizabeth Street	C7-C8
Falmouth Road	C2-C3
Field Street	C3
Freckleton Street	C5
General Street	B8
George Street	C7-C8
Gorton Street	C8
Grasmere Road	C4
Grosvenor Street	C7
Haig Road	B2
Harrison Street	C5
Henry Street	C3
High Street	B8
Hill Street	B1
Hornby Road	B6-C6
Hull Road	B6
Kay Street	B5
Kent Road	B5-C5-C4
Keswick Road	C4-C5
King Street	C7
Larkhill Street	C8
Leamington Road	C7
Leopold Grove	B7-B6-C6
Lincoln Road	C6-C7
Livingstone Road	C5-C6
Lonsdale Road	B3
Lord Street	B8
Lune Grove	C4
Lunedale Avenue	C2
Lytham Road	B1-B2-B3-B4
Market Street	B7
Maudland Road	B3-C3
Milbourne Street	C7-C8
Montague Street	B1
Montrose Avenue	B5-C5
Moore Street	B1
New Bonny Street	B5-B6
Palatine Road	B5-C5-C6
Palmer Avenue	C3
Park Road	C5-C6-C7
Princes Street	B4-B5-C5
Promenade	B1-B2-B3-B4-B5-B6-A6-A7-B7-B8
Queen Street	B7-B8
Queen Victoria Road	C3-C4
Raikes Parade	C6-C7
Rawcliffe Street	B1
Reads Avenue	B5-C5-C6
Regent Road	C6-C7
Ribble Road	C5
Rigby Road	B4-C4
Rydal Avenue	C5
St Annes Road	C1-C2
St Bede's Avenue	B2
St Chad's Road	B3
St Heliers Road	C2-C3
Salthouse Avenue	C4
Saville Road	C2-C3
Shannon Street	B5
Shaw Road	B2
Sheppard Street	B6
Shetland Road	C2-C3
South King Street	C6-C7
Springfield Road	B8

Station Road	B1
Station Terrace	B1
Talbot Road	B7-B8-C8
Topping Street	B7
Tyldesley Road	B4
Vance Road	B6
Victoria Street	B6
Victory Road	C8
Waterloo Road	B2-C2
Wellington Road	B3
Westmorland Avenue	C4
Withnell Road	B1
Woodfield Road	B3
Woolman Road	C5
Yorkshire Street	B5

Fleetwood

Abbots Walk	A3
Adelaide Street	B3-C3-C2
Addison Road	A1
Albert Street	C2-C3
Ash Street	A1-A2
Aughton Street	C3
Balmoral Terrace	B4
Belmont Road	A1
Blakiston Street	A2-B2-B3
Bold Street	B4-C4
Burns Road	A3
Byron Street	A3
Chaucer Road	A2
Church Street	C2
Cop Lane	A1-B1-B2
Copse Road	A1
Custom House Lane	C3
Dock Road	B1
Dock Street	B1-B2-C2
Dryden Road	A2-A3
Elm Street	A1-A2
Harris Street	A2-A3-B3
Hesketh Place	B3
Kemp Street	B2-B3
Kent Street	B3-C3
London Street	B3
Lord Street	A1-A2-B2-C2-C3
Lower Lune Street	C3
Milton Street	A2-A3
Mount Road	A3-B3
Mount Street	A2-B2
North Albert Street	C3-C4
North Albion Street	A1-A2
North Church Street	B3-B4
North Street	B3
Oak Street	A1
Outer Promenade	A4-B4
Pharos Street	B3-C3-C4
Poulton Road	A2
Poulton Street	A2
Preston Street	B2
Promenade Road	A3-A4
Queen's Terrace	C3-C4
Radcliffe Road	A1
Rhyl Street	B3
St Peters Place	B2-B3
Seabank Road	A2-A3

Lytham

Agnew Street	B2-B3
Alder Grove	A3-B3
Ballam Road	B2-B3-B4-C4
Bath Street	B2
Beach Street	B2
Bellingham Road	C4
Bleasdale Road	C3
Brook Road	C3
Calcroft Place	A3-B4
Cecil Street	A2-A3
Central Beach	B2-C2
Church Road	A2-B2
Cleveland Road	B3-C3
Clifton Street	B2-C2
East Beach	C2
Forest Drive	A3-B3
Gregory Place	A3
Hastings Place	B2-B3
Henry Street	B2
Holcroft Place	A3
Lilac Avenue	B4
Longacre Place	A3
Lowther Terrace	A2
Market Square	B2
Moorfield Drive	B3
Mythop Avenue	C3
Mythop Road	C3
Norfolk Road	C4
North Clifton Street	B2-C2
North Warton Street	C2
Park Street	B2
Parkview Road	C2-C3-C4
Queen Street	B2
Reedy Acre Place	A3-A4
Ring Dyke Way	A3
Rogerly Close	A3
South Clifton Street	B2-C2
South-Holme	C3
South Park	A3-B3
South Warton Street	C2
Starfield Close	B3
Station Road	C2
Talbot Road	C4
Upper Westby Street	A2-B2
Warton Street	C2
West Beach	A2-B2
Westby Street	B2-C2
Westwood Mews	A2
Westwood Road	A2

Siding Road	A1
Station Road	A1
Styan Street	A2-A1-B1
Tennyson Road	A2
The Esplanade	A3-A4-B4
Upper Lune Street	C4
Victoria Street	B3-C3
Walmsley Street	A3-A2-B2
Warrenhurst Road	A1
Warren Street	B3-B2-C2
Warwick Place	A3
Willow Street	A1
Windsor Terrace	B4

Woodville Terrace	A2
Wykeham Road	C3-C4

ATH

135

Street Index with Grid Reference

Bournemouth

Albert Road	C3-D3
Avenue Road	B3-C3
Bath Road	D2-E2-E3-E4-F4
Beacon Road	C1
Bodorgan Road	C4
Bourne Avenue	B3-C3
Bradbourne Road	B3
Braidley Road	B3-B4
Branksome Wood Gardens	A4
Branksome Wood Road	A4
Cambridge Road	A2-A3
Central Drive	B4
Chine Crescent	A1
Chine Crescent Road	A1-A2
Christchurch Road	F4
Commercial Road	B2
Cotlands Road	F4
Cranbourne Road	B2-C2
Crescent Road	A3-B3
Cumnor Road	E4
Dean Park Crescent	C4-D4
Dean Park Road	C4
Durley Chine Road	A1-A2
Durley Chine Road South	A1
Durley Gardens	A1-A2
Durley Road	A1-A2-B1
Durrant Road	B4
East Overcliff Drive	E2-F2-F3
Exeter Crescent	C2
Exeter Park Road	C2-D2
Exeter Road	C2-D2
Fir Vale Road	D3-D4
Gervis Place	C3-D3
Gervis Road	E3-F3
Glenfern Road	D3-E3-E4
Grove Road	E3-F3
Hahnemann Road	A1-B1-B2
Hinton Road	D2-D3-E2
Holdenhurst Road	F4
Kensington Drive	A4
Kerley Road	C1
Lansdowne Road	E4-F4
Lorne Park Road	E4
Madeira Road	D4-E4
Marlborough Road	A2
Meyrick Road	F3-F4
Norwich Avenue	A2
Norwich Avenue West	A3
Norwich Road	A2-B2
Old Christchurch Road	D3-D4-E4-F4
Orchard Street	C2-C3
Parsonage Road	D3-E3
Poole Hill	A2-B2
Poole Road	A2
Post Office Road	C3
Priory Road	C1-C2
Purbeck Road	B2
Richmond Gardens	C4
Richmond Hill	C3-C4
Richmond Hill Drive	C4
Russell Cotes Road	E2
Somerville Road	A2
St Michael's Road	B2-B1-C1
St Peter's Road	D3-E3
St Stephen's Road	B3-B4-C4-C3
St Stephen's Way	C4
Stafford Road	E4
Suffolk Road	A3-B3
Surrey Road	A3
Terrace Road	B2-C2
The Triangle	B2-B3
Tregonwell Road	B2-C2-C1
Trinity Road	E4
Undercliffe Drive	D1-D2-E1-E2-F2
Upper Hinton Road	D2-D3-E2
Upper Norwich Road	A2-B2
Upper Terrace Road	B2-C2
Wessex Way	A3-A4-B4-C4-D4-E4
West Cliff Gardens	B1
West Cliff Promenade	B1-C1-D1-C1
West Cliff Road	A1-B1
Westhill Road	A2-B2-B1
Westover Road	D2-D3
West Promenade	C1-D1
Wimborne Road	C4
Wootton Gardens	E3-E4
Wootton Mount	E4
Yelverton Road	C3-D3

Christchurch

Albion Road	A4
Arcadia Road	A4
Arthur Road	B3
Avenue Road	A3-B3
Avon Road West	A3-A4-B4
Bargates	B2-B3
Barrack Road	A4-A3-B2-B3
Beaconsfield Road	B2-B3
Bridge Street	C2
Bronte Avenue	B4
Canberra Road	A4
Castle Street	B2-C2
Christchurch By-Pass	B2-C2-C3
Clarendon Road	A3-B3
Douglas Avenue	A2-B2
Endfield Road	A4
Fairfield	B3
Fairfield Drive	A2
Fairmile Road	A4-B4-B3
Flambard Avenue	B4
Gardner Road	A3-A4
Gleadows Avenue	A2-B2
Grove Road East	A3-B3
Grove Road West	A3
High Street	B2
Iford Lane	A1
Jumpers Avenue	A4
Jumpers Road	A3-A4-B4
Kings Avenue	A2-B2
Manor Road	B2
Milhams Street	B2-C2
Mill Road	B3-B4
Portfield Road	A3-B3
Queens Avenue	B1
Quay Road	B1
River Lea Road	B2
Soapers Lane	B1
Saxonbury Road	A1
St John's Road	A2
St Margarets Avenue	B1
Sopers Lane	B1-B2
South View Road	A1-B1
Stony Lane	C4-C3-C2
Stour Road	B3-B2-A1-A2
Stourbank Road	B2
The Grove	A4
Tuckton Road	A1
Twynham Avenue	B2-B3
Walcott Avenue	A4-B4
Waterloo Place	C2
Wickfield Avenue	B1-B2
Wick Lane	A1-B1-B2
Willow Drive	A1-B1
Willow Way	A1-B1
Windsor Road	A3

Poole

Ballard Road	B1-C1
Church Street	A1
Dear Hay Lane	A2-B2
Denmark Road	C3
East Quay Road	B1
East Street	B1
Elizabeth Road	C3
Emerson Road	B1-B2
Esplanade	B3
Garland Road	C4
Green Road	B2-B1-C1
Heckford Road	C3-C4
High Street	A1-B1-B2
Hill Street	B2
Johns Road	C3-C4
Jolliffe Road	C4
Kingland Road	B2-C2
Kingston Road	C3-C4
Lagland Street	B1-B2
Longfleet Road	C3
Maple Road	C3-C4
Mount Pleasant Road	C2-C3
Newfoundland Drive	C1
New Orchard	A1-A2
North Street	B2
Old Orchard	B1
Parkstone Road	C1-C2
Perry Gardens	B1
Poole Bridge	A1
Sandbourne Road	C4
St Mary's Road	C3
Seldown Lane	C2-C3
Shaftesbury Road	C3
Skinner Street	B1
South Road	B2
Stanley Road	B1
Sterte Avenue	A4-B4
Sterte Road	B2-B3-B4
Stokes Avenue	B4-C4
Strand Street	A1-B1
Tatnam Road	B4-C4
The Quay	A1-B1
Towngate Bridge	B2-B3
West Quay Road	A1-A2-B2
West Street	A1-A2-B2
Wimborne Road	B3-C3-C4

Swanage

Argyle Road	A2
Atlantic Road	A1-B1
Battlemead	B4
Beach Gardens	B4
Bon Accord Road	B1
Broad Road	C1
Cauldron Avenue	B4
Cauldron Barn Road	A4-B4
Cauldron Crescent	A4
Church Hill	A2
Clifton Road	B4
Cluny Crescent	B1-C1
Court Hill	A2
Court Road	A2
Cowlease	A1-A2
Cranborne Road	B2
De Moulham Road	B3-B4
D'uberville Drive	A4-B4
Eldon Terrace	B2
Encombe Road	C1
Exeter Road	B1-C1
Gannets Park	B3
Gilbert Road	A2-B2
Gordon Road	B1
Grosvenor Road	C1
Hanbury Road	A2
High Street	A2-B3
Ilminster Road	B2-B3
Institute Road	B2-B2
Kings Road	A2-B2
Kings Road East	B2
Kings Road West	A2
Locarno Road	A2
Manor Road	B1-C1
Manwell Drive	A1
Manwell Road	A1
Mariners Drive	A1
Marshall Row	C1
Mount Pleasant Lane	B1-B2
Mountscar	A1
Newton Road	B1
Northbrook Road	A2-A3-B3-B4
Osborne Road	A1
Park Road	C1
Princess Road	A2
Prospect Crescent	A3
Peveril Heights	C1
Peveril Point Road	C1
Priests Road	C1
Queens Mead	B1
Queens Road	A1-B1-C1
Rabling Road	A3-B3
Rempstone Road	B2-B3
Richmond Road	A1
St Vast's Road	B1
Sentry Road	C1
Seymer Road	C1
Shore Road	B3-B4
Springfield Road	B2
Stafford Road	B1-B2
Station Road	B2
Sunridge Close	B1
Taunton Road	C1
The Parade	C2
Townsend Road	A1
Ulwell Road	B4
Victoria Avenue	A3-B3
Vivian Park	B4
Walrond Road	A3-B3

LEGEND

AA Recommended roads	
Other roads	
Restricted roads	
Buildings of interest	Sta
AA Centre	AA
Churches	+
Car parks	P
One Way streets	
Parks and open spaces	

Bournemouth

Until the beginning of the 19th-century the landscape was open heath. Bournemouth's rise began in Victorian times when the idea of seaside holidays was very new. In the next 50 years it had become a major resort. Holidaymakers today enjoy miles of sandy beaches, a mild climate and beautiful setting, along with a tremendous variety of amenities, including some of the best shopping in the south. Entertainments range from variety shows, cinemas, opera and the world famous Bournemouth Symphony Orchestra.

Christchurch is situated at the confluence of the rivers Avon and Stour which flow into Christchurch Harbour at Mudeford. The Priory Church dominates the town with its many attractive walks and old buildings.

Poole is famous for the large natural harbour and Poole Quay with its unique historical interest.

The Maritime Museum illustrates the town's associations with the sea since prehistoric times and the famous Poole Pottery offers guided tours of its workshops with exhibits of pottery past and present.

Swanage is one of Dorset's most popular holiday resorts that has still retained much of its Victorian influence. Dramatic coastal scenery with cliff top walks and many places of interest are within easy reach.

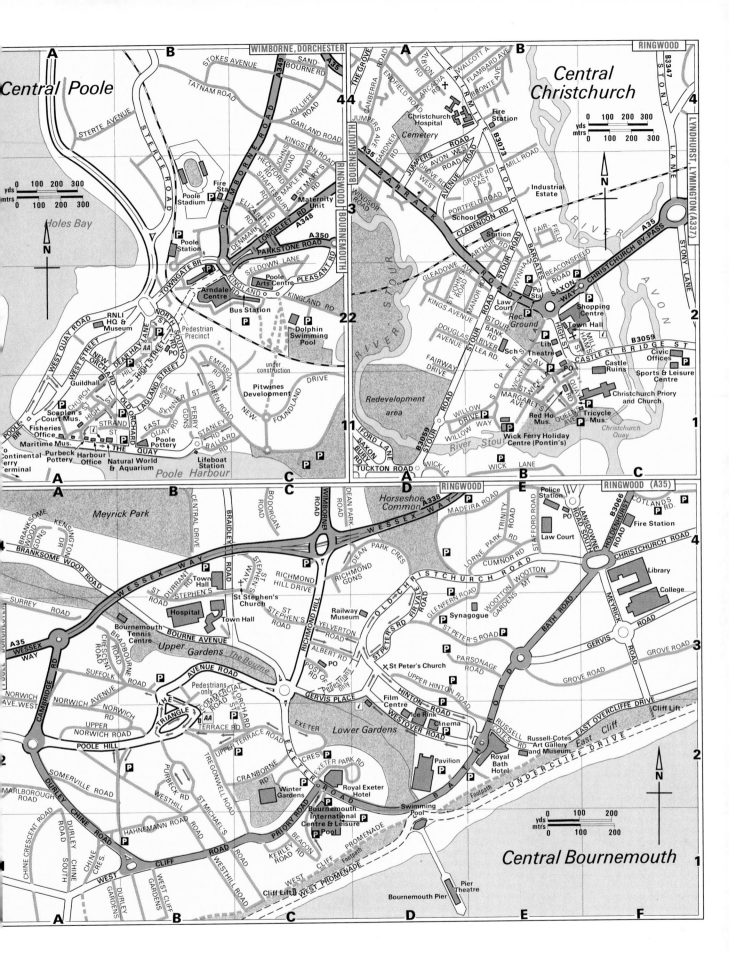

Central Poole

Holes Bay

Poole Stadium
Fire Sta
Poole Station
Poole Arts Centre
Arndale Centre
Bus Station
Poole Pottery
Dolphin Swimming Pool
RNLI HQ & Museum
Guildhall
Pedestrian Precinct
Pitwines Development
under construction
Scaplen's Court Mus.
Fisheries Office
Maritime Mus.
Purbeck Pottery
Harbour Office
Natural World & Aquarium
Lifeboat Station
Poole Harbour
Continental Ferry Terminal

STOKES AVENUE
TATNAM ROAD
SAND-BOURNE RD
JOLLIFFE ROAD
GARLAND ROAD
KINGSTON ROAD
STERTE AVENUE
STERTE ROAD
WIMBORNE ROAD
HECKFORD ROAD
MAPLE ROAD
ST MARY'S
SHAFTSBURY
ST JOHN'S
DENMARK
ELIZABETH RD
LONGFLEET RD
PARKSTONE ROAD
A348
A350
A349
SELDOWN LANE
PLEASANT RD
KINGLAND
KINGLAND RD
PLEASANT RD
TOWNGATE BR
NORTH ST
SOUTH RD
HIGH STREET
DEAR HAY LANE
HILL ST
NEW ORCHARD
OLD ORCHARD
CHURCH
HIGH ST
STRAND ST
LAGLAND STREET
SKINNER ST
EAST ST
EMERSON RD
GREEN ROAD
PERRY GDNS
STANLEY RD
QUAY RD
BALLARD RD
NEW
FOUNDLAND
DRIVE
THE QUAY
WEST QUAY ROAD
WESTSTREET
POOLE BR

Central Christchurch

RINGWOOD
B3347
STONY LANE
LYNDHURST, LYMINGTON (A337)
Christchurch Hospital
Cemetery
Fire Station
School
Station
Industrial Estate
Law Court
Pol Sta
Rec. Ground
Shopping Centre
Town Hall
Library
Civic Offices
Castle Ruins
Sports & Leisure Centre
Christchurch Priory and Church
Red Ho. Mus.
Tricycle Mus.
Christchurch Quay
Wick Ferry Holiday Centre (Pontin's)
Redevelopment area

THE GROVE
WALCOTT A
ABION RD
CANBERRA ROAD
ENDFIELD ROAD
ARCADIA RD
FLAMBARD AVE
BRONTE AVE
JUMPERS AVE
GARDNER RD
GROVE RD EAST
AVON
WEST
ROAD
WINDSOR ROAD
PORTFIELD ROAD
CLARENDON RD
ARTHUR RD
BARRACK ROAD
STOUR ROAD
BARGATES
BEACONSFIELD ROAD
SAXON WAY
FAIR-FIELD
HIGH ST
CASTLE ST
BRIDGE ST
MILL ROAD
B3073
B3059
GLEADOWE AVE
ST JOHN'S ROAD
MANOR RD
KINGS AVENUE
DOUGLAS AVENUE
STOUR RD
STOUR
BANK RD
RIVER
STLEA RD
FAIRWAY DRIVE
SUPER
ST WICK LANE
ST MARGARET'S AVE
WILLOW DRIVE
WILLOW WAY
WICKFIELD AV
QUEENS AVE
IFORD LANE
SAXONBURY RD
TUCKTON ROAD
STOUR RD
WICK LA
WICK LANE
B3059
River Stour
RIVER STOUR
RIVER AVON
A35 BY-PASS
A35

Central Bournemouth

RINGWOOD
RINGWOOD (A35)
B3066
COTLANDS RD
Police Station
Fire Station
Law Court
Library
College
Meyrick Park
Horseshoe Common
Richmond Gdns
Railway Museum
Synagogue
St Peter's Church
St Stephen's Church
Town Hall
Hospital
Bournemouth Tennis Centre
Upper Gardens
The Bourne
The Triangle
Winter Gardens
Royal Exeter Hotel
Bournemouth International Centre & Leisure Pool
Film Centre
Ice Rink
Cinema
Lower Gardens
Pavilion
Royal Bath Hotel
Russell-Cotes Art Gallery and Museum
East Cliff
Cliff Lift
Swimming Pool
Pier Theatre
Bournemouth Pier
West Promenade

WIMBORNE ROAD
DEAN PARK
DEAN PARK CRES
RICHMOND HILL DRIVE
RICHMOND HILL
WESSEX WAY
MADEIRA ROAD
LORNE PARK RD
TRINITY RD
CUMNOR RD
STAFFORD RD
LANSDOWNE ROAD SOUTH
HOLDENHURST ROAD
CHRISTCHURCH ROAD
BRANKSOME WOOD ROAD
BRANKSOME WOOD
KENSINGTON DR
GDNS
CENTRAL DRIVE
BRAIDLEY ROAD
BODORGAN ROAD
SURREY ROAD
ST DURRANT RD
ST STEPHEN'S WAY
ST STEPHEN'S ROAD
BOURNE AVENUE
BRADBOURNE RD
CRESCENT ROAD
SUFFOLK ROAD
AVENUE ROAD
COMMERCIAL ROAD
ORCHARD ST
TERRACE RD
OLD CHRISTCHURCH ROAD
FIRVALE ROAD
GLENFERN ROAD
WOOTTON GDNS
WOOTTON MT
ST PETER'S ROAD
ST PETER'S RD
PARSONAGE ROAD
UPPER HINTON ROAD
HINTON ROAD
WESTOVER ROAD
GERVIS PLACE
YELVERTON ROAD
ALBERT RD
POST OFFICE RD
EXETER CRES
EXETER ROAD
EXETER PARK RD
NORWICH AVE. WEST
NORWICH AVENUE
NORWICH RD
UPPER NORWICH ROAD
CAMBRIDGE RD
POOLE HILL
SOMERVILLE ROAD
MARLBOROUGH ROAD
DURLEY CHINE ROAD
CHINE CRESCENT ROAD
CHINE CRES
CHINE SOUTH
DURLEY GARDENS
WEST CLIFF GARDENS
WEST CLIFF ROAD
WESTHILL ROAD
HAHNEMANN ROAD
ST MICHAEL'S ROAD
PURBECK RD
WESTHILL RD
TREGONWELL ROAD
CRANBORNE RD
PRIORY ROAD
KERLEY RD
BEACON RD
BATH ROAD
RUSSELL COTES RD
EAST OVERCLIFFE DRIVE
UNDERCLIFFE DRIVE
GERVIS ROAD
BATH ROAD
MEYRICK ROAD
GROVE ROAD
WEST PROMENADE
WEST CLIFF
Footpath
N
A35
WESSEX WAY

yds / mtrs 0 100 200 300

BOURNEMOUTH
The pier, safe sea-bathing, golden sands facing south and sheltered by steep cliffs, and plenty of amenities for the holiday maker make Bournemouth one of the most popular resorts on the south coast of England.

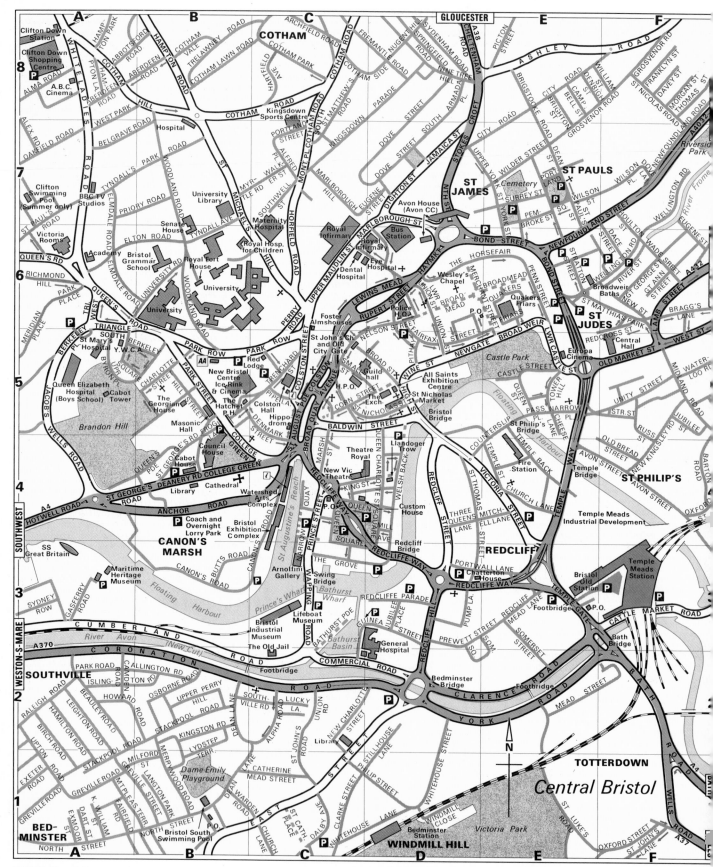

Bristol

One of Britain's most historic seaports, Bristol retains many of its visible links with the past, despite terrible damage inflicted during bombing raids in World War II. Most imposing is the cathedral, founded as an abbey church in 1140. Perhaps even more famous than the cathedral is the Church of St Mary Redcliffe. Ranking among the finest churches in the country, it owes much of its splendour to 14th- and 15th-century merchants who bestowed huge sums of money on it.

The merchant families brought wealth to the whole of Bristol, and their trading links with the world are continued in today's modern aerospace and technological industries. Much of the best of Bristol can be seen in the area of the Floating Harbour. Several of the old warehouses have been converted into museums, galleries and exhibition centres. Among them are genuinely picturesque old pubs, the best known which is the Llandoger Trow. It is a timbered 17th-century house, the finest of its kind in Bristol. Further up the same street - King Street - is the Theatre Royal, built in 1766 and the oldest theatre in the country. In Corn Street, the heart of the business area, is a magnificent 18th-century corn exchange. In front of it are the four pillars known as the 'nails', on which merchants used to make cash transactions, hence to 'pay on the nail';

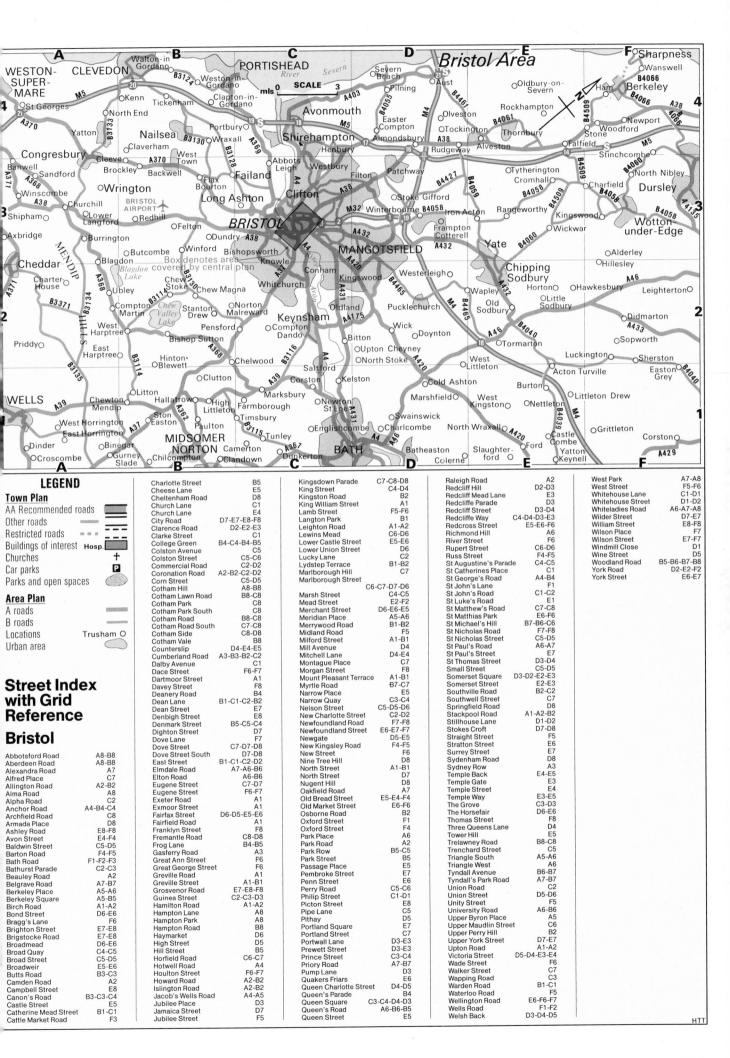

LEGEND

Town Plan

AA Recommended roads
Other roads
Restricted roads
Buildings of interest   Hosp.
Churches   †
Car parks   P
Parks and open spaces

Area Plan

A roads
B roads
Locations   Trusham ○
Urban area

Street Index with Grid Reference

Bristol

Abbotsford Road	A8-B8
Aberdeen Road	A8-B8
Alexandra Road	A7
Alfred Place	C7
Allington Road	A2-B2
Alma Road	A8
Alpha Road	C2
Anchor Road	A4-B4-C4
Archfield Road	C8
Armada Place	D8
Ashley Road	E8-F8
Avon Street	E4-F4
Baldwin Street	C5-D5
Barton Road	F4-F5
Bath Road	F1-F2-F3
Bathurst Parade	C2-C3
Beauley Road	A2
Belgrave Road	A7-B7
Berkeley Place	A5-A6
Berkeley Square	A5-B5
Birch Road	A1-A2
Bond Street	D6-E6
Bragg's Lane	F6
Brighton Street	E7-E8
Brigstocke Road	E7-E8
Broadmead	D6-E6
Broad Quay	C4-C5
Broad Street	C5-D5
Broadweir	E5-E6
Butts Road	B3-C3
Camden Road	A2
Campbell Street	E8
Canon's Road	B3-C3-C4
Castle Street	E5
Catherine Mead Street	B1-C1
Cattle Market Road	F3
Charlotte Street	B5
Cheese Lane	E5
Cheltenham Road	D8
Church Lane	C1
Church Lane	E4
City Road	D7-E7-E8-F8
Clarence Road	D2-E2-E3
Clarke Street	C1
College Green	B4-C4-B4-B5
Colston Avenue	C5
Colston Street	C5-C6
Commercial Road	C2-D2
Coronation Road	A2-B2-C2-D2
Corn Street	C5-D5
Cotham Hill	A8-B8
Cotham Lawn Road	B8-C8
Cotham Park	C8
Cotham Park South	C8
Cotham Road	B8-C8
Cotham Road South	C7-C8
Cotham Side	C8-D8
Cotham Vale	B8
Countership	D4-E4-E5
Cumberland Road	A3-B3-B2-C2
Dalby Avenue	C1
Dace Street	F6-F7
Dartmoor Street	A1
Davey Street	F8
Deanery Road	B4
Dean Lane	B1-C1-C2-B2
Dean Street	E7
Denbigh Street	E8
Denmark Street	B5-C5-C4
Dighton Street	D7
Dove Lane	F7
Dove Street	C7-D7-D8
Dove Street South	D7-D8
East Street	B1-C1-C2-D2
Elmdale Road	A7-A6-B6
Elton Road	A6-B6
Eugene Street	C7-D7
Eugene Street	F6-F7
Exeter Road	A1
Exmoor Street	A1
Fairfax Street	D6-D5-E5-E6
Fairfield Road	A1
Franklyn Street	F8
Fremantle Road	C8-D8
Frog Lane	B4-B5
Gasferry Road	A3
Great Ann Street	F6
Great George Street	F6
Greville Road	A1
Greville Street	A1-B1
Grosvenor Road	E7-E8-F8
Guinea Street	C2-C3-D3
Hamilton Road	A1-A2
Hampton Lane	A8
Hampton Park	A8
Hampton Road	B8
Haymarket	D6
High Street	D5
Hill Street	B5
Horfield Road	C6-C7
Hotwell Road	A4
Houlton Street	F6-F7
Howard Road	A2-B2
Islington Road	A2-B2
Jacob's Wells Road	A4-A5
Jubilee Place	D3
Jamaica Street	D7
Jubilee Street	F5
Kingsdown Parade	C7-C8-D8
King Street	C4-D4
Kingston Road	B2
King William Street	A1
Lamb Street	F5-F6
Langton Park	B1
Leighton Road	A1-A2
Lewins Mead	C6-D6
Lower Castle Street	E5-E6
Lower Union Street	D6
Lucky Lane	C2
Lydstep Terrace	B1-B2
Marlborough Hill	C7
Marlborough Street	C6-C7-D7-D6
Marsh Street	C4-C5
Mead Street	E2-F2
Merchant Street	D6-E6-E5
Meridian Place	A5-A6
Merrywood Road	B1-B2
Midland Road	F5
Milford Street	A1-B1
Mill Avenue	D4
Mitchell Lane	E4-E4
Montague Place	C7
Morgan Street	F8
Mount Pleasant Terrace	A1-B1
Myrtle Road	B7-C7
Narrow Place	E5
Narrow Quay	C3-C4
Nelson Street	C5-D5-D6
New Charlotte Street	C2-D2
Newfoundland Road	F7-F8
Newfoundland Street	E6-E7-F7
Newgate	D5-E5
New Kingsley Road	F4-F5
New Street	F6
Nine Tree Hill	D8
North Street	A1-B1
North Street	D7
Nugent Hill	D8
Oakfield Road	A7
Old Bread Street	E5-E4-F4
Old Market Street	E6-F6
Osborne Road	B2
Oxford Street	F1
Oxford Street	F4
Park Place	A6
Park Road	A2
Park Row	B5-C5
Park Street	B5
Passage Place	E5
Pembroke Street	E7
Penn Street	E6
Perry Road	C5-C6
Philip Street	C1-D1
Picton Street	E8
Pipe Lane	C5
Pithay	D5
Portland Square	E7
Portland Street	C7
Portwall Lane	D3-E3
Prewett Street	D3-E3
Prince Street	C3-C4
Priory Road	A7-B7
Pump Lane	D3
Quakers Friars	E6
Queen Charlotte Street	D4-D5
Queen's Parade	B4
Queen Square	C3-C4-D4-D3
Queen's Road	A6-B6-B5
Queen Street	E5
Raleigh Road	A2
Redcliff Hill	D2-D3
Redcliff Mead Lane	E3
Redcliffe Parade	D3
Redcliff Street	D3-D4
Redcliff Way	C4-D4-D3-E3
Redcross Street	E5-E6-F6
Richmond Hill	A6
River Street	F6
Rupert Street	C6-D6
Russ Street	F4-F5
St Augustine's Parade	C4-C5
St Catherines Place	C1
St George's Road	A4-B4
St John's Lane	F1
St John's Road	C1-C2
St Luke's Road	E1
St Matthew's Road	C7-C8
St Matthias Park	E6-F6
St Michael's Hill	B7-B6-C6
St Nicholas Road	F7-F8
St Nicholas Street	C5-D5
St Paul's Road	A6-A7
St Paul's Street	E7
St Thomas Street	D3-D4
Small Street	C5-D5
Somerset Square	D3-D2-E2-E3
Somerset Street	E2-E3
Southville Road	B2-C2
Southwell Street	C7
Springfield Road	D8
Stackpool Road	A1-A2-B2
Stillhouse Lane	D1-D2
Stokes Croft	D7-D8
Straight Street	F5
Stratton Street	E6
Surrey Street	E7
Sydenham Road	D8
Sydney Row	A3
Temple Back	E4-E5
Temple Gate	E3
Temple Street	E4
Temple Way	E3-E5
The Grove	C3-D3
The Horsefair	D6-E6
Thomas Street	F8
Three Queens Lane	D4
Tower Hill	E5
Trelawney Road	B8-C8
Trenchard Street	C5
Triangle South	A5-A6
Triangle West	A6
Tyndall Avenue	B6-B7
Tyndall's Park Road	A7-B7
Union Road	C2
Union Street	D5-D6
Unity Street	F5
University Road	A6-B6
Upper Byron Place	A5
Upper Maudlin Street	C6
Upper Perry Hill	B2
Upper York Street	D7-E7
Upton Road	A1-A2
Victoria Street	D5-D4-E3-E4
Wade Street	F6
Walker Street	C7
Wapping Road	C3
Warden Road	B1-C1
Waterloo Road	F5
Wellington Road	E6-F6-F7
Wells Road	F1-F2
Welsh Back	D3-D4-D5
West Park	A7-A8
West Street	F5-F6
Whitehouse Lane	C1-D1
Whitehouse Street	D1-D2
Whiteladies Road	A6-A7-A8
Wilder Street	D7-E7
William Street	E8-F8
Wilson Place	F7
Wilson Street	E7-F7
Windmill Close	D1
Wine Street	D5
Woodland Road	B5-B6-B7-B8
York Road	D2-E2-F2
York Street	E6-E7

139

HTT

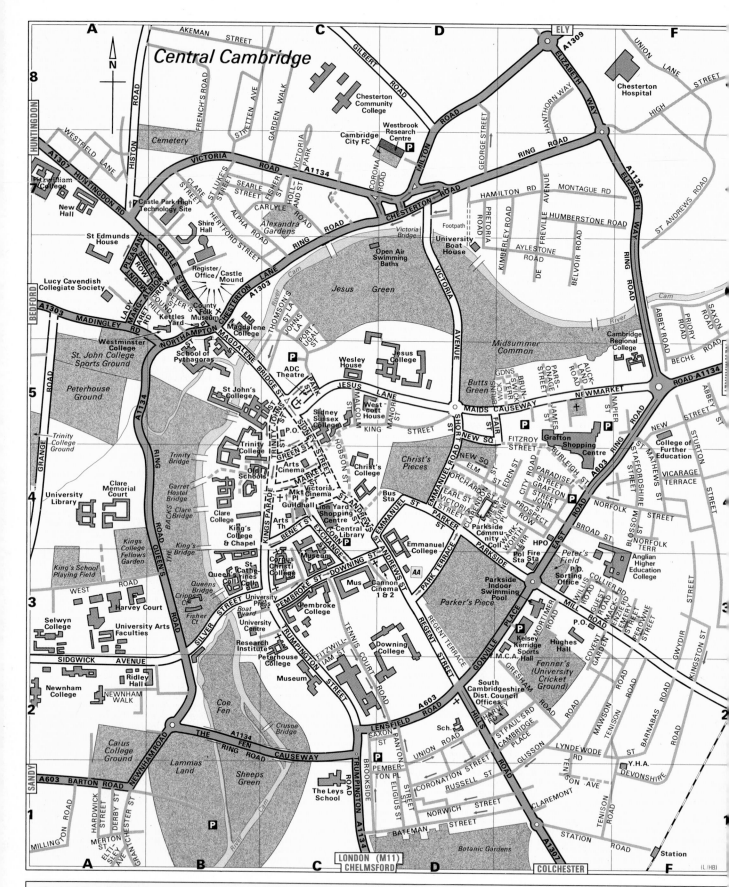

Cambridge

Few views in England, perhaps even in Europe, are as memorable as that from Cambridge's Backs towards the colleges. Dominating the scene, in every sense, is King's College Chapel. One of the finest Gothic buildings anywhere, it was built in three stages from 1446 to 1515.

No one would dispute that the chapel is Cambridge's masterpiece, but there are dozens of buildings here that would be the finest in any other town or city. Most are colleges, or are attached to colleges, and it is the university which permeates every aspect of Cambridge's landscape and life. In all there are 33 university colleges in the city, and nearly all have buildings and features of great interest. Guided tours of the colleges are available.

Cambridge can provide a complete history of English architecture. The oldest surviving building is the tower of St Benet's Church dating back to before the Norman Conquest, and its most famous church is the Church of the Holy Sepulchre, one of only four round churches of its kind.

Of the many notable museums in Cambridge, the Fitzwilliam Museum contains some of the best collections of ceramics, paintings, coins, medals and Egyptian, Greek and Roman antiquities outside London.

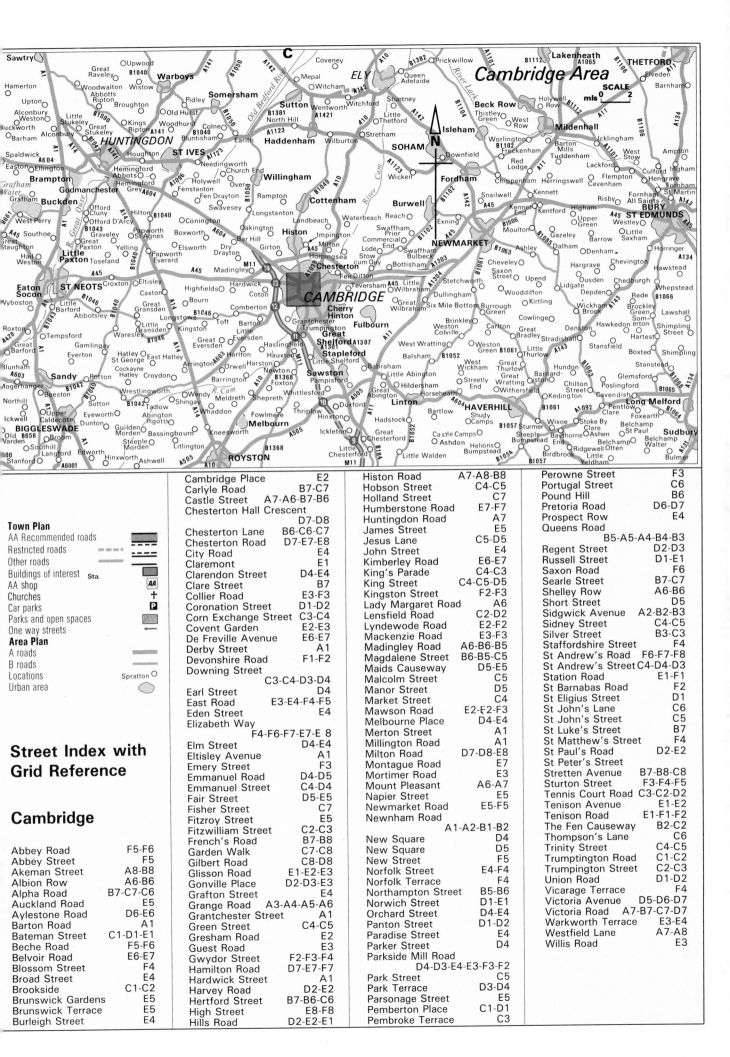

Street Index with Grid Reference

Town Plan

AA Recommended roads
Restricted roads
Other roads
Buildings of interest   Sta.
AA shop   AA
Churches   †
Car parks   P
Parks and open spaces
One way streets

Area Plan

A roads
B roads
Locations   Spratton ○
Urban area

Cambridge

Abbey Road	F5-F6
Abbey Street	F5
Akeman Street	A8-B8
Albion Row	A6-B6
Alpha Road	B7-C7-C6
Auckland Road	E5
Aylestone Road	D6-E6
Barton Road	A1
Bateman Street	C1-D1-E1
Beche Road	F5-F6
Belvoir Road	E6-E7
Blossom Street	F4
Broad Street	E4
Brookside	C1-C2
Brunswick Gardens	E5
Brunswick Terrace	E5
Burleigh Street	E4
Cambridge Place	E2
Carlyle Road	B7-C7
Castle Street	A7-A6-B7-B6
Chesterton Hall Crescent	D7-D8
Chesterton Lane	B6-C6-C7
Chesterton Road	D7-E7-E8
City Road	E4
Claremont	E1
Clarendon Street	D4-E4
Clare Street	B7
Collier Road	E3-F3
Coronation Street	D1-D2
Corn Exchange Street	C3-C4
Covent Garden	E2-E3
De Freville Avenue	E6-E7
Derby Street	A1
Devonshire Road	F1-F2
Downing Street	C3-C4-D3-D4
Earl Street	D4
East Road	E3-E4-F4-F5
Eden Street	E4
Elizabeth Way	F4-F6-F7-E7-E 8
Elm Street	D4-E4
Eltisley Avenue	A1
Emery Street	F3
Emmanuel Road	D4-D5
Emmanuel Street	C4-D4
Fair Street	D5-E5
Fisher Street	C7
Fitzroy Street	E5
Fitzwilliam Street	C2-C3
French's Road	B7-B8
Garden Walk	C7-C8
Gilbert Road	C8-D8
Glisson Road	E1-E2-E3
Gonville Place	D2-D3-E3
Grafton Street	E4
Grange Road	A3-A4-A5-A6
Grantchester Street	A1
Green Street	C4-C5
Gresham Road	E2
Guest Road	E3
Gwydor Street	F2-F3-F4
Hamilton Road	D7-E7-F7
Hardwick Street	A1
Harvey Road	D2-E2
Hertford Street	B7-B6-C6
High Street	E8-F8
Hills Road	D2-E2-E1
Histon Road	A7-A8-B8
Hobson Street	C4-C5
Holland Street	C7
Humberstone Road	E7-F7
Huntingdon Road	A7
James Street	E5
Jesus Lane	C5-D5
John Street	E4
Kimberley Road	E6-E7
King's Parade	C4-C3
King Street	C4-C5-D5
Kingston Street	F2-F3
Lady Margaret Road	A6
Lensfield Road	C2-D2
Lyndewode Road	E2-F2
Mackenzie Road	E3-F3
Madingley Road	A6-B6-B5
Magdalene Street	B6-B5-C5
Maids Causeway	D5-E5
Malcolm Street	C5
Manor Street	D5
Market Street	C4
Mawson Road	E2-F2-F3
Melbourne Place	D4-E4
Merton Street	A1
Millington Road	A1
Milton Road	D7-D8-E8
Montague Road	E7
Mortimer Road	E3
Mount Pleasant	A6-A7
Napier Street	E5
Newmarket Road	E5-F5
Newnham Road	A1-A2-B1-B2
New Square	D4
New Square	D5
New Street	F5
Norfolk Street	E4-F4
Norfolk Terrace	F4
Northampton Street	B5-B6
Norwich Street	D1-E1
Orchard Street	D4-E4
Panton Street	D1-D2
Paradise Street	E4
Parker Street	D4
Parkside Mill Road	D4-D3-E4-E3-F3-F2
Park Street	C5
Park Terrace	D3-D4
Parsonage Street	E5
Pemberton Place	C1-D1
Pembroke Terrace	C3
Perowne Street	F3
Portugal Street	C6
Pound Hill	B6
Pretoria Road	D6-D7
Prospect Row	E4
Queens Road	B5-A5-A4-B4-B3
Regent Street	D2-D3
Russell Street	D1-E1
Saxon Road	F6
Searle Street	B7-C7
Shelley Row	A6-B6
Short Street	D5
Sidgwick Avenue	A2-B2-B3
Sidney Street	C4-C5
Silver Street	B3-C3
Staffordshire Street	F4
St Andrew's Road	F6-F7-F8
St Andrew's Street	C4-D4-D3
Station Road	E1-F1
St Barnabas Road	F2
St Eligius Street	D1
St John's Lane	C6
St John's Street	C5
St Luke's Street	B7
St Matthew's Street	C4
St Paul's Road	D2-E2
St Peter's Street	
Stretten Avenue	B7-B8-C8
Sturton Street	F3-F4-F5
Tennis Court Road	C3-C2-D2
Tenison Avenue	E1-E2
Tenison Road	E1-F1-F2
The Fen Causeway	B2-C2
Thompson's Lane	C6
Trinity Street	C4-C5
Trumptington Road	C1-C2
Trumpington Street	C2-C3
Union Road	D1-D2
Vicarage Terrace	F4
Victoria Avenue	D5-D6-D7
Victoria Road	A7-B7-C7-D7
Warkworth Terrace	E3-E4
Westfield Lane	A7-A8
Willis Road	E3

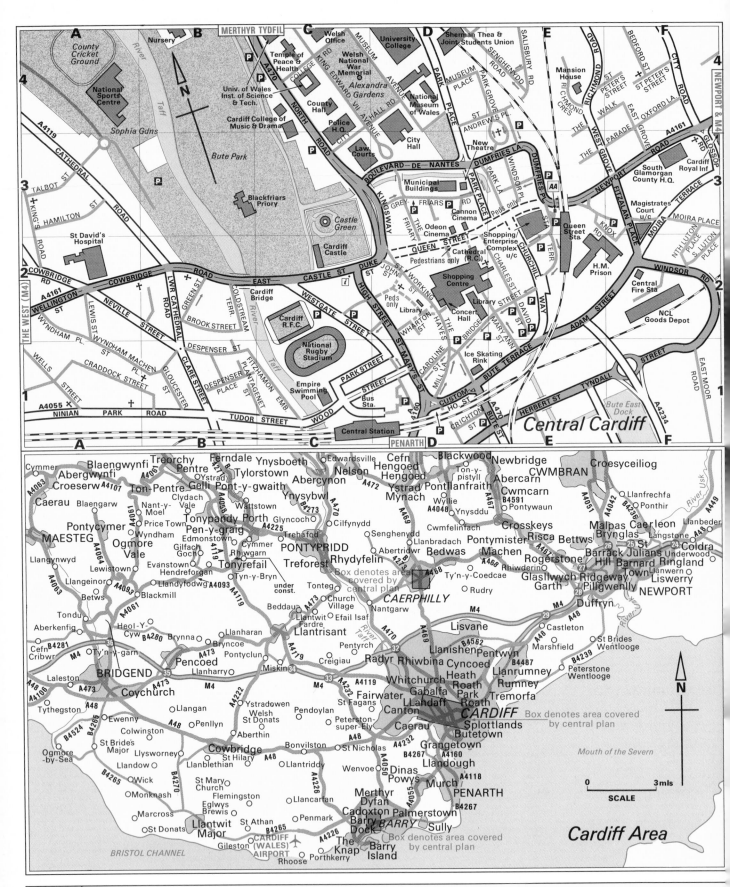

Cardiff

Strategically important to both the Romans and the Normans, Cardiff slipped from prominence in medieval times and remained a quiet market town in a remote area until it was transformed – almost overnight – by the effects of the Industrial Revolution. The valleys of South Wales were a principal source of iron and coal – raw materials which helped to change the shape and course of

the 19th-century world. Cardiff became a teeming export centre; by the end of the 19th century it was the largest coal-exporting city in the world.

Close to the castle – an exciting place with features from Roman times to the 19th century – is the city's civic centre – a fine concourse of buildings dating largely from the early part of the 20th century. Among them is the National Museum of Wales – a superb collection of art and antiquities from Wales and around the world.

Barry has sandy beaches, landscaped gardens and parks, entertainment arcades and funfairs. Like Cardiff it grew as a result of the demand for coal and steel, but now its dock complex is involved in the petrochemical and oil industries.

Caerphilly is famous for two things – a castle and cheese. The cheese is no longer made here, but the 13th-century castle, slighted by Cromwell, still looms above its moat. No castle in Britain – except Windsor – is larger.

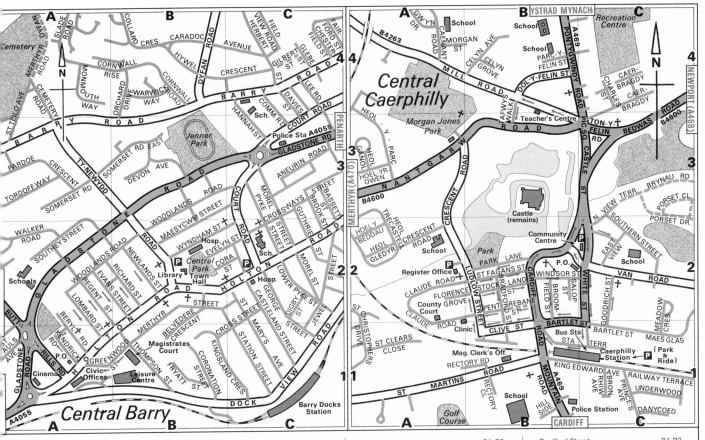

Central Caerphilly

Central Barry

LEGEND

Town Plan
AA recommended route
Restricted roads
Other roads
Buildings of interest — Cinema 🅿
Car parks 🅿
Parks and open spaces
One way streets

Area Plan
A roads
B roads
Locations — Glyncoch ◯
Urban area

Street Index with Grid Reference

Cardiff

Adam Street	E1-E2-F2
Bedford Street	F4
Boulevard de Nantes	C3-D3
Bridge Street	D1-D2-E2
Brook Street	B2
Bute Street	D1-E1
Bute Terrace	D1-E1
Caroline Street	D1
Castle Street	C2
Cathedral Street	A4-A3-B3-B2-A2
Charles Street	D2-E2
Churchill Way	E2-E3
City Hall Road	C3-C4-D4
City Road	F4
Clare Street	B1
Coldstream Terrace	B2
College Road	C4
Cowbridge Road	A2
Cowbridge Road East	A2-B2-C2
Craddock Street	A1-B1
Crichton Street	D1
Customhouse Street	D1
David Street	E2
Despenser Place	B1
Despenser Street	B1
Duke Street	C2-D2
Dumfries Lane	D3-E3
Dumfries Place	E3
East Grove	F4-F3
East Moor Road	F1
Fitzalan Place	F3-F2
Fitzhamon Embankment	B1-C1
Glossop Road	F3
Gloucester Street	B1

Green Street	B2
Greyfriars Road	D3
Hamilton Street	A3
Herbert Street	E1
High Street	C2-D2
King Edward VII Avenue	C4-D4-D3-C3
King's Road	A2-A3
Kingsway	C3-D3-D2
Knox Road	E3-F3-F2
Lewis Street	A2
Lower Cathedral Road	B1-B2
Machen Place	A1-B1
Mary Ann Street	E1-E2
Mill Lane	D1
Moira Place	F3
Moira Terrace	F2-F3
Museum Avenue	C4-D4
Museum Place	D4
Neville Street	A2-B2-B1
Newport Road	A1-B1
Ninian Park Road	A1
North Luton Place	F2-F3
North Road	B4-C4-C3
Oxford Lane	F4
Park Grove	D4-E4
Park Lane	D3-E3
Park Place	D4-D3-E3
Park Street	C1-D1
Plantagenet Street	B1-C1
Queen Street	D2-D3
Richmond Crescent	E4
Richmond Road	E4
St Andrew's Place	D4-E4
St John Street	D2
St Mary's Street	D1-D2
St Peter's Street	E4-F4
Salisbury Road	E4
Senghenydd Road	D4-E4
South Luton Place	F2-F3
Station Terrace	E2-E3
The Friary	D2-D3
The Hayes	D1-D2
The Parade	E3-F3-F4
The Walk	E3-E4-F4
Talbot Street	A3
Tudor Street	B1-C1
Tyndall Street	E1-F1
Wellington Street	A2
Wells Street	A1
Westgate Street	C2-D2-D1
West Grove	E4-E3-F3
Wharton Street	D2
Windsor Place	E3
Windsor Road	F2
Wood Street	C1-D1
Working Street	D2
Wyndham Place	A2
Wyndham Street	A1-A2

Barry

Aneurin Road	C3
Barry Road	A3-A4-B3-B4-C4
Bassett Street	C2-C3
Belvedere Crescent	B1-B2
Beryl Road	A1-A2
Brook Street	C2-C3
Buttrills Road	A1-A2
Caradoc Avenue	B4-C4

Castleland Street	C1-C2
Cemetery Road	A3-A4
Chesterfield Street	C4
Collard Crescent	B4
Commercial Road	C3-C4
Cora Street	B2-C2
Cornwall Rise	A3-A4
Cornwall Road	B4
Coronation Street	B1
Cross Street	B1-C1-C2
Crossways Street	C2-C3
Court Road	C2-C3-C4
Davies Street	C3-C4
Devon Avenue	B3
Digby Street	C2
Dock View Road	B1-C1-C2
Dyfan Road	B4
Evans Street	A2-B2
Evelyn Street	B2-C2
Fairford Street	C4
Field View Road	C4
Fryatt Street	B1
George Street	C4
Gilbert Street	C1-C2
Gladstone Road	A1-A2-B2-B3-C3
Glebe Street	C4
Greenwood Street	A1-B1
Guthrie Street	C3-C2
Hannah Street	C4-C3
Herbert Street	C4
Holton Road	A1-B1-B2-C2
Hywell Crescent	B4-C4
Jewel Street	C1-C2
Kendrick Road	A1
Kingsland Crescent	B1-C1
Lee Road	C4
Lombard Street	A1-A2
Lower Pyke Street	C2
Maesycwm Street	B2-B3-C3
Merthyr Dyfan Road	A4
Merthyr Street	B1-B2-C2
Monmouth Way	A4
Morel Street	C2-C3
Newlands Street	B2
Orchard Drive	B3-B4
Pardoe Crescent	A3
Pyke Street	C3-C2
Regent Street	A2-B2
Richard Street	A2-B2
St Mary's Avenue	C1-C2
St Pauls Avenue	A1
St Teilo Avenue	A3-A4
Slade Road	A4
Somerset Road	A3
Somerset Road East	A3-B3
Southey Street	A2-A3
Station Street	C1
Thompson Street	B1
Tordoff Way	A3
Ty-Newydd Road	A3-B3-B2
Walker Road	A2
Warwick Way	B4
Woodlands Road	A2-B2-B3-C3
Wyndham Street	B2-C2

Caerphilly

Bartlet Street	B2-B1-C1
Bedwas Road	C3-C4

Bradford Street	B1-B2
Broomfield Street	B2
Bronrhiw Avenue	C1
Brynau Road	C3
Caenant Road	A4
Caer Bragdy	C4
Cardiff Road	B1-B2
Castle Street	C3
Celyn Avenue	B4
Celyn Grove	B4
Charles Street	C4
Claude Road	A1-A2-B2
Clive Street	B1-B2
Crescent Rod	A2-A3-B3
Danycoed	C1
Dol-y-Felen Street	B4
East View	C2
Florence Grove	A2-B2
Goodrich Street	C1-C2
Gwyn Drive	A4
Heol Ganol	A3
Heol Gledyr	A2
Heol Trecastell	A2-A3
Hillside	B1
Heol y Beddau	A2
Heol-yr-Owen	A3
King Edward Avenue	B1-C1
Ludlow Street	A2-B2-B1
Maes Glas	C1
Meadow Crescent	C1-C2
Mill Road	A4-B4-B3
Morgan Street	A4-B4
Mountain Road	B1
Nantgarw Road	A3-B3
North View Terrace	C2-C3
Parc-y-Felin Street	B4
Park Lane	B2
Pentrebone Street	B2
Piccadilly Square	C3
Pontygwindy Road	B4-C4
Porset Close	C3
Porset Drive	C2-C3
Prince's Avenue	C1
Railway Terrace	C1
Rectory Road	A1-B1
Rectory Close	B1
St Christopher's Drive	A1-A2
St Clears Close	A1
St Fagans Street	B2
St Martins Road	A1-B1
Salop Street	B2
Southern Street	C2-C3
Station Terrace	B1-C1
Stockland Street	B2
Tafwy Walk	B3-B4
Ton-y-Felin Road	C3
Underwood	C1
Van Road	C2
White Street	C2
Windsor Street	B2

143

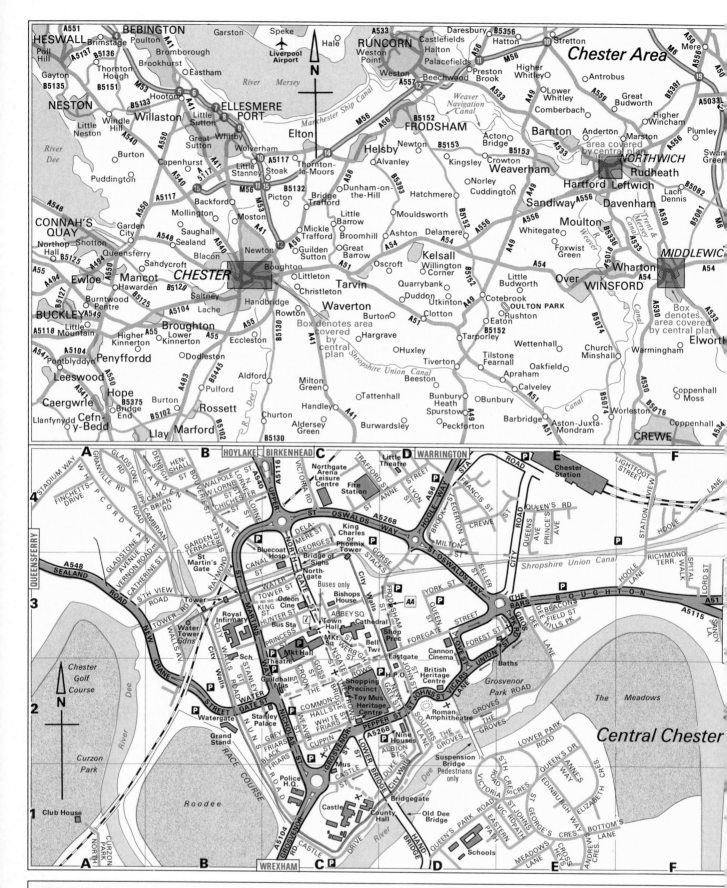

Chester

Chester is the only English city to have preserved the complete circuit of its Roman and medieval walls. On the west side, the top of the walls is now at pavement level, but on the other three sides the walk along the ramparts is remarkable. Two of the old watchtowers contain small museums: the Water Tower, built to protect the old river port, displays relics of medieval Chester; King Charles's

Tower, from which Charles I watched the defeat of the Royalist army at the Battle of Rowton Moor in 1645, portrays Chester's role in the Civil War.

Looking down from the top of the Eastgate, crowned with the ornate and gaily-coloured Jubilee Clock erected in 1897, the view down the main street, the old Roman *Via Principalis*, reveals a dazzling display of the black-and-white timbered buildings for which Chester is famous. One of these, Providence House, bears the inscription

'God's Providence is Mine Inheritance', carved in thanks for sparing the survivors of the plague of 1647 that ravaged the city.

On either side of Eastgate, Watergate and Bridge Street are the Rows, a feature unique to Chester, and dating back at least to the 13th century. These covered galleries of shops, raised up at first-floor level, protected pedestrians from weather and traffic. Chester's magnificent cathedral has beautifully carved choir stalls.

144

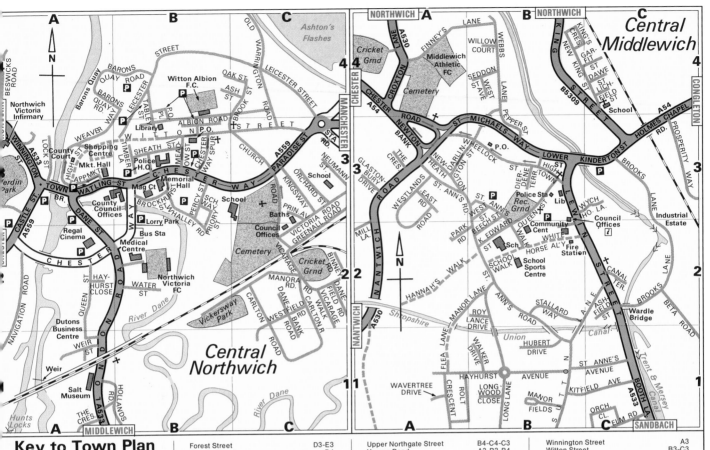

Key to Town Plan and Area Plan

Town Plan

AA Recommended roads	
Other roads	
Restricted roads	
Buildings of interest	College
AA Service Centre	AA
Car Parks	P
Parks and open spaces	
Churches	+

Area Plan

A roads	
B roads	
Locations	DuddonO
Urban area	
Locks	

Street Index with Grid Reference

Chester

Abbey Square	C3
Albion Street	D2
Andrews Crescent	E1
Anne's Way	E2-E1
Beaconsfield Street	E3
Black Friars	E1-F1
Bottom's Lane	E3-F3
Boughton	E3-F3
Bouverie Street	B4
Bridge Street	C2
Brook Street	D4
Cambrian Road	A4-B4
Canal Street	B3-C3
Castle Drive	C1
Castle Street	C1
Catherine Street	A3-B3
Chichester Street	B4-C4
City Road	E3-E4
City Walls Road	B3-B2
Commonhall Street	C2
Crewe Street	D4-E4
Crook Street	C2
Cross Heys	E1
Cuppin Street	C2
Curzon Park North	A1
Dee Hills Park	E3
Dee Lane	E3
Delamere Street	C4
Denbigh Street	B4
Duke Street	D1-D2
Eastern Path	D1-E1
Edinburgh Way	E1
Egerton Street	D4
Elizabeth Crescent	E1-E2
Finchetts Drive	A4
Foregate Street	D3

Forest Street	D3-E3
Francis Street	D4
Frodsham Street	D3
Garden Lane	A4-B4
Garden Terrace	B3-B4
George Street	C3-C4
Gladstone Avenue	A3-A4
Gladstone Road	A4
Gorse Stacks	C4-C3-D3
Goss Street	C2
Granville Road	A4
Grey Friars	C2
Grosvenor Park Road	E3
Grosvenor Road	C1
Grosvenor Street	C1-C2
Groves Road	D2-E2
Handbridge	D1
Henshall Street	B4
Hoole Lane	F3-F4
Hoole Way	D4
Hunter Street	B3-C3
King Street	B3-C3
Lightfoot Street	E4-F4
Lord Street	F3
Lorne Street	B4
Lower Bridge Street	C2-C1-D1
Lower Park Road	D2-E2
Love Street	D3
Lyon Street	D4
Meadows Lane	E1
Milton Street	D4
New Crane Street	A3-B3-B2
Newgate Street	D2
Nicholas Street	C2-C1
Northgate Street	C3-C2
North Lorne Street	B4
Nuns Road	B2-B1-C1
Pepper Street	C2-D2
Princess Street	C3
Prince's Avenue	E4
Queens Avenue	E4
Queen's Drive	E1-E2
Queen's Park Road	D1-E1
Queen's Road	E4
Queen Street	D3
Raymond Street	B3-B4
Richmond Terrace	F4
St Anne Street	C4-C4
St Georges Crescent	E1
St Johns Road	E1
St Johns Street	D2
St John Street	D3-D2
St Martins Way	B4-B3-C3-B2-C2
St Oswalds Way	C4-D4-D3
St Werburgh Street	C3
Sealand Road	A3
Sellier Street	D3
Souters Lane	D2
South Crescent Road	D2-E2-E1
South View Road	A3-B3
Spittal Walk	F4-F3
Stadium Way	A4
Stanley Street	B2
Station Road	D4-E4
Station View	F4
The Bars	E3
The Groves	D2-E2
The Rows	C2
Tower Road	B3
Trafford Street	C4-D4
Union Street	D2-D3-E3
Upper Cambrian Road	A4-B4-B3

Upper Northgate Street	B4-C4-C3
Vernon Road	A3-B3-B4
Vicars Lane	D2
Victoria Crescent	D1-E1
Victoria Path	D1-E1
Victoria's Road	C4
Walls Avenue	B3-B2
Walpole Street	B4
Watergate Street	B2-C2
Water Tower Street	B3-C3
Weaver Street	C2
West Lorne Street	B4
White Friars	C2
Whipcord Lane	A4-B4
York Street	D3

Northwich

Albion Road	B3
Apple Market	A3
Ash Street	B4-C4
Barons Quay Road	A4-B4
Beswicks Road	A4
Binney Road	B3
Brockhurst Street	C2
Brook Street	B3-C3-C4
Carlton Road	C2-C1
Castle Street	A2-A3
Chester Way	A2-B2-B3-C3
Chester Way Spur	B3
Church Road	C3
Danebank Road	C2-C1
Danefield Road	C2
Dane Street	A3-A2
Greenall Road	C2-C3
Hayhurst Close	A2
High Street	A3
Hollands Road	A1-B1
Kingsway	C3
Leicester Street	B3-B4
Lock Street	A3
London Road	A1-A2-B2
Manora Road	C2
Meadow Street	B3
Navigation Road	A1-A2
Neumann Street	C3
Oak Street	B4-C4
Old Warrington Road	C4-C3
Orchard Street	C3
Paradise Street	B3
Percy Street	B4-B3
Post Office Place	B3
Princes Avenue	C3
Priory Street	B2-B3
Queen Street	A2
School Way	B3
Sheath Street	B3
Station Road	C3
The Crescent	A1
Tabley Street	B4-B3
Timber Lane	B3
Town Bridge	A3
Vicarage Road	C2
Vicarage Walk	C2
Victoria Road	C2-C3
Water Street	B2
Watling Street	A3-B3
Weaver Way	A3-B3-B4
Weir Street	A1
Wesley Place	C3
Westfield Road	C2
Whalley Road	B3-B2

Winnington Street	A3
Witton Street	B3-C3

Middlewich

Ashfield Street	C2
Beech Street	B2-B3
Beta Road	C2-C1
Booth Lane	C1
Brooks Lane	C3-C2
Canal Terrace	C2
Chester Road	A4-A3
Croxton Lane	A4
Darlington Street	A3-B3
Dawe Street	C4
Dierdene Terrace	B3
East Road	A3
Elm Road	C1
Finney's Lane	A4-B4
Flea Lane	A1
Garfit Street	B4-C4
Glastonbury Drive	A3
Hannah's Walk	A2-B2
Hauhurst Avenue	A1-B1
High Town	B3
Holmes Chapel Road	C3-C4
Hubert Drive	B1
Kinderton Street	B3-C3
King Edward Street	B2
King's Crescent	B4-C4
King Street	B4-C4-C3
Kittfield Avenue	B1-C1
Lewin Street	B3-B2-C2-C1
Lichfield Street	B2
Long Lane	B1
Longwood Close	B2
Lower Street	B3
Manor Fields	B1
Manor Lane	A2
Mill Lane	A2-B2
Nantwich Road	A1-A2-A3
New King Street	B4-C4
Newton Bank	A4-A3
Newton Heath	A3
Orchard Close	C1
Park Road	A2-B2
Pepper Street	B4-B3
Prosperity Way	C3
Queen Street	B2-B3
Rolt Crescent	A1-B1
Roy Lance Drive	B2
St Anne's Avenue	B1-C1
St Ann's Road	A3-B3-B2-B1
St Ann's Walk	B2-B3
St Michaels Way	A3-B3
School Walk	B2
Seddon Street	B4
Southway	B3
Stallard Way	B2
Sutton Lane	B1-B2-C2
The Crescent	A3
Walker Drive	B1
Wavertree Drive	A1
Webbs Lane	B4
West Lane	B4
Westlands Road	A3-A2
West Street	B3
Wheelock Street	A3-B3
White Horse Alley	B2
Willow Court	B4
Wych House Lane	B3-C3

145

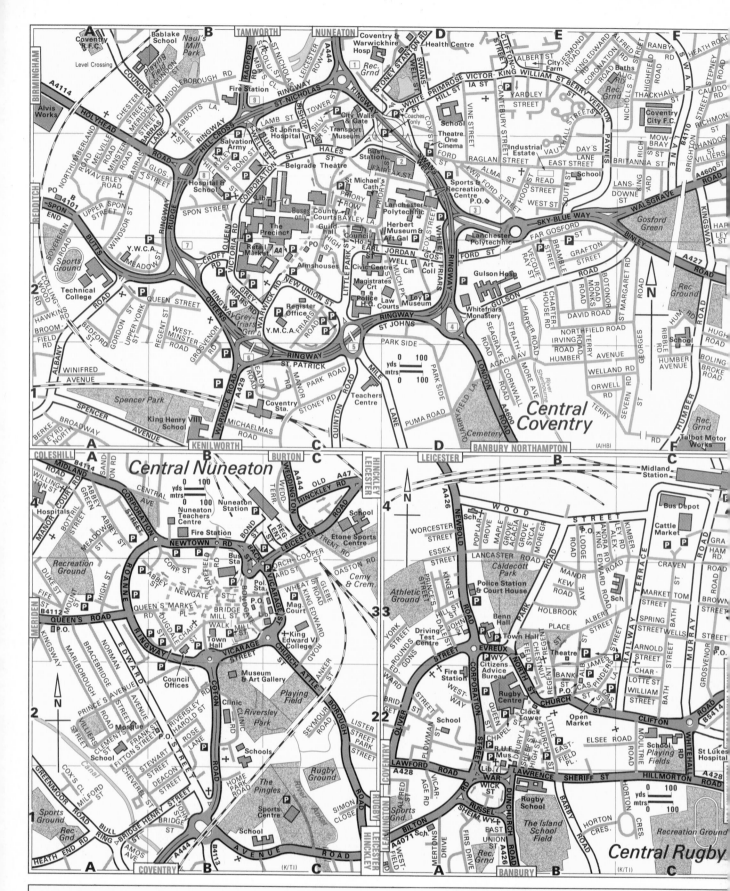

Coventry

Few British towns were as battered by the Blitz as Coventry. A raid in November 1940 flattened most of the city and left the lovely cathedral church a gaunt shell with only the tower and spire still standing. Rebuilding started almost immediately. Symbolising the creation of the new from the ashes of the old is Sir Basil Spence's cathedral, completed in 1962 beside the bombed ruins.

A few medieval buildings have survived intact in the city. St Mary's Guildhall is a finely restored 14th-century building with an attractive minstrels' gallery. Whitefriars Monastery now serves as a local museum. The Herbert Art Gallery and Museum has several collections. Coventry is an important manufacturing centre – most notably for cars – and it is also a university city with the fine campus of the University of Warwick some four miles from the centre.

Nuneaton is an industrial town to the north of Coventry with two distinguished old churches – St Nicholas' and St Mary's. Like Coventry it was badly damaged in the war and its centre has been rebuilt.

Rugby was no more than a sleepy market town until the arrival of the railway. Of course it did have the famous Rugby School, founded in 1567 and one of the country's foremost educational establishments. The railway brought industry – still the town's mainstay.

146

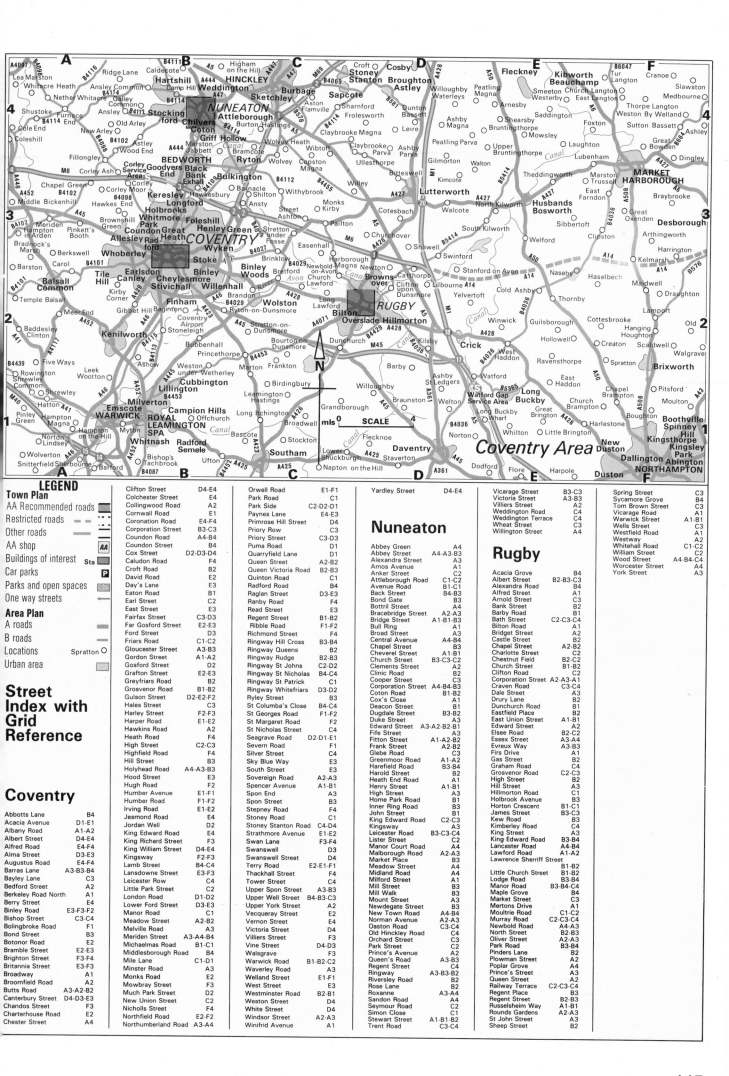

LEGEND

Town Plan

- AA Recommended roads
- Restricted roads
- Other roads
- AA shop — **AA**
- Buildings of interest — Sta
- Car parks — **P**
- Parks and open spaces
- One way streets

Area Plan

- A roads
- B roads
- Locations — Spratton ○
- Urban area

Street Index with Grid Reference

Coventry

Abbotts Lane	B4
Acacia Avenue	D1-E1
Albany Road	A1-A2
Albert Street	D4-E4
Alfred Road	E4-F4
Alma Street	D3-E3
Augustus Road	E4-F4
Barras Lane	A3-B3-B4
Bayley Lane	C3
Bedford Street	A2
Berkeley Road North	A1
Berry Street	E4
Binley Road	E3-F3-F2
Bishop Street	C3-C4
Bolingbroke Road	F1
Bond Street	B3
Botonor Road	E2
Bramble Street	E2-E3
Brighton Street	F3-F4
Britannia Street	E3-F3
Broadway	A1
Broomfield Road	A2
Butts Road	A3-A2-B2
Canterbury Street	D4-D3-E3
Chandos Street	F3
Charterhouse Road	E2
Chester Street	A4
Clifton Street	D4-E4
Colchester Street	E4
Collingwood Road	A2
Cornwall Road	E1
Coronation Road	E4-F4
Corporation Street	B3-C3
Coundon Road	A4-B4
Coundon Street	B4
Cox Street	D2-D3-D4
Caludon Road	F4
Croft Road	B2
David Road	E2
Day's Lane	E3
Eaton Road	B1
Earl Street	C2
East Street	E3
Fairfax Street	C3-D3
Far Gosford Street	E2-E3
Ford Street	D3
Friars Road	C1-C2
Gloucester Street	A3-B3
Gordon Street	A1-A2
Gosford Street	D2
Grafton Street	E2-E3
Greyfriars Road	B2
Grosvenor Road	B1-B2
Gulson Street	D2-E2-F2
Hales Street	C3
Harley Street	F2-F3
Harper Road	E1-E2
Hawkins Road	A2
Heath Road	F4
High Street	C2-C3
Highfield Road	F4
Hill Street	B3
Holyhead Road	A4-A3-B3
Hood Street	E3
Hugh Road	F2
Humber Avenue	E1-F1
Humber Road	F1-F2
Irving Road	E1-E2
Jesmond Road	E4
Jordan Well	D2
King Edward Road	E4
King Richard Street	F3
King William Street	D4-E4
Kingsway	F2-F3
Lamb Street	B4-C4
Lansdowne Street	E3-F3
Leicester Row	C4
Little Park Street	C2
London Road	D1-D2
Lower Ford Street	D3-E3
Manor Road	C1
Meadow Street	A2-B2
Melville Road	A3
Meriden Street	A3-A4-B4
Michaelmas Road	B1-C1
Mile Lane	C1-D1
Minster Road	A3
Monks Road	E2
Mowbray Street	F3
Much Park Street	D2
New Union Street	C2
Nicholls Street	F4
Northfield Road	E2-F2
Northumberland Road	A3-A4
Orwell Road	E1-F1
Park Road	C1
Park Side	C2-D2-D1
Paynes Lane	E4-E3
Primrose Hill Street	D4
Priory Row	C3
Priory Street	C3-D3
Puma Road	D1
Quarryfield Lane	E1
Queen Street	A2-B2
Queen Victoria Road	B2-B3
Quinton Road	C1
Radford Road	B4
Raglan Street	D3-E3
Ranby Road	F4
Read Street	E3
Regent Street	B1-B2
Ribble Road	F1-F2
Richmond Street	F4
Ringway Hill Cross	B3-B4
Ringway Queens	B2
Ringway Rudge	B2-B3
Ringway St Johns	C2-D2
Ringway St Nicholas	B4-C4
Ringway St Patrick	C3
Ringway Whitefriars	D3-D2
Ryley Street	B3
St Columba's Close	B4-C4
St Georges Road	F1-F2
St Margaret Road	F2
St Nicholas Street	C4
Seagrave Road	D2-D1-E1
Severn Road	F1
Silver Street	C4
Sky Blue Way	E3
South Street	E3
Sovereign Road	A2-A3
Spencer Avenue	A1-B1
Spon End	A3
Spon Street	B3
Stepney Road	F4
Stoney Road	C1
Stoney Stanton Road	C4-D4
Strathmore Avenue	E1-E2
Swan Lane	F3-F4
Swanswell	D3
Swanswell Street	D4
Terry Road	E2-E1-F1
Thackhall Street	F4
Tower Street	C4
Upper Spon Street	A3-B3
Upper Well Street	B4-B3-C3
Upper York Street	A2
Vecqueray Street	E2
Vernon Street	E4
Victoria Street	D4
Villiers Street	F3
Vine Street	D4-D3
Walsgrave	F4
Warwick Road	B1-B2-C2
Waverley Road	A3
Welland Street	E1-F1
West Street	E3
Westminster Road	B2-B1
Weston Street	D4
White Street	D4
Windsor Street	A2-A3
Winifrid Avenue	A1
Yardley Street	D4-E4

Nuneaton

Abbey Green	A4
Abbey Street	A4-A3-B3
Alexandra Street	A3
Amos Avenue	A1
Anker Street	C2
Attleborough Road	C1-C2
Avenue Road	B1-C1
Back Street	B4-B3
Bond Gate	B3
Bottril Street	A4
Bracebridge Street	A2-A3
Bridge Street	A1-B1-B3
Bull Ring	A1
Broad Street	A3
Central Avenue	A4-B4
Chapel Street	B3
Cheverel Street	A1-B1
Church Street	B3-C3-C2
Clements Street	C2-D2
Clinic Road	B2
Cooper Street	C2
Corporation Street	A4-B4-B3
Coton Road	B1-B2
Cox's Close	A1
Deacon Street	B1
Dugdale Street	B3-B2
Duke Street	A3
Edward Street	A3-A2-B2-B1
Fife Street	A3
Fitton Street	A1-A2-B2
Frank Street	A2-B2
Glebe Road	B2
Greenmoor Road	A1-A2
Harefield Road	B3-B4
Harold Street	B2
Heath End Road	A1
Henry Street	A1-B1
High Street	A3
Home Park Road	B1
Inner Ring Road	B3
John Street	B1
King Edward Road	C2-C3
Kingsway	A3
Leicester Road	B3-C3-C4
Lister Street	C2
Manor Court Road	A4
Malborough Road	A2-A3
Market Place	B3
Meadow Street	A4
Midland Road	A4
Milford Street	A1
Mill Street	B3
Mill Walk	B3
Mount Street	A3
Newdegate Street	B3
New Town Road	A4-B4
Norman Avenue	A2-A3
Oaston Road	C3-C4
Old Hinckley Road	A3
Orchard Street	C3
Park Street	C2
Prince's Avenue	A2
Queen's Road	A3-B3
Regent Street	C4
Ringway	A3-B3-B2
Riversley Road	B2
Rose Lane	B2
Roxanne	A3-A4
Sandon Road	A4
Seymour Road	C2
Simon Close	C1
Stewart Street	A1-B1-B2
Trent Road	C3-C4
Vicarage Street	B3-C3
Victoria Street	A3-B3
Villiers Street	A2
Weddington Road	C4
Weddington Terrace	C4
Wheat Street	C3
Willington Street	A4

Rugby

Acacia Grove	B4
Albert Street	B2-B3-C3
Alexandra Road	B4
Alfred Street	A1
Arnold Street	C3
Bank Street	B2
Barby Road	B1
Bath Street	C2-C3-C4
Bilton Road	A1
Bridget Street	A2
Castle Street	B2
Chapel Street	A2-B2
Charlotte Street	C2
Chestnut Field	B2-C2
Church Street	B1-B2
Clifton Road	C2
Corporation Street	A2-A3-A1
Craven Road	C3-C4
Dale Street	A3
Drury Lane	B2
Dunchurch Road	B1
Eastfield Place	B2
East Union Street	A1-B1
Edward Street	A2
Elsee Road	B2-C2
Essex Street	A3-A4
Evreux Way	A3-B3
Firs Drive	A1
Gas Street	B2
Graham Road	C4
Grosvenor Road	C2-C3
High Street	B2
Hill Street	A3
Hillmorton Road	C1
Holbrook Avenue	B3
Horton Crescent	B1-C1
James Street	B3-C3
Kew Road	B3
Kimberley Road	C4
King Street	A3
King Edward Road	B3-B4
Lancaster Road	A4-B4
Lawford Road	A1-A2
Lawrence Sherriff Street	B1-B2
Little Church Street	B1-B2
Lodge Road	B3-B4
Manor Road	B3-B4-C4
Maple Grove	B4
Market Street	C3
Mertons Drive	A1
Moultrie Road	C1-C2
Murray Road	C2-C3-C4
Newbold Road	A4-A3
North Street	B2-B3
Oliver Street	A2-A3
Park Road	B3-B4
Pinders Lane	B2
Plowman Street	A4
Poplar Grove	A4
Prince's Street	A2
Queen Street	B2
Railway Terrace	C2-C3-C4
Regent Place	B3
Regent Street	B2
Russelsheim Way	A1-B1
Rounds Gardens	A2-A3
St John Street	A3
Sheep Street	B2
Spring Street	C3
Sycamore Grove	B4
Tom Brown Street	C3
Vicarage Road	C3
Warwick Street	A1-B1
Wells Street	C3
Westfield Road	A1
Westway	C2
Whitehall Road	C1-C2
William Street	C2
Wood Street	A4-B4-C4
Worcester Street	A4
York Street	A3

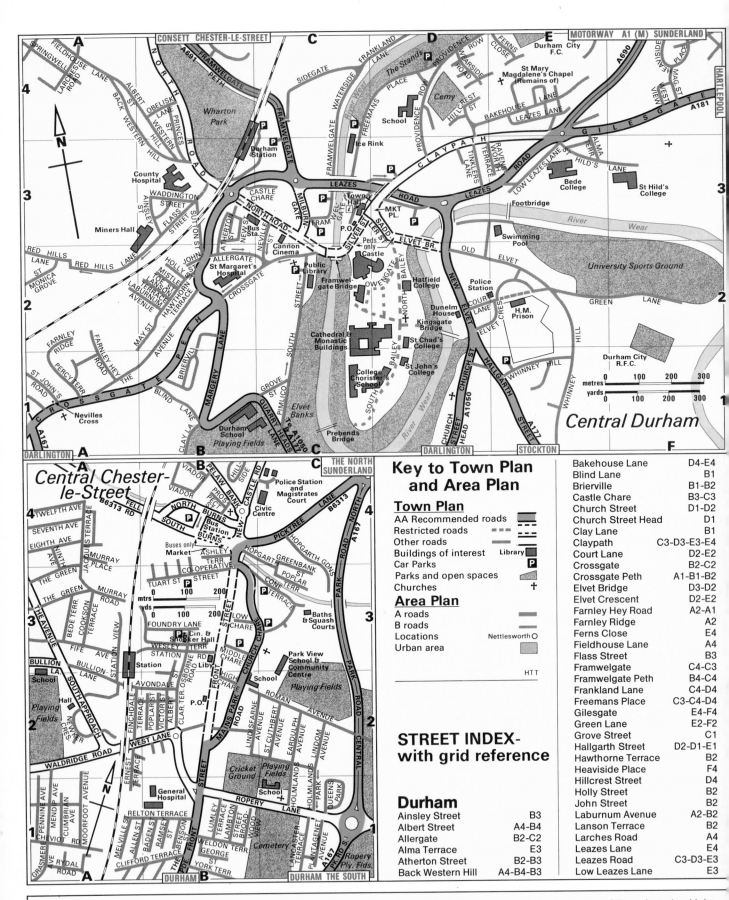

Durham

The castle and the cathedral stand side by side high above the city like sentinels, dramatically symbolising the military and religious power Durham wielded in the past. Its origins date from about 995 when the remains of St Cuthbert arrived from Lindisfarne and his shrine was a popular centre of pilgrimage. Soon after that early fortifications were built, later replaced by a stone castle which became the residence of the Prince-Bishops of Durham – powerful feudal rulers appointed by the King. Today the city's university, the oldest in England after Oxford and Cambridge, occupies the castle and most of the buildings around peaceful, secluded Palace Green. The splendid Norman cathedral, sited on the other side of the Green, is considered to be one of the finest in Europe. Its combination of strength and size, tempered with grace and beauty, is awe-inspiring.

Under the shadow of these giants the old city streets, known as vennels, ramble down the bluff past the 17th-century Bishop Cosin's House and the old grammar school, to the thickly-wooded banks of the Wear. Here three historic bridges link the city's heart with the pleasant Georgian suburbs on the other side of the river.

Although Durham is not an industrial city, it has become the venue for the North-East miners' annual Gala Day in July.

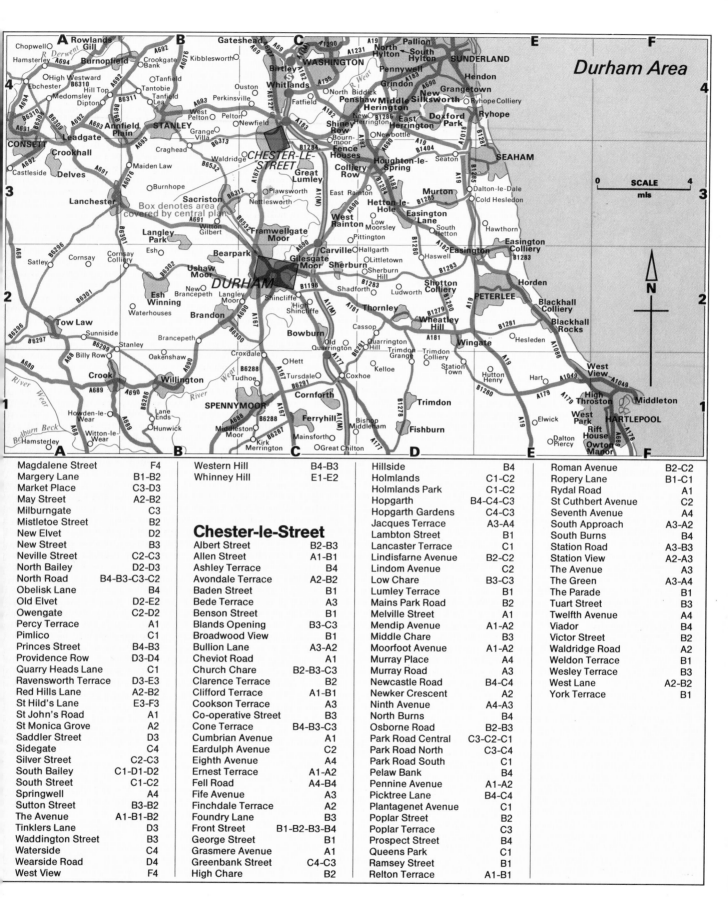

Durham Area

SCALE 4
mls

N

Magdalene Street	F4	Western Hill	B4-B3	Hillside	B4
Margery Lane	B1-B2	Whinney Hill	E1-E2	Holmlands	C1-C2
Market Place	C3-D3			Holmlands Park	C1-C2
May Street	A2-B2			Hopgarth	B4-C4-C3
Milburngate	C3	**Chester-le-Street**		Hopgarth Gardens	C4-C3
Mistletoe Street	B2	Albert Street	B2-B3	Jacques Terrace	A3-A4
New Elvet	D2	Allen Street	A1-B1	Lambton Street	B1
New Street	B3	Ashley Terrace	B4	Lancaster Terrace	C1
Neville Street	C2-C3	Avondale Terrace	A2-B2	Lindisfarne Avenue	B2-C2
North Bailey	D2-D3	Baden Street	B1	Lindom Avenue	C2
North Road	B4-B3-C3-C2	Bede Terrace	A3	Low Chare	B3-C3
Obelisk Lane	B4	Benson Street	B1	Lumley Terrace	B1
Old Elvet	D2-E2	Blands Opening	B3-C3	Mains Park Road	B2
Owengate	C2-D2	Broadwood View	B1	Melville Street	A1
Percy Terrace	A1	Bullion Lane	A3-A2	Mendip Avenue	A1-A2
Pimlico	C1	Cheviot Road	A1	Middle Chare	B3
Princes Street	B4-B3	Church Chare	B2-B3-C3	Moorfoot Avenue	A1-A2
Providence Row	D3-D4	Clarence Terrace	B2	Murray Place	A4
Quarry Heads Lane	C1	Clifford Terrace	A1-B1	Murray Road	A3
Ravensworth Terrace	D3-E3	Cookson Terrace	A3	Newcastle Road	B4-C4
Red Hills Lane	A2-B2	Co-operative Street	B3	Newker Crescent	A2
St Hild's Lane	E3-F3	Cone Terrace	B4-B3-C3	Ninth Avenue	A4-A3
St John's Road	A1	Cumbrian Avenue	A1	North Burns	B4
St Monica Grove	A2	Eardulph Avenue	C2	Osborne Road	B2-B3
Saddler Street	D3	Eighth Avenue	A4	Park Road Central	C3-C2-C1
Sidegate	C4	Ernest Terrace	A1-A2	Park Road North	C3-C4
Silver Street	C2-C3	Fell Road	A4-B4	Park Road South	C1
South Bailey	C1-D1-D2	Fife Avenue	A3	Pelaw Bank	B4
South Street	C1-C2	Finchdale Terrace	A2	Pennine Avenue	A1-A2
Springwell	A4	Foundry Lane	B3	Picktree Lane	B4-C4
Sutton Street	B3-B2	Front Street	B1-B2-B3-B4	Plantagenet Avenue	C1
The Avenue	A1-B1-B2	George Street	B1	Poplar Street	B2
Tinklers Lane	D3	Grasmere Avenue	A1	Poplar Terrace	C3
Waddington Street	B3	Greenbank Street	C4-C3	Prospect Street	B4
Waterside	C4	High Chare	B2	Queens Park	C1
Wearside Road	D4			Ramsey Street	B1
West View	F4			Relton Terrace	A1-B1

Roman Avenue	B2-C2
Ropery Lane	B1-C1
Rydal Road	A1
St Cuthbert Avenue	C2
Seventh Avenue	A4
South Approach	A3-A2
South Burns	B4
Station Road	A3-B3
Station View	A2-A3
The Avenue	A3
The Green	A3-A4
The Parade	B1
Tuart Street	B3
Twelfth Avenue	A4
Viador	B4
Victor Street	B2
Waldridge Road	A2
Weldon Terrace	B1
Wesley Terrace	B3
West Lane	A2-B2
York Terrace	B1

DURHAM
High above the wooded banks of the River Wear, Durham's castle and cathedral crown the steep hill on which the city is built. They share the site with several of the university's attractive old buildings.

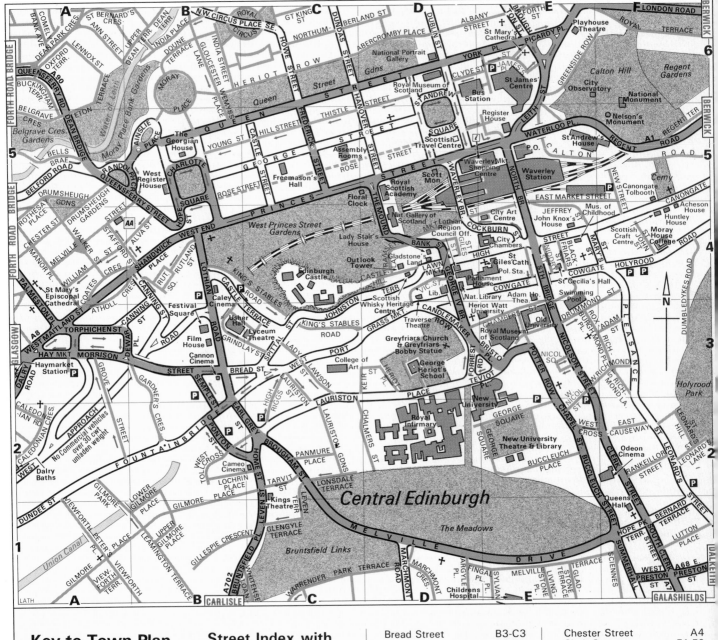

Key to Town Plan and Area Plan

Town Plan

A A Recommended roads	
Other roads	
Restricted roads	
Buildings of intrest	Gallery
Car Parks	P
Parks and open spaces	
A A Service Centre	AA
Churches	†

Area Plan

A roads	
B roads	
Locations	Newcraighall O
Urban area	

Street Index with Grid Reference

Edinburgh

Abercromby Place	C6-D6
Adam Street	F3
Ainslie Place	B5
Albany Street	D6-E6
Alva Street	A4-B4
Ann Street	A6
Argyle Place	D1
Athol Crescent	A3-A4-B4
Bank Street	D4
Belford Road	A5
Belgrave Crescent	A4
Bells Brae	A5
Bernard Terrace	F1
Blackfriars Street	E4

Bread Street	B3-C3
Bristo Place	D3-E3
Brougham Street	C2
Broughton Street	E6
Bruntsfield Place	B1-C1
Buccleuch Place	E2
Buccleuch Street	E2-F2-F1
Buckingham Terrace	A5-A6
Caledonian Crescent	A2
Caledonian Road	A2
Calton Road	E4-F4
Candlemaker Row	D3
Canning Street	A3-B3-B4
Canongate	E4-F4-F5
Castle Hill	D4
Castle Street	C5
Castle Terrace	B4-B3-C3
Chalmers Street	C2-D2
Chambers Street	D3-E3
Charlotte Square	B4-B5
Chapel Street	E2

Chester Street	A4
Clerk Street	F1-F2
Clyde Street	D6-E6
Coates Crescent	A4-B4
Cockburn Street	D4-E4
Comely Bank Avenue	A6
Cowgate	D4-E4-F4
Dalry Road	A3
Dean Bridge	A5
Dean Park Crescent	A6
Dean Terrace	B4
Dewar Place	A3-B3
Doune Terrace	B6
Drummond Street	E3-F3-F4
Drumsheugh Gardens	A4-A5
Dublin Street	D6
Dumbiedykes Road	F3-F4
Dundas Street	C6
Dundee Street	A1-A2
Earl Grey Street	B2-C2
East Cross Causeway	F2

Edinburgh

Scotland's ancient capital, dubbed the "Athens of the North", is one of the most splendid cities in the whole of Europe. Its buildings, its history and its cultural life give it an international importance which is celebrated every year in its world-famous festival. The whole city is overshadowed by the craggy castle which seems to grow out of the rock itself. There has been a fortress here since the 7th century and most of the great figures of Scottish history have been associated with it. The old town grew up around the base of Castle Rock within the boundaries of the defensive King's Wall and, unable to spread outwards, grew upwards in a maze of tenements. However, during the 18th century new prosperity from the shipping trade resulted in the building of the New Town and the regular, spacious layout of the Georgian development makes a striking contrast with the old hotch-potch of streets. Princes Street is the main east-west thoroughfare with excellent shops on one side and Princes Street Gardens with their famous floral clock on the south side.

As befits such a splendid capital city there are numerous museums and art galleries packed with priceless treasures. Among these are the famous picture gallery in 16th-century Holyroodhouse, the present Royal Palace, and the fascinating and unusual Museum of Childhood.

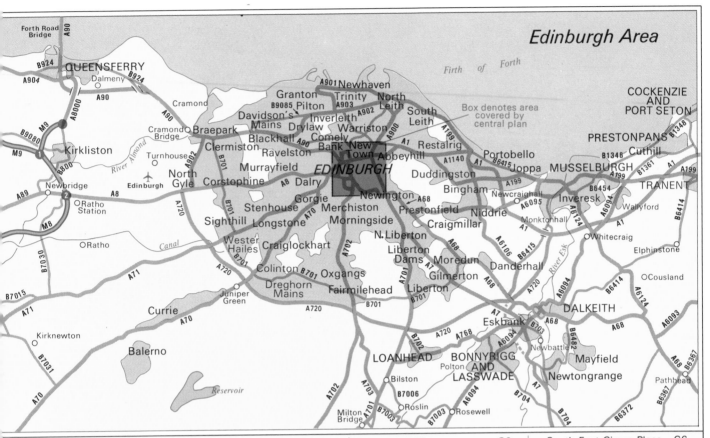

Edinburgh Area

Firth of Forth

Box denotes area covered by central plan

(Map labels: Forth Road Bridge, QUEENSFERRY, Dalmeny, Cramond, Kirkliston, Newbridge, Ratho Station, Ratho, Turnhouse, Edinburgh, Braepark, Cramond Bridge, Clermiston, Davidson's Mains, Blackhall, Ravelston, Murrayfield, North Gyle, Corstophine, Stenhouse, Sighthill, Longstone, Wester Hailes, Craiglockhart, Colinton, Dreghorn Mains, Juniper Green, Currie, Kirknewton, Balerno, Reservoir, Loanhead, Bilston, Milton Bridge, Roslin, Rosewell, Bonnyrigg and Lasswade, Polton, Newbattle, Newtongrange, Mayfield, Pathhead, Cousland, Elphinstone, Whitecraig, Dalkeith, Eskbank, Tranent, Wallyford, Inveresk, Musselburgh, Monktonhall, Newcraighall, Bingham, Joppa, Portobello, Cuthill, Prestonpans, Cockenzie and Port Seton, Duddingston, Craigmillar, Niddrie, Moredun, Gilmerton, Danderhall, Liberton, Liberton Dams, N. Liberton, Fairmilehead, Oxgangs, Prestonfield, Newington, EDINBURGH, Dalry, Gorgie, Merchiston, Morningside, New Town, Abbeyhill, Comely Bank, Restalrig, Granton, Pilton, Inverleith, Drylaw, Warriston, Trinity, North Leith, South Leith, Newhaven)

East Market Street	E5-E4-F4-F5	Kier Street	C3-D3
East Preston Street	F1	King's Stables Road	B4-C4-C3
Eton Terrace	A5-A6	Lady Lawson Street	C3
Fingal Place	D1-E1	Lauriston Gardens	C2
Forrest Road	D3	Lauriston Place	C2-C3-D3
Fountain Bridge	A2-B2-B3-C3	Lauriston Street	C2-C3
Frederick Street	C5	Lawn Market	D4
Forth Street	E6	Leamington Terrace	A1-B1
Gardeners Crescent	B2-B3	Leith Street	E4-E6
George IV Bridge	D3-D4	Lennox Street	A6
George Square	E2	Leven Street	C1-C2
George Street	B5-C5-D5	Leven Terrace	C1-C2
Gillespie Crescent	B1-C1	Livingtone Place	E1
Gilmore Park	A1-A2	Lochrin Place	B2-C2
Gilmore Place	A1-B1-B2-C2	London Road	F6
Gladstone Terrace	E1	Lonsdale Terrace	C2
Glengyle Terrace	C1	Lothian Road	B3-B4
Gloucester Lane	B6	Lower Gilmore Place	B1-B2
Grass Market	D3	Lutton Place	F1
Great King Street	C6	Manor Place	A4
Greenside Row	E6-F6	Marchmont Crescent	D1
Grindley Street	B3-C3	Marchmont Road	D1
Grove Street	A2-A3	Market Street	D4-D4
Hanover Street	C6-D6-D5	Melville Drive	C2-C1-D1-E1-F1
Hay Market	A3	Melville Street	A4-B4-B5
Heriot Place	D3	Melville Terrace	E1-F1
High Riggs	C2-C3	Moray Place	B5-B6
High Street	D4-E4	Morriston Street	A3-B3
Hill Street	C5	New Street	F4-F5
Holyrood Road	F4	Nicolson Square	E3
Home Street	C2	Nicolson Street	E3-E2-F2
Hope Park Terrace	F1	Niddry Street	E4
Hope Street	B4	North Bridge	E4-E5
Howe Street	C6	North West Circus Place	B6
India Place	B6	Northumberland Street	C6-D6
India Street	B6	Oxford Terrace	A6
Jeffrey Street	E4	Palmerston Place	A3-A4
Johnston Terrace	C3-C4-D4		

Panmure Place	C2	South East Circus Place	C6
Picardy Place	E6	Spittal Street	C3
Pleasance	F3-F4	Stafford Street	A4-B4
Ponton Street	B2-C2	Summerhall	F1
Potter Row	E2-E3	Sylvan Place	E1
Princes Street	B4-C4-C5-D5-E5	The Mound	D4-D5
Queen Street	B5-C5-C6-D6	Tarvit Street	C2
Queensferry Road	A5-A6	Teviot Place	D3-E3
Queensferry Street	A5-B5-B4	Thistle Street	C5-D5-D6
Ramsy Lane	D4	Torphichen Street	A3
Randoplph Crescent	A5-B5	Upper Dean Terrace	B6
Rankeillor Street	F2	Upper Gilmore Place	B1
Regent Road	E5-F5	Victoria Street	D4
Regent Terrace	F5	Viewforth	A1-B1
Richmond Lane	F2-F3	viewforth Terrace	A1
Richmond Place	E3-F3	Walker Street	A4-A5
Rose Street	B5-C5-D5	Warrender Park Terr	D1
Rothesay Place	A4-A5	Waterloo Place	E5
Roxbury Place	E3	Waverley Bridge	D4-D5
Royal Circus	B6-C6	Wemyss Place	B5-B6
Royal Terrace	E6-F6	West Approach Road	A2-A3-B3
Rutland Square	B4	West Cross-Causeway	E2
Rutland Street	B4	West End	B4
St Andrew Square	D5-D6	West Nicolson Street	E2-E3
St Bernard's Crescent	A6-B6	West Maitland Street	A3-A4
St Giles Street	D4	West Port	C3
St James's Place	E6	West Preston Street	F1
St John Street	F4	West Richmond Street	E3-F3
St Leonards Hill	F2	West Tollcross	B2
St Leonards Lane	F2	Whitehouse Loan	B1-C1
St Leonards Street	F1-F2	William Street	A4
St Mary's Street	E4-F4	York Place	D6-E6
St Peter Place	A1	Young Street	B5-C5
Sciennes	F1		
Semples Street	B2-B3		
Shandwick Place	B4		
South Bridge	E3-E4		
South Clerk Street	F1		

EDINBURGH
Holyrood Palace orginated as a guest house for the Abbey of Holyrood in the 16th century, but most of the present building was built for Charles II. Mary Queen of Scots was one of its most famous inhabitants.

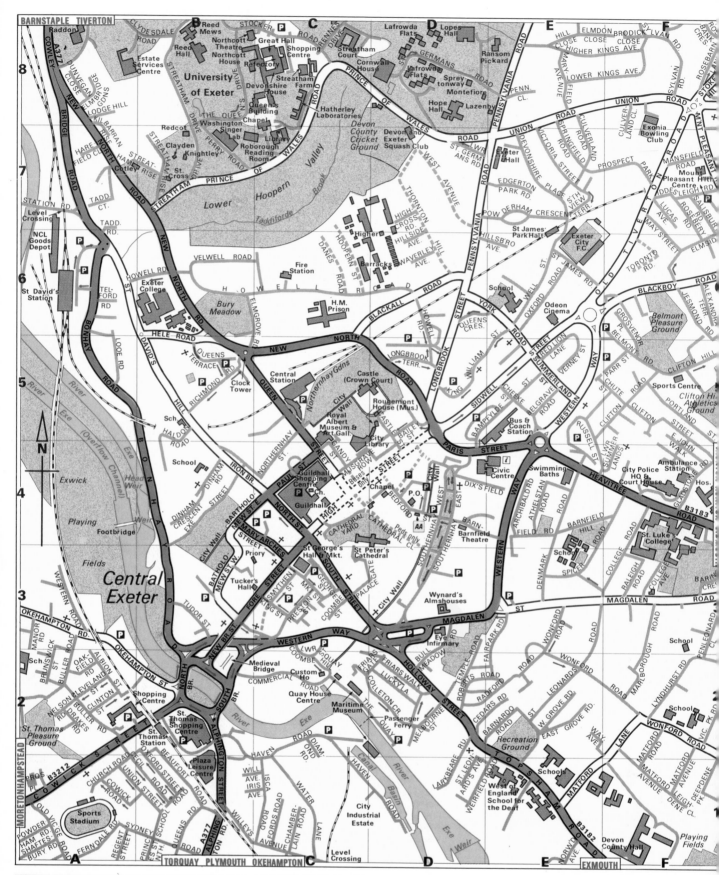

Exeter

The cathedral is Exeter's greatest treasure. Founded in 1050, but rebuilt by the Normans during the 12th-century and again at the end of the 13th-century, it has many beautiful and outstanding features - especially the exquisite rib-vaulting of the nave. Most remarkable, perhaps, is the fact that it still stood after much around it was flattened during the bombing raids in World War II.

There are still plenty of reminders of Old Exeter; Roman and medieval walls circle parts of the city;

14th-century underground passages can be explored; the Guildhall is 15th-century; and Sir Francis Drake is said to have met his explorer companions at Mol's Coffee House. Of the city's ancient churches the most interesting are St Mary Steps, St Mary Arches and St Martin's. The extensive Maritime Museum has over 100 boats from all over the world. Other museums include the Rougemont House, the Devonshire Regiment and the Royal Albert Memorial Museum and Art Gallery.

Exmouth has a near- perfect position at the

mouth of the Exe estuary. On each side it has expanses of sandy beach, on another a wide estuary alive with wildfowl and small boats, while inland is beautiful Devon countryside.

Honiton is famous for traditional hand-made lace and pottery which can still be bought in the busy town.

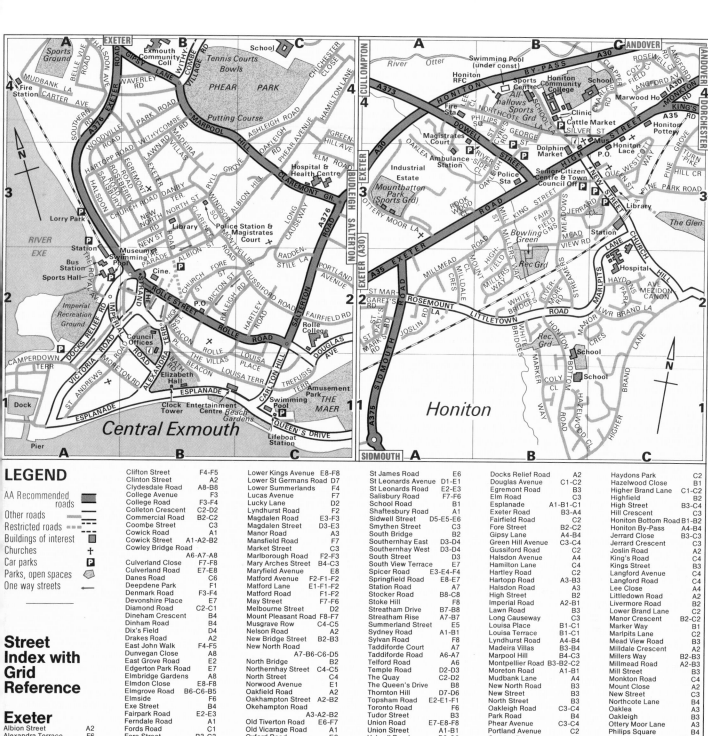

Central Exmouth

Honiton

LEGEND

AA Recommended roads
Other roads
Restricted roads
Buildings of interest
Churches
Car parks
Parks, open spaces
One way streets

Street Index with Grid Reference

Exeter

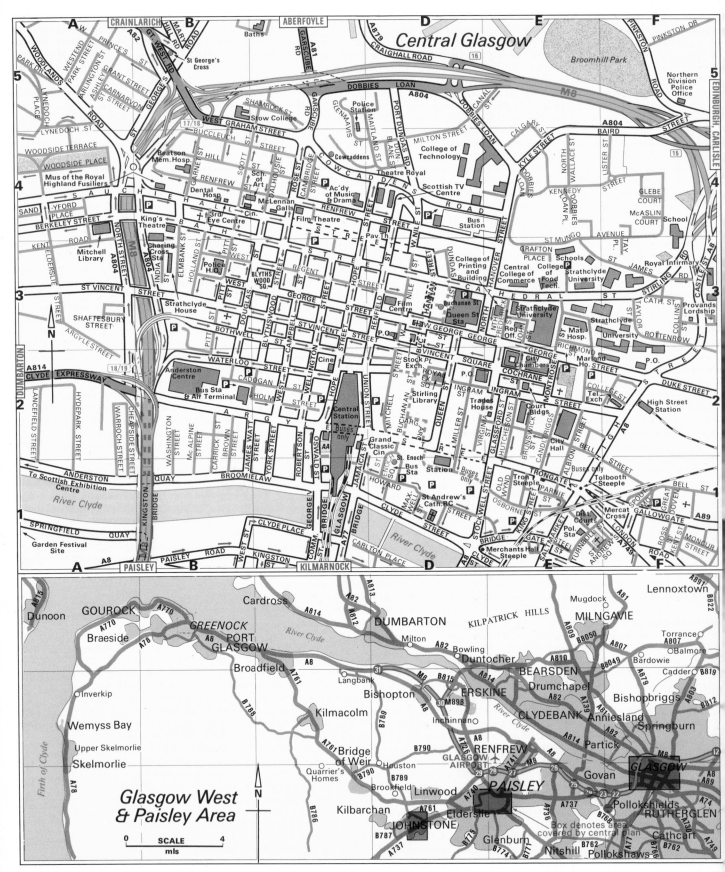

Glasgow

Although much of Glasgow is distinctly Victorian in character, its roots go back very many centuries. It's best link with the past is the Cathedral, in High Street. Founded in the 6th-century, it has features from many succeeding centuries, including an exceptional 13th-century crypt. Nearby is Provand's Lordship, the city's oldest house. It dates from 1471 and is now a museum. Two much larger museums are to be found a little out of the centre - the Art Gallery and Museum contains one of the finest collections of paintings in Britain, while the Hunterian Museum, attached to the University, covers geology, archaeology, ethnography and more general subjects. On Glasgow Green is People's Palace - a museum of city life. Most imposing of the Victorian buildings are the City Chambers and City Hall which was built in 1841 as a concert hall. A new International Concert Hall has now been built.

Paisley is famous for the lovely fabric pattern to which it gives its name. It was taken from fabrics brought from the Near East in the early 19th-century, and its manufacture, along with the production of thread, is still important. Coats Observatory is one of the best equipped in the country.

Johnstone grew rapidly as a planned industrial town in the 19th-century, but suffered from the effects of the Industrial Revolution. Today, engineering is the main industry.

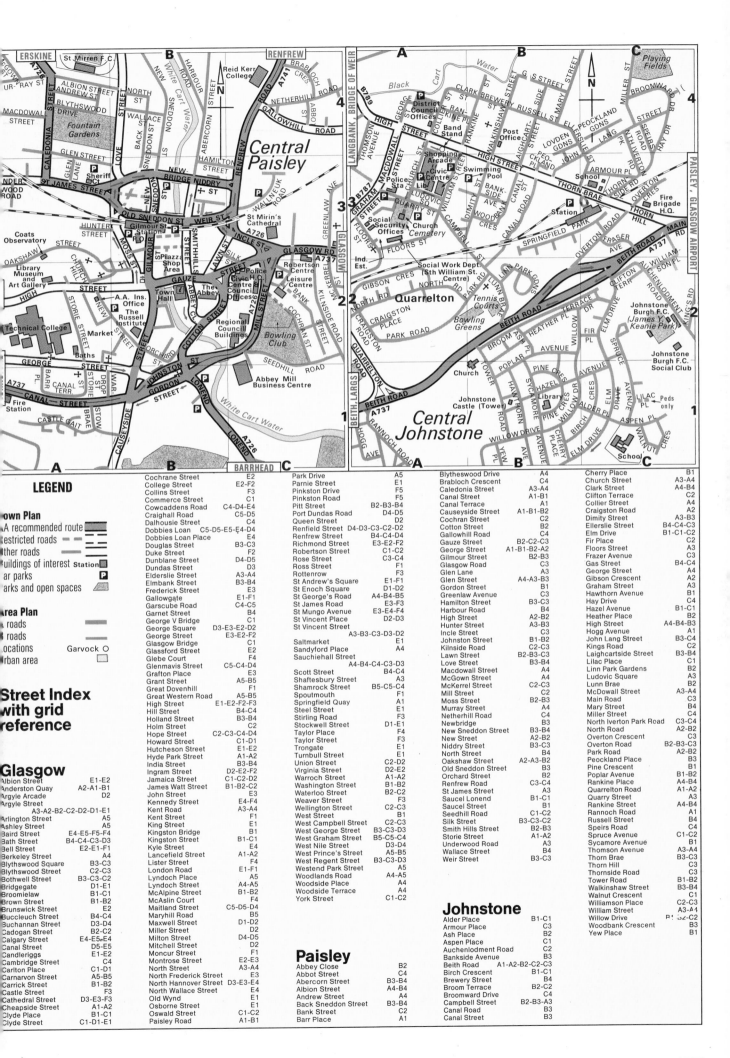

LEGEND

Town Plan
- A recommended route
- restricted roads
- other roads
- buildings of interest — Station
- car parks — P
- parks and open spaces

Area Plan
- A roads
- B roads
- locations — Garvock O
- urban area

Street Index with grid reference

Glasgow

Albion Street	E1-E2
Anderston Quay	A2-A1-B1
Argyle Arcade	D2
Argyle Street	A3-A2-B2-C2-D2-D1-E1
Arlington Street	A5
Ashley Street	A5
Baird Street	E4-E5-F5-F4
Bath Street	B4-C4-C3-D3
Bell Street	E2-E1-F1
Berkeley Street	A4
Blythswood Square	B3-C3
Blythswood Street	C2-C3
Bothwell Street	B3-C3-C2
Bridgegate	D1-E1
Broomielaw	B1-C1
Brown Street	B1-B2
Brunswick Street	E2
Buccleuch Street	B4-C4
Buchanan Street	D3-D4
Cadogan Street	B2-C2
Calgary Street	E4-E5-E4
Canal Street	D5-E5
Candleriggs	E1-E2
Cambridge Street	C4
Carlton Place	C1-D1
Carnarvon Street	A5-B5
Carrick Street	B1-B2
Castle Street	F3
Cathedral Street	D3-E3-F3
Cheapside Street	A1-A2
Clyde Place	B1-C1
Clyde Street	C1-D1-E1
Cochrane Street	E2
College Street	E2-F2
Collins Street	C1
Commerce Street	C1
Cowcaddens Road	C4-D4-E4
Craighall Road	C5-D5
Dalhousie Street	C4
Dobbies Loan	C5-D5-E5-E4-D4
Dobbies Loan Place	E4
Douglas Street	B3-C3
Duke Street	F2
Dunblane Street	D4-D5
Dundas Street	D3
Elderslie Street	A3-A4
Elmbank Street	B3-B4
Frederick Street	E3
Gallowgate	E3
Garscube Road	C4-C5
Garnet Street	C1
George V Bridge	C1
George Square	D3-E3-E2-D2
George Street	E3-E2-F2
Glasgow Bridge	C1
Glassford Street	E2
Glebe Court	E3
Glenmavis Street	C5-C4-D4
Grafton Place	E3
Grant Street	A5-B5
Great Dovenhill	F1
Great Western Road	A5-B5
High Street	E1-E2-F2-F3
Hill Street	B4-C4
Holland Street	B3-B4
Holm Street	C2
Hope Street	C2-C3-C4-D4
Howard Street	C1-D1
Hutcheson Street	E1-E2
Hyde Park Street	A1-A2
India Street	B3-B4
Ingram Street	D2-E2-F2
Jamaica Street	C1-C2-D2
James Watt Street	B1-B2-C2
John Street	E3
Kennedy Street	E4-F4
Kent Road	A3-A4
Kent Street	F1
King Street	E1
Kingston Bridge	B1
Kingston Street	B1-C1
Kyle Street	E4
Lancefield Street	A1-A2
Lister Street	F4
London Road	E1-F1
Lyndoch Place	A5
Lyndoch Street	A4-A5
McAlpine Street	B1-B2
McAslin Court	F4
Maitland Street	C5-D5-D4
Maryhill Road	B5
Maxwell Street	D1-D2
Miller Street	D2
Milton Street	D4-D5
Mitchell Street	D2
Moncur Street	F1
Montrose Street	E2-E3
North Street	A3-A4
North Frederick Street	E3
North Hannover Street	D3-E3-E4
North Wallace Street	E4
Old Wynd	E1
Osborne Street	E1
Paisley Road	A1-B1
Park Drive	A5
Parnie Street	E1
Pinkston Drive	F5
Pinkston Road	F5
Pitt Street	B2-B3-B4
Port Dundas Road	D4-D5
Queen Street	D2
Renfield Street	D4-D3-C3-C2-D2
Renfrew Street	B4-C4-D4
Richmond Street	E3-E2-F2
Robertson Street	C1-C2
Rose Street	C3-C4
Ross Street	F1
Rottenrow	F3
St Andrew's Square	E1-F1
St Enoch Square	D1-D2
St George's Road	A4-B4-B5
St James Road	E3-F3
St Mungo Avenue	E3-E4-F4
St Vincent Place	D2-D3
St Vincent Street	A3-B3-C3-D3-D2
Saltmarket	E1
Sandyford Place	A4
Sauchiehall Street	A4-B4-C4-C3-D3
Scott Street	B4-C4
Shaftesbury Street	A3
Shamrock Street	B5-C5-C4
Spoutmouth	F1
Springfield Quay	A1
Steel Street	E1
Stirling Road	F3
Stockwell Street	D1-E1
Taylor Place	F4
Taylor Street	F3
Trongate	E1
Turnbull Street	E1
Union Street	C2-D2
Virginia Street	D2-E2
Warroch Street	A1-A2
Washington Street	B1-B2
Waterloo Street	B2-C2
Weaver Street	F3
Wellington Street	C2-C3
West Street	B1
West Campbell Street	C2-C3
West George Street	B3-C3-D3
West Graham Street	B5-C5-C4
West Nile Street	D3-D4
West Prince's Street	A5-B5
West Regent Street	B3-C3-D3
Westend Park Street	A4
Woodlands Road	A4-A5
Woodside Place	A4
Woodside Terrace	A4
York Street	C1-C2

Paisley

Abbey Close	B2
Abbot Street	C4
Abercorn Street	B3-B4
Albion Street	A4-B4
Andrew Street	A4
Back Sneddon Street	B3-B4
Bank Street	C2
Barr Place	A1
Blytheswood Drive	A4
Brabloch Crescent	C4
Caledonia Street	A3-A4
Canal Street	A1-B1
Canal Terrace	A1
Causeyside Street	A1-B1-B2
Cochran Street	C2
Cotton Street	B2
Gallowhill Road	C3
Gauze Street	C4
George Street	A1-B1-B2-A2
Gilmour Street	B2-B3
Glasgow Road	C3
Glen Lane	A3
Glen Street	A4-A3-B3
Gordon Street	B1
Greenlaw Avenue	C3
Hamilton Street	B3-C3
Harbour Road	B4
High Street	A2-B2
Hunter Street	A3-B3
Incle Street	C3
Johnston Street	B1-B2
Kilnside Road	C2-C3
Lawn Street	B2-B3-C3
Love Street	B3-B4
Macdowall Street	A4
McGown Street	A4
McKerrel Street	C2-C3
Mill Street	C2
Moss Street	B2-B3
Murray Street	A4
Netherhill Road	C4
Newbridge	B3
New Sneddon Street	B3-B4
New Street	B3-C3
Niddry Street	B3-C3
North Street	B4
Oakshaw Street	A2-A3-B2
Old Sneddon Street	B3
Orchard Street	B2
Renfrew Road	C3-C4
St James Street	A3
Saucel Lonend	B1-C1
Saucel Street	B1
Seedhill Road	C1-C2
Silk Street	B3-C3-C2
Smith Hills Street	B2-B3
Storie Street	A1-A2
Underwood Road	A3
Wallace Street	B4
Weir Street	B3-C3
Cherry Place	B1
Church Street	A3-A4
Clark Street	A4-B4
Clifton Terrace	C2
Collier Street	A4
Craigston Road	A2
Dimity Street	A3-B3
Ellerslie Street	B4-C4-C3
Elm Drive	B1-C1-C2
Fir Place	C2
Floors Street	A3
Frazer Avenue	C3
Gas Street	B4-C4
George Street	A4
Gibson Crescent	A2
Graham Street	A3
Hawthorn Avenue	B1
Hay Drive	C4
Hazel Avenue	B1-C1
Heather Place	B2
High Street	A4-B4-B3
Hogg Avenue	A1
John Lang Street	B3-C4
Kings Road	C2
Laighcartside Street	B3-B4
Lilac Place	C1
Linn Park Gardens	B2
Ludovic Square	A3
Lunn Brae	B2
McDowall Street	A3-A4
Main Road	C3
Mary Street	B4
Miller Street	C2
North Iverton Park Road	C3-C4
North Road	A2-B2
Overton Crescent	C3
Overton Road	B2-B3-C2
Park Road	A2-B2
Peockland Place	B3
Pine Crescent	B1
Poplar Avenue	B1-B2
Rankine Place	A4-B4
Quarrelton Road	A1-A2
Quarry Street	A3
Rankine Street	A4-B4
Rannoch Road	A1
Russell Street	B4
Speirs Road	C4
Spruce Avenue	C1-C2
Sycamore Avenue	B1
Thomson Avenue	A3-A4
Thorn Brae	B3-C3
Thorn Hill	C3
Thornside Road	C3
Tower Road	B1-B2
Walkinshaw Street	B3-B4
Walnut Crescent	C1
Williamson Place	C2-C3
William Street	A3-A4
Willow Drive	B1-B2-C2
Woodbank Crescent	B3
Yew Place	B1

Johnstone

Alder Place	B1-C1
Armour Place	C3
Ash Place	B2
Aspen Place	C1
Auchenlodment Road	C2
Bankside Avenue	B3
Beith Road	A1-A2-B2-C2-C3
Birch Crescent	B1-C1
Brewery Street	B4
Broom Terrace	B2-C2
Broomward Drive	C4
Campbell Street	B2-B3-A3
Canal Road	B3
Canal Street	B3

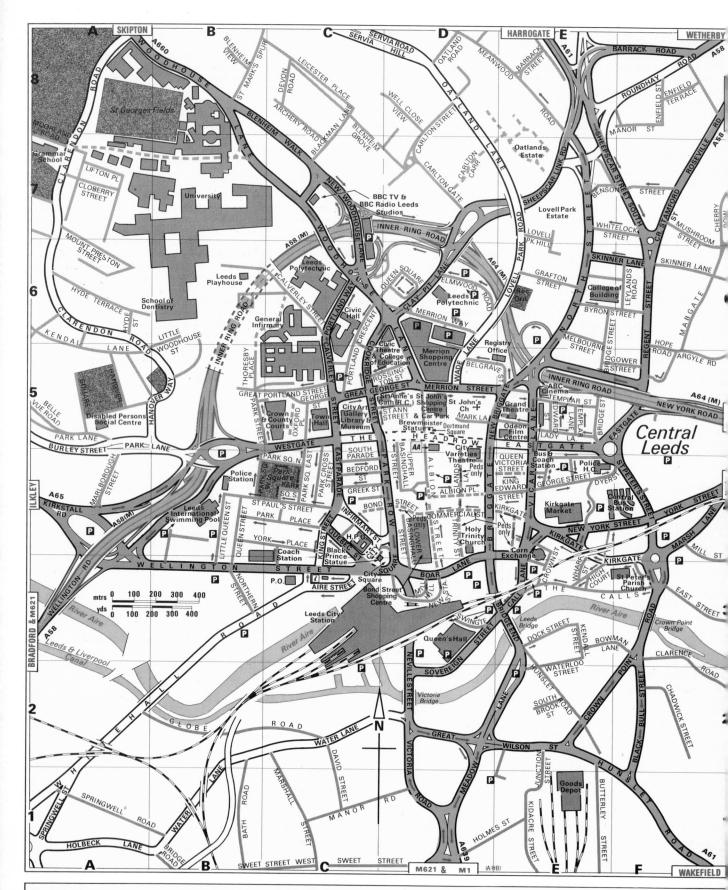

Leeds

In the centre of Leeds is its town hall – a monumental piece of architecture with a 225ft clock-tower. It was opened by Queen Victoria in 1858, and has been a kind of mascot for the city ever since. It exudes civic pride; such buildings could only have been created in the heyday of Victorian prosperity and confidence. Leeds' staple industry has always been the wool trade, but it only became a boom town towards the end of the 18th century, when textile mills were introduced. Today, the wool trade and ready-made clothing (Mr Hepworth and Mr Burton began their work here) are still important, though industries like paper, leather, furniture and electrical equipment are prominent.

Across Calverley Street from the town hall is the City Art Gallery, Library and Museum. Its collections include sculpture by Henry Moore, who was a student at Leeds School of Art. Nearby is the Headrow, Leeds' foremost shopping thoroughfare. On it is the City Varieties Theatre, venue for many years of the famous television programme 'The Good Old Days'. Off the Headrow are several shopping arcades, of which Leeds has many handsome examples. Leeds has a good number of interesting churches; perhaps the finest is St John's, unusual in that it dates from 1634, a time when few churches were built.

156

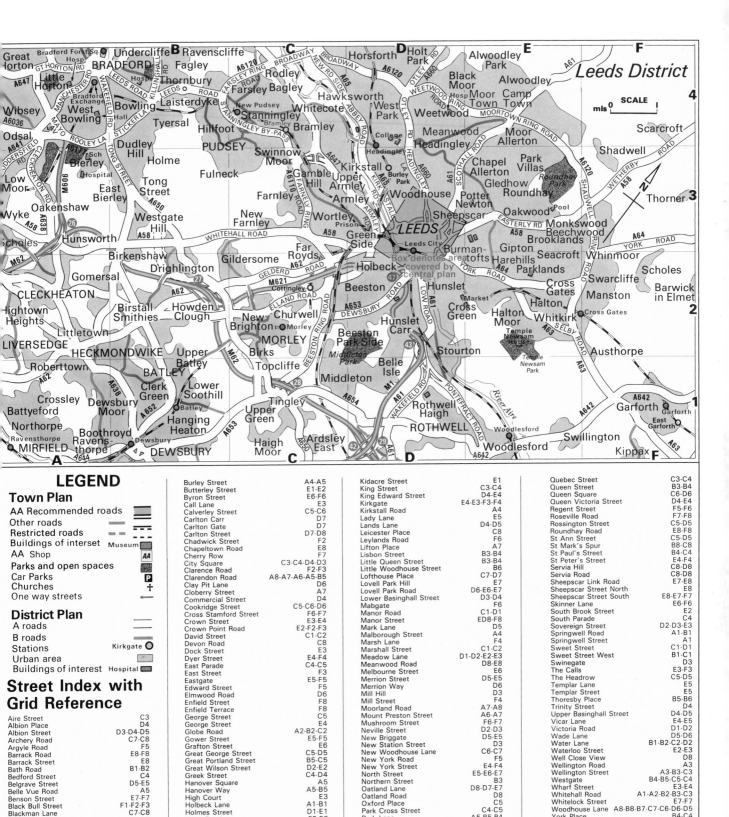

Leeds District

SCALE
mls 0 [   ] l

LEGEND

Town Plan

AA Recommended roads	
Other roads	
Restricted roads	
Buildings of interset	Museum
AA Shop	AA
Parks and open spaces	
Car Parks	P
Churches	+
One way streets	←

District Plan

A roads	
B roads	
Stations	Kirkgate
Urban area	
Buildings of interest	Hospital

Street Index with Grid Reference

Aire Street	C3
Albion Place	D4
Albion Street	D3-D4-D5
Archery Road	C7-C8
Argyle Road	F5
Barrack Road	E8-F8
Barrack Street	E8
Bath Road	B1-B2
Bedford Street	C4
Belgrave Street	D5-E5
Belle Vue Road	A5
Benson Street	E7-F7
Black Bull Street	F1-F2-F3
Blackman Lane	C7-C8
Blenheim Grove	C8-C7-D7
Blenheim View	B8
Blenheim Walk	B8-C8-C7
Boar Lane	D3-D4
Bond Street	C4-D4
Bowman Lane	E3-F3
Bridge End	D3-E3
Bridge Road	B1
Bridge Street	E5-E6
Briggate	D3-D4-D5

Burley Street	A4-A5
Butterley Street	E1-E2
Byron Street	E6-F6
Call Lane	E3
Calverley Street	C5-C6
Carlton Carr	D7
Carlton Gate	D7
Carlton Street	D7-D8
Chadwick Street	F2
Chapeltown Road	E8
Cherry Row	F7
City Square	C3-C4-D4-D3
Clarence Road	F2-F3
Clarendon Road	A8-A7-A6-A5-B5
Clay Pit Lane	D6
Cloberry Street	A7
Commercial Street	D4
Cookridge Street	C5-C6-D6
Cross Stamford Street	F6-F7
Crown Street	E3-E4
Crown Point Road	E2-F2-F3
David Street	C1-C2
Devon Road	C8
Dock Street	E3
Dyer Street	E4-F4
East Parade	C4-C5
East Street	F3
Eastgate	E5-F5
Edward Street	F5
Elmwood Road	D6
Enfield Street	F8
Enfield Terrace	F8
George Street	C5
George Street	E4
Globe Road	A2-B2-C2
Gower Street	E5-F5
Grafton Street	E6
Great George Street	C5-D5
Great Portland Street	B5-C5
Great Wilson Street	D2-E2
Greek Street	C4-D4
Hanover Square	A5
Hanover Way	A5-B5
High Court	E3
Holbeck Lane	D1-E1
Holmes Street	E3
Hope Road	F5-F6
Hunslett Road	E3-E2-E1-F1-F2
Hyde Street	A6
Hyde Terrace	A6
Infirmary Street	C4-D4
Inner Ring Road	B5-B6-C6-C7-D7-D6-E6-E5-F5
Junction Street	E1-E2
Kendal Lane	A5-A6
Kendal Street	E3

Kidacre Street	E1
King Street	C3-C4
King Edward Street	D4-E4
Kirkgate	E4-E3-F3-F4
Kirkstall Road	A4
Lady Lane	E5
Lands Lane	D4-D5
Leicester Place	C8
Leylands Road	F6
Lifton Place	A7
Lisbon Street	B3-B4
Little Queen Street	B3-B4
Little Woodhouse Street	B6
Lofthouse Place	C7-D7
Lovell Park Hill	E7
Lovell Park Road	D6-E6-E7
Lower Basinghall Street	D3-D4
Mabgate	F6
Manor Road	C1-D1
Manor Street	ED8-F8
Mark Lane	D5
Malborough Street	A4
Marsh Lane	F4
Marshall Street	C1-C2
Meadow Lane	D1-D2-E2-E3
Meanwood Road	D8-E8
Melbourne Street	E6
Merrion Street	D5-E5
Merrion Way	D6
Mill Hill	D3
Mill Street	F4
Moorland Road	A7-A8
Mount Preston Street	A6-A7
Mushroom Street	F6-F7
Neville Street	D2-D3
New Briggate	D5-E5
New Station Street	D3
New Woodhouse Lane	C6-C7
New York Road	F5
New York Street	E4-F4
North Street	E5-E6-E7
Northern Street	B3
Oatland Lane	D8-D7-E7
Oatland Road	D8
Oxford Place	C5
Park Cross Street	C4-C5
Park Lane	A5-B5-B4
Park Place	B4-C4
Park Row	C4-C5-D5-D4
Park Square East	C4
Park Square North	B4-C4
Park Square South	C4
Park Square West	B4
Park Street	B5-C5
Portland Crescent	C5-C6
Portland Way	C6

Quebec Street	C3-C4
Queen Street	B3-B4
Queen Square	C6-D6
Queen Victoria Street	D4-E4
Regent Street	F5-F6
Roseville Road	F7-F8
Rossington Street	C5-D5
Roundhay Road	E8-F8
St Ann Street	C5-D5
St Mark's Spur	B8-C8
St Paul's Street	B4-C4
St Peter's Street	E4-F4
Servia Hill	C8-D8
Servia Road	C8-D8
Sheepscar Link Road	E7-E8
Sheepscar Street North	E8
Sheepscar Street South	E8-E7-F7
Skinner Lane	E6-F6
South Brook Street	E2
South Parade	C4
Sovereign Street	D2-D3-E3
Springwell Road	A1-B1
Springwell Street	A1
Sweet Street	C1-D1
Sweet Street West	B1-C1
Swinegate	D3
The Calls	E3-F3
The Headrow	C5-D5
Templar Lane	E5
Templar Street	E5
Thoresby Place	B5-B6
Trinity Street	D4
Upper Basinghall Street	D4-D5
Vicar Lane	E4-E5
Victoria Road	D1-D2
Wade Lane	D5-D6
Water Lane	B1-B2-C2-D2
Waterloo Street	E2-E3
Well Close View	D8
Wellington Road	A3
Wellington Street	A3-B3-C3
Westgate	B4-B5-C5-C4
Wharf Street	E3-E4
Whitehall Road	A1-A2-B2-B3-C3
Whitelock Street	E7-F7
Woodhouse Lane	A8-B8-B7-C7-C6-D6-D5
York Place	B4-C4
York Street	F4

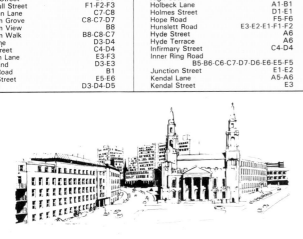

LEEDS

Offices now occupy the handsome twin-towered Civic Hall which stands in Calverley Street in front of the new buildings of Leeds Polytechnic. This area of the city – the commercial centre – has been extensively redeveloped

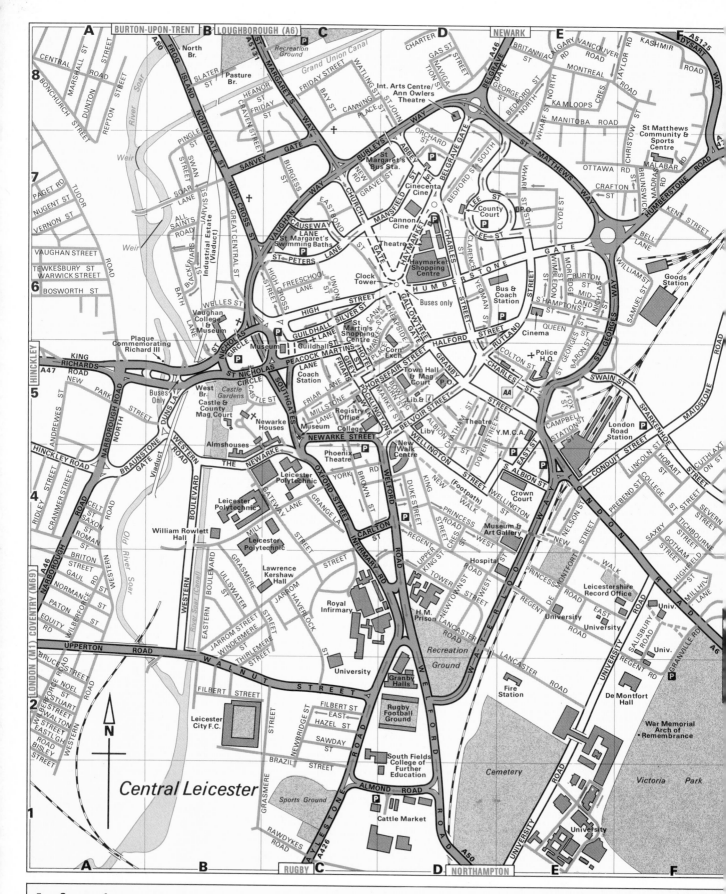

Leicester

A regional capital in Roman times, Leicester has retained many buildings from its eventful and distinguished past. Today the city is a thriving modern place, a centre for industry and commerce, serving much of the Midlands. Among the most outstanding monuments from the past is the Jewry Wall, a great bastion of Roman masonry. Close by are remains of the Roman baths and

several other contemporary buildings. Attached is a museum covering all periods from prehistoric times to 1500. Numerous other museums include the Wygston's House Museum of Costume, with displays covering the period 1769 to 1924; Newarke House, with collections showing changing social conditions in Leicester through four hundred years; and Leicestershire Museum and Art Gallery, with collections of drawings, paintings, ceramics, geology and natural history.

The medieval Guildhall has many features of interest, including a great hall, library and police cells. Leicester's castle, although remodelled in the 17th century, retains a 12th-century great hall. The Church of St Mary de Castro, across the road from the castle, has features going back at least as far as Norman times; while St Nicholas's Church is even older, with Roman and Saxon foundations. St Martin's Cathedral dates mainly from the 13th to 15th centuries and has a notable Bishop's throne.

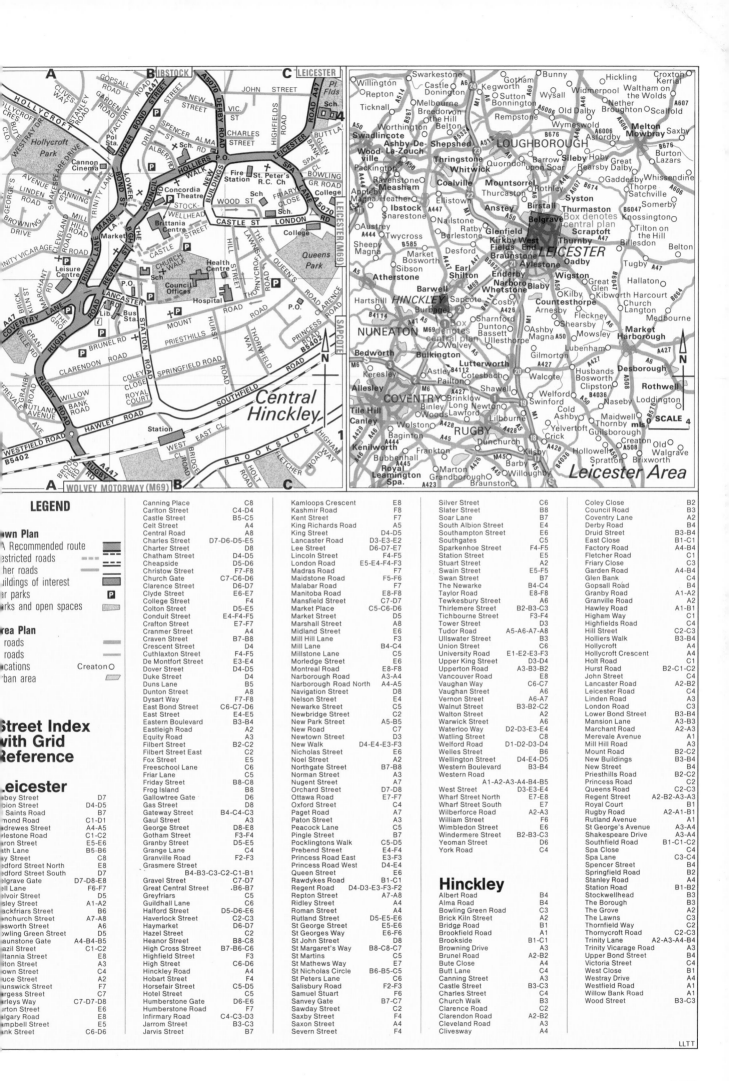

LEGEND

Town Plan
- Recommended route
- Restricted roads
- Other roads
- Buildings of interest
- Car parks — P
- Parks and open spaces

Area Plan
- roads
- roads
- locations — Creton O
- urban area

Street Index with Grid Reference

Leicester

Abbey Street	D7
Albion Street	D4-D5
All Saints Road	B7
Almond Road	C1-D1
Andrewes Street	A4-A5
Aylestone Road	C1-C2
Bedford Street North	E8
Bedford Street South	D7
Belgrave Gate	D7-D8-E8
Bell Lane	F6-F7
Belvoir Street	D5
Bisley Street	A1-A2
Blackfriars Street	B6
Bonchurch Street	A7-A8
Bosworth Street	A6
Bowling Green Street	D5
Braunstone Gate	A4-B4-B5
Brazil Street	C1-C2
Britannia Street	E8
Bruton Street	A3
Bruce Street	C4
Bruswick Street	A2
Burgess Street	F7
Burleys Way	C7
Burton Street	C7-D7-D8
Calgary Road	E6
Campbell Street	E8
Canning Street	E5
	C6-D6

Canning Place	C8
Carlton Street	C4-D4
Castle Street	B5-C5
Celt Street	A4
Central Road	A8
Charles Street	D7-D6-D5-E5
Charter Street	D8
Chatham Street	D4-D5
Cheapside	D5-D6
Christow Street	F7-F8
Church Gate	C7-C6-D6
Clarence Street	D6-D7
Clyde Street	E6-E7
College Street	F4
Colton Street	D5-E5
Conduit Street	E4-F4-F5
Crafton Street	E7-F7
Cranmer Street	A4
Craven Street	B7-B8
Crescent Street	D4
Cuthlaxton Street	F4-F5
De Montfort Street	E3-E4
Dover Street	D4-D5
Duke Street	D4
Duns Lane	B5
Dunton Street	A8
Dysart Way	F7-F8
East Bond Street	C6-C7-D6
East Street	E4-E5
Eastern Boulevard	B3-B4
Eastleigh Road	A2
Equity Road	A3
Filbert Street	B2-C2
Filbert Street East	C2
Fox Street	E5
Freeschool Lane	C6
Friar Lane	C5
Friday Street	B8-C8
Frog Island	B8
Gallowtree Gate	D6
Gas Street	D8
Gateway Street	B4-C4-C3
Gaul Street	A3
George Street	D8-E8
Gotham Street	F3-F4
Granby Street	D5-E5
Grange Lane	C4
Granville Road	F2-F3
Grasmere Street	B4-B3-C3-C2-C1-B1
Gravel Street	C7-D7
Great Central Street	B6-B7
Greyfriars	C5
Guildhall Lane	C5
Halford Street	D5-D6-E6
Haverlock Street	C2-C3
Haymarket	D6-D7
Hazel Street	C2
Heanor Street	B8
High Cross Street	B7-B6-C6
Highfield Street	F3
High Street	C6-D6
Hinckley Road	A4
Hobart Street	F4
Horsefair Street	C5-D5
Hotel Street	C5
Humberstone Gate	D6-E6
Humberstone Road	F7
Infirmary Road	C4-C3-D3
Jarrom Street	B3-C3
Jarvis Street	B7

Kamloops Crescent	E8
Kashmir Road	F8
Kent Street	F7
King Richards Road	A5
King Street	D4-D5
Lancaster Road	D3-E3-E2
Lee Street	D6-D7-E7
Lincoln Street	F4-F5
London Road	E5-E4-F4-F3
Madras Road	F7
Maidstone Road	F5-F6
Malabar Road	F7
Manitoba Road	E8-F8
Mansfield Street	C7-D7
Market Place	C5-C6-D6
Market Street	D5
Marshall Street	A8
Midland Street	E6
Mill Hill Lane	F3
Mill Lane	B4-C4
Millstone Lane	C5
Morledge Street	E6
Montreal Road	E8-F8
Narborough Road	A3-A4
Narborough Road North	A4-A5
Navigation Street	D8
Nelson Street	E4
Newarke Street	C5
Newbridge Street	C2
New Park Street	A5-B5
New Road	C7
Newtown Street	D3
New Walk	D4-E4-E3-F3
Nicholas Street	E6
Noel Street	A2
Northgate Street	B7-B8
Norman Street	A3
Nugent Street	A7
Orchard Street	D7-D8
Ottawa Road	E7-F7
Oxford Street	C4
Paget Road	A7
Paton Street	A3
Peacock Lane	C5
Pingle Street	B7
Pocklingtons Walk	C5-D5
Prebend Street	E4-F4
Princess Road East	E3-F3
Princess Road West	D4-E4
Queen Street	E6
Rawdykes Road	B1-C1
Regent Road	D4-D3-E3-F3-F2
Repton Street	A7-A8
Ridley Street	A4
Roman Street	A4
Rutland Street	D5-E5-E6
St George Street	E5-E6
St Georges Way	E6-F6
St John Street	D8
St Margaret's Way	B8-C8-C7
St Martins	C5
St Mathews Way	E7
St Nicholas Circle	B6-B5-C5
St Peters Lane	C6
Salisbury Road	F2-F3
Samuel Stuart	F6
Sanvey Gate	B7-C7
Saxby Street	F4
Saxon Street	A4
Sawday Street	C2
Severn Street	F4

Silver Street	C6
Slater Street	B8
Soar Lane	B7
South Albion Street	E4
Southampton Street	E6
Southgates	C5
Sparkenhoe Street	F4-F5
Station Street	E5
Stuart Street	A2
Swain Street	E5-F5
Swan Street	B7
The Newarke	B4-C4
Taylor Road	E8-F8
Tewkesbury Street	A6
Thirlemere Street	B2-B3-C3
Tichbourne Street	F3-F4
Tower Street	D3
Tudor Road	A5-A6-A7-A8
Ullswater Street	B3
Union Street	C6
University Road	E1-E2-E3-F3
Upper King Street	D3-D4
Upperton Road	A3-B3-B2
Vancouver Road	E8
Vaughan Way	C6-C7
Vaughan Street	A6
Vernon Street	A6-A7
Walnut Street	B3-B2-C2
Walton Street	A2
Warwick Street	A6
Waterloo Way	D2-D3-E3-E4
Watling Street	C8
Welford Road	D1-D2-D3-D4
Welles Street	B6
Wellington Street	D4-E4-D5
Western Boulevard	B3-B4
Western Road	A1-A2-A3-A4-B4-B5
West Street	D3-E3-E4
Wharf Street North	E7-E8
Wharf Street South	E7
Wilberforce Road	A2-A3
William Street	F6
Wimbledon Street	E6
Windermere Street	B2-B3-C3
Yeoman Street	D6
York Road	C4

Hinckley

Albert Road	B4
Alma Road	B4
Bowling Green Road	C3
Brick Kiln Street	A2
Bridge Road	B1
Brookfield Road	A1
Brookside	B1-C1
Browning Drive	A3
Brunel Road	A2-B2
Bute Close	A4
Butt Lane	C4
Canning Street	A3
Castle Street	B3-C3
Charles Street	C4
Church Walk	B3
Clarence Road	C2
Clarendon Road	A2-B2
Cleveland Road	A3
Clivesway	A4

Coley Close	B2
Council Road	B3
Coventry Lane	A2
Derby Road	B4
Druid Street	B3-B4
East Close	B1-C1
Factory Road	A4-B4
Fletcher Road	C1
Friary Close	C3
Garden Road	A4-B4
Glen Bank	C4
Gopsall Road	B4
Granby Road	A1-A2
Granville Road	A2
Hawley Road	A1-B1
Higham Way	C1
Highfields Road	C4
Hill Street	C2-C3
Holliers Walk	B3-B4
Hollycroft	A4
Hollycroft Crescent	A4
Holt Road	C6
Hurst Road	B2-C1-C2
John Street	C4
Lancaster Road	A2-B2
Leicester Road	C4
Linden Road	A3
London Road	C3
Lower Bond Street	B3-B4
Mansion Lane	A3-B3
Marchant Road	A2-A3
Merevale Avenue	A1
Mill Hill Road	A3
Mount Road	B2-C2
New Buildings	B3-B4
New Street	B4
Priesthills Road	B2-C2
Princess Road	C2
Queens Road	C2-C3
Regent Street	A2-B2-A3-A3
Royal Court	B1
Rugby Road	A2-A1-B1
Rutland Avenue	A1
St George's Avenue	A3-A4
Shakespeare Drive	A3-A4
Southfield Road	B1-C1-C2
Spa Close	C4
Spa Lane	C3-C4
Spencer Street	B4
Springfield Road	B2
Stanley Road	A4
Station Road	B1-B2
Stockwellhead	B3
The Borough	B3
The Grove	A2
The Lawns	C3
Thornfield Way	C1
Thornycroft Road	C2-C3
Trinity Lane	A2-A3-A4-B4
Trinity Vicarage Road	A3
Upper Bond Street	B4
Victoria Street	C4
West Close	B1
Westray Drive	A4
Westfield Road	A1
Willow Bank Road	A1
Wood Street	B3-C3

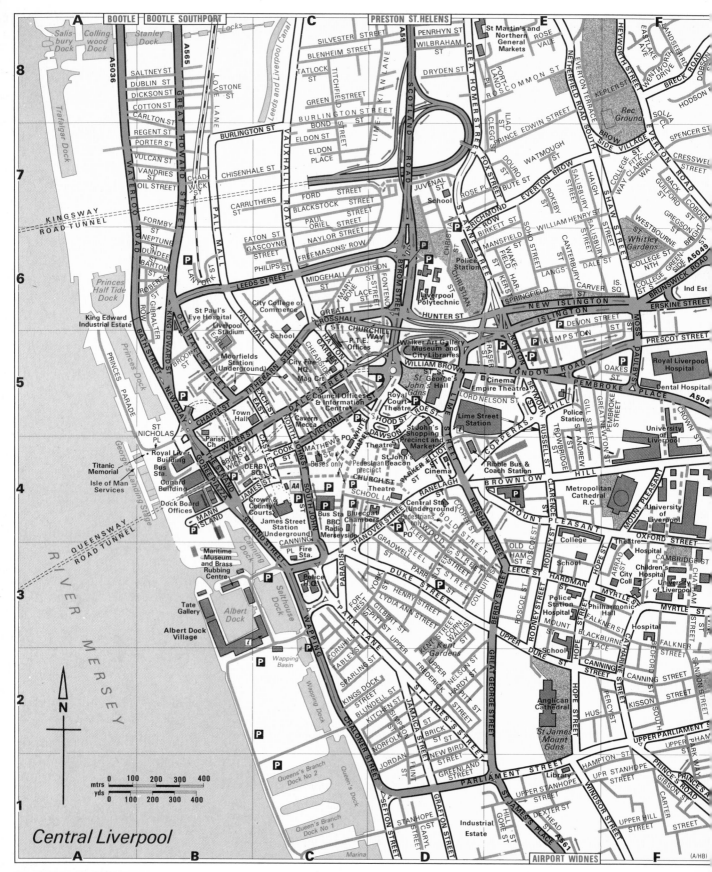

Liverpool

Although its dock area has been much reduced, Liverpool was at one time second only to London in pre-eminence as a port. Formerly the centrepiece of the docks area are three monumental buildings - the Dock Board Offices, built in 1907 with a huge copper-covered dome; the Cunard Building, dating from 1912 and decorated with an abundance of ornamental carving; and best-known of all, the world-famous Royal Liver Building, with the two 'liver birds' crowning its twin cupolas.

Some of the city's best industrial buildings have fallen into disuse in recent years, but some have been preserved as monuments of the idustrial age. One has become a maritime museum housing full-sized craft and a workshop where maritime crafts are demonstrated. Other museums and galleries include the Walker Art Gallery, with excellent collections of European painting and sculpture; Liverpool City Libraries, one of the oldest and largest public libraries in Britain, with a vast collection of books and manuscripts; and Bluecoat

Chambers, a Queen Anne building now used as a gallery and concert hall. Liverpool has two outstanding cathedrals: the Roman Catholic, completed in 1967 in an uncompromising controversial style; and the Protestant, constructed in the great tradition of Gothic architecture, but begun in 1904 and only recently completed.

160

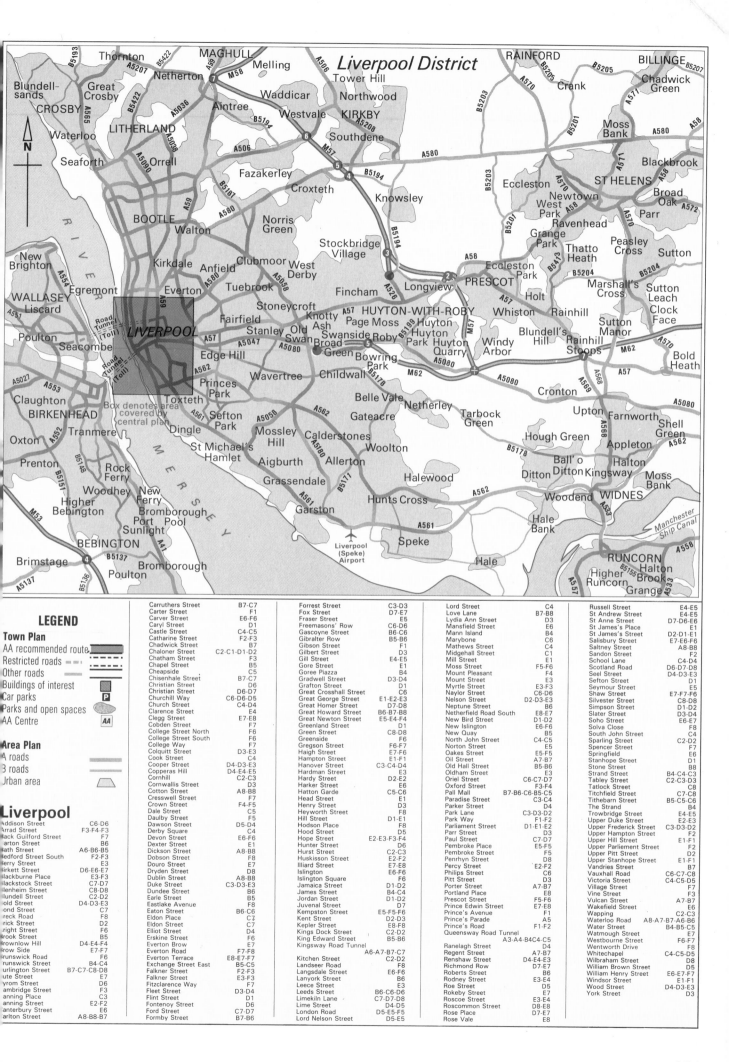

Liverpool District

LEGEND

Town Plan

- AA recommended route
- Restricted roads
- Other roads
- Buildings of interest
- Car parks
- Parks and open spaces
- AA Centre

Area Plan

- A roads
- B roads
- Urban area

Liverpool

Addison Street	C6-D6
Arrad Street	F3-F4-F3
Back Guilford Street	F7
Barton Street	B6
Bath Street	A6-B6-B5
Bedford Street South	F2-F3
Berry Street	E3
Birkett Street	D6-E6-E7
Blackburne Place	F3-F3
Blackstock Street	C7-D7
Blenheim Street	C8-D8
Blundell Street	C2-D2
Bold Street	D4-D3-E3
Bond Street	C7
Breck Road	F8
Brick Street	D2
Bright Street	F6
Brook Street	B5
Brownlow Hill	D4-E4-F4
Brow Side	E7-F7
Brunswick Road	F6
Brunswick Street	B4-C4
Burlington Street	B7-C7-C8-D8
Bute Street	E7
Byrom Street	D6
Cambridge Street	F3
Canning Place	C3
Canning Street	E2-F2
Canterbury Street	E6
Carlton Street	A8-B8-B7
Carruthers Street	B7-C7
Carter Street	F1
Carver Street	E6-F6
Caryl Street	D1
Castle Street	C4-C5
Catharine Street	F2-F3
Chadwick Street	B7
Chaloner Street	C2-C1-D1-D2
Chatham Street	F3
Chapel Street	B5
Cheapside	C5
Chisenhale Street	B7-C7
Christian Street	D6
Christian Street	D6-D7
Churchill Way	C6-D6-D5
Church Street	C4-D4
Clarence Street	E4
Clegg Street	E7-E8
Cobden Street	F7
College Street North	F6
College Street South	F6
College Way	F7
Colquitt Street	D3-E3
Cook Street	C4
Cooper Street	D4-D3-E3
Copperas Hill	D4-E4-E5
Cornhill	C2-C3
Cornwallis Street	D3
Cotton Street	A8-B8
Cresswell Street	F7
Crown Street	F4-F5
Dale Street	C5
Daulby Street	F5
Dawson Street	D5-D4
Derby Square	C4
Devon Street	E6-F6
Dexter Street	E1
Dickson Street	A8-B8
Dobson Street	F8
Douro Street	E7
Dryden Street	D8
Dublin Street	B5
Duke Street	C3-D3-E3
Dundee Street	B5
Earle Street	B5
Eastlake Avenue	F8
Eaton Street	B6-C6
Eldon Place	C7
Eldon Street	C7
Elliot Street	D4
Erskine Street	F6
Everton Brow	E7
Everton Road	F7-F8
Everton Terrace	E8-E7-F7
Exchange Street East	B5-C5
Falkner Street	F2-F3
Falkner Street	E3-F3
Fitzclarence Way	F7
Fleet Street	D3-D4
Flint Street	D1
Fontenoy Street	D6
Ford Street	C7-D7
Formby Street	B7-B6
Forrest Street	C3-D3
Fox Street	D7-E7
Fraser Street	E5
Freemasons' Row	C6-D6
Gascoyne Street	B6-C6
Gibralter Row	B5-B6
Gibson Street	F1
Gilbert Street	D3
Gill Street	E4-E5
Gore Street	E1
Goree Piazza	B4
Gradwell Street	D3-D4
Grafton Street	D1
Great Crosshall Street	C6
Great George Street	E1-E2-E3
Great Homer Street	D7-D8
Great Howard Street	B6-B7-B8
Great Newton Street	E5-E4-F4
Greenland Street	D1
Green Street	C8-D8
Greenside	F6
Gregson Street	F6-F7
Haigh Street	E7-F6
Hampton Street	E1-F1
Hanover Street	C3-C4-D4
Hardman Street	E3
Hardy Street	D2-E2
Harker Street	E6
Hatton Garde	C5-C6
Head Street	E1
Henry Street	D3
Heyworth Street	F8
Hill Street	D1-E1
Hodson Place	F8
Hood Street	D5
Hope Street	E2-E3-F3-F4
Hunter Street	D6
Hurst Street	C2-C3
Huskisson Street	E2-F2
Illiard Street	E7-E8
Islington	E6-F6
Islington Square	F6
Jamaica Street	D1-D2
James Street	B4-C4
Jordan Street	D1-D2
Juvenal Street	D7
Kempston Street	E5-F5-F6
Kent Street	D2-D3
Kepler Street	E8-F8
Kings Dock Street	C2-D2
King Edward Street	B5-B6
Kingsway Road Tunnel	A6-A7-B7-C7
Kitchen Street	C2-D2
Landseer Road	F8
Langsdale Street	E6-F6
Lanyork Street	B6
Leece Street	E3
Leeds Street	B6-C6-D6
Lime Street	D4-D5
Limekiln Lane	C7-D7-D8
London Road	D5-E5-F5
Lord Nelson Street	D5-E5
Lord Street	C4
Love Lane	B7-B8
Lydia Ann Street	D3
Mansfield Street	E6
Mann Island	B4
Marybone	C6
Mathews Street	C4
Midghehall Street	C1
Mill Street	E1
Moss Street	F5-F6
Mount Pleasant	F4
Mount Street	E3
Myrtle Street	E3-F3
Naylor Street	C6-D6
Nelson Street	D2-D3-E3
Neptune Street	B6
Netherfield Road South	E8-E7
New Bird Street	D1-D2
New Islington	E6-F6
New Quay	B5
North John Street	C4-C5
Norton Street	E5
Oakes Street	E5-F5
Oil Street	A7-B7
Old Hall Street	B5-B6
Oldham Street	E3
Oriel Street	C6-C7-D7
Oxford Street	F3-F4
Pall Mall	B7-B6-C6-B5-C5
Paradise Street	C3-C4
Parker Street	D4
Park Lane	C3-D3-D2
Park Way	F1-F2
Parliament Street	D1-E1-E2
Parr Street	D3
Paul Street	C7-D7
Pembroke Place	E5-F5
Pembroke Street	F5
Penrhyn Street	D8
Percy Street	E2-F2
Philips Street	C6
Pitt Street	D3
Porter Street	A7-B7
Portland Place	E8
Prescot Street	F5-F6
Prince Edwin Street	E7-E8
Prince's Avenue	F1
Prince's Parade	A5
Prince's Road	F1-F2
Queensway Road Tunnel	A3-A4-B4C4-C5
Ranelagh Street	D4
Regent Street	A7-B7
Renshaw Street	D4-E4-E3
Richmond Row	D7-E7
Roberts Street	B6
Rodney Street	E3-E4
Roe Street	D5
Rokeby Street	E7
Roscoe Street	E3-E4
Roscommon Street	D8-E8
Rose Place	D7-E7
Rose Vale	E8
Russell Street	E4-E5
St Andrew Street	E4-E5
St Anne Street	D7-D6-E6
St James's Place	E1
St James's Street	D2-D1-E1
Salisbury Street	E7-E6-F6
Saltney Street	A8-B8
Sandon Street	F2
School Lane	C4-D4
Scotland Road	D6-D7-D8
Seel Street	D4-D3-E3
Sefton Street	E5
Seymour Street	E5
Shaw Street	E7-F7-F6
Silvester Street	C8-D8
Simpson Street	D1-D2
Slater Street	D3-D4
Soho Street	E6-E7
Solva Close	F8
South John Street	C4
Sparling Street	C2-D2
Spencer Street	F7
Springfield	E6
Stanhope Street	D1
Stone Street	B8
Strand Street	B4-C4-C3
Tabley Street	C2-C3-D3
Tatlock Street	C8
Titchfield Street	C7-C8
Tithebarn Street	B5-C5-C6
The Strand	B4
Trowbridge Street	E4-E5
Upper Duke Street	E2-E3
Upper Frederick Street	C3-D3-D2
Upper Hampton Street	F2
Upper Hill Street	E1-F1
Upper Parliement Street	F2
Upper Pitt Street	D2
Upper Stanhope Street	E1-F1
Vandries Street	B7
Vauxhall Road	C6-C7-C8
Victoria Street	C4-C5-D5
Village Street	F7
Vine Street	F3
Vulcan Street	A7-B7
Wakefield Street	E6
Wapping	C2-C3
Waterloo Road	A8-A7-B7-A6-B6
Water Street	B4-B5-C5
Watmough Street	E7
Westbourne Street	F6-F7
Wentworth Drive	B7
Whitechapel	C4-C5-D5
Wilbraham Street	D5
William Brown Street	D5
William Henry Street	E6-E7-F7
Windsor Street	E1-F1
Wood Street	D4-D3-E3
York Street	D3

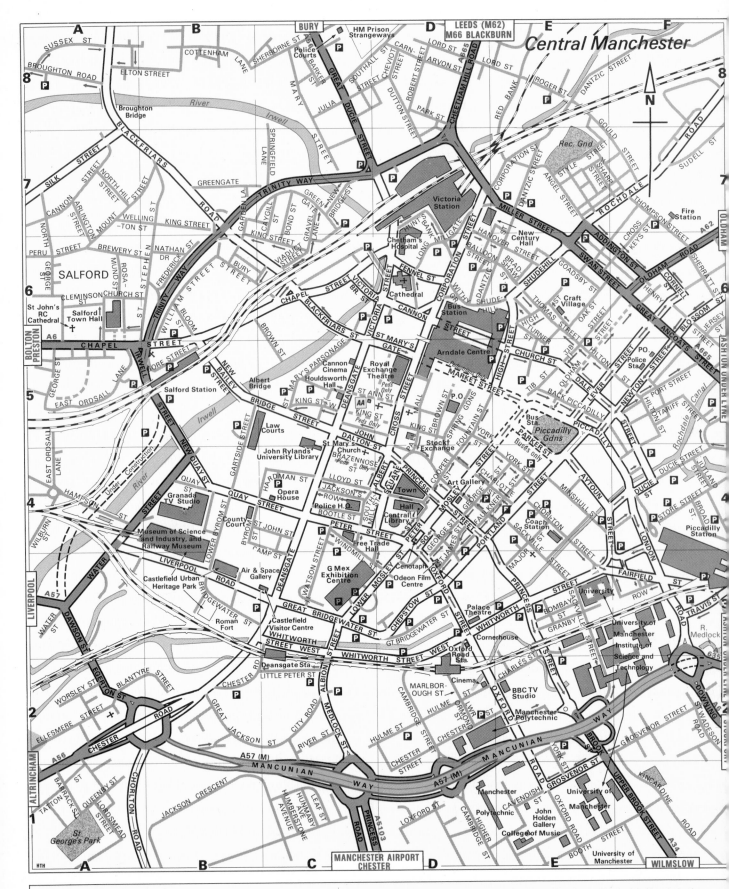

Manchester

The gigantic conurbation called Greater Manchester covers a staggering 60 square miles, reinforcing Manchester's claim to be Britain's second city. Commerce and industry are vital aspects of the city's character, but it is also an important cultural centre - the Halle Orchestra has its home at the Free Trade Hall (a venue for many concerts besides classical music), there are several theatres, a library (the John Rylands) which houses one of the most important collections of books in the world, and a number of museums and galleries, including the Whitworth Gallery with its lovely watercolours.

Like many great cities it suffered badly during the bombing raids of World War II, but some older buildings remain, including the town hall, a huge building designed in Gothic style by Alfred Waterhouse and opened in 1877. Manchester Cathedral dates mainly from the 15th century and is noted for its fine tower and outstanding carved woodwork. Nearby is Chetham's Hospital, also 15th-century and now housing a music school. Much new development has taken place, and more is planned. Shopping precincts cater for the vast population, and huge hotels have provided services up to international standards. The Museum of Science and Industry opened in 1980, inside the worlds first passenger railway station, with exhibits from the Industrial Revolution to the Space Age.

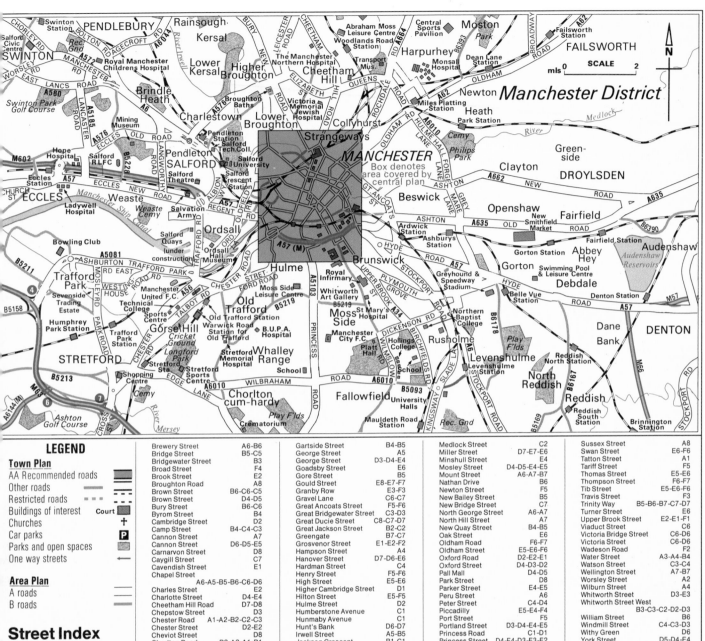

LEGEND

Town Plan

AA Recommended roads	━━
Other roads	━━
Restricted roads	┅ ┅
Buildings of interest	Court ▪
Churches	†
Car parks	Ⓟ
Parks and open spaces	▨
One way streets	←

Area Plan

A roads	━━
B roads	━━

Street Index with Grid Reference

Manchester

Addington Street	E7-E6-F6
Albert Square	C4-D4
Albion Street	C2-C3
Angel Street	E7
Arlington Street	A7
Aytoun Street	E4-F4-F3-E3
Back Piccadilly	E5-F5-F4
Balloon Street	D6-E6
Barker Street	C8
Barrack Street	A1
Blackfriars Road	A8-A7-B7-B6-C6
Blackfriars Street	C5-C6
Bloom Street	B6
Blossom Street	F6
Bombay Street	E3
Bond Street	C7
Booth Street	E1-F1
Bootle Street	C4
Bradshaw Street	E6
Brazennose Street	C4-D4

Brewery Street	A6-B6
Bridge Street	B5-C5
Bridgewater Street	B3
Broad Street	F4
Brook Street	E2
Broughton Road	A8
Brown Street	B6-C6-C5
Brown Street	D4-D5
Bury Street	B6-C6
Byrom Street	B4
Cambridge Street	D2
Camp Street	B4-C4-C3
Cannon Street	A7
Cannon Street	D6-D5-E5
Carnarvon Street	D8
Caygill Street	C7
Cavendish Street	E1
Chapel Street	A6-A5-B5-B6-C6-D6
Charles Street	E2
Charlotte Street	D4-E4
Cheetham Hill Road	D7-D8
Chepstow Street	D3
Chester Road	A1-A2-B2-C2-C3
Chester Street	D2-E2
Cheviot Street	D8
Chorlton Road	B2-A2-A1-B1
Chorlton Street	E3-E4
Church Street	A6-B6
Church Street	E5
Cleminson Street	A6
City Road	C2
Cooper Street	D4
Cornell Street	F6
Corporation Street	D6-D7-E7
Cottenham Lane	B8
Cross Keys Street	F6-F7
Cross Street	D4-D5-D6
Dale Street	E5-F5-F4
Dantzig Street	D6-E6-E7-E8-F8
Dawson Street	A3
Deansgate	C3-C4-C5
Downing Street	F2
Ducie Street	F4
Dutton Street	D7-D8
East Ordsall Lane	A4-A5
Egerton Street	A2
Ellesmere Street	A2
Elton Street	A8-B2
Fairfield Street	F3
Faulkner Street	D4-E4
Fennel Street	D6
Fountain Street	D4-D5
Frederick Street	B6
Garden Lane	B6-B7

Gartside Street	B4-B5
George Street	A5
George Street	D3-D4-E4
Goadsby Street	E6
Gore Street	B5
Gould Street	E8-E7-F7
Granby Row	E3-F3
Gravel Lane	C6-C7
Great Ancoats Street	F5-F6
Great Bridgewater Street	C3-D3
Great Ducie Street	C8-C7-D7
Great Jackson Street	B2-C2
Greengate	B7-C7
Grosvenor Street	E1-E2-F2
Hampson Street	A4
Hanover Street	D7-D6-E6
Hardman Street	C4
Henry Street	F5-F6
High Street	E5-E6
Higher Cambridge Street	D1
Hilton Street	E5-F5
Hulme Street	D2
Humberstone Avenue	C1
Hunmaby Avenue	C1
Hunt's Bank	D6-D7
Irwell Street	A5-B5
Jackson Crescent	B1-C1
Jackson's Row	C4
Jersey Street	F6
John Dalton Street	C5-C4-D4-D5
Julia Street	C8-D8
Jutland Street	F4
Kincardine Road	F1-F2
King Street	A7-B7-B6-C6
King Street	C5-D5
King St West	C5
Leaf Street	C1
Lever Street	E5-F5-F6
Little Peter Street	B2-C2
Liverpool Road	A4-A3-B4-B3-C3
Lloyd Street	C4
London Road	F3-F4
Long Millgate	D6-D7
Lord Street	D8-E8
Lordsmead Street	A1
Lower Byrom Street	B3-B4
Lower Mosley Street	C3-D3-D4
Lower Ormond Street	D2
Loxford Street	D1
Major Street	E3-E4
Mancunian Way	B2-B1-C2-C1-D1-D2-E2-F2
Market Street	D5-E5
Marlborough Street	D2
Mary Street	C7-C8

Medlock Street	C2
Miller Street	D7-E7-E6
Minshull Street	E4
Mosley Street	D4-D5-E4-E5
Mount Street	A6-A7-B7
Nathan Drive	B6
Newton Street	F5
New Bailey Street	B5
New Bridge Street	C7
North George Street	A6-A7
North Hill Street	A7
New Quay Street	B4-B5
Oak Street	E6
Oldham Road	F6-F7
Oldham Street	E5-E6-F6
Oxford Road	D2-E2-E1
Oxford Street	D4-D3-D2
Pall Mall	D4-D5
Park Street	D8
Parker Street	E4-E5
Peru Street	A6
Peter Street	C4-D4
Piccadilly	E5-E4-F4
Port Street	F5
Portland Street	D3-D4-E4-E5
Princess Road	C1-D1
Princess Street	D4-E4-D3-E3-E2
Quay Street	B4-C4
Queenby Street	A1
Red Bank	E7-E8
River Street	C2
Robert Street	D8
Rochdale Road	E7-F7-F8
Roger Street	E8
Rosamund Street	A6
St Ann Street	C5-D5
St Mary's Gate	C5-C6-D5-D6
St Mary's Parsonage	C5-C6
St James Street	D3-D4
St John Street	B4-C4
St Peter Square	D4
St Stephen Street	A6-B6-B7
Sackville Street	E2-E3-E4
Sharp Street	E7
Sherrat Street	F6
Sherborne Street	B8-C8
Shudehill	D6-E6
Silk Street	A7
Southall Street	C8-D8
Southmill Street	C4
Spring Gardens	D4-D5
Springfield Lane	C7-C8
Store Street	F4
Style Street	E7-E8
Sudell Street	F7-F8

Sussex Street	A8
Swan Street	E6-F6
Tatton Street	A1
Tariff Street	F5
Thomas Street	E5-E6
Thompson Street	F6-F7
Tib Street	E5-E6-F6
Travis Street	F3
Trinity Way	B5-B6-B7-C7-D7
Turner Street	E6
Upper Brook Street	E2-E1-F1
Viaduct Street	C6
Victoria Bridge Street	C6-D6
Victoria Street	C6-D6
Wadeson Road	F2
Water Street	A3-A4-B4
Watson Street	C3-C4
Wellington Street	A7-B7
Worsley Street	A2
Wilburn Street	A4
Whitworth Street	D3-E3
Whitworth Street West	B3-C3-C2-D2-D3
William Street	B6
Windmill Street	C4-C3-D3
Withy Green	D6
York Street	D5-D4-E4

MANCHESTER
The Barton Swing Bridge carries the Bridgewater Canal over the Manchester Ship Canal, which links Manchester with the sea nearly 40 miles away. Completed in 1894, the canal is navigable by vessels up to 15,000 tons.

163

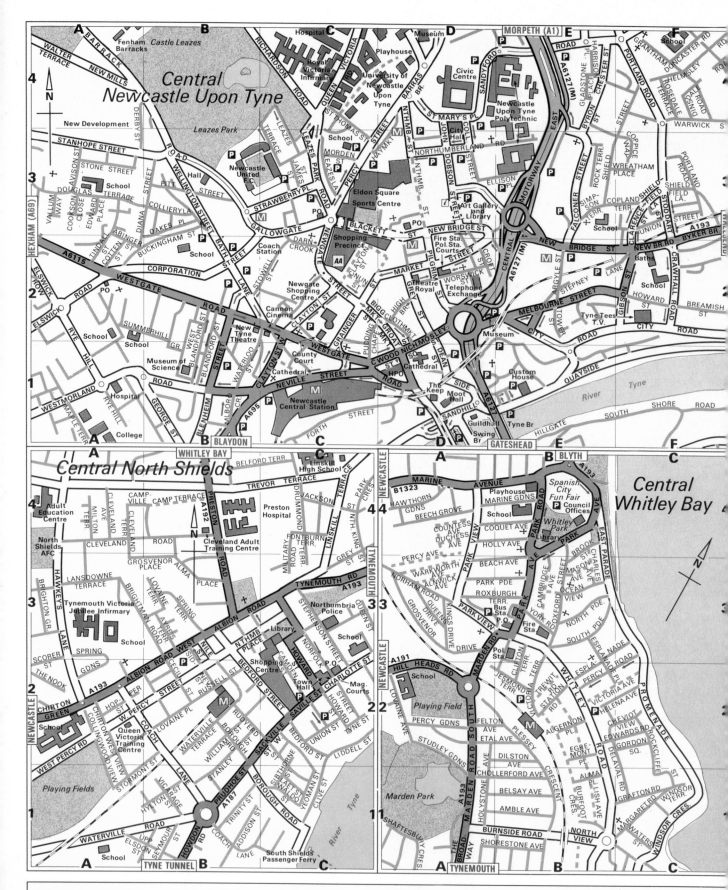

Newcastle

Six bridges span the Tyne at Newcastle; they all help to create a striking scene, but the most impressive is the High Level Bridge, built by Robert Stephenson in 1845-49 and consisting of two levels, one for the railway and one for the road. It is from the river that some of the best views of the city can be obtained. Grey Street is Newcastle's most handsome thoroughfare. It dates from the

time, between 1835 and 1840, when much of this part of the city was replanned and rebuilt. Elegant façades curve up to Grey's Monument. Close to the Monument is the Eldon Centre, combining sports facilities and shopping centre to form an integrated complex which is one of the largest of its kind in Europe. Newcastle has many museums. The industrial background of the city is traced in the Museum of Science and Engineering, while the Laing Art Gallery and Museum covers painting,

costumes and local domestic history. The Hancock Museum has an exceptional natural history collection and the John George Joicey Museum has period displays in a 17th-century almshouse. In Black Gate is one of Britain's most unusual museums – a collection of over 100 sets of bagpipes. Within the University precincts are three further museums. Of the city's open spaces, Town Moor is the largest. At nearly 1,000 acres it is big enough to feel genuinely wild.

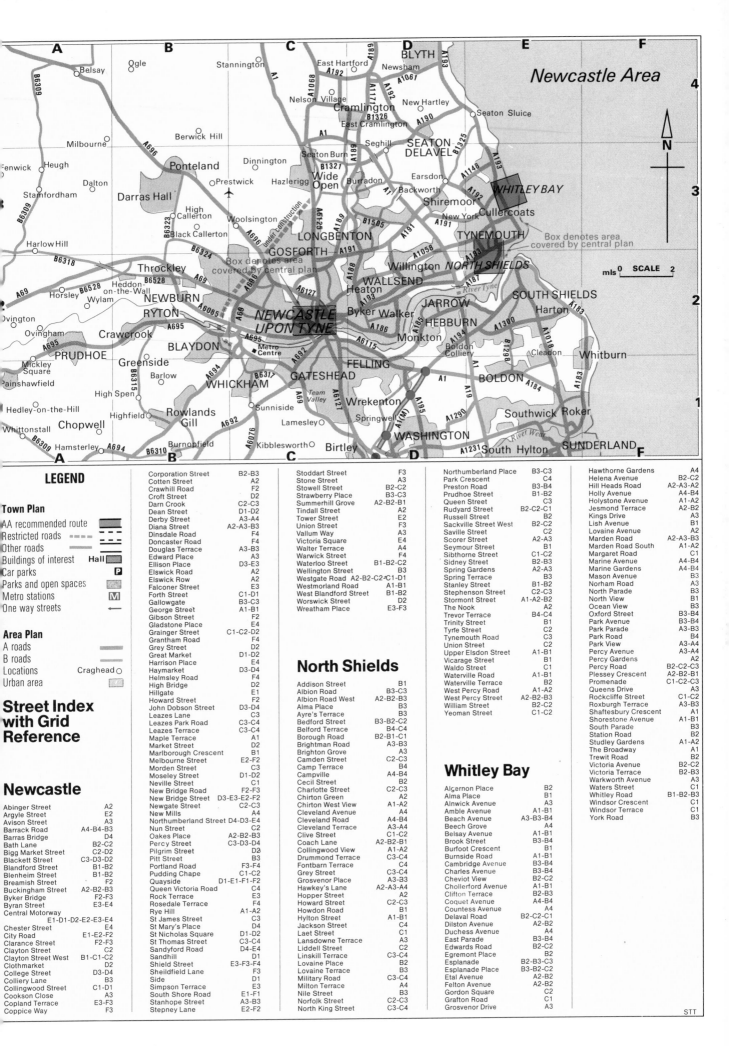

Newcastle Area

Box denotes area covered by central plan

mls 0 SCALE 2

LEGEND

Town Plan

AA recommended route	
Restricted roads	
Other roads	
Buildings of interest	Hall
Car parks	P
Parks and open spaces	
Metro stations	M
One way streets	←

Area Plan

A roads	
B roads	
Locations	Craghead ○
Urban area	

Street Index with Grid Reference

Newcastle

Abinger Street	A2
Argyle Street	E2
Avison Street	A3
Barrack Road	A4-B4-B3
Barras Bridge	D4
Bath Lane	B2-C2
Bigg Market Street	C2-D2
Blackett Street	C3-D3-D2
Blandford Street	B1-B2
Blenheim Street	B1-B2
Breamish Street	F2
Buckingham Street	A2-B2-B3
Byker Bridge	F2-F3
Byran Street	E3-E4
Central Motorway	E1-D1-D2-E2-E3-E4
Chester Street	E4
City Road	E1-E2-F2
Clarance Street	F2-F3
Clayton Street	C2
Clayton Street West	B1-C1-C2
Clothmarket	D2
College Street	D3-D4
Colliery Lane	B3
Collingwood Street	C1-D1
Cookson Close	A3
Copland Terrace	E3-F3
Coppice Way	F3
Corporation Street	B2-B3
Cotten Street	A2
Crawhill Road	F2
Croft Street	D2
Darn Crook	C2-C3
Dean Street	D1-D2
Derby Street	A3-A4
Diana Street	A2-A3-B3
Dinsdale Road	F4
Doncaster Road	F4
Douglas Terrace	A3-B3
Edward Place	A3
Ellison Place	D3-E3
Elswick Road	A2
Elswick Row	A2
Falconer Street	E3
Forth Street	C1-D1
Gallowgate	B3-C3
George Street	A1-B1
Gibson Street	E4
Gladstone Place	E4
Grainger Street	C1-C2-D2
Grantham Road	F4
Grey Street	D2
Great Market	D1-D2
Harrison Place	E4
Haymarket	D3-D4
Helmsley Road	F2
High Bridge	D2
Hillgate	E1
Howard Street	F2
John Dobson Street	D3-D4
Leazes Lane	C3
Leazes Park Road	C3-C4
Leazes Terrace	C3-C4
Maple Terrace	A1
Market Street	D2
Marlborough Crescent	B1
Melbourne Street	E2-F2
Morden Street	C3
Moseley Street	D1-D2
Neville Street	C1
New Bridge Road	F2-F3
New Bridge Street	D3-E3-E2-F2
Newgate Street	C2-C3
New Mills	A4
Northumberland Street	D4-D3-E4
Nun Street	C2
Oakes Place	A2-B2-B3
Percy Street	C3-D3-D4
Pilgrim Street	D2
Pitt Street	B3
Portland Road	F3-F4
Pudding Chape	C1-C2
Quayside	D1-E1-F1-F2
Queen Victoria Road	C4
Rock Terrace	E3
Rosedale Terrace	F4
Rye Hill	A1-A2
St James Street	C3
St Mary's Place	D4
St Nicholas Square	D1-D2
St Thomas Street	C3-C4
Sandyford Road	D4-E4
Sandhill	D1
Shield Street	E3-F3-F4
Sheildfield Lane	F3
Side	D1
Simpson Street	E3
South Shore Road	E1-F1
Stanhope Street	A3-B3
Stepney Lane	E2-F2
Stoddart Street	F3
Stone Street	A3
Stowell Street	B2-C2
Strawberry Place	B3-C3
Summerhill Grove	A2-B2-B1
Tindall Street	A2
Tower Street	E2
Union Street	F3
Vallum Way	A3
Victoria Square	E4
Walter Terrace	A4
Warwick Street	F4
Waterloo Street	B1-B2-C2
Wellington Street	B3
Westgate Road	A2-B2-C2-C1-D1
Westmorland Road	A1-B1
West Blandford Street	B1-B2
Worswick Street	D2
Wreatham Place	E3-F3

North Shields

Addison Street	B1
Albion Road	B3-C3
Albion Road West	A2-B2-B3
Alma Place	B3
Ayre's Terrace	B3
Bedford Street	B3-B2-C2
Belford Terrace	B4-C4
Borough Road	B2-B1-C1
Brightman Road	A3-B3
Brighton Grove	A3
Camden Street	C2-C3
Camp Terrace	B4
Campville	A4-B4
Cecil Street	B2
Charlotte Street	C2-C3
Chirton Green	A2
Chirton West View	A1-A2
Cleveland Avenue	A4
Cleveland Road	A4-B4
Cleveland Terrace	A3-A4
Clive Street	C1-C2
Coach Lane	A2-B2-B1
Collingwood View	A1-A2
Drummond Terrace	C3-C4
Fontbarn Terrace	C4
Grey Street	C3-C4
Grosvenor Place	A3-B3
Hawkey's Lane	A2-A3-A4
Hopper Street	A2
Howard Street	C2-C3
Howdon Road	B1
Hylton Street	A1-B1
Jackson Street	C4
Laet Street	C1
Lansdowne Terrace	A3
Liddell Street	C2
Linskill Terrace	C3-C4
Lovaine Place	B2
Lovaine Terrace	B3
Military Road	C3-C4
Milton Terrace	A4
Nile Street	B3
Norfolk Street	C2-C3
North King Street	C3-C4
Northumberland Place	B3-C3
Park Crescent	C4
Preston Road	B3-B4
Prudhoe Street	B1-B2
Queen Street	C3
Rudyard Street	B2-C2-C1
Russell Street	B2
Sackville Street West	B2-C2
Saville Street	C2
Scorer Street	A2-A3
Seymour Street	B1
Sibthorne Street	C1-C2
Sidney Street	B2-B3
Spring Gardens	A2-A3
Spring Terrace	B3
Stanley Street	B1-B2
Stephenson Street	C2-C3
Stormont Street	A1-A2-B2
The Nook	A2
Trevor Terrace	B4-C4
Trinity Street	B1
Tyrfe Street	C2
Tynemouth Road	C3
Union Street	C2
Upper Elsdon Street	A1-B1
Vicarage Street	B1
Waldo Street	C1
Waterville Road	A1-B1
Waterville Terrace	B2
West Percy Road	A1-A2
West Percy Street	A2-B2-B3
William Street	B2-C2
Yeoman Street	C1-C2

Whitley Bay

Algernon Place	B2
Alma Place	B1
Alnwick Avenue	A3
Amble Avenue	A1-B1
Beach Avenue	A3-B3-B4
Beech Grove	A4
Belsay Avenue	A1-B1
Brook Street	B3-B4
Burfoot Crescent	B1
Burnside Road	A1-B1
Cambridge Avenue	B3-B4
Charles Avenue	B3-B4
Cheviot View	B2-C2
Chollerford Avenue	A1-B1
Clifton Terrace	B2-B3
Coquet Avenue	A4-B4
Countess Avenue	A4
Delaval Road	B2-C2-C1
Dilston Avenue	A2-B2
Duchess Avenue	A4
East Parade	B3-B4
Edwards Road	B2-C2
Egremont Place	B2
Esplanade	B2-B3-C3
Esplanade Place	B3-B2-C2
Etal Avenue	A2-B2
Felton Avenue	A2-B2
Gordon Square	C2
Grafton Road	C1
Grosvenor Drive	A3
Hawthorne Gardens	A4
Helena Avenue	B2-C2
Hill Heads Road	A2-A3-A2
Holly Avenue	A4-B4
Holystone Avenue	A1-A2
Jesmond Terrace	A2-B2
Kings Drive	A3
Lish Avenue	B1
Lovaine Avenue	A2
Marden Road	A2-A3-B3
Marden Road South	A1-A2
Margaret Road	C1
Marine Avenue	A4-B4
Marine Gardens	A4-B4
Mason Avenue	B3
Norham Road	A3
North Parade	B3
North View	B1
Ocean View	B3
Oxford Street	B3-B4
Park Avenue	B3-B4
Park Parade	A3-B3
Park Road	B4
Park View	A3-A4
Percy Avenue	A3-A4
Percy Gardens	A4
Percy Road	B2-C2-C3
Plessey Crescent	A2-B2-B1
Promenade	C1-C2-C3
Queens Drive	A3
Rockcliffe Street	C1-C2
Roxburgh Terrace	A3-B3
Shaftesbury Crescent	A1
Shorestone Avenue	A1-B1
South Parade	B3
Station Road	B2
Studley Gardens	A1-A2
The Broadway	A1
Trewit Road	B2
Victoria Avenue	B2-C2
Victoria Terrace	B2-B3
Warkworth Avenue	A3
Waters Street	C1
Whitley Road	B1-B2-B3
Windsor Crescent	C1
Windsor Terrace	C1
York Road	B3

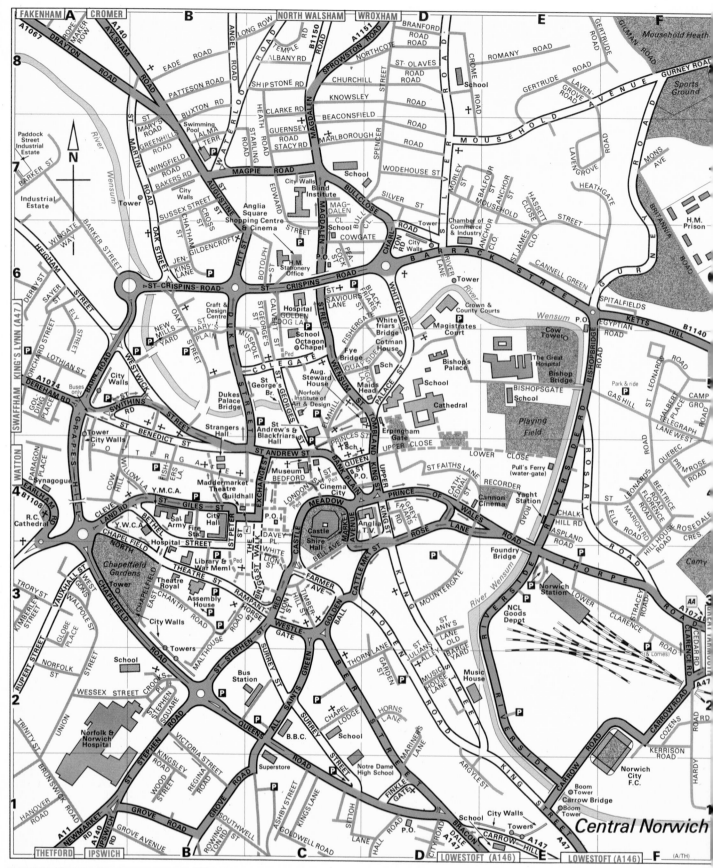

Norwich

Fortunately the heart has not been ripped out of Norwich to make way for some bland precinct, so its ancient character has been preserved. Narrow alleys run between the streets – sometimes opening out into quiet courtyards, sometimes into thoroughfares packed with people, sometimes into lanes which seem quite deserted. It is a unique place, with something of interest on every corner.

The cathedral was founded in 1096 by the city's first bishop, Herbert de Losinga. Among its most notable features are the nave, with its huge pillars, the bishop's throne (a Saxon survival unique in Europe) and the cloisters with their matchless collection of roof bosses. Across the city is the great stone keep of the castle, set on a mound and dominating all around it. It dates from Norman times, but was refaced in 1834. The keep now forms part of Norwich Castle Museum – an extensive and

fascinating collection. Other museums are Bridewell Museum – collections relating to local crafts and industries within a 14th-century building – and Strangers' Hall, a genuinely 'old world' house, rambling and full of surprises, both in its tumble of rooms and in the things which they contain. Especially picturesque parts of the city are Elm Hill – a street of ancient houses; Tombland – with two gateways into the Cathedral Close; and Pull's Ferry – a watergate by the river.

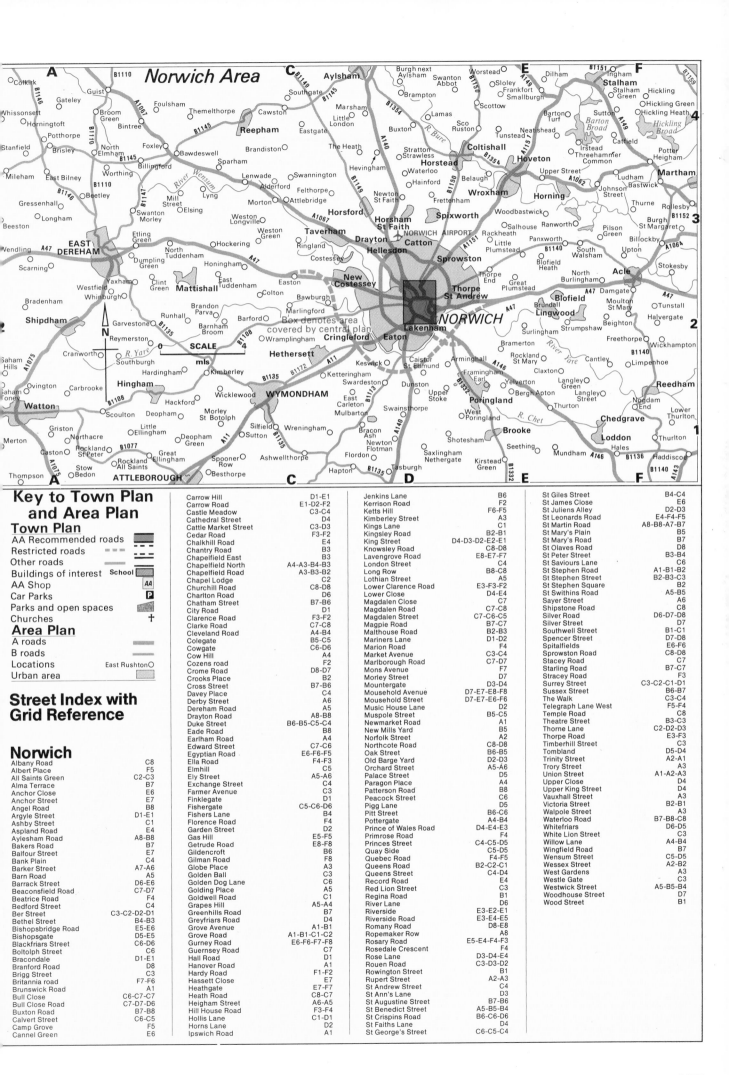

Norwich Area

Box denotes area covered by central plan

Key to Town Plan and Area Plan

Town Plan

AA Recommended roads
Restricted roads
Other roads
Buildings of interest — School
AA Shop — AA
Car Parks — P
Parks and open spaces
Churches — †

Area Plan

A roads
B roads
Locations — East Rushton○
Urban area

Street Index with Grid Reference

Norwich

Albany Road	C8
Albert Place	F5
All Saints Green	C2-C3
Alma Terrace	B7
Anchor Close	E6
Anchor Street	E7
Angel Road	B8
Argyle Street	D1-E1
Ashby Street	C1
Aspland Road	E4
Aylesham Road	A8-B8
Bakers Road	B7
Balfour Street	E7
Bank Plain	C4
Barker Street	A7-A6
Barn Road	A5
Barrack Street	D6-E6
Beaconsfield Road	C7-D7
Beatrice Road	C7
Bedford Street	C4
Ber Street	C3-C2-D2-D1
Bethel Street	B4-B3
Bishopsbridge Road	E5-E6
Bishopsgate	D5-E5
Blackfriars Street	C6-D6
Boltolph Street	C6
Bracondale	D1-E1
Branford Road	D8
Brigg Street	C3
Britannia road	F7-F6
Brunswick Road	A1
Bull Close	C6-C7-C8
Bull Close Road	C7-D7-D6
Buxton Road	B7-B8
Calvert Street	C6-C5
Camp Grove	F5
Cannel Green	E6

Carrow Hill	D1-E1
Carrow Road	E1-D2-F2
Castle Meadow	C3-C4
Cathedral Street	D4
Cattle Market Street	C3-D3
Cedar Road	F3-F2
Chalkhill Road	E4
Chantry Road	B3
Chapelfield East	B3
Chapelfield North	A4-A3-B4-B3
Chapelfield Road	A3-B3-B2
Chapel Lodge	C2
Churchill Road	C8-D8
Charlton Road	D6
Chatham Street	B7-B6
City Road	D1
Clarence Road	F3-F2
Clarke Road	C7-C8
Cleveland Road	A4-B4
Colegate	B5-C5
Cowgate	C6-D6
Cow Hill	A4
Cozens road	F2
Crome Road	B2
Crooks Place	B3
Cross Street	B7-B6
Davey Place	C4
Derby Street	A6
Dereham Road	A5
Drayton Road	A8-B8
Duke Street	B6-B5-C5-C4
Eade Road	B8
Earlham Road	A4
Edward Street	C7-C6
Egyptian Road	F4-F3
Ella Road	F4-F3
Elmhill	C5
Ely Street	A5-A6
Exchange Street	C4
Farmer Avenue	C3
Finklegate	D1
Fishergate	C5-C6-D6
Fishers Lane	B4
Florence Road	F4
Garden Street	D2
Gas Hill	E5-F5
Getrude Road	E8-F8
Gildencroft	B6
Gilman Road	F8
Globe Place	A3
Golden Ball	C3
Golden Dog Lane	C6
Golding Place	A5
Goldwell Road	B1
Grapes Hill	A5-A4
Greenhills Road	B7
Greyfriars Road	D4
Grove Avenue	A1-B1
Grove Road	A1-B1-C1-C2
Gurney Road	E6-F6-F7-F8
Guernsey Road	C7
Hall Road	D1
Hanover Road	A1
Hardy Road	F1-F2
Hassett Close	E7
Heathgate	E7-F7
Heath Road	C8-C7
Heigham Street	A6-A5
Hill House Road	F3-F4
Hollis Lane	C1-D1
Horns Lane	D2
Ipswich Road	A1

Jenkins Lane	B6
Kerrison Road	F2
Ketts Hill	F6-F5
Kimberley Street	A3
Kings Lane	C1
Kingsley Road	B2-B1
King Street	D4-D3-D2-E2-E1
Knowsley Road	C8-D8
Lavengrove Road	E8-E7-F7
London Street	C4
Long Row	B8-C8
Lothian Street	A5
Lower Clarence Road	E3-F3-F2
Lower Close	D4-E4
Magdalen Close	C7
Magdalen Road	C7-C8
Magdalen Street	C7-C6-C5
Magpie Road	B7-C7
Malthouse Road	B2-B3
Mariners Lane	D1-D2
Marion Road	F4
Market Avenue	C3-C4
Marlborough Road	C7-D7
Mons Avenue	F7
Morley Street	D7
Mountergate	D3-D4
Mousehold Avenue	D7-E7-E8-F8
Mousehold Street	D7-E7-E6-F6
Music House Lane	D2
Muspole Street	B5-C5
Newmarket Road	A1
New Mills Yard	B5
Norfolk Street	A2
Northcote Road	C8-D8
Oak Street	B6-B5
Old Barge Yard	D2-D3
Orchard Street	A5-A6
Palace Street	D5
Paragon Place	A4
Patterson Road	B8
Peacock Street	C6
Pigg Lane	D5
Pitt Street	B6-C6
Pottergate	A4-B4
Prince of Wales Road	D4-E4-E3
Primrose Road	F4
Princes Street	C4-C5-D5
Quay Side	C5-D5
Quebec Road	F4-F5
Queens Road	B2-C2-C1
Queens Street	C4-D4
Record Road	E4
Red Lion Street	C3
Regina Road	B1
River Lane	D6
Riverside	E3-E2-E1
Riverside Road	E3-E4-E5
Romany Road	D8-E8
Ropemaker Row	A8
Rosary Road	E5-E4-F4-F3
Rosedale Crescent	F4
Rose Lane	D3-D4-E4
Rouen Road	C3-D3-D2
Rowington Street	B1
Rupert Street	A2-A3
St Andrew Street	C4
St Ann's Lane	D3
St Augustine Street	B7-B6
St Benedict Street	A5-B5-B4
St Crispins Road	B6-C6-D6
St Faiths Lane	D4
St George's Street	C6-C5-C4

St Giles Street	B4-C4
St James Close	E6
St Juliens Alley	D2-D3
St Leonards Road	E4-F4-F5
St Martin Road	A8-B8-A7-B7
St Mary's Plain	B5
St Mary's Road	B7
St Olaves Road	D8
St Peter Street	B3-B4
St Saviours Lane	C6
St Stephen Road	A1-B1-B2
St Stephen Street	B2-B3-C3
St Stephen Square	B2
St Swithins Road	A5-B5
Sayer Street	A6
Shipstone Road	C8
Silver Road	D6-D7-D8
Silver Street	D7
Southwell Street	B1-C1
Spencer Street	D7-D8
Spitalfields	E6-F6
Sprowston Road	C8-D8
Stacey Road	C7
Starling Road	B7-C7
Stracey Road	F3
Surrey Street	C3-C2-C1-D1
Sussex Street	B6-B7
The Walk	C3-C4
Telegraph Lane West	F5-F4
Temple Road	C8
Theatre Street	B3-C3
Thorne Lane	C2-D2-D3
Thorpe Road	E3-F3
Timberhill Street	C3
Tombland	D5-D4
Trinity Street	A2-A1
Trory Street	A3
Union Street	A1-A2-A3
Upper Close	D4
Upper King Street	D4
Vauxhall Street	A3
Victoria Street	B2-B1
Walpole Street	A3
Waterloo Road	B7-B8-C8
Whitefriars	D6-D5
White Lion Street	C3
Willow Lane	A4-B4
Wingfield Road	B7
Wensum Street	C5-D5
Wessex Street	A2-B2
West Gardens	A3
Westle Gate	C3
Westwick Street	A5-B5-B4
Woodhouse Street	D7
Wood Street	B1

167

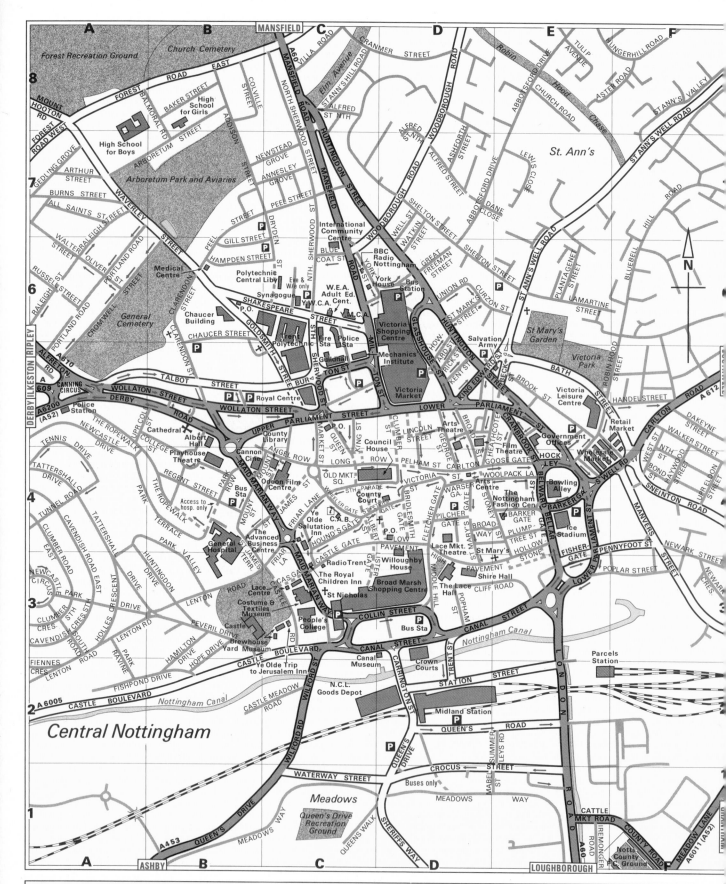

Nottingham

Hosiery and lace were the foundations upon which Nottingham's prosperity was built. The stockings came first – a knitting machine for these had been invented by a Nottinghamshire man as early as 1589 – but a machine called a 'tickler', which enabled simple patterns to be created in the stocking fabric, prompted the development of machine-made lace. The earliest fabric was produced in 1768, and an example from not much later than that is kept in the city's Castlegate Costume and Textile Museum. In fact, the entire history of lacemaking is beautifully explained in this converted row of Georgian terraces. The Industrial Museum at Wollaton Park has many other machines and exhibits tracing the development of the knitting industry, as well as displays on the other industries which have brought wealth to the city – tobacco, pharmaceuticals, engineering and printing. At Wollaton Hall is a natural history museum, while nearer the centre are the Canal Museum and the Brewhouse Yard Museum, a marvellous collection which shows items from daily life in the city up to the present day. Nottingham is not complete without mention of Robin Hood, the partly mythical figure whose statue is in the castle grounds. Although the castle itself has Norman foundations, the present structure is largely Victorian. It is now a museum.

168

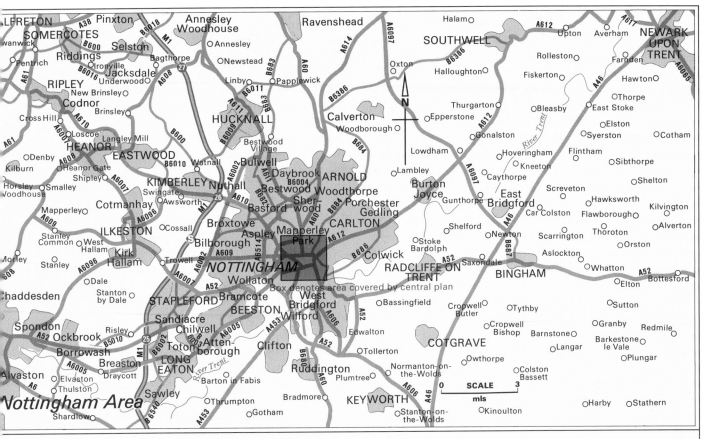

Key to Town Plan and Area Plan
Town Plan

AA Recommended roads	▬▬
Restricted roads	--- ▬
Other roads	▬
Buildings of interest	Theatre ▮
Car Parks	P
Parks and open spaces	▨
Churches	†
One Way Streets	→

Area Plan

A roads	▬
B roads	▬
Locations	Bagthorpe○
Urban area	▨

Street Index with Grid Reference

Nottingham

Abbotsford Drive	D6-D7-D7-E7-E8
Addison Street	B8-B7
Albert Street	C4
Alfred Street	D7
Alfred Street North	C8, D7-D8
Alfreton Road	A5-A6
All Saints Street	A7
Angel Row	B5-B4-C4
Annesley Grove	B7-C7
Ashforth Street	D7-D8
Aster Road	E8-F8
Arboretum Street	A7-B7-B8
Arthur Street	A7
Baker Street	B8
Balmoral Road	A8-B8-B7
Barker Gate	E4
Bath Street	E5-F5
Beck Street	E5
Bellar Gate	E4
Belward Street	E4
Bluebell Hill Road	F6-F7
Bluecoat Street	C6
Bond Street	F4
Bridlesmith Gate	D4
Broad Street	D4-D5
Broadway	D4-E4
Brook Street	E5
Burns Street	A7
Burton Street	C5
Canal Street	C3-D3-E3
Canning Circus	A5
Carlton Road	F5
Carlton Street	D4
Carrington Street	D2-D3
Castle Boulevard	A2-B2-B3-C3
Castle Gate	C3-C4
Castle Meadow Road	B2-C2
Castle Road	C3
Cattle Market Road	E1-F1
Cavendish Crescent South	A3
Cavendish Road East	A3-A4
Chaucer Street	B5-B6
Church Road	E8
Clarendon Street	B5-B6
Cliff Road	D3-E3
Clumber Crescent South	A3
Clumber Road East	A3-A4
Clumber Street	D4-D5
College Street	A5-B5-B4
Collin Street	C3-D3
Colville Street	B8
County Road	F1
Cranbrook Street	E4-E5
Cranmer Street	C8-D8
Crocus Street	D1-E1
Cromwell Street	A5-A6-B6
Curzon Street	D6-E6
Dane Close	D7-E7
Dakeyne Street	F5
Derby Road	A5-B5
Dryden Street	C6-C7
Fienness Crescent	A2
Fishergate	E3-E4
Fishpond Drive	A2-B2
Fletcher Gate	D4
Forest Road East	A8-B8-C8
Forest Road West	A7-A8
Friar Lane	C3-C4
Gedling Grove	A7
George Street	D4-D5
Glasshouse Street	D5-D6
Gill Street	B6-C6
Goldsmith Street	B6-C6-C5
Goose Gate	D4-E4
Great Freeman Street	D6
Hamilton Drive	B2-B3
Hampden Street	B6-C6
Handel Street	E5-F5
Haywood Street	F4-F5
Heathcote Street	D4-D5-E5
High Pavement	D4-D3-E3
Hockley	E4
Holles Crescent	A3
Hollowstone	E3-E4
Hope Drive	B2-B3
Hound's Gate	C4
Howard Street	D5-D6
Hungerhill Road	E8-F8
Huntingdon Drive	A4-A3-B3
Huntingdon Street	C8-D7-D6-E5
Iremonger Road	E1
Kent Street	D5
King Edward Street	D5-E5
King Street	C4-C5
Lamartine Street	E6-F6
Lenton Road	A2-A3-B3
Lewis Close	E7
Lincoln Street	D5
Lister Gate	C3-C4
London Road	E1-E2-E3
Long Row	C4-D4
Lower Parliament Street	D5-E4-E3
Low Pavement	C4-D4
Mabel Street	E1
Maid Marian Way	B4-C4-C3
Mansfield Road	C6-C7-C8
Manvers Street	F3-F4
Market Street	C4-C5
Meadow Lane	F1
Meadows Way	B1-C1-D1-E1
Middle Hill	D3-D4
Milton Street	C6-C5-D5
Mount Hooton Road	A8
Mount Street	B4-C4
Newark Crescent	F3
Newark Street	F3-F4
Newcastle Circus	A3
Newcastle Drive	A4-A5
Newstead Grove	B7-C7
North Street	F4-F5
North Sherwood Street	C6-C7-C8
Old Market Square	C4
Oliver Street	A6
Park Drive	A3-B3
Park Ravine	A2-A3
Park Row	B4
Park Terrace	A4-B4
Park Valley	A4-B4-B3
Peel Street	B6-B7-C7
Pelham Street	D4
Pennyfoot Street	E4-F4
Peveril Drive	B3
Pilcher Gate	D4
Plantagenet Street	E6
Plumptree Street	E4
Popham Street	D3
Poplar Street	E3-F3
Portland Road	A5-A6-A7
Queen's Drive	B1-C1, D1-D2
Queen's Road	D2-E2
Queen Street	C4-C5
Queen's Walk	C1
Raleigh Street	A6-A7
Regent Street	B4
Rick Street	D5
Robin Hood Street	E5-F5-F6
Russell Street	A6
St Ann's Hill Road	C8
St Ann's Valley	F7-F8
St Ann's Well Road	E5-E6-E7-F7-F8
St James Street	C4
St James Terrace	B4-B3-C3
St Mark's Street	D6
St Mary's Gate	D3-D4
St Peters Gate	C4-D4
Shakespeare Street	B6-C6
Shelton Street	D7-D6-E6
Sheriff's Way	D1
Sneinton Road	F4
South Parade	C4-D4
South Road	A3
South Sherwood Street	C5-C6
Southwell Road	E4-F4
Station Street	D2-E2
Stony Street	D4-E4
Summer Leys Road	E1
Talbot Street	A5-B5-C5
Tattershall Drive	A4-A3-B3
Tennis Drive	A4-A5-A4
The Ropewalk	A5-A4-B4
Trent Street	D2-D3
Tulip Avenue	E8
Tunnel Road	A4
Union Road	D6
Upper College Street	A5-B5
Upper Eldon Street	F4
Upper Parliament Street	B5-C5-D5
Victoria Street	D4
Villa Road	C8
Walker Street	F4-F5
Walter Street	A6-A7
Warser Gate	D4
Waterway Street	C1-D1
Watkin Street	D6-D7
Waverely Street	A8-A7-B7-B6
Wellington Street	D6-D7
West Street	F4-F5
Wheeler Gate	C4
Wilford Road	C1-C2
Wilford Street	C2-C3
Wollaton Street	A5-B5-C5
Woodborough Road	C6-C7-D7-D8
Woolpack Lane	D4-E4
York Street	C6-D6

LBTT

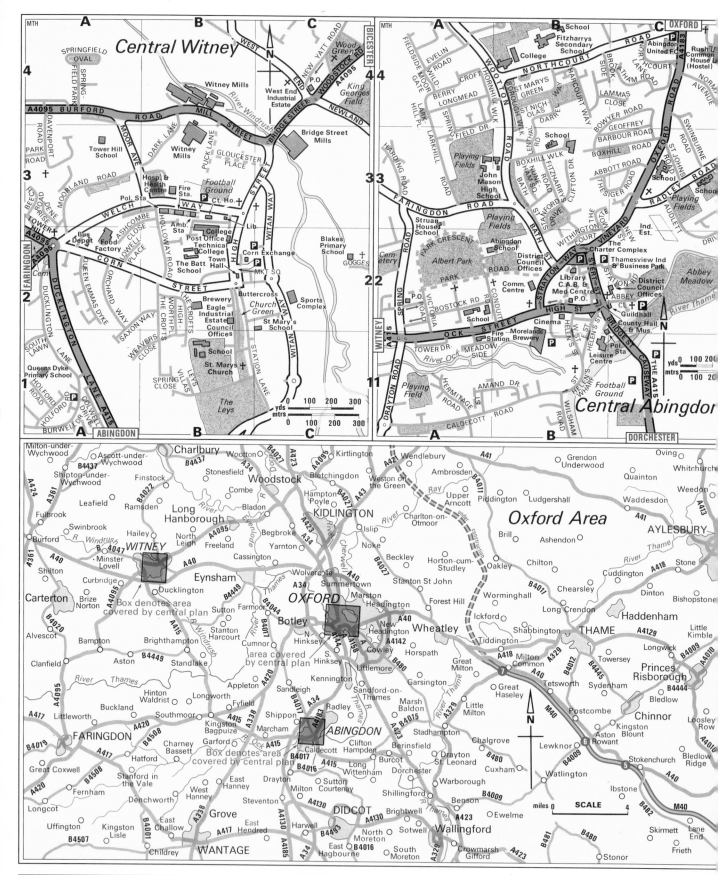

Oxford

From Carfax (at the centre of the city) round to Magdalen Bridge stretches High Street, one of England's best and most interesting thoroughfares. Shops rub shoulders with churches and colleges, alleyways lead to ancient inns and to a large covered market, and little streets lead to views of some of the finest architecture to be seen anywhere. Catte Street, beside St Mary's Church (whose lovely tower gives a panoramic view of Oxford), opens out into Radcliffe Square, dominated by the Radcliffe Camera, a great round structure built in 1749. Close by is the Bodleian Library, one of the finest collections of books and manuscripts in the world. All around are ancient college buildings. Close to Magdalen Bridge is Magdalen College, founded in 1448 and certainly not to be missed. Across the High Street are the Botanical Gardens, founded in 1621 and the oldest such foundation in England. Footpaths lead through Christ Church Meadow to Christ Church College and the cathedral. Tom Tower is the college's most notable feature; the cathedral is actually its chapel and is the smallest cathedral in England. Among much else not to be missed in Oxford is the Ashmolean Museum, whose vast collections of precious and beautiful objects from all over the world repay many hours of study; perhaps the loveliest treasure is the 9th-century Alfred Jewel.

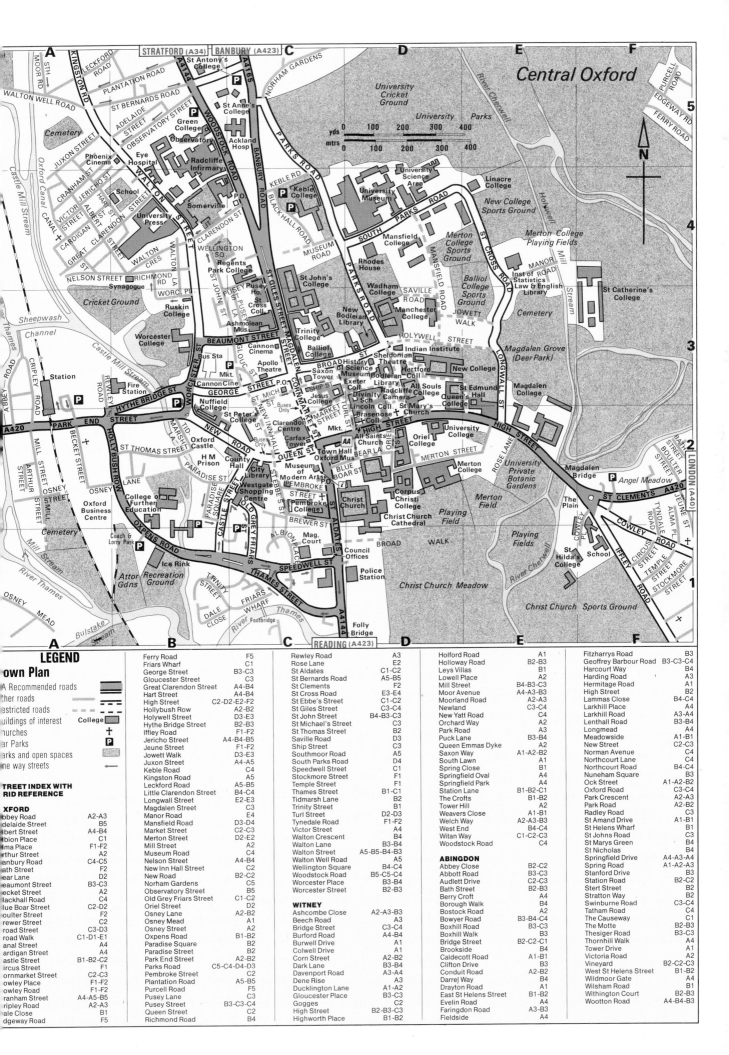

Central Oxford

STRATFORD (A34) · BANBURY (A423) · READING (A423) · LONDON (A40)

University Cricket Ground · University Parks · University Science Area · University Museum

Scale: yds 0 100 200 300 400 / mtrs 0 100 200 300 400

LEGEND

Town Plan

- Recommended roads
- Other roads
- Restricted roads
- Buildings of interest — College
- Churches — †
- Car Parks — P
- Parks and open spaces
- One way streets — ⟵

STREET INDEX WITH GRID REFERENCE

OXFORD

Abbey Road	A2-A3
Adelaide Street	B5
Albert Street	A4-B4
Albion Place	C1
Alma Place	F1-F2
Arthur Street	A2
Banbury Road	C4-C5
Bath Street	F2
Bear Lane	D2
Beaumont Street	B3-C3
Becket Street	C2
Blackhall Road	C4
Blue Boar Street	C2-D2
Boulter Street	F2
Brewer Street	C2
Broad Walk	C1-D1-E1
Canal Street	A4
Cardigan Street	A4
Castle Street	B1-B2-C2
Circus Street	F1
Cornmarket Street	C2-C3
Cowley Place	F1-F2
Cowley Road	F1-F2
Cranham Street	A4-A5-B5
Cripley Road	A2-A3
Dale Close	B1
Edgeway Road	F5
Ferry Road	F5
Friars Wharf	C1
George Street	B3-C3
Gloucester Street	C3
Great Clarendon Street	A4-B4
Hart Street	A4
High Street	C2-D2-E2-F2
Hollybush Row	A2-B2
Holywell Street	D3-E3
Hythe Bridge Street	B2-B3
Iffley Road	F1-F2
Jericho Street	A4-B4-B5
Jeune Street	F1-F2
Jowett Walk	D3-E3
Juxon Street	A4-A5
Keble Road	C4
Kingston Road	A5
Leckford Road	A5-B5
Little Clarendon Street	B4-C4
Longwall Street	E2-E3
Magdalen Street	C3
Manor Road	E4
Mansfield Road	D3-D4
Market Street	C2-C3
Merton Street	D2-E2
Mill Street	C4
Museum Road	C4
Nelson Street	A4-B4
New Inn Hall Street	C2
New Road	B2-C2
Norham Gardens	C5
Observatory Street	B5
Old Grey Friars Street	C1-C2
Oriel Street	D2
Osney Lane	A2-B2
Osney Mead	A1
Osney Street	A2
Oxpens Road	B1-B2
Paradise Square	B2
Paradise Street	B2
Park End Street	A2-B2
Parks Road	C5-C4-D4-D3
Pembroke Street	C2
Plantation Road	A5-B5
Purcell Road	F5
Pusey Lane	C3
Pusey Street	B3-C3-C4
Queen Street	C2
Richmond Road	B4
Rewley Road	A3
Rose Lane	E2
St Aldates	C1-C2
St Bernards Road	A5-B5
St Clements	F2
St Cross Road	E3-E4
St Ebbe's Street	C1-C2
St Giles Street	C3-C4
St John Street	B4-B3-C3
St Michael's Street	C3
St Thomas Street	B2
Saville Road	D3
Ship Street	C3
Southmoor Road	A5
South Parks Road	D4
Speedwell Street	C1
Stockmore Street	F1
Temple Street	F1
Thames Street	B1-C1
Tidmarsh Lane	B2
Trinity Street	B1
Turl Street	D2-D3
Tynedale Road	F1-F2
Victor Street	A4
Walton Crescent	B4
Walton Lane	B3-B4
Walton Street	A5-B5-B4-B3
Walton Well Road	A5
Wellington Square	B4-C4
Woodstock Road	B5-C5-C4
Worcester Place	B3-B4
Worcester Street	B2-B3

WITNEY

Ashcombe Close	A2-A3-B3
Beech Road	A3
Bridge Street	C3-C4
Burford Road	A4-B4
Burwell Drive	A1
Colwell Drive	A1
Corn Street	B3-B4
Dark Lane	B3-B4
Davenport Road	A3-A4
Dene Rise	A3
Ducklington Lane	A1-A2
Gloucester Place	B3-C3
Gogges	C2
High Street	B2-B3-C3
Highworth Place	B1-B2
Holford Road	A1
Holloway Road	B2-B3
Leys Villas	B1
Lowell Place	A2
Mill Street	B4-B3-C3
Moor Avenue	A4-A3-B3
Moorland Road	A2-A3
Newland	C3-C4
New Yatt Road	C4
Orchard Way	A2
Park Road	A3
Puck Lane	B3-B4
Queen Emmas Dyke	A2
Saxon Way	A1-A2-B2
South Lawn	A1
Spring Close	B1
Springfield Oval	A4
Springfield Park	A4
Station Lane	B1-B2-C1
The Crofts	B1-B2
Tower Hill	A2
Weavers Close	A1-B1
Welch Way	A2-A3-B3
West End	B4-C4
Witan Way	C1-C2-C3
Woodstock Road	C4

ABINGDON

Abbey Close	B2-C2
Abbott Road	B3-C3
Audlett Drive	C2-C3
Bath Street	B2-B3
Berry Croft	A4
Borough Walk	B4
Bostock Road	A2
Bowyer Road	B3-B4-C4
Boxhill Road	B3-C3
Boxhill Walk	B3
Bridge Street	B2-C2-C1
Brookside	A1-B1
Caldecott Road	A1-B1
Clifton Drive	B3
Conduit Road	A2-B2
Darrel Way	B4
Drayton Road	A1
East St Helens Street	B1-B2
Evelin Road	A4
Faringdon Road	A3-B3
Fieldside	A4
Fitzharrys Road	B3
Geoffrey Barbour Road	B3-C3-C4
Harcourt Way	B4
Harding Road	A3
Hermitage Road	A1
High Street	B2
Lammas Close	B4-C4
Larkhill Place	A4
Larkhill Road	A3-A4
Lenthall Road	B3-B4
Longmead	A4
Meadowside	A1-B1
New Street	C2-C3
Norman Avenue	C4
Northcourt Lane	C4
Northcourt Road	B4-C4
Nuneham Square	B3
Ock Street	A1-A2-B2
Oxford Road	C3-C4
Park Crescent	A2-A3
Park Road	A2-B2
Radley Road	C3
St Amand Drive	A1-B1
St Helens Wharf	B1
St Johns Road	C3
St Marys Green	B4
St Nicholas	B4
Springfield Drive	A4-A3-A4
Spring Road	A1-A2-A3
Stanford Drive	B3
Station Road	B2-C2
Stert Street	B2
Stratton Way	B2
Swinburne Road	C3-C4
Tatham Road	C4
The Causeway	C1
The Motte	B2-B3
Thesiger Road	B3-C3
Thornhill Walk	A4
Tower Drive	A1
Victoria Road	A2
Vineyard	B2-C2-C3
West St Helens Street	B1-B2
Wildmoor Gate	A4
Wilsham Road	B1
Withington Court	B2-B3
Wootton Road	A4-B4-B3

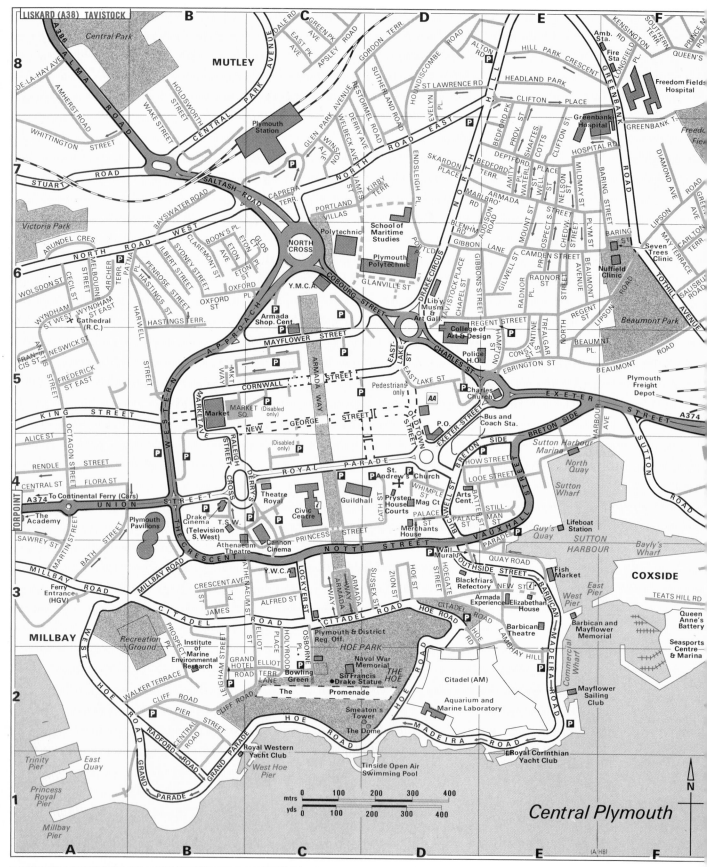

Plymouth

Ships, sailors and the sea permeate every aspect of Plymouth's life and history. Its superb natural harbour - Plymouth Sound - has ensured its importance as a port, yachting centre and naval base (latterly at Devonport) over many centuries. Sir Francis Drake is undoubtedly the city's most famour sailor. His stratue stands on the Hoe - where he really did play bowls before tackling the Spanish Armada. Also on the Hoe are Smeaton's

Tower, which once formed the upper part of the third Eddystone Lighthouse, and the impressive Royal Naval War Memorial. Just east of the Hoe is the Royal Citidel, an imposing fortress built in 1666 by order of Charles II. North is Sutton Harbour, perhaps the most atmospheric part of Plymouth. Here fishing boats bob up and down in a harbour whose quays are lined with attractive old houses, inns and warehouses. One of the memorials on Mayflower Quay just outside the harbour commemorates the sailing of the *Mayflower* from

here in 1620. Plymouth's shopping centre was built after the old centre was badly damaged in World War II. Nearby is the 200ft-high tower of the impressive modern Civic Centre. Some buildings escaped destruction, including the Elizabethan House and the 500-year-old Prysten House. Next door is St Andrew's Church, with stained glass by John Piper.

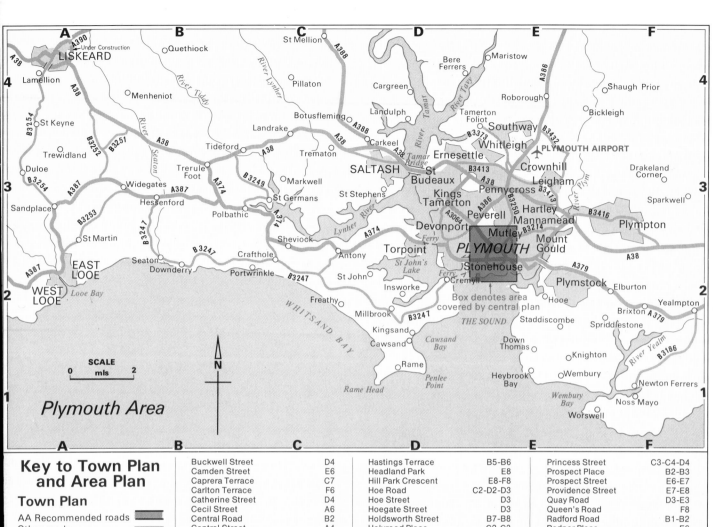

Plymouth Area

SCALE
0 mls 2

N

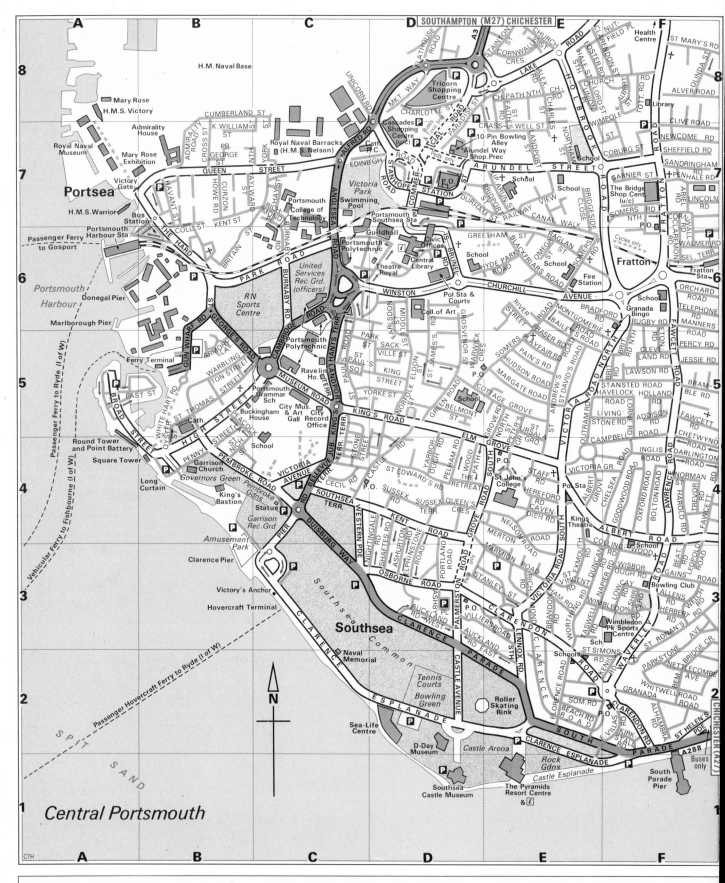

Portsmouth

Richard the Lionheart first recognised the strategic importance of Portsea Island and ordered the first docks, and later the town to be built. Succeeding monarchs improved the defences and extended the docks which now cover some 300 acres - as befits Britain's premier naval base. Of the defensive fortifications, Fort Widley and the Round Tower are the best preserved remains. Three famous ships

rest in Portsmouth; HMS Victory, the Mary Rose and HMS Warrior. The former, Lord Nelson's flagship, has been fully restored and the adjacent Royal Naval museum houses numerous relics of Trafalgar. The Mary Rose, built by Henry VIII, lay on the sea bed off Southsea until she was spectacularly raised in 1982. She has now been put on display and there is an exhibition of artefacts that have been recovered from her. HMS Warrior is the worlds first iron hulled warship.

Portsmouth suffered greatly from bombing in World War II and the centre has been almost completely rebuilt. However, the old town clustered around the harbour mouth, escaped severe damage and, now restored, forms an attractive and fashionable area of the city.

Southsea, Portsmouth's near neighbour, developed in the 19th century as an elegant seaside resort with fine houses and terraces, an esplanade and an extensive seafront common.

174

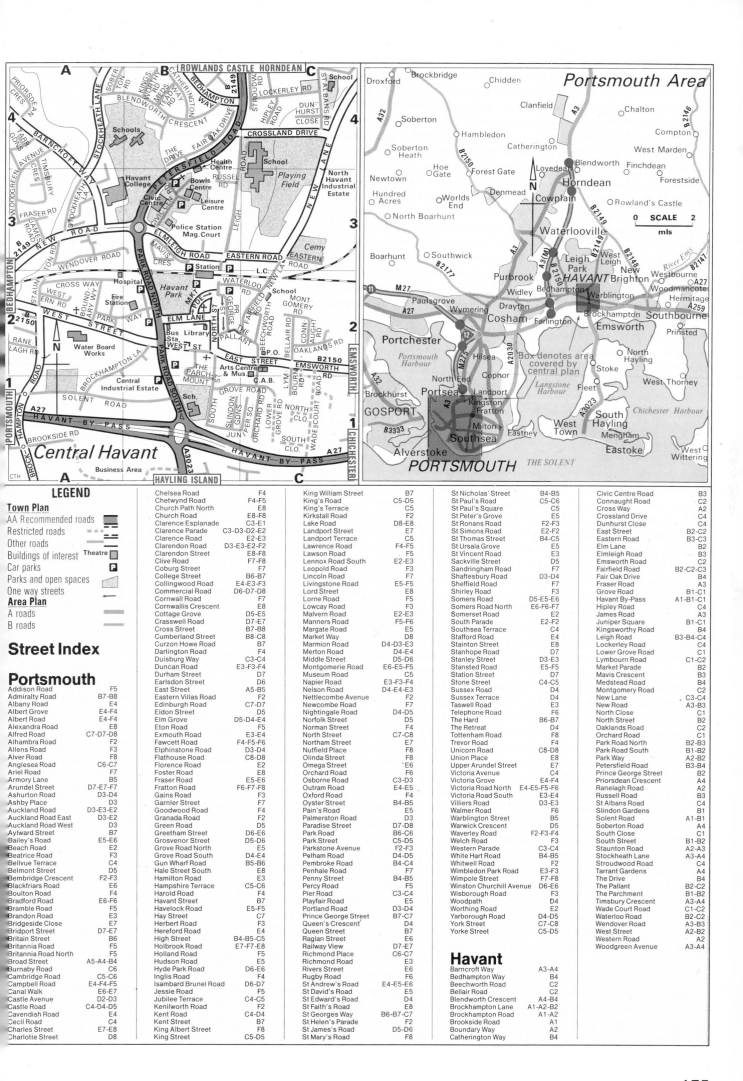

Central Havant map and **Portsmouth Area** map

LEGEND

Town Plan
- AA Recommended roads
- Restricted roads
- Other roads
- Buildings of interest — Theatre
- Car parks — P
- Parks and open spaces
- One way streets
Area Plan
- A roads
- B roads

Street Index

Portsmouth

Addison Road	F5
Admiralty Road	B7-B8
Albany Road	E4
Albert Grove	E4-F4
Albert Road	E4-F4
Alexandra Road	E8
Alfred Road	C7-D7-D8
Alhambra Road	F2
Allens Road	F3
Alver Road	F8
Anglesea Road	C6-C7
Ariel Road	F7
Armory Lane	B5
Arundel Street	D7-E7-F7
Ashurton Road	D3-D4
Ashby Place	D3
Auckland Road	D3-E3-E2
Auckland Road East	D3-E2
Auckland Road West	D3
Aylward Street	B7
Bailey's Road	E5-E6
Beach Road	E2
Beatrice Road	F3
Bellvue Terrace	C4
Belmont Street	D5
Bembridge Crescent	F2-F3
Blackfriars Road	E6
Boulton Road	F4
Bradford Road	E6-F6
Bramble Road	F5
Brandon Road	E3
Bridgeside Close	E7
Bridport Street	D7-E7
Britain Street	B6
Britannia Road	F5
Britannia Road North	F5
Broad Street	A5-A4-B4
Burnaby Road	C6
Cambridge Road	C5-C6
Campbell Road	E4-F4-F5
Canal Walk	E6-E7
Castle Avenue	D2-D3
Castle Road	C4-D4-D5
Cavendish Road	E4
Cecil Road	C4
Charles Street	E7-E8
Charlotte Street	D8

Chelsea Road	F4
Chetwynd Road	F4-F5
Church Path North	E8
Church Road	E8-F8
Clarence Esplanade	C3-E1
Clarence Parade	C3-D3-D2-E2
Clarence Road	E2-E3
Clarendon Road	D3-E3-E2-F2
Clarendon Street	E8-F8
Clive Road	F7-F8
Coburg Street	F7
College Street	B6-B7
Collingwood Road	E4-E3-F3
Commercial Road	D6-D7-D8
Cornwall Road	F7
Cornwallis Crescent	E8
Cottage Grove	D5-E5
Crasswell Road	D7-E7
Cross Street	B7-B8
Cumberland Street	B8-C8
Curzon Howe Road	B7
Darlington Road	F4
Duisburg Way	C3-C4
Duncan Road	E3-F3-F4
Durham Street	D7
Earlsdon Street	D6
East Street	A5-B5
Eastern Villas Road	F2
Edinburgh Road	C7-D7
Eldon Street	D5
Elm Grove	D5-D4-E4
Eton Road	F5
Exmouth Road	E3-E4
Fawcett Road	F4-F5-F6
Elphinstone Road	D3-D4
Flathouse Road	C8-D8
Florence Road	E2
Foster Road	E8
Fraser Road	B5
Fratton Road	F6-F7-F8
Gains Road	F3
Garnier Street	F7
Goodwood Road	F4
Granada Road	F2
Green Road	D5
Greetham Street	D6-E6
Grosvenor Street	D5-D6
Grove Road North	E5
Grove Road South	D4-E4
Gun Wharf Road	B5-B6
Hale Street South	E8
Hamilton Road	E3
Hampshire Terrace	C5-C6
Harold Road	F4
Havant Street	B7
Havelock Road	E5-F5
Hay Street	C7
Herbert Road	F3
Hereford Road	E4
High Street	B4-B5-C5
Holbrook Road	E7-F7-F8
Holland Road	F5
Hudson Road	E6
Hyde Park Road	D6-E6
Inglis Road	F4
Isambard Brunel Road	D6-D7
Jessie Road	F5
Jubilee Terrace	C4-C5
Kenilworth Road	F2
Kent Road	C4-D4
Kent Street	B7
King Albert Street	F8
King Street	C5-D5

King William Street	B7
King's Road	C5-D5
King's Terrace	C5
Kirkstall Road	F2
Lake Road	D8-E8
Landport Street	E7
Landport Terrace	C5
Lawrence Road	F4-F5
Lawson Road	F5
Lennox Road South	E2-E3
Leopold Road	F3
Lincoln Road	F7
Livingstone Road	E5-F5
Lord Street	E8
Lorne Road	F5
Lowcay Road	F3
Malvern Road	E2-E3
Manners Road	F5-F6
Margate Road	E5
Market Way	D8
Marmion Road	D4-D3-E3
Merton Road	D4-E4
Middle Street	D5-D6
Montgomerie Road	E6-E5-F5
Museum Road	C5
Napier Road	E3-F3-F4
Nelson Road	D4-E4-E3
Nettlecombe Avenue	F2
Newcombe Road	F7
Nightingale Road	D4-D5
Norfolk Street	D5
Norman Street	F4
North Street	C7-C8
Northam Street	E7
Nutfield Place	F8
Olinda Street	F8
Omega Street	E6
Orchard Road	F6
Osborne Road	C3-D3
Outram Road	E4-E5
Oxford Road	F4
Oyster Street	B4-B5
Pain's Road	D3
Palmerston Road	D3
Paradise Street	D7-D8
Park Road	B6-C6
Park Street	C5-D5
Parkstone Avenue	F2-F3
Pelham Road	D4-D5
Pembroke Road	B4-C4
Penhale Road	F7
Penny Street	B4-B5
Percy Road	F5
Pier Road	C3-C4
Playfair Road	E6
Portland Road	D3-D4
Prince George Street	B7-C7
Queen's Crescent	D4
Queen Street	B7
Raglan Street	E6
Railway View	D7-E7
Richmond Place	C6-C7
Richmond Road	E3
Rivers Street	E6
Rugby Road	F5
St Andrew's Road	E4-E5-E6
St David's Road	E5
St Edward's Road	D4
St Faith's Road	E8
St Georges Way	B6-B7-C7
St Helen's Parade	F2
St James's Road	D5-D6
St Mary's Road	F8

St Nicholas' Street	B4-B5
St Paul's Road	C5-C6
St Paul's Square	C5
St Peter's Grove	E5
St Ronans Road	F2-F3
St Simons Road	E2-F2
St Thomas Street	B4-C5
St Ursala Grove	E5
St Vincent Road	E3
Sackville Street	D5
Sandringham Road	F7
Shaftesbury Road	D3-D4
Sheffield Road	F7
Shirley Road	F3
Somers Road	D5-E5-E6
Somers Road North	E6-F6-F7
Somerset Road	E2
South Parade	E2-F2
Southsea Terrace	C4
Stafford Road	E4
Stainton Street	E8
Stanhope Road	D7
Stanley Street	D3-E3
Stansted Road	E5-F5
Station Street	D7
Stone Street	C4-C5
Sussex Road	D4
Sussex Terrace	D4
Taswell Road	E3
Telephone Road	F6
The Hard	B6-B7
The Retreat	D4
Tottenham Road	F8
Trevor Road	F4
Unicorn Road	C8-D8
Union Place	E8
Upper Arundel Street	E7
Victoria Avenue	C4
Victoria Grove	F4
Victoria Road North	E4-E5-F5-F6
Victoria Road South	E3-E4
Villiers Road	D3-E3
Walmer Road	F6
Warblington Street	B5
Warwick Crescent	D5
Waverley Road	F2-F3-F4
Welch Road	F3
Western Parade	C3-C4
White Hart Road	B4-B5
Whitwell Road	F2
Wimbledon Park Road	E3-F3
Wimpole Street	F7-F8
Winston Churchill Avenue	D6-E6
Wisborough Road	F3
Woodpath	D4
Worthing Road	E2
Yarborough Road	D4-D5
York Street	C7-C8
Yorke Street	C5-D5

Havant

Barncroft Way	A3-A4
Bedhampton Way	B4
Beechworth Road	C2
Bellair Road	C2
Blendworth Crescent	A4-B4
Brockhampton Lane	A1-A2-B2
Brockhampton Road	A1-A2
Brookside Road	A1
Boundary Way	A2
Catherington Way	B4

Civic Centre Road	B3
Connaught Road	C2
Cross Way	A2
Crossland Drive	C4
Dunhurst Close	C4
East Street	B2-C2
Eastern Road	B3-C3
Elm Lane	B2
Elmleigh Road	B3
Emsworth Road	C2
Fairfield Road	B2-C2-C3
Fair Oak Drive	B4
Fraser Road	A3
Grove Road	B1-C1
Havant By-Pass	A1-B1-C1
Hipley Road	C4
James Road	A3
Juniper Square	B1-C1
Kingsworthy Road	B4
Leigh Road	B3-B4-C4
Lockerley Road	C4
Lower Grove Road	C1
Lymbourn Road	C1-C2
Market Parade	B2
Mavis Crescent	B3
Medstead Road	B4
Montgomery Road	C2
New Lane	C3-C4
New Road	A3-B3
North Close	C1
North Street	B2
Oaklands Road	C2
Orchard Road	C1
Park Road North	B2-B3
Park Road South	B1-B2
Park Way	A2-B2
Petersfield Road	B3-B4
Prince George Street	B2
Priorsdean Crescent	A4
Ranelagh Road	A2
Russell Road	B3
St Albans Road	C4
Slindon Gardens	B1
Solent Road	A1-B1
Soberton Road	A4
South Close	C1
South Street	B1-B2
Staunton Road	A2-A3
Stockheath Lane	A3-A4
Stroudwood Road	A4
Tarrant Gardens	A4
The Drive	B4
The Pallant	B2-C2
The Parchment	B1-B2
Timsbury Crescent	A3-A4
Wade Court Road	C1-C2
Waterloo Road	B2-C2
Wendover Road	A3-B3
West Street	A2-B2
Western Road	A2
Woodgreen Avenue	A3-A4

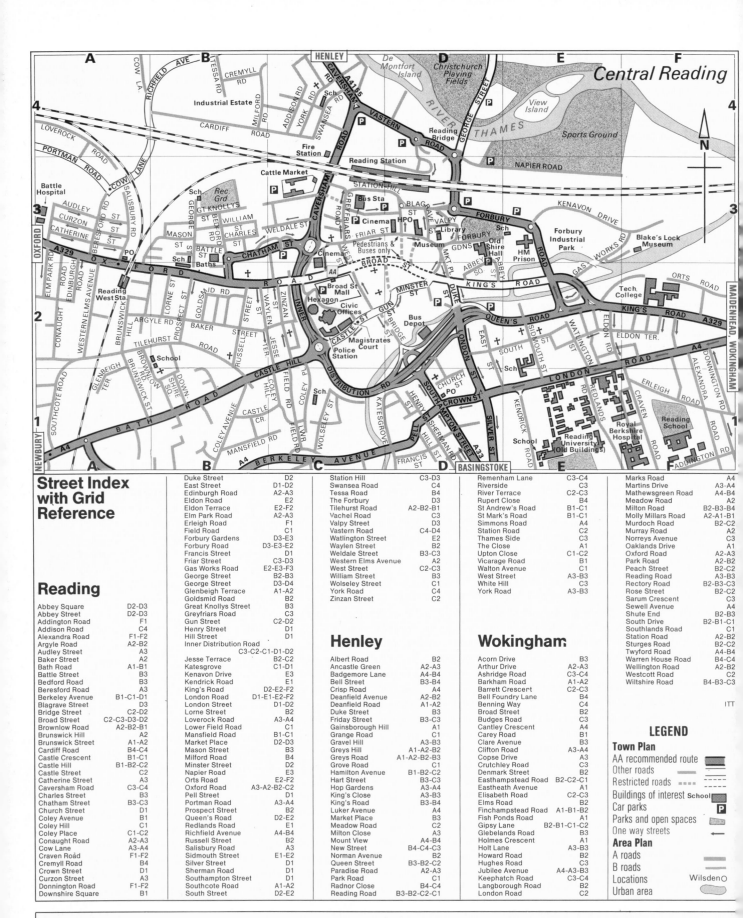

Street Index with Grid Reference

Reading

Abbey Square	D2-D3
Abbey Street	D2-D3
Addington Road	F1
Addison Road	C4
Alexandra Road	F1-F2
Argyle Road	A2-B2
Audley Street	A3
Baker Street	A2
Bath Road	A1-B1
Battle Street	B3
Bedford Road	B3
Beresford Road	A3
Berkeley Avenue	B1-C1-D1
Blagrave Street	D3
Bridge Street	C2-D2
Broad Street	C2-C3-D3-D2
Brownlow Road	A2-B2-B1
Brunswick Hill	A2
Brunswick Street	A1-A2
Cardiff Road	B4-C4
Castle Crescent	B1-C1
Castle Hill	B1-B2-C2
Castle Street	C2
Catherine Street	A3
Caversham Road	C3-C4
Charles Street	B3
Chatham Street	B3-C3
Church Street	D1
Coley Avenue	B1
Coley Hill	C1
Coley Place	C1-C2
Conaught Road	A2-A3
Cow Lane	A3-A4
Craven Road	F1-F2
Cremyll Road	B4
Crown Street	D1
Curzon Street	A3
Donnington Road	F1-F2
Downshire Square	B1

Duke Street	D2
East Street	D1-D2
Edinburgh Road	A2-A3
Eldon Road	E2
Eldon Terrace	E2-F2
Elm Park Road	A2-A3
Erleigh Road	F1
Field Road	C1
Forbury Gardens	D3-E3
Forbury Road	D3-E3-E2
Francis Street	D1
Friar Street	C3-D3
Gas Works Road	E2-E3-F3
George Street	B2-B3
George Street	D3-D4
Glenbeigh Terrace	A1-A2
Goldsmid Road	B2
Great Knollys Street	B3
Greyfriars Road	C3
Gun Street	C2-D2
Henry Street	D1
Hill Street	D1
Inner Distribution Road	
	C3-C2-C1-D1-D2
Jesse Terrace	B2-C2
Katesgrove	C1-D1
Kenavon Drive	E3
Kendrick Road	E1
King's Road	D2-E2-F2
London Road	D1-E1-E2-F2
London Street	D1-D2
Lorne Street	B2
Loverock Road	A3-A4
Lower Field Road	C1
Mansfield Road	B1-C1
Market Place	D2-D3
Mason Street	B3
Milford Road	B4
Minster Street	D2
Napier Road	E3
Orts Road	E2-F2
Oxford Road	A3-A2-B2-C2
Pell Street	D1
Portman Road	A3-A4
Prospect Street	B2
Queen's Road	D2-E2
Redlands Road	E1
Richfield Avenue	A4-B4
Russell Street	B2
Salisbury Road	A3
Sidmouth Street	E1-E2
Silver Street	D1
Sherman Road	D1
Southampton Street	D1
Southcote Road	A1-A2
South Street	D2-E2

Station Hill	C3-D3
Swansea Road	C4
Tessa Road	B4
The Forbury	D3
Tilehurst Road	A2-B2-B1
Vachel Road	C3
Valpy Street	D3
Vastern Road	C4-D4
Watlington Street	E2
Waylen Street	B2
Weldale Street	B3-C3
Western Elms Avenue	A2
West Street	C2-C3
William Street	B3
Wolseley Street	C1
York Road	C4
Zinzan Street	C2

Henley

Albert Road	B2
Ancastle Green	A2-A3
Badgemore Lane	A4-B4
Bell Street	B3-B4
Crisp Road	A4
Deanfield Avenue	A2-B2
Deanfield Road	A1-A2
Duke Street	B3
Friday Street	B3-C3
Gainsborough Hill	A1
Grange Road	C1
Gravel Hill	A3-B3
Greys Hill	A1-A2-B2
Greys Road	A1-A2-B2-B3
Grove Road	C1
Hamilton Avenue	B1-B2-C2
Hart Street	B3-C3
Hop Gardens	A3-A4
King's Close	A3-B3
King's Road	B3-B4
Luker Avenue	A4
Market Place	B3
Meadow Road	C1
Milton Close	A3
Mount View	A4-B4
New Street	B4-C4-C3
Norman Avenue	B2
Queen Street	B3-B2-C2
Paradise Road	A2-A3
Park Road	C1
Radnor Close	B4-C4
Reading Road	B3-B2-C2-C1

Wokingham

Acorn Drive	B3
Arthur Drive	A2-A3
Ashridge Road	C3-C4
Barkham Road	A1-A2
Barrett Crescent	C2-C3
Bell Foundry Lane	B4
Benning Way	C4
Broad Street	B2
Budges Road	C3
Cantley Crescent	A4
Carey Road	B1
Clare Avenue	B3
Clifton Road	A3-A4
Copse Drive	A3
Crutchley Road	C3
Denmark Street	B2
Easthampstead Road	B2-C2-C1
Eastheath Avenue	A1
Elisabeth Road	C2-C3
Elms Road	B2
Finchampstead Road	A1-B1-B2
Fish Ponds Road	A1
Gipsy Lane	B2-B1-C1-C2
Glebelands Road	B3
Holmes Crescent	A1
Holt Lane	A3-B3
Howard Road	B2
Hughes Road	C3
Jubilee Avenue	A4-A3-B3
Keephatch Road	C3-C4
Langborough Road	B2
London Road	C2

Marks Road	A4
Martins Drive	A3-A4
Mathewsgreen Road	A4-B4
Meadow Road	A2
Milton Road	B2-B3-B4
Molly Millars Road	A2-A1-B1
Murdoch Road	B2-C2
Murray Road	A2
Norreys Avenue	C3
Oaklands Drive	A1
Oxford Road	A2-A3
Park Road	A2-B2
Peach Street	B2-C2
Reading Road	A3-B3
Rectory Road	B2-B3-C3
Rose Street	B2-C2
Sarum Crescent	C3
Sewell Avenue	A4
Shute End	B2-B3
South Drive	B2-B1-C1
Southlands Road	C1
Station Road	A2-B2
Sturges Road	B2-C2
Twyford Road	A4-B4
Warren House Road	B4-C4
Wellington Road	A2-B2
Westcott Road	C2
Wiltshire Road	B4-B3-C3

ITT

LEGEND

Town Plan

AA recommended route	
Other roads	
Restricted roads	
Buildings of interest	School
Car parks	P
Parks and open spaces	
One way streets	←

Area Plan

A roads	
B roads	
Locations	Wilsden○
Urban area	

Reading

Shopping and light industry first spring to mind when thinking of Reading, but the town actually has a long and important history. Its rise to significance began in 1121 when Henry I founded an abbey here which became the third most important in England. However, after the Dissolution of the Monasteries, only a few ruins were left. Reading also used to be one of the major centres of the medieval cloth trade, but, already declining in the early 17th century, this source of income was reduced still further as a result of Civil War disturbances.

A fascinating collection of all types of farm implements and domestic equipment can be found in the extremely comprehensive Museum of English Rural Life, situated in the University Campus at Whiteknights Park. The town's own museum has major displays about nearby Silchester – the powerful Roman town of *Calleva*.

Henley-on-Thames, famous for its annual rowing regatta, is a lovely old town, well-provided with old coaching inns, Georgian façades and numerous listed buildings.

Wokingham has been a market town for centuries and over the years has been known for its silk industry and its bell-foundry. Half-timbered gabled houses can be seen in the town centre, although modern development surrounds it.

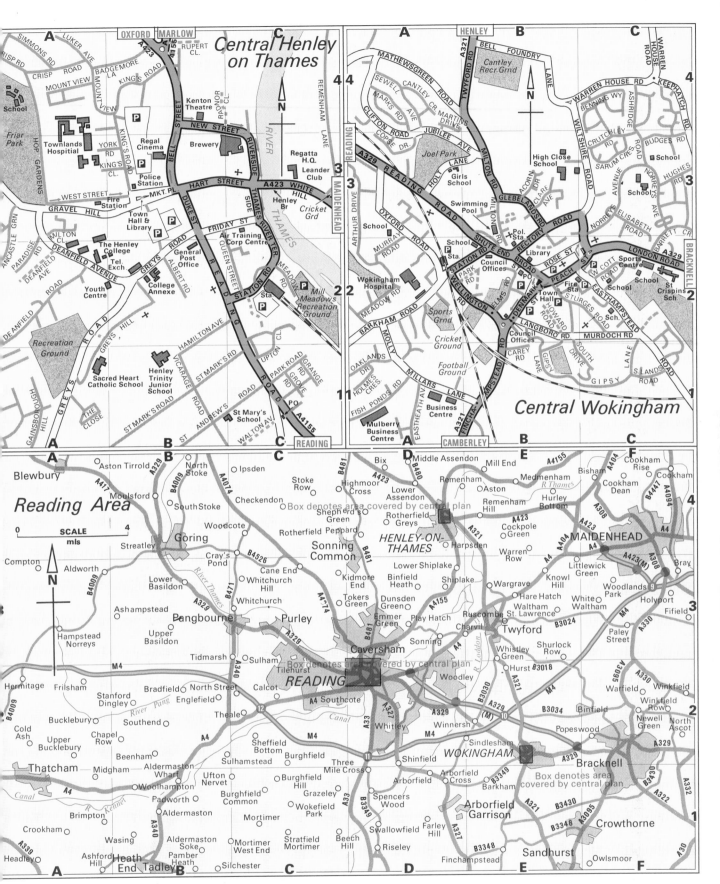

READING
Whiteknights, which consists of 300 acres of landscaped parkland, provides Reading's modern university with an incomparable campus setting and includes a conservation area and a biological reserve for research purposes.

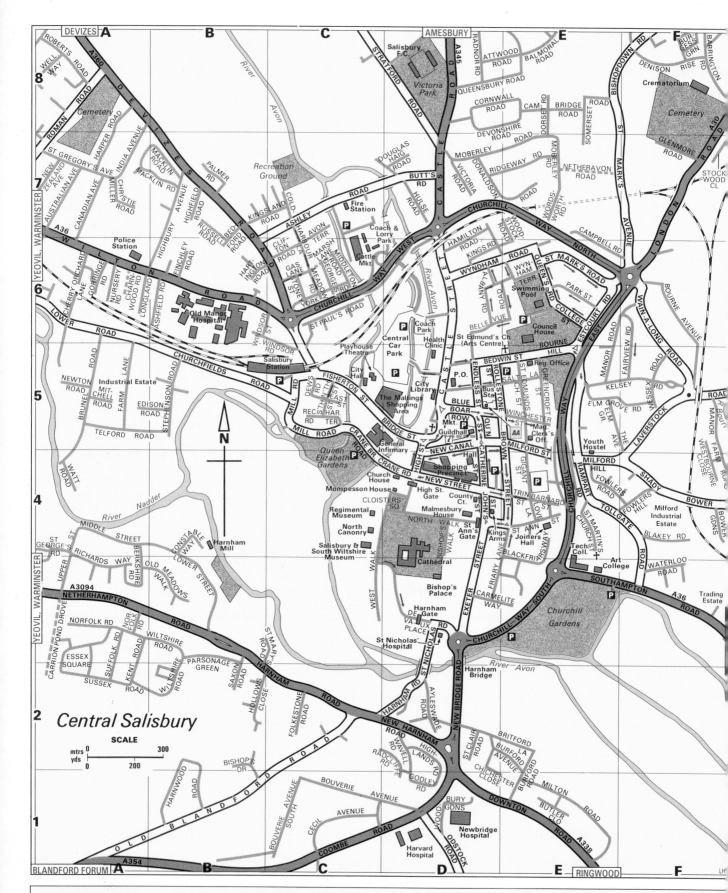

Salisbury

Its attractive site where the waters of the Avon and Nadder meet, its beautiful cathedral and its unspoilt centre put Salisbury among England's finest cities. In 1220 the people of the original settlement at Old Sarum, two miles to the north, moved down to the plain and laid the first stone of the cathedral.

Within 38 years it was completed and the result is a superb example of Early English architecture. The cloisters are the largest in England and the spire the tallest in Britain. All the houses within the Cathedral Close were built for cathedral functionaries, and although many have Georgian facades, most date back to the 13th century. Mompesson House is one of the handsome mansions here and as it belongs to the National Trust, its equally fine interior can be seen. Another building houses the Museum of the Duke of Edinburgh's Royal Regiment. At one time, relations between the clergy and the citizens of Salisbury were not always harmonious, so the former built a protective wall around the Close.

The streets of the modern city follow the medieval grid pattern of squares, or 'chequers', and the tightly-packed houses provide a very pleasing townscape. Salisbury was granted its first charter in 1227 and flourished as a market and wool centre; there is still a twice-weekly market in the spacious square.

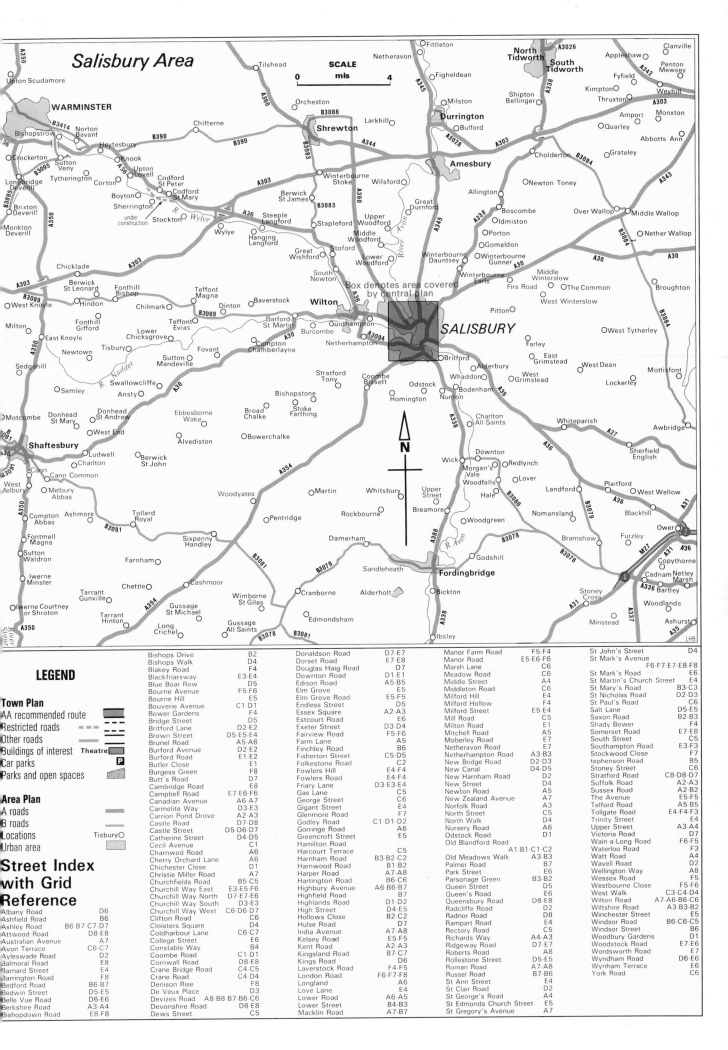

Salisbury Area

LEGEND

Town Plan

AA recommended route
Restricted roads
Other roads
Buildings of interest — Theatre [P]
Car parks — P
Parks and open spaces

Area Plan

A roads
B roads
Locations — Tisbury
Urban area

Street Index with Grid Reference

Albany Road	D6	Bishops Drive	B2	Donaldson Road	D7-E7	Manor Farm Road	F5-F4
Ashfield Road	B6	Bishops Walk	D4	Dorset Road	E7-E8	Manor Road	E5-E6-F6
Ashley Road	B6-B7-C7-D7	Blakey Road	F4	Douglas Haig Road	D7	Marsh Lane	C6
Attwood Road	D8-E8	Blackfriarsway	E3-E4	Downton Road	D1-E1	Meadow Road	C6
Australian Avenue	A7	Blue Boar Row	D5	Edison Road	A5-B5	Middle Street	A4
Avon Terrace	C6-C7	Bourne Avenue	F5-F6	Elm Grove	E5	Middleton Road	C6
Ayleswade Road	D2	Bourne Hill	E5	Elm Grove Road	E5-F5	Milford Hill	E4
Balmoral Road	E8	Bouverie Avenue	C1-D1	Endless Street	D5	Milford Hollow	F4
Barnard Street	E4	Bower Gardens	F4	Essex Square	A2-A3	Milford Street	E5-E4
Barrington Road	F8	Bridge Street	D5	Estcourt Road	E6	Mill Road	C5
Bedford Road	B6-B7	Britford Lane	D2-E2	Exeter Street	D3-D4	Milton Road	E1
Bedwin Street	D5-E5	Brown Street	D5-E5-E4	Fairview Road	F5-F6	Mitchell Road	A5
Belle Vue Road	D6-E6	Brunel Road	A5-A6	Farm Lane	A5	Moberley Road	E7
Berkshire Road	A3-A4	Burford Avenue	D2-E2	Finchley Road	B6	Netheravon Road	E7
Bishopdown Road	E8-F8	Burford Road	E1-E2	Fisherton Street	C5-D5	Netherhampton Road	A3-B3
		Butler Close	E1	Folkestone Road	C2	New Bridge Road	D2-D3
		Burgess Green	F8	Fowlers Hill	E4-F4	New Canal	D4-D5
		Butt's Road	D7	Fowlers Road	E4-F4	New Harnham Road	D2
		Cambridge Road	E8	Friary Lane	D3-E3-E4	New Street	D4
		Campbell Road	E7-E6-F6	Gas Lane	C5	Newton Road	A5
		Canadian Avenue	A6-A7	George Street	C6	New Zealand Avenue	A7
		Carmelite Way	D3-E3	Gigant Street	E4	Norfolk Road	A3
		Carrion Pond Drove	A2-A3	Glenmore Road	F7	North Street	C5
		Castle Road	D7-D8	Godley Road	C1-D1-D2	North Walk	D4
		Castle Street	D5-D6-D7	Gorringe Road	A6	Nursery Road	A6
		Catherine Street	D4-D5	Greencroft Street	E5	Odstock Road	D1
		Cecil Avenue	C1	Hamilton Road		Old Blandford Road	A1-B1-C1-C2
		Charnwood Road	A6	Harcourt Terrace	C5	Old Meadows Walk	A3-B3
		Cherry Orchard Lane	A6	Harnham Road	B3-B2-C2	Palmer Road	B7
		Chichester Close	D1	Harnwood Road	B1-B2	Park Street	E6
		Christie Miller Road	A7	Harper Road	A7-A8	Parsonage Green	B3-B2
		Churchfields Road	B5-C5	Hartington Road	B6-C6	Queen Street	D5
		Churchill Way East	E3-E5-F6	Highbury Avenue	A6-B6-B7	Queen's Road	E6
		Churchill Way North	D7-E7-E6	Highfield Road	B7	Queensbury Road	D8-E8
		Churchill Way South	D3-E3	Highlands Road	D1-D2	Radcliffe Road	D2
		Churchill Way West	C6-D6-D7	High Street	D4-E5	Radnor Road	D8
		Clifton Road	C6	Hollows Close	B2-C2	Rampart Road	E4
		Cloisters Square	D4	Hulse Road	D7	Rectory Road	C5
		Coldharbour Lane	C6-C7	India Avenue	A7-A8	Richards Way	A4-A3
		College Street	E6	Kelsey Road	E5-F5	Ridgeway Road	D7-E7
		Constable Way	B4	Kent Road	A2-A3	Roberts Road	A8
		Coombe Road	C1-D1	Kingsland Road	B7-C7	Rollestone Street	D5-E5
		Cornwall Road	D8-E8	Kings Road	D6	Roman Road	A7-A8
		Crane Bridge Road	C4-C5	Laverstock Road	F4-F5	Russel Road	B7-B6
		Crane Road	C4-D4	London Road	F6-F7-F8	St Ann Street	E4
		Denison Rise	F8	Longland	A6	St Clair Road	D2
		De Veux Place	D3	Love Lane	E4	St George's Lane	A4
		Devizes Road	A8-B8-B7-B6-C6	Lower Road	A6-A5	St Edmonds Church Street	E5
		Devonshire Road	D8-E8	Lower Street	B4-B3	St Gregory's Avenue	A7
		Dews Street	C5	Macklin Road	A7-B7		

St John's Street	D4
St Mark's Avenue	F6-F7-E7-E8-F8
St Mark's Road	E6
St Martin's Church Street	E4
St Mary's Road	B3-C3
St Nicholas Road	D2-D3
St Paul's Road	C6
Salt Lane	D5-E5
Saxon Road	B2-B3
Shady Bower	F4
Somerset Road	E7-E8
South Street	C5
Southampton Road	E3-F3
Stockwood Close	F7
tephenson Road	B5
Stoney Street	C6
Stratford Road	C8-D8-D7
Suffolk Road	A2-A3
Sussex Road	A2-B2
The Avenue	E5-F5
Telford Road	A5-B5
Tollgate Road	E4-F4-F3
Trinity Street	E4
Upper Street	A3-A4
Victoria Road	D7
Wain-a-Long Road	F6-F5
Waterloo Road	F3
Watt Road	A4
Wavell Road	D2
Wellington Way	A8
Wessex Road	F5
Westbourne Close	F5-F6
West Walk	C3-C4-D4
Wilton Road	A7-A6-B6-C6
Wiltshire Road	A3-B3-B2
Winchester Street	D5
Windsor Road	B6-C6-C5
Windsor Street	B6
Woodbury Gardens	D1
Woodstock Road	E7-E6
Wordsworth Road	E7
Wyndham Road	D6-E6
Wynham Terrace	B6
York Road	C6

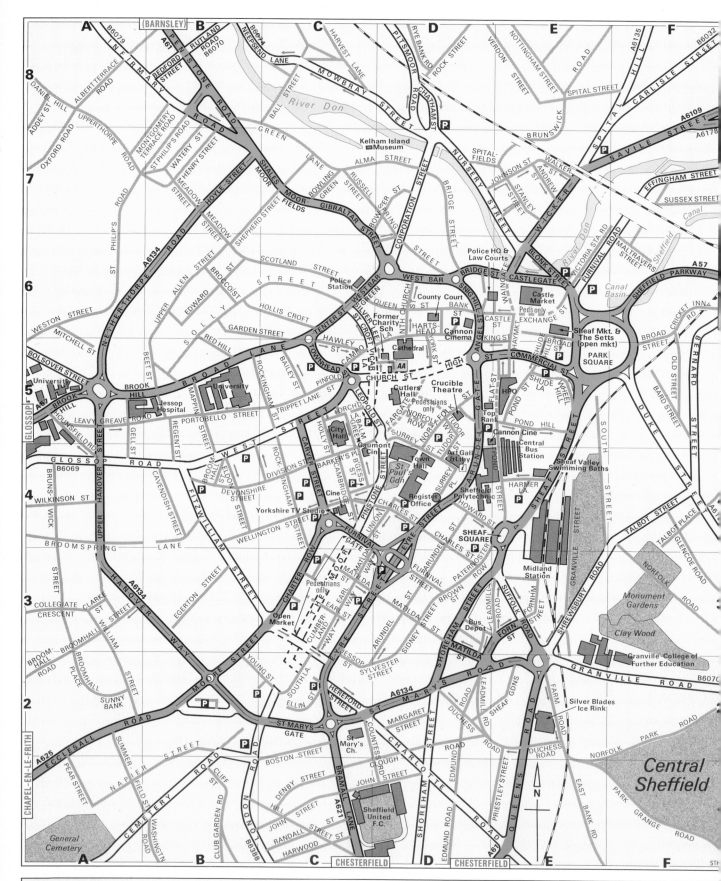

Sheffield

Cutlery – which has made the name of Sheffield famous throughout the world – has been manufactured here since at least as early as the time of Chaucer. The god of blacksmiths, Vulcan, is the symbol of the city's industry, and he crowns the town hall, which was opened in 1897 by Queen Victoria. At the centre of the industry, however, is Cutlers' Hall, the headquarters of the Company of Cutlers. This society was founded in 1624 and has the right to grant trade marks to articles of a sufficiently high standard. In the hall is the company's collection of silver, with examples of craftsmanship dating back every year to 1773. A really large collection of cutlery is kept in the city museum. Steel production, a vital component of the industry, was greatly improved when the crucible process was invented here in 1740. At Abbeydale Industrial Hamlet, 3½ miles south-west of the city centre, is a complete restored site open as a museum and showing 18th-century methods of steel production. Sheffield's centre, transformed since World War II, is one of the finest and most modern in Europe. There are no soot-grimed industrial eyesores here, for the city has stringent pollution controls and its buildings are carefully planned and set within excellent landscaping projects. Many parks are set in and around the city, and the Pennines are within easy reach.

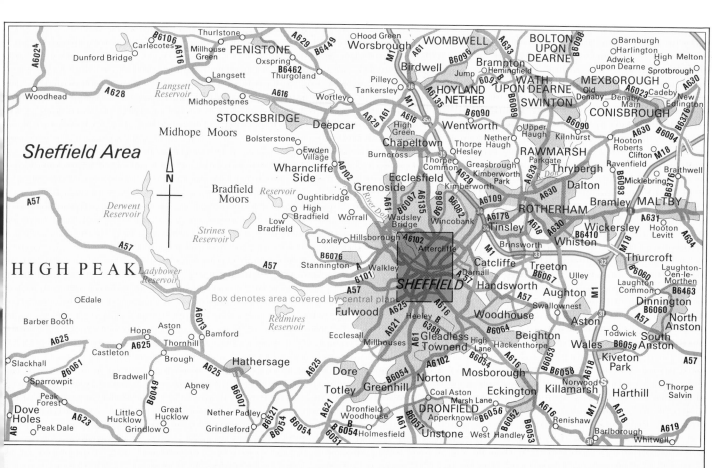

Sheffield Area

LEGEND

Town Plan
AA Recommended roads
Other roads
Restricted roads
Buildings of interest
One Way streets
Car Parks   P
Parks and open spaces

Area Plan
A roads
B roads
Locations   Hartshead ○
Urban area

Street Index with grid reference

Sheffield

Addey Street	A7-A8
Albert Terrace Road	A8
Alma Street	C7 D7
Andrew Street	E7
Angel Street	D5-D6
Arundel Gate	D4-D5
Arundel Street	C2-D2-D3-D4
Bailey Street	C5
Ball Street	C8
Balm Green	C4-C5
Bank Street	D6
Bard Street	F5
Barker's Pool	C4-C5-D5
Bedford Street	B8
Beet Street	B5
Bernard Street	F4-F5-F6
Blonk Street	E6
Bolsover Street	A5
Boston Street	C7-D7
Bower Road	C7
Bowling Green	C7
Bramall Lane	C1-C2
Bridge Street	D7-D6-E6
Broad Lane	B5-C5-C6
Broad Street	E6-F5-F6
Brocco Street	B6
Brook Hill	A5-B5
Broomhall Place	A2
Broomhall Road	A2
Broomhall Street	A2-A3-B4
Broomspring Lane	A4-B4
Brown Street	D3

Brunswick Street	A3-A4
Brunswick Road	E7-E8
Burgess Street	C4
Cambridge Street	C4
Campo Lane	C5-D5-D6
Carlisle Street	F8
Carver Street	C4-C5
Castle Street	D6-E6
Castlegate	E6
Cavendish Street	B4
Cemetery Road	A1-B1-B2
Charles Street	D3-D4
Charlotte Road	C2-D2-D1-E1
Charter Row	C3-C4
Chatham Street	D7-D8
Church Street	C5-D5
Clarke Street	A3
Cliff Street	B1
Clough Road	C1-D1-D2
Club Garden Road	B1
Collegiate Crescent	A3
Commercial Street	E5
Corporation Street	D6-D7
Countess Road	C2-D2-D1
Cricket Inn Road	F6
Cumberland Way	C3
Daniel Hill	A8
Denby Street	C1
Devonshire Street	B4-C4
Division Street	C4
Duchess Road	D2-E2
Duke Street	F4-F5
Earl Street	C3
Earl Way	C3
East Bank Road	E1-E2
Ecclesall Road	A1-A2-B2
Edmund Road	D1-D2
Edward Street	B6
Effingham Street	F7
Egerton Street	B3
Eldon Street	B4
Ellin Street	C2
Eyre Street	C2-C3-D3-D4
Exchange Street	E6
Fargate	D5
Farm Road	E2
Fitzwilliam Street	B4-B3-C3
Flat Street	E5
Fornham Street	E3
Furnival Gate	C3-C4-D3-D4
Furnival Road	E6-F6-F7
Furnival Street	D3
Garden Street	B6-C6-C5
Gell Street	A4-A5
Gibraltar Street	C7-C6-D6
Glencoe Road	F3-F4
Glossop Road	A4-B4
Granville Road	E2-F2
Granville Street	E3-E4
Green Lane	B8-C8-C7
Hanover Way	A3-B3-B2
Harmer Lane	E4
Hartshead	D6
Harwood Street	C1
Harvest Lane	C8

Hawley Street	C5
Haymarket	E5-E6
Henry Street	B7
Hereford Street	C2
High Street	D5-E5
Hill Street	B1-C1
Hollis Croft	B6-C6
Holly Street	C4-C5
Hounsfield Road	A4-A5
Howard Street	D4-E4
Hoyle Street	B7
Infirmary Road	A8-B8 B7
Jessop Street	C2
John Street	C1-D1
Johnson Street	D7-E7
King Street	D5-E5-E6
Leadmill Road	D2-D3-E3
Leavy Greave Road	A5-B5
Lee Croft	C5-C6
Leopold Street	C5-D5
London Road	C1-B1-B2-C2
Maltravers Street	F6
Mappin Street	B4-B5
Margaret Street	D2
Matilda Street	C3-D3-D2
Matilda Way	C3
Meadow Street	B6-B7
Mitchell Street	A5-A6
Montgomery Terrace Road	A7-B7-B8
Moorfields	C7
Moore Street	B2-B3-C3
Mowbray Street	C8-D8-D7
Napier Street	A1-B1-B2
Neepsend Lane	B8-C8-C7
Netherthorpe Road	A5-A6-B6-B7
Norfolk Park Road	E1-E2-F2
Norfolk Road	F3-F4
Norfolk Row	D5
Norfolk Street	D4-D5
North Church Street	D6
Nottingham Street	E8
Nursery Street	D7-E7-E6
Old Street	F5-F6
Orchard Lane	C5
Oxford Road	A7-A8
Park Grange Road	E1-F1
Park Square	E5-E6-F6-F5
Paternoster Row	D3-D4-E4
Pear Street	A1
Penistone Road	B7-B8
Pinfold Street	C5
Pinstone Street	C4-D4-D5
Pitsmoor Road	D8
Pond Hill	E5
Pond Street	E4-E5
Portobello Street	B5-C5
Priestley Street	D1-E1-E2
Queen Street	C6-D6
Queen's Road	E1-E2
Randall Street	C1
Red Hill	B5-B6
Regent Street	B4-B5
Rock Street	D8
Rockingham Street	B5-C5-C4
Russell Street	C7

Rutland Road	B8
Rye Bank Road	D8
St Mary's Gate	C2
St Mary's Road	C2-D2-E2
St Philip's Road	A6-A7-B7-B8
Savile Street	E7-F7-F8
Scotland Street	B6-C6
Shales Moor	B7-C7
Sheaf Gardens	D2-E2
Sheaf Street	E4-E5
Sheffield Parkway	F6
Shepherd Street	B6-B7-C7
Shoreham Street	D1-D2-D3-E3
Shrewsbury Road	E3-E4-F3-F4
Shude Lane	E5
Shude Hill	E5-E6
Sidney Street	D3
Silver Street	C6
Snig Hill	D6
Solly Street	B5-B6-C6
South Lane	C3
South Street	E4-E5
Spital Hill	E7-E8-F8
Spital Street	E8-F8
Spitalfields	D7-E7
Spring Street	D6-D7
Stanley Street	E7
Suffolk Road	E3
Summerfield Street	A2-A1-B1
Sunny Bank	A2
Surrey Place	D4
Surrey Street	D4-D5
Sussex Street	F7
Sylvester Street	C2-D2
Talbot Place	F4
Talbot Street	F4
Tenter Street	C6
The Moor	C3-C4
Townhead Street	C5
Trippet Lane	C5
Tudor Street	D4-D5
Tudor Way	D5
Union Street	C4-D4
Upper Allen Street	B6
Upper Hanover Street	A3-A4-A5
Upperthorpe Road	A7-A8
Verdon Street	D8-E8
Vicar Lane	C5-D5
Victoria Station Road	E6-E7-F7
Waingate	E6
Walker Street	E7
Washington Road	B1
Watery Street	B7-B8
Wellington Street	B4-C4
West Bar	D6
West Bar Green	C6-D6
West Street	B4-B5-C5
Weston Street	A5-A6
Wheel Hill	E5
Wicker	E6-E7
Wilkinson Street	A4
William Street	A2-A3
York Street	D5-D6
Young Street	B2-C2

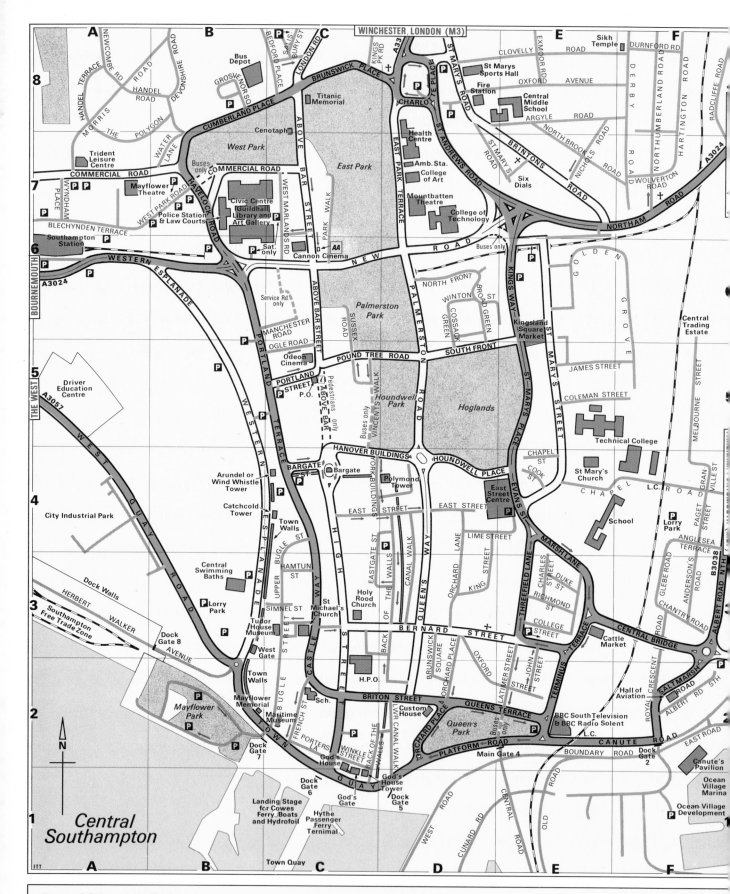

Southampton

In the days of the great ocean-going liners, Southampton was Britain's premier passenger port. Today container traffic is more important, but cruise liners still berth there. A unique double tide caused by the Solent waters, and protection from the open sea by the Isle of Wight, has meant that Southampton has always been a superb and important port. Like many great cities it was devastated by bombing raids during World War II. However, enough survives to make the city a fascinating place to explore. Outstanding are the town walls, which stand to their original height in some places, especially along Western Esplanade. The main landward entrance to the walled town was the Bargate – a superb medieval gateway with a Guildhall (now a museum) on its upper floor. The best place to appreciate old Southampton is in and around St Michael's Square. Here is St Michael's Church, oldest in the city and founded in 1070. Opposite is Tudor House Museum, a lovely gabled building housing much of interest. Down Bugle Street are old houses, with the town walls, pierced by the 13th-century West Gate, away to the right. At the corner of Bugle Street is the Wool House Maritime Museum, contained in a 14th-century warehouse. On the quayside is God's House Tower, part of the town's defences and now an archaeological museum.

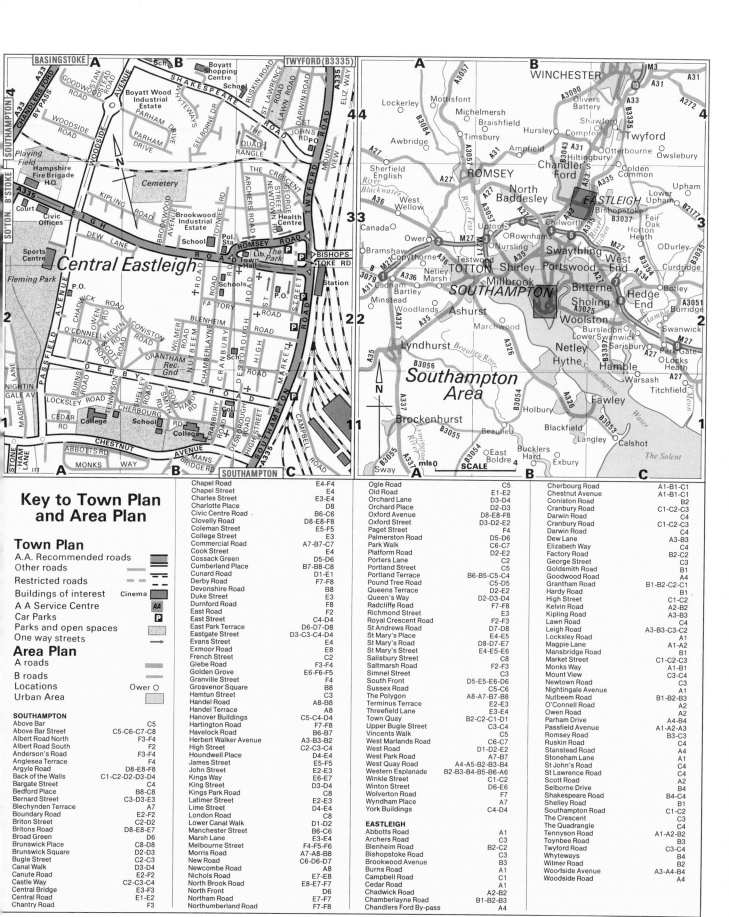

Key to Town Plan and Area Plan

Town Plan

A.A. Recommended roads
Other roads
Restricted roads
Buildings of interest — Cinema
A A Service Centre — AA
Car Parks — P
Parks and open spaces
One way streets

Area Plan

A roads
B roads
Locations — Ower O
Urban Area

SOUTHAMPTON	
Above Bar	C5
Above Bar Street	C5-C6-C7-C8
Albert Road North	F3-F4
Albert Road South	F2
Anderson's Road	F3-F4
Anglesea Terrace	F4
Argyle Road	D8-E8-F8
Back of the Walls	C1-C2-D2-D3-D4
Bargate Street	C4
Bedford Place	B8-C8
Bernard Street	C3-D3-E3
Blechynden Terrace	A7
Boundary Road	E2-F2
Briton Street	C2-D2
Britons Road	D8-E8-E7
Broad Green	D6
Brunswick Place	C8-D8
Brunswick Square	D2-D3
Bugle Street	C2-C3
Canal Walk	D3-D4
Canute Road	E2-F2
Castle Way	C2-C3-C4
Central Bridge	E3-F3
Central Road	E1-E2
Chantry Road	F3

Chapel Road	E4-F4
Chapel Street	E4
Charles Street	E3-E4
Charlotte Place	D8
Civic Centre Road	B6-C6
Clovelly Road	D8-E8-F8
Coleman Street	E5-F5
College Street	E3
Commercial Road	A7-B7-C7
Cook Street	E4
Cossack Green	D5-D6
Cumberland Place	B7-B8-C8
Cunard Road	D1-E1
Derby Road	F7-F8
Devonshire Road	B8
Duke Street	E3
Durnford Road	F8
East Road	F2
East Street	C4-D4
East Park Terrace	D6-D7-D8
Eastgate Street	D3-C3-C4-D4
Evans Street	E4
Exmoor Road	E8
French Street	C2
Glebe Road	F3-F4
Golden Grove	E6-F6-F5
Granville Street	F4
Grosvenor Square	B8
Hamtun Street	C3
Handel Road	A8-B8
Handel Terrace	A8
Hanover Buildings	C5-C4-D4
Hartington Road	F7-F8
Havelock Road	B6-B7
Herbert Walker Avenue	A3-B3-B2
High Street	C2-C3-C4
Houndwell Place	D4-E4
James Street	E5-F5
John Street	E2-E3
Kings Way	E6-E7
King Street	D3-D4
Kings Park Road	C8
Latimer Street	E2-E3
Lime Street	D4-E4
London Road	C8
Lower Canal Walk	D1-D2
Manchester Street	B6-C6
Marsh Lane	E3-E4
Melbourne Street	F4-F5-F6
Morris Road	A7-A8-B8
New Road	C6-D6-D7
Newcombe Road	A8
Nichols Road	E7-E8
North Brook Road	E8-E7-F7
North Front	D6
Northam Road	E7-F7
Northumberland Road	F7-F8

Ogle Road	C5
Old Road	E1-E2
Orchard Lane	D3-D4
Orchard Place	D2-D3
Oxford Avenue	D8-E8-F8
Oxford Street	D3-D2-E2
Paget Street	F4
Palmerston Road	D5-D6
Park Walk	C6-C7
Platform Road	D2-E2
Porters Lane	C2
Portland Street	C5
Portland Terrace	B6-B5-C5-C4
Pound Tree Road	C5-D5
Queens Terrace	D2-E2
Queen's Way	D2-D3-D4
Radcliffe Road	F7-F8
Richmond Street	E3
Royal Crescent Road	F2-F3
St Andrews Road	D7-D8
St Mary's Place	E4-E5
St Mary's Road	D8-D7-E7
St Mary's Street	E4-E5-E6
Salisbury Street	C8
Saltmarsh Road	F2-F3
Simnel Street	C3
South Front	D5-E5-E6-D6
Sussex Road	C5-C6
The Polygon	A8-A7-B7-B8
Terminus Terrace	E2-E3
Threefield Lane	E3-E4
Town Quay	B2-C2-C1-D1
Upper Bugle Street	C3-C4
Vincents Walk	C5
West Marlands Road	C6-C7
West Road	A7-B7
West Park Road	A7-B7
West Quay Road	A4-A5-B2-B3-B4
Western Esplanade	B2-B3-B4-B5-B6-A6
Winkle Street	C1-C2
Winton Street	D6-E6
Wolverton Road	F7
Wyndham Place	A7
York Buildings	C4-D4

EASTLEIGH	
Abbotts Road	A1
Archers Road	C3
Blenheim Road	B2-C2
Bishopstoke Road	C3
Brookwood Avenue	B3
Burns Road	A1
Campbell Road	C1
Cedar Road	A1
Chadwick Road	A2-B2
Chamberlayne Road	B1-B2-B3
Chandlers Ford By-pass	A4

Cherbourg Road	A1-B1-C1
Chestnut Avenue	A1-B1-C1
Coniston Road	B2
Cranbury Road	C1-C2-C3
Darwin Road	C4
Cranbury Road	C1-C2-C3
Darwin Road	C4
Dew Lane	A3-B3
Elizabeth Way	C4
Factory Road	B2-C2
George Street	C3
Goldsmith Road	B1
Goodwood Road	A4
Grantham Road	B1-B2-C2-C1
Hardy Road	B1
High Street	C1-C2
Kelvin Road	A2-B2
Kipling Road	A3-B3
Lawn Road	C4
Leigh Road	A3-B3-C3-C2
Locksley Road	A1
Magpie Lane	A1-A2
Mansbridge Road	B1
Market Street	C1-C2-C3
Monks Way	A1-B1
Mount View	C3-C4
Newtown Road	C3
Nightingale Avenue	A1
Nutbeem Road	B1-B2-B3
O'Connell Road	A2
Owen Road	A2
Parham Drive	A4-B4
Passfield Avenue	A1-A2-A3
Romsey Road	B3-C3
Ruskin Road	C4
Stanstead Road	A4
Stoneham Lane	A1
St John's Road	C4
St Lawrence Road	C4
Scott Road	A2
Selborne Drive	B4
Shakespeare Road	B4-C4
Shelley Road	B1
Southampton Road	C1-C2
The Crescent	C3
The Quadrangle	C4
Tennyson Road	A1-A2-B2
Toynbee Road	B3
Twyford Road	C3-C4
Whyteways	B4
Wilmer Road	B2
Woodside Avenue	A3-A4-B4
Woodside Road	A4

SOUTHAMPTON
Although liners still use Southampton's docks which handled all the great ocean-going passenger ships before the age of air travel replaced sea travel, the port is chiefly used by commercial traffic today.

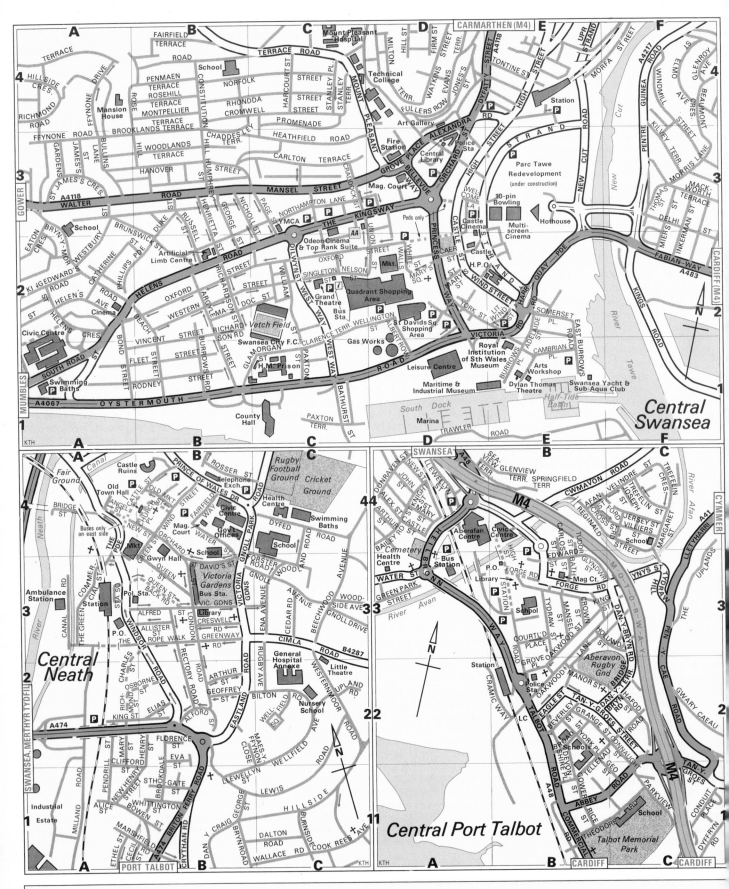

Swansea

Like nearly all towns in the valleys and along the coast of Glamorgan, Swansea grew at an amazing speed during the Industrial Revolution. Ironworks, non-ferrous metal smelting works and mills and factories of every kind were built to produce the goods which were exported from the city's docks. There had been a settlement here from very early times - the city's name is derived from Sweyn's Ea

- Ea means island, and Sweyn was a Viking pirate who had a base here. Heavy industry is still pre-eminent in the area, but commerce is of increasing importance and the university exerts a strong influence. Hundreds of acres of parkland and open space lie in and around the city, and just to the west is the Gower, one of the most beautiful areas of Wales. The history of Swansea is traced in the Maritime and Industrial Museum and Royal Institution of South Wales Museum, while the Glynn Vivian Art Gallery contains notable paintings and

porcelain.

Neath and *Port Talbot* are, like Swansea, dominated by heavy industry. Neath was once a Roman station, and later had a castle and an abbey, ruins of which can still be seen. Port Talbot has been an industrial centre since 1770, when a copper-smelting works was built. Steelworks and petrochemical works stretch for miles around Swansea Bay.

184

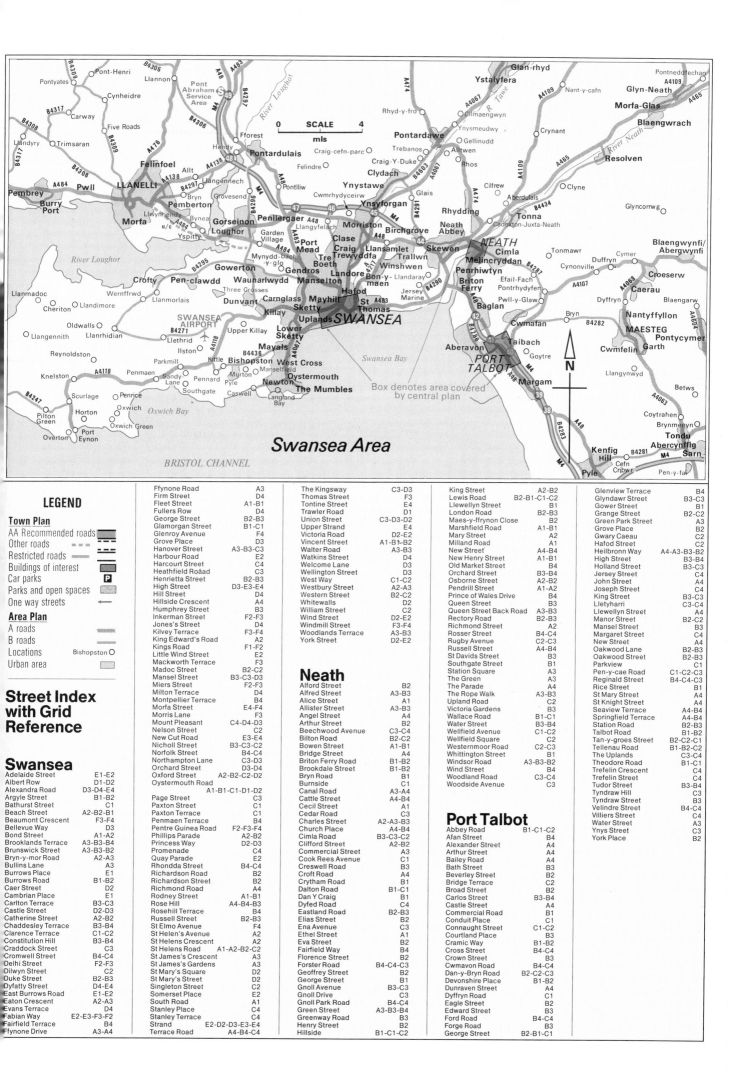

Swansea Area

BRISTOL CHANNEL

Box denotes area covered by central plan

LEGEND

Town Plan
- AA Recommended roads
- Other roads
- Restricted roads
- Buildings of interest
- Car parks
- Parks and open spaces
- One way streets

Area Plan
- A roads
- B roads
- Locations   Bishopston ○
- Urban area

Street Index with Grid Reference

Swansea

Adelaide Street	E1-E2
Albert Row	D1-D2
Alexandra Road	D3-D4-E4
Argyle Row	B1-B2
Bathurst Street	C1
Beach Street	A2-B2-B1
Beaumont Crescent	F3-F4
Bellevue Way	D3
Bond Street	A1-A2
Brooklands Terrace	A3-B3-B4
Brunswick Street	A3-B3-B2
Bryn-y-mor Road	A2-A3
Bullins Lane	A3
Burrows Place	E1
Burrows Road	B1-B2
Caer Street	D2
Cambrian Place	E1
Carlton Terrace	B3-C3
Castle Street	D2-D3
Catherine Street	A2-B2
Chaddesley Terrace	B3-B4
Clarence Terrace	C1-C2
Constitution Hill	B3-B4
Craddock Street	C3
Cromwell Street	B4-C4
Delhi Street	F2-F3
Dilwyn Street	C2
Duke Street	B2-B3
Dyfatty Street	D4-E4
East Burrows Road	E1-E2
Eaton Crescent	A2-A3
Evans Terrace	D4
Fabian Way	E2-E3-F3-F2
Fairfield Terrace	B4
Ffynone Drive	A3-A4
Ffynone Road	A3
Firm Street	D4
Fleet Street	A1-B1
Fullers Row	D4
George Street	B2-B3
Glamorgan Street	B1-C1
Glenroy Avenue	F4
Grove Place	D3
Hanover Street	A3-B3-C3
Harbour Road	E2
Harcourt Street	C4
Heathfield Roāad	C3
Henrietta Street	B2-B3
High Street	D3-E3-E4
Hill Street	D4
Hillside Crescent	A4
Humphrey Street	B3
Inkerman Street	F2-F3
Jones's Street	D4
Kilvey Terrace	F3-F4
King Edward's Road	A2
Kings Road	F1-F2
Little Wind Street	E2
Mackworth Terrace	F3
Madoc Street	B2-C2
Mansel Street	B3-C3-D3
Miers Street	F2-F3
Milton Terrace	D4
Montpellier Terrace	B4
Morfa Street	E4-F4
Morris Lane	F3
Mount Pleasant	C4-D4-D3
Nelson Street	C2
New Cut Road	E3-E4
Nicholl Street	B3-C3-C2
Norfolk Street	B4-C4
Northampton Lane	C3-D3
Orchard Street	D3-D4
Oxford Street	A2-B2-C2-D2
Oystermouth Road	A1-B1-C1-D1-D2
Page Street	C3
Paxton Street	C1
Paxton Terrace	C1
Penmaen Terrace	B4
Pentre Guinea Road	F2-F3-F4
Phillips Parade	A2-B2
Princess Way	D2-D3
Promenade	C4
Quay Parade	E2
Rhondda Street	B4-C4
Richardson Road	B2
Richardson Street	B2
Richmond Road	A4
Rodney Street	A1-B1
Rose Hill	A4-B4-B3
Rosehill Terrace	B4
Russell Street	B2-B3
St Elmo Avenue	F4
St Helen's Avenue	A2
St Helens Crescent	A2
St Helens Road	A1-A2-B2-C2
St James's Crescent	A3
St James's Gardens	A3
St Mary's Square	D2
St Mary's Street	D2
Singleton Street	C2
Somerset Place	E2
South Road	A1
Stanley Place	C4
Stanley Terrace	C4
Strand	E2-D2-D3-E3-E4
Terrace Road	A4-B4-C4

The Kingsway	C3-D3
Thomas Street	F3
Tontine Street	E4
Trawler Road	D1
Union Street	C3-D3-D2
Upper Strand	E4
Victoria Road	D2-E2
Vincent Street	A1-B1-B2
Walter Road	A3-B3
Watkins Street	D4
Welcome Lane	D3
Wellington Street	D3
West Way	C1-C2
Westbury Street	A2-A3
Western Street	B2-C2
Whitewalls	D2
William Street	C2
Wind Street	D2-E2
Windmill Street	F3-F4
Woodlands Terrace	A3-B3
York Street	D2-E2

Neath

Alford Street	B2
Alfred Street	A3-B3
Alice Street	A1
Allister Street	A3-B3
Angel Street	A4
Arthur Street	B2
Beechwood Avenue	C3-C4
Bilton Road	B2-C2
Bowen Street	A1-B1
Bridge Street	A4
Briton Ferry Road	B1-B2
Brookdale Street	B1-B2
Bryn Road	B1
Burnside	C1
Canal Road	A3-A4
Cattle Street	A4-B4
Cecil Street	A1
Cedar Road	C3
Charles Street	A2-A3-B3
Church Place	A4-B4
Cimla Road	B3-C3-C2
Clifford Street	A2-B2
Commercial Street	A3
Cook Rees Avenue	C1
Creswell Road	B3
Croft Road	A4
Crytham Road	B1
Dalton Road	B1-C1
Dan Y Craig	B1
Dyfed Road	C4
Eastland Road	B2-B3
Elias Street	B2
Ena Avenue	C3
Ethel Street	A1
Eva Street	B2
Fairfield Way	B2
Florence Street	B2
Forster Road	B4-C4-C3
Geoffrey Street	B2
George Street	B1
Gnoll Avenue	B3-C3
Gnoll Drive	C3
Gnoll Park Road	B4-C4
Green Street	A3-B3-B4
Greenway Road	B3
Henry Street	B2
Hillside	B1-C1-C2

King Street	A2-B2
Lewis Road	B2-B1-C1-C2
Llewellyn Street	B1
London Road	B2-B3
Maes-y-ffrynon Close	B2
Marshfield Road	A1-B1
Mary Street	A2
Milland Road	A1
New Street	A4-B4
New Henry Street	A1-B1
Old Market Street	B4
Orchard Street	B3-B4
Osborne Street	A2-B2
Pendrill Street	A1-A2
Prince of Wales Drive	B4
Queen Street	B3
Queen Street Back Road	A3-B3
Rectory Road	B2-B3
Richmond Street	A2
Rosser Street	B4-C4
Rugby Avenue	C2-C3
Russell Street	A4-B4
St Davids Street	B3
Southgate Street	B1
Station Square	A3
The Green	A3
The Parade	A4
The Rope Walk	A3-B3
Upland Road	C2
Victoria Gardens	B3
Wallace Road	B1-C1
Water Street	B3-B4
Wellfield Avenue	C1-C2
Wellfield Square	C2
Westernmoor Road	C2-C3
Whittington Street	B1
Windsor Road	A3-B3-B2
Wind Street	B4
Woodland Road	C3-C4
Woodside Avenue	C3

Port Talbot

Abbey Road	B1-C1-C2
Afan Street	B4
Alexander Street	A4
Arthur Street	A4
Bailey Road	A4
Bath Street	B3
Beverley Street	B2
Bridge Terrace	C2
Broad Street	B2
Carlos Street	B3-B4
Castle Street	A4
Commercial Road	B1
Conduit Place	C1
Connaught Street	C1-C2
Courtland Place	B3
Cramic Way	B1-B2
Cross Street	B4-C4
Crown Street	B3
Cwmavon Road	B4-C4
Dan-y-Bryn Road	B2-C2-C3
Devonshire Place	B1-B2
Dunraven Street	A4
Dyffryn Road	C1
Eagle Street	B2
Edward Street	B3
Ford Road	B4-C4
Forge Road	B3
George Street	B2-B1-C1

Glenview Terrace	B4
Glyndawr Street	B3-C3
Gower Street	B1
Grange Street	B2-C2
Green Park Street	A3
Grove Place	B2
Gwary Caeau	C2
Hafod Street	C2
Heilbronn Way	A4-A3-B3-B2
High Street	B3-B4
Holland Street	B3-C3
Jersey Street	A4
John Street	C4
Joseph Street	C4
King Street	B3-C3
Lletyharri	C3-C4
Llewellyn Street	A4
Manor Street	B2-C2
Mansel Street	B3
Margaret Street	C4
New Street	A4
Oakwood Lane	B2-B3
Oakwood Street	B2-B3
Parkview	C1
Pen-y-cae Road	C1-C2-C3
Reginald Street	B4-C4-C3
Rice Street	B1
St Mary Street	A4
St Knight Street	A4
Seaview Terrace	A4-B4
Springfield Terrace	A4-B4
Station Road	B2-B3
Talbot Road	B1-B2
Tan-y-groes Street	B2-C2-C1
Tellenau Road	B1-B2-C2
The Uplands	B3
Theodore Road	B1-C1
Trefelin Crescent	C4
Trefelin Street	C4
Tudor Street	B3-B4
Tyndraw Hill	C3
Tyndraw Street	B3
Velindre Street	B4-C4
Villiers Street	C4
Water Street	A3
Ynys Street	C3
York Place	B2

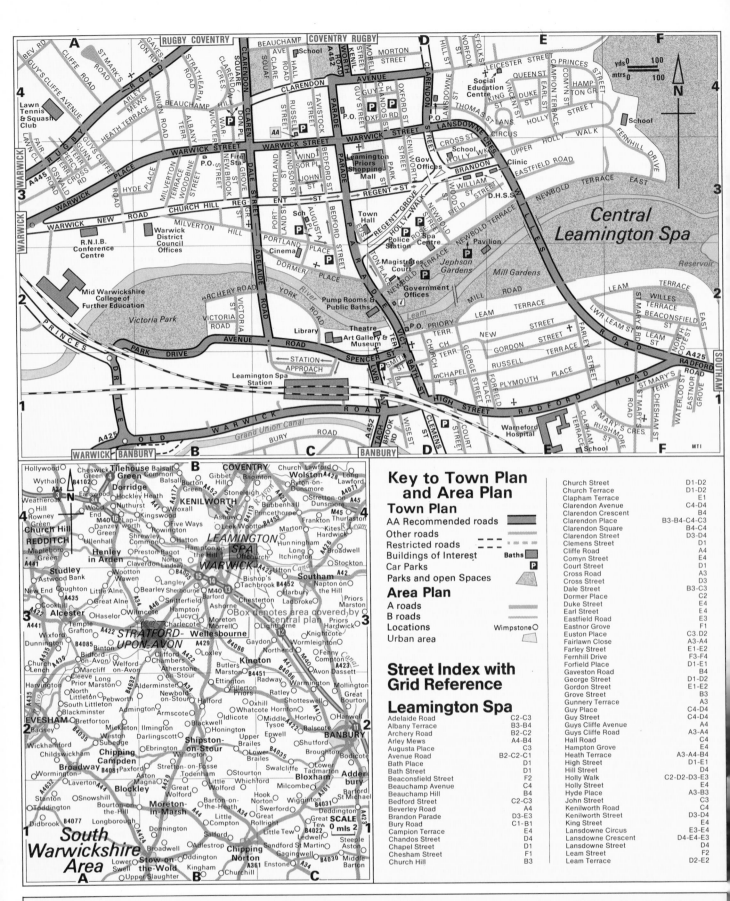

Warwick

The old county town of the shire, Warwick lies in the shadow of its massive, historic castle which occupies the rocky ridge above the River Avon. Thomas Beauchamp and his son built the huge towers and curtain walls in the 14th century, but it was the Jacobean holders of the earldom, the Grevilles, who transformed the medieval stronghold into a nobleman's residence. In 1694, the heart of the town was almost completely destroyed by fire and the few medieval buildings that survived lie on the outskirts of the present 18th-century centre. Of these Oken House, now a doll museum, and Lord Leycester's Hospital, almshouses dating back to the 14th century, are particularly striking.

Stratford-upon-Avon, as the birthplace of William Shakespeare, England's most famous poet and playwright, is second only to London as a tourist attraction. This charming old market town is a living memorial to him; his plays are performed in the Royal Shakespeare Theatre which dominates the river bank, a waxwork museum specialises in scenes from his works, and his childhood home in Henley Street is a museum.

Leamington Spa, an inland spa on the River Leam, gained the prefix 'Royal' after Queen Victoria had visited it in 1838, and the town has been a fashionable health resort ever since.

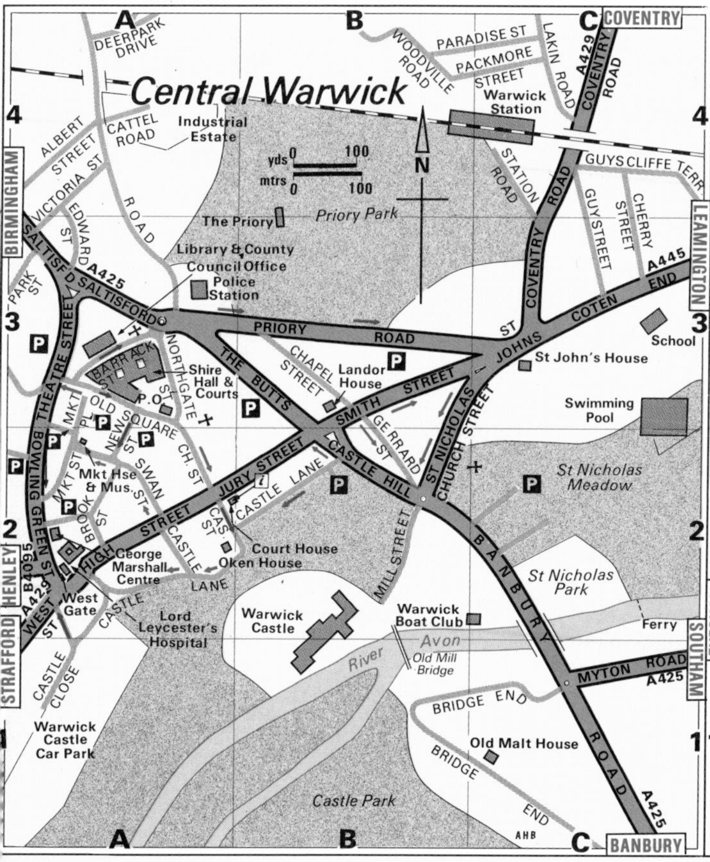

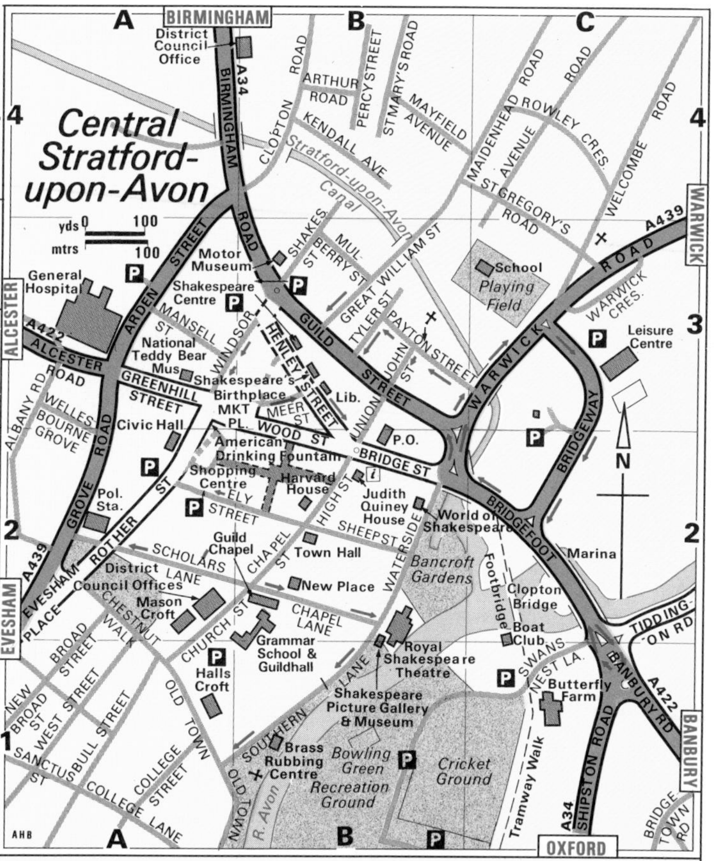

Leam Terrace East	E2-F2-F1
Leicester Street	D4-E4-F4
Lower Avenue	D1
Lower Leam Street	E2-F2
Mill Road	D2-E2
Milverton Hill	B3-C3
Milverton Terrace	B3
Morrell Street	C4-D4
Morton Street	D4
New Street	D2-E2
Newbold Street	D3
Newbold Terrace	D2-D3-E3
Newbold Terrace East	E3-F3
New Brook Street	B3
Norfolk Street	D4
Northcote Street	F1-F2
Old Warwick Road	A1-B1-C1-D1
Oswald Road	A3
Oxford Road	D4
Oxford Street	D4
Parade	C4-C3-C2-D2
Park Drive	A2-B2-B1-B2
Park Street	D3
Percy Terrace	A3
Plymouth Place	E1
Princes Drive	A1-A2
Princes Street	E4
Priory Terrace	D2
Portland Place	C2-C3
Portland Street	C3
Queen Street	E4
Radford Road	E1-F1
Regent Grove	C3-D3
Regent Street	B3-C3-D3
Rosefield Street	D2-D3-E3
Rugby Road	A3-A4-B4
Rushmore Street	E1-F1
Russell Street	C4
Russell Terrace	D1-E1-E2-F2
St Mark's Road	A4
St Mary's Crescent	E1-F1
St Mary's Road	F1-F2
St Mary's Terrace	F1
Satchwell Street	C3-D3
Smith Street	D1
Spencer Street	C1-D1-D2
Station Approach	C1
Strathearn Road	B4
Suffolk Street	D4
Tachbrook Road	D1
Tavistock Street	C4

Thomas Street	D4-E4
Union Road	B3-B4
Upper Holly Walk	E3-E4-F4
Victoria Road	B2
Victoria Street	B2
Victoria Terrace	D1-D2
Vincent Street	E4
Warwick New Road	A3-B3
Warwick Place	A3-B3
Warwick Street	B3-C3-C4-D4
Warwick Terrace	B3-B4
Waterloo Street	F1
Willes Road	E3-E2-F2-F1
Willes Terrace	F2
William Street	D3-E3
Windsor Place	C3
Windsor Street	C3
Wise Street	D1
Woodbine Street	B3
Wood Street	D3
York Road	C2

Warwick

Albert Street	A4
Banbury Road	B2-C2-C1
Barrack Street	A3
Bowling Green Street	A2
Bridge End	C1-B1-C1
Brook Street	A2
Cape Road	A3-A4
Castle Close	A1
Castle Hill	B2
Castle Lane	A1-A2-B2
Castle Street	A2
Chapel Street	B3
Cherry Street	C3-C4
Church Street	A2-A3
Coten End	C3
Coventry Road	C3-C4
Deerpark Drive	A4
Edward Street	A3-A4
Gerrard Street	B2-B3
Guys Cliffe Terrace	C4
Guy Street	C3-C4
High Street	A2
Jury Street	A2-B2
Lakin Road	C4
Market Place	A2-A3
Market Street	A2
Mill Street	B2
Myton Road	C1
New Street	A2-A3
Northgate Street	A3
North Rock	A3
Old Square	A3
Packmore Street	B4-C4
Paradise Street	B4-C4
Parkes Street	A3
Priory Road	A3-B3-C3
St Johns	C3
St Nicholas Church Street	B2-B3-C3
Saltisford	A3-A4
Smith Street	B2-B3-C3
Station Road	C4
Swan Street	A2
Theatre Street	A3
The Butts	A3-B3
Victoria Street	A3-A4
West Street	A1-A2
Woodville Road	B4

Stratford-upon-Avon

Albany Road	A2-A3
Alcester Road	A3
Arden Street	A3-A4
Arthur Road	B4
Avenue Road	C3-C4
Banbury Road	C1
Birmingham Road	A4-B4-B3
Bridgefoot	B2-C2
Bridge Street	B2
Bridgetown Road	C1
Bridgeway	C2-C3
Broad Street	A1-A2
Bull Street	A1
Chapel Lane	B2
Chapel Street	B2
Chestnut Walk	A1-A2
Church Street	A1-A2-B2
Clopton Road	B4
College Lane	A1
College Street	A1
Ely Street	A2-B2
Evesham Place	A1-A2
Great William Street	B3-B4
Greenhill Street	A3
Grove Road	A2-A3
Guild Street	B3
Henley Street	B2-B3
High Street	B2
John Street	B3
Kendall Avenue	B4
Maidenhead Road	B4-C4
Mansell Street	A3
Market Place	A3-B3
Mayfield Avenue	B4
Mulberry Street	B3
New Broad Street	A1
Old Town	A1-B1-A1
Payton Street	B3-C3
Percy Street	B4
Rother Street	A2-A3
Rowley Crescent	C4
St Gregory's Road	B4-C4-C3
St Mary's Road	B4
Sanctus Street	A1
Scholars Lane	A2-B2
Shakespeare Street	B3-B4
Sheep Street	B2
Shipston Road	C1
Southern Lane	A1-B1-B2
Swans Nest Lane	C1
Tiddington Road	C2
Tyler Street	B3
Union Street	B2-B3
Warwick Crescent	C3
Warwick Road	B3-C3-C4
Waterside	B2
Welcombe Road	C3-C4
Wellesbourne Grove	A2-A3
West Street	A1-A2
Windsor Street	A3-B3
Wood Street	B2-B3

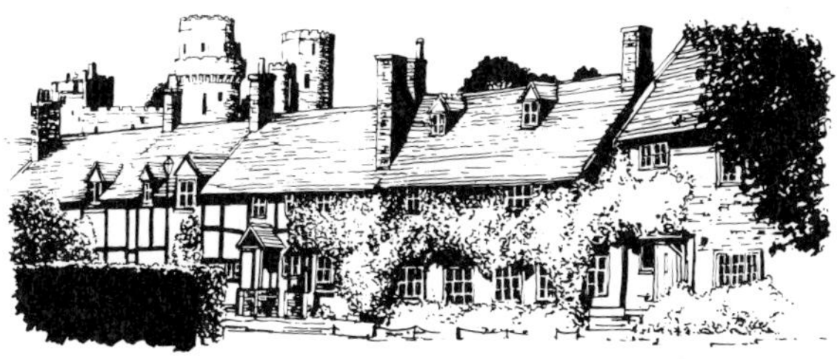

WARWICK
These pretty brick and timbered cottages standing in the shadow of the great medieval towers of Warwick Castle are among the few buildings in the town that survived a devastating fire in the late 17th century.

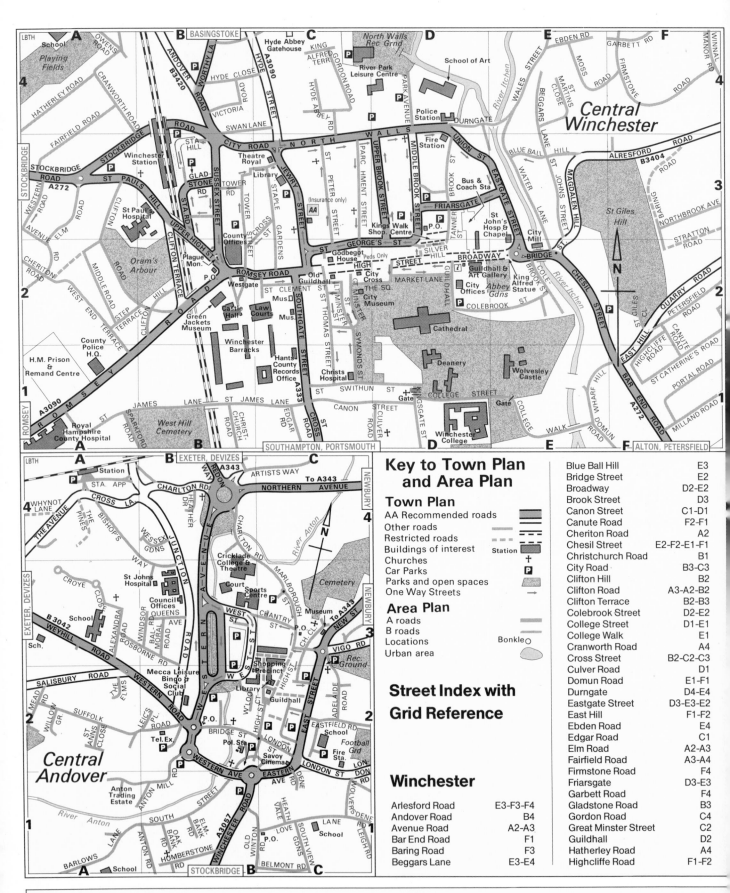

Key to Town Plan and Area Plan

Town Plan

AA Recommended roads	▬▬
Other roads	───
Restricted roads	─ ─ ─
Buildings of interest	Station
Churches	+
Car Parks	P
Parks and open spaces	
One Way Streets	→

Area Plan

A roads	
B roads	
Locations	Bonkle○
Urban area	

Street Index with Grid Reference

Winchester

Arlesford Road	E3-F3-F4
Andover Road	B4
Avenue Road	A2-A3
Bar End Road	F1
Baring Road	F3
Beggars Lane	E3-E4

Blue Ball Hill	E3
Bridge Street	E2
Broadway	D2-E2
Brook Street	D3
Canon Street	C1-D1
Canute Road	F2-F1
Cheriton Road	A2
Chesil Street	E2-F2-E1-F1
Christchurch Road	B1
City Road	B3-C3
Clifton Hill	B2
Clifton Road	A3-A2-B2
Clifton Terrace	B2-B3
Colebrook Street	D2-E2
College Street	D1-E1
College Walk	E1
Cranworth Road	A4
Cross Street	B2-C2-C3
Culver Road	D1
Domun Road	E1-F1
Durngate	D4-E4
Eastgate Street	D3-E3-E2
East Hill	F1-F2
Ebden Road	E4
Edgar Road	C1
Elm Road	A2-A3
Fairfield Road	A3-A4
Firmstone Road	F4
Friarsgate	D3-E3
Garbett Road	F4
Gladstone Road	B3
Gordon Road	C4
Great Minster Street	C2
Guildhall	D2
Hatherley Road	A4
Highcliffe Road	F1-F2

Winchester

King Alfred designated Winchester capital of England, a status it retained until after the Norman Conquest. Although gradually eclipsed by London, the city maintained close links with the Crown until the reign of Charles II.

Tucked away unobtrusively in the heart of Winchester is the impressive cathedral which encompasses Norman, and all the later Gothic styles of architecture. William of Wykeham was a bishop here in the 14th century and it was he who founded Winchester College, one of the oldest and most famous public schools in England. The buildings lie just outside the peaceful, shady Close where Pilgrims' Hall can be visited. Nearby are the Bishop's Palace and remains of Wolvesley Castle, one of Winchester's two Norman castles. Of the other, only the Great Hall, just outside the Westgate survives. Here hangs the 14th-century Round Table associated with the legend of King Arthur.

The streets of the city, which cover a remarkably small area, are lined with many charming old buildings of different periods. A walk along the pedestrianised High Street takes you past the former Guildhall - now a bank - and the old Butter Cross, into the Broadway where a statue of King Alfred stands near the River Itchen. A delightful path follows the river alongside the remnants of the old city walls.

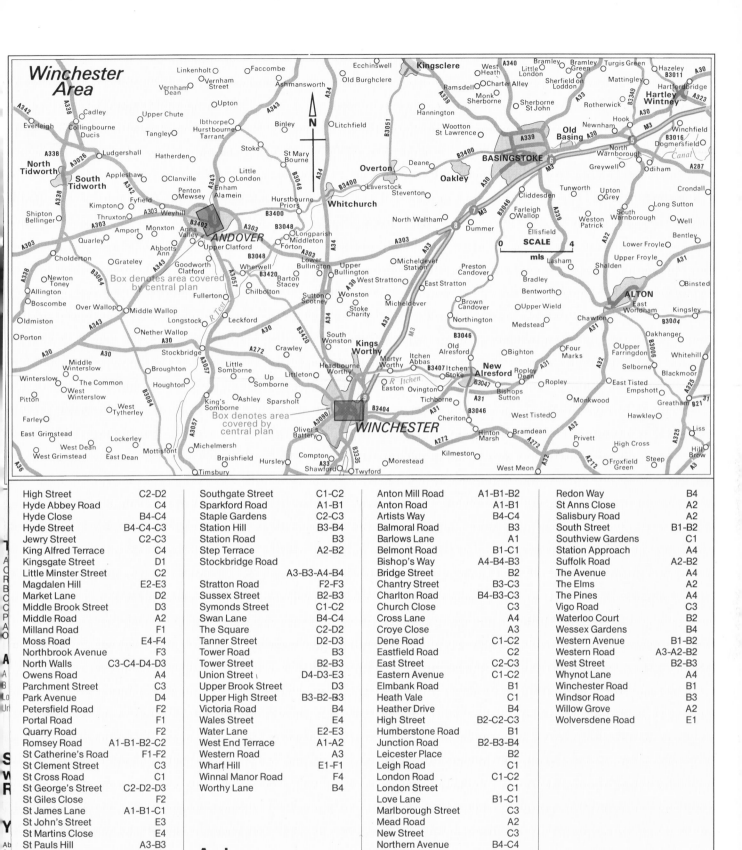

Winchester Area

WINCHESTER
Standing on the site of the old Hall of Court in the Broadway is the city's Guildhall. Built in 1873, its style was influenced by Northampton Town Hall. It is now a centre for culture and the arts.

London

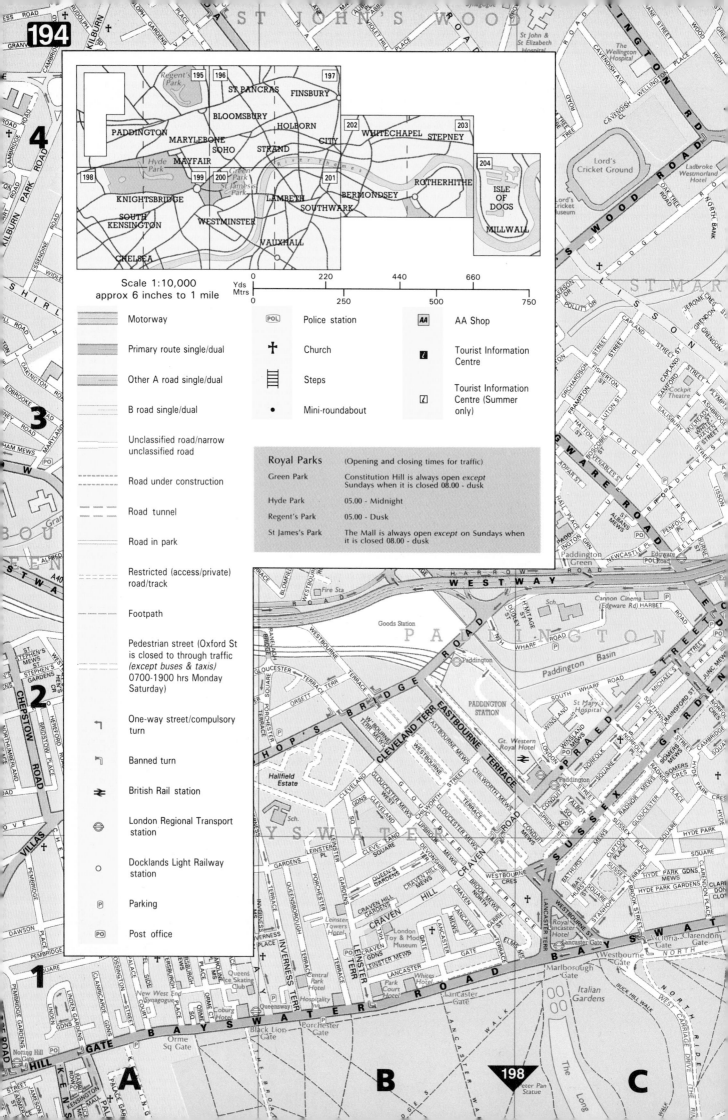

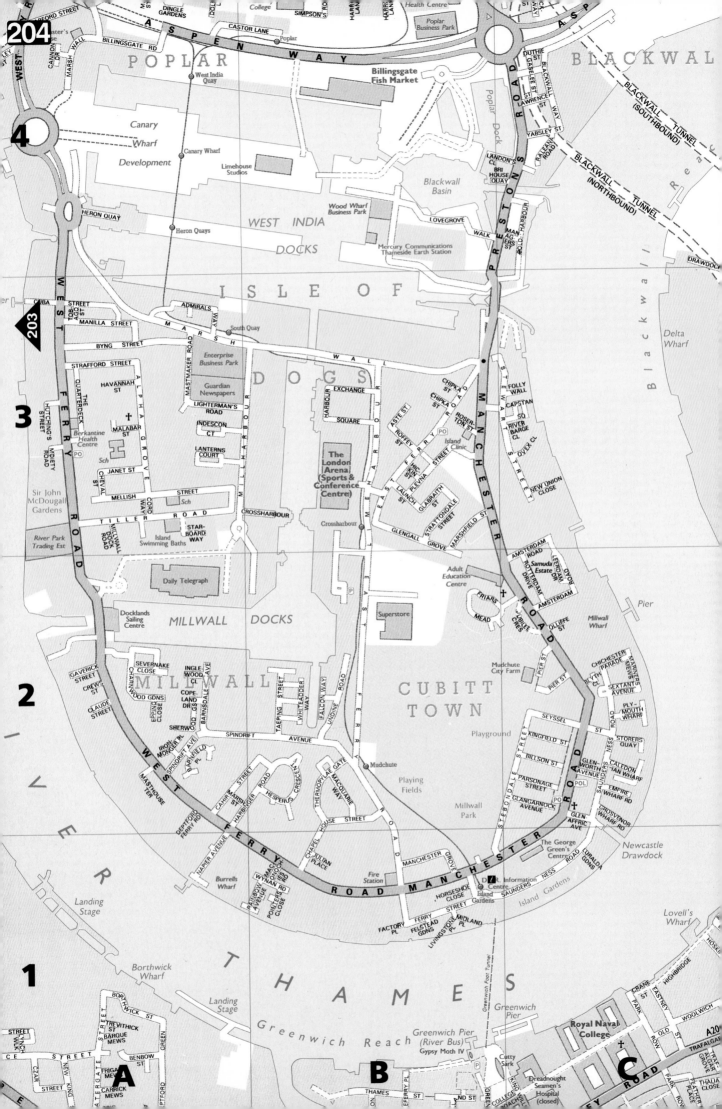

London street index

In the index, the street names are listed in alphabetical order and written in full, but may be abbreviated on the map. Postal codes are listed where information is available. Each entry is followed by its map page number in bold type and an arbitrary letter and figure grid reference eg Exhibition Road SW7 **198** C3. **Turn to page '198'. The letter 'C' refers to the grid square located at the bottom of the page. The figure '3' refers to the grid square located at the lefthand side of the page.** Exhibition Road **is found within the intersecting square.** SW7 **refers to the postcode.**

bbey Orchard Way — Bond Way

ɔey Orchard Street
'1 **200** B3
ɔey Street SE1 **202** A1
ɔots Lane SE1 **202** A2
:hurch Lane EC4 **197** F1
ərdour Street SE1 **201** F2
ngdon Road W8 **198** A3
ngdon Street SW1 **200** B3
ngdon Villas W8 **198** A3
nilles Way W1 **199** E4
kroyd Drive E3 **203** F4
ɔrn Walk SE16 **203** F2
:on Street WC1 **196** C4
am And Eve Mews W8 **198** A3
am Street WC2 **196** B1
am's Row W1 **195** E1
dington Street SE1 **200** C3
dle Hill EC4 **197** E1
dle Street EC2 **197** E2
əlina Grove E1 **202** D4
əline Place WC1 **196** B2
er Street E1 **202** B4
miral Place SE16 **203** E2
ɔar Street W2 **194** C3
rian Mews SW10 **198** A1
ar Street WC2 **196** B1
atha Close E1 **202** C2
don Street EC1 **197** D3
nes Street E14 **203** F4
Street W1 **196** A1
ska Street SE1 **200** C4
any Mews SE5 **201** E1
any Road SE5 **201** E1
any Street NW1 **195** F4
atross Way SE16 **203** D1
emarle Street W1 **195** F1
ert Court SW7 **198** C3
ert Embankment SE1 **200** B1
ert Gardens E1 **203** D3
ert Hall Mansions
'7 **198** C3
ert Mews W8 **198** B3
ert Place W8 **198** B3
erta Street SE17 **201** D1
ion Close W2 **195** D1
ion Mews W2 **195** D1
ion Place EC1 **197** D3
ion Street SE16 **203** D1
ion Street W2 **195** D1
enham Street NW1 **196** A4
ermanbury EC2 **197** E2
erney Street SW1 **199** F2
ersgate Street EC1 **197** E3
ford Street W1 **195** E1
gate EC3 **202** A3
gate High Street EC3 **202** A3
wych WC2 **196** C1
xander Place SW7 **198** C2
xander Square SW3 **198** C2
red Mews W1 **196** A3
red Place WC1 **196** A3
ce Street SE1 **201** F3
Street E1 **202** B3
Hallows Lane EC4 **197** F1
en Street W8 **198** A3

Allington Street SW1 **199** F3
Allsop Place NW1 **195** D3
Alpha Place SW3 **199** D1
Alsace Road SE17 **201** F1
Alscot Road SE1 **202** B1
Alvey Street SE17 **201** F2
Ambergate Street SE17 **201** D1
Ambrosden Avenue SW1 **200** A3
Amelia Street SE17 **201** E2
Amen Corner EC4 **197** D2
Amen Court EC4 **197** D2
America Square EC3 **202** A3
Amoy Place E14 **203** F3
Ampton Place WC1 **196** C4
Ampton Street WC1 **196** C4
Amwell Street EC1 **196** C4
Anderson Street SW3 **199** D2
Angel Court EC2 **197** F2
Angel Passage EC4 **197** F1
Angel Street EC1 **197** E2
Ansdell Street W8 **198** A3
Antill Terrace E1 **203** D4
Apple Tree Yard SW1 **196** A1
Appold Street EC2 **197** F3
Aquinas Street SE1 **201** D4
Arbour Square E1 **203** D4
Archangel Street SE16 **203** E1
Archer Street W1 **196** A1
Argyle Square WC1 **196** B4
Argyle Street WC1 **161** B4
Argyle Walk WC1 **196** B4
Argyll Road W8 **198** A3
Argyll Street W1 **195** F2
Arlington Street SW1 **199** F4
Arlington Way EC1 **197** D4
Arne Street WC2 **196** B2
Arneway Street SW1 **200** A2
Arnside Street SE17 **201** E1
Arthur Street EC4 **197** F1
Artichoke Hill E1 **202** C3
Artillery Lane E1 **202** A4
Artillery Row SW1 **200** A3
Arundel Street WC2 **196** C1
Ashbridge Street NW8 **194** C3
Ashburn Gardens SW7 **198** B2
Ashburn Mews SW7 **198** B2
Ashburn Place SW7 **198** B2
Ashby Street EC1 **197** D4
Asher Drive E1 **202** B3
Ashfield Street E1 **202** C4
Ashfield Street E1 **202** C4
Ashland Place W1 **194** E3
Ashley Place SW1 **199** F3
Ashmill Street NW1 **194** C3
Aske Street N1 **197** F4
Assam Street E1 **202** B4
Assembly Passage E1 **203** D4
Astell Street SW3 **199** D2
Aston Street E14 **203** E4
Astwood Mews SW7 **198** B2
Atherstone Mews SW7 **198** B2
Atterbury Street SW1 **200** B2
Attneave Street WC1 **196** C4
Auckland Street SE11 **200** C1
Augustus Street NW1 **195** F4

Aulton Place SE11 **201** D1
Austin Friars EC2 **197** F2
Austral Street SE11 **201** D2
Ave Maria Lane EC4 **197** E2
Aveline Street SE11 **200** C1
Avery Row W1 **195** F1
Avis Square E1 **203** E4
Avon Place SE1 **201** E3
Avonmouth Street SE1 **201** E3
Aybrook Street W1 **195** E2
Aylesbury Road SE17 **201** F1
Aylesbury Street EC1 **197** D3
Aylesford Street SW1 **200** A1
Aylward Street E1 **203** D4
Ayres Street SE1 **201** E4

Bacchus Walk N1 **197** F4
Bache's Street N1 **197** F4
Back Church Lane E1 **202** B4
Back Hill EC1 **197** D3
Bacon Grove SE1 **202** A1
Bainbridge Street WC1 **196** B2
Baker Street W1&NW1 **195** D3
Baker's Mews W1 **195** E2
Baker's Row EC1 **197** F3
Balcombe Street NW1 **195** D3
Balderton Street W1 **195** E1
Baldwin Street EC1 **197** F4
Baldwin's Gardens EC1 **196** C3
Balfe Street N1 **196** B4
Balfour Mews W1 **195** E1
Balfour Place W1 **195** E1
Balfour Street SE17 **201** F2
Balneil Gate SW1 **200** A1
Baltic Street EC1 **197** E3
Balvaird Place SW1 **200** B2
Bancroft Road E1 **200** C1
Bank End SE1 **201** E4
Bankside SE1 **197** E1
Banner Street EC1 **197** E3
Banyard Road SE16 **202** C1
Barge House Street SE1 **197** D1
Barkston Gardens SW5 **198** A2
Barleycorn Way E14 **203** F3
Barlow Place W1 **195** F1
Barlow Street SE17 **201** F2
Barnardo Street E1 **203** D3
Barnby Street NW1 **196** A4
Barnes Street E14 **203** E4
Barnham Street SE1 **202** A2
Baron's Place SE1 **201** D3
Barrett Street W1 **195** E2
Barrie Street W2 **194** B1
Barter Street WC1 **196** B2
Barth Lane EC2 **197** F2
Bartholomew Close EC1 **197** E2
Bartholomew Square EC1 **197** E3
Bartholomew Street SE1 **201** F2
Barton Street SW1 **200** B3
Basil Street SW3 **199** D3
Basinghall Avenue EC2 **197** E2
Basinghall Street EC2 **197** E2
Bastwick Street EC1 **197** E3
Bate Street E14 **203** F3

Bateman Street W1 **196** A2
Bath Place N1 **197** F4
Bath Street EC1 **197** E4
Bath Terrace SE1 **201** E3
Bathurst Mews W2 **194** C1
Bathurst Street W2 **194** C1
Battle Bridge Lane SE1 **201** F4
Batty Street E1 **202** B4
Bayley Street WC1 **196** A2
Baylis Road SE1 **200** C3
Bayswater Road W2 **194** A1
Baythorne Street E3 **174** F1
Beaconsfield Road SE17 **201** F1
Beak Street W1 **196** A1
Bear Gardens SE1 **197** E1
Bear Lane SE1 **201** D4
Beauchamp Place SW3 **199** D3
Beaufort Gardens SW3 **199** D3
Beaufort Street SW3 **198** B1
Beaumont Mews W1 **195** E2
Beaumont Place W1 **196** A3
Beaumont Street W1 **195** E3
Beccles Street E14 **203** F3
Beckway Street SE17 **201** F2
Bedford Avenue WC1 **196** B2
Bedford Court WC2 **196** B1
Bedford Gardens W8 **198** A4
Bedford Place WC1 **196** B3
Bedford Row WC1 **196** C3
Bedford Square WC1 **196** B2
Bedford Street WC2 **196** B1
Bedford Way WC1 **196** B3
Bedfordbury WC2 **196** B1
Beech Street EC2 **197** E3
Beeston Place SW1 **199** F3
Belgrave Mews North
SW1 **199** E3
Belgrave Mews South
SW1 **199** E3
Belgrave Mews West
SW1 **199** E3
Belgrave Place SW1 **199** E3
Belgrave Road SW1 **199** F2
Belgrave Square SW1 **199** E3
Belgrave Street E1 **203** E3
Belgrove Street WC1 **196** B4
Bell Lane E1 **202** A4
Bell Street NW1 **194** C3
Bell Yard WC2 **196** C2
Belvedere Buildings SE1 **201** E3
Belvedere Road SE1 **200** C4
Ben Jonson Road E1 **203** E4
Ben Smith Way SE16 **202** C1
Bendall Mews W1 **195** D3
Bentinck Street W1 **195** E2
Bere Street E1 **203** E3
Berkeley Gardens W8 **198** A4
Berkeley Mews W1 **16** E1
Berkeley Square W1 **195** F1
Berkeley Street W1 **195** F1
Bermondsey Street SE1 **202** A2
Bermondsey Wall East
SE16 **202** B1
Bermondsey Wall West
SE16 **202** B2

Bernard Street WC1 **196** B3
Berners Mews W1 **196** A2
Berners Street W1 **196** A2
Berry Street EC1 **197** E3
Berryfield Road SE17 **201** E1
Berwick Street W1 **196** A2
Bessborough Gardens
SW1 **200** B2
Bessborough Place SW1 **200** A1
Bessborough Street SW1 **200** A1
Betterton Street WC2 **196** B2
Betts Street E1 **202** C3
Bevenden Street N1 **197** F4
Bevin Close SE16 **203** E2
Bevin Way WC1 **196** C4
Bevington Street SE16 **202** B1
Bevis Marks EC3 **202** A4
Bewley Street E1 **202** C3
Bickenhall Street W1 **195** D3
Bidborough Street WC1 **196** B4
Bigland Street E1 **202** C3
Billiter Street EC3 **202** A3
Bina Gardens SW5 **198** B2
Bingham Place W1 **195** E3
Binney Street W1 **195** E1
Birchfield Street E14 **203** E3
Birchin Lane EC3 **197** F1
Bird Street W1 **195** E2
Birdcage Walk SW1 **200** A3
Birkenhead Street WC1 **196** B4
Bishop's Terrace SE11 **201** D2
Bishops Bridge Road W2 **194** B2
Bishopsgate EC2 **197** F2
Bittern Street SE1 **201** E3
Black Prince Road
SE1&SE11 **200** C2
Black Swan Yard SE1 **202** A2
Blackall Street EC2 **197** F3
Blackburne's Mews W1 **195** E1
Blackfriars Bridge
EC4&SE1 **197** D1
Blackfriars Lane EC4 **197** D1
Blackfriars Passage EC4 **197** D1
Blackfriars Road SE1 **201** D4
Blacklands Terrace SW3 **199** D2
Blackwood Street SE17 **201** F1
Blandford Square NW1 **195** D3
Blandford Street W1 **195** E2
Bletchley Street N1 **197** E4
Blithfield Street W8 **198** A3
Blomfield Street EC2 **197** F2
Blomfield Villas W2 **194** B2
Bloomfield Terrace SW1 **199** E2
Bloomsbury Square WC1 **196** B2
Bloomsbury Street WC1 **196** B2
Bloomsbury Way WC1 **196** B2
Blount Street E14 **203** E4
Blue Anchor Yard E1 **202** B3
Bolsover Street W1 **195** F3
Bolt Court EC4 **197** D2
Bolton Gardens Mews
SW10 **198** B1
Bolton Gardens SW5 **198** A2
Bolton Street W1 **199** F4
Bond Way SW8 **200** B1

Bonhill Street

Cramer Stre

Bonhill Street EC2 **197** F3
Bonnington Square SW8 **200** C1
Booker Close E14 **203** F4
Boot Street N1 **197** F4
Borough High Street SE1 **201** E3
Borough Road SE1 **201** E3
Borrett Close SE17 **201** E1
Boscobel Place SW1 **199** E2
Boscobel Street NW8 **194** C3
Boss Street SE1 **202** A2
Boston Place NW1 **194** D3
Boswell Street WC1 **196** B3
Botolph Lane EC3 **197** F1
Boulcott Street E1 **203** E3
Boundary Lane SE17 **201** E1
Boundary Road SE1 **201** D4
Bourdon Street W1 **195** F1
Bourlet Close W1 **195** F2
Bourne Street SW1 **199** E2
Bouverie Street EC4 **197** D1
Bow Lane EC4 **197** E1
Bow Street WC2 **196** B2
Bowden Street SE11 **201** D1
Bower Street E1 **203** D3
Bowley Street E14 **203** F3
Bowling Green Lane EC1 **197** D3
Bowling Green Street SE11 **200** C1
Bowling Green Walk N1 **197** F4
Boyd Street E1 **202** B3
Boyfield Street SE1 **201** D3
Boyson Road SE17 **201** E1
Brackley Street EC1 **197** E3
Brad Street SE1 **201** D4
Braganza Street SE17 **201** D1
Braham Street E1 **202** B3
Braidwood Street SE1 **202** A2
Bramerton Street SW3 **198** C1
Bramham Gardens SW5 **198** A2
Branch Road E14 **203** E3
Brandon Street SE17 **201** E2
Brangton Road SE11 **200** C1
Brass Tally Alley SE16 **203** E1
Bray Crescent SE16 **203** D2
Bray Place SW3 **199** D2
Bread Street EC4 **197** E1
Bream's Buildings EC **196** C2
Brechin Place SW7 **198** B2
Breezer's Hill E1 **202** C3
Bremner Road SW7 **198** B3
Brendon Street W1 **195** D2
Brenton Street E14 **203** E4
Bressenden Place SW1 **199** F3
Brettell Street SE17 **201** F1
Brewer Street W1 **196** A1
Brewhouse Lane E1 **202** C2
Brewhouse Walk SE16 **203** E2
Brick Street W1 **199** E4
Bride Lane EC4 **197** D2
Bridewell Place EC4 **197** D1
Bridford Mews W1 **195** F3
Bridge Place SW1 **199** F2
Bridge Street SW1 **200** B3
Bridge Yard SE1 **201** F4
Bridgeway Street NW1 **196** A2
Bridle Lane W1 **196** A1
Brightlingsea Place E14 **203** F3
Brill Place NW1 **196** A4
Briset Street EC1 **197** D3
Britannia Street WC1 **196** C4
Britannia Walk N1 **197** F4
Britten Street SW3 **198** C1
Britton Street EC1 **197** D3
Broad Court WC2 **196** B2
Broad Sanctuary SW1 **200** B3
Broad Walk W2 **199** E4
Broadbent Street W1 **195** F1
Broadley Street NW8 **194** C4
Broadley Terrace NW1 **195** D3
Broadstone Place W1 **195** E2
Broadwall SE1 **201** D4
Broadway SW1 **200** A3
Broadwick Street W1 **196** A1
Brockham Street SE1 **201** E3
Brodlove Lane E1 **203** D3
Bromley Street E1 **203** E4
Brompton Place SW3 **199** D3
Brompton Road SW3 **199** D3
Brompton Square SW3 **198** C3
Bronti Close SE17 **201** E1
Brook Drive SE11 **201** D2
Brook Mews North W2 **194** B1
Brook Street W1 **195** E1
Brook Street W2 **194** C1
Brook's Mews W1 **195** F1
Brooke Street EC1 **197** D2
Brooke's Court EC1 **196** C2
Brown Hart Gardens W1 **195** E1
Brown Street W1 **195** D2
Browning Street SE17 **201** E2
Brownlow Mews WC1 **196** C3
Brownlow Street WC1 **196** C2
Brune Street E1 **202** A4
Brunel Road SE16 **203** D1
Brunswick Gardens W8 **198** A4
Brunswick Mews W1 **195** D2
Brunswick Place N1 **197** F4
Brunswick Quay SE16 **203** E1
Brunswick Square WC1 **196** B3
Brunton Place E14 **203** E3
Brushfield Street E1 **202** A4
Bruton Lane W1 **195** F1
Bruton Place W1 **195** F1
Bruton Street W1 **195** F1
Bryan Road SE16 **203** F2
Bryanston Mews East W1 **195** D2
Bryanston Mews West W1 **195** D2
Bryanston Place W1 **195** D2
Bryanston Square W1 **195** D2
Bryanston Street W1 **195** D2
Buck Hill Walk W2 **194** C1
Buck Street WC2 **196** B1
Buckingham Gate SW1 **199** F3
Buckingham Palace Road SW1 **199** F2
Buckingham Place SW1 **199** F3
Buckland Street N1 **197** F4
Buckle Street E1 **202** B4
Bucklersbury EC4 **197** E2
Bucknall Street WC2 **196** B2
Buckters Rents SE16 **203** E2
Budge's Walk W2 **194** B4
Bullwharf Lane EC4 **197** E1
Bulstrode Street W1 **195** E2
Bunhill Row EC1 **197** F3
Bunhouse Place SW1 **199** E2
Burbage Close SE1 **201** F3
Burdett Street SE1 **201** D3
Burgess Street E14 **203** F4
Burleigh Street WC2 **196** B1
Burlington Arcade W1 **195** F1
Burlington Gardens W1 **195** F1
Burne Street NW1 **194** C3
Burnsall Street SW3 **199** D1
Burr Cose E1 **202** B2
Burrell Street SE1 **201** D4
Burrows Mews SE1 **201** D4
Burslem Street E1 **202** C3
Burton Grove SE17 **201** F1
Burton Street WC1 **196** B4
Burwell Close E1 **202** C3
Burwood Place W2 **195** D2
Bury Court EC3 **202** A4
Bury Place WC1 **196** B2
Bury Street EC3 **202** A3
Bury Street SW1 **200** A4
Bury Walk SW3 **198** C2
Bush Lane EC4 **197** E1
Butcher Row E1 **203** E3
Bute Street SW7 **198** C1
Buttesland Street N1 **197** F4
Byng Place WC1 **196** A3
Byward Street EC3 **202** A3
Bywater Place SE16 **203** E2
Bywater Street SW3 **199** D2

Cabbell Street NW1 **194** C2
Cable Street E1 **202** B3
Cadiz Street SE17 **201** E1
Cadogan Gardens SW3 **199** D2
Cadogan Gate SW1 **199** D2
Cadogan Lane SW1 **199** E3
Cadogan Place SW1 **199** E2
Cadogan Square SW1 **199** D2
Cadogan Street SW3 **199** D2
Caledonia Street N1 **196** B4
Cale Street SW3 **198** C2
Caledonian Road N1&N7 **196** B4
Callingham Close E14 **203** F4
Callow Street SW3 **198** B1
Calthorpe Street WC1 **196** C3
Camberwell Road SE5 **201** E1
Cambridge Circus WC2 **196** B1
Cambridge Gate NW1 **195** F3
Cambridge Place W8 **198** B3
Cambridge Square W2 **194** C2
Cambridge Street SW1 **199** F2
Camdenhurst Street E14 **203** E4
Camera Place SW10 **198** B1
Cameron Place E1 **202** C4
Camomile Street EC3 **202** A4
Campden Green W8 **198** A4
Campden Hill Road W8 **198** A3
Camperdown Street E1 **202** B3
Canada Street SE16 **203** E1
Canal Street SE5 **201** F1
Canning Passage W8 **198** B3
Canning Place W8 **198** B3
Cannon Beck Road SE16 **203** D2
Cannon Drive E14 **203** F3
Cannon Row SW1 **200** B3
Cannon Street EC4 **197** E2
Cannon Street Road E1 **202** C3
Canterbury Place SE17 **201** E2
Canvey Street SE1 **201** E4
Cape Yard E1 **202** B3
Capland Street NW8 **194** C3
Capper Street WC1 **196** A3
Capstan Way SE16 **203** E2
Carbis Road E14 **203** F4
Carburton Street W1 **195** F3
Cardigan Street SE11 **200** C1
Cardington Street NW1 **196** A4
Carey Lane EC2 **197** E2
Carey Street WC2 **196** C2
Carlisle Avenue EC3 **202** A3
Carlisle Lane SE1 **200** C3
Carlisle Place SW1 **199** F2
Carlisle Street W1 **196** A2
Carlos Place W1 **195** E1
Carlton Gardens SW1 **200** A4
Carlton House Terrace SW17 **200** A4
Carlyle Square SW3 **198** C1
Carmelite Street EC4 **197** D1
Carnaby Street W1 **196** A1
Caroline Place Mews W2 **194** A1
Caroline Street E1 **203** E3
Caroline Terrace SW1 **199** E2
Carpenter Street W1 **195** E1
Carr Street E14 **203** E4
Carter Lane EC4 **197** E2
Carter Place SE17 **201** E1
Carter Street SE17 **201** E1
Caroline Street E1 **203** E3
Caroline Terrace SW1 **199** E2
Carpenter Street W1 **195** E1
Carr Street E14 **203** E4
Carter Lane EC4 **197** E2
Carter Place SE17 **201** E1
Carter Street SE17 **201** E1
Carteret Street SW1 **200** A3
Carthusian Street EC1 **197** E3
Carting Lane WC2 **196** C1
Cartwright Gardens WC1 **196** B4
Cartwright Street E1 **202** B3
Casson Street E1 **202** B4
Castle Baynard Street EC4 **197** E1
Castle Lane SW1 **200** A3
Castle Yard SE1 **201** D4
Catesby Street SE17 **201** F2
Cathay Street SE16 **202** C1
Cathcart Road SW10 **198** B1
Cathedral Piazza SW1 **199** F3
Catherine Place SW1 **199** F3
Catherine Street WC2 **196** C1
Catherine Wheel Alley E1 **202** A4
Catton Street WC1 **196** C2
Causton Street SW1 **200** B2
Cavaye Place SW10 **198** B1
Cavell Street E1 **202** C4
Cavendish Avenue NW8 **194** C4
Cavendish Close NW8 **194** C4
Cavendish Place W1 **195** F2
Cavendish Square W1 **195** F2
Caversham Street SW3 **199** D1
Caxton Street SW1 **200** A3
Cayton Street EC1 **197** E4
Centaur Street SE1 **200** C3
Central Street EC1 **197** E4
Chadbourn Street E14 **24** D1
Chadwell Street EC1 **197** D4
Chadwick Street SW1 **200** A3
Chagford Street NW1 **195** D3
Chalton Street NW1 **196** A4
Chamber Street E1 **202** B3
Chambers Street SE16 **202** B1
Chancel Street SE1 **201** D4
Chancery Lane WC2 **196** C2
Chandler Street E1 **202** C2
Chandos Place WC2 **196** B1
Chandos Street W1 **195** F2
Chapel Place W1 **195** F2
Chapel Side W2 **194** A1
Chapel Street NW1 **194** C2
Chapel Street SW1 **199** E3
Chapman Street E1 **202** C3
Chapter Road SE17 **201** E1
Chapter Street SW1 **200** A2
Chapter Terrace SE17 **201** D1
Chargrove Close SE16 **203** D2
Charing Cross Road WC2 **196** B2
Charles II Street SW1 **200** A4
Charles Square N1 **197** F4
Charles Street W1 **199** F4
Charleston Street SE17 **201** E2
Charlotte Road EC2 **197** F4
Charlotte Street W1 **196** A3
Charlwood Street SW1 **200** A1
Chart Street N1 **197** F4
Charterhouse Square EC1 **197** E2
Charterhouse Street EC1 **197** D2
Chaseley Street E14 **203** E4
Chatham Street SE17 **201** F2
Cheapside EC4 **197** E2
Chelsea Bridge Road SW1 **199** E1
Chelsea Bridge SW1 & SW8 **199** E1
Chelsea Embankment SW3 **199** D1
Chelsea Manor Gardens SW3 **199** D1
Chelsea Manor Street SW3 **199** D1
Chelsea Park Gardens SW3 **198** C1
Chelsea Square SW3 **198** C1
Cheltenham Terrace SW3 **199** D2
Chenies Mews WC1 **196** A3
Chenies Street WC1 **196** E3
Cheniston Gardens W8 **198** A3
Chequer Street EC1 **197** E3
Cherbury Street N1 **197** F4
Cherry Garden Street SE16 **202** C1
Chesham Place SW1 **199** E3
Chesham Street SW1 **199** E3
Chester Close South NW1 **195** F4
Chester Gate NW1 **195** F4
Chester Mews SW1 **199** E3
Chester Place NW1 **195** F4
Chester Row SW1 **199** E2
Chester Square SW1 **199** E2
Chester Street SW1 **199** E3
Chester Terrace NW1 **195** F4
Chester Way SE11 **201** D2
Chesterfield Gardens W1 **199** E4
Chesterfield Hill W1 **195** E1
Chesterfield Street W1 **199** E4
Cheval Place SW7 **199** D3
Cheyne Gardens SW3 **198** D1
Cheyne Walk SW3 & SW10 **198** C1
Chicheley Street SE1 **200** C4
Chichester Street SW1 **200** A1
Chicksand Street E1 **202** B4
Child's Place SW5 **198** A2
Child's Street SW5 **198** A2
Chiltern Street W1 **195** E3
Chilworth Mews W2 **194** B2
Chilworth Street W2 **194** B2
Chiswell Street EC1 **197** E3
Chitty Street W1 **196** A3
Christchurch Street SW3 **199** D1
Christian Street E1 **202** C3
Christopher Street EC2 **197** F3
Chudleigh Street E1 **203** E4
Chumleigh Street SE5 **201** F1
Church Street NW8 **194** C3
Church Yard Row SE11 **201** D2
Churchill Gardens Road SW1 **199** F1
Churchway NW1 **196** A4
Churton Street SW1 **200** A2
Cinnamon Street E1 **202** C2
City Garden Row N1 **197** E4
City Road EC1 **197** F3
Clabon Mews SW1 **199** D2
Clack Street SE16 **203** D1
Clanricarde Gardens W2 **194** A1
Clare Market WC2 **196** C2
Claremont Close N1 **197** D4
Claremont Square N1 **197** D4
Clarence Gardens NW1 **195** F4
Clarendon Close W2 **194** C1
Clarendon Place W2 **194** C1
Clarendon Street SW1 **199** F1
Clareville Grove SW7 **198** B2
Clareville Street SW7 **198** B2
Clarges Mews W1 **199** F4
Clarges Street W1 **199** F4
Clark Street E1 **202** C4
Clark's Orchard SE16 **202** C1
Clave Street E1 **202** C2
Claverton Street SW1 **200** A1
Clay Street W1 **195** D2
Clayton Street SE11 **200** C1
Clearbrook Way E1 **203** D4
Cleaver Square SE11 **201** D1
Cleaver Street SE11 **201** D1
Clegg Street E1 **202** C2
Clemence Street E14 **203** F4
Clement's Inn WC2 **196** C2
Clement's Road SE16 **202** C1
Clements Lane EC4 **197** F1
Clenston Mews W1 **195** D2
Clere Street EC2 **197** F3
Clerkenwell Close EC1 **197** D3
Clerkenwell Green EC1 **197** D3
Clerkenwell Road EC1 **196** C3
Cleveland Gardens W2 **194** B2
Cleveland Mews W1 **195** F3
Cleveland Row SW1 **200** A4
Cleveland Square W2 **194** B2
Cleveland Street W1 **195** F3
Cleveland Terrace W2 **194** B2
Clifford Street W1 **195** F1
Clifton Place W2 **194** C1
Clifton Street EC2 **197** F3
Clink Street SE1 **201** E4
Clipstone Mews W1 **195** F3
Clipstone Street W1 **195** F3
Cliveden Place SW1 **199**
Cloak Lane EC4 **197**
Cloth Fair EC1 **197**
Cloth Street EC1 **197**
Cluny Place SE1 **201**
Cobb Street E1 **202**
Cobourg Street NW1 **196**
Cock Lane EC1 **197**
Cockpit Yard WC1 **196**
Cockspur Street SW1 **200**
Codling Close E1 **202**
Coin Street SE1 **201**
Coke Street E1 **202**
Colbeck Mews SW7 **198**
Cole Street SE1 **201**
Colebrooke Row N1 **197**
Coleherne Mews SW10 **200**
Coleherne Road SW10 **198**
Coleman Street EC2 **197**
Coley Street WC1 **196**
College Street EC4 **197**
Collett Road SE16 **202**
Collier Street N1 **196**
Collingham Gardens SW5 **198**
Collingham Place SW4 **198**
Collingham Road SW5 **198**
Collinson Street SE1 **201**
Colnbrook Street SE1 **201**
Colombo Street SE1 **201**
Colonnade WC1 **196**
Colworth Grove SE17 **201**
Commercial Road E1 & E14 **202**
Commercial Street E1 **202**
Compton Passage EC1 **197**
Compton Place WC1 **196**
Compton Street EC1 **197**
Comus Place SE17 **201**
Concert Hall Approach SE1 **200**
Conduit Mews W2 **194**
Conduit Place W2 **194**
Conduit Street W1 **195**
Congreve Street SE17 **201**
Connaught Place W2 **195**
Connaught Square W2 **195**
Connaught Street W2 **194**
Cons Street SE1 **201**
Constitution Hill SW1 **199**
Content Street SE17 **201**
Conway Street W1 **195**
Cook's Road SE17 **201**
Cookham Crescent SE16 **203**
Coombs Street N1 **197**
Cooper Close SE1 **201**
Cooper's Row EC3 **202**
Cope Place W8 **198**
Copenhagen Place E14 **203**
Copley Close SE17 **201**
Copperfield Street SE1 **201**
Copthall Avenue EC2 **197**
Coptic Street WC1 **196**
Coral Street SE1 **201**
Coram Street WC1 **196**
Cork Street W1 **195**
Cornhill EC3 **197**
Cornwall Gardens SW7 **198**
Cornwall Gardens Walk SW7 **198**
Cornwall Mews South SW7 **198**
Cornwall Mews West SW7 **198**
Cornwall Road SE1 **200**
Cornwall Street E1 **202**
Cornwall Terrace NW1 **195**
Cornwood Drive E1 **203**
Coronet Street N1 **197**
Corporation Row EC1 **197**
Corsham Street N1 **197**
Cosser Street SE1 **200**
Cosway Street NW1 **195**
Cotham Street SE17 **201**
Cottesmore Gardens W8 **198**
Cottingham Close SE11 **201**
Cottington Street SE11 **201**
Cottons Lane SE1 **201**
Counter Street SE1 **201**
County Street SE1 **201**
Court Street E1 **202**
Courtenay Square SE11 **200**
Courtenay Street SE11 **200**
Courtfield Gardens SW5 **198**
Courtfield Road SW7 **198**
Cousin Lane EC4 **197**
Coventry Street W1 **196**
Coverley Close E1 **202**
Cowcross Street EC1 **197**
Cowley Street SW1 **200**
Cowper Street EC2 **197**
Coxon Place SE1 **202**
Crace Street NW1 **196**
Crail Row SE17 **201**
Cramer Street W1 **195**

Crampton Street Gloucester Terrace

Crampton Street SE17 201 C2
Cranbourn Street WC2 196 B1
Cranford Street E1 203 E3
Cranley Gardens SW7 198 B2
Cranley Mews SW7 198 B2
Cranley Place SW7 198 C2
Cranmer Court SW3 199 D2
Cranwood Street EC1 197 F4
Craven Hill Gardens W2 194 B1
Craven Hill Mews W2 194 B1
Craven Hill W2 194 B1
Craven Road W2 194 B1
Craven Street WC2 196 B1
Craven Terrace W2 194 B1
Crawford Passage EC1 197 D3
Crawford Place W1 195 D2
Crawford Street W1 195 D2
Creechurch Lane EC3 202 A3
Creechurch Place EC3 202 A3
Creed Lane EC4 197 E2
Crescent Place SW3 199 D2
Crescent Row EC1 197 E3
Cresswell Place SW10 198 B1
Cressy Place E1 203 D4
Crestfield Street WC1 196 B4
Crimscott Street SE1 202 A1
Crispin Street E1 202 A4
Crofts StreetE1 202 B3
Cromer Street WC1 196 B3
Cromwell Mews SW7 198 C2
Cromwell Place SW7 198 C2
Cromwell Road SW7 & SW5 198 A1
Crondall Street N1 197 F4
Crosby Row SE1 201 F3
Cross Lane EC3 202 A3
Crosslet Street SE17 201 F2
Crosswall EC3 202 A3
Crowder Street E1 202 C3
Crown Court WC2 196 B2
Crown Office Row EC4 197 D1
Crucifix Lane SE1 202 A2
Cruikshank Street WC1 196 C4
Crutched Friars EC3 202 A3
Cuba Street E14 203 F2
Cubitt Street WC1 196 C4
Culford Gardens SW3 199 D2
Culling Road SE16 203 D1
Cullum Street EC3 202 A3
Culross Street W1 195 E1
Culworth Street NW8 194 C4
Cumberland Gate W1 & W2 195 D1
Cumberland Market NW1 195 F4
Cumberland Street SW1 199 F1
Cumberland Terrace NW1 195 E4
Cumming Street N1 196 C4
Cundy Street SW1 199 E2
Cureton Street SW1 200 B2
Curlew Street SE1 202 B2
Cursitor Street EC4 196 C2
Curzon Gate W1 199 E4
Curzon Place W1 199 E4
Curzon Street W1 199 E4
Cuthbert Street W2 194 C3
Cutler Street E1 202 A4
Cynthia Street N1 196 C4
Cyrus Street EC1 197 D3

D'arblay Street W1 196 A2
D'oyley Street SW1 199 E2
Dacre Street SW1 200 A3
Dalgleish Street E14 203 E4
Dallington Street EC1 197 D3
Damien Street E1 202 C4
Dane Street WC1 196 C2
Dante Road SE11 201 D2
Daplyn Street E1 202 B4
Dartford Street SE17 201 E1
Dartmouth Street SW1 200 A3
Darwin Street SE17 201 F2
Date Street SE17 201 E1
Davenant Street E1 202 B4
Daventry Street NW1 194 C3
Davidge Street SE1 201 D3
Davies Mews W1 195 E1
Davies Street W1 195 E1
Dawes Street SE17 201 F2
De Laune Street SE17 201 D1
De Vere Gardens W8 198 B3
Deacon Way SE17 201 E2
Deal Porters Way SE16 203 D1
Deal Street E1 202 B4
Dean Bradley Street SW1 200 B2
Dean Close SE16 203 E2
Dean Farrar Street SW1 200 A3
Dean Ryle Street SW1 200 B2
Dean Street W1 196 A2
Dean Trench Street SW1 200 B3
Dean's Buildings SE17 201 F2
Dean's Mews W1 195 F2
Deancross Street E1 202 C3
Deanery Street W1 199 E4
Decima Street SE1 201 F3
Deck Close SE16 203 E2
Dellow Street E1 202 C3
Delverton Road SE17 201 E1
Denbigh Street SW1 200 A2
Denman Street W1 196 A1
Denmark Street WC2 196 B2
Denny Crescent SE11 201 D2
Denny Street SE11 201 D2
Denyer Street SW3 199 D2
Derby Gate SW1 200 B3
Derby Street W1 199 E4
Dering Street W1 195 F2
Deverell Street SE1 201 F3
Devonport Street E1 203 D3
Devonshire Close W1 195 F3
Devonshire Mews South W1 195 E3
Devonshire Mews West W1 195 E3
Devonshire Place Mews W1 195 E3
Devonshire Place W1 195 E3
Devonshire Row EC2 202 A4
Devonshire Square EC2 202 A4
Devonshire Street W1 195 E3
Devonshire Terrace W2 194 B1
Diana Place NW1 195 F3
Dickens Square SE1 201 E3
Dilke Street SW3 199 D1
Dingley Place EC1 197 E4
Dingley Road EC1 197 E4
Disney Place SE1 201 E3
Distaff Lane EC4 197 E1
Distin Street SE11 200 C2
Dock Hill Avenue SE16 203 E2
Dock Street E1 202 B3
Dockhead SE1 202 B1
Dockley Road SE16 202 B1
Dod Street E14 203 F4
Doddington Grove SE17 201 D1
Doddington Place SE17 201 D1
Dodson Street SE1 201 D3
Dolben Street SE1 201 D4
Dolland Street SE11 200 C1
Dolphin Close SE16 203 D2
Dombey Street WC1 196 C3
Dominion Street EC2 197 F2
Donegal Street N1 196 C4
Donne Place SW3 199 D2
Doon Street SE1 200 C4
Dora Street E14 203 F4
Doric Way NW1 196 A4
Dorset Close NW1 195 D3
Dorset Mews SW1 199 E3
Dorset Rise EC4 197 D1
Dorset Square NW1 195 D3
Dorset Street W1 195 D2
Doughty Mews WC1 196 C3
Doughty Street WC1 196 C3
Douglas Street SW1 200 A2
Douro Place W8 198 B3
Dove Mews SW5 198 B2
Dove Walk SW1 199 E2
Dovehouse Street SW3 198 C1
Dover Street W1 195 F1
Dowgate Hill EC4 197 F1
Down Street W1 199 E4
Downing Street SW1 200 B4
Downton Road SE16 203 E2
Draco Street SE17 201 E1
Drake Street WC1 196 C2
Draycott Avenue SW3 199 D2
Draycott Place SW3 199 D2
Draycott Terrace SW3 199 D2
Drayson Mews W8 198 A3
Drayton Gardens SW10 198 B1
Druid Street SE1 202 A2
Drum Street E1 202 B4
Drummond Crescent NW1 196 A4
Drummond Gate SW1 200 A1
Drummond Road SE16 202 C1
Drummond Street NW1 195 F3
Drury Lane WC2 196 B2
Dryden Court SE11 201 D2
Duchess Mews W1 195 F2
Duchess Street W1 195 F2
Duchy Street SE1 201 D4
Dudley Street W2 194 B2
Dudmaston Mews SW3 198 C2
Dufferin Street EC1 197 E3
Dufour's Place W1 196 A4
Duke Of Wellington Place SW1 199 E3
Duke Of York Street SW1 196 A1
Duke Street Hill SE1 201 F4
Duke Street W1 195 E2
Duke's Lane W8 198 A4
Duke's Place EC3 202 A4
Duke's Road WC1 196 B4
Duncannon Street WC2 196 B1
Dundee Street E1 202 C2
Dunelm Street D1 203 D4
Dunlop Place SE16 202 B1
Dunraven Street W1 195 E1
Dunstable Mews W1 195 E3
Dunster Court EC3 202 A3
Dunsterville Way SE1 201 F3
Duplex Ride SW1 199 E3
Dupont Street E14 203 E4
Durham House Street WC2 196 B1
Durham Row E1 203 E4
Durham Street SE11 200 C1
Durward Street E1 202 C4
Dyott Street WC1 196 B2
Dysart Street EC2 197 F3

Eagle Court EC1 197 D3
Eagle Street WC2 196 C2
Eardley Crescent SW5 198 A1
Earl Street EC2 197 F3
Earl's Court Gardens SW5 198 A2
Earl's Court Square SW5 198 A1
Earlham Street WC2 196 B2
Earls Court Road W8 198 A2
Earnshaw Street WC2 196 B2
East Arbour Street E1 203 D4
East Harding Street EC4 197 D2
East Lane SE16 202 B1
East Road N1 197 F4
East Smithfield E1 202 B3
East Street SE17 201 E1
East Tenter Street E1 202 B3
Eastbourne Mews W2 194 B2
Eastbourne Terrace W2 194 B2
Eastcastle Street W1 196 A2
Eastcheap EC3 197 F1
Easton Street WC1 196 C3
Eaton Gate SW1 199 E2
Eaton Mews North SW1 199 E2
Eaton Mews South SW1 199 E2
Eaton Place SW1 199 E2
Eaton Square SW1 199 E2
Eaton Terrace SW1 199 E2
Ebbisham Drive SW8 200 C1
Ebenezer Street N1 197 F4
Ebury Bridge Road SW1 199 E1
Ebury Bridge SW1 199 E2
Ebury Mews East SW1 199 E2
Ebury Mews SW1 199 E2
Ebury Square SW1 199 E2
Ebury Street SW1 199 E2
Eccleston Bridge SW1 199 F2
Eccleston Mews SW1 199 E3
Eccleston Place SW1 199 E2
Eccleston Square Mews SW1 199 F2
Eccleston Square SW1 199 F2
Eccleston Street SW1 199 E2
Edge Street W8 198 A4
Edgware Road W2 194 C3
Edward Mews W1 195 E2
Edward Street NW1 195 F4
Egerton Crescent SW3 199 D2
Egerton Gardens SW3 198 C2
Egerton Terrace SW3 199 D3
Elba Place SE17 201 E2
Eldon Road W8 198 B3
Eldon Street EC2 197 F2
Elephant And Castle SE1 201 E2
Elephant Lane SE16 202 C2
Elephant Road SE17 201 E2
Elf Row E1 203 D3
Elgar Street SE16 203 F1
Elia Street N1 197 D4
Elim Street SE1 201 F3
Elizabeth Bridge SW1 199 F2
Elizabeth Street SW1 199 E2
Ellen Street E1 202 B3
Elliott Road SE9 201 D2
Ellis Street SW1 199 E2
Elm Park Gardens SW10 198 C1
Elm Park Lane SW3 198 B1
Elm Park Road SW3 198 B1
Elm Place SW7 198 C1
Elm Street WC1 196 C3
Elm Tree Close NW8 194 C4
Elm Tree Road NW8 194 C4
Elmos Road SE16 203 E1
Elms Mews W2 194 C1
Elsa Street E1 203 E4
Elsted Street SE17 201 F2
Elvaston Mews SW7 198 B3
Elvaston Place SW7 198 B3
Elverton Street SW1 200 A2
Ely Place EC1 197 D2
Elystan Place SW3 199 D2
Elystan Street SW3 198 C2
Emba Street SE16 202 C1
Embankment Gardens SW3 199 D1
Embankment Place WC2 200 B4
Emerald Street WC1 196 C3
Emerson Street SE1 201 E4
Emery Hill Street SW1 200 A2
Emery Street SE1 201 D3
Emmett Street E14 203 F3
Emperor's Gate SW7 198 B2
Empress Place SW6 198 A1
Empress Street SE17 201 E1
Endell Street WC2 196 B2
Endsleigh Gardens WC1 196 A3
Endsleigh Place WC1 196 A3
Endsleigh Street WC1 196 A3
Enford Street W1 195 D3
Enid Street SE16 202 B1
Ennismore Garden Mews SW7 198 C3
Ennismore Gardens SW7 198 C3
Ennismore Mews SW7 198 C3
Ennismore Street SW7 198 C3
Ensign Street E1 202 B3
Ensor Mews SW7 198 B1
Epworth Street EC2 197 F3
Erasmus Street SW1 200 B2
Errol Street EC1 197 E3
Essex Street WC2 196 C1
Esterbrooke Street SW1 200 A2
Ethel Street SE17 201 E2
Europa Place EC1 197 E4
Euston Road NW1 195 F3
Euston Square NW1 196 A4
Euston Street NW1 196 A4
Evelyn Gardens SW7 200 B1
Evelyn Walk N1 197 F4
Eversholt Street NW1 196 A4
Ewer Street SE1 201 E4
Exeter Street WC2 196 B1
Exhibition Road SW7 198 C3
Exmouth Market EC1 197 D3
Exmouth Street E1 203 D4
Exon Street SE17 201 F2
Exton Street SE1 200 C4
Eyre Street Hill EC1 197 D3

Fair Street SE1 202 A2
Fairclough Street E1 202 B3
Falcon Close SE1 201 E4
Falmouth Road SE1 201 E3
Fann Street EC1 197 E3
Fanshaw Street N1 197 F4
Farm Street W1 195 E1
Farmer Street W8 198 A4
Farncombe Street SE16 202 C1
Farnell Mews SW5 198 A1
Farnham Place SE1 201 E4
Farnham Royal SE11 200 C1
Farrance Street E14 203 F3
Farringdon Lane EC1 197 D3
Farringdon Road EC1 196 C3
Farringdon Street EC4 197 D2
Farrins Rents SE16 203 E2
Farrow Place SE16 203 E1
Fashion Street E1 202 B4
Faunce Street SE17 201 D1
Fawcett Street SW10 198 B1
Featherstone Street EC1 197 F3
Fen Court EC3 202 A3
Fenchurch Avenue EC3 202 A3
Fenchurch Street EC3 197 F1
Fendall Street SE1 202 A1
Fernsbury Street WC1 196 C4
Fetter Lane EC4 197 D2
Field Street WC1 196 C4
Fieldgate Street E1 202 B4
Fielding Street SE17 201 E1
Finborough Road SW10 198 A1
Finch Lane EC3 197 F2
Finland Street SE16 203 E1
Finsbury Avenue EC2 197 F2
Finsbury Circus EC2 197 F2
Finsbury Pavement EC2 197 F3
Finsbury Square EC2 197 F3
Finsbury Street EC2 197 F3
First Street SW3 199 D2
Firtree Close SE16 203 E2
Fish Street Hill EC3 197 F1
Fisher Street WC1 196 C2
Fishermans Drive SE16 203 E2
Fisherton Street NW8 194 C3
Fitzalan Street SE11 200 C2
Fitzhardinge Street W1 195 E2
Fitzmaurice Place W1 195 F1
Fitzroy Square W1 195 F3
Fitzroy Street WC1 195 F3
Flamborough Street E14 203 E3
Flank Street E1 202 B3
Flaxman Terrace WC1 196 B4
Fleet Lane EC4 197 D2
Fleet Square WC1 196 C4
Fleet Street EC4 197 D2
Fleming Road SE17 201 D1
Flint Street SE17 201 F2
Flitcroft Street WC2 196 B2
Flood Street SW3 199 D1
Flood Walk SW3 199 D1
Floral Street WC2 196 B1
Foley Street W1 195 F2
Forbes Street E1 202 B3
Ford Square E1 202 C4
Fordham Street E1 202 C4
Fore Street Avenue EC2 197 E2
Fore Street EC2 197 E2
Forset Street W1 195 D2
Forsyth Gardens SE17 201 D1
Fortune Street EC1 197 E3
Foster Lane EC2 197 E2
Foubert's Place W1 195 F1
Foulis Terrace SW7 198 C2
Foundry Close SE16 203 E2
Fournier Street E1 202 B4
Fowey Close E1 202 C2
Frampton Street NW8 194 C3
Francis Street SW1 200 A2
Franklin's Row SW3 199 D1
Frazier Street SE1 200 C3
Frean Street SE16 202 B1
Frederick Close W2 195 D1
Frederick Street WC1 196 C4
Fremantle Street SE17 201 F2
Friday Street EC4 197 E1
Friend Street EC1 197 D4
Frith Street W1 196 A2
Frying Pan Alley E1 202 A4
Fulbourne Street E1 202 C4
Fulford Street SE16 202 C1
Fulham Road SW3,SW6 & SW10 198 C1
Furnival Street EC4 197 D2
Fynes Street SW1 200 A2

Gainsford Street SE1 202 A2
Galen Place WC1 196 B2
Galway Street EC1 197 E4
Gambia Street SE1 201 D4
Ganton Street W1 196 A1
Gard Street EC1 197 E4
Garden Row SE1 201 D3
Garford Street E14 203 F3
Garlick Hill EC4 197 F1
Garnault Mews EC1 197 D4
Garnet Street E1 202 C3
Garrett Street EC1 197 E3
Garrick Street WC2 196 B1
Gasholder Place SE11 200 C1
Gaspar Close SW5 198 B2
Gaspar Mews SW5 198 B2
Gate Street WC2 196 C2
Gateway SE17 201 E1
Gatliff Road SW1 199 E1
Gaunt Street SE1 201 E3
Gayfere Street SW1 200 B3
Gaywood Street SE1 201 D3
Gaza Street SE17 201 D1
Gedling Place SE1 202 B1
Gee Street EC1 197 E3
Gees Court W1 195 E2
George Mews NW1 196 A4
George Row SE16 202 B1
George Street W1 195 D2
George Yard EC3 197 F1
George Yard W1 195 E1
Gerald Road SW1 199 E2
Geraldine Street SE11 201 D3
Gerrard Street W1 196 A1
Gerridge Street SE1 201 D3
Gibson Road SE11 201 D3
Gilbert Place WC1 196 B2
Gilbert Road SE11 201 D2
Gilbert Street W1 195 E1
Gildea Street W1 195 F2
Gill Street E14 203 F3
Gillingham Street SW1 199 F2
Gillison Walk SE16 202 C1
Gilston Road SW10 198 B1
Giltspur Street EC1 197 D2
Gladstone Street SE1 201 D3
Glamis Place E1 203 D3
Glamis Road E1 203 D3
Glasgow Terrace SW1 199 F1
Glasshill Street SE1 201 E3
Glasshouse Fields E1 203 D3
Glasshouse Street W1 196 A1
Glasshouse Walk SE11 200 B1
Glebe Place SW3 198 C1
Gledhow Gardens SW5 198 B2
Glendower Place SW7 198 C2
Glentworth Street NW1 195 D3
Globe Pond Road SE16 203 E2
Globe Street SE1 201 E3
Gloucester Court EC3 202 A3
Gloucester Mews W2 194 B2
Gloucester Mews West W2 194 B2
Gloucester Place Mews W1 195 D2
Gloucester Place NW1 & W1 195 D3
Gloucester Road SW7 198 B3
Gloucester Square W2 194 C2
Gloucester Street SW1 199 F1
Gloucester Terrace W2 194 B2

208

Ormond Yard
Silk Street

Ormond Yard SW1 196 A1
Ormonde Gate SW3 199 D1
Orsett Street SE11 200 C2
Orsett Terrace W2 194 B2
Osbert Street SW1 200 A2
Osborne Street E1 202 B4
Osnaburgh Street NW1 195 F3
Ossington Street W2 194 A1
Ossulston Street NW1 196 A4
Osten Mews SW7 198 B2
Oswin Street SE11 201 D2
Othello Close SE1 201 D2
Otto Street SE17 201 D1
Oval Way SE11 200 C1
Ovington Gardens SW3 199 D3
Ovington Square SW3 199 D3
Ovington Street SW3 199 D2
Owen Street EC1 197 D4
Oxford Square W2 194 C2
Oxford Street W1 195 E1

Paddington Green W2 194 C3
Paddington Street W1 195 E3
Page Street SW1 200 B2
Paget Street EC1 197 D4
Pakenham Street WC1 196 C3
Palace Avenue W8 198 A4
Palace Court W2 194 A1
Palace Gardens Mews W8 198 A4
Palace Gardens Terrace W8 198 A4
Palace Gate W8 198 B3
Palace Street SW1 199 F3
Pall Mall East SW1 196 B1
Pall Mall SW1 200 A4
Palmer Street SW1 200 A3
Pancras Lane EC4 197 E2
Panton Street SW1 196 A1
Paradise Street SE16 202 C1
Paradise Walk SW3 199 D1
Pardoner Street SE1 201 F3
Parfetts Street E1 202 C4
Paris Garden SE1 201 D4
Park Approach SE16 202 C1
Park Crescent Mews East W1 195 F3
Park Crescent Mews West W1 195 E3
Park Crescent W1 195 E3
Park Lane W1 195 E1
Park Place SW1 199 F4
Park Road NW1-NW8 195 D4
Park Square East NW1 195 F3
Park Square West NW1 195 E3
Park Street SE1 201 D4
Park Street W1 196 B2
Park Walk SW10 198 B1
Park West Place W2 195 D2
Parker Street WC2 196 B2
Parkers Row SE1 202 B1
Parliament Square SW1 200 B3
Parliament Street SW1 200 B4
Parnham Street E14 203 E4
Parry Street SW8 200 B1
Passmore Street SW1 199 E2
Pastor Street SE11 201 D2
Pater Street W8 198 A3
Paternoster Row EC4 197 E2
Paternoster Square EC4 197 E2
Paul Street EC2 197 F3
Paultons Square SW3 198 C1
Paveley Street NW8 194 C4
Pavilion Road SW1 199 D2
Pavilion Street SW1 199 D3
Peabody Avenue SW1 199 F1
Peacock Street SE17 201 E2
Pear Tree Court EC1 197 D3
Pear Tree Street EC1 197 E3
Pearl Street E1 202 C2
Pearman Street SE1 201 D3
Peartree Lane E1 203 D3
Peerless Street EC1 197 E4
Pelham Crescent SW7 198 C2
Pelham Place SW7 198 C2
Pelham Street SW7 198 C2
Pelier Street SE17 201 E1
Pelling Street E14 203 F4
Pemberton Row EC4 197 D2
Pembridge Gardens W2 194 A1
Pembridge Road W11 194 A1
Pembridge Square W2 194 A1
Penang Street E1 202 C2
Penfold Place NW1 194 C3
Penfold Street NW1 & NW8 194 C3
Pennant Mews W8 198 A2
Pennington Street E1 202 C3
Penrose Grove SE17 201 E1
Penrose Street SE17 201 E1
Penryn Street NW1 198 A2
Penton Place SE17 201 D2
Penton Rise WC1 196 C4
Pentonville Road N1 196 C4

Pepper Street SE1 201 E4
Pepys Street EC3 202 A3
Percival Street EC1 197 D3
Percy Circus WC1 196 C4
Percy Street W1 196 A2
Perkin's Rents SW1 200 A3
Perryn Road SE16 202 C1
Peter Street W1 196 A1
Peter's Lane EC1 197 D3
Petersham Lane SW7 198 B3
Petersham Mews SW7 198 B3
Petersham Place SW7 198 B3
Peto Place NW1 195 F3
Petty France SW1 200 A3
Petyward SW3 199 D2
Phelp Street SE17 201 F1
Phene Street SW3 199 D1
Philchurch Place E1 202 B3
Phillimore Walk W8 198 A3
Philpot Lane EC3 197 F1
Philpot Street E1 202 C4
Phipp Street EC2 197 F3
Phoenix Place WC1 196 C3
Phoenix Road NW1 196 A4
Piccadilly W1 199 F4
Pickard Street EC1 197 E4
Pickwick Street SE1 201 E3
Picton Place W1 195 E2
Piggot Street E14 203 F3
Pilgrim Street EC4 197 D2
Pilgrimage Street SE1 201 F3
Pimlico Road SW1 199 E2
Pinchin Street E1 202 B3
Pindar Street EC2 197 F3
Pine Street EC1 197 D3
Pitfield Street N1 197 F4
Pitsea Place E1 203 E3
Pitsea Street E1 203 E3
Pitt Street W8 198 A3
Pitt's Head Mews W1 199 E4
Pixley Street E14 203 F4
Platina Street EC2 197 F3
Playhouse Yard EC4 197 D1
Plover Way SE16 203 E1
Plumber's Row E1 203 B4
Plumtree Court EC4 197 D2
Plympton Street NW8 194 C3
Pocock Street SE1 201 D3
Poland Street W1 196 A2
Pollitt Drive NW8 194 C3
Polygon Road NW1 196 A4
Pomwell Way E1 202 B4
Pond Place SW3 198 C2
Ponler Street E1 202 C3
Ponsonby Place SW1 200 B2
Ponsonby Terrace SW1 200 B2
Pont Street Mews SW1 199 D3
Pont Street SW1 199 D3
Poolmans Street SE16 203 D2
Poonah Street E1 203 D3
Pope Street SE1 202 A1
Porchester Place W2 195 D2
Porchester Square W2 194 B2
Porchester Terrace W2 194 B1
Porchester Terrace W2 194 B2
Porlock Street SE1 201 F3
Porter Street W1 195 E3
Portland Place W1 195 F2
Portland Street SE17 201 F1
Portman Close W1 195 E2
Portman Mews South W1 195 E2
Portman Square W1 195 E2
Portman Street W1 195 E2
Portpool Lane EC1 196 C3
Portsea Place W2 195 D2
Portsoken Street EC3 202 B3
Portugal Street WC2 196 C2
Potier Street SE1 201 F3
Potter's Fields SE1 202 A2
Pottery Street SE16 202 C1
Poultry EC2 197 E2
Praed Street W2 194 C2
Pratt Walk SE11 200 C2
Prescot Street E1 202 B3
Presidents Drive E1 202 C2
Price's Street SE1 201 D4
Prideaux Place WC1 196 C4
Primrose Street EC2 202 A4
Prince Albert Road NW1 & NW1 194 C4
Prince Consort Road SW7 198 C3
Prince's Gardens SW7 198 C3
Prince's Gate Mews SW7 198 C3
Prince's Gate SW7 198 C3
Princelet Street E1 202 B4
Princes Street EC2 197 F2
Princes Street W1 195 F2
Princess Street SE1 201 D3
Princeton Street WC1 196 C2
Printer Street EC4 197 D2
Prioress Street SE1 201 F3
Priory Walk SW10 198 B1
Priter Road SE16 202 B1
Procter Street WC1 196 C2

Prospect Place E1 203 D2
Prospect Street SE16 202 C1
Providence Court W1 195 E1
Provost Street N1 197 F4
Prusom Street E1 202 C2
Pudding Lane EC3 197 F1
Puddle Dock EC4 196 D1
Puma Court E1 202 B4
Purbrook Street SE1 202 A1

Quebec Way SE16 203 E1
Queen Anne Street W1 195 E2
Queen Anne's Gate SW1 200 A3
Queen Elizabeth Street SE1 202 A2
Queen Square WC1 196 B3
Queen Street EC4 197 E1
Queen Street Place EC4 197 E1
Queen Street W1 197 F4
Queen Victoria Street EC4 197 D1
Queen's Gardens SW1 199 F3
Queen's Gardens W2 194 B1
Queen's Gate Gardens SW7 198 B2
Queen's Gate Mews SW7 198 B3
Queen's Gate Place Mews SW7 198 B2
Queen's Gate Place SW7 198 B3
Queen's Gate SW7 198 B3
Queen's Gate Terrace SW7 198 B3
Queen's Row SE17 201 E1
Queen's Walk SW1 199 F4
Queenhithe EC4 197 E1
Queensberry Mews West SW7 198 B2
Queensberry Place SW7 198 C2
Queensborough Terrace W2 194 B1
Queensway W2 194 A1
Quick Street N1 197 D4

Rabbit Row W8 198 A4
Radcot Street SE11 201 D1
Radley Court SE16 203 E2
Radley Mews W8 198 A2
Radnor Mews W2 194 C2
Radnor Place W2 194 C2
Radnor Street EC1 197 D3
Radnor Walk SW3 199 D1
Railway Approach SE1 201 F4
Railway Avenue SE16 203 D2
Raine Street E1 202 C2
Rainsford Street W2 194 C2
Ralston Street SW3 199 D1
Ramillies Place W1 195 F2
Ramillies Street W1 196 A2
Rampart Street E1 202 C4
Rampayne Street SW1 200 A2
Randall Road SE11 200 C2
Randall Row SE11 200 C2
Ranelagh Bridge W2 194 B2
Ranelagh Grove SW1 199 E2
Ranelagh Road SW1 200 A1
Ranston Street NW1 194 C3
Raphael Street SW7 199 D3
Ratcliff Grove EC1 197 E4
Ratcliffe Cross Street E1 203 E3
Ratcliffe Lane E14 203 E3
Rathbone Street W1 196 A2
Raven Row E1 202 C4
Ravensdon Street SE11 201 D1
Ravent Road SE11 200 C2
Ravey Street EC2 197 F3
Rawlings Street SW3 199 D2
Rawstorne Street EC1 197 D4
Ray Street EC1 197 D3
Reardon Path E1 202 C2
Reardon Street E1 202 C2
Rebecca Terrace SE16 203 D1
Rectory Square E1 203 E4
Red Lion Row SE17 201 E1
Red Lion Square WC1 196 C2
Red Lion Street WC1 196 C2
Redburn Street SW3 199 D1
Redcastle Close E1 203 D3
Redcliffe Gardens SW10 & SW5 198 A1
Redcliffe Mews SW10 198 B1
Redcliffe Place SW10 198 B1
Redcliffe Road SW10 198 B1
Redcliffe Square SW10 198 A1
Redcliffe Street SW10 198 A1
Redcross Way SE1 201 E4
Redesdale Street SW3 199 D1
Redfield Lane SW5 198 A2
Redhill Street NW1 195 F4
Redman's Road E1 203 D4
Redriff Road SE16 203 E1
Redwood Close SE16 203 E2
Reece Mews SW7 198 C1

Reedworth Street SE11 201 D2
Reeves Mews W1 195 E1
Regal Close E1 202 C4
Regan Way N1 197 F4
Regency Street SW1 200 A2
Regent Square WC1 196 B4
Regent Street W1 & SW1 195 F2
Relton Mews SW7 199 D3
Remington Street N1 197 E4
Renforth Street SE16 203 D1
Renfrew Road SE11 201 D2
Rennie Street SE1 197 E1
Rephidim Street SE1 201 F3
Repton Street E14 203 E4
Reston Place SW7 198 B3
Reveley Close SE16 203 E1
Rex Place W1 195 E1
Rhodeswell Road E14 203 F4
Rich Lane SW5 198 A1
Rich Street E14 203 F3
Richard Street E1 202 C3
Richard's Place SW3 199 D2
Richmond Mews W1 196 A2
Richmond Terrace SW1 200 B4
Rickett Street SW6 198 A1
Ridgmount Gardens WC1 196 A3
Ridgmount Street WC1 196 A3
Riding House Street W1 195 F2
Riley Road SE1 202 A1
Risborough Street SE1 201 E4
Risdon Street SE16 203 D1
River Street EC1 197 D4
Riverside Walk SE1 200 C4
Rivington Street EC2 197 F3
Robert Adam Street W1 195 E2
Robert Dashwood Way SE17 201 E2
Robert Street NW1 195 F4
Robert Street WC2 196 B1
Rochester Row SW1 200 A2
Rochester Street SW1 200 A2
Rockingham Street SE1 201 E3
Rocliffe Street N1 197 E4
Roding Mews E1 202 B2
Rodmarton Street W1 195 D2
Rodney Place SE17 201 E2
Rodney Road SE17 201 E2
Roger Street WC1 196 C3
Roland Gardens SW7 198 B1
Roland Way SE17 201 F1
Roland Way SW7 198 B1
Rolls Buildings EC4 197 D2
Rolls Passage EC4 196 C2
Romford Street E1 202 C4
Romilly Street W1 196 A1
Romney Street SW1 200 B2
Ronald Street E1 203 D3
Rood Lane EC3 197 F1
Rope Street SE16 203 E1
Ropemaker Road SE16 203 E1
Ropemaker Street EC2 197 F3
Ropemaker's Fields E14 203 F3
Roper Lane SE1 202 A1
Rosary Gardens SW7 198 B2
Roscoe Street EC1 197 E3
Rose Alley SE1 201 E4
Rosebery Avenue EC1 199 D3
Rosemoor Street SW3 199 D2
Rosoman Street EC1 197 D4
Rossmore Road NW1 195 D3
Rotary Street SE1 201 D3
Rotherhithe Street SE16 203 D2
Rotherhithe Tunnel Approach E3 203 E3
Rotherhithe Tunnel Approach SE16 203 F1
Rothsay Street SE1 201 F3
Rotten Row SW7 & SW1 198 C4
Rouel Road SE16 202 B1
Roupell Street SE1 201 D4
Roxby Place SW6 198 A1
Royal Avenue SW3 199 D1
Royal Hospital Road SW3 199 D1
Royal Mint Place E1 202 B3
Royal Mint Street E1 202 B3
Royal Opera Arcade SW1 200 A4
Royal Road SE17 201 D1
Royal Street SE1 200 C3
Rufus Street N1 197 F4
Rugby Street WC1 196 C3
Rugg Street E14 203 F3
Rum Close E1 202 C3
Rupack Street SE16 203 D1
Rupert Street W1 196 A1
Rushworth Street SE1 201 D3
Russell Square WC1 196 B3
Russell Street WC2 196 C1
Russia Dock Road SE16 203 E2
Russia Row EC2 197 E2
Russia Walk SE16 203 E1
Rutherford Street SW1 200 A2
Rutland Gardens SW7 199 D3
Rutland Gate SW7 198 C3
Rutland Place EC1 197 E3

Rutland Street SW7 198 C
Rysbrack Street SW3 199 D

Sackville Street W1 196 A
Saffron Hill EC1 197 D
Saffron Street EC1 197 D
Sage Street E1 202 C
Sage Way WC1 196 C
Sail Street SE11 200 C
Salamanca Place SE1 200 C
Salamanca Street SE1?SE11 200 C
Salisbury Close SE17 201 F
Salisbury Court EC4 197 D
Salisbury Place W1 195 D
Salisbury Street NW8 194 C
Salmon Lane E14 203 E
Salter Road SE16 203 E
Salter Street E14 203 F
Samford Street NW8 194 C
Sampson Street E1 202 C
Sancroft Street SE11 200 C
Sandell Street SE1 201 D
Sandland Street WC1 196 C
Sandwich Street WC1 196 B
Sandys Row E1 202 A
Sans Walk EC1 199 D
Sardinia Street WC2 196 C
Savile Row W1 195 F
Savoy Place WC2 196 B
Savoy Street WC2 196 C
Savoy Way WC2 196 C
Sawyer Street SE1 201 E
Scala Street W1 196 A
Scandrett Street E1 202 C
Scarborough Street E1 202 B
Scarsdale Place W8 198 A
Scarsdale Villas W8 198 A
School House Lane E1 203 D
Schooner Close SE16 203 D
Scoresby Street SE1 201 D
Scott Lidgett Crescent SE16 202 B
Scovell Road SE1 201 E
Scrutton Street EC2 197 F
Seacoal Lane EC4 197 D
Seager Place E3 203 F
Seagrave Road SW6 198 A
Searles Road SE1 201 F
Seaton Close SE11 201 D
Sebastian Street EC1 197 D
Secker Street SE1 200 C
Sedan Way SE17 201 F
Seddon Street WC1 196 C
Seething Lane EC3 202 A
Sekforde Street EC1 197 D
Sellon Mews SE11 200 C
Selsey Street E14 203 F
Selwood Place SW7 198 C
Semley Place SW1 199 E
Senrab Street E1 203 D
Serle Street WC2 196 C
Serpentine Road W2 198 C
Seth Street SE16 203 D
Settles Street E1 202 C
Seven Dials WC2 196 B
Seward Street EC1 197 E
Seymour Mews W1 195 E
Seymour Place W1 195 D
Seymour Street W2 195 D
Seymour Walk SW10 198 B
Shad Thames SE1 202 A
Shadwell Pier Head E1 203 D
Shadwell Place E1 202 C
Shaftesbury Avenue W1 & WC2 196 A
Shafto Mews SW1 199 D
Shand Street SE1 202 A
Sharsted Street SE17 201 D
Shawfield Street SW3 199 D
Sheffield Terrace W8 198 A
Shelmerdine Close E3 203 F
Shelton Street WC2 196 B
Shepherd Market W1 199 F
Shepherd Street W1 199 E
Shepherdess Walk N1 197 E
Sherlock Mews W1 195 E
Sherwood Street W1 196 A
Shillibeer Place W1 195 D
Shipwright Road SE16 203 E
Shoe Lane EC4 197 D
Short Street SE1 201 D
Short's Gardens WC2 196 B
Shoulder Of Mutton Alley E14 203 F
Shouldham Street W1 195 D
Shroton Street NW1 194 C
Siddons Lane NW1 195 D
Sidmouth Street WC1 196 C
Sidney Square E1 203 D
Sidney Street E1 202 C
Silex Street SE1 201 D
Silk Street EC2 197 E

Waley Street E1	203	E4
Wallgrave Road SW5	198	A2
Wallwood Street E14	203	F4
Walnut Tree Walk SE11	200	C2
Walpole Street SW3	199	D2
Walton Place SW3	199	D3
Walton Street SW3	199	D2
Walworth Place SE17	201	E1
Walworth Road SE1 & SE17	201	E2
Wansey Street SE17	201	E2
Wapping Dock Street E1	202	C2
Wapping High Street E1	202	B2
Wapping Lane E1	202	C3
Wapping Wall E1	203	D2
Wardour Street W1	196	A2
Warner Street EC1	196	C3
Warren Street W1	195	F3
Warwick House Street SW1	200	B4
Warwick Lane EC4	197	E2
Warwick Row SW1	199	F3
Warwick Square EC4	199	F2
Warwick Square SW1	197	D2
Warwick Street W1	196	A1
Warwick Way SW1	199	F2
Waterloo Bridge WC2 & SE1	196	C1
Waterloo Place SW1	200	A4
Waterloo Road SE1	200	C4
Waterman Way E1	202	C2
Waterside Close SE16	202	B1
Watling Street EC4	197	E2
Watney Street E1	202	C3
Watson's Street SE8	202	C2
Waveney Close E1	202	B2
Waverton Street W1	199	E4
Weavers Lane SE1	202	A2
Webb Street SE1	201	F3
Webber Row SE1	201	D3
Webber Street SE1	201	D3
Webster Road SE16	202	C1
Weighouse Street W1	195	E1
Welbeck Street W1	195	E2
Welbeck Way W1	195	E2

Welland Mews E1	202	C1
Wellclose Square E1	202	B3
Weller Street SE1	201	E3
Wellesley Street E1	203	D4
Wellesley Terrace N1	197	E4
Wellington Place NW8	194	C4
Wellington Road NW8	194	C4
Wellington Square SW3	199	D1
Wellington Street WC2	196	C1
Wells Mews W1	196	A2
Wells Square WC1	196	C4
Wells Street W1	195	F2
Wendover Street SE17	201	F1
Wenlock Road N1	197	E4
Wenlock Street N1	197	E4
Wentworth Street E1	202	B4
Werrington Street NW1	196	A4
Wesley Close SE17	201	D2
West Arbour Street E1	203	D4
West Eaton Place SW1	199	D2
West Ferry Road E14	203	F2
West Gardens E1	202	C3
West Halkin Street SW1	199	E3
West India Dock Road E14	203	F3
West Lane SE16	202	C1
West Road SW4	199	D1
West Smithfield EC1	197	D2
West Square SE11	201	D2
West Street WC2	196	B1
West Tenter Street E1	202	B3
Westbourne Crescent W2	194	B1
Westbourne Street W2	194	C1
Westbourne Terrace Mews W2	194	B2
Westbourne Terrace Road W2	194	B2
Westbourne Terrace W2	194	B2
Westcott Road SE17	201	D1
Western Place SE16	203	D2
Westgate Terrace SW10	198	A1
Westland Place N1	197	F4
Westminster Bridge Road SE1	200	F3
Westminster Bridge SW1		

& SE1	200	B3
Westmoreland Place SW1	199	F1
Westmoreland Road SE17	201	E1
Westmoreland Street W1	195	E2
Westmoreland Terrace SW1	199	F1
Weston Rise WC1	196	C4
Weston Street SE1	201	F3
Westport Street E1	203	E4
Westway W12	194	B2
Wetherby Gardens SW5	198	B2
Wetherby Place SW7	198	B2
Weymouth Mews W1	195	F2
Weymouth Street W1	195	E2
Wharf Road N1	197	E4
Wharfedale Street SW10	198	A1
Wharton Street WC1	196	C4
Whetstone Park WC2	196	C2
Whidborne Street WC1	196	B4
Whiskin Street EC1	197	D4
Whitcomb Street WC2	196	A1
White Church Lane E1	202	B4
White Hart Street SE11	201	D2
White Horse Lane E1	203	E4
White Horse Road E1	203	E3
White Horse Street W1	199	F4
White Kennet Street E1	202	A4
White Lion Hill EC4	197	E1
White's Grounds SE1	202	A1
White's Row E1	202	A4
Whitechapel High Street E1	202	B4
Whitechapel Road E1	202	B4
Whitecross Place EC2	197	F3
Whitecross Street EC1	197	E3
Whitefriars Street EC4	197	D2
Whitehall Court SW1	200	B4
Whitehall Place SW1	200	B4
Whitehall SW1	200	B4
Whitehaven Street NW8	194	C3
Whitehead's Grove SW3	199	D2
Whitfield Street W1	196	A3
Whitgift Street SE11	200	C2
Whittaker Street SW1	199	E2
Whittlesey Street SE1	201	D4

Wickham Street SE11	200	C1
Wicklow Street WC1	196	C4
Wigmore Place W1	195	E2
Wigmore Street W1	195	E2
Wilbraham Place SW1	199	E2
Wilcox Place SW1	200	A3
Wild Court WC2	196	C2
Wild Street WC2	196	B2
Wild's Rents SE1	201	F3
Wilfred Street SW1	199	F3
Wilkes Street E1	202	B4
William IV Street WC2	196	B1
William Mews SW1	199	E3
William Road NW1	195	F4
William Street SW1	199	D3
Willow Place SW1	200	A2
Willow Street EC2	197	F3
Wilmington Square WC1	197	D4
Wilmington Street WC1	197	D4
Wilson Grove SE16	202	C1
Wilson Street EC2	197	F2
Wilson's Place E14	203	F3
Wilton Crescent SW1	199	E3
Wilton Mews SW1	199	E3
Wilton Place SW1	199	E3
Wilton Road SW1	199	F2
Wilton Row SW1	199	E3
Wilton Street SW1	199	E3
Wilton Terrace SW1	199	E3
Wimpole Mews W1	195	E2
Wimpole Street W1	195	E2
Winchester Close SE17	201	D2
Winchester Street SW1	199	F2
Winchester Walk SE1	201	F4
Wincott Street SE11	201	D2
Windmill Row SE11	201	D1
Windmill Street W1	196	A2
Windmill Walk SE1	201	D4
Windrose Close SE16	203	D2
Windsor Terrace N1	197	E4
Wine Close E1	202	C2
Wine Office Court EC4	197	D2
Winsland Mews W2	194	C2
Winsland Street W2	194	C2
Winsley Street W1	196	A2

Winterton Place SW10	198	B1
Woburn Place WC1	196	B3
Woburn Square WC1	196	B3
Wolfe Crescent SE16	203	D1
Wolseley Street SE1	202	B1
Wood Street EC2	197	E2
Wood's Mews W1	195	E1
Wood's Place SE1	202	A1
Woodbridge Street EC1	197	D3
Woodfall Street SW3	199	D1
Woodstock Street W1	195	E2
Woolaston Close SE1	201	E2
Wooler Street SE17	201	F1
Wootton Street SE1	201	D4
Worgan Street SE11	200	C2
Wormwood Street EC2	197	F2
Worship Street EC2	197	F3
Wren Street WC1	196	C3
Wright's Lane W8	198	A3
Wyclif Street EC1	197	D4
Wyndham Place W1	195	D2
Wyndham Street W1	195	D2
Wynnstay Gardens W8	198	A3
Wynyard Terrace SE11	200	C1
Wynyatt Street EC1	197	D4
Wythburn Place W1	195	D2
Yardley Street WC1	196	C4
Yarmouth Place W1	199	E4
Yeoman's Row SW3	199	D3
York Buildings WC2	196	B1
York Gate NW1	195	E3
York House Place W8	198	A4
York Road SE1	200	C3
York Square E14	203	E4
York Street W1	195	D3
York Terrace East NW1	195	E3
York Terrace West NW1	195	E3
Yorkshire Road E14	203	E3
Young Street W8	198	A3
Zoar Street SE1	201	E4

212

Index to atlas

Each placename entry in this index is identified by its county or region name. These are shown in italics. A list of the abbreviated forms used is given below.

To locate a placename in the atlas turn to the map page number indicated in bold type in the index and use the 4 figure grid reference.

e g Hythe Kent **29** TR16**3**4 is found on page '**29**'. The two letters 'TR' refer to the National Grid. To pin point our example the first bold figure '**1**' is found along the bottom edge of the page. The following figure '**6**' indicates how many imaginary tenths to move east of line '**1**'. The next bold figure'**3**' is found along the left hand side of the page. The last figure '**4**' shows how many imaginary tenths to move north of line '**3**'. You will locate Hythe where these two lines intersect.

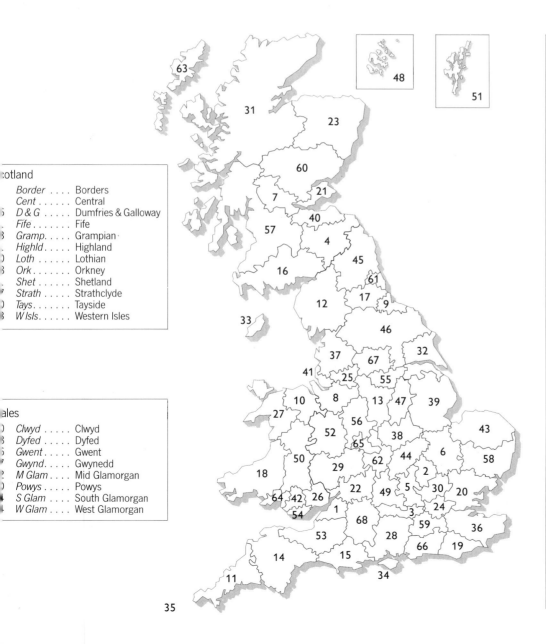

Scotland

Border	Borders
Cent	Central
D & G	Dumfries & Galloway
Fife	Fife
Gramp.	Grampian
Highld	Highland
Loth	Lothian
Ork	Orkney
Shet	Shetland
Strath	Strathclyde
Tays	Tayside
W Isls	Western Isles

Wales

Clwyd	Clwyd
Dyfed	Dyfed
Gwent	Gwent
Gwynd.	Gwynedd
M Glam	Mid Glamorgan
Powys	Powys
S Glam	South Glamorgan
W Glam	West Glamorgan

England

1	*Avon*	Avon
2	*Beds*	Bedfordshire
3	*Berks*	Berkshire
5	*Bucks*	Buckinghamshire
6	*Cambs*	Cambridgeshire
8	*Ches*	Cheshire
9	*Cleve.*	Cleveland
11	*Cnwll.*	Cornwall
12	*Cumb.*	Cumbria
13	*Derbys*	Derbyshire
14	*Devon*	Devon
15	*Dorset.*	Dorset
17	*Dur.*	Durham
19	*E.Susx.*	East Sussex
20	*Essex*	Essex
22	*Gloucs.*	Gloucestershire
24	*Gt Lon.*	Greater London
25	*Gt Man*	Greater Manchester
28	*Hants*	Hampshire
29	*H & W*	Hereford & Worcester
30	*Herts.*	Hertfordshire
32	*Humb*	Humberside
33	*IOM*	Isle of Man
34	*IOW.*	Isle of Wight
35	*IOS*	Isles of Scilly
36	*Kent*	Kent
37	*Lancs*	Lancashire
38	*Leics*	Leicestershire
39	*Lincs.*	Lincolnshire
41	*Mersyd*	Merseyside
43	*Norfk*	Norfolk
44	*Nhants*	Northamptonshire
45	*Nthumb.*	Northumberland
46	*N York*	North Yorkshire
47	*Notts.*	Nottinghamshire
49	*Oxon.*	Oxfordshire
52	*Shrops*	Shropshire
53	*Somset*	Somerset
55	*S York*	South Yorkshire
56	*Staffs*	Staffordshire
58	*Suffk*	Suffolk
59	*Surrey*	Surrey
61	*T & W.*	Tyne & Wear
62	*Warwks*	Warwickshire
65	*W Mids*	West Midland
66	*W Susx*	West Sussex
67	*W York*	West Yorkshire
68	*Wilts*	Wiltshire

A'Chill Appleby Parva

A'Chill Highld 84 NG2705
Ab Kettleby Leics 40 SK7223
Abbas Combe Somset 9 ST7022
Abberley H & W 28 SO7567
Abberley Common H & W 28 SO7467
Abberton H & W 28 SO9953
Abberton Essex 25 TM0019
Abbess Roding Essex 24 TL5711
Abbey Dore H & W 27 SO3830
Abbey Green Staffs 48 SJ9757
Abbey St. Bathans Border 76 NT7661
Abbey Town Cumb 67 NY1750
Abbey Village Lancs 54 SD6422
Abbey Wood Gt Lon 23 TQ4779
Abbeydale S York 49 SK3281
Abbeylands IOM 52 SC4585
Abbeystead Lancs 53 SD5654
Abbot's Salford Warwks 28 SP0650
Abbotrule Border 68 NT6113
Abbots Bickington Devon 6 SS3813
Abbots Bromley Staffs 38 SK0724
Abbots Deuglie Tays 82 NO1111
Abbots Langley Herts 22 TL0901
Abbots Leigh Avon 19 ST5474
Abbots Morton H & W 28 SP0255
Abbots Ripton Cambs 31 TL2377
Abbots Worthy Hants 10 SU4932
Abbotsbury Dorset 8 SY5785
Abbotsford Border 76 NT5034
Abbotsham Devon 6 SS4226
Abbotskerswell Devon 5 SX8568
Abbotsley Cambs 31 TL2256
Abbott Street Dorset 9 ST9800
Abbotts Ann Hants 21 SU3243
Abdon Shrops 37 SO5786
Aber Gwynd 45 SH6572
Aberaeron Dyfed 34 SN4562
Aberaman M Glam 18 SO0100
Aberangell Powys 35 SH8410
Aberarder Highld 92 NH6225
Aberargie Tays 82 NO1615
Aberarth Dyfed 34 SN4763
Aberavon W Glam 18 SS7489
Abercanaid M Glam 18 SO0503
Abercairny Tays 82 NN9222
Abercarn Gwent 19 ST2194
Abercastle Dyfed 16 SM8533
Abercegir Powys 35 SH8001
Aberchalder Lodge Highld 86 NH3403
Aberchirder Gramp 94 NJ6252
Abercraf Powys 26 SN8212
Abercregan W Glam 18 SS8496
Abercrombie Fife 83 NO5102
Abercwmboi M Glam 18 ST0299
Abercych Dyfed 17 SN2441
Abercynon M Glam 18 ST0794
Aberdalgie Tays 82 NO0720
Aberdare Powys 18 SO0002
Aberdaron Gwynd 44 SH1726
Aberdeen Gramp 89 NJ9306
Aberdour Fife 82 NT1985
Aberdovey Gwynd 35 SN6196
Aberdulais W Glam 18 SS7799
Aberedw Powys 26 SO0847
Abereiddy Dyfed 16 SM7931
Abererch Gwynd 44 SH3936
Aberfan M Glam 18 SO0700
Aberfeldy Tays 87 NN8549
Aberffraw Gwynd 44 SH3569
Aberford W York 55 SE4337
Aberfoyle Cent 81 NN5200
Abergavenny Gwent 27 SO2914
Abergele Clwyd 45 SH9477
Abergorlech Dyfed 17 SN5833
Abergwesyn Powys 26 SN8552
Abergwili Dyfed 17 SN4320
Abergwynfi W Glam 18 SS8995
Aberkenfig M Glam 18 SS8984
Aberlady Loth 83 NT4679
Aberlemno Tays 89 NO5255
Aberllefenni Gwynd 35 SH7609
Aberllynfi Powys 27 SO1737
Aberlour Gramp 94 NJ2642
Abermule Powys 36 SO1594
Abernant Dyfed 17 SN3323
Abernethy Tays 82 NO1816
Abernyte Tays 83 NO2531
Aberporth Dyfed 17 SN2651
Abersoch Gwynd 44 SH3127
Abersychan Gwent 19 SO2603
Aberthin S Glam 18 ST0074
Abertillery Gwent 27 SO2104
Abertridwr Powys 36 SJ0319
Abertridwr M Glam 18 ST1289
Aberuthven Tays 82 NN9815
Aberystwyth Dyfed 34 SN5881
Abingdon Oxon 21 SU4997
Abinger Surrey 12 TQ1145
Abinger Hammer Surrey 12 TQ0947
Abington Strath 75 NS9323
Abington Nhants 30 SP7861
Abington Pigotts Cambs 31 TL3044
Ablington Gloucs 28 SP1007
Abney Derbys 48 SK1980
Aboyne Gramp 89 NO5298
Abram Gt Man 47 SD6001
Abriachan Highld 92 NH5535
Abridge Essex 23 TQ4696
Abson Avon 20 ST7074
Abthorpe Nhants 29 SP6446
Aby Lincs 51 TF4078
Acaster Malbis N York 56 SE5845
Acaster Selby N York 56 SE5741
Accrington Lancs 54 SD7628
Acha Strath 78 NM1854
Achahoish Strath 71 NR7877
Achalader Tays 88 NO1245
Achaleven Strath 80 NM9233
Achanalt Highld 92 NH2661
Achandunie Highld 92 NH6472
Achany Highld 96 NC5602
Acharacle Highld 79 NM6767
Acharn Tays 87 NN7543
Achavanich Highld 100 ND1842
Achduart Highld 91 NC0403
Achfary Highld 98 NC2939
Achiltibuie Highld 91 NC0208
Achinhoan Strath 72 NR7516
Achintee Highld 85 NG9441
Achlain Highld 92 NH2812
Achmelvich Highld 98 NC0524
Achmore W Isls 102 NB3029
Achmore Highld 85 NG8533
Achnacarnin Highld 98 NC0432
Achnacarry Highld 86 NN1787
Achnacloich Highld 84 NG5908
Achnacloich Strath 80 NM9534
Achnaconeran Highld 92 NH4118
Achnacroish Strath 79 NM8541
Achnadrish Lodge Strath 79 NM4652
Achnafauld Tays 82 NN8736
Achnagarron Highld 93 NH6870
Achnaha Highld 79 NM4668
Achnahaird Highld 98 NC0013
Achnairn Highld 96 NC5512
Achnalea Highld 79 NM8561
Achnamara Strath 71 NR7887
Achnasheen Highld 92 NH1658
Achnashellach Station Highld 91 NH0048
Achnastank Gramp 94 NJ2733
Achosnich Highld 79 NM4467
Achranich Highld 79 NM7047
Achreamie Highld 100 ND0166
Achriabhach Highld 86 NN1468
Achriesgill Highld 98 NC2554
Achtoty Highld 99 NC6762
Achurch Nhants 40 TL0283
Achvaich Highld 97 NH7194
Ackergill Highld 100 ND3553
Acklam Cleve 62 NZ4817
Acklam N York 56 SE7861
Ackleton Shrops 37 SO7698
Acklington Nthumb 69 NU2301
Ackton W York 55 SE4121
Ackworth Moor Top W York 55 SE4316
Acle Norfk 43 TG4010
Acock's Green W Mids 38 SP1283
Acol Kent 15 TR3067
Acomb Nthumb 68 NY9366
Acomb N York 56 SE5651
Aconbury H & W 27 SO5133
Acton Ches 47 SJ6352
Acton Staffs 38 SJ8241
Acton H & W 28 SO8467
Acton Suffk 32 TL8945
Acton Gt Lon 23 TQ2080
Acton Beauchamp H & W 28 SO6850
Acton Bridge Ches 47 SJ6075
Acton Burnell Shrops 37 SJ5302
Acton Green H & W 28 SO6950
Acton Park Clwyd 46 SJ3451
Acton Round Shrops 37 SO6395
Acton Scott Shrops 36 SO4589
Acton Trussell Staffs 38 SJ9318
Acton Turville Avon 20 ST8080
Adbaston Staffs 37 SJ7627
Adber Dorset 9 ST5920
Adbolton Notts 49 SK5938
Adderbury Oxon 29 SP4735
Adderley Shrops 37 SJ6640
Addiewell Loth 75 NS9962
Addingham W York 55 SE0749
Addington Bucks 30 SP7428
Addington Kent 14 TQ6559
Addiscombe Gt Lon 23 TQ3366
Addlestone Surrey 22 TQ0564
Addlestonemore Surrey 22 TQ0565
Addlethorpe Lincs 51 TF5468
Adeyfield Herts 22 TL0708
Adfa Powys 36 SJ0601
Adforton H & W 36 SO4071
Adisham Kent 15 TR2253
Adlestrop Gloucs 29 SP2426
Adlingfleet Humb 56 SE8421
Adlington Lancs 54 SD6013
Admaston Shrops 37 SJ6313
Admaston Staffs 38 SK0423
Admington Warwks 29 SP2045
Adsborough Somset 8 ST2729
Adscombe Somset 19 ST1837
Adstock Bucks 30 SP7329
Adversane W Susx 12 TQ0723
Advie Highld 93 NJ1234
Adwick Le Street S York 56 SE5308
Adwick upon Dearne S York 49 SE4701
Ae D & G 66 NX9889
Ae Bridgend D & G 66 NY0186
Affleck Gramp 94 NJ5540
Affpuddle Dorset 9 SY8093
Affric Lodge Highld 92 NH1822
Afton Bridgend Strath 66 NS6213
Agglethorpe N York 61 SE0885
Aigburth Mersyd 46 SJ3886
Aike Humb 57 TA0446
Aiketgate Cumb 67 NY4846
Aikton Cumb 67 NY2753
Ailey H & W 27 SO3348
Ailsworth Cambs 40 TL1198
Ainderby Quernhow N York 62 SE3480
Ainderby Steeple N York 62 SE3392
Aingers Green Essex 25 TM1120
Ainsdale Mersyd 53 SD3112
Ainstable Cumb 67 NY5246
Ainthorpe N York 62 NZ7007
Aird W Isls 102 NB5635
Aird Strath 79 NM7600
Aird D & G 64 NX0960
Aird of Kinloch Strath 79 NM5228
Aird of Sleat Highld 84 NG5900
Airdeny Strath 80 NM9929
Airdrie Strath 74 NS7565
Airdriehill Strath 74 NS7867
Airds Bay Strath 80 NM9932
Airds of Kells D & G 65 NX6770
Airieland D & G 65 NX7556
Airmyn Humb 56 SE7224
Airntully Tays 82 NO0935
Airor Highld 85 NG7205
Airth Cent 82 NS9087
Airton N York 54 SD9059
Aisby Lincs 50 SK8692
Aisby Lincs 40 TF0138
Aish Devon 5 SX6960
Aish Devon 5 SX8458
Aiskew N York 61 SE2788
Aislaby Cleve 62 NZ4012
Aislaby N York 63 NZ8608
Aislaby N York 63 SE7785
Aisthorpe Lincs 50 SK9480
Aith Shet 103 HU3455
Akeld Nthumb 77 NT9529
Akeley Bucks 30 SP7037
Akenham Suffk 33 TM1449
Albaston Devon 4 SX4270
Alberbury Shrops 36 SJ3614
Albourne W Susx 12 TQ2516
Albrighton Shrops 37 SJ4918
Albrighton Shrops 37 SJ8004
Alburgh Norfk 33 TM2687
Albury Herts 31 TL4324
Albury Surrey 12 TQ0447
Albury Heath Surrey 12 TQ0646
Alcaig Highld 92 NH5657
Alcaston Shrops 36 SO4587
Alcester Warwks 28 SP0857
Alciston E Susx 13 TQ5005
Alconbury Cambs 31 TL1875
Alconbury Weston Cambs 31 TL1777
Aldborough N York 55 SE4066
Aldborough Norfk 43 TG1834
Aldbourne Wilts 21 SU2676
Aldbrough Humb 57 TA2438
Aldbury Herts 30 SP9612
Aldcliffe Cumb 53 SD4660
Aldclune Tays 87 NN8964
Aldeburgh Suffk 33 TM4656
Aldeby Norfk 43 TM4493
Aldenham Herts 22 TQ1498
Alderbury Wilts 10 SU1827
Alderholt Dorset 10 SU1212
Alderley Gloucs 20 ST7690
Alderley Edge Ches 47 SJ8478
Aldermaston Berks 21 SU5965
Alderminster Warwks 29 SP2348
Aldershot Hants 22 SU8650
Alderton Gloucs 28 SP0033
Alderton Nhants 30 SP7446
Alderton Wilts 20 ST8482
Alderton Suffk 33 TM3441
Alderwasley Derbys 49 SK3053
Aldfield N York 55 SE2669
Aldford Ches 46 SJ4159
Aldgate Leics 40 SK9804
Aldham Essex 24 TL9126
Aldham Suffk 32 TM0545
Aldingbourne W Susx 11 SU9205
Aldingham Cumb 53 SD2870
Aldington H & W 28 SP0644
Aldington Kent 15 TR0736
Aldington Corner Kent 15 TR0636
Aldivalloch Gramp 94 NJ3526
Aldochlay Strath 80 NS3591
Aldreth Cambs 31 TL4473
Aldridge W Mids 38 SK0500
Aldringham Suffk 33 TM4461
Aldsworth Gloucs 28 SP1509
Aldunie Gramp 94 NJ3626
Aldwark N York 55 SE4663
Aldwark Derbys 48 SK2257
Aldwick W Susx 11 SZ9198
Aldwincle Nhants 40 TL0081
Aldworth Berks 21 SU5579
Alexandria Strath 80 NS3979
Aley Somset 19 ST1838
Alfington Devon 8 SY1197
Alfold Surrey 12 TQ0333
Alfold Crossways Surrey 12 TQ0335
Alford Gramp 94 NJ5715
Alford Somset 9 ST6032
Alford Lincs 51 TF4575
Alfreton Derbys 49 SK4155
Alfrick H & W 28 SO7453
Alfrick Pound H & W 28 SO7452
Alfriston E Susx 13 TQ5103
Algarkirk Lincs 41 TF2935
Alhampton Somset 9 ST6234
Alkborough Humb 56 SE8821
Alkerton Gloucs 28 SO7705
Alkham Kent 15 TR2542
Alkmonton Derbys 48 SK1838
All Cannings Wilts 20 SU0661
All Saints South Elmham Suffk 33 TM3482
All Stretton Shrops 36 SO4595
Allaleigh Devon 5 SX8053
Allanaquoich Gramp 88 NO1291
Allanbank Strath 74 NS8458
Allanton Strath 74 NS7454
Allanton Strath 74 NS8457
Allanton Border 77 NT8654
Allardice Gramp 89 NO8173
Allaston Gloucs 27 SO6304
Allbrook Hants 10 SU4521
Allen End Warwks 38 SP1696
Allen's Green Herts 31 TL4516
Allendale Town Nthumb 68 NY8355
Allenheads Nthumb 68 NY8645
Allensmore H & W 27 SO4635
Allenton Derbys 39 SK3732
Aller Devon 7 SS7625
Aller Somset 8 ST4029
Allerby Cumb 58 NY0839
Allercombe Devon 7 SY0494
Allerford Somset 7 SS9046
Allerston N York 63 SE8782
Allerthorpe Humb 56 SE7847
Allerton W York 55 SE1234
Allerton Mersyd 46 SJ3987
Allerton Bywater W York 55 SE4227
Allerton Mauleverer N York 55 SE4157
Allesley W Mids 39 SP3080
Allestree Derbys 49 SK3439
Allexton Leics 40 SK8100
Allgreave Ches 48 SJ9767
Allhallows Kent 24 TQ8377
Alligin Shuas Highld 91 NG8357
Allington Lincs 50 SK8540
Allington Wilts 20 ST8975
Allington Wilts 20 SU0663
Allington Wilts 10 SU2039
Allington Dorset 8 SY4693
Allithwaite Cumb 59 SD3876
Alloa Cent 82 NS8892
Allonby Cumb 58 NY0842
Alloway Strath 73 NS3318
Allowenshay Somset 8 ST3913
Alltchaorunn Highld 86 NN1951
Alltmawr Powys 26 SO0746
Alltwalis Dyfed 17 SN4431
Alltwen W Glam 18 SN7303
Alltyblaca Dyfed 17 SN5245
Allweston Dorset 9 ST6614
Almeley H & W 27 SO3351
Almeley Wooton H & W 27 SO3352
Almer Dorset 9 SY9199
Almholme S York 56 SE5808
Almington Staffs 37 SJ7034
Almondbank Tays 82 NO0625
Almondbury W York 55 SE1614
Almondsbury Avon 19 ST6084
Alness Highld 93 NH6569
Alnham Nthumb 68 NT9810
Alnmouth Nthumb 69 NU2410
Alnwick Nthumb 69 NU1813
Alperton Gt Lon 23 TQ1883
Alphamstone Essex 24 TL8735
Alpheton Suffk 32 TL8750
Alphington Devon 5 SX9190
Alport Derbys 48 SK2264
Alpraham Ches 47 SJ5859
Alresford Essex 25 TM0621
Alrewas Staffs 38 SK1614
Alsager Ches 47 SJ7955
Alshot Somset 8 ST1935
Alsop en le Dale Derbys 48 SK1554
Alston Cumb 68 NY7146
Alston Devon 8 ST3002
Alston Sutton Somset 19 ST4151
Alstone Gloucs 28 SO9832
Alstonefield Staffs 48 SK1355
Alswear Devon 7 SS7222
Altandhu Highld 98 NB9812
Altarnun Cnwll 4 SX2281
Altass Highld 96 NC5000
Altcreich Strath 79 NM6938
Altgaltraig Strath 80 NS0473
Althorne Essex 24 TQ9198
Althorpe Humb 56 SE8309
Altnabreac Station Highld 100 ND0045
Altnacraig Strath 79 NM8429
Altnaharra Highld 99 NC5635
Alton Staffs 48 SK0741
Alton Derbys 49 SK3664
Alton Hants 11 SU7139
Alton Barnes Wilts 20 SU1062
Alton Pancras Dorset 9 ST7002
Alton Priors Wilts 20 SU1162
Altrincham Gt Man 47 SJ7687
Alva Cent 82 NS8897
Alvanley Ches 46 SJ4974
Alvaston Derbys 39 SK3833
Alvechurch H & W 38 SP0272
Alvecote Warwks 39 SK2404
Alvediston Wilts 9 ST9723
Alveley Shrops 37 SO7584
Alverdiscott Devon 6 SS5225
Alverstoke Hants 11 SZ6098
Alverstone IOW 11 SZ5785
Alverthorpe W York 55 SE3121
Alverton Notts 50 SK7942
Alves Gramp 93 NJ1362
Alvescot Oxon 29 SP2704
Alveston Warwks 29 SP2356
Alveston Avon 19 ST6388
Alvie Highld 93 NH8609
Alvingham Lincs 51 TF3691
Alvington Gloucs 19 SO6000
Alwalton Cambs 40 TL1396
Alwinton Nthumb 68 NT9106
Alwoodley W York 55 SE2840
Alyth Tays 88 NO2448
Amberley Gloucs 20 SO8501
Amberley W Susx 12 TQ0213
Amble Nthumb 69 NU2604
Amblecote W Mids 38 SO8985
Ambler Thorn W York 55 SE0929
Ambleside Cumb 59 NY3704
Ambleston Dyfed 16 SN0025
Amcotts Humb 56 SE8514
Amersham Bucks 22 SU9597
Amesbury Wilts 20 SU1541
Amisfield Town D & G 66 NY0082
Amlwch Gwynd 44 SH4492
Ammanford Dyfed 17 SN6212
Amotherby N York 63 SE7473
Ampfield Hants 10 SU4023
Ampleforth N York 62 SE5878
Ampney Crucis Gloucs 20 SP0601
Ampney St. Mary Gloucs 20 SP0802
Ampney St. Peter Gloucs 20 SP0801
Amport Hants 21 SU3044
Ampthill Beds 30 TL0337
Ampton Suffk 32 TL8671
Amroth Dyfed 17 SN1608
Amwell Herts 31 TL1613
Anaheilt Highld 79 NM8162
Ancaster Lincs 50 SK9843
Anchor Shrops 36 SO1785
Ancroft Nthumb 77 NT9945
Ancrum Border 76 NT6224
Anderby Lincs 51 TF5275
Anderson Dorset 9 SY8897
Andover Hants 21 SU3645
Andoversford Gloucs 28 SP0219
Andreas IOM 52 SC4199
Anerley Gt Lon 23 TQ3369
Anfield Mersyd 46 SJ3692
Angarrack Cnwll 2 SW5838
Angelbank Shrops 37 SO5776
Angersleigh Somset 8 ST1918
Angle Dyfed 16 SM8603
Angmering W Susx 12 TQ0604
Angram N York 55 SE5248
Ankerville Highld 97 NH8174
Anlaby Humb 56 TA0328
Anmer Norfk 42 TF7429
Anmore Hants 11 SU6611
Anna Valley Hants 21 SU3543
Annan D & G 67 NY1966
Annat Highld 91 NG8954
Annat Strath 80 NN0322
Annathill Strath 74 NS7270
Annbank Strath 73 NS4023
Annesley Notts 49 SK5053
Annesley Woodhouse Notts 49 SK4953
Annfield Plain Dur 69 NZ1651
Anniesland Strath 74 NS5368
Ansdell Lancs 53 SD3428
Ansford Somset 9 ST6433
Ansley Warwks 39 SP3091
Anslow Staffs 39 SK2125
Anslow Gate Staffs 39 SK1924
Anstey Leics 39 SK5508
Anstey Herts 31 TL4033
Anstruther Fife 83 NO5703
Anstruther Easter Fife 83 NO5704
Ansty Warwks 39 SP4083
Ansty Wilts 9 ST9526
Ansty W Susx 12 TQ2923
Anthorn Cumb 67 NY1958
Antingham Norfk 43 TG2533
Antony Cnwll 4 SX4054
Antrobus Ches 47 SJ6480
Anwick Lincs 50 TF1150
Anwoth D & G 65 NX5856
Aperfield Gt Lon 23 TQ4158
Apethorpe Nhants 40 TL0295
Apley Lincs 50 TF1075
Apperknowle Derbys 49 SK3878
Apperley Gloucs 28 SO8628
Appin Strath 86 NM9346
Appleby D & G 64 NX4140
Appleby Humb 56 SE9514
Appleby Magna Leics 39 SK3109
Appleby Parva Leics 39 SK3008

Appleby-in-Westmorland Bacup

Appleby-in-Westmorland *Cumb* **60** NY6820
Applecross *Highld* **91** NG7144
Appledore *Devon* **6** SS4630
Appledore *Devon* **7** ST0614
Appledore *Kent* **14** TQ9529
Appleford *Oxon* **21** SU5293
Applegarth Town *D & G* **67** NY1084
Appleshaw *Hants* **21** SU3048
Appleton *Ches* **46** SJ5186
Appleton *Oxon* **21** SP4401
Appleton Roebuck *N York* **56** SE5542
Appleton Wiske *N York* **62** NZ3804
Appleton-le-Moors *N York* **63** SE7387
Appleton-le-Street *N York* **63** SE7373
Appletreehall *Border* **76** NT5117
Appletreewick *N York* **55** SE0560
Appley *Somset* **7** ST0721
Appley Bridge *Lancs* **53** SD5209
Apse Heath *IOW* **11** SZ5683
Apsley End *Beds* **30** TL1232
Apuldram *W Susx* **11** SU8403
Arbirlot *Tays* **83** NO6040
Arboll *Highld* **97** NH8781
Arborfield *Berks* **22** SU7567
Arborfield Cross *Berks* **22** SU7666
Arbory *IOM* **52** SC2470
Arbroath *Tays* **89** NO6441
Arbuthnott *Gramp* **89** NO8074
Archdeacon Newton *Dur* **61** NZ2517
Archencarroch *Strath* **81** NS4182
Archiestown *Gramp* **94** NJ2244
Arclid Green *Ches* **47** SJ7861
Ard a'Chapuill *Strath* **80** NS0179
Ardaily *Strath* **72** NR6450
Ardalanish *Strath* **78** NM3619
Ardanaiseig Hotel *Strath* **80** NN0824
Ardarroch *Highld* **85** NG8339
Ardarroch *Strath* **80** NS2494
Ardbeg *Strath* **70** NR4146
Ardbeg *Strath* **72** NS0766
Ardbeg *Strath* **80** NS1583
Ardcharnich *Highld* **96** NH1788
Ardchiavaig *Strath* **78** NM3818
Ardchonnel *Strath* **80** NM9812
Ardchullarie More *Cent* **81** NN5813
Ardechive *Highld* **86** NN1490
Ardeer *Strath* **73** NS2740
Ardeley *Herts* **31** TL3027
Ardelve *Highld* **85** NG8627
Arden *Strath* **80** NS3684
Ardens Grafton *Warwks* **28** SP1154
Ardentinny *Strath* **80** NS1887
Ardersier *Highld* **93** NH7855
Ardessie *Highld* **91** NH0689
Ardfen *Strath* **79** NM8004
Ardgay *Highld* **97** NH5990
Ardgour *Highld* **86** NN0163
Ardgowan *Strath* **80** NS2073
Ardhallow *Strath* **80** NS1674
Ardhasig *W Isls* **102** NB1202
Ardheslaig *Highld* **91** NG7855
Ardindrean *Highld* **96** NH1588
Ardingly *W Susx* **12** TQ3429
Ardington *Oxon* **21** SU4388
Ardlamont *Strath* **71** NR9865
Ardleigh *Essex* **25** TM0529
Ardleigh Heath *Essex* **25** TM0430
Ardler *Tays* **88** NO2642
Ardley *Oxon* **29** SP5427
Ardley End *Essex* **31** TL5214
Ardlui *Strath* **80** NN3115
Ardlussa *Strath* **71** NR6487
Ardmaddy *Strath* **80** NN0837
Ardmair *Highld* **96** NH1198
Ardmaleish *Strath* **72** NS0768
Ardminish *Strath* **72** NR6448
Ardmolich *Highld* **85** NM7172
Ardmore *Highld* **97** NH7086
Ardmore *Strath* **80** NS3178
Ardnadam *Strath* **80** NS1780
Ardnagrask *Highld* **92** NH5249
Ardnarff *Highld* **85** NG8935
Ardnastang *Highld* **79** NM8061
Ardno *Strath* **80** NN1508
Ardochy House *Highld* **86** NH2002
Ardpatrick *Strath* **71** NR7660
Ardpeaton *Strath* **80** NS2185
Ardrishaig *Strath* **71** NR8585
Ardrossan *Strath* **73** NS2342
Ardshealach *Highld* **79** NM6867
Ardsley East *W York* **55** SE3025
Ardslignish *Highld* **79** NM5661
Ardtalla *Strath* **70** NR4654
Ardtalnaig Hotel *Tays* **81** NN7039
Ardtoe *Highld* **79** NM6270
Arduaine *Strath* **79** NM7910
Ardvasar *Highld* **84** NG6303
Ardverikie *Highld* **87** NN5087
Ardvorlich *Tays* **81** NN6322
Ardvourlie *W Isls* **102** NB1810
Ardwell *D & G* **64** NX1045
Ardwick *Gt Man* **47** SJ8597
Arevegaig *Highld* **79** NM6568
Arford *Hants* **11** SU8236
Argoed *Gwent* **19** ST1799
Aribrauch *W Isls* **102** NB2417
Aridhglas *Strath* **78** NM3123
Arileod *Strath* **78** NM1655
Arinacrinachd *Highld* **91** NG7458
Arinagour *Strath* **78** NM2257
Ariogan *Strath* **79** NM8627
Arisaig *Highld* **85** NM6586
Arisaig House *Highld* **85** NM6984
Arkendale *N York* **55** SE3861
Arkesden *Essex* **31** TL4834
Arkholme *Lancs* **54** SD5871
Arkleton *D & G* **67** NY3791
Arkley *Gt Lon* **23** TQ2295
Arksey *S York* **56** SE5807
Arkwright Town *Derbys* **49** SK4270
Arle *Gloucs* **28** SO9223
Arlecdon *Cumb* **58** NY0419
Arlesey *Beds* **31** TL1936
Arleston *Shrops* **37** SJ6609
Arley *Ches* **47** SJ6680
Arley *Warwks* **39** SP2890
Arlingham *Gloucs* **28** SO7010
Arlington *Devon* **6** SS6140
Arlington *E Susx* **13** TQ5407
Armadale *Highld* **99** NC7864
Armadale *Loth* **75** NS9368
Armaside *Cumb* **58** NY1527
Armathwaite *Cumb* **67** NY5046
Arminghall *Norfk* **43** TG2504
Armitage *Staffs* **38** SK0715
Armley *W York* **55** SE2833
Armston *Nhants* **40** TL0685
Armthorpe *S York* **56** SE6204
Arnabost *Strath* **78** NM2159
Arncliffe *N York* **54** SD9371
Arncroach *Fife* **83** NO5105
Arndilly House *Gramp* **94** NJ2847
Arne *Dorset* **9** SY9788
Arnesby *Leics* **39** SP6192
Arngask *Tays* **82** NO1410
Arnicle *Strath* **72** NR7138
Arnisdale *Highld* **85** NG8410
Arnish *Highld* **90** NG5948
Arniston *Loth* **75** NT3362
Arnol *W Isls* **102** NB3148
Arnold *Notts* **49** SK5845
Arnold *Humb* **57** TA1241
Arnprior *Cent* **81** NS6194
Arnside *Cumb* **59** SD4578
Aros *Strath* **79** NM5645
Arrad Foot *Cumb* **58** SD3080
Arram *Humb* **56** TA0344
Arrathorne *N York* **61** SE2093
Arreton *IOW* **11** SZ5386
Arrington *Cambs* **31** TL3250
Arriundle *Highld* **79** NM8264
Arrochar *Strath* **80** NN2904
Arrow *Warwks* **28** SP0856
Arscott *Shrops* **36** SJ4307
Artafallie *Highld* **92** NH6349
Arthington *W York* **55** SE2644
Arthingworth *Nhants* **40** SP7581
Arthrath *Gramp* **95** NJ9636
Artrochie *Gramp* **95** NK0031
Arundel *W Susx* **12** TQ0106
Asby *Cumb* **58** NY0620
Ascog *Strath* **73** NS1062
Ascot *Berks* **22** SU9268
Ascott-under-Wychwood *Oxon* **29** SP3018
Asenby *N York* **62** SE3975
Asfordby *Leics* **40** SK7019
Asfordby Hill *Leics* **40** SK7219
Asgarby *Lincs* **50** TF1145
Asgarby *Lincs* **51** TF3366
Ash *Somset* **8** ST4720
Ash *Surrey* **22** SU9051
Ash *Kent* **14** TQ6064
Ash *Kent* **15** TR2858
Ash Green *Warwks* **39** SP3384
Ash Green *Surrey* **22** SU9049
Ash Magna *Shrops* **37** SJ5739
Ash Mill *Devon* **7** SS7823
Ash Parva *Shrops* **37** SJ5739
Ash Priors *Somset* **8** ST1529
Ash Street *Suffk* **32** TM0146
Ash Thomas *Devon* **7** ST0010
Ash Vale *Surrey* **22** SU8951
Ashampstead *Berks* **21** SU5676
Ashampstead Green *Berks* **21** SU5677
Ashbocking *Suffk* **33** TM1754
Ashbocking Green *Suffk* **33** TM1854
Ashbourne *Derbys* **48** SK1746
Ashbrittle *Somset* **7** ST0521
Ashburton *Devon* **5** SX7570
Ashbury *Oxon* **21** SU2685
Ashbury *Devon* **6** SX5098
Ashby *Humb* **56** SE8908
Ashby Folville *Leics* **40** SK7012
Ashby Magna *Leics* **39** SP5690
Ashby Parva *Leics* **39** SP5288
Ashby Puerorum *Lincs* **51** TF3271
Ashby St. Ledgers *Nhants* **29** SP5768
Ashby St. Mary *Norfk* **43** TG3202
Ashby by Partney *Lincs* **51** TF4266
Ashby cum Fenby *Humb* **51** TA2500
Ashby de la Launde *Lincs* **50** TF0555
Ashby-de-la-Zouch *Leics* **39** SK3516
Ashchurch *Gloucs* **28** SO9233
Ashcombe *Avon* **19** ST3361
Ashcombe *Devon* **5** SX9179
Ashcott *Somset* **19** ST4336
Ashdon *Essex* **31** TL5842
Ashe *Hants* **21** SU5350
Asheldham *Essex* **25** TL9701
Ashen *Essex* **32** TL7442
Ashendon *Bucks* **30** SP7014
Asheridge *Bucks* **22** SP9304
Ashfield *Cent* **81** NN7803
Ashfield *Suffk* **33** TM2062
Ashfield Green *Suffk* **33** TM2573
Ashford *Derbys* **48** SK1969
Ashford *Devon* **6** SS5335
Ashford *Devon* **5** SX6948
Ashford *Surrey* **22** TQ0771
Ashford *Kent* **15** TR0142
Ashford Bowdler *Shrops* **27** SO5170
Ashford Carbonel *Shrops* **27** SO5270
Ashford Hill *Hants* **21** SU5562
Ashgill *Strath* **74** NS7850
Ashill *Devon* **7** ST0811
Ashill *Somset* **8** ST3217
Ashill *Norfk* **42** TF8804
Ashingdon *Essex* **24** TQ8693
Ashington *Nthumb* **69** NZ2687
Ashington *Somset* **8** ST5621
Ashington *W Susx* **12** TQ1315
Ashkirk *Border* **76** NT4722
Ashleworth *Gloucs* **28** SO8125
Ashleworth Quay *Gloucs* **28** SO8125
Ashley *Staffs* **37** SJ7636
Ashley *Ches* **47** SJ7784
Ashley *Nhants* **40** SP7990
Ashley *Devon* **7** SS6511
Ashley *Wilts* **20** ST8268
Ashley *Gloucs* **20** ST9394
Ashley *Hants* **10** SU3831
Ashley *Hants* **10** SZ2595
Ashley *Cambs* **32** TL6961
Ashley *Kent* **15** TR3048
Ashley Green *Bucks* **22** SP9705
Ashmansworth *Hants* **21** SU4157
Ashmansworthy *Devon* **6** SS3418
Ashmore *Dorset* **9** ST9117
Ashmore Green *Berks* **21** SU5069
Ashorne *Warwks* **29** SP3057
Ashover *Derbys* **49** SK3463
Ashow *Warwks* **29** SP3170
Ashperton *H & W* **27** SO6441
Ashprington *Devon* **5** SX8157
Ashreigney *Devon* **7** SS6313
Ashtead *Surrey* **23** TQ1857
Ashton *Ches* **46** SJ5069
Ashton *H & W* **27** SO5164
Ashton *Nhants* **30** SP7649
Ashton *Cnwll* **2** SW6028
Ashton *Devon* **5** SX8584
Ashton *Nhants* **40** TL0588
Ashton Common *Wilts* **20** ST8958
Ashton Keynes *Wilts* **20** SU0494
Ashton under Hill *H & W* **28** SO9937
Ashton-under-Lyne *Gt Man* **48** SJ9399
Ashurst *Hants* **10** SU3310
Ashurst *W Susx* **12** TQ1715
Ashurst *Kent* **13** TQ5138
Ashurstwood *W Susx* **13** TQ4136
Ashwater *Devon* **6** SX3895
Ashwell *Leics* **40** SK8613
Ashwell *Herts* **31** TL2639
Ashwell End *Herts* **31** TL2540
Ashwellthorpe *Norfk* **43** TM1497
Ashwick *Somset* **19** ST6348
Ashwicken *Norfk* **42** TF7018
Askam in Furness *Cumb* **58** SD2177
Askern *S York* **56** SE5613
Askerswell *Dorset* **8** SY5292
Askett *Bucks* **22** SP8105
Askham *Cumb* **59** NY5123
Askham *Notts* **50** SK7374
Askham Bryan *N York* **56** SE5548
Askham Richard *N York* **56** SE5347
Asknish *Strath* **71** NR9391
Askrigg *N York* **61** SD9491
Askwith *N York* **55** SE1648
Aslackby *Lincs* **40** TF0830
Aslacton *Norfk* **33** TM1590
Aslockton *Notts* **50** SK7440
Aspatria *Cumb* **58** NY1441
Aspenden *Herts* **31** TL3528
Aspley Guise *Beds* **30** SP9335
Aspley Heath *Beds* **30** SP9334
Aspull *Gt Man* **47** SD6108
Asselby *Humb* **56** SE7127
Assington *Suffk* **25** TL9338
Assington Green *Suffk* **32** TL7751
Astbury *Ches* **47** SJ8461
Astcote *Nhants* **30** SP6753
Asterby *Lincs* **51** TF2679
Asterley *Shrops* **36** SJ3707
Asterton *Shrops* **36** SO3991
Asthall *Oxon* **29** SP2811
Asthall Leigh *Oxon* **29** SP3013
Astle *Highld* **97** NH7391
Astley *Gt Man* **47** SD7000
Astley *Shrops* **37** SJ5218
Astley *H & W* **28** SO7867
Astley *Warwks* **39** SP3189
Astley Abbots *Shrops* **37** SO7096
Astley Bridge *Gt Man* **54** SD7111
Astley Cross *H & W* **28** SO8069
Aston *Clwyd* **46** SJ3067
Aston *Shrops* **37** SJ5328
Aston *Ches* **47** SJ5578
Aston *Shrops* **37** SJ6109
Aston *Ches* **47** SJ6146
Aston *Staffs* **37** SJ7541
Aston *Staffs* **38** SJ8923
Aston *Staffs* **38** SJ9130
Aston *Derbys* **48** SK1783
Aston *S York* **49** SK4685
Aston *H & W* **36** SO4671
Aston *Shrops* **37** SO8093
Aston *Oxon* **21** SP3403
Aston *Berks* **22** SU7884
Aston *Herts* **31** TL2722
Aston Abbotts *Bucks* **30** SP8420
Aston Botterell *Shrops* **37** SO6384
Aston Cantlow *Warwks* **28** SP1460
Aston Clinton *Bucks* **30** SP8812
Aston Crews *H & W* **28** SO6723
Aston End *Herts* **31** TL2724
Aston Eyre *Shrops* **37** SO6594
Aston Fields *H & W* **28** SO9669
Aston Flamville *Leics* **39** SP4692
Aston Ingham *H & W* **28** SO6823
Aston Magna *Gloucs* **29** SP1935
Aston Pigott *Shrops* **36** SJ3305
Aston Rogers *Shrops* **36** SJ3406
Aston Rowant *Oxon* **22** SU7299
Aston Somerville *H & W* **28** SP0438
Aston Subedge *Gloucs* **28** SP1441
Aston Tirrold *Oxon* **21** SU5586
Aston Upthorpe *Oxon* **21** SU5586
Aston le Walls *Nhants* **29** SP4950
Aston on Clun *Shrops* **36** SO3981
Aston-in-Makerfield *Gt Man* **47** SJ5798
Aston-on-Trent *Derbys* **39** SK4129
Astwick *Beds* **31** TL2138
Astwood *H & W* **28** SO9365
Astwood *Bucks* **30** SP9547
Astwood Bank *H & W* **28** SP0462
Aswarby *Lincs* **40** TF0639
Aswardby *Lincs* **51** TF3770
Atch Lench *H & W* **28** SP0350
Atcham *Shrops* **37** SJ5409
Athelhampton *Dorset* **9** SY7694
Athelington *Suffk* **33** TM2171
Athelney *Somset* **8** ST3428
Athelstaneford *Loth* **76** NT5377
Atherington *Devon* **6** SS5922
Atherstone *Warwks* **39** SP3097
Atherstone on Stour *Warwks* **29** SP2051
Atherton *Gt Man* **47** SD6703
Atlow *Derbys* **48** SK2248
Attadale *Highld* **85** NG9238
Atterby *Lincs* **50** SK9792
Attercliffe *S York* **49** SK3788
Atterton *Leics* **39** SP3598
Attleborough *Warwks* **39** SP3790
Attleborough *Norfk* **42** TM0495
Attlebridge *Norfk* **43** TG1216
Attleton Green *Suffk* **32** TL7454
Attonburn *Border* **76** NT8122
Atwick *Humb* **57** TA1850
Atworth *Wilts* **20** ST8565
Aubourn *Lincs* **50** SK9262
Auchagallon *Strath* **72** NR8934
Auchedly *Gramp* **95** NJ8933
Auchenblae *Gramp* **89** NO7279
Auchenbowie *Cent* **81** NS7987
Auchencairn *D & G* **66** NX7951
Auchencairn *D & G* **66** NX9884
Auchencrow *Border* **77** NT8560
Auchendinny *Loth* **75** NT2561
Auchengray *Strath* **75** NS9954
Auchenhalrig *Gramp* **94** NJ3761
Auchenheath *Strath* **74** NS8043
Auchenhessnane *D & G* **66** NX8096
Auchenlochan *Strath* **71** NR9772
Auchenmade *Strath* **73** NS3548
Auchenmalg *D & G* **64** NX2352
Auchentibber *Strath* **74** NS6755
Auchentiber *Strath* **73** NS3647
Auchentroig *Cent* **81** NS5493
Auchindrean *Highld* **96** NH1980
Auchininna *Gramp* **94** NJ6546
Auchinleck *Strath* **74** NS5521
Auchinloch *Strath* **74** NS6570
Auchinstarry *Strath* **74** NS7176
Auchintore *Highld* **86** NN0972
Auchiries *Gramp* **95** NK0737
Auchlee *Gramp* **89** NO8996
Auchleven *Gramp* **94** NJ6224
Auchlochan *Strath* **74** NS7937
Auchlossan *Gramp* **89** NJ5601
Auchlyne *Cent* **81** NN5129
Auchmacoy *Gramp* **95** NJ9931
Auchmillan *Strath* **74** NS5129
Auchmithie *Tays* **89** NO6743
Auchmuirbridge *Fife* **82** NO2101
Auchnacree *Tays* **89** NO4663
Auchnagatt *Gramp* **95** NJ9241
Auchnangoul *Strath* **80** NN0605
Auchnotteroch *D & G* **64** NW9960
Auchroisk *Gramp* **94** NJ3351
Auchronie *Tays* **88** NO4480
Auchterarder *Tays* **82** NN9412
Auchteraw *Highld* **92** NH3507
Auchterblair *Highld* **93** NH9222
Auchtercairn *Highld* **91** NG8077
Auchterhouse *Tays* **83** NO3337
Auchterless *Gramp* **95** NJ7141
Auchtermuchty *Fife* **83** NO2311
Auchterneed *Highld* **92** NH4959
Auchtertool *Fife* **82** NT2190
Auchtertyre *Highld* **85** NG8427
Auchtoo *Cent* **81** NN5520
Auckengill *Highld* **100** ND3663
Auckley *S York* **49** SE6400
Audenshaw *Gt Man* **48** SJ9197
Audlem *Ches* **47** SJ6543
Audley *Staffs* **47** SJ7950
Audley End *Essex* **31** TL5337
Audley End *Suffk* **32** TL8553
Aughertree *Cumb* **58** NY2538
Aughton *Lancs* **46** SD3905
Aughton *Lancs* **53** SD5567
Aughton *Humb* **56** SE7038
Aughton *S York* **49** SK4586
Aughton *Wilts* **21** SU2356
Aughton Park *Lancs* **46** SD4006
Auldallan *Tays* **88** NO3158
Auldearn *Highld* **93** NH9255
Aulden *H & W* **27** SO4654
Auldgirth *D & G* **66** NX9186
Auldhame *Loth* **83** NT5984
Auldhouse *Strath* **74** NS6250
Ault Hucknall *Derbys* **49** SK4665
Ault a' chruinn *Highld* **85** NG9420
Aultbea *Highld* **91** NG8789
Aultgrishin *Highld* **91** NG7485
Aultguish Inn *Highld* **92** NH3570
Aultmore *Gramp* **94** NJ4053
Aultnagoire *Highld* **92** NH5423
Aultnamain Inn *Highld* **97** NH6681
Aunsby *Lincs* **40** TF0438
Aust *Avon* **19** ST5788
Austerfield *Notts* **49** SK6694
Austrey *Warwks* **39** SK2906
Austwick *N York* **54** SD7668
Authorpe *Lincs* **51** TF3980
Avebury *Wilts* **20** SU1069
Aveley *Essex* **24** TQ5680
Avening *Gloucs* **20** ST8898
Averham *Notts* **50** SK7654
Aveton Gifford *Devon* **5** SX6947
Aviemore *Highld* **93** NH8913
Avington *Berks* **21** SU3767
Avoch *Highld* **93** NH7055
Avon *Dorset* **10** SZ1498
Avon Dassett *Warwks* **29** SP4150
Avonbridge *Cent* **75** NS9172
Avonmouth *Avon* **19** ST5178
Avonwick *Devon* **5** SX7158
Awliscombe *Devon* **8** ST1301
Awre *Gloucs* **28** SO7008
Awsworth *Notts* **49** SK4844
Axbridge *Somset* **19** ST4354
Axford *Wilts* **21** SU2370
Axford *Hants* **21** SU6043
Axminster *Devon* **8** SY2998
Axmouth *Devon* **8** SY2591
Aycliffe *Dur* **61** NZ2822
Aylburton *Gloucs* **19** SO6101
Aylesbeare *Devon* **5** SY0392
Aylesbury *Bucks* **30** SP8213
Aylesby *Humb* **57** TA2007
Aylesford *Kent* **14** TQ7359
Aylesham *Kent* **15** TR2452
Aylestone *Leics* **39** SK5700
Aylmerton *Norfk* **43** TG1839
Aylsham *Norfk* **43** TG1926
Aylton *H & W* **27** SO6537
Aylworth *Gloucs* **28** SP1021
Aymestrey *H & W* **27** SO4265
Aynho *Nhants* **29** SP5133
Ayot Green *Herts* **31** TL2214
Ayot St. Lawrence *Herts* **31** TL1916
Ayot St. Peter *Herts* **31** TL2115
Ayr *Strath* **73** NS3321
Aysgarth *N York* **61** SE0088
Ayshford *Devon* **7** ST0415
Ayside *Cumb* **59** SD3983
Ayston *Leics* **40** SK8600
Aythorpe Roding *Essex* **24** TL5815
Ayton *Border* **77** NT9260
Azerley *N York* **61** SE2574

B

Babbacombe *Devon* **5** SX9265
Babbs Green *Herts* **31** TL3916
Babcary *Somset* **8** ST5628
Babington *Somset* **20** ST7051
Babraham *Cambs* **31** TL5150
Babworth *Notts* **49** SK6880
Back of Keppoch *Highld* **85** NM6587
Backaland *Ork* **103** HY5630
Backfolds *Gramp* **95** NK0252
Backford *Ches* **46** SJ3971
Backies *Highld* **97** NC8302
Backlass *Highld* **100** ND2053
Backwell *Avon* **19** ST4968
Baconsthorpe *Norfk* **43** TG1236
Bacton *H & W* **27** SO3732
Bacton *Norfk* **43** TG3433
Bacton *Suffk* **32** TM0567
Bacup *Lancs* **54** SD8622

Badachro
Beddgelert

Badachro Highld 91 NG7873
Badbury Wilts 21 SU1980
Badby Nhants 29 SP5658
Badcall Highld 98 NC1541
Badcall Highld 98 NC2455
Badcaul Highld 91 NH0291
Baddesley Clinton Warwks 29 SP2070
Baddesley Ensor Warwks 39 SP2798
Baddidarroch Highld 98 NC0822
Badenscoth Gramp 95 NJ6938
Badenyon Gramp 94 NJ3319
Badger Shrops 37 SO7699
Badgeworth Gloucs 28 SO9019
Badgworth Somset 19 ST3952
Badicaul Highld 85 NG7529
Badingham Suffk 33 TM3068
Badlesmere Kent 15 TR0153
Badlieu Border 75 NT0518
Badlipster Highld 100 ND2448
Badluachrach Highld 91 NG9994
Badninish Highld 97 NH7594
Badrallach Highld 91 NH0691
Badsey H & W 28 SP0743
Badshot Lea Surrey 22 SU8648
Badsworth W York 55 SE4614
Badwell Ash Suffk 32 TL9868
Bag Enderby Lincs 51 TF3571
Bagber Dorset 9 ST7513
Bagby N York 62 SE4680
Bagillt Clwyd 46 SJ2175
Baginton Warwks 39 SP3474
Baglan W Glam 18 SS7492
Bagley Shrops 36 SJ4027
Bagley Somset 19 ST4645
Bagmore Hants 21 SU6544
Bagnall Staffs 48 SJ9250
Bagot Shrops 37 SO5873
Bagshot Surrey 22 SU9063
Bagstone Avon 20 ST6987
Bagworth Leics 39 SK4408
Bagwy Llydiart H & W 27 SO4426
Baildon W York 55 SE1539
Baildon Green W York 55 SE1439
Baile Mor Strath 78 NM2824
Baillieston Strath 74 NS6764
Bainbridge N York 61 SD9390
Bainshole Gramp 94 NJ6035
Bainton Humb 56 SE9652
Bainton Cambs 40 TF0906
Baintown Fife 83 NO3503
Bairnkine Border 76 NT6515
Bakewell Derbys 48 SK2168
Bala Gwynd 45 SH9235
Balallan W Isls 102 NB2920
Balbeg Highld 92 NH4431
Balbeggie Tays 82 NO1629
Balblair Highld 92 NH5145
Balblair Highld 93 NH7066
Balby S York 49 SE5600
Balcary D & G 66 NX8149
Balchraggan Highld 92 NH5343
Balchrick Highld 98 NC1960
Balcombe W Susx 12 TQ3130
Balcomie Links Fife 83 NO6209
Balcurvie Fife 83 NO3400
Baldersby N York 62 SE3578
Baldersby St. James N York 62 SE3676
Balderstone Lancs 54 SD6332
Balderton Notts 50 SK8151
Baldinnie Fife 83 NO4211
Baldinnies Tays 82 NO0216
Baldock Herts 31 TL2434
Baldovie Tays 83 NO4533
Baldslow E Susx 14 TQ8013
Bale Norfk 42 TG0136
Baledgarno Tays 83 NO2730
Balemartine Strath 78 NL9841
Balerno Loth 75 NT1666
Balfarg Fife 83 NO2803
Balfield Tays 89 NO5468
Balfour Ork 103 HY4716
Balfron Cent 81 NS5489
Balgaveny Gramp 94 NJ6540
Balgavies Tays 89 NO5451
Balgonar Fife 82 NT0293
Balgowan Highld 87 NN6494
Balgowan D & G 64 NX1142
Balgown Highld 90 NG3868
Balgracie D & G 64 NW9860
Balgray Tays 83 NO4038
Balhalgardy Gramp 95 NJ7523
Balham Gt Lon 23 TQ2873
Balhary Tays 88 NO2646
Balholmie Tays 82 NO1436
Baligill Highld 99 NC8565
Balintore Highld 97 NH8675
Balintore Tays 88 NO2859
Balintraid Highld 93 NH7370
Balivanich W Isls 102 NF7755
Balk N York 62 SE4780
Balkeerie Tays 88 NO3244
Balkholme Humb 56 SE7828
Balkissock Strath 64 NX1482
Ballachgair Strath 72 NR7727
Ballachulish Highld 86 NN0858
Ballantrae Strath 64 NX0882
Ballasalla IOM 52 SC2870
Ballater Gramp 88 NO3695
Ballaugh IOM 52 SC3493
Ballchraggan Highld 97 NH7675
Ballechin Tays 87 NN9353
Ballencrieff Loth 83 NT4878
Ballevullin Strath 78 NL9546
Ballidon Derbys 48 SK2054
Balliekine Strath 72 NR8739
Balliemore Strath 80 NS1099
Balligmorrie Strath 64 NX2290
Ballimore Cent 81 NN5317
Ballimore Strath 71 NR9283
Ballindalloch Gramp 94 NJ1636
Ballindean Tays 83 NO2529
Ballinger Common Bucks 22 SP9103
Ballingham H & W 27 SO5731
Ballingry Fife 82 NT1797
Ballinluig Tays 88 NN9752
Ballinshoe Tays 88 NO4153
Ballintuim Tays 88 NO1055
Balloch Highld 93 NH7247
Balloch Tays 82 NN8419
Balloch Strath 64 NX3295
Ballochroy Strath 71 NR7352
Ballogie Gramp 89 NO5795
Balls Cross W Susx 12 SU9826
Balls Green E Susx 13 TQ4936
Ballygown Strath 79 NM4343
Ballygrant Strath 70 NR3966
Ballygroggan Strath 72 NR6219
Ballyhaugh Strath 78 NM1758
Ballymenoch Strath 80 NS3086
Ballymichael Strath 72 NR9231
Balmacara Highld 85 NG8028
Balmaclellan D & G 65 NX6579
Balmacneil Tays 88 NN9750
Balmae D & G 65 NX6844
Balmaha Cent 81 NS4290
Balmalcolm Fife 83 NO3208
Balmangan D & G 65 NX6445
Balmedie Gramp 95 NJ9618
Balmerino Fife 83 NO3524
Balmore Strath 74 NS5973
Balmuchy Highld 97 NH8678
Balmuir Tays 89 NO5648
Balmule Fife 82 NT2088
Balmullo Fife 83 NO4220
Balnaboth Tays 88 NO3166
Balnacoil Lodge Highld 97 NC8011
Balnacroft Gramp 88 NO2894
Balnafoich Highld 93 NH6835
Balnaguard Tays 87 NN9451
Balnahard Strath 79 NM4534
Balnahard Strath 70 NR4199
Balnain Highld 92 NH4430
Balnakeil Highld 98 NC3968
Balnapaling Highld 93 NH7969
Balquharn Tays 82 NO0235
Balquhidder Cent 81 NN5320
Balruddery House Tays 83 NO3132
Balsall W Mids 39 SP2376
Balsall Heath W Mids 38 SP0784
Balscote Oxon 29 SP3942
Balsham Cambs 31 TL5850
Baltasound Shet 103 HP6208
Baltersan D & G 64 NX4261
Balthangie Gramp 95 NJ8351
Baltonsborough Somset 8 ST5434
Balvicar Strath 79 NM7616
Balvraid Highld 85 NG8416
Balvraid Highld 93 NH8231
Bamber Bridge Lancs 53 SD5625
Bamber's Green Essex 24 TL5722
Bamburgh Nthumb 77 NU1734
Bamff Tays 88 NO2251
Bamford Derbys 48 SK2083
Bampton Cumb 59 NY5118
Bampton Oxon 21 SP3103
Bampton Devon 7 SS9522
Bampton Grange Cumb 59 NY5218
Banavie Highld 86 NN1177
Banbury Oxon 29 SP4540
Bancffosfelem Dyfed 17 SN4811
Banchory Gramp 89 NO6995
Banchory-Devenick Gramp 89 NJ9002
Bancycapel Dyfed 17 SN4214
Bancyfelin Dyfed 17 SN3218
Bandirran Tays 82 NO2030
Banff Gramp 95 NJ6863
Bangor Gwynd 44 SH5772
Bangor-is-y-coed Clwyd 46 SJ3845
Bangors Cnwll 6 SX2099
Banham Norfk 32 TM0687
Bank Hants 10 SU2807
Bankend Strath 74 NS8033
Bankend D & G 66 NY0268
Bankfoot Tays 82 NO0635
Bankglen Strath 66 NS5912
Bankhead Gramp 95 NJ9009
Bankhead Strath 73 NS3739
Banknock Cent 81 NS7779
Banks Lancs 53 SD3920
Bankshill D & G 67 NY1982
Banningham Norfk 43 TG2129
Bannister Green Essex 24 TL6920
Bannockburn Cent 82 NS8190
Banstead Surrey 23 TQ2559
Bantham Devon 5 SX6643
Banton Strath 81 NS7480
Banwell Avon 19 ST3959
Bapchild Kent 14 TQ9263
Bapton Wilts 20 ST9938
Bar Hill Cambs 31 TL3863
Barassie Strath 73 NS3232
Barbaraville Highld 93 NH7472
Barbieston Strath 73 NS4317
Barbon Cumb 60 SD6282
Barbrook Devon 18 SS7147
Barby Nhants 29 SP5470
Barcaldine Strath 86 NM9641
Barcheston Warwks 29 SP2639
Barcombe E Susx 13 TQ4114
Barcombe Cross E Susx 13 TQ4115
Barden N York 61 SE1493
Barden Park Kent 13 TQ5746
Bardfield End Green Essex 24 TL6231
Bardfield Saling Essex 24 TL6826
Bardney Lincs 50 TF1269
Bardon Leics 39 SK4412
Bardon Mill Nthumb 68 NY7764
Bardowie Strath 74 NS5873
Bardrainney Strath 80 NS3373
Bardsea Cumb 58 SD3074
Bardsey W York 55 SE3643
Bardwell Suffk 32 TL9473
Bare Lancs 53 SD4564
Barfad D & G 64 NX3266
Barford Warwks 29 SP2760
Barford Norfk 43 TG1107
Barford St. John Oxon 29 SP4433
Barford St. Martin Wilts 10 SU0531
Barford St. Michael Oxon 29 SP4332
Barfrestone Kent 15 TR2650
Bargeddie Strath 74 NS6964
Bargoed M Glam 19 ST1599
Bargrennan D & G 64 NX3577
Barham Cambs 30 TL1375
Barham Suffk 33 TM1451
Barham Kent 15 TR2050
Barholm Lincs 40 TF0810
Barkby Leics 39 SK6309
Barkby Thorpe Leics 39 SK6309
Barkestone-le-Vale Leics 40 SK7734
Barkham Berks 22 SU7766
Barking Suffk 32 TM0753
Barking Gt Lon 23 TQ4484
Barking Tye Suffk 32 TM0652
Barkingside Gt Lon 23 TQ4489
Barkisland W York 55 SE0519
Barkla Shop Cnwll 2 SW7350
Barkston N York 55 SE4936
Barkston Lincs 50 SK9341
Barkway Herts 31 TL3835
Barlaston Staffs 48 SJ8938
Barlavington W Susx 12 SU9716
Barlborough Derbys 49 SK4777
Barlestone Leics 39 SK4205
Barley Lancs 54 SD8240
Barley Herts 31 TL4038
Barleythorpe Leics 40 SK8409
Barling Essex 25 TQ9389
Barlings Lincs 50 TF0774
Barlochan D & G 66 NX8157
Barlow T & W 69 NZ1561
Barlow N York 56 SE6428
Barlow Derbys 49 SK3474
Barmby Moor Humb 56 SE7748
Barmby on the Marsh Humb 56 SE6928
Barmer Norfk 42 TF8133
Barmollack Strath 72 NR8043
Barmouth Gwynd 35 SH6116
Barmpton Dur 62 NZ3118
Barmston Humb 57 TA1659
Barnacabber Strath 80 NS1789
Barnacarry Strath 80 NS0094
Barnack Cambs 40 TF0705
Barnard Castle Dur 61 NZ0516
Barnard Gate Oxon 29 SP4010
Barnardiston Suffk 32 TL7148
Barnbarroch D & G 66 NX8456
Barnburgh S York 55 SE4803
Barnby Suffk 33 TM4789
Barnby Dun S York 56 SE6109
Barnby Moor Notts 49 SK6684
Barnby in the Willows Notts 50 SK8552
Barncorkrie D & G 64 NX0935
Barnes Gt Lon 23 TQ2276
Barnes Street Kent 13 TQ6447
Barnet Gt Lon 23 TQ2496
Barnetby le Wold Humb 57 TA0509
Barney Norfk 42 TF9932
Barnham W Susx 12 SU9503
Barnham Suffk 32 TL8779
Barnham Broom Norfk 42 TG0807
Barnhead Tays 89 NO6657
Barnhill Gramp 93 NJ1457
Barnhill Tays 83 NO4731
Barnhills D & G 64 NW9871
Barningham Dur 61 NZ0810
Barningham Suffk 32 TL9676
Barnoldby le Beck Humb 57 TA2303
Barnoldswick Lancs 54 SD8746
Barns Green W Susx 12 TQ1226
Barnsley S York 55 SE3406
Barnsley Gloucs 28 SP0704
Barnsole Kent 15 TR2756
Barnstaple Devon 6 SS5633
Barnston Mersyd 46 SJ2783
Barnston Essex 24 TL6419
Barnstone Notts 40 SK7335
Barnt Green H & W 38 SP0173
Barnton Loth 75 NT1874
Barnton Ches 47 SJ6375
Barnwell All Saints Nhants 40 TL0484
Barnwell St. Andrew Nhants 40 TL0584
Barnwood Gloucs 28 SO8518
Barr Strath 64 NX2794
Barrachan D & G 64 NX3649
Barrapoll Strath 78 NL9442
Barrasford Nthumb 68 NY9173
Barrhead Strath 74 NS4958
Barrhill Strath 64 NX2382
Barrington Somset 8 ST3818
Barrington Cambs 31 TL3849
Barripper Cnwll 2 SW6338
Barrmill Strath 73 NS3651
Barrnacarry Bay Strath 79 NM8122
Barrock Highld 100 ND2570
Barrow Lancs 54 SD7338
Barrow Leics 40 SK8815
Barrow Gloucs 28 SO8824
Barrow Somset 9 ST7231
Barrow Suffk 32 TL7663
Barrow Burn Nthumb 68 NT8610
Barrow Gurney Avon 19 ST5268
Barrow Haven Humb 57 TA0622
Barrow upon Soar Leics 39 SK5717
Barrow upon Trent Derbys 39 SK3528
Barrow-in-Furness Cumb 53 SD2068
Barrow-upon-Humber Humb 57 TA0620
Barrowby Lincs 40 SK8736
Barrowden Leics 40 SK9400
Barrowford Lancs 54 SD8539
Barry Tays 83 NO5334
Barry S Glam 18 ST1268
Barsby Leics 40 SK6911
Barsham Suffk 33 TM3989
Barskimmings Strath 73 NS4825
Barston W Mids 39 SP2078
Bartestree H & W 27 SO5640
Barthol Chapel Gramp 95 NJ8133
Bartholomew Green Essex 24 TL7221
Barthomley Ches 47 SJ7652
Bartley Hants 10 SU3012
Bartley Green W Mids 38 SP0081
Bartlow Cambs 31 TL5845
Barton N York 61 NZ2208
Barton Lancs 53 SD3509
Barton Lancs 53 SD5137
Barton Ches 46 SJ4454
Barton Gloucs 28 SP0925
Barton Oxon 29 SP5507
Barton Devon 5 SX9167
Barton Cambs 31 TL4055
Barton Bendish Norfk 42 TF7105
Barton End Gloucs 20 ST8498
Barton Hartshorn Bucks 29 SP6430
Barton Mills Suffk 32 TL7173
Barton Seagrave Nhants 30 SP8877
Barton St. David Somset 8 ST5432
Barton Stacey Hants 21 SU4341
Barton Town Devon 7 SS6840
Barton Waterside Humb 56 TA0222
Barton in Fabis Notts 39 SK5132
Barton in the Beans Leics 39 SK3906
Barton in the Clay Beds 30 TL0830
Barton on Sea Hants 10 SZ2393
Barton-Upon-Humber Humb 56 TA0221
Barton-le-Street N York 63 SE7274
Barton-le-Willows N York 56 SE7163
Barton-on-the-Heath Warwks 29 SP2532
Barton-under-Needwood Staffs 38 SK1818
Barvas W Isls 102 NB3649
Barway Cambs 31 TL5575
Barwell Leics 39 SP4496
Barwick Devon 6 SS5907
Barwick Somset 8 ST5513
Barwick in Elmet W York 55 SE4037
Baschurch Shrops 36 SJ4221
Bascote Warwks 29 SP4063
Bashall Eaves Lancs 54 SD6943
Basildon Berks 21 SU6078
Basildon Essex 24 TQ7189
Basingstoke Hants 21 SU6352
Baslow Derbys 48 SK2572
Bason Bridge Somset 19 ST3446
Bassaleg Gwent 19 ST2786
Bassendean Border 76 NT6245
Bassenthwaite Cumb 58 NY2332
Bassett Hants 10 SU4216
Bassingbourn Cambs 31 TL3343
Bassingham Lincs 50 SK9060
Bassingthorpe Leics 40 SK9628
Bassus Green Herts 31 TL3025
Baston Lincs 40 TF1113
Bastwick Norfk 43 TG4217
Batchworth Herts 22 TQ0694
Batcombe Somset 20 ST6938
Batecombe Dorset 9 ST6103
Batford Herts 30 TL1415
Bath Avon 20 ST7464
Bath Side Essex 25 TM2532
Bathampton Avon 20 ST7766
Bathealton Somset 7 ST0823
Batheaston Avon 20 ST7767
Bathford Avon 20 ST7866
Bathgate Loth 75 NS9768
Bathley Notts 50 SK7759
Bathpool Somset 8 ST2526
Bathpool Cnwll 4 SX2874
Bathville Loth 75 NS9367
Bathway Somset 19 ST5952
Batley W York 55 SE2224
Batsford Gloucs 29 SP1833
Battersby N York 62 NZ5907
Battersea Gt Lon 23 TQ2776
Battisford Tye Suffk 32 TM0354
Battle Powys 26 SO0130
Battle E Susx 14 TQ7515
Battledykes Tays 88 NO4555
Battlesbridge Essex 24 TQ7894
Battleton Somset 7 SS9127
Baughton H & W 28 SO8841
Baughurst Hants 21 SU5860
Baulds Gramp 89 NO6093
Baulking Oxon 21 SU3191
Baumber Lincs 51 TF2274
Baunton H & W 28 SP0104
Baverstock Wilts 9 SU0332
Bawburgh Norfk 43 TG1508
Bawdeswell Norfk 42 TG0420
Bawdrip Somset 19 ST3439
Bawdsey Suffk 33 TM3440
Bawtry Notts 49 SK6493
Baxenden Lancs 54 SD7726
Baxterley Warwks 39 SP2896
Bayble W Isls 102 NB5231
Baybridge Hants 11 SU5223
Baycliff Cumb 53 SD2872
Baydon Wilts 21 SU2878
Bayford Somset 9 ST7229
Bayford Herts 23 TL3108
Bayhead W Isls 102 NF7468
Baylham Suffk 33 TM1051
Baysham H & W 27 SO5727
Bayston Hill Shrops 37 SJ4808
Baythorne End Essex 32 TL7242
Bayton H & W 37 SO6973
Bayworth Oxon 21 SP4901
Beachampton Bucks 30 SP7736
Beachamwell Norfk 42 TF7505
Beacon Devon 8 ST1805
Beacon End Essex 25 TL9524
Beacon's Bottom Bucks 22 SU7895
Beaconsfield Bucks 22 SU9490
Beacontree Gt Lon 23 TQ4786
Beadlam N York 62 SE6584
Beadlow Beds 30 TL1038
Beadnell Nthumb 77 NU2229
Beaford Devon 6 SS5515
Beal Nthumb 77 NU0642
Beal N York 56 SE5325
Bealsmill Cnwll 4 SX3576
Beaminster Dorset 8 ST4701
Beamish Dur 69 NZ2253
Beamsley N York 55 SE0752
Beanacre Wilts 20 ST9066
Beanley Nthumb 77 NU0818
Beardon Devon 4 SX5184
Beare Devon 7 SS9901
Beare Green Surrey 12 TQ1742
Bearley Warwks 29 SP1860
Bearpark Dur 69 NZ2343
Bearsbridge Nthumb 68 NY7857
Bearsden Strath 74 NS5372
Bearstead Kent 14 TQ8055
Bearstone Shrops 37 SJ7239
Bearwood W Mids 38 SP0286
Beattock D & G 66 NT0802
Beauchamp Roding Essex 24 TL5809
Beaufort Gwent 27 SO1611
Beaulieu Hants 10 SU3802
Beauly Highld 92 NH5246
Beaumaris Gwynd 44 SH6076
Beaumont Jersey 101 JS0000
Beaumont Cumb 67 NY3459
Beaumont Essex 25 TM1624
Beausale Warwks 29 SP2470
Beauworth Hants 11 SU5726
Beaver Green Kent 15 TR0041
Beaworthy Devon 6 SX4699
Beazley End Essex 24 TL7429
Bebington Mersyd 46 SJ3383
Beccles Suffk 33 TM4289
Becconsall Lancs 53 SD4523
Beck Row Suffk 32 TL6977
Beck Side Cumb 58 SD2382
Beckbury Shrops 37 SJ7601
Beckenham Gt Lon 23 TQ3769
Beckering Lincs 50 TF1280
Beckermet Cumb 58 NY0106
Beckfoot Cumb 67 NY0949
Beckford H & W 28 SO9736
Beckhampton Wilts 20 SU0868
Beckingham Notts 50 SK7789
Beckingham Lincs 50 SK8753
Beckington Somset 20 ST8051
Beckjay Shrops 36 SO3977
Beckley Oxon 29 SP5611
Beckley E Susx 14 TQ8523
Beckton Gt Lon 23 TQ4381
Beckwithshaw N York 55 SE2653
Becquet Vincent Jersey 101 JS0000
Bedale N York 61 SE2688
Bedchester Dorset 9 ST8517
Beddau M Glam 18 ST0585
Beddgelert Gwynd 44 SH5948

Brandis Corner

Buckland in the Moor

Brandis Corner *Devon* 6 SS4104
Brandiston *Norfk* 43 TG1421
Brandon *Dur* 61 NZ2340
Brandon *Lincs* 50 SK9048
Brandon *Warwks* 39 SP4176
Brandon *Suffk* 32 TL7886
Brandon Parva *Norfk* 42 TG0708
Brandsby *N York* 56 SE5872
Brandy Wharf *Lincs* 50 TF0196
Branksome *Dorset* 10 SZ0492
Branksome Park *Dorset* 10 SZ0590
Bransbury *Hants* 21 SU4242
Bransby *Lincs* 50 SK8978
Branscombe *Devon* 8 SY1988
Bransford *H & W* 28 SO7952
Bransgore *Hants* 10 SZ1897
Bransley *Shrops* 37 SO6575
Branston *Staffs* 39 SK2221
Branston *Leics* 40 SK8129
Branston *Lincs* 50 TF0166
Branston Booths *Lincs* 50 TF0668
Branstone *IOW* 11 SZ5583
Brant Broughton *Lincs* 50 SK9154
Brantham *Suffk* 25 TM1034
Branthwaite *Cumb* 58 NY0525
Branthwaite *Cumb* 58 NY2937
Brantingham *Humb* 56 SE9429
Branton *Nthumb* 77 NU0416
Branton *S York* 49 SE6401
Branton Green *N York* 55 SE4362
Branxton *Nthumb* 77 NT8937
Brassington *Derbys* 48 SK2254
Brasted *Kent* 23 TQ4755
Brasted Chart *Gt Lon* 13 TQ4653
Brathens *Gramp* 89 NO6798
Bratoft *Lincs* 51 TF4764
Brattleby *Lincs* 50 SK9481
Bratton *Wilts* 20 ST9152
Bratton Clovelly *Devon* 4 SX4691
Bratton Fleming *Devon* 7 SS6437
Bratton Seymour *Somset* 9 ST6729
Braughing *Herts* 31 TL3925
Braunston *Leics* 40 SK8306
Braunston *Nhants* 29 SP5466
Braunstone *Leics* 39 SK5502
Braunton *Devon* 6 SS4836
Brawby *N York* 63 SE7378
Brawl *Highld* 99 NC8166
Brawlbin *Highld* 100 ND0757
Bray *Berks* 22 SU9079
Bray Shop *Cnwll* 4 SX3374
Braybrooke *Nhants* 40 SP7684
Brayford *Devon* 7 SS6834
Braythorn *N York* 55 SE2449
Brayton *N York* 56 SE6030
Braywick *Berks* 22 SU8979
Braywoodside *Berks* 22 SU8775
Breachwood Green *Herts* 30 TL1522
Breadsall *Derbys* 49 SK3639
Breadstone *Gloucs* 20 SO7000
Breage *Cnwll* 2 SW6128
Breakachy *Highld* 92 NH4644
Breamore *Hants* 10 SU1517
Brean *Somset* 19 ST2956
Brearton *N York* 55 SE3261
Breasclete *W Isls* 102 NB2135
Breaston *Derbys* 39 SK4533
Brechfa *Dyfed* 17 SN5230
Brechin *Tays* 89 NO6060
Breckles *Norfk* 42 TL9594
Breckonside *D & G* 66 NX8489
Brecon *Powys* 26 SO0428
Bredbury *Gt Man* 48 SJ9291
Brede *E Susx* 14 TQ8218
Bredenbury *H & W* 27 SO6056
Bredfield *Suffk* 33 TM2653
Bredgar *Kent* 14 TQ8860
Bredhurst *Kent* 14 TQ7962
Bredon *H & W* 28 SO9236
Bredon's Hardwick *H & W* 28 SO9135
Bredon's Norton *H & W* 28 SO9339
Bredwardine *H & W* 27 SO3344
Breedon on the Hill *Leics* 39 SK4022
Breich *Loth* 75 NS9560
Breightmet *Gt Man* 54 SD7409
Breighton *Humb* 56 SE7033
Breinton *H & W* 27 SO4739
Bremhill *Wilts* 20 ST9773
Brenchley *Kent* 14 TQ6741
Brendon *Devon* 18 SS7748
Brenfield *Strath* 71 NR8482
Brenish *W Isls* 102 NA9925
Brent Eleigh *Suffk* 32 TL9448
Brent Knoll *Somset* 19 ST3350
Brent Mill *Devon* 5 SX6959
Brent Pelham *Herts* 31 TL4330
Brentford *Gt Lon* 23 TQ1777
Brentingby *Leics* 40 SK7818
Brentwood *Essex* 24 TQ5993
Brenzett *Kent* 15 TR0027
Brenzett Green *Kent* 15 TR0128
Brereton Green *Ches* 47 SJ7764
Bressingham *Norfk* 32 TM0780
Bretabister *Shet* 103 HU4857
Bretby *Derbys* 39 SK2922
Bretford *Warwks* 39 SP4377
Bretforton *H & W* 28 SP0944
Bretherdale Head *Cumb* 59 NY5705
Bretherton *Lancs* 53 SD4720
Brettenham *Norfk* 32 TL9383
Brettenham *Suffk* 32 TL9654
Bretton *Clwyd* 46 SJ3563
Brewood *Staffs* 38 SJ8808
Briantspuddle *Dorset* 9 SY8193
Brick Houses *S York* 49 SK3081
Bricket Wood *Herts* 22 TL1202
Bricklehampton *H & W* 28 SO9742
Bride *IOM* 52 NX4401
Bridekirk *Cumb* 58 NY1133
Bridestowe *Devon* 4 SX5189
Brideswell *Gramp* 94 NJ5738
Bridford *Devon* 5 SX8186
Bridge *Cnwll* 2 SW6744
Bridge *Kent* 15 TR1854
Bridge Hewick *N York* 55 SE3370
Bridge Sollers *H & W* 27 SO4142
Bridge Street *Suffk* 32 TL8749
Bridge Trafford *Ches* 46 SJ4571
Bridge of Alford *Gramp* 94 NJ5617
Bridge of Avon *Gramp* 94 NJ1835
Bridge of Balgie *Tays* 87 NN5746
Bridge of Brewlands *Tays* 88 NO1961
Bridge of Brown *Highld* 93 NJ1120
Bridge of Cally *Tays* 88 NO1351
Bridge of Canny *Gramp* 89 NO6597
Bridge of Craigisla *Tays* 88 NO2553
Bridge of Dee *D & G* 65 NX7359
Bridge of Don *Gramp* 95 NJ9409
Bridge of Dulsie *Highld* 93 NH9341
Bridge of Dye *Gramp* 89 NO6586
Bridge of Earn *Tays* 82 NO1318
Bridge of Ericht *Tays* 87 NN5258
Bridge of Feugh *Gramp* 89 NO7094
Bridge of Forss *Highld* 100 ND0368
Bridge of Gairn *Gramp* 88 NO3597
Bridge of Gaur *Tays* 87 NN5056
Bridge of Orchy *Strath* 80 NN2939
Bridge of Tilt *Tays* 87 NN8765
Bridge of Tynet *Gramp* 94 NJ3861
Bridge of Walls *Shet* 103 HU2752
Bridge of Weir *Strath* 73 NS3965
Bridge of Westfield *Highld* 100 ND0664
Bridgehampton *Somset* 8 ST5624
Bridgehill *Dur* 68 NZ0951
Bridgemary *Hants* 11 SU5803
Bridgend *Gramp* 94 NJ3731
Bridgend *Gramp* 94 NJ5135
Bridgend *Gramp* 95 NJ7249
Bridgend *Tays* 82 NO1224
Bridgend *Fife* 83 NO3911
Bridgend *Tays* 89 NO5368
Bridgend *Strath* 70 NR3362
Bridgend *Loth* 75 NT0475
Bridgend *D & G* 66 NT0708
Bridgend *Border* 76 NT5235
Bridgend *M Glam* 18 SS9079
Bridgend *Devon* 4 SX5548
Bridgerule *Devon* 6 SS2702
Bridgetown *Somset* 7 SS9233
Bridgham *Norfk* 32 TL9685
Bridgnorth *Shrops* 37 SO7193
Bridgtown *Staffs* 38 SJ9808
Bridgwater *Somset* 19 ST2937
Bridlington *Humb* 57 TA1866
Bridport *Dorset* 8 SY4692
Bridstow *H & W* 27 SO5824
Brierfield *Lancs* 54 SD8436
Brierley *W York* 55 SE4010
Brierley *Gloucs* 27 SO6215
Brierley Hill *W Mids* 28 SO9169
Brig o'Turk *Cent* 81 NN5306
Brigg *Humb* 56 TA0007
Briggate *Norfk* 43 TG3127
Briggswath *N York* 63 NZ8608
Brigham *Cumb* 58 NY0830
Brigham *Humb* 57 TA0753
Brighouse *W York* 55 SE1422
Brighstone *IOW* 10 SZ4282
Brighthampton *Oxon* 21 SP3803
Brightley *Devon* 6 SX6097
Brightling *E Susx* 14 TQ6820
Brightlingsea *Essex* 25 TM0817
Brighton *E Susx* 12 TQ3104
Brighton le Sands *Mersyd* 46 SJ3098
Brightons *Cent* 75 NS9277
Brightwalton *Berks* 21 SU4279
Brightwell *Oxon* 21 SU5790
Brightwell *Suffk* 33 TM2543
Brightwell Baldwin *Oxon* 21 SU6595
Brightwell Upperton *Oxon* 21 SU6594
Brignall *Dur* 61 NZ0712
Brigsley *Humb* 51 TA2501
Brigsteer *Cumb* 59 SD4889
Brigstock *Nhants* 40 SP9485
Brill *Bucks* 29 SP6513
Brill *Cnwll* 2 SW7229
Brilley *H & W* 27 SO2648
Brimfield *H & W* 27 SO5267
Brimfield Cross *H & W* 27 SO5368
Brimington *Derbys* 49 SK4073
Brimley *Devon* 5 SX8077
Brimpsfield *Gloucs* 28 SO9312
Brimpton *Berks* 21 SU5564
Brimscombe *Gloucs* 20 SO8702
Brimstage *Mersyd* 46 SJ3082
Brincliffe *S York* 49 SK3284
Brind *Humb* 56 SE7430
Brindister *Shet* 103 HU2857
Brindle *Lancs* 54 SD5924
Brineton *Staffs* 37 SJ8013
Bringhurst *Leics* 40 SP8492
Brington *Cambs* 30 TL0875
Briningham *Norfk* 42 TG0434
Brinkhill *Lincs* 51 TF3773
Brinkley *Cambs* 32 TL6354
Brinklow *Warwks* 39 SP4379
Brinkworth *Wilts* 20 SU0184
Brinscall *Lancs* 54 SD6221
Brinsley *Notts* 49 SK4548
Brinton *Norfk* 42 TG0335
Brinyan *Ork* 103 HY4327
Brisley *Norfk* 42 TF9421
Brislington *Avon* 19 ST6270
Brissenden Green *Kent* 14 TQ9439
Bristol *Avon* 19 ST5972
Briston *Norfk* 42 TG0632
Britford *Wilts* 10 SU1627
Brithdir *Gwynd* 35 SH7618
Brithdir *M Glam* 18 SO1401
British Legion Village *Kent* 14 TQ7257
Briton Ferry *W Glam* 18 SS7394
Britwell Salome *Oxon* 22 SU6792
Brixham *Devon* 5 SX9255
Brixton *Devon* 4 SX5552
Brixton *Gt Lon* 23 TQ3175
Brixton Deverill *Wilts* 20 ST8638
Brixworth *Nhants* 30 SP7470
Brize Norton *Oxon* 29 SP2907
Broad Alley *H & W* 28 SO8867
Broad Blunsdon *Wilts* 20 SU1491
Broad Campden *Gloucs* 28 SP1537
Broad Carr *W York* 55 SE0919
Broad Chalke *Wilts* 9 SU0325
Broad Green *H & W* 28 SO7756
Broad Green *Suffk* 32 TL7859
Broad Green *Essex* 24 TL8823
Broad Haven *Dyfed* 16 SM8613
Broad Hinton *Wilts* 20 SU1075
Broad Laying *Hants* 21 SU4362
Broad Marston *H & W* 28 SP1446
Broad Oak *Mersyd* 46 SJ5395
Broad Oak *H & W* 27 SO4821
Broad Oak *E Susx* 14 TQ8219
Broad Street *Kent* 14 TQ8356
Broad Street *E Susx* 14 TQ8616
Broad Street *Kent* 15 TR1139
Broad Town *Wilts* 20 SU0977
Broad's Green *Essex* 24 TL6912
Broadbridge *W Susx* 11 SU8105
Broadbridge Heath *W Susx* 12 TQ1431
Broadclyst *Devon* 7 SX9897
Broadfield *Strath* 80 NS3373
Broadford *Highld* 85 NG6423
Broadford Bridge *W Susx* 12 TQ0921
Broadgairhill *Border* 67 NT2010
Broadgrass Green *Suffk* 32 TL9663
Broadhaugh *Border* 77 NT8655
Broadheath *Gt Man* 47 SJ7689
Broadhembury *Devon* 8 ST1004
Broadhempston *Devon* 5 SX8066
Broadland Row *E Susx* 14 TQ8319
Broadley *Gramp* 94 NJ3961
Broadmayne *Dorset* 9 SY7286
Broadmoor *Dyfed* 16 SN0906
Broadoak *Dorset* 8 SY4396
Broadoak *E Susx* 13 TQ6022
Broadoak *Kent* 15 TR1761
Broadstairs *Kent* 15 TR3967
Broadstone *Shrops* 37 SO5489
Broadstone *Dorset* 9 SZ0095
Broadwater *Herts* 31 TL2422
Broadwater *W Susx* 12 TQ1404
Broadwaters *H & W* 38 SO8477
Broadway *H & W* 28 SP0937
Broadway *Somset* 8 ST3215
Broadwell *Gloucs* 29 SP2027
Broadwell *Oxon* 29 SP2504
Broadwell *Warwks* 29 SP4565
Broadwindsor *Dorset* 8 ST4302
Broadwood Kelly *Devon* 6 SS6106
Broadwoodwidger *Devon* 4 SX4189
Brochel *Highld* 90 NG5846
Brockamin *H & W* 28 SO7753
Brockbridge *Hants* 11 SU6118
Brockdish *Norfk* 33 TM2179
Brockenhurst *Hants* 10 SU3002
Brocketsbrae *Strath* 74 NS8239
Brockford Street *Suffk* 33 TM1167
Brockhall *Nhants* 29 SP6362
Brockham *Surrey* 12 TQ1949
Brockhampton *H & W* 27 SO5931
Brockhampton *Gloucs* 28 SP0322
Brockholes *W York* 55 SE1510
Brocklesby *Lincs* 57 TA1311
Brockley *Avon* 19 ST4666
Brockley *Suffk* 32 TL8371
Brockley Green *Suffk* 32 TL7247
Brockley Green *Suffk* 32 TL8254
Brockton *Shrops* 36 SJ3104
Brockton *Staffs* 37 SJ8131
Brockton *Shrops* 36 SO3285
Brockton *Shrops* 37 SO5794
Brockweir *Gwent* 19 SO5401
Brockworth *Gloucs* 28 SO8916
Brocton *Staffs* 38 SJ9619
Brodick *Strath* 72 NS0135
Brodie *Gramp* 93 NH9757
Brodsworth *S York* 55 SE5007
Brogaig *Highld* 90 NG4767
Brokenborough *Wilts* 20 ST9189
Brokerswood *Wilts* 20 ST8352
Bromborough *Mersyd* 46 SJ3582
Brome *Suffk* 33 TM1376
Brome Street *Suffk* 33 TM1576
Bromeswell *Suffk* 33 TM3050
Bromfield *Cumb* 67 NY1746
Bromfield *Shrops* 37 SO4876
Bromham *Wilts* 20 ST9665
Bromham *Beds* 30 TL0051
Bromley *Shrops* 37 SO7395
Bromley *Gt Lon* 23 TQ4069
Brompton *N York* 62 SE3796
Brompton *N York* 63 SE9482
Brompton *Kent* 14 TQ7668
Brompton Ralph *Somset* 7 ST0832
Brompton Regis *Somset* 7 SS9531
Brompton-on-Swale *N York* 61 SE2199
Bromsberrow *Gloucs* 28 SO7433
Bromsberrow Heath *Gloucs* 28 SO7333
Bromsgrove *H & W* 28 SO9670
Bromyard *H & W* 27 SO6554
Bronant *Dyfed* 35 SN6467
Brongest *Dyfed* 17 SN3245
Bronington *Clwyd* 37 SJ4839
Bronllys *Powys* 26 SO1434
Bronwydd Arms *Dyfed* 17 SN4123
Bronygarth *Shrops* 36 SJ2637
Brook *Hants* 10 SU2714
Brook *Surrey* 11 SU9237
Brook *IOW* 10 SZ3983
Brook *Kent* 15 TR0644
Brook Hill *Hants* 10 SU2714
Brook Street *Suffk* 32 TL8248
Brook Street *W Susx* 12 TQ3026
Brook Street *Essex* 24 TQ5793
Brook Street *Kent* 14 TQ9333
Brooke *Leics* 40 SK8405
Brooke *Norfk* 43 TM2899
Brookfield *Strath* 73 NS4164
Brookhampton *Somset* 9 ST6327
Brookhampton *Hants* 11 SU7106
Brookhouse *Lancs* 53 SD5464
Brookhouse *S York* 49 SK5188
Brookhouse Green *Ches* 47 SJ8161
Brookhouses *Derbys* 48 SK0388
Brookland *Kent* 15 TQ9926
Brooklands *Gt Man* 47 SJ7890
Brookmans Park *Herts* 23 TL2404
Brookthorpe *Gloucs* 28 SO8312
Brookwood *Surrey* 22 SU9557
Broom *S York* 49 SK4491
Broom *Warwks* 28 SP0853
Broom *Beds* 31 TL1742
Broom Hill *S York* 49 SE4102
Broom Hill *Notts* 49 SK5447
Broom Hill *H & W* 38 SO9175
Broom Street *Kent* 15 TR0462
Broome *Shrops* 36 SO4080
Broome *H & W* 38 SO9078
Broome *Norfk* 33 TM3591
Broomedge *Ches* 47 SJ7085
Broomfield *Somset* 8 ST2232
Broomfield *Essex* 24 TL7010
Broomfield *Kent* 14 TQ8452
Broomfield *Kent* 15 TR1966
Broomfleet *Humb* 56 SE8727
Broomhaugh *Nthumb* 68 NZ0261
Broomhill *Nthumb* 69 NU2401
Brora *Highld* 97 NC9103
Broseley *Shrops* 37 SJ6701
Brotherlee *Dur* 60 NY9237
Brotherstone *Border* 76 NT6135
Brotherton *N York* 55 SE4825
Brotton *Cleve* 62 NZ6819
Broubster *Highld* 100 ND0359
Brough *Shet* 103 HU5665
Brough *Highld* 100 ND2273
Brough *Cumb* 60 NY7914
Brough *Humb* 56 SE9326
Brough *Notts* 50 SK8458
Brough Lodge *Shet* 103 HU5892
Brough Sowerby *Cumb* 60 NY7912
Broughall *Shrops* 37 SJ5741
Broughton *Border* 75 NT1136
Broughton *Lancs* 53 SD5234
Broughton *Gt Man* 47 SD8201
Broughton *N York* 54 SD9451
Broughton *N York* 63 SE7673
Broughton *Humb* 56 SE9608
Broughton *Clwyd* 46 SJ3363
Broughton *Staffs* 37 SJ7634
Broughton *Oxon* 29 SP4138
Broughton *Nhants* 30 SP8375
Broughton *Bucks* 30 SP8939
Broughton *S Glam* 18 SS9270
Broughton *Hants* 10 SU3033
Broughton *Cambs* 31 TL2878
Broughton Astley *Leics* 39 SP5292
Broughton Gifford *Wilts* 20 ST8763
Broughton Green *H & W* 28 SO9561
Broughton Hackett *H & W* 28 SO9254
Broughton Mains *D & G* 65 NX4545
Broughton Mills *Cumb* 58 SD2290
Broughton Moor *Cumb* 58 NY0533
Broughton Poggs *Oxon* 21 SP2303
Broughton-in-Furness *Cumb* 58 SD2187
Broughty Ferry *Tays* 83 NO4630
Brown Candover *Hants* 11 SU5739
Brown Edge *Staffs* 48 SJ9053
Brownhill *Gramp* 95 NJ8640
Brownhills *Fife* 83 NO5215
Brownhills *W Mids* 38 SK0405
Browninghill Green *Hants* 21 SU5859
Brownmuir *Gramp* 89 NO7377
Brownsham *Devon* 6 SS2826
Brownston *Devon* 5 SX6952
Brox *Surrey* 22 TQ0263
Broxa *N York* 63 SE9491
Broxbourne *Herts* 23 TL3606
Broxburn *Loth* 75 NT0872
Broxburn *Loth* 76 NT6977
Broxted *Essex* 24 TL5727
Broxwood *H & W* 27 SO3654
Bruan *Highld* 100 ND3139
Bruar *Tays* 87 NN8265
Brucefield *Highld* 97 NH9386
Bruchag *Strath* 73 NS1157
Bruisyard *Suffk* 33 TM3266
Bruisyard Street *Suffk* 33 TM3365
Brumby *Humb* 56 SE8909
Brund *Staffs* 48 SK1061
Brundall *Norfk* 43 TG3308
Brundish *Suffk* 33 TM2769
Brundish Street *Suffk* 33 TM2671
Brunthwaite *W York* 55 SE0546
Bruntingthorpe *Leics* 39 SP6089
Brunton *Fife* 83 NO3220
Brunton *Nthumb* 77 NU2024
Brunton *Wilts* 21 SU2456
Brushford *Somset* 7 SS9225
Brushford Barton *Devon* 7 SS6707
Bruton *Somset* 9 ST6835
Bryan's Green *H & W* 28 SO8868
Bryanston *Dorset* 9 ST8607
Bryant's Bottom *Bucks* 22 SU8599
Brydekirk *D & G* 67 NY1870
Brympton *Somset* 8 ST5115
Bryn *W Glam* 18 SS8192
Bryn Du *Gwynd* 44 SH3472
Bryn Gates *Lancs* 47 SD5901
Bryn Saith Marchog *Clwyd* 46 SJ0750
Bryn-coch *W Glam* 18 SS7499
Bryn-henllan *Dyfed* 16 SN0139
Bryn-mawr *Gwynd* 44 SH2433
Bryn-y-maen *Clwyd* 45 SH8376
Brynaman *Dyfed* 26 SN7114
Brynberian *Dyfed* 16 SN1035
Bryncir *Gwynd* 44 SH4844
Bryncroes *Gwynd* 44 SH2231
Bryncrug *Gwynd* 35 SH6103
Bryneglwys *Clwyd* 46 SJ1447
Brynford *Clwyd* 46 SJ1774
Bryngwran *Gwynd* 44 SH3577
Bryngwyn *Powys* 27 SO1849
Bryngwyn *Gwent* 27 SO3909
Brynhoffnant *Dyfed* 17 SN3351
Brynithel *Gwent* 19 SO2101
Brynmawr *Gwent* 27 SO1911
Brynmenyn *M Glam* 18 SS9084
Brynmill *W Glam* 17 SS6392
Brynna *M Glam* 18 SS9883
Brynrefail *Gwynd* 44 SH5562
Brynsadler *M Glam* 18 ST0280
Brynsiencyn *Gwynd* 44 SH4867
Bualintur *Highld* 84 NG4020
Bubbenhall *Warwks* 39 SP3672
Bubwith *Humb* 56 SE7136
Buchanan Smithy *Cent* 81 NS4689
Buchanhaven *Gramp* 95 NK1247
Buchanty *Tays* 82 NN9328
Buchany *Cent* 81 NN7102
Buchlyvie *Cent* 81 NS5793
Buck's Cross *Devon* 6 SS3522
Buck's Mills *Devon* 6 SS3523
Buckabank *Cumb* 67 NY3749
Buckden *N York* 61 SD9477
Buckden *Cambs* 31 TL1967
Buckenham *Norfk* 43 TG3505
Buckerell *Devon* 8 ST1200
Buckfast *Devon* 5 SX7467
Buckfastleigh *Devon* 5 SX7366
Buckhaven *Fife* 83 NT3598
Buckholm *Border* 76 NT4738
Buckholt *Gwent* 27 SO5016
Buckhorn Weston *Dorset* 9 ST7524
Buckhurst Hill *Essex* 23 TQ4194
Buckie *Gramp* 94 NJ4265
Buckingham *Bucks* 30 SP6933
Buckland *Gloucs* 28 SP0835
Buckland *Bucks* 30 SP8812
Buckland *Oxon* 21 SU3498
Buckland *Devon* 5 SX6743
Buckland *Herts* 31 TL3533
Buckland *Surrey* 12 TQ2150
Buckland *Kent* 15 TR3042
Buckland Brewer *Devon* 6 SS4220
Buckland Common *Bucks* 22 SP9207
Buckland Dinham *Somset* 20 ST7551
Buckland Filleigh *Devon* 6 SS4609
Buckland Monachorum *Devon* 4 SX4968
Buckland Newton *Dorset* 9 ST6805
Buckland Ripers *Dorset* 9 SY6582
Buckland St. Mary *Somset* 8 ST2613
Buckland in the Moor *Devon* 5 SX7273

Buckland-Tout-Saints
Cardigan

Buckland-Tout-Saints *Devon* 5 SX7645
Bucklebury *Berks* 21 SU5570
Bucklerheads *Tays* 83 NO4636
Bucklers Hard *Hants* 10 SU4000
Bucklesham *Suffk* 33 TM2441
Buckley *Clwyd* 46 SJ2763
Bucklow Hill *Ches* 47 SJ7383
Buckminster *Leics* 40 SK8722
Bucknall *Staffs* 48 SJ9047
Bucknall *Lincs* 50 TF1668
Bucknell *Shrops* 36 SO3574
Bucknell *Oxon* 29 SP5625
Buckpool *Gramp* 94 NJ4165
Bucks Green *W Susx* 12 TQ0833
Bucks Horn Oak *Hants* 11 SU8041
Bucksburn *Gramp* 95 NJ8909
Buckton *Nthumb* 77 NU0838
Buckton *Humb* 57 TA1872
Buckworth *Cambs* 30 TL1476
Budbrooke *Warwks* 29 SP2665
Budby *Notts* 49 SK6169
Budd's Titson *Cnwll* 6 SS2401
Buddon *Tays* 83 NO5232
Bude *Cnwll* 6 SS2105
Budge's Shop *Cnwll* 4 SX3259
Budleigh Salterton *Devon* 5 SY0682
Budock Water *Cnwll* 2 SW7831
Buerton *Ches* 47 SJ6843
Bugbrooke *Nhants* 30 SP6757
Bugle *Cnwll* 3 SX0158
Bugley *Dorset* 9 ST7824
Bugthorpe *Humb* 56 SE7757
Buildwas *Shrops* 37 SJ6204
Builth Wells *Powys* 26 SO0350
Bulbridge *Wilts* 10 SU0830
Buldoo *Highld* 100 ND0067
Bulford *Wilts* 20 SU1643
Bulkeley *Ches* 46 SJ5354
Bulkington *Warwks* 39 SP3986
Bulkington *Wilts* 20 ST9458
Bulkworthy *Devon* 6 SS3914
Bull's Green *Herts* 31 TL2717
Bullbrook *Berks* 22 SU8869
Bullington *Hants* 21 SU4541
Bullington *Lincs* 50 TF0877
Bullwood *Strath* 80 NS1675
Bulmer *N York* 56 SE6967
Bulmer *Essex* 32 TL8440
Bulmer Tye *Essex* 24 TL8438
Bulphan *Essex* 24 TQ6385
Bulwark *Gramp* 95 NJ9345
Bulwell *Notts* 49 SK5343
Bulwick *Nhants* 40 SP9694
Bumble's Green *Essex* 23 TL4005
Bunacaimb *Highld* 85 NM6588
Bunarkaig *Highld* 86 NN1887
Bunbury *Ches* 47 SJ5657
Bunchrew *Highld* 92 NH6246
Bundalloch *Highld* 85 NG8927
Bunessan *Strath* 78 NM3821
Bungay *Suffk* 33 TM3389
Bunnahabhainn *Strath* 70 NR4173
Bunny *Notts* 39 SK5829
Buntait *Highld* 92 NH4030
Buntingford *Herts* 31 TL3629
Bunwell *Norfk* 33 TM1292
Bunwell Street *Norfk* 43 TM1193
Burbage *Leics* 39 SP4492
Burbage *Wilts* 21 SU2261
Burchett's Green *Berks* 22 SU8481
Burcombe *Wilts* 10 SU0730
Burcott *Bucks* 30 SP8823
Bures *Suffk* 24 TL9034
Burford *H & W* 27 SO5868
Burford *Oxon* 29 SP2512
Burg *Strath* 78 NM3845
Burgates *Hants* 11 SU7728
Burgess Hill *W Susx* 12 TQ3218
Burgh *Suffk* 33 TM2351
Burgh Castle *Norfk* 43 TG4805
Burgh Heath *Surrey* 23 TQ2457
Burgh Le Marsh *Lincs* 51 TF5065
Burgh St. Margaret *Norfk* 43 TG4413
Burgh St. Peter *Norfk* 43 TM4693
Burgh by Sands *Cumb* 67 NY3259
Burgh next Aylsham *Norfk* 43 TG2125
Burgh on Bain *Lincs* 51 TF2186
Burghclere *Hants* 21 SU4761
Burghead *Gramp* 93 NJ1168
Burghfield *Berks* 22 SU6668
Burghfield Common *Berks* 21 SU6566
Burghill *H & W* 27 SO4844
Burghwallis *S York* 56 SE5311
Burham *Kent* 14 TQ7262
Buriton *Hants* 11 SU7419
Burland *Ches* 47 SJ6153
Burlawn *Cnwll* 3 SW9970
Burleigh *Gloucs* 20 SO8601
Burleigh *Berks* 22 SU9169
Burlescombe *Devon* 7 ST0716
Burleston *Dorset* 9 SY7794
Burley *Leics* 40 SK8810
Burley *Hants* 10 SU2102
Burley Gate *H & W* 27 SO5947
Burley Street *Hants* 10 SU2004
Burley Wood Head *W York* 55 SE1544
Burley in Wharfedale *W York* 55 SE1646
Burleydam *Ches* 37 SJ6042
Burlingham Green *Norfk* 43 TG3610
Burlton *Shrops* 36 SJ4526
Burmarsh *Kent* 15 TR1032
Burmington *Warwks* 29 SP2637
Burn *N York* 56 SE5928
Burn of Cambus *Cent* 81 NN7102
Burnage *Gt Man* 47 SJ8692
Burnaston *Derbys* 39 SK2832
Burnbrae *Strath* 74 NS8759
Burnby *Humb* 56 SE8346
Burneside *Cumb* 59 SD5095
Burneston *N York* 61 SE3084
Burnett *Avon* 20 ST6665
Burnfoot *Tays* 82 NN9904
Burnfoot *Border* 67 NT4113
Burnfoot *Border* 76 NT5116
Burnfoot *D & G* 66 NX9791
Burnfoot *D & G* 67 NY3388
Burnfoot *D & G* 67 NY3996
Burnham *Bucks* 22 SU9282
Burnham Deepdale *Norfk* 42 TF8044
Burnham Green *Herts* 31 TL2616
Burnham Market *Norfk* 42 TF8342
Burnham Norton *Norfk* 42 TF8343
Burnham Overy *Norfk* 42 TF8442
Burnham Thorpe *Norfk* 42 TF8541
Burnham-on-Crouch *Essex* 25 TQ9496
Burnham-on-Sea *Somset* 19 ST3049
Burnhaven *Gramp* 95 NK1244
Burnhead *D & G* 66 NX8695
Burnhervie *Gramp* 95 NJ7319
Burnhill Green *Staffs* 37 SJ7800
Burnhope *Dur* 69 NZ1948
Burnhouse *Strath* 73 NS3850
Burniston *N York* 63 TA0193
Burnley *Lancs* 54 SD8432
Burnmouth *Border* 77 NT9560
Burnopfield *Dur* 69 NZ1757
Burnsall *N York* 55 SE0361
Burnside *Gramp* 94 NJ1769
Burnside *Fife* 82 NO1608
Burnside *Tays* 88 NO4259
Burnside *Tays* 89 NO5050
Burnside *Fife* 75 NT0575
Burnside of Duntrune *Tays* 83 NO4434
Burnt Hill *Berks* 21 SU5774
Burnt Yates *N York* 55 SE2561
Burntisland *Fife* 83 NT2385
Burntwood *Staffs* 38 SK0509
Burnworthy *Somset* 8 ST1915
Burpham *Surrey* 12 TQ0152
Burpham *W Susx* 12 TQ0308
Burradon *Nthumb* 68 NT9806
Burrafirth *Shet* 103 HP6113
Burravoe *Shet* 103 HU5180
Burrells *Cumb* 60 NY6718
Burrelton *Tays* 82 NO2037
Burridge *Devon* 8 ST3106
Burridge *Hants* 11 SU5110
Burrill *N York* 61 SE2387
Burringham *Humb* 56 SE8309
Burrington *H & W* 36 SO4472
Burrington *Devon* 7 SS6416
Burrington *Avon* 19 ST4859
Burrough Green *Cambs* 32 TL6355
Burrough on the Hill *Leics* 40 SK7510
Burrow *Somset* 7 SS9342
Burrow Bridge *Somset* 8 ST3530
Burrowhill *Surrey* 22 SU9762
Burry Port *Dyfed* 17 SN4400
Burrygreen *W Glam* 17 SS4591
Burscough *Lancs* 53 SD4310
Burscough Bridge *Lancs* 53 SD4412
Bursea *Humb* 56 SE8033
Bursledon *Hants* 10 SU4809
Burslem *Staffs* 47 SJ8649
Burstall *Suffk* 33 TM0944
Burstock *Dorset* 8 ST4202
Burston *Norfk* 33 TM1383
Burstow *Surrey* 12 TQ3141
Burstwick *Humb* 57 TA2227
Burtersett *N York* 60 SD8989
Burtholme *Cumb* 67 NY5463
Burthorpe Green *Suffk* 32 TL7764
Burtoft *Lincs* 41 TF2635
Burton *Ches* 46 SJ3174
Burton *Ches* 46 SJ5063
Burton *Lincs* 50 SK9574
Burton *Dyfed* 16 SM9805
Burton *Somset* 19 ST1944
Burton *Wilts* 20 ST8179
Burton *Dorset* 10 SZ1694
Burton Agnes *Humb* 57 TA1062
Burton Bradstock *Dorset* 8 SY4889
Burton Coggles *Lincs* 40 SK9725
Burton Dassett *Warwks* 29 SP3951
Burton End *Essex* 31 TL5323
Burton Fleming *Humb* 57 TA0871
Burton Hastings *Warwks* 39 SP4189
Burton Joyce *Notts* 49 SK6443
Burton Latimer *Nhants* 30 SP9074
Burton Lazars *Leics* 40 SK7716
Burton Leonard *N York* 55 SE3263
Burton Overy *Leics* 39 SP6798
Burton Pedwardine *Lincs* 50 TF1142
Burton Pidsea *Humb* 57 TA2431
Burton Salmon *N York* 55 SE4927
Burton in Lonsdale *N York* 54 SD6572
Burton on the Wolds *Leics* 39 SK5821
Burton upon Stather *Humb* 56 SE8717
Burton upon Trent *Staffs* 39 SK2323
Burton's Green *Essex* 24 TL8226
Burton-in-Kendal *Cumb* 59 SD5376
Burtonwood *Ches* 47 SJ5692
Burwardsley *Ches* 46 SJ5156
Burwarton *Shrops* 37 SO6185
Burwash *E Susx* 14 TQ6724
Burwash Common *E Susx* 13 TQ6323
Burwash Weald *E Susx* 13 TQ6523
Burwell *Lincs* 51 TF3579
Burwell *Cambs* 31 TL5866
Burwen *Gwynd* 44 SH4293
Burwick *Ork* 103 ND4484
Bury *Gt Man* 54 SD8011
Bury *Somset* 7 SS9427
Bury *Cambs* 41 TL2883
Bury *W Susx* 12 TQ0113
Bury Green *Herts* 31 TL4521
Bury St. Edmunds *Suffk* 32 TL8564
Burythorpe *N York* 56 SE7964
Busby *Strath* 74 NS5756
Buscot *Wilts* 21 SU2298
Bush *Gramp* 89 NO7565
Bush Bank *H & W* 27 SO4551
Bush Hill Park *Gt Lon* 23 TQ3395
Bushbury *W Mids* 38 SJ9202
Bushey *Herts* 22 TQ1395
Bushey Heath *Herts* 22 TQ1494
Bushley *H & W* 28 SO8734
Bushton *Wilts* 20 SU0677
Bussex *Somset* 8 ST3535
Butcher's Pasture *Essex* 24 TL6024
Butcombe *Avon* 19 ST5161
Butleigh *Somset* 8 ST5233
Butleigh Wootton *Somset* 8 ST5035
Butlers Marston *Warwks* 29 SP3250
Butley *Suffk* 33 TM3650
Buttercrambe *N York* 56 SE7358
Butterdean *Border* 76 NT7964
Butterknowle *Dur* 61 NZ1025
Butterleigh *Devon* 7 SS9708
Buttermere *Cumb* 58 NY1717
Buttershaw *W York* 55 SE1329
Butterstone *Tays* 88 NO0645
Butterton *Staffs* 38 SJ8242
Butterton *Staffs* 48 SK0756
Butterwick *Humb* 63 SE7277
Butterwick *N York* 56 SE9871
Butterwick *Lincs* 51 TF3845
Buttington *Powys* 36 SJ2408
Buttonoak *Shrops* 37 SO7578
Buxhall *Suffk* 32 TM0057
Buxted *E Susx* 13 TQ4923
Buxton *Derbys* 48 SK0572
Buxton *Norfk* 43 TG2322
Buxton Heath *Norfk* 43 TG1821
Bwlch *Powys* 27 SO1522
Bwlch-y-cibau *Powys* 36 SJ1717
Bwlch-y-ffridd *Powys* 36 SO0795
Bwlch-y-groes *Dyfed* 17 SN2436
Bwlch-y-sarnau *Powys* 36 SO0374
Bwlchgwyn *Clwyd* 46 SJ2653
Bwlchllan *Dyfed* 34 SN5758
Bwlchtocyn *Gwynd* 34 SH3125
Byers Green *Dur* 61 NZ2233
Byfield *Nhants* 29 SP5152
Byfleet *Surrey* 22 TQ0661
Byford *H & W* 27 SO3942
Byker *T & W* 69 NZ2764
Bylchau *Clwyd* 45 SH9762
Byley *Ches* 47 SJ7269
Byrewalls *Border* 76 NT6642
Byrness *Nthumb* 68 NT7602
Bystock *Devon* 5 SY0283
Bythorn *Cambs* 30 TL0575
Byton *H & W* 27 SO3764
Bywell *Nthumb* 68 NZ0461
Byworth *W Susx* 12 SU9821

C

Cabourne *Lincs* 50 TA1401
Cabrach *Gramp* 94 NJ3826
Cabrach *Strath* 70 NR4964
Cabus *Lancs* 53 SD4948
Cabvie Lodge *Highld* 92 NH1567
Cadbury *Devon* 7 SS9105
Cadder *Strath* 74 NS6072
Caddington *Beds* 30 TL0619
Caddonfoot *Border* 76 NT4535
Cade Street *E Susx* 13 TQ6020
Cadeby *S York* 49 SE5100
Cadeby *Leics* 39 SK4202
Cadeleigh *Devon* 7 SS9108
Cadgwith *Cnwll* 2 SW7214
Cadham *Fife* 83 NO2801
Cadishead *Gt Man* 47 SJ7091
Cadle *W Glam* 17 SS6296
Cadley *Lancs* 53 SD5231
Cadley *Wilts* 21 SU2066
Cadley *Wilts* 21 SU2453
Cadmore End *Bucks* 22 SU7892
Cadnam *Hants* 10 SU3013
Cadney *Humb* 56 TA0103
Cadoxton *S Glam* 18 ST1269
Cadoxton Juxta-Neath *W Glam* 18 SS7598
Caeathro *Gwynd* 44 SH5061
Caenby *Lincs* 50 SK9989
Caeo *Dyfed* 26 SN6740
Caer Farchell *Dyfed* 16 SM7927
Caerau *M Glam* 18 SS8694
Caerau *S Glam* 18 ST1375
Caergeiliog *Gwynd* 44 SH3178
Caergwrle *Clwyd* 46 SJ3057
Caerlanrig *Border* 67 NT3904
Caerleon *Gwent* 19 ST3490
Caernarfon *Gwynd* 44 SH4862
Caerphilly *M Glam* 19 ST1587
Caersws *Powys* 36 SO0392
Caerwedros *Dyfed* 34 SN3755
Caerwent *Gwent* 19 ST4790
Caerwys *Clwyd* 46 SJ1272
Cairnbaan *Strath* 71 NR8390
Cairnbrogie *Gramp* 95 NJ8527
Cairnbulg *Gramp* 95 NK0365
Cairncross *Border* 77 NT8963
Cairncurran *Strath* 73 NS3170
Cairndow *Strath* 80 NN1810
Cairneyhill *Fife* 82 NT0486
Cairnfield *D & G* 64 NX3848
Cairnfield House *Gramp* 94 NJ4162
Cairngarroch *D & G* 64 NX0549
Cairngrassie *Gramp* 89 NO9095
Cairnhall *D & G* 66 NX9086
Cairnie *Gramp* 94 NJ4844
Cairnorrie *Gramp* 95 NJ8641
Cairnryan *D & G* 64 NX0668
Cairnty *Gramp* 94 NJ3352
Cairnwhin *Strath* 64 NX2491
Caister-on-Sea *Norfk* 43 TG5112
Caistor *Lincs* 50 TA1101
Caistor St. Edmund *Norfk* 43 TG2303
Caistron *Nthumb* 68 NT9901
Calbourne *IOW* 10 SZ4286
Calcot *Clwyd* 46 SJ1674
Calcot *Gloucs* 28 SP0810
Calcot Row *Berks* 22 SU6771
Calcots *Gramp* 94 NJ2563
Caldbeck *Cumb* 58 NY3240
Caldecote *Cambs* 40 TL1488
Caldecote *Herts* 31 TL2338
Caldecote *Cambs* 31 TL3456
Caldecote Highfields *Cambs* 31 TL3559
Caldecott *Leics* 40 SP8693
Caldecott *Nhants* 30 SP9868
Caldecott *Oxon* 21 SU4996
Calder Bridge *Cumb* 58 NY0306
Calder Grove *W York* 55 SE3016
Calder Vale *Lancs* 53 SD5345
Calderbank *Strath* 74 NS7663
Caldercruix *Strath* 74 NS8167
Caldermill *Strath* 74 NS6641
Caldicot *Gwent* 19 ST4888
Caldwell *N York* 61 NZ1613
Calfsound *Ork* 103 HY5738
Calgary *Strath* 78 NM3751
Califer *Gramp* 93 NJ0857
California *Cent* 74 NS9076
California *Derbys* 39 SK3335
California *Norfk* 43 TG5115
Calke *Derbys* 39 SK3721
Callander *Cent* 81 NN6207
Callanish *W Isls* 102 NB2133
Callert Cottage *Highld* 86 NN1060
Callestick *Cnwll* 2 SW7750
Calligarry *Highld* 84 NG6203
Callington *Cnwll* 4 SX3669
Callow *H & W* 27 SO4934
Callow End *H & W* 28 SO8350
Callow Hill *Wilts* 20 SU0384
Calmore *Hants* 10 SU3414
Calmsden *Gloucs* 28 SP0508
Calne *Wilts* 20 ST9971
Calshot *Hants* 10 SU4701
Calstock *Cnwll* 4 SX4368
Calstone Wellington *Wilts* 20 SU0268
Calthorpe *Norfk* 43 TG1831
Calthorpe Street *Norfk* 43 TG4025
Calthwaite *Cumb* 59 NY4640
Calton *N York* 54 SD9059
Calton *Staffs* 48 SK1049
Calveley *Ches* 47 SJ5958
Calver *Derbys* 48 SK2374
Calverhall *Shrops* 37 SJ6037
Calverleigh *Devon* 7 SS9214
Calverton *Notts* 49 SK6149
Calverton *Bucks* 30 SP7939
Calvine *Tays* 87 NN8065
Calvo *Cumb* 67 NY1453
Calzeat *Border* 75 NT1135
Cam *Gloucs* 20 ST7599
Camas Luinie *Highld* 85 NG9428
Camasachoirce *Highld* 79 NM7660
Camasine *Highld* 79 NM7561
Camastianavaig *Highld* 84 NG5039
Camasunary *Highld* 84 NG5118
Camault Muir *Highld* 92 NH5040
Camber *E Susx* 15 TQ9618
Camberley *Surrey* 22 SU8860
Camberwell *Gt Lon* 23 TQ3276
Camblesforth *N York* 56 SE6425
Cambo *Nthumb* 68 NZ0285
Camborne *Cnwll* 2 SW6440
Cambridge *Gloucs* 20 SO7403
Cambridge *Cambs* 31 TL4558
Cambrose *Cnwll* 2 SW6845
Cambus *Cent* 82 NS8594
Cambus O' May *Gramp* 88 NO4198
Cambusavie Platform *Highld* 97 NH7696
Cambusbarron *Cent* 81 NS7792
Cambuskenneth *Cent* 81 NS8094
Cambusmoon *Strath* 81 NS4285
Cambuswallace *Strath* 75 NT0438
Camden Town *Gt Lon* 23 TQ2883
Cameley *Avon* 19 ST6157
Camelford *Cnwll* 3 SX1083
Camelon *Cent* 82 NS8680
Camer's Green *H & W* 28 SO7735
Camerory *Highld* 93 NJ0131
Camerton *Cumb* 58 NY0330
Camerton *Avon* 20 ST6857
Camghouran *Tays* 87 NN5556
Cammachmore *Gramp* 89 NO9195
Cammeringham *Lincs* 50 SK9482
Camore *Highld* 97 NH7889
Campbeltown *Strath* 72 NR7120
Cample *D & G* 66 NX8993
Campmuir *Tays* 82 NO2137
Camps *Loth* 75 NT0968
Camps End *Cambs* 31 TL6142
Campsall *S York* 56 SE5413
Campsie *Strath* 81 NS6079
Campsie Ash *Suffk* 33 TM3356
Campton *Beds* 30 TL1238
Camptown *Border* 68 NT6813
Camrose *Dyfed* 16 SM9220
Camserney *Tays* 87 NN8149
Camster *Highld* 100 ND2642
Camusnagaul *Highld* 91 NH0589
Camusnagaul *Highld* 86 NN0874
Camusteel *Highld* 91 NG7042
Camusterrach *Highld* 85 NG7141
Canada *Hants* 10 SU2818
Candacraig *Gramp* 88 NO3499
Candlesby *Lincs* 51 TF4567
Candyburn *Strath* 75 NT0741
Cane End *Oxon* 22 SU6779
Canewdon *Essex* 24 TQ9094
Canfield End *Essex* 24 TL5821
Canford Cliffs *Dorset* 10 SZ0589
Canford Magna *Dorset* 9 SZ0398
Canisbay *Highld* 100 ND3472
Canley *W Mids* 39 SP3077
Cann *Dorset* 9 ST8721
Cannich *Highld* 92 NH3331
Canning Town *Gt Lon* 23 TQ4081
Cannington *Somset* 19 ST2539
Cannock *Staffs* 38 SJ9810
Cannon Bridge *H & W* 27 SO4340
Canon Frome *H & W* 27 SO6443
Canon Pyon *H & W* 27 SO4548
Canonbie *D & G* 67 NY3976
Canons Ashby *Nhants* 29 SP5750
Canonstown *Cnwll* 2 SW5335
Canterbury *Kent* 15 TR1457
Cantley *S York* 49 SE6202
Cantley *Norfk* 43 TG3704
Canton *S Glam* 19 ST1676
Cantraywood *Highld* 93 NH7847
Cantsfield *Lancs* 54 SD6272
Canvey Island *Essex* 24 TQ7983
Canwick *Lincs* 50 SK9869
Canworthy Water *Cnwll* 4 SX2291
Caol *Highld* 86 NN1175
Caoles *Strath* 78 NM0848
Caonich *Highld* 86 NN0692
Capel *Surrey* 12 TQ1740
Capel *Kent* 13 TQ6344
Capel Bangor *Dyfed* 35 SN6580
Capel Betws Lleucu *Dyfed* 34 SN6058
Capel Coch *Gwynd* 44 SH4682
Capel Curig *Gwynd* 45 SH7258
Capel Dewi *Dyfed* 17 SN4542
Capel Dewi *Dyfed* 17 SN4720
Capel Garmon *Gwynd* 45 SH8155
Capel Gwynfe *Dyfed* 26 SN7222
Capel Hendre *Dyfed* 17 SN5911
Capel Iwan *Dyfed* 17 SN2936
Capel Mawr *Gwynd* 44 SH4171
Capel Seion *Dyfed* 35 SN6379
Capel St. Andrew *Suffk* 33 TM3748
Capel St. Mary *Suffk* 25 TM0838
Capel le Ferne *Kent* 15 TR2539
Capel-Dewi *Dyfed* 35 SN6282
Capelles *Guern* 101 GN0000
Capelulo *Gwynd* 45 SH7476
Capenhurst *Ches* 46 SJ3673
Capheaton *Nthumb* 68 NZ0380
Caplaw *Strath* 73 NS4458
Cappercleuch *Border* 75 NT2423
Capton *Somset* 7 ST0839
Capton *Devon* 5 SX8353
Caputh *Tays* 82 NO0840
Car Colston *Notts* 49 SK7142
Carbeth Inn *Cent* 81 NS5279
Carbis Bay *Cnwll* 2 SW5238
Carbost *Highld* 84 NG3731
Carbost *Highld* 90 NG4248
Carbrook *S York* 49 SK3889
Carbrooke *Norfk* 42 TF9402
Carcary *Tays* 89 NO6455
Cardenden *Fife* 82 NT2195
Cardiff *S Glam* 19 ST1876
Cardigan *Dyfed* 17 SN1746

Cardinal's Green

Chewton Mendip

Cardinal's Green *Cambs* **31** TL6146
Cardington *Shrops* **37** SO5095
Cardington *Beds* **30** TL0847
Cardinham *Cnwll* **3** SX1268
Cardow *Gramp* **94** NJ1943
Cardrain *D & G* **64** NX1231
Cardrona *Border* **75** NT3038
Cardross *Strath* **80** NS3477
Cardryne *D & G* **64** NX1132
Cardurnock *Cumb* **67** NY1758
Careby *Lincs* **40** TF0216
Careston *Tays* **89** NO5260
Carew *Dyfed* **16** SN0403
Carew Cheriton *Dyfed* **16** SN0402
Carew Newton *Dyfed* **16** SN0404
Carey *H & W* **27** SO5730
Carfin *Strath* **74** NS7759
Carfraemill *Border* **76** NT5053
Cargate Green *Norfk* **43** TG3912
Cargen *D & G* **66** NX9672
Cargenbridge *D & G* **66** NX9575
Cargill *Tays* **82** NO1536
Cargo *Cumb* **67** NY3659
Cargreen *Cnwll* **4** SX4362
Carham *Nthumb* **76** NT7938
Carhampton *Somset* **7** ST0042
Carharrack *Cnwll* **2** SW7341
Carie *Tays* **87** NN6257
Carinish *W Isls* **102** NF8260
Carisbrooke *IOW* **10** SZ4888
Cark *Cumb* **59** SD3676
Carkeel *Cnwll* **4** SX4160
Carlbury *Dur* **61** NZ2115
Carlby *Lincs* **40** TF0413
Carlcroft *Nthumb* **68** NT8311
Carleen *Cnwll* **2** SW6130
Carleton *N York* **54** SD9749
Carleton Forehoe *Norfk* **43** TG0905
Carleton Rode *Norfk* **43** TM1093
Carleton St. Peter *Norfk* **43** TG3402
Carlincraig *Gramp* **95** NJ6743
Carlingcott *Avon* **20** ST6958
Carlisle *Cumb* **67** NY3956
Carlops *Border* **75** NT1656
Carloway *W Isls* **102** NB2043
Carlton *Cleve* **62** NZ3921
Carlton *N York* **62** NZ5004
Carlton *N York* **61** SE0684
Carlton *W York* **55** SE3327
Carlton *S York* **55** SE3610
Carlton *N York* **62** SE6086
Carlton *N York* **56** SE6423
Carlton *Leics* **39** SK3904
Carlton *Notts* **49** SK6041
Carlton *Beds* **30** SP9555
Carlton *Cambs* **32** TL6452
Carlton *Suffk* **33** TM3764
Carlton Colville *Suffk* **33** TM5189
Carlton Curlieu *Leics* **40** SP6997
Carlton Green *Cambs* **32** TL6451
Carlton Husthwaite *N York* **62** SE4976
Carlton Miniott *N York* **62** SE3981
Carlton Scroop *Lincs* **50** SK9445
Carlton in Lindrick *Notts* **49** SK5883
Carlton-le-Moorland *Lincs* **50** SK9058
Carlton-on-Trent *Notts* **50** SK7963
Carluke *Strath* **74** NS8450
Carmacoup *Strath* **74** NS7927
Carmarthen *Dyfed* **17** SN3919
Carmel *Gwynd* **44** SH4954
Carmel *Dyfed* **17** SN5816
Carmunnock *Strath* **74** NS5957
Carmyle *Strath* **74** NS6462
Carmyllie *Tays* **89** NO5442
Carn Brea *Cnwll* **2** SW6841
Carn-gorm *Highld* **85** NG9520
Carnaby *Humb* **57** TA1465
Carnach *W Isls* **102** NG2297
Carnbee *Fife* **83** NO5206
Carnbo *Tays* **82** NO0503
Carndu *Highld* **85** NG8827
Carnduff *Strath* **74** NS6646
Carnell *Strath* **73** NS4731
Carnforth *Lancs* **53** SD4970
Carnhell Green *Cnwll* **2** SW6137
Carnie *Gramp* **89** NJ8005
Carnkie *Cnwll* **2** SW7134
Carno *Powys* **35** SN9696
Carnoch *Highld* **85** NM8696
Carnock *Fife* **82** NT0489
Carnon Downs *Cnwll* **2** SW7940
Carnousie *Gramp* **94** NJ6650
Carnoustie *Tays* **83** NO5534
Carnwath *Strath* **75** NS9846
Carol Green *W Mids* **39** SP2577
Carperby *N York* **61** SE0089
Carr Gate *W York* **55** SE3123
Carr Shield *Nthumb* **68** NY8047
Carradale *Strath* **72** NR8138
Carrbridge *Highld* **93** NH9022
Carrefour *Jersey* **101** JS0000
Carreglefn *Gwynd* **44** SH3889
Carrhouse *Humb* **56** SE7706
Carrick *Fife* **83** NO4422
Carrick *Strath* **71** NR9086
Carrick Castle *Strath* **80** NS1994
Carriden *Cent* **82** NT0181
Carrington *Loth* **75** NT3160
Carrington *Gt Man* **47** SJ7492
Carrog *Clwyd* **46** SJ1043
Carron *Gramp* **94** NJ2241
Carron *Cent* **82** NS8882
Carron Bridge *Cent* **81** NS7483
Carronbridge *D & G* **66** NX8698
Carronshore *Cent* **82** NS8983
Carruth House *Strath* **73** NS3566
Carrutherstown *D & G* **67** NY1071
Carrville *Dur* **69** NZ3043
Carsaig *Strath* **79** NM5421
Carscreugh *D & G* **64** NX2260
Carse Gray *Tays* **88** NO4553
Carseriggan *D & G* **64** NX3167
Carsethorn *D & G* **66** NX9959
Carshalton *Gt Lon* **23** TQ2764
Carsie *Tays* **88** NO1742
Carsington *Derbys* **48** SK2553
Carskey *Strath* **72** NR6508
Carsluith *D & G* **65** NX4854
Carsphairn *D & G* **65** NX5693
Carstairs *Strath* **75** NS9345
Carstairs Junction *Strath* **75** NS9545
Carter Bar *Border* **68** NT6907
Carterton *Oxon* **29** SP2806
Carthew *Cnwll* **3** SX0056
Carthorpe *N York* **61** SE3083
Cartland *Strath* **74** NS8646
Cartmel *Cumb* **59** SD3878
Carway *Dyfed* **17** SN4606
Cashe's Green *Gloucs* **28** SO8205
Cassington *Oxon* **29** SP4511
Cassop Colliery *Dur* **62** NZ3438
Castel *Guern* **101** GN0000
Casterton *Lancs* **60** SD6279
Castle Acre *Norfk* **42** TF8115
Castle Ashby *Nhants* **30** SP8659
Castle Bolton *N York* **61** SE0391
Castle Bromwich *W Mids* **38** SP1489
Castle Bytham *Lincs* **40** SK9818
Castle Caereinion *Powys* **36** SJ1605
Castle Camps *Cambs* **32** TL6242
Castle Carrock *Cumb* **67** NY5455
Castle Cary *Somset* **9** ST6432
Castle Combe *Wilts* **20** ST8477
Castle Donington *Leics* **39** SK4427
Castle Douglas *D & G* **65** NX7662
Castle Eaton *Wilts* **20** SU1496
Castle Eden *Dur* **62** NZ4238
Castle Frome *H & W* **28** SO6645
Castle Gresley *Derbys* **39** SK2717
Castle Hedingham *Essex* **24** TL7835
Castle Hill *Suffk* **33** TM1446
Castle Kennedy *D & G* **64** NX1159
Castle Lachlan *Strath* **80** NS0195
Castle O'er *D & G* **67** NY2492
Castle Pulverbatch *Shrops* **36** SJ4202
Castle Rising *Norfk* **42** TF6624
Castle Stuart *Highld* **93** NH7449
Castlebay *W Isls* **102** NL6698
Castlebythe *Dyfed* **16** SN0229
Castlecary *Strath* **81** NS7878
Castlecraig *Highld* **93** NH8269
Castleford *W York* **55** SE4225
Castlehill *Highld* **100** ND1968
Castlehill *Strath* **74** NS8451
Castlehill *Border* **75** NT2135
Castlemartin *Dyfed* **16** SR9198
Castlemilk *D & G* **67** NY1577
Castlemorton *H & W* **28** SO7937
Castleside *Dur* **68** NZ0748
Castlethorpe *Bucks* **30** SP8044
Castleton *Border* **67** NY5189
Castleton *N York* **62** NZ6807
Castleton *Gt Man* **54** SD8810
Castleton *Derbys* **48** SK1582
Castleton *Gwent* **19** ST2583
Castletown *Highld* **100** ND1967
Castletown *T & W* **69** NZ3658
Castletown *IOM* **52** SC2667
Castley *N York* **55** SE2646
Caston *Norfk* **42** TL9597
Castor *Cambs* **40** TL1298
Cat's Ash *Gwent* **19** ST3790
Catacol *Strath* **72** NR9149
Catchall *Cnwll* **2** SW4228
Catcliffe *S York* **49** SK4288
Catcomb *Wilts* **20** SU0076
Catcott *Somset* **19** ST3939
Catcott Burtle *Somset* **19** ST4043
Caterham *Surrey* **23** TQ3455
Catfield *Norfk* **43** TG3821
Catfirth *Shet* **103** HU4354
Catford *Gt Lon* **23** TQ3773
Catforth *Lancs* **53** SD4735
Cathcart *Strath* **74** NS5860
Cathedine *Powys* **26** SO1425
Catherington *Hants* **11** SU6914
Catherston Leweston *Dorset* **8** SY3694
Cathpair *Border* **76** NT4646
Catisfield *Hants* **11** SU5506
Catlodge *Highld* **87** NN6392
Catmere End *Essex* **31** TL4939
Catmore *Berks* **21** SU4580
Caton *Lancs* **53** SD5364
Caton Green *Lancs* **53** SD5565
Catrine *Strath* **74** NS5225
Catsfield *E Susx* **14** TQ7213
Catshill *H & W* **38** SO9573
Cattadale *Strath* **72** NR6710
Cattal *N York* **55** SE4454
Cattawade *Suffk* **25** TM1033
Catterall *Lancs* **53** SD4942
Catterick *N York* **61** SE2397
Catterick Bridge *N York* **61** SE2299
Catterlen *Cumb* **59** NY4833
Catterton *N York* **55** SE5145
Catteshall *Surrey* **12** SU9844
Catthorpe *Leics* **39** SP5578
Cattistock *Dorset* **9** SY5999
Catton *Cumb* **68** NY8257
Catton *N York* **62** SE3678
Catton *Norfk* **43** TG2312
Catwick *Humb* **57** TA1345
Catworth *Cambs* **30** TL0873
Caudle Green *Gloucs* **28** SO9410
Caulcott *Oxon* **29** SP5024
Cauldcots *Tays* **89** NO6547
Cauldhame *Cent* **81** NS6493
Cauldmill *Border* **76** NT5315
Cauldon *Staffs* **48** SK0749
Cauldside *D & G* **67** NY4480
Cauldwell *Derbys* **39** SK2517
Caulkerbush *D & G* **66** NX9257
Caundle Marsh *Dorset* **9** ST6713
Caunton *Notts* **50** SK7460
Causeway End *D & G* **64** NX4260
Causeway End *Essex* **24** TL6819
Causewayend *Strath* **75** NT0336
Causewayhead *Cent* **81** NS8095
Causey Park *Nthumb* **69** NZ1794
Causeyend *Gramp* **95** NJ9419
Cavendish *Suffk* **32** TL8046
Cavenham *Suffk* **32** TL7670
Caversfield *Oxon* **29** SP5825
Caversham *Berks* **22** SU7274
Caverswall *Staffs* **48** SJ9542
Caverton Mill *Border* **76** NT7425
Cawdor *Highld* **93** NH8450
Cawood *N York* **56** SE5737
Cawsand *Cnwll* **4** SX4350
Cawston *Norfk* **43** TG1323
Cawthorne *S York* **55** SE2808
Caxton *Cambs* **31** TL3058
Caynham *Shrops* **37** SO5573
Caythorpe *Notts* **49** SK6845
Caythorpe *Lincs* **50** SK9348
Cayton *N York* **63** TA0583
Ceannacroc Lodge *Highld* **92** NH2211
Cefn *Gwent* **19** ST2788
Cefn Cribwr *M Glam* **18** SS8582
Cefn-brith *Clwyd* **45** SH9350
Cefn-mawr *Clwyd* **36** SJ2842
Cefn-y-pant *Dyfed* **17** SN1925
Cefngorwydd *Powys* **26** SN9045
Cellarhead *Staffs* **48** SJ9547
Cemaes *Gwynd* **44** SH3793
Cemmaes *Powys* **35** SH8406
Cemmaes Road *Powys* **35** SH8104
Cenarth *Dyfed* **17** SN2641
Ceres *Fife* **83** NO4011
Cerne Abbas *Dorset* **9** ST6601
Cerney Wick *Gloucs* **20** SU0796
Cerrigceinwen *Gwynd* **44** SH4274
Cerrigydrudion *Clwyd* **45** SH9548
Ceunant *Gwynd* **44** SH5361
Chaceley *Gloucs* **28** SO8530
Chacewater *Cnwll* **2** SW7544
Chackmore *Bucks* **30** SP6835
Chacombe *Nhants* **29** SP4944
Chadbury *H & W* **28** SP0146
Chadderton *Gt Man* **54** SD9005
Chaddesden *Derbys* **39** SK3836
Chaddesley Corbett *H & W* **38** SO8973
Chaddlehanger *Devon* **4** SX4678
Chaddleworth *Berks* **21** SU4178
Chadlington *Oxon* **29** SP3321
Chadshunt *Warwks* **29** SP3453
Chadwell *Leics* **40** SK7824
Chadwell Heath *Gt Lon* **23** TQ4888
Chadwell St. Mary *Essex* **24** TQ6478
Chadwick *H & W* **28** SO8369
Chadwick End *W Mids* **39** SP2073
Chaffcombe *Somset* **8** ST3510
Chagford *Devon* **5** SX7087
Chailey *E Susx* **13** TQ3919
Chainhurst *Kent* **14** TQ7248
Chaldon *Surrey* **23** TQ3155
Chaldon Herring or East Chaldon *Dorset* **9** SY7983
Chale *IOW* **10** SZ4877
Chale Green *IOW* **10** SZ4879
Chalfont Common *Bucks* **22** TQ0092
Chalfont St. Giles *Bucks* **22** SU9893
Chalfont St. Peter *Bucks* **22** TQ0090
Chalford *Gloucs* **20** SO8802
Chalford *Wilts* **20** ST8650
Chalgrove *Oxon* **21** SU6396
Chalk *Kent* **14** TQ6773
Chalkwell *Kent* **14** TQ8963
Challacombe *Devon* **7** SS6940
Challoch *D & G* **64** NX3866
Challock Lees *Kent* **15** TR0050
Chalton *Hants* **11** SU7315
Chalton *Beds* **30** TL0326
Chalvey *Berks* **22** SU9679
Chalvington *E Susx* **13** TQ5109
Chandler's Cross *Herts* **22** TQ0698
Chandler's Ford *Hants* **10** SU4319
Chantry *Somset* **20** ST7146
Chantry *Suffk* **33** TM1443
Chapel *Fife* **83** NT2593
Chapel Allerton *W York* **55** SE3037
Chapel Allerton *Somset* **19** ST4050
Chapel Amble *Cnwll* **3** SW9975
Chapel Brampton *Nhants* **30** SP7266
Chapel Chorlton *Staffs* **37** SJ8137
Chapel Green *Warwks* **29** SP4660
Chapel Haddlesey *N York* **56** SE5826
Chapel Hall *Strath* **73** NS1369
Chapel Hill *Gramp* **95** NK0635
Chapel Hill *N York* **55** SE3446
Chapel Hill *Gwent* **37** SO5399
Chapel Hill *Lincs* **51** TF2054
Chapel Lawn *Shrops* **36** SO3176
Chapel Leigh *Somset* **8** ST1229
Chapel Rossan *D & G* **64** NX1044
Chapel Row *Berks* **21** SU5769
Chapel St. Leonards *Lincs* **51** TF5672
Chapel Stile *Cumb* **58** NY3205
Chapel le Dale *N York* **60** SD7377
Chapel of Garioch *Gramp* **95** NJ7124
Chapel-en-le-Frith *Derbys* **48** SK0580
Chapelend Way *Essex* **32** TL7039
Chapelhall *Strath* **74** NS7862
Chapelhill *Tays* **82** NO0030
Chapelknowe *D & G* **67** NY3173
Chapelton *Tays* **89** NO6247
Chapelton *Strath* **74** NS6848
Chapelton *Devon* **6** SS5726
Chapeltown *Gramp* **94** NJ2320
Chapeltown *Lancs* **54** SD7315
Chapeltown *S York* **49** SK3596
Chapmans Well *Devon* **4** SX3593
Chapmanslade *Wilts* **20** ST8247
Chapmore End *Herts* **31** TL3216
Chappel *Essex* **24** TL8928
Chard *Somset* **8** ST3208
Chard Junction *Somset* **8** ST3404
Chardleigh Green *Somset* **8** ST3110
Chardstock *Devon* **8** ST3004
Charfield *Avon* **20** ST7292
Charing *Kent* **14** TQ9549
Charingworth *Gloucs* **29** SP1939
Charlbury *Oxon* **29** SP3519
Charlcombe *Avon* **20** ST7467
Charlcutt *Wilts* **20** ST9875
Charlecote *Warwks* **29** SP2656
Charles *Devon* **7** SS6832
Charles Tye *Suffk* **32** TM0252
Charleston *Tays* **88** NO3845
Charlestown *Highld* **91** NG8174
Charlestown *Highld* **92** NH6448
Charlestown *Gramp* **89** NJ9300
Charlestown *Fife* **82** NT0683
Charlestown *Gt Man* **47** SD8100
Charlestown *W York* **54** SD9726
Charlestown *W York* **55** SE1638
Charlestown *Cnwll* **3** SX0351
Charlesworth *Derbys* **48** SK0092
Charlinch *Somset* **19** ST2338
Charlton *Nthumb* **68** NY8184
Charlton *Shrops* **37** SJ5911
Charlton *H & W* **28** SP0045
Charlton *Nhants* **29** SP5335
Charlton *Somset* **20** ST2926
Charlton *Wilts* **9** ST9022
Charlton *Wilts* **20** ST9588
Charlton *Wilts* **20** SU1156
Charlton *Wilts* **10** SU1723
Charlton *Oxon* **21** SU4088
Charlton *W Susx* **11** SU8812
Charlton *Gt Lon* **23** TQ4178
Charlton Abbots *Gloucs* **28** SP0324
Charlton Adam *Somset* **8** ST5328
Charlton Horethorne *Somset* **9** ST6623
Charlton Kings *Gloucs* **28** SO9621
Charlton Mackrell *Somset* **8** ST5328
Charlton Marshall *Dorset* **9** ST9004
Charlton Musgrove *Somset* **9** ST7229
Charlton on the Hill *Dorset* **9** ST8903
Charlton-on-Otmoor *Oxon* **29** SP5616
Charlwood *Hants* **11** SU6731
Charlwood *Surrey* **12** TQ2441
Charminster *Dorset* **9** SY6792
Charmouth *Dorset* **8** SY3693
Charndon *Bucks* **30** SP6724
Charney Bassett *Oxon* **21** SU3894
Charnock Richard *Lancs* **53** SD5515
Charsfield *Suffk* **33** TM2556
Chart Sutton *Kent* **14** TQ8049
Charter Alley *Hants* **21** SU5958
Charterhall *Border* **76** NT7647
Charterhouse *Somset* **19** ST4955
Chartershall *Cent* **81** NS7990
Chartham *Kent* **15** TR1054
Chartham Hatch *Kent* **15** TR1056
Chartridge *Bucks* **22** SP9303
Charwelton *Nhants* **29** SP5356
Chastleton *Oxon* **29** SP2429
Chasty *Devon* **6** SS3402
Chatburn *Lancs* **54** SD7644
Chatcull *Staffs* **37** SJ7934
Chatham *Kent* **14** TQ7567
Chatham Green *Essex* **24** TL7115
Chathill *Nthumb* **77** NU1827
Chattenden *Kent* **14** TQ7572
Chatteris *Cambs* **41** TL3985
Chatterton *Lancs* **54** SD7918
Chattisham *Suffk* **33** TM0942
Chatto *Border* **76** NT7717
Chatton *Nthumb* **77** NU0528
Chawleigh *Devon* **7** SS7112
Chawton *Hants* **11** SU7037
Cheadle *Gt Man* **47** SJ8688
Cheadle *Staffs* **48** SK0043
Cheadle Hulme *Gt Man* **47** SJ8786
Cheam *Gt Lon* **23** TQ2463
Chearsley *Bucks* **22** SP7110
Chebsey *Staffs* **38** SJ8528
Checkendon *Oxon* **22** SU6683
Checkley *Ches* **47** SJ7346
Checkley *Staffs* **48** SK0237
Chedburgh *Suffk* **32** TL7957
Cheddar *Somset* **19** ST4553
Cheddington *Bucks* **30** SP9217
Cheddleton *Staffs* **48** SJ9752
Cheddon Fitzpaine *Somset* **8** ST2427
Chedgrave *Norfk* **43** TM3699
Chedington *Dorset* **8** ST4805
Chediston *Suffk* **33** TM3577
Chedworth *Gloucs* **28** SP0512
Chedzoy *Somset* **19** ST3437
Cheetham Hill *Gt Man* **47** SD8401
Cheetwood *Gt Man* **47** SJ8399
Cheldon *Devon* **7** SS7313
Chelford *Ches* **47** SJ8174
Chellaston *Derbys* **39** SK3730
Chellington *Beds* **30** SP9555
Chelmarsh *Shrops* **37** SO7288
Chelmondiston *Suffk* **25** TM2037
Chelmorton *Derbys* **48** SK1169
Chelmsford *Essex* **24** TL7007
Chelmsley Wood *W Mids* **38** SP1887
Chelsea *Gt Lon* **23** TQ2778
Chelsfield *Gt Lon* **23** TQ4864
Chelsworth *Suffk* **32** TL9748
Cheltenham *Gloucs* **28** SO9422
Chelveston *Nhants* **30** SP9969
Chelvey *Avon* **19** ST4668
Chelwood *Avon* **19** ST6361
Chelwood Gate *E Susx* **13** TQ4130
Chelworth Lower Green *Wilts* **20** SU0892
Chelworth Upper Green *Wilts* **20** SU0893
Cheney Longville *Shrops* **36** SO4284
Chenies *Bucks* **22** TQ0198
Chepstow *Gwent* **19** ST5393
Cherhill *Wilts* **20** SU0370
Cherington *Warwks* **29** SP2936
Cherington *Gloucs* **20** ST9098
Cheriton *W Glam* **17** SS4593
Cheriton *Hants* **11** SU5828
Cheriton *Kent* **15** TR2037
Cheriton Bishop *Devon* **5** SX7793
Cheriton Fitzpaine *Devon* **7** SS8606
Cheriton or Stackpole Elidor *Dyfed* **16** SR9897
Cherrington *Shrops* **37** SJ6619
Cherry Burton *Humb* **56** SE9841
Cherry Hinton *Cambs* **31** TL4856
Cherry Orchard *H & W* **28** SO8553
Cherry Willingham *Lincs* **50** TF0272
Chertsey *Surrey* **22** TQ0466
Cheselbourne *Dorset* **9** SY7699
Chesham *Gt Man* **54** SD8012
Chesham *Bucks* **22** SP9601
Chesham Bois *Bucks* **22** SU9699
Cheshunt *Herts* **23** TL3502
Cheslyn Hay *Staffs* **38** SJ9707
Chessetts Wood *Warwks* **38** SP1873
Chessington *Surrey* **23** TQ1863
Chester *Ches* **46** SJ4066
Chester Moor *Dur* **69** NZ2649
Chester-le-Street *T & W* **69** NZ2751
Chesterblade *Somset* **20** ST6641
Chesterfield *Derbys* **49** SK3871
Chesterhill *Loth* **76** NT3764
Chesters *Border* **76** NT6022
Chesters *Border* **68** NT6210
Chesterton *Shrops* **37** SO7897
Chesterton *Gloucs* **20** SP0100
Chesterton *Oxon* **29** SP5621
Chesterton *Cambs* **40** TL1295
Chesterton *Cambs* **31** TL4660
Chesterton Green *Warwks* **29** SP3558
Chesterwood *Nthumb* **68** NY8364
Chestfield *Kent* **15** TR1365
Cheston *Devon* **5** SX6858
Cheswardine *Shrops* **37** SJ7130
Cheswick *Nthumb* **77** NU0346
Chetnole *Dorset* **9** ST6008
Chettisham *Cambs* **41** TL5483
Chettle *Dorset* **9** ST9513
Chetton *Shrops* **37** SO6690
Chetwode *Bucks* **29** SP6429
Chetwynd *Shrops* **37** SJ7321
Chetwynd Aston *Shrops* **37** SJ7517
Cheveley *Cambs* **32** TL6861
Chevening *Kent* **23** TQ4857
Chevington *Suffk* **32** TL7859
Chevington Drift *Nthumb* **69** NZ2598
Chevithorne *Devon* **7** SS9715
Chew Magna *Avon* **19** ST5763
Chew Stoke *Avon* **19** ST5561
Chewton Keynsham *Avon* **19** ST6566
Chewton Mendip *Somset* **19** ST5953

Chicheley Cock Clarks

Chicheley *Bucks* 30 SP9046
Chichester *W Susx* 11 SU8604
Chickerell *Dorset* 9 SY6480
Chicklade *Wilts* 9 ST9134
Chidden *Hants* 11 SU6517
Chiddingfold *Surrey* 12 SU9635
Chiddingly *E Susx* 13 TQ5414
Chiddingstone *Kent* 13 TQ5045
Chiddingstone Causeway *Kent* 13 TQ5246
Chideock *Dorset* 8 SY4292
Chidham *W Susx* 11 SU7903
Chidswell *W York* 55 SE2623
Chieveley *Berks* 21 SU4774
Chignall Smealy *Essex* 24 TL6611
Chignall St. James *Essex* 24 TL6610
Chigwell *Essex* 23 TQ4494
Chigwell Row *Essex* 23 TQ4693
Chilbolton *Hants* 21 SU3940
Chilcomb *Hants* 10 SU5028
Chilcombe *Dorset* 8 SY5291
Chilcompton *Somset* 19 ST6451
Chilcote *Leics* 39 SK2811
Child Okeford *Dorset* 9 ST8312
Child's Ercall *Shrops* 37 SJ6625
Childer Thornton *Ches* 46 SJ3677
Childrey *Oxon* 21 SU3687
Childswickham *H & W* 28 SP0738
Childwall *Mersyd* 46 SJ4189
Childwick Green *Herts* 22 TL1410
Chilfrome *Dorset* 9 SY5898
Chilgrove *W Susx* 11 SU8314
Chilham *Kent* 15 TR0653
Chillaton *Devon* 4 SX4381
Chillenden *Kent* 15 TR2753
Chillerton *IOW* 10 SZ4883
Chillesford *Suffk* 33 TM3852
Chillingham *Nthumb* 77 NU0525
Chillington *Somset* 8 ST3811
Chillington *Devon* 5 SX7942
Chilmark *Wilts* 9 ST9732
Chilmington Green *Kent* 15 TQ9840
Chilson *Oxon* 29 SP3119
Chilsworthy *Devon* 6 SS3206
Chilsworthy *Cnwll* 4 SX4172
Chilthorne Domer *Somset* 8 ST5219
Chiltington *E Susx* 13 TQ3815
Chilton *Bucks* 22 SP6811
Chilton *Oxon* 21 SU4885
Chilton Candover *Hants* 21 SU5940
Chilton Cantelo *Somset* 8 ST5722
Chilton Foliat *Wilts* 21 SU3170
Chilton Polden *Somset* 19 ST3740
Chilton Street *Suffk* 32 TL7546
Chilton Trinity *Somset* 19 ST2939
Chilworth *Hants* 10 SU4018
Chimney *Oxon* 21 SP3501
Chineham *Hants* 21 SU6555
Chingford *Gt Lon* 23 TQ3894
Chinley *Derbys* 48 SK0482
Chinnor *Oxon* 22 SP7501
Chipnall *Shrops* 37 SJ7231
Chippenham *Wilts* 20 ST9173
Chippenham *Cambs* 32 TL6669
Chipperfield *Herts* 22 TL0401
Chipping *Lancs* 54 SD6243
Chipping *Herts* 31 TL3531
Chipping Campden *Gloucs* 28 SP1539
Chipping Norton *Oxon* 29 SP3127
Chipping Ongar *Essex* 24 TL5503
Chipping Sodbury *Avon* 20 ST7282
Chipping Warden *Nhants* 29 SP4948
Chipstable *Somset* 7 ST0427
Chipstead *Surrey* 23 TQ2756
Chipstead *Kent* 23 TQ5056
Chirbury *Shrops* 36 SO2698
Chirk *Clwyd* 36 SJ2837
Chirnside *Border* 77 NT8756
Chirnsidebridge *Border* 77 NT8556
Chirton *Wilts* 20 SU0757
Chisbury *Wilts* 21 SU2766
Chiselborough *Somset* 8 ST4614
Chiseldon *Wilts* 21 SU1880
Chisholme *Border* 67 NT4112
Chislehampton *Oxon* 21 SU5999
Chislehurst *Gt Lon* 23 TQ4470
Chislet *Kent* 15 TR2264
Chisley *W York* 54 SE0028
Chiswellgreen *Herts* 22 TL1304
Chiswick *Gt Lon* 23 TQ2078
Chisworth *Derbys* 48 SJ9991
Chithurst *W Susx* 11 SU8423
Chittering *Cambs* 31 TL4969
Chitterne *Wilts* 20 ST9843
Chittlehamholt *Devon* 7 SS6520
Chittlehampton *Devon* 7 SS6325
Chittlehampton *Devon* 7 SS6511
Chittoe *Wilts* 20 ST9566
Chivelstone *Devon* 5 SX7838
Chlenry *D & G* 64 NX1260
Chobham *Surrey* 22 SU9762
Cholderton *Wilts* 21 SU2242
Cholesbury *Bucks* 22 SP9307
Chollerton *Nthumb* 68 NY9372
Cholsey *Oxon* 21 SU5886
Cholstrey *H & W* 27 SO4659
Chop Gate *N York* 62 SE5599
Choppington *T & W* 69 NZ2484
Chopwell *T & W* 69 NZ1158
Chorley *Lancs* 54 SD5817
Chorley *Ches* 47 SJ5751
Chorley *Shrops* 37 SO6983
Chorleywood *Herts* 22 TQ0396
Chorleywood West *Herts* 22 TQ0296
Chorlton *Ches* 47 SJ7250
Chorlton Lane *Ches* 46 SJ4547
Chorlton-cum-Hardy *Gt Man* 47 SJ8193
Choulton *Shrops* 36 SO3788
Chowley *Ches* 46 SJ4756
Chrishall *Essex* 31 TL4439
Chrisswell *Strath* 80 NS2274
Christchurch *Dorset* 10 SZ1592
Christchurch *Cambs* 41 TL4996
Christian Malford *Wilts* 20 ST9678
Christleton *Ches* 46 SJ4465
Christmas Common *Oxon* 22 SU7193
Christon *Avon* 19 ST3757
Christon Bank *Nthumb* 77 NU2123
Christow *Devon* 5 SX8385
Christskirk *Gramp* 94 NJ6027
Chudleigh *Devon* 5 SX8679
Chudleigh Knighton *Devon* 5 SX8477
Chulmleigh *Devon* 7 SS6814
Church *Lancs* 54 SD7429
Church Ashton *Shrops* 37 SJ7317
Church Brampton *Nhants* 30 SP7165
Church Broughton *Derbys* 39 SK2033
Church Crookham *Hants* 22 SU8051
Church Eaton *Staffs* 38 SJ8417
Church End *Hants* 22 SU6756
Church End *Beds* 31 TL1937
Church End *Herts* 31 TL4422
Church End *Essex* 24 TL7228
Church End *Gt Lon* 23 TQ2490
Church Enstone *Oxon* 29 SP3725
Church Fenton *N York* 55 SE5136
Church Green *Devon* 8 SY1796
Church Hanborough *Oxon* 29 SP4213
Church Hill *Ches* 47 SJ6465
Church Houses *N York* 62 SE6697
Church Knowle *Dorset* 9 SY9481
Church Langton *Leics* 40 SP7293
Church Lawford *Warwks* 39 SP4576
Church Lawton *Staffs* 47 SJ8255
Church Leigh *Staffs* 38 SK0235
Church Lench *H & W* 28 SP0251
Church Mayfield *Staffs* 48 SK1544
Church Minshull *Ches* 47 SJ6660
Church Norton *W Susx* 11 SZ8795
Church Preen *Shrops* 37 SO5498
Church Pulverbatch *Shrops* 36 SJ4303
Church Stoke *Powys* 36 SO2794
Church Stowe *Nhants* 29 SP6357
Church Street *Kent* 14 TQ7174
Church Stretton *Shrops* 36 SO4593
Church Village *M Glam* 18 ST0885
Church Warsop *Notts* 49 SK5668
Churcham *Gloucs* 28 SO7618
Churchdown *Gloucs* 28 SO8819
Churchend *Essex* 25 TR0093
Churchfield *W Mids* 38 SP0192
Churchill *H & W* 38 SO8879
Churchill *H & W* 28 SO9253
Churchill *Oxon* 29 SP2824
Churchill *Devon* 8 ST2902
Churchill *Avon* 19 ST4459
Churchinford *Devon* 8 ST2112
Churchover *Warwks* 39 SP5180
Churchstanton *Somset* 8 ST1914
Churchstow *Devon* 5 SX7145
Churchtown *Lancs* 53 SD4843
Churchtown *Derbys* 49 SK2662
Churston Ferrers *Devon* 5 SX9056
Churt *Surrey* 11 SU8538
Churton *Ches* 46 SJ4156
Churwell *W York* 55 SE2729
Chwilog *Gwynd* 44 SH4338
Chyandour *Cnwll* 2 SW4731
Cilcain *Clwyd* 46 SJ1765
Cilcennin *Dyfed* 34 SN5260
Cilfrew *W Glam* 18 SN7700
Cilfynydd *M Glam* 18 ST0891
Cilgerran *Dyfed* 17 SN1942
Cilgwyn *Dyfed* 26 SN7429
Cilmaengwyn *W Glam* 26 SN7405
Cilmery *Powys* 26 SO0051
Cilrhedyn *Dyfed* 17 SN2834
Cilsan *Dyfed* 17 SN5922
Ciltalgarth *Gwynd* 45 SH8940
Cilycwm *Dyfed* 26 SN7539
Cimla *W Glam* 18 SS7696
Cinderford *Gloucs* 27 SO6514
Cippenham *Bucks* 22 SU9480
Cirencester *Gloucs* 20 SP0201
Clabhach *Strath* 78 NM1858
Clachaig *Strath* 80 NS1181
Clachan *Highld* 84 NG5436
Clachan *Strath* 79 NM7819
Clachan *Strath* 79 NM8543
Clachan *Strath* 71 NR7656
Clachan *S Glam* 14 NR7656
Clachan Mor *Strath* 78 NL9847
Clachan-Seil *Strath* 79 NM7718
Clachan-a-Luib *W Isls* 102 NF8163
Clachaneasy *D & G* 64 NX3574
Clachnaharry *Highld* 92 NH6446
Clachtoll *Highld* 98 NC0427
Clackavoid *Tays* 88 NO1463
Clackmannan *Cent* 82 NS9191
Clackmarass *Gramp* 94 NJ2458
Clacton-on-Sea *Essex* 25 TM1715
Cladich *Strath* 80 NN0921
Cladswell *H & W* 28 SP0558
Claggan *Highld* 79 NM7049
Claigan *Highld* 90 NG2354
Clanfield *Oxon* 21 SP2801
Clanfield *Hants* 11 SU6916
Clanville *Somset* 9 ST6233
Clanville *Hants* 21 SU3148
Claonaig *Strath* 71 NR8656
Clapgate *Herts* 31 TL4424
Clapham *N York* 54 SD7469
Clapham *Beds* 30 TL0352
Clapham *W Susx* 12 TQ0906
Clapham *Gt Lon* 23 TQ2975
Clapton *Somset* 8 ST4106
Clapton *Somset* 19 ST6453
Clapton *Somset* 20 ST6852
Clapton-in-Gordano *Avon* 19 ST4773
Clapton-on-the-Hill *Gloucs* 28 SP1617
Claravale *T & W* 69 NZ1364
Clarbeston *Dyfed* 16 SN0521
Clarbeston Road *Dyfed* 16 SN0121
Clarborough *Notts* 50 SK7383
Clare *Suffk* 32 TL7745
Clarebrand *D & G* 65 NX7665
Clarencefield *D & G* 67 NY0968
Clarewood *Nthumb* 68 NZ0169
Clarilaw *Border* 76 NT5218
Clarkston *Strath* 74 NS5757
Clashmore *Highld* 98 NC0331
Clashmore *Highld* 97 NH7489
Clashnessie *Highld* 98 NC0530
Clashnoir *Gramp* 94 NJ2222
Clathy *Tays* 82 NN9920
Clathymore *Tays* 82 NO0121
Clatt *Gramp* 94 NJ5326
Clatter *Powys* 35 SN9994
Clatworthy *Somset* 7 ST0531
Claughton *Lancs* 53 SD5342
Claughton *Lancs* 53 SD5566
Claughton *Mersyd* 46 SJ3088
Claverdon *Warwks* 29 SP1965
Claverham *Avon* 19 ST4566
Clavering *Essex* 31 TL4731
Claverley *Shrops* 37 SO7993
Claverton *Avon* 20 ST7864
Clawdd-coch *S Glam* 18 ST0577
Clawdd-newydd *Clwyd* 46 SJ0852
Clawton *Devon* 6 SX3599
Claxby *Lincs* 50 TF1194
Claxton *N York* 56 SE6959
Claxton *Norfk* 43 TG3303
Clay Coton *Nhants* 39 SP5976
Clay Cross *Derbys* 49 SK3963
Clay End *Herts* 31 TL3024
Claybrooke Magna *Leics* 39 SP4988
Claydon *Oxon* 29 SP4549
Claydon *Suffk* 33 TM1349
Claygate *D & G* 67 NY3979
Claygate *Surrey* 22 TQ1563
Claygate *Kent* 14 TQ7144
Clayhanger *Devon* 7 ST0222
Clayhidon *Devon* 8 ST1615
Clayhill *E Susx* 14 TQ8323
Clayock *Highld* 100 ND1659
Claypits *Gloucs* 28 SO7606
Cock Marling *E Susx* 14 TQ8718
Cockayne Hatley *Beds* 31 TL2649
Cockburnspath *Border* 76 NT7770
Cockenzie and Port Seton *Loth* 76 NT4075
Cockerham *Lancs* 53 SD4651
Cockermouth *Cumb* 58 NY1230
Cockernhoe Green *Herts* 30 TL1223
Cockett *W Glam* 17 SS6394
Cockfield *Dur* 61 NZ1224
Cockfield *Suffk* 32 TL9054
Cockfosters *Gt Lon* 23 TQ2796
Cocking *W Susx* 11 SU8717
Cocking Causeway *W Susx* 11 SU8819
Cockington *Devon* 5 SX8963
Cocklake *Somset* 19 ST4449
Cockley Beck *Cumb* 58 NY2501
Cockley Cley *Norfk* 42 TF7904
Cockpole Green *Berks* 22 SU7981
Cockshutt *Shrops* 36 SJ4328
Cockthorpe *Norfk* 42 TF9842
Cockwood *Devon* 5 SX9780
Cockyard *Derbys* 48 SK0479
Coddenham *Suffk* 33 TM1354
Coddington *Notts* 50 SK8354
Coddington *H & W* 28 SO7142
Codford St. Mary *Wilts* 20 ST9739
Codford St. Peter *Wilts* 20 ST9639
Codicote *Herts* 31 TL2118
Codmore Hill *W Susx* 12 TQ0520
Codnor *Derbys* 49 SK4149
Codrington *Avon* 20 ST7278
Codsall *Staffs* 38 SJ8603
Codsall Wood *Staffs* 38 SJ8404
Coed Talon *Clwyd* 46 SJ2659
Coed-y-paen *Gwent* 19 ST3398
Coedana *Gwynd* 44 SH4382
Coedpoeth *Clwyd* 46 SJ2851
Coffinswell *Devon* 5 SX8968
Cofton Hackett *H & W* 38 SP0075
Cogan *S Glam* 19 ST1771
Cogenhoe *Nhants* 30 SP8260
Coggeshall *Essex* 24 TL8522
Coignafearn *Highld* 93 NH7018
Coilantogle *Cent* 81 NN5907
Coilcreach *Gramp* 88 NO3296
Coillore *Highld* 84 NG3537
Coiltry *Highld* 86 NH3506
Coity *M Glam* 18 SS9281
Col *W Isls* 102 NB4739
Colaboll *Highld* 96 NC5610
Colan *Cnwll* 3 SW8661
Colaton Raleigh *Devon* 5 SY0787
Colbost *Highld* 90 NG2148
Colburn *N York* 61 SE1999
Colby *Cumb* 60 NY6620
Colby *IOM* 52 SC2370
Colby *Norfk* 43 TG2231
Colchester *Essex* 25 TL9925
Cold Ash *Berks* 21 SU5169
Cold Ashby *Nhants* 39 SP6576
Cold Ashton *Avon* 20 ST7572
Cold Aston *Gloucs* 28 SP1219
Cold Brayfield *Bucks* 30 SP9252
Cold Hanworth *Lincs* 50 TF0383
Cold Hesledon *Dur* 69 NZ4146
Cold Hiendley *W York* 55 SE3714
Cold Higham *Nhants* 30 SP6653
Cold Kirby *N York* 62 SE5384
Cold Norton *Essex* 24 TL8500
Cold Overton *Leics* 40 SK8010
Coldbackie *Highld* 99 NC6160
Coldean *E Susx* 12 TQ3308
Coldeast *Devon* 5 SX8174
Colden *W York* 54 SD9628
Colden Common *Hants* 10 SU4822
Coldfair Green *Suffk* 33 TM4360
Coldharbour *Surrey* 12 TQ1443
Coldingham *Border* 77 NT9065
Claypole *Lincs* 50 SK8449
Clayton *W York* 55 SE1231
Clayton *S York* 55 SE4507
Clayton *W Susx* 12 TQ2914
Clayton West *W York* 55 SE2510
Clayton-le-Moors *Lancs* 54 SD7530
Clayton-le-Woods *Lancs* 53 SD5622
Clayworth *Notts* 50 SK7387
Cleadale *Highld* 84 NM4789
Cleadon *T & W* 69 NZ3862
Clearbrook *Devon* 4 SX5265
Clearwell *Gloucs* 27 SO5608
Cleasby *N York* 61 NZ2512
Cleat *Ork* 103 ND4584
Cleatlam *Dur* 61 NZ1118
Cleator *Cumb* 58 NY0113
Cleator Moor *Cumb* 58 NY0115
Cleckheaton *W York* 55 SE1825
Clee St. Margaret *Shrops* 37 SO5684
Cleehill *Shrops* 37 SO5975
Cleekhimin *Strath* 74 NS7658
Cleethorpes *Humb* 57 TA3008
Cleeton St. Mary *Shrops* 37 SO6178
Cleeve *Avon* 19 ST4666
Cleeve *Oxon* 21 SU6081
Cleeve Hill *Gloucs* 28 SO9827
Cleeve Prior *H & W* 28 SP0849
Clehonger *H & W* 27 SO4637
Cleish *Tays* 82 NT0998
Cleland *Strath* 74 NS7958
Clenamacrie *Strath* 80 NM9228
Clenchwarton *Norfk* 41 TF5920
Clent *H & W* 38 SO9279
Clenterty *Gramp* 95 NJ7760
Cleobury Mortimer *Shrops* 37 SO6775
Cleobury North *Shrops* 37 SO6286
Cleongart *Strath* 72 NR6734
Clephanton *Highld* 93 NH8150
Clerkhill *D & G* 67 NY2697
Cleuch Head *Border* 67 NT5910
Cleuch-head *D & G* 66 NS8200
Clevancy *Wilts* 20 SU0575
Clevedon *Avon* 19 ST4171
Cleveleys *Lancs* 53 SD3143
Cleverton *Wilts* 20 ST9785
Clewer *Somset* 19 ST4351
Cley next the Sea *Norfk* 42 TG0444
Cliburn *Cumb* 59 NY5725
Cliddesden *Hants* 21 SU6349
Cliff End *E Susx* 14 TQ8813
Cliffe *Dur* 61 NZ2115
Cliffe *N York* 56 SE6631
Cliffe *Kent* 14 TQ7376
Clifford *W York* 55 SE4344
Clifford *H & W* 27 SO2445
Clifford Chambers *Warwks* 29 SP1952
Clifford's Mesne *Gloucs* 28 SO7023
Clifton *Cent* 80 NN3231
Clifton *Cumb* 59 NY5326
Clifton *Lancs* 53 SD4630
Clifton *W York* 55 SE1622
Clifton *W York* 55 SE1948
Clifton *N York* 56 SE5953
Clifton *Derbys* 48 SK1644
Clifton *S York* 49 SK5296
Clifton *Notts* 39 SK5434
Clifton *H & W* 28 SO8446
Clifton *Oxon* 29 SP4931
Clifton *Avon* 19 ST5773
Clifton *Beds* 31 TL1639
Clifton Campville *Staffs* 39 SK2510
Clifton Hampden *Oxon* 21 SU5495
Clifton Reynes *Bucks* 30 SP9051
Clifton upon Dunsmore *Warwks* 39 SP5376
Clifton upon Teme *H & W* 28 SO7161
Cliftonville *Kent* 15 TR3771
Climping *W Susx* 12 SU9902
Clink *Somset* 20 ST7948
Clint *N York* 55 SE2659
Clint Green *Norfk* 42 TG0210
Clinterty *Gramp* 95 NJ8311
Clintmains *Border* 76 NT6132
Clippesby *Norfk* 43 TG4214
Clipsham *Leics* 40 SK9716
Clipston *Notts* 39 SK6334
Clipston *Nhants* 40 SP7181
Clipstone *Notts* 49 SK6064
Clipstone *Beds* 30 SP9426
Clitheroe *Lancs* 54 SD7441
Clive *Shrops* 37 SJ5124
Cloatley *Wilts* 20 ST9890
Clocaenog *Clwyd* 46 SJ0854
Clochan *Gramp* 94 NJ4060
Clochtow *Tays* 89 NO4852
Clodock *H & W* 27 SO3227
Clola *Gramp* 95 NK0043
Clophill *Beds* 30 TL0838
Clopton *Nhants* 40 TL0680
Clopton *Suffk* 33 TM2253
Clopton Corner *Suffk* 33 TM2254
Clos du Valle *Guern* 101 GN0000
Closeburn *D & G* 66 NX8992
Closeburnmill *D & G* 66 NX9094
Closworth *Somset* 8 ST5610
Clothall *Herts* 31 TL2731
Clotton *Ches* 46 SJ5264
Clough Foot *W York* 54 SD9123
Clough Head *W York* 55 SE0918
Cloughton *N York* 63 TA0194
Clousta *Shet* 103 HU3057
Clova *Tays* 88 NO3273
Clovelly *Devon* 6 SS3124
Clovenfords *Border* 76 NT4536
Clovulin *Highld* 86 NN0063
Clow Bridge *Lancs* 54 SD8228
Clowne *Derbys* 49 SK4875
Clows Top *H & W* 37 SO7172
Cluanie Inn *Highld* 85 NH0711
Cluanie Lodge *Highld* 85 NH0910
Clugston *D & G* 64 NX3557
Clun *Shrops* 36 SO3080
Clunas *Highld* 93 NH8846
Clunbury *Shrops* 36 SO3780
Clune *Highld* 93 NH7925
Clunes *Highld* 86 NN1988
Clungunford *Shrops* 36 SO3978
Clunie *Gramp* 94 NJ6350
Clunie *Tays* 88 NO1043
Clunton *Shrops* 36 SO3381
Clutton *Ches* 46 SJ4654
Clutton *Avon* 19 ST6259
Clutton Hill *Avon* 19 ST6359
Clydach *W Glam* 18 SN6800
Clydach *Gwent* 27 SO2213
Clydach Vale *M Glam* 18 SS9792
Clydebank *Strath* 74 NS4970
Clydey *Dyfed* 17 SN2535
Clyffe Pypard *Wilts* 20 SU0777
Clynder *Strath* 80 NS2484
Clynderwen *Dyfed* 16 SN1219
Clyne *W Glam* 18 SN8000
Clynelish *Highld* 97 NC8905
Clynnog-fawr *Gwynd* 44 SH4149
Clyro *Powys* 27 SO2143
Clyst Honiton *Devon* 5 SX9893
Clyst Hydon *Devon* 7 ST0301
Clyst St. George *Devon* 5 SX9888
Clyst St. Lawrence *Devon* 7 ST0200
Clyst St. Mary *Devon* 5 SX9791
Clyth *Highld* 100 ND2835
Cnwch Coch *Dyfed* 35 SN6774
Coad's Green *Cnwll* 4 SX2976
Coalburn *Strath* 74 NS8134
Coalburns *T & W* 69 NZ1260
Coaley *Gloucs* 20 SO7701
Coalhill *Essex* 24 TQ7597
Coalpit Heath *Avon* 20 ST6780
Coalport *Shrops* 37 SJ6902
Coalsnaughton *Cent* 82 NS9195
Coaltown of Balgonie *Fife* 83 NT2999
Coaltown of Wemyss *Fife* 83 NT3295
Coalville *Leics* 39 SK4214
Coanwood *Nthumb* 68 NY6859
Coat *Somset* 8 ST4520
Coatbridge *Strath* 74 NS7365
Coatdyke *Strath* 74 NS7465
Coate *Wilts* 20 SU0462
Coate *Wilts* 21 SU1882
Coates *Lincs* 50 SK9083
Coates *Gloucs* 20 SO9701
Coates *W Susx* 12 SU9917
Coates *Cambs* 41 TL3097
Cobbaton *Devon* 6 SS6126
Coberley *Gloucs* 28 SO9616
Cobham *Surrey* 22 TQ1060
Cobham *Kent* 14 TQ6768
Cobnash *H & W* 27 SO4560
Cobo *Guern* 101 GN0000
Coburby *Gramp* 95 NJ9164
Cock Bridge *Gramp* 94 NJ2509
Cock Clarks *Essex* 24 TL8102

Cock Green

Craigdarroch

Cock Green *Essex* 24 TL6919
Cock Marling *E Susx* 14 TQ8718
Cockayne Hatley *Beds* 31 TL2649
Cockburnspath *Border* 76 NT7770
Cockenzie and Port Seton *Loth* 76 NT4075
Cockerham *Lancs* 53 SD4651
Cockermouth *Cumb* 58 NY1230
Cockernhoe Green *Herts* 30 TL1223
Cockett *W Glam* 17 SS6394
Cockfield *Dur* 61 NZ1224
Cockfield *Suffk* 32 TL9054
Cockfosters *Gt Lon* 23 TQ2796
Cocking *W Susx* 11 SU8717
Cocking Causeway *W Susx* 11 SU8819
Cockington *Devon* 5 SX8963
Cocklake *Somset* 19 ST4449
Cockley Beck *Cumb* 58 NY2501
Cockley Cley *Norfk* 42 TF7904
Cockpole Green *Berks* 22 SU7981
Cockshutt *Shrops* 36 SJ4328
Cockthorpe *Norfk* 42 TF9842
Cockwood *Devon* 5 SX9780
Cockyard *Derbys* 48 SK0479
Coddenham *Suffk* 33 TM1354
Coddington *Notts* 50 SK8354
Coddington *H & W* 28 SO7142
Codford St. Mary *Wilts* 20 ST9739
Codford St. Peter *Wilts* 20 ST9639
Codicote *Herts* 31 TL2118
Codmore Hill *W Susx* 12 TQ0520
Codnor *Derbys* 49 SK4149
Codrington *Avon* 20 ST7278
Codsall *Staffs* 38 SJ8603
Codsall Wood *Staffs* 38 SJ8404
Coed Talon *Clwyd* 46 SJ2659
Coed-y-paen *Gwent* 19 ST3398
Coedana *Gwynd* 44 SH4382
Coedpoeth *Clwyd* 46 SJ2851
Coffinswell *Devon* 5 SX8968
Cofton Hackett *H & W* 38 SP0075
Cogan *S Glam* 19 ST1771
Cogenhoe *Nhants* 30 SP8260
Coggeshall *Essex* 24 TL8522
Coignafearn *Highld* 93 NH7018
Coilantogle *Cent* 81 NN5907
Coilcreach *Gramp* 88 NO3296
Coillore *Highld* 84 NG3537
Coiltry *Highld* 86 NH3506
Coity *M Glam* 18 SS9281
Col *W Isls* 102 NB4739
Colaboll *Highld* 96 NC5610
Colan *Cnwll* 3 SW8661
Colaton Raleigh *Devon* 5 SY0787
Colbost *Highld* 90 NG2148
Colburn *N York* 61 SE1999
Colby *Cumb* 60 NY6620
Colby *IOM* 52 SC2370
Colby *Norfk* 43 TG2231
Colchester *Essex* 25 TL9925
Cold Ash *Berks* 21 SU5169
Cold Ashby *Nhants* 39 SP6576
Cold Ashton *Avon* 20 ST7572
Cold Aston *Gloucs* 28 SP1219
Cold Brayfield *Bucks* 30 SP9252
Cold Hanworth *Lincs* 50 TF0383
Cold Hesledon *Dur* 69 NZ4146
Cold Hiendley *W York* 55 SE3714
Cold Higham *Nhants* 30 SP6653
Cold Kirby *N York* 62 SE5384
Cold Norton *Essex* 24 TL8500
Cold Overton *Leics* 40 SK8010
Coldbackie *Highld* 99 NC6160
Coldean *E Susx* 12 TQ3308
Coldeast *Devon* 5 SX8174
Colden *W York* 54 SD9628
Colden Common *Hants* 10 SU4822
Coldfair Green *Suffk* 33 TM4360
Coldharbour *Surrey* 12 TQ1443
Coldingham *Border* 77 NT9065
Coldmeece *Staffs* 38 SJ8532
Coldred *Kent* 15 TR2747
Coldridge *Devon* 7 SS6907
Coldstream *Border* 77 NT8439
Coldwaltham *W Susx* 12 TQ0216
Coldwell *H & W* 27 SO4235
Coldwells *Gramp* 95 NJ9538
Coldwells *Gramp* 95 NK1039
Cole *Somset* 9 ST6733
Cole Green *Herts* 23 TL2811
Colebatch *Shrops* 36 SO3187
Colebrook *Devon* 7 ST0006
Colebrooke *Devon* 7 SX7699
Coleby *Humb* 56 SE8919
Coleby *Lincs* 50 SK9760
Coleby *Lincs* 50 SK9760
Coleford *Gloucs* 27 SO5710
Coleford *Devon* 7 SS7701
Coleford *Somset* 20 ST6848
Coleford Water *Somset* 8 ST1133
Colegate End *Norfk* 33 TM1987
Colehill *Dorset* 9 SU0201
Coleman's Hatch *E Susx* 13 TQ4433
Colemere *Shrops* 36 SJ4332
Colemore *Hants* 11 SU7030
Colenden *Tays* 82 NO1029
Colerne *Wilts* 20 ST8271
Colesbourne *Gloucs* 28 SP0013
Coleshill *Warwks* 39 SP2089
Coleshill *Oxon* 21 SU2393
Coleshill *Bucks* 22 SU9495
Coley *Avon* 19 ST5855
Colgate *W Susx* 12 TQ2332
Colgrain *Strath* 80 NS3280
Colinsburgh *Fife* 83 NO4703
Colinton *Loth* 75 NT2168
Colintraive *Strath* 80 NS0374
Colkirk *Norfk* 42 TF9126
Collace *Tays* 82 NO2032
Collafirth *Shet* 103 HU3482
Collaton *Devon* 5 SX7139
Collaton St. Mary *Devon* 5 SX8660
College Town *Berks* 22 SU8560
College of Roseisle *Gramp* 93 NJ1466
Collessie *Fife* 83 NO2813
Collier Row *Gt Lon* 23 TQ5091
Collier Street *Kent* 14 TQ7145
Collier's End *Herts* 31 TL3720
Collieston *Gramp* 95 NK0328
Collin *D & G* 66 NY0276
Collingbourne Ducis *Wilts* 21 SU2453
Collingbourne Kingston *Wilts* 21 SU2355
Collingham *W York* 55 SE3945
Collington *H & W* 27 SO6460
Collingtree *Nhants* 30 SP7555
Collins Green *Ches* 47 SJ5594
Colliston *Tays* 89 NO6045
Colliton *Devon* 7 ST0804
Collyweston *Nhants* 40 SK9902
Colmonell *Strath* 64 NX1485
Colmworth *Beds* 30 TL1058
Coln Rogers *Gloucs* 28 SP0809
Coln St. Aldwyns *Gloucs* 28 SP1405
Coln St. Dennis *Gloucs* 28 SP0810
Colnbrook *Gt Lon* 22 TQ0277
Colne *Lancs* 54 SD8939
Colne *Cambs* 31 TL3775
Colne Engaine *Essex* 24 TL8430
Colney *Norfk* 43 TG1807
Colney Heath *Herts* 23 TL2005
Colney Street *Herts* 22 TL1502
Colpy *Gramp* 94 NJ6432
Colquhar *Border* 75 NT3341
Colsterworth *Lincs* 40 SK9324
Colston Bassett *Notts* 40 SK7033
Colt's Hill *Kent* 13 TQ6443
Coltfield *Gramp* 93 NJ1163
Coltishall *Norfk* 43 TG2719
Colton *Cumb* 58 SD3185
Colton *W York* 55 SE3732
Colton *N York* 56 SE5444
Colton *Staffs* 38 SK0420
Colton *Norfk* 43 TG1009
Colva *Powys* 27 SO1952
Colvend *D & G* 66 NX8654
Colwall *H & W* 28 SO7542
Colwell *Nthumb* 68 NY9575
Colwich *Staffs* 38 SK0121
Colwinston *S Glam* 18 SS9375
Colworth *W Susx* 11 SU9103
Colwyn Bay *Clwyd* 45 SH8578
Colyford *Devon* 8 SY2592
Colyton *Devon* 8 SY2494
Combe *H & W* 27 SO3463
Combe *Oxon* 29 SP4116
Combe *Berks* 21 SU3760
Combe Fishacre *Devon* 5 SX8465
Combe Florey *Somset* 8 ST1531
Combe Hay *Avon* 20 ST7359
Combe Martin *Devon* 6 SS5846
Combe Moor *H & W* 27 SO3663
Combe Raleigh *Devon* 8 ST1502
Combe St. Nicholas *Somset* 8 ST3011
Combeinteignhead *Devon* 5 SX9071
Comberbach *Ches* 47 SJ6477
Comberford *Staffs* 39 SK1907
Comberton *H & W* 27 SO4968
Comberton *Cambs* 31 TL3856
Combrook *Warwks* 29 SP3051
Combs *Derbys* 48 SK0478
Combs *Suffk* 32 TM0456
Combs *Suffk* 32 TM0456
Combs Ford *Suffk* 32 TM0457
Combwich *Somset* 19 ST2542
Comers *Gramp* 95 NJ6707
Comhampton *H & W* 28 SO8367
Commercial *Dyfed* 16 SN1416
Commins Coch *Powys* 35 SH8402
Common Moor *Cnwll* 4 SX2469
Common The *Wilts* 10 SU2432
Commondale *N York* 62 NZ6610
Compstall *Gt Man* 48 SJ9690
Compstonend *D & G* 65 NX6652
Compton *Staffs* 38 SO8284
Compton *Wilts* 20 SU1351
Compton *Hants* 10 SU4625
Compton *Berks* 21 SU5280
Compton *W Susx* 11 SU7714
Compton *Surrey* 12 SU9546
Compton *Devon* 5 SX8664
Compton Abbas *Dorset* 9 ST8618
Compton Abdale *Gloucs* 28 SP0516
Compton Bassett *Wilts* 20 SU0372
Compton Beauchamp *Oxon* 21 SU2786
Compton Bishop *Somset* 19 ST3955
Compton Chamberlayne *Wilts* 9 SU0229
Compton Dando *Avon* 19 ST6464
Compton Dundon *Somset* 8 ST4932
Compton Durville *Somset* 8 ST4117
Compton Greenfield *Avon* 19 ST5681
Compton Martin *Avon* 19 ST5457
Compton Pauncefoot *Somset* 9 ST6426
Compton Valence *Dorset* 9 SY5993
Comrie *Tays* 81 NN7722
Comrie *Fife* 82 NT0289
Conaglen House *Highld* 86 NN0268
Conchra *Highld* 85 NG8827
Concraigie *Tays* 88 NO0944
Conderton *H & W* 28 SO9637
Condicote *Gloucs* 28 SP1528
Condorrat *Strath* 74 NS7373
Condover *Shrops* 37 SJ4905
Coney Hill *Gloucs* 28 SO8517
Coney Weston *Suffk* 32 TL9578
Coneyhurst Common *W Susx* 12 TQ1023
Coneysthorpe *N York* 56 SE7171
Congdon's Shop *Cnwll* 4 SX2878
Congerstone *Leics* 39 SK3605
Congham *Norfk* 42 TF7123
Congleton *Ches* 47 SJ8562
Congresbury *Avon* 19 ST4363
Conheath *D & G* 66 NX9969
Conicavel *Gramp* 93 NH9853
Conichan *Tays* 82 NN8432
Coningsby *Lincs* 51 TF2257
Conington *Cambs* 40 TL1885
Conington *Cambs* 31 TL3266
Conisbrough *S York* 49 SK5098
Conisholme *Lincs* 51 TF4095
Coniston *Cumb* 58 SD3097
Coniston *Humb* 57 TA1434
Coniston Cold *N York* 54 SD9054
Conistone *N York* 54 SD9867
Connah's Quay *Clwyd* 46 SJ2969
Connel *Strath* 80 NM9134
Connel Park *Strath* 66 NS6012
Connor Downs *Cnwll* 2 SW5939
Conon Bridge *Highld* 92 NH5455
Cononley *N York* 54 SD9846
Consall *Staffs* 48 SJ9848
Consett *Dur* 68 NZ1051
Constable Burton *N York* 61 SE1690
Constantine *Cnwll* 2 SW7329
Contin *Highld* 92 NH4556
Conwy *Gwynd* 45 SH7877
Conyer's Green *Suffk* 32 TL8867
Cooden *E Susx* 14 TQ7107
Coodham *Strath* 73 NS3932
Cook's Green *Essex* 25 TM1818
Cookbury *Devon* 6 SS4006
Cookham *Berks* 22 SU8985
Cookham Dean *Berks* 22 SU8685
Cookham Rise *Berks* 22 SU8885
Cookhill *Warwks* 28 SP0558
Cookley *H & W* 38 SO8480
Cookley *Suffk* 33 TM3475
Cookley Green *Oxon* 22 SU6990
Cookney *Gramp* 89 NO8693
Cooks Green *Suffk* 32 TL9753
Cooksmill Green *Essex* 24 TL6306
Coolham *W Susx* 12 TQ1122
Cooling *Kent* 14 TQ7575
Coombe *Gloucs* 20 ST7694
Coombe *Hants* 11 SU6620
Coombe *Devon* 5 SX9373
Coombe *Devon* 5 SX9373
Coombe *Devon* 8 SY1091
Coombe Bissett *Wilts* 10 SU1026
Coombe Cellars *Devon* 5 SX9072
Coombe End *Somset* 7 ST0329
Coombe Hill *Gloucs* 28 SO8826
Coombe Keynes *Dorset* 9 SY8484
Coombe Pafford *Devon* 5 SX9166
Coombe Street *Somset* 9 ST7631
Cooperhill *Gramp* 93 NH9953
Coopersale Common *Essex* 23 TL4702
Coopersale Street *Essex* 23 TL4701
Cop Street *Kent* 23 TQ2959
Copdock *Suffk* 33 TM1242
Copford Green *Essex* 24 TL9222
Copgrove *N York* 55 SE3463
Copister *Shet* 103 HU4879
Cople *Beds* 30 TL1048
Copley *Dur* 61 NZ0825
Copmanthorpe *N York* 56 SE5646
Copmere End *Staffs* 37 SJ8029
Copp *Lancs* 53 SD4239
Coppathorne *Cnwll* 6 SS2000
Coppenhall *Staffs* 38 SJ9019
Copperhouse *Cnwll* 2 SW5637
Coppingford *Cambs* 40 TL1679
Copplestone *Devon* 7 SS7702
Coppull *Lancs* 53 SD5614
Copsale *W Susx* 12 TQ1724
Copster Green *Lancs* 54 SD6733
Copston Magna *Warwks* 39 SP4588
Copt Hewick *N York* 55 SE3471
Copthall Green *Essex* 23 TL4201
Copthorne *W Susx* 12 TQ3139
Copy's Green *Norfk* 42 TF9439
Copythorne *Hants* 10 SU3014
Corbets Tay *Gt Lon* 24 TQ5685
Corbiere *Jersey* 101 JS0000
Corbridge *Nthumb* 68 NY9964
Corby *Nhants* 40 SP8988
Corby Glen *Lincs* 40 TF0024
Cordon *Strath* 72 NS0230
Coreley *Shrops* 37 SO6173
Corfe *Somset* 8 ST2319
Corfe Castle *Dorset* 9 SY9681
Corfe Mullen *Dorset* 9 SY9798
Corfton *Shrops* 37 SO4985
Corgarff *Gramp* 94 NJ2708
Corhampton *Hants* 11 SU6120
Corley *Warwks* 39 SP3085
Corley Ash *Warwks* 39 SP2986
Cormuir *Tays* 88 NO3066
Cornard Tye *Suffk* 32 TL9041
Cornforth *Dur* 62 NZ3134
Cornhill *Gramp* 94 NJ5858
Cornhill-on-Tweed *Nthumb* 77 NT8639
Cornholme *W York* 54 SD9126
Cornoigmore *Strath* 78 NL9846
Cornsay *Dur* 69 NZ1443
Cornsay Colliery *Dur* 69 NZ1643
Corntown *Highld* 92 NH5556
Corntown *M Glam* 18 SS9177
Cornwell *Oxon* 29 SP2727
Cornwood *Devon* 5 SX6059
Cornworthy *Devon* 5 SX8255
Corpach *Highld* 86 NN0976
Corpusty *Norfk* 43 TG1129
Corrachree *Gramp* 89 NJ4604
Corran *Highld* 85 NG8409
Corran *Highld* 86 NN0263
Corrie *Strath* 72 NS0242
Corrie *D & G* 67 NY2086
Corriecravie *Strath* 72 NR9223
Corriegour *Highld* 86 NN2692
Corriemoille *Highld* 92 NH3663
Corrimony *Highld* 92 NH3730
Corringham *Lincs* 50 SK8691
Corringham *Essex* 24 TQ7083
Corris *Gwynd* 35 SH7508
Corris Uchaf *Gwynd* 35 SH7408
Corrow *Strath* 80 NN1800
Corry *Highld* 85 NG6424
Corrygills *Strath* 72 NS0335
Corscombe *Dorset* 8 ST5105
Corscombe *Devon* 6 SX6296
Corse *Gramp* 94 NJ6040
Corse Lawn *Gloucs* 28 SO8330
Corsham *Wilts* 20 ST8770
Corsindae *Gramp* 95 NJ6808
Corsley *Wilts* 20 ST8246
Corsley Heath *Wilts* 20 ST8245
Corsock *D & G* 65 NX7675
Corston *Avon* 20 ST6965
Corston *Wilts* 20 ST9283
Corstorphine *Loth* 75 NT1972
Cortachy *Tays* 88 NO3959
Cortachy *Tays* 88 NO3959
Corton *Wilts* 20 ST9340
Corton *Suffk* 43 TM5497
Corton Denham *Somset* 9 ST6322
Coruanan Lodge *Highld* 86 NN0668
Corvallie *IOM* 52 SC1968
Corwar *Strath* 64 NX2780
Corwen *Clwyd* 46 SJ0743
Coryton *Devon* 4 SX4583
Coryton *Essex* 24 TQ7382
Cosby *Leics* 39 SP5495
Coseley *W Mids* 38 SO9494
Cosgrove *Nhants* 30 SP7942
Cosham *Hants* 11 SU6505
Cosheston *Dyfed* 16 SN0003
Coshieville *Tays* 87 NN7749
Cossall *Notts* 49 SK4842
Cossington *Leics* 39 SK6013
Cossington *Somset* 19 ST3540
Costessey *Norfk* 43 TG1711
Costock *Notts* 39 SK5726
Coston *Leics* 40 SK8422
Coston *Norfk* 42 TG0506
Cote *Oxon* 21 SP3502
Cotebrook *Ches* 47 SJ5765
Cotehill *Cumb* 67 NY4650
Cotes *Leics* 39 SK5520
Cotesbach *Leics* 39 SP5382
Cotgrave *Notts* 39 SK6435
Cotham *Notts* 50 SK7947
Cotherstone *Dur* 61 NZ0119
Cothill *Oxon* 21 SU4699
Cotleigh *Devon* 8 ST2002
Coton *Staffs* 37 SJ8120
Coton *Nhants* 30 SP6771
Coton *Cambs* 31 TL4058
Coton Clanford *Staffs* 38 SJ8723
Coton Hill *Shrops* 37 SJ4813
Coton in the Elms *Derbys* 39 SK2415
Cott *Devon* 5 SX7861
Cottage End *Hants* 21 SU4143
Cottam *Lancs* 53 SD5032
Cottam *Notts* 50 SK8179
Cottenham *Cambs* 31 TL4467
Cottered *Herts* 31 TL3129
Cotterstock *Nhants* 40 TL0490
Cottesbrooke *Nhants* 30 SP7173
Cottesmore *Leics* 40 SK9013
Cottingham *Nhants* 40 SP8490
Cottingham *Humb* 57 TA0432
Cottingley *W York* 55 SE1137
Cottisford *Oxon* 29 SP5831
Cotton *Suffk* 32 TM0666
Cottown *Gramp* 94 NJ5026
Cottown *Gramp* 95 NJ7615
Cottown *Gramp* 95 NJ8140
Cotts *Devon* 4 SX4365
Coughton *Warwks* 28 SP0860
Coulaghailtro *Strath* 71 NR7165
Coulags *Highld* 91 NG9645
Coull *Gramp* 89 NJ5102
Coulport *Strath* 80 NS2187
Coulsdon *Gt Lon* 23 TQ2959
Coulter *Strath* 75 NT0234
Coulton *N York* 62 SE6373
Coultra *Fife* 83 NO3523
Cound *Shrops* 37 SJ5505
Coundon *Dur* 61 NZ2329
Countersett *N York* 60 SD9187
Countess Wear *Devon* 5 SX9489
Countesthorpe *Leics* 39 SP5895
Countisbury *Devon* 18 SS7449
Coupar Angus *Tays* 82 NO2239
Coupland *Nthumb* 77 NT9330
Cour *Strath* 72 NR8248
Courance *D & G* 66 NY0590
Court Henry *Dyfed* 17 SN5522
Courteachan *Highld* 85 NM6897
Courteenhall *Nhants* 30 SP7653
Courtsend *Essex* 25 TR0293
Courtway *Somset* 8 ST2033
Cousland *Loth* 76 NT3768
Cousley Wood *E Susx* 13 TQ6533
Cove *Highld* 91 NG8191
Cove *Gramp* 89 NJ9501
Cove *Strath* 80 NS2282
Cove *Devon* 7 SS9619
Cove *Hants* 22 SU8555
Covehithe *Suffk* 33 TM5282
Coven *Staffs* 38 SJ9106
Coveney *Cambs* 41 TL4882
Covenham St. Bartholomew *Lincs* 51 TF3394
Covenham St. Mary *Lincs* 51 TF3394
Coventry *W Mids* 39 SP3378
Coverack *Cnwll* 2 SW7818
Coverack Bridges *Cnwll* 2 SW6630
Coverham *N York* 61 SE1086
Coverham *N York* 61 SE1086
Covington *Cambs* 30 TL0570
Cow Honeybourne *H & W* 28 SP1143
Cowan Bridge *Lancs* 60 SD6376
Cowbeech *E Susx* 13 TQ6114
Cowbit *Lincs* 41 TF2518
Cowbridge *S Glam* 18 SS9974
Cowden *Kent* 13 TQ4640
Cowdenbeath *Fife* 82 NT1691
Cowdenburn *Border* 75 NT2052
Cowers Lane *Derbys* 49 SK3046
Cowes *IOW* 10 SZ4996
Cowesby *N York* 62 SE4689
Cowfold *W Susx* 12 TQ2122
Cowhill *Avon* 19 ST6091
Cowie *Cent* 82 NS8389
Cowley *Gloucs* 28 SO9614
Cowley *Oxon* 29 SP5304
Cowley *Devon* 7 SX9095
Cowley *Gt Lon* 22 TQ0582
Cowling *Lancs* 54 SD5917
Cowling *N York* 54 SD9643
Cowling *N York* 61 SE2387
Cowlinge *Suffk* 32 TL7154
Cowpen *Nthumb* 69 NZ2981
Cowplain *Hants* 11 SU6810
Cowshill *Dur* 60 NY8540
Cowslip Green *Avon* 19 ST4861
Cowthorpe *N York* 55 SE4252
Coxbank *Ches* 37 SJ6541
Coxbench *Derbys* 49 SK3743
Coxford *Cnwll* 6 SX1696
Coxford *Norfk* 42 TF8529
Coxheath *Kent* 14 TQ7451
Coxhoe *Dur* 62 NZ3136
Coxley *Somset* 19 ST5343
Coxley Wick *Somset* 19 ST5243
Coxtie Green *Essex* 24 TQ5696
Coxwold *N York* 62 SE5377
Coychurch *M Glam* 18 SS9379
Coylton *Strath* 73 NS4219
Coylumbridge *Highld* 93 NH9111
Coytrahen *M Glam* 18 SS8885
Crabbs Cross *H & W* 28 SP0465
Crabtree *W Susx* 12 TQ2125
Crackenthorpe *Cumb* 60 NY6622
Crackington Haven *Cnwll* 6 SX1496
Crackleybank *Shrops* 37 SJ7611
Cracoe *N York* 54 SD9760
Craddock *Devon* 7 ST0812
Cradley *H & W* 28 SO7347
Cradoc *Powys* 26 SO0130
Crafthole *Cnwll* 4 SX3654
Crafton *Bucks* 30 SP8819
Cragg *W York* 54 SE0023
Craggan *Highld* 93 NJ0226
Craghead *Dur* 69 NZ2150
Crai *Powys* 26 SN8924
Craibstone *Gramp* 94 NJ4959
Craibstone *Gramp* 95 NJ8710
Craichie *Tays* 89 NO5047
Craig Llangiwg *W Glam* 26 SN7204
Craigburn *Border* 75 NT2354
Craigdam *Gramp* 95 NJ8430
Craigdarroch *Strath* 66 NS6306
Craigdarroch *D & G* 65 NX7391

D

Dalton in Furness
Duddlestone

Dalton in Furness Cumb 58 SD2274
Dalton-le-Dale Dur 69 NZ4048
Dalton-on-Tees N York 61 NZ2907
Dalvadie D & G 64 NX0851
Dalveen D & G 66 NS8806
Dalveich Cent 81 NN6124
Dalwhinnie Highld 87 NN6384
Dalwood Devon 8 ST2400
Damerham Hants 10 SU1016
Damgate Norfk 43 TG4009
Danbury Essex 24 TL7805
Danby N York 62 NZ7008
Danby Wiske N York 62 SE3398
Dandaleith Gramp 94 NJ2846
Danderhall Loth 75 NT3069
Dane End Herts 31 TL3321
Dane Hills Leics 39 SK5604
Dane Street Kent 15 TR0552
Danebridge Ches 48 SJ9665
Danehill E Susx 13 TQ4027
Danshillock Gramp 95 NJ7157
Danskine Loth 76 NT5667
Darenth Kent 14 TQ5671
Daresbury Ches 47 SJ5882
Darfield S York 55 SE4104
Dargate Kent 15 TR0861
Darite Cnwll 4 SX2569
Darlaston W Mids 38 SO9796
Darlaston Green W Mids 38 SO9797
Darley N York 55 SE2059
Darley Abbey Derbys 49 SK3538
Darley Bridge Derbys 49 SK2661
Darley Green Warwks 38 SP1874
Darley Head N York 55 SE1959
Darleyhall Herts 30 TL1422
Darlingscott Warwks 29 SP2342
Darlington Dur 61 NZ2814
Darlton Notts 50 SK7773
Darowen Powys 35 SH8201
Darra Gramp 95 NJ7447
Darracott Devon 6 SS2317
Darracott Devon 6 SS4739
Darrington W York 55 SE4820
Darsham Suffk 33 TM4169
Dartford Kent 23 TQ5474
Dartington Devon 5 SX7862
Dartmouth Devon 5 SX8751
Darton S York 55 SE3110
Darvel Strath 74 NS5637
Darwen Lancs 54 SD6922
Datchet Berks 22 SU9877
Datchworth Herts 31 TL2619
Datchworth Green Herts 31 TL2718
Daubhill Gt Man 47 SD7007
Dauntsey Wilts 20 ST9782
Dauntsey Green Wilts 20 ST9981
Dava Highld 93 NJ0038
Davenham Ches 47 SJ6571
Daventry Nhants 29 SP5762
Davidson's Mains Loth 75 NT2175
Davidstow Cnwll 4 SX1587
Davington D & G 67 NT2302
Davington Hill Kent 15 TR0161
Daviot Highld 93 NH7239
Daviot Gramp 95 NJ7428
Daviot House Highld 93 NH7240
Davoch of Grange Gramp 94 NJ4751
Dawesgreen Surrey 12 TQ2147
Dawley Shrops 37 SJ6808
Dawlish Devon 5 SX9576
Dawlish Warren Devon 5 SX9778
Dawn Clwyd 45 SH8672
Daybrook Notts 49 SK5744
Daylesford Gloucs 29 SP2425
Deal Kent 15 TR3752
Dean Cumb 58 NY0725
Dean Oxon 29 SP3422
Dean Devon 18 SS7048
Dean Somset 20 ST6743
Dean Hants 10 SU4431
Dean Hants 11 SU5619
Dean Devon 5 SX7364
Dean Bottom Kent 14 TQ5868
Dean Court Oxon 29 SP4705
Dean Prior Devon 5 SX7363
Deanburnhaugh Border 67 NT3911
Deancombe Devon 5 SX7264
Deane Gt Man 47 SD6907
Deane Hants 21 SU5450
Deanhead W York 55 SE0415
Deanland Dorset 9 ST9918
Deanraw Nthumb 68 NY8162
Deanscales Cumb 58 NY0926
Deanshanger Nhants 30 SP7639
Deanshaugh Gramp 94 NJ3550
Deanshaugh Gramp 94 NJ3550
Deanston Cent 81 NN7101
Dearham Cumb 58 NY0736
Debach Suffk 33 TM2454
Debden Green Essex 23 TQ4398
Debenham Suffk 33 TM1763
Deblin's Green H & W 28 SO8148
Dechmont Loth 75 NT0370
Dechmont Road Loth 75 NT0269
Deddington Oxon 29 SP4631
Dedham Essex 25 TM0533
Dedworth Berks 22 SU9476
Deene Nhants 40 SP9492
Deenethorpe Nhants 40 SP9591
Deeping Gate Lincs 40 TF1509
Deeping St. James Lincs 40 TF1609
Deeping St. Nicholas Lincs 41 TF2115
Deerhurst Gloucs 28 SO8730
Defford H & W 28 SO9143
Defynnog Powys 26 SN9227
Deganwy Gwynd 45 SH7779
Degnish Strath 79 NM7812
Deighton N York 62 NZ3801
Deighton N York 56 SE6244
Deiniolen Gwynd 44 SH5763
Delabole Cnwll 3 SX0683
Delamere Ches 47 SJ5668
Delfrigs Gramp 95 NJ9620
Dell Quay W Susx 11 SU8302
Delliefure Highld 93 NJ0730
Delnabo Gramp 93 NJ1517
Delnashaugh Hotel Gramp 94 NJ1835
Delny Highld 93 NH7372
Delves Dur 69 NZ1149
Delvine Tays 82 NO1240
Dembleby Lincs 40 TF0437
Denaby S York 49 SK4899
Denbigh Clwyd 45 SJ0566
Denbrae Fife 83 NO3818
Denbury Devon 5 SX8268
Denby Derbys 49 SK3946
Denby Dale W York 55 SE2208
Denchworth Oxon 21 SU3891
Dendron Cumb 53 SD2470
Denfield Tays 82 NN9517
Denford Nhants 30 SP9976
Dengie Essex 25 TL9802
Denham Suffk 32 TL7561
Denham Suffk 33 TM1974
Denham Bucks 22 TQ0487
Denham Green Bucks 22 TQ0488
Denhead Gramp 95 NJ9952
Denhead Fife 83 NO4613
Denhead of Gray Tays 83 NO3531
Denholm Border 76 NT5718
Denholme W York 55 SE0734
Denmead Hants 11 SU6512
Denmore Gramp 95 NJ9411
Dennington Suffk 33 TM2867
Denny Cent 81 NS8082
Dennyloanhead Cent 81 NS8080
Denside Gramp 89 NO8095
Densole Kent 15 TR2141
Denston Suffk 32 TL7652
Denstone Staffs 48 SK0940
Denstroude Kent 15 TR1061
Dent Cumb 60 SD7086
Dent-de-Lion Kent 15 TR3269
Denton Dur 61 NZ2118
Denton N York 55 SE1448
Denton Gt Man 48 SJ9295
Denton Lincs 40 SK8632
Denton Nhants 30 SP8358
Denton Cambs 40 TL1587
Denton Norfk 33 TM2788
Denton E Susx 13 TQ4502
Denton Kent 15 TR2147
Denver Norfk 41 TF6001
Denwick Nthumb 69 NU2014
Deopham Norfk 42 TG0400
Deopham Green Norfk 42 TM0499
Deptford Wilts 20 SU0138
Deptford Gt Lon 23 TQ3777
Derby Derbys 39 SK3536
Derbyhaven IOM 52 SC2867
Derculich Tays 87 NN8852
Deri M Glam 18 SO1201
Derringstone Kent 15 TR2049
Derrington Staffs 38 SJ8922
Derry Hill Wilts 20 ST9670
Derrythorpe Humb 56 SE8208
Dersingham Norfk 42 TF6830
Dervaig Strath 79 NM4352
Derwen Clwyd 46 SJ0750
Derwenlas Powys 35 SN7298
Desborough Nhants 40 SP8083
Desford Leics 39 SK4703
Deskford Gramp 94 NJ5061
Detling Kent 14 TQ7958
Devauden Gwent 19 ST4898
Devil's Bridge Dyfed 35 SN7376
Devizes Wilts 20 SU0061
Devonport Devon 4 SX4554
Devonside Cent 82 NS9196
Devoran Cnwll 2 SW7939
Dewarton Loth 76 NT3763
Dewlish Dorset 9 SY7798
Dewsbury W York 55 SE2421
Deytheur Powys 36 SJ2317
Dhoon IOM 52 SC3784
Dial Green W Susx 11 SU9227
Dial Post W Susx 12 TQ1519
Dibden Hants 10 SU4008
Dibden Purlieu Hants 10 SU4106
Dickleburgh Norfk 33 TM1682
Didbrook Gloucs 28 SP0531
Didcot Oxon 21 SU5290
Diddington Cambs 31 TL1965
Diddlebury Shrops 37 SO5085
Didling W Susx 11 SU8318
Didmarton Gloucs 20 ST8287
Didsbury Gt Man 47 SJ8491
Digby Lincs 50 TF0854
Digg Highld 90 NG4668
Diggle Gt Man 54 SE0007
Digmore Lancs 46 SD4905
Dihewyd Dyfed 34 SN4855
Dilham Norfk 43 TG3325
Dilhorne Staffs 48 SJ9743
Dillington Cambs 30 TL1365
Dilston Nthumb 68 NY9763
Dilton Wilts 20 ST8548
Dilton Marsh Wilts 20 ST8449
Dilwyn H & W 27 SO4154
Dinas Gwynd 44 SH2735
Dinas Dyfed 16 SN0138
Dinas Powys S Glam 19 ST1571
Dinas-Mawddwy Gwynd 35 SH8515
Dinder Somset 19 ST5744
Dinedor H & W 27 SO5336
Dingle Mersyd 46 SJ3687
Dingley Nhants 40 SP7787
Dingwall Highld 92 NH5458
Dinnet Gramp 88 NO4598
Dinnington T & W 69 NZ2073
Dinnington Somset 8 ST4012
Dinorwic Gwynd 44 SH5961
Dinton Bucks 22 SP7610
Dinton Wilts 9 SU0131
Dinwoodie D & G 67 NY1190
Dinworthy Devon 6 SS3015
Dipford Somset 8 ST2021
Dippen Strath 72 NR7937
Dippertown Devon 4 SX4284
Dippin Strath 72 NS0422
Dipple Gramp 94 NJ3258
Dipple Strath 73 NS2002
Diptford Devon 5 SX7256
Dipton Dur 69 NZ1554
Dirleton Loth 83 NT5184
Dirt Pot Nthumb 68 NY8545
Diseworth Leics 39 SK4524
Dishforth N York 62 SE3873
Disley Ches 48 SJ9784
Diss Norfk 33 TM1180
Distington Cumb 58 NY0023
Ditchampton Wilts 10 SU0831
Ditchburn Nthumb 77 NU1320
Ditcheat Somset 19 ST6236
Ditchingham Norfk 33 TM3391
Ditchling E Susx 12 TQ3215
Ditherington Shrops 37 SJ5014
Ditteridge Wilts 20 ST8169
Dittisham Devon 5 SX8655
Ditton Ches 46 SJ4986
Ditton Kent 14 TQ7158
Ditton Green Cambs 32 TL6558
Ditton Priors Shrops 37 SO6089
Dixton Gwent 27 SO5113
Dixton Gloucs 28 SO9830
Dobcross Gt Man 54 SD9906
Dobwalls Cnwll 4 SX2165
Doccombe Devon 5 SX7786
Dochgarroch Highld 92 NH6140
Docker Lancs 59 SD5774
Docking Norfk 42 TF7636
Docklow H & W 27 SO5657
Dockray Cumb 59 NY3921
Dod's Leigh Staffs 38 SK0134
Dodd's Green Ches 47 SJ6043
Doddinghurst Essex 24 TQ5999
Doddington Nthumb 77 NT9932
Doddington Lincs 50 SK8970
Doddington Shrops 37 SO6176
Doddington Cambs 41 TL4090
Doddington Kent 14 TQ9357
Doddiscombsleigh Devon 5 SX8586
Dodford H & W 38 SO9373
Dodford Nhants 29 SP6160
Dodington Somset 19 ST1740
Dodington Avon 20 ST7580
Dodleston Ches 46 SJ3661
Dodside Strath 74 NS5053
Dodworth S York 55 SE3105
Dog Village Devon 7 SX9896
Dogdyke Lincs 51 TF2055
Dogmersfield Hants 22 SU7852
Dolanog Powys 36 SJ0612
Dolbenmaen Gwynd 44 SH5043
Dolfor Powys 36 SO1087
Dolgarrog Gwynd 45 SH7767
Dolgellau Gwynd 35 SH7217
Doll Highld 97 NC8803
Dollar Cent 82 NS9698
Dollarbeg Cent 82 NS9796
Dollarfield Cent 82 NS9697
Dolphin Clwyd 46 SJ1973
Dolphinholme Lancs 53 SD5253
Dolphinston Border 76 NT6815
Dolphinton Strath 75 NT1046
Dolton Devon 6 SS5712
Dolwen Clwyd 45 SH8874
Dolwyddelan Gwynd 45 SH7352
Domgay Powys 36 SJ2818
Doncaster S York 56 SE5703
Donhead St. Andrew Wilts 9 ST9124
Donhead St. Mary Wilts 9 ST9024
Donibristle Fife 82 NT1688
Doniford Somset 7 ST0842
Donington Lincs 41 TF2035
Donington on Bain Lincs 51 TF2382
Donisthorpe Leics 39 SK3113
Donnington Shrops 37 SJ5708
Donnington Shrops 37 SJ7114
Donnington Gloucs 29 SP1928
Donnington Berks 21 SU4668
Donnington W Susx 11 SU8501
Donyatt Somset 8 ST3314
Doonfoot Strath 73 NS3219
Doonholm Strath 73 NS3317
Doonholm Strath 73 NS3317
Dorback Lodge Highld 93 NJ0716
Dorchester Oxon 21 SU5794
Dorchester Dorset 9 SY6990
Dordon Warwks 39 SK2500
Dore S York 49 SK3181
Dores Highld 92 NH5934
Dorking Surrey 12 TQ1649
Dorlin House Highld 85 NM6671
Dormans Land Surrey 13 TQ4041
Dormington H & W 27 SO5840
Dormston H & W 28 SO9857
Dornal Strath 64 NX2976
Dorney Berks 22 SU9378
Dornie Highld 85 NG8826
Dornoch Highld 97 NH7989
Dornock D & G 67 NY2366
Dorrery Highld 100 ND0754
Dorridge W Mids 38 SP1775
Dorrington Shrops 37 SJ4702
Dorrington Shrops 37 SJ7340
Dorrington Lincs 50 TF0852
Dorsington Warwks 28 SP1349
Dorstone H & W 27 SO3141
Dorton Bucks 30 SP6814
Douganhill D & G 66 NX8155
Douglas Strath 74 NS8330
Douglas IOM 52 SC3775
Douglas Castle Strath 74 NS8431
Douglas Hill Gwynd 44 SH6065
Douglas Pier Strath 80 NS1999
Douglas Water Strath 74 NS8736
Douglas West Strath 74 NS8231
Douglas and Angus Tays 83 NO4233
Douglastown Tays 88 NO4147
Dougarie Strath 72 NR8837
Dounby Ork 103 HY2920
Doune Highld 96 NC4400
Doune Cent 81 NN7201
Dounepark Strath 64 NX1897
Dounie Highld 96 NH5690
Dounreay Highld 100 ND0065
Dousland Devon 4 SX5369
Dove Holes Derbys 48 SK0777
Dovenby Cumb 58 NY0933
Dover Kent 15 TR3141
Dovercourt Essex 25 TM2431
Doverdale H & W 28 SO8666
Doveridge Derbys 38 SK1133
Doversgreen Surrey 12 TQ2548
Dowally Tays 88 NO0048
Dowdeswell Gloucs 28 SP0019
Dowhill Strath 73 NS2003
Dowlais M Glam 26 SO0607
Dowland Devon 6 SS5610
Dowlish Wake Somset 8 ST3712
Down Ampney Gloucs 20 SU0996
Down Hatherley Gloucs 28 SO8622
Down St. Mary Devon 7 SS7404
Down Thomas Devon 4 SX5050
Downderry Cnwll 4 SX3154
Downe Gt Lon 23 TQ4361
Downend Avon 19 ST6577
Downend Gloucs 20 ST8398
Downfield Tays 83 NO3932
Downgate Cnwll 4 SX2871
Downgate Cnwll 4 SX3672
Downham Lancs 54 SD7844
Downham Cambs 41 TL5284
Downham Gt Lon 23 TQ3871
Downham Essex 24 TQ7296
Downham Market Norfk 41 TF6103
Downhead Somset 8 ST5625
Downhead Somset 20 ST6945
Downhill Tays 82 NO0930
Downholme N York 61 SE1197
Downies Gramp 89 NO9294
Downley Bucks 22 SU8495
Downside Surrey 22 TQ1057
Downton Wilts 10 SU1821
Downton Hants 10 SZ2693
Downton on the Rock H & W 36 SO4273
Dowsby Lincs 40 TF1129
Doynton Avon 20 ST7274
Draethen M Glam 19 ST2287
Draffan Strath 74 NS7945
Drakeholes Notts 49 SK7090
Drakemyre Strath 73 NS2950
Drakes Broughton H & W 28 SO9248
Draughton N York 55 SE0352
Draughton Nhants 30 SP7676
Drax N York 56 SE6726
Draycote Warwks 29 SP4470
Draycott Derbys 39 SK4433
Draycott Gloucs 29 SP1835
Draycott Somset 19 ST4751
Draycott in the Clay Staffs 38 SK1528
Draycott in the Moors Staffs 48 SJ9840
Drayton H & W 38 SO8975
Drayton Oxon 29 SP4241
Drayton Leics 40 SP8392
Drayton Somset 8 ST4024
Drayton Oxon 21 SU4894
Drayton Hants 11 SU6705
Drayton Norfk 43 TG1813
Drayton Bassett Staffs 39 SK1900
Drayton Beauchamp Bucks 22 SP9011
Drayton Parslow Bucks 30 SP8328
Drayton St Leonard Oxon 21 SU5996
Dreenhill Dyfed 16 SM9214
Drefach Dyfed 17 SN3538
Drefach Dyfed 17 SN4945
Drefach Dyfed 17 SN5213
Dreghorn Strath 73 NS3538
Drellingore Kent 15 TR2441
Drem Loth 83 NT5079
Drewsteignton Devon 5 SX7391
Driffield Gloucs 20 SU0799
Driffield Humb 56 TA0257
Drift Cnwll 2 SW4328
Drigg Cumb 58 SD0699
Drighlington W York 55 SE2228
Drimnin Highld 79 NM5554
Drimpton Dorset 8 ST4104
Drimsallie Highld 85 NM9578
Drimsynie Strath 80 NN1901
Dringhouses N York 56 SE5849
Drinkstone Suffk 32 TL9561
Drinkstone Green Suffk 32 TL9660
Driver's End Herts 31 TL2220
Drointon Staffs 38 SK0226
Droitwich Spa H & W 28 SO8963
Dron Tays 82 NO1416
Dronfield Derbys 49 SK3578
Drongan Strath 73 NS4418
Dronley Tays 83 NO3435
Droop Dorset 9 ST7508
Droxford Hants 11 SU6018
Droylsden Gt Man 48 SJ9097
Druid Clwyd 45 SJ0443
Druidston Dyfed 16 SM8616
Druimachoish Highld 86 NN1246
Druimarbin Highld 86 NN0770
Druimdrishaig Strath 71 NR7370
Druimindarroch Highld 85 NM6884
Drum Tays 82 NO0400
Drum Strath 71 NR9276
Drumalbin Strath 74 NS9038
Drumbeg Highld 98 NC1232
Drumblade Gramp 94 NJ5840
Drumblair House Gramp 94 NJ6343
Drumbreddon D & G 64 NX0843
Drumbuie Highld 85 NG7730
Drumburgh Cumb 67 NY2659
Drumburn D & G 66 NX8854
Drumchapel Strath 74 NS5270
Drumchastle Tays 87 NN6858
Drumclog Strath 74 NS6438
Drumeldrie Fife 83 NO4403
Drumelzier Border 75 NT1334
Drumfearn Highld 85 NG6716
Drumfrennie Gramp 89 NO7298
Drumgask Highld 87 NN6193
Drumhead Gramp 89 NO6092
Drumin Gramp 94 NJ1830
Drumjohn D & G 65 NX5297
Drumlamford Strath 64 NX2876
Drumlasie Gramp 89 NJ6405
Drumleaning Cumb 67 NY2751
Drumlemble Strath 72 NR6619
Drumlithie Gramp 89 NO7880
Drummoddie D & G 64 NX3845
Drummond Highld 92 NH6065
Drummore D & G 64 NX1336
Drummore D & G 66 NX9074
Drummuir Gramp 94 NJ3843
Drumnadrochit Highld 92 NH5030
Drumnagorrach Gramp 94 NJ5252
Drumore Strath 72 NR7022
Drumpark D & G 66 NX8779
Drumrunie Lodge Highld 96 NC1604
Drumshang Strath 73 NS2514
Drumtroddan D & G 64 NX3645
Drumuie Highld 90 NG4546
Drumvaich Cent 81 NN6704
Drumvillie Highld 93 NH9420
Drumwalt D & G 64 NX3053
Drumwhirn D & G 65 NX7480
Drunzie Tays 82 NO1308
Dry Doddington Lincs 50 SK8546
Dry Drayton Cambs 31 TL3861
Drybeck Cumb 60 NY6615
Drybridge Gramp 94 NJ4362
Drybridge Strath 73 NS3536
Drybrook Gloucs 27 SO6417
Dryburgh Border 76 NT5932
Dryhope Border 75 NT2624
Drym Cnwll 2 SW6133
Drymen Cent 81 NS4788
Drymuir Gramp 95 NJ9046
Drynoch Highld 84 NG4031
Dryton Shrops 37 SJ5905
Dubford Gramp 95 NJ7963
Duchally Highld 96 NC3817
Duck Street Hants 21 SU3249
Ducklington Oxon 29 SP3507
Duddingston Loth 75 NT2872
Duddington Nhants 40 SK9800
Duddlestone Somset 8 ST2321

Duddlewick
Eaton

Duddlewick *Shrops* 37 SO6583
Duddo *Nthumb* 77 NT9342
Duddon *Ches* 46 SJ5164
Dudleston *Shrops* 36 SJ3438
Dudley *T & W* 69 NZ2573
Dudley *W Mids* 38 SO9490
Dudley Port *W Mids* 38 SO9691
Dudsbury *Dorset* 10 SZ0798
Duffield *Derbys* 49 SK3443
Duffryn *M Glam* 18 SS8495
Dufftown *Gramp* 94 NJ3240
Duffus *Gramp* 94 NJ1668
Dufton *Cumb* 60 NY6825
Duggleby *N York* 56 SE8767
Duirinish *Highld* 85 NG7831
Duisdalemore *Highld* 85 NG7013
Duisky *Highld* 85 NN0076
Duke Street *Suffk* 32 TM0742
Dukinfield *Gt Man* 48 SJ9397
Dulcote *Somset* 19 ST5644
Dulford *Devon* 7 ST0706
Dull *Tays* 87 NN8049
Dullatur *Strath* 74 NS7476
Dullingham *Cambs* 32 TL6357
Dullingham Ley *Cambs* 32 TL6456
Dulnain Bridge *Highld* 93 NH9925
Duloe *Cnwll* 4 SX2358
Duloe *Beds* 30 TL1560
Dulverton *Somset* 7 SS9127
Dulwich *Gt Lon* 23 TQ3373
Dumbarton *Strath* 80 NS3975
Dumbleton *Gloucs* 28 SP0135
Dumcrieff *D & G* 67 NT1003
Dumfries *D & G* 66 NX9776
Dumgoyne *Cent* 81 NS5283
Dummer *Hants* 21 SU5846
Dumpton *Kent* 15 TR3966
Dun *Tays* 89 NO6659
Dunalastair *Tays* 87 NN7158
Dunan *Highld* 84 NG5828
Dunan *Tays* 87 NN4757
Dunan *Strath* 80 NS1571
Dunans *Strath* 80 NS0491
Dunavourd *Tays* 88 NN9657
Dunaverty *Strath* 72 NR6807
Dunball *Somset* 19 ST3141
Dunbar *Loth* 83 NT6778
Dunbeath *Highld* 100 ND1629
Dunbeg *Strath* 79 NM8833
Dunblane *Cent* 81 NN7801
Dunbog *Fife* 83 NO2817
Duncanston *Highld* 92 NH5856
Duncanstone *Gramp* 94 NJ5726
Dunchideock *Devon* 5 SX8787
Dunchurch *Warwks* 39 SP4871
Duncow *D & G* 66 NX9683
Duncrievie *Tays* 82 NO1309
Duncton *W Susx* 12 SU9617
Dundee *Tays* 83 NO4030
Dundon *Somset* 8 ST4832
Dundonald *Strath* 73 NS3634
Dundonnell *Highld* 91 NH0987
Dundraw *Cumb* 67 NY2149
Dundreggan *Highld* 92 NH3214
Dundrennan *D & G* 65 NX7447
Dundry *Avon* 19 ST5666
Dunecht *Gramp* 95 NJ7509
Dunfermline *Fife* 82 NT0987
Dunfield *Gloucs* 20 SU1497
Dungavel *Strath* 74 NS6537
Dunglass *Loth* 76 NT7671
Dunham *Notts* 50 SK8074
Dunham Town *Gt Man* 47 SJ7387
Dunham Woodhouses *Gt Man* 47 SJ7287
Dunham-on-the-Hill *Ches* 46 SJ4772
Dunhampton *H & W* 28 SO8466
Dunholme *Lincs* 50 TF0279
Dunino *Fife* 83 NO5311
Dunipace *Cent* 81 NS8083
Dunk's Green *Kent* 13 TQ6152
Dunkeld *Tays* 88 NO0242
Dunkerton *Avon* 20 ST7159
Dunkeswell *Devon* 8 ST1407
Dunkeswick *W York* 55 SE3047
Dunkirk *Avon* 20 ST7885
Dunkirk *Kent* 15 TR0759
Dunlappie *Tays* 89 NO5867
Dunley *H & W* 28 SO7869
Dunlop *Strath* 73 NS4049
Dunmaglass *Highld* 92 NH5922
Dunmore *Strath* 71 NR7961
Dunmore *Cent* 82 NS8989
Dunnet *Highld* 100 ND2171
Dunnichen *Tays* 89 NO5048
Dunning *Tays* 82 NO0114
Dunnington *N York* 56 SE6652
Dunnington *Warwks* 28 SP0654
Dunnington *Warwks* 28 SP0654
Dunnington *Humb* 57 TA1551
Dunnockshaw *Lancs* 54 SD8127
Dunoon *Strath* 80 NS1776
Dunphail *Gramp* 93 NJ0048
Dunragit *D & G* 64 NX1557
Dunrod *Strath* 80 NS2273
Duns *Border* 76 NT7853
Duns Tew *Oxon* 29 SP4528
Dunsby *Lincs* 40 TF1026
Dunscore *D & G* 66 NX8684
Dunsdale *Cleve* 62 NZ6019
Dunsden Green *Oxon* 22 SU7377
Dunsdon *Devon* 6 SS3008
Dunsfold *Surrey* 12 TQ0035
Dunsford *Devon* 5 SX8189
Dunshelt *Fife* 83 NO2410
Dunshillock *Gramp* 95 NJ9848
Dunsill *Notts* 49 SK4661
Dunsley *N York* 63 NZ8511
Dunsley *Staffs* 38 SO8583
Dunsmore *Bucks* 22 SP8605
Dunsop Bridge *Lancs* 54 SD6649
Dunstable *Beds* 30 TL0122
Dunstall *Staffs* 38 SK1820
Dunstan *Nthumb* 77 NU2419
Dunster *Somset* 7 SS9943
Dunston *T & W* 69 NZ2362
Dunston *Staffs* 38 SJ9217
Dunston *Lincs* 50 TF0662
Dunston *Norfk* 43 TG2202
Dunstone *Devon* 5 SX5951
Dunstone *Devon* 5 SX7175
Dunswell *Humb* 57 TA0735
Dunsyre *Strath* 75 NT0748
Dunterton *Devon* 4 SX3779
Duntisbourne Abbots *Gloucs* 28 SO9607
Duntisbourne Rouse *Gloucs* 28 SO9805
Duntish *Dorset* 9 ST6906
Duntocher *Strath* 74 NS4973
Dunton *Bucks* 30 SP8224
Dunton *Norfk* 42 TF8830
Dunton *Beds* 31 TL2344
Dunton Bassett *Leics* 39 SP5490
Dunton Green *Kent* 23 TQ5157
Duntulm *Highld* 90 NG4174
Dunure *Strath* 73 NS2515
Dunvant *W Glam* 17 SS5993
Dunvegan *Highld* 90 NG2547
Dunwich *Suffk* 33 TM4770
Durgan *Cnwll* 2 SW7727
Durham *Dur* 61 NZ2742
Durisdeer *D & G* 66 NS8903
Durisdeermill *D & G* 66 NS8804
Durleigh *Somset* 19 ST2736
Durley *Wilts* 21 SU2364
Durley *Hants* 11 SU5116
Durley Street *Hants* 11 SU5217
Durlock *Kent* 15 TR2757
Durlock *Kent* 15 TR3164
Durmgley *Tays* 88 NO4250
Durness *Highld* 98 NC4068
Duror *Highld* 86 NM9754
Durran *Highld* 100 ND1963
Durrington *Wilts* 20 SU1544
Durrington *W Susx* 12 TQ1105
Dursley *Gloucs* 20 ST7598
Dursley Cross *Gloucs* 28 SO6920
Durston *Somset* 8 ST2928
Durweston *Dorset* 9 ST8508
Duston *Nhants* 30 SP7261
Duthil *Highld* 93 NH9324
Dutton *Ches* 47 SJ5779
Duxford *Oxon* 21 SP3600
Duxford *Cambs* 31 TL4846
Dwygyfylchi *Gwynd* 45 SH7376
Dwyran *Gwynd* 44 SH4465
Dyce *Gramp* 95 NJ8812
Dye House *Nthumb* 68 NY9358
Dyffryn Ardudwy *Gwynd* 34 SH5823
Dyffryn Cellwen *W Glam* 26 SN8510
Dyke *Gramp* 93 NH9858
Dyke *Lincs* 40 TF1022
Dykehead *Tays* 88 NO2453
Dykehead *Tays* 88 NO3859
Dykehead *Cent* 81 NS5997
Dykehead *Strath* 74 NS8759
Dykelands *Gramp* 89 NO7068
Dykends *Tays* 88 NO2557
Dykeside *Gramp* 95 NJ7243
Dymchurch *Kent* 15 TR1029
Dymock *Gloucs* 28 SO7031
Dyrham *Avon* 20 ST7475
Dysart *Fife* 83 NT3093
Dyserth *Clwyd* 45 SJ0578

E

Eagland Hill *Lancs* 53 SD4345
Eagle *Lincs* 50 SK8766
Eaglescliffe *Cleve* 62 NZ4215
Eaglesfield *Cumb* 58 NY0928
Eaglesfield *D & G* 67 NY2374
Eaglesham *Strath* 74 NS5751
Eagley *Gt Man* 54 SD7112
Eakring *Notts* 49 SK6762
Ealand *Humb* 56 SE7811
Ealing *Gt Lon* 23 TQ1780
Eals *Nthumb* 68 NY6756
Eamont Bridge *Cumb* 59 NY5228
Earby *Lancs* 54 SD9046
Eardington *Shrops* 37 SO7290
Eardisland *H & W* 27 SO4158
Eardisley *H & W* 27 SO3149
Eardiston *Shrops* 36 SJ3725
Eardiston *H & W* 28 SO6968
Earith *Cambs* 31 TL3875
Earl Shilton *Leics* 39 SP4697
Earl Soham *Suffk* 33 TM2363
Earl Sterndale *Derbys* 48 SK0966
Earl's Croome *H & W* 28 SO8642
Earlestown *Mersyd* 47 SJ5795
Earley *Berks* 22 SU7472
Earlish *Highld* 90 NG3861
Earls Barton *Nhants* 30 SP8563
Earls Colne *Essex* 24 TL8528
Earls Common *H & W* 28 SO9559
Earlsdon *W Mids* 39 SP3278
Earlsferry *Fife* 83 NO4800
Earlsfield *Gt Lon* 23 TQ2573
Earlsford *Gramp* 95 NJ8334
Earlsheaton *W York* 55 SE2621
Earlston *Strath* 73 NS4035
Earlston *Border* 76 NT5738
Earlswood *Warwks* 38 SP1174
Earlswood *Surrey* 12 TQ2749
Earnley *W Susx* 11 SZ8196
Earsdon *Nthumb* 69 NZ1993
Earsdon *T & W* 69 NZ3272
Earsham *Norfk* 33 TM3288
Eartham *W Susx* 11 SU9309
Easby *N York* 62 NZ5708
Easebourne *W Susx* 11 SU9023
Easenhall *Warwks* 39 SP4679
Eashing *Surrey* 12 SU9443
Easington *Dur* 69 NZ4143
Easington *Cleve* 63 NZ7417
Easington *Bucks* 22 SP6810
Easington *Humb* 57 TA3919
Easington Colliery *Dur* 69 NZ4344
Easingwold *N York* 55 SE5269
Eassie and Nevay *Tays* 88 NO3344
East Aberthaw *S Glam* 18 ST0366
East Allington *Devon* 5 SX7748
East Anstey *Devon* 7 SS8626
East Appleton *N York* 61 SE2395
East Ashley *IOW* 11 SZ5888
East Ashling *W Susx* 11 SU8107
East Ayton *N York* 63 SE9985
East Barkwith *Lincs* 50 TF1681
East Barming *Kent* 14 TQ7254
East Barnby *N York* 63 NZ8212
East Barnet *Gt Lon* 23 TQ2795
East Barns *Loth* 76 NT7176
East Barsham *Norfk* 42 TF9133
East Beckham *Norfk* 43 TG1639
East Bedfont *Gt Lon* 22 TQ0873
East Bergholt *Suffk* 25 TM0734
East Bilney *Norfk* 42 TF9519
East Blanerne *Border* 77 NT8457
East Blatchington *E Susx* 13 TQ4800
East Boldon *T & W* 69 NZ3661
East Boldre *Hants* 10 SU3700
East Bradenham *Norfk* 42 TF9308
East Brent *Somset* 19 ST3451
East Bridgford *Notts* 49 SK6943
East Buckland *Devon* 7 SS6831
East Budleigh *Devon* 5 SY0684
East Butterwick *Humb* 56 SE8306
East Calder *Loth* 75 NT0867
East Carleton *Norfk* 43 TG1701
East Carlton *W York* 55 SE2143
East Carlton *Nhants* 40 SP8389
East Challow *Oxon* 21 SU3888
East Charleton *Devon* 5 SX7642
East Chelborough *Dorset* 8 ST5505
East Chiltington *E Susx* 13 TQ3715
East Chinnock *Somset* 8 ST4913
East Chisenbury *Wilts* 20 SU1452
East Clandon *Surrey* 12 TQ0651
East Claydon *Bucks* 30 SP7325
East Coker *Somset* 8 ST5412
East Combe *Somset* 8 ST1631
East Compton *Somset* 19 ST6141
East Cornworthy *Devon* 5 SX8455
East Cottingwith *Humb* 56 SE7042
East Coulston *Wilts* 20 ST9554
East Cowes *IOW* 10 SZ5095
East Cowick *Humb* 56 SE6620
East Cowton *N York* 61 NZ3003
East Cranmore *Somset* 20 ST6743
East Creech *Dorset* 9 SY9382
East Dean *H & W* 27 SO6520
East Dean *Hants* 10 SU2726
East Dean *W Susx* 11 SU9012
East Dean *E Susx* 13 TV5598
East Dereham *Norfk* 42 TF9913
East Down *Devon* 6 SS6041
East Drayton *Notts* 50 SK7775
East Dulwich *Gt Lon* 23 TQ3375
East Dundry *Avon* 19 ST5766
East Ella *Humb* 57 TA0529
East End *Oxon* 29 SP3915
East End *Somset* 20 ST6746
East End *Hants* 21 SU4161
East End *Hants* 10 SZ3696
East End *Kent* 14 TQ8335
East Everleigh *Wilts* 21 SU2053
East Farleigh *Kent* 14 TQ7353
East Farndon *Nhants* 40 SP7184
East Ferry *Lincs* 50 SK8199
East Fortune *Loth* 83 NT5479
East Garston *Berks* 21 SU3576
East Goscote *Leics* 39 SK6413
East Grafton *Wilts* 21 SU2560
East Grange *Gramp* 93 NJ0961
East Grimstead *Wilts* 10 SU2227
East Grinstead *W Susx* 13 TQ3938
East Guldeford *E Susx* 14 TQ9321
East Haddon *Nhants* 30 SP6668
East Hagbourne *Oxon* 21 SU5288
East Halton *Humb* 57 TA1319
East Ham *Gt Lon* 23 TQ4283
East Hanney *Oxon* 21 SU4193
East Hanningfield *Essex* 24 TL7701
East Hardwick *W York* 55 SE4618
East Harling *Norfk* 32 TL9986
East Harlsey *N York* 62 SE4299
East Harnham *Wilts* 10 SU1428
East Harptree *Avon* 19 ST5655
East Hartburn *Cleve* 62 NZ4217
East Hartford *Nthumb* 69 NZ2679
East Harting *W Susx* 11 SU7919
East Hatch *Wilts* 9 ST9228
East Hatley *Cambs* 31 TL2850
East Hauxwell *N York* 61 SE1693
East Haven *Tays* 83 NO5836
East Heckington *Lincs* 50 TF1944
East Hedleyhope *Dur* 61 NZ1540
East Helmsdale *Highld* 97 ND0315
East Hendred *Oxon* 21 SU4588
East Heslerton *N York* 63 SE9276
East Hewish *Avon* 19 ST4064
East Hoathly *E Susx* 13 TQ5216
East Holme *Dorset* 9 SY8986
East Horndon *Essex* 24 TQ6389
East Horrington *Somset* 19 ST5846
East Horsley *Surrey* 12 TQ0952
East Howe *Dorset* 10 SZ0795
East Huntspill *Somset* 19 ST3445
East Hyde *Beds* 30 TL1217
East Ilsley *Berks* 21 SU4980
East Keal *Lincs* 51 TF3863
East Kennett *Wilts* 20 SU1167
East Keswick *W York* 55 SE3644
East Kilbride *Strath* 74 NS6354
East Kirkby *Lincs* 51 TF3362
East Knighton *Dorset* 9 SY8185
East Knoyle *Wilts* 9 ST8830
East Kyloe *Nthumb* 77 NU0639
East Lambrook *Somset* 8 ST4318
East Langdon *Kent* 15 TR3346
East Langton *Leics* 40 SP7292
East Laroch *Highld* 86 NN0858
East Lavant *W Susx* 11 SU8608
East Lavington *W Susx* 12 SU9416
East Layton *N York* 61 NZ1609
East Leake *Notts* 39 SK5526
East Leigh *Devon* 7 SS6905
East Leigh *Devon* 5 SX7657
East Lexham *Norfk* 42 TF8517
East Linton *Loth* 76 NT5877
East Lockinge *Oxon* 21 SU4287
East Lound *Humb* 50 SK7899
East Lulworth *Dorset* 9 SY8682
East Lutton *N York* 56 SE9469
East Lydford *Somset* 8 ST5731
East Malling *Kent* 14 TQ7056
East Marden *W Susx* 11 SU8014
East Markham *Notts* 50 SK7373
East Martin *Hants* 10 SU0719
East Marton *N York* 54 SD9050
East Meon *Hants* 11 SU6822
East Mersea *Essex* 25 TM0414
East Molesey *Surrey* 22 TQ1467
East Morden *Dorset* 9 SY9194
East Morton *D & G* 66 NS8800
East Morton *W York* 55 SE0942
East Ness *N York* 62 SE6978
East Norton *Leics* 40 SK7800
East Ogwell *Devon* 5 SX8370
East Orchard *Dorset* 9 ST8317
East Ord *Nthumb* 77 NT9751
East Peckham *Kent* 14 TQ6648
East Pennar *Dyfed* 16 SM9602
East Pennard *Somset* 19 ST5937
East Perry *Cambs* 30 TL1566
East Poringland *Norfk* 43 TG2701
East Portlemouth *Devon* 5 SX7538
East Prawle *Devon* 5 SX7836
East Preston *W Susx* 12 TQ0602
East Pulham *Dorset* 9 ST7209
East Putford *Devon* 6 SS3616
East Quantoxhead *Somset* 18 ST1343
East Rainton *T & W* 69 NZ334
East Ravendale *Lincs* 51 TF2399
East Raynham *Norfk* 42 TF8825
East Rigton *W York* 55 SE3743
East Rounton *N York* 62 NZ4203
East Rudham *Norfk* 42 TF8228
East Runton *Norfk* 43 TG1942
East Ruston *Norfk* 43 TG3427
East Saltoun *Loth* 76 NT4767
East Sheen *Gt Lon* 23 TQ2075
East Shefford *Berks* 21 SU3874
East Stoke *Notts* 50 SK7549
East Stoke *Dorset* 9 SY8686
East Stour *Dorset* 9 ST8022
East Stourmouth *Kent* 15 TR2662
East Stowford *Devon* 7 SS6326
East Stratton *Hants* 21 SU5440
East Taphouse *Cnwll* 3 SX1863
East Taphouse *Cnwll* 3 SX1863
East Thirston *Nthumb* 61 NZ1900
East Tilbury *Essex* 24 TQ6877
East Tisted *Hants* 11 SU7032
East Torrington *Lincs* 50 TF1483
East Tuddenham *Norfk* 42 TG0711
East Tytherley *Hants* 10 SU2929
East Tytherton *Wilts* 20 ST9674
East Village *Devon* 7 SS8405
East Wall *Shrops* 37 SO5293
East Walton *Norfk* 42 TF7416
East Water *Somset* 19 ST5350
East Week *Devon* 5 SX6692
East Wellow *Hants* 10 SU3020
East Wemyss *Fife* 83 NT3497
East Whitburn *Loth* 75 NS9665
East Wickham *Gt Lon* 23 TQ4677
East Williamston *Dyfed* 16 SN0904
East Winch *Norfk* 42 TF6916
East Winterslow *Wilts* 10 SU2434
East Wittering *W Susx* 11 SZ7997
East Witton *N York* 61 SE1486
East Woodburn *Nthumb* 68 NY9086
East Woodhay *Hants* 21 SU4061
East Worldham *Hants* 11 SU7538
East Wretham *Norfk* 32 TL9190
East Youlstone *Devon* 6 SS2715
Eastbourne *Dur* 61 NZ3013
Eastbourne *E Susx* 13 TV6199
Eastbridge *Suffk* 33 TM4566
Eastburn *W York* 54 SE0144
Eastbury *Berks* 21 SU3477
Eastbury *Herts* 22 TQ1092
Eastby *N York* 54 SE0154
Eastchurch *Kent* 15 TQ9871
Eastcombe *Gloucs* 28 SO8904
Eastcote *W Mids* 39 SP1979
Eastcote *Nhants* 30 SP6853
Eastcote *Gt Lon* 22 TQ1088
Eastcott *Wilts* 20 SU0255
Eastcourt *Wilts* 20 ST9792
Eastcourt *Wilts* 21 SU2361
Eastend *Strath* 75 NS9537
Eastend *Essex* 25 TQ9492
Easter Balmoral *Gramp* 88 NO2694
Easter Compton *Avon* 19 ST5782
Easter Dalziel *Highld* 93 NH7550
Easter Elchies *Gramp* 94 NJ2744
Easter Howgate *Tays* 75 NT2463
Easter Kinkell *Highld* 92 NH5755
Easter Lednathie *Tays* 88 NO3463
Easter Moniack *Highld* 92 NH5543
Easter Ord *Gramp* 89 NJ8304
Easter Pitkierie *Fife* 83 NO5606
Easter Skeld *Shet* 103 HU3144
Eastergate *W Susx* 12 SU9405
Easterhouse *Strath* 74 NS6865
Eastern Green *W Mids* 39 SP2879
Easterton *Wilts* 20 SU0254
Eastertown *Strath* 74 NS8622
Eastfield *Strath* 74 NS7475
Eastfield *Cent* 74 NS8964
Eastfield *N York* 63 TA0484
Eastgate *Dur* 61 NY9538
Eastgate *Norfk* 43 TG1423
Easthampstead *Berks* 22 SU8667
Easthampton *H & W* 27 SO4063
Easthope *Shrops* 37 SO5695
Easthorpe *Essex* 24 TL9121
Eastington *Gloucs* 28 SP1213
Eastington *Devon* 7 SS7408
Eastlands *D & G* 66 NX8172
Eastleach Martin *Gloucs* 29 SP2004
Eastleach Turville *Gloucs* 29 SP1905
Eastleigh *Devon* 6 SS4827
Eastleigh *Hants* 10 SU4519
Eastling *Kent* 15 TQ9656
Eastney *Hants* 11 SZ6698
Eastnor *H & W* 28 SO7237
Eastoft *Humb* 56 SE8016
Easton *Cumb* 67 NY2759
Easton *Lincs* 40 SK9326
Easton *Somset* 19 ST5147
Easton *Wilts* 20 ST8970
Easton *Hants* 11 SU5132
Easton *Devon* 5 SX7289
Easton *Dorset* 9 SY6971
Easton *Norfk* 43 TG1310
Easton *Cambs* 30 TL1371
Easton *Suffk* 33 TM2858
Easton Grey *Wilts* 20 ST8887
Easton Maudit *Nhants* 30 SP8858
Easton Royal *Wilts* 21 SU2060
Easton on the Hill *Nhants* 40 TF0104
Easton-in-Gordano *Avon* 19 ST5175
Eastrea *Cambs* 41 TL2997
Eastriggs *D & G* 67 NY2466
Eastrington *Humb* 56 SE7929
Eastrop *Wilts* 21 SU2092
Eastry *Kent* 15 TR3054
Eastville *Lincs* 51 TF4056
Eastwell *Leics* 40 SK7728
Eastwick *Herts* 23 TL4311
Eastwood *W York* 54 SD9726
Eastwood *Notts* 49 SK4646
Eastwood *Essex* 24 TQ8688
Eathorpe *Warwks* 29 SP3969
Eaton *Ches* 47 SJ5763
Eaton *Ches* 47 SJ8765
Eaton *Notts* 49 SK7077
Eaton *Leics* 40 SK7928
Eaton *Shrops* 37 SO5089
Eaton *Oxon* 21 SP4403

Eaton

Farnham

Eaton Norfk 43 TG2006
Eaton Bray Beds 30 SP9720
Eaton Constantine Shrops 37 SJ5906
Eaton Green Beds 30 SP9621
Eaton Hastings Oxon 21 SU2598
Eaton Mascott Shrops 37 SJ5305
Eaton Socon Beds 31 TL1759
Eaton upon Tern Shrops 37 SJ6523
Ebberston N York 63 SE8982
Ebbesborne Wake Wilts 9 ST9924
Ebbw Vale Gwent 27 SO1609
Ebchester Dur 68 NZ1055
Ebford Devon 5 SX9887
Ebley Gloucs 28 SO8205
Ebnal Ches 46 SJ4948
Ebrington Gloucs 29 SP1840
Ebsworthy Town Devon 4 SX5090
Ecchinswell Hants 21 SU4959
Ecclaw Loth 76 NT7568
Ecclefechan D & G 67 NY1974
Eccles Border 76 NT7641
Eccles Gt Man 47 SJ7798
Eccles Kent 14 TQ7360
Eccles Road Norfk 32 TM0189
Ecclesall S York 49 SK3284
Ecclesfield S York 49 SK3593
Ecclesgreig Gramp 89 NO7465
Eccleshall Staffs 38 SJ8329
Eccleshill W York 55 SE1736
Ecclesmachan Loth 75 NT0573
Eccleston Lancs 53 SD5217
Eccleston Ches 46 SJ4162
Eccleston Mersyd 46 SJ4895
Echt Gramp 89 NJ7405
Eckford Border 76 NT7026
Eckington Derbys 49 SK4379
Eckington H & W 28 SO9241
Ecton Nhants 30 SP8263
Edale Derbys 48 SK1285
Edburton W Susx 12 TQ2311
Edderton Highld 97 NH7084
Eddleston Border 75 NT2447
Eddlewood Strath 74 NS7153
Edenbridge Kent 13 TQ4446
Edenfield Lancs 54 SD8019
Edenhall Cumb 59 NY5632
Edenham Lincs 40 TF0621
Edensor Derbys 48 SK2469
Edentaggart Strath 80 NS3293
Edenthorpe S York 56 SE6206
Ederline Strath 79 NM8702
Edern Gwynd 44 SH2739
Edgbaston W Mids 38 SP0684
Edgcott Bucks 30 SP6722
Edgcott Devon 7 SS8438
Edge Shrops 36 SJ3908
Edge Gloucs 28 SO8409
Edgefield Norfk 43 TG0934
Edgefield Green Norfk 43 TG0934
Edgertown W York 55 SE1317
Edgeworth Gloucs 28 SO9406
Edgmond Shrops 37 SJ7119
Edgton Shrops 36 SO3885
Edgware Gt Lon 23 TQ1991
Edgworth Lancs 54 SD7416
Edinample Cent 81 NN6022
Edinbane Highld 90 NG3451
Edinburgh Loth 75 NT2573
Edingale Staffs 39 SK2111
Edingham D & G 66 NX8363
Edingley Notts 49 SK6655
Edingthorpe Norfk 43 TG3132
Edingthorpe Green Norfk 43 TG3031
Edington Border 77 NT8956
Edington Nthumb 69 NZ1582
Edington Somset 19 ST3839
Edington Wilts 20 ST9253
Edington Burtle Somset 19 ST3943
Edingworth Somset 19 ST3653
Edith Weston Leics 40 SK9205
Edithmead Somset 19 ST3249
Edlesborough Bucks 30 SP9719
Edlingham Nthumb 69 NU1109
Edlington Lincs 51 TF2371
Edmondsham Dorset 10 SU0611
Edmondsley Dur 69 NZ2349
Edmondthorpe Leics 40 SK8517
Edmonton Gt Lon 23 TQ3492
Edmundbyers Dur 68 NZ0150
Ednam Border 76 NT7337
Edradynate Tays 87 NN8751
Edrom Border 77 NT8255
Edstaston Shrops 37 SJ5132
Edstone Warwks 29 SP1962
Edwinstowe Notts 49 SK6266
Edworth Beds 31 TL2241
Edwyn Ralph H & W 27 SO6457
Edzell Tays 89 NO6068
Efail Isaf M Glam 18 ST0884
Efail-fach W Glam 18 SS7895
Efailnewydd Gwynd 44 SH3535
Efailwen Dyfed 16 SN1325
Efenechtyd Clwyd 46 SJ1155
Effgill D & G 67 NY3092
Effingham Surrey 12 TQ1153
Efford Devon 7 SS8901
Egerton Gt Man 54 SD7014
Egerton Kent 14 TQ9147
Eggesford Devon 7 SS6811
Eggington Beds 30 SP9525
Egginton Derbys 39 SK2628
Egglescliffe Cleve 62 NZ4113
Eggleston Dur 61 NY9923
Egham Surrey 22 TQ0071
Egleton Leics 40 SK8707
Eglingham Nthumb 77 NU1019
Egloshayle Cnwll 3 SX0072
Egloskerry Cnwll 4 SX2786
Eglwys Cross Clwyd 37 SJ4740
Eglwysbach Gwynd 45 SH8070
Eglwyswrw Dyfed 16 SN1438
Egmanton Notts 50 SK7368
Egremont Cumb 58 NY0110
Egremont Mersyd 46 SJ3192
Egton N York 63 NZ8006
Egton Bridge N York 63 NZ8004
Eight Ash Green Essex 25 TL9425
Eilanreach Highld 85 NG8018
Elan Village Powys 35 SN9364
Elberton Avon 19 ST6088
Elburton Devon 4 SX5353
Elcombe Wilts 20 SU1280
Eldersfield H & W 28 SO7931
Elderslie Strath 73 NS4463
Eldon Dur 61 NZ2328
Elfhill Gramp 89 NO8085
Elford Staffs 38 SK1810
Elgin Gramp 94 NJ2162
Elgol Highld 84 NG5213
Elham Kent 15 TR1744
Elie Fife 83 NO4900
Elim Gwynd 44 SH3584
Eling Hants 10 SU3612
Elkesley Notts 49 SK6975
Elkstone Gloucs 28 SO9612
Ella Gramp 94 NJ6459
Ellanbeich Strath 79 NM7417
Elland W York 55 SE1120
Ellary Strath 71 NR7376
Ellastone Staffs 48 SK1143
Ellel Lancs 53 SD4856
Ellemford Border 76 NT7260
Ellen's Green Surrey 12 TQ0935
Ellenhall Staffs 38 SJ8426
Ellerbeck N York 62 SE4396
Ellerby N York 63 NZ7914
Ellerdine Heath Shrops 37 SJ6122
Elleric Strath 86 NN0448
Ellerker Humb 56 SE9229
Ellerton N York 61 SE2598
Ellerton Humb 56 SE7039
Ellesborough Bucks 22 SP8306
Ellesmere Shrops 36 SJ3934
Ellesmere Port Ches 46 SJ4076
Ellingham Nthumb 77 NU1725
Ellingham Norfk 33 TM3592
Ellingstring N York 61 SE1783
Ellington Nthumb 69 NZ2791
Ellington Cambs 31 TL1671
Ellington Thorpe Cambs 31 TL1670
Elliots Green Somset 20 ST7945
Ellisfield Hants 21 SU6446
Ellishader Highld 90 NG5065
Ellon Gramp 95 NJ9530
Ellonby Cumb 59 NY4235
Elloughton Humb 56 SE9428
Ellwood Gloucs 27 SO5908
Elm Park Gt Lon 23 TQ5385
Elmbridge H & W 28 SO9068
Elmdon W Mids 38 SP1783
Elmdon Essex 31 TL4639
Elmers End Gt Lon 23 TQ3668
Elmesthorpe Leics 39 SP4696
Elmhurst Staffs 38 SK1112
Elmley Castle H & W 28 SO9841
Elmley Lovett H & W 28 SO8769
Elmore Gloucs 28 SO7815
Elmore Back Gloucs 28 SO7616
Elmsett Suffk 32 TM0546
Elmstead Market Essex 25 TM0624
Elmsted Court Kent 15 TR1144
Elmstone Kent 15 TR2660
Elmstone Hardwicke Gloucs 28 SO9125
Elmswell Humb 56 SE9958
Elmswell Suffk 32 TL9964
Elmton Derbys 49 SK5073
Elphin Highld 96 NC2111
Elphinstone Loth 76 NT3970
Elrick Gramp 89 NJ8106
Elrig D & G 64 NX3248
Elrington Nthumb 68 NY8563
Elsdon Nthumb 68 NY9393
Elsenham Essex 31 TL5326
Elsfield Oxon 29 SP5410
Elsham Humb 56 TA0312
Elsick House Gramp 89 NO8894
Elsing Norfk 42 TG0516
Elslack N York 54 SD9349
Elson Hants 11 SU6002
Elsrickle Strath 75 NT0643
Elstead Surrey 11 SU9043
Elsted W Susx 11 SU8119
Elston Notts 50 SK7647
Elstone Devon 7 SS6716
Elstow Beds 30 TL0546
Elstree Herts 23 TQ1795
Elstronwick Humb 57 TA2232
Elswick T & W 69 NZ2263
Elswick Lancs 53 SD4238
Elsworth Cambs 31 TL3163
Elterwater Cumb 58 NY3204
Eltham Gt Lon 23 TQ4274
Eltisley Cambs 31 TL2759
Elton Cleve 62 NZ4017
Elton Ches 46 SJ4575
Elton Derbys 48 SK2260
Elton Notts 40 SK7638
Elton H & W 27 SO4570
Elton Cambs 40 TL0893
Eltringham Nthumb 68 NZ0762
Elvaston Derbys 39 SK4032
Elveden Suffk 32 TL8280
Elvingston Loth 76 NT4674
Elvington N York 56 SE7047
Elvington Kent 15 TR2750
Elwick Cleve 62 NZ4532
Elworth Ches 47 SJ7361
Elworthy Somset 7 ST0834
Ely S Glam 18 ST1476
Ely Cambs 41 TL5480
Emberton Bucks 30 SP8849
Embleton Nthumb 77 NU2322
Embo Highld 97 NH8192
Embo Street Highld 97 NH8091
Emborough Somset 19 ST6151
Embsay N York 54 SE0053
Emery Down Hants 10 SU2808
Emley W York 55 SE2413
Emmington Oxon 22 SP7402
Emneth Cambs 41 TF4807
Emneth Hungate Norfk 41 TF5107
Empingham Leics 40 SK9508
Empshott Hants 11 SU7531
Emsworth Hants 11 SU7406
Enborne Berks 21 SU4365
Enborne Row Hants 21 SU4463
Encombe Dorset 9 SY9478
Enderby Leics 39 SP5399
Endmoor Cumb 59 SD5384
Endon Staffs 48 SJ9253
Endon Bank Staffs 48 SJ9253
Enfield Gt Lon 23 TQ3597
Enfield Lock Gt Lon 23 TQ3698
Enfield Wash Gt Lon 23 TQ3598
Enford Wilts 20 SU1351
Engine Common Avon 20 ST6984
Englefield Berks 21 SU6272
Englefield Green Surrey 22 SU9971
Englesea-brook Ches 47 SJ7551
English Bicknor Gloucs 27 SO5815
English Frankton Shrops 36 SJ4529
Englishcombe Avon 20 ST7162
Enham-Alamein Hants 21 SU3649
Enmore Somset 8 ST2435
Enmore Green Dorset 9 ST8523
Ennerdale Bridge Cumb 58 NY0615
Enochdhu Tays 88 NO0662
Ensay Strath 78 NM3648
Ensbury Dorset 10 SZ0896
Ensdon Shrops 36 SJ4017
Ensis Devon 6 SS5626
Enstone Oxon 29 SP3724
Enterkinfoot D & G 66 NS8504
Enville Staffs 38 SO8286
Epney Gloucs 28 SO7611
Epperstone Notts 49 SK6548
Epping Essex 23 TL4502
Epping Green Herts 23 TL2906
Epping Green Essex 23 TL4305
Epping Upland Essex 23 TL4404
Eppleby N York 61 NZ1713
Epsom Surrey 23 TQ2160
Epwell Oxon 29 SP3540
Epworth Humb 56 SE7803
Erbistock Clwyd 36 SJ3541
Erdington W Mids 38 SP1191
Ericstane D & G 66 NT0711
Eridge Green E Susx 13 TQ5535
Erines Strath 71 NR8575
Eriswell Suffk 32 TL7278
Erith Gt Lon 23 TQ5177
Erlestoke Wilts 20 ST9653
Ermington Devon 5 SX6353
Erpingham Norfk 43 TG1931
Errogie Highld 92 NH5622
Errol Tays 83 NO2422
Erskine Strath 73 NS4770
Ervie D & G 64 NX0067
Erwarton Suffk 25 TM2234
Eryholme N York 62 NZ3208
Eryrys Clwyd 46 SJ2057
Escomb Dur 61 NZ1830
Escrick N York 56 SE6242
Esgairgeiliog Powys 35 SH7606
Esh Dur 69 NZ1944
Esh Winning Dur 61 NZ1942
Esher Surrey 22 TQ1364
Eshott Nthumb 69 NZ2097
Eskadale Highld 92 NH4540
Eskbank Loth 75 NT3266
Eskdale Green Cumb 58 NY1400
Eskdalemuir D & G 67 NY2597
Esprick Lancs 53 SD4036
Essendine Leics 40 TF0412
Essendon Herts 23 TL2708
Essich Highld 92 NH6439
Essington Staffs 38 SJ9603
Esslemont Gramp 95 NJ9229
Esthorpe Lincs 40 TF0623
Eston Cleve 62 NZ5418
Etal Nthumb 77 NT9339
Etchilhampton Wilts 20 SU0460
Etchingham E Susx 14 TQ7126
Etchinghill Staffs 38 SK0218
Etchinghill Kent 15 TR1639
Etloe Gloucs 28 SO6806
Eton Wick Berks 22 SU9478
Etruria Staffs 47 SJ8647
Etteridge Highld 87 NN6892
Ettersgill Dur 60 NY8829
Ettiley Heath Ches 47 SJ7360
Ettingshall W Mids 38 SO9396
Ettington Warwks 29 SP2749
Etton Humb 56 SE9743
Etton Cambs 40 TF1406
Ettrick Border 67 NT2714
Ettrick Hill Border 67 NT2514
Ettrickbridge Border 76 NT3824
Etwall Derbys 39 SK2631
Euston Suffk 32 TL8979
Euxton Lancs 53 SD5519
Evanton Highld 92 NH6066
Evedon Lincs 50 TF0947
Evelith Shrops 37 SJ7405
Evelix Highld 97 NH7790
Evenjobb Powys 27 SO2662
Evenley Oxon 29 SP5834
Evenlode Gloucs 29 SP2129
Evenwood Dur 61 NZ1524
Evercreech Somset 19 ST6438
Everingham Humb 56 SE8042
Everleigh Wilts 21 SU2053
Eversholt Beds 30 SP9833
Evershot Dorset 8 ST5704
Eversley Hants 22 SU7762
Eversley Cross Hants 22 SU7961
Everthorpe Humb 56 SE9031
Everton Mersyd 46 SJ3491
Everton Notts 49 SK6990
Everton Hants 10 SZ2894
Everton Beds 31 TL2051
Evertown D & G 67 NY3576
Evesbatch H & W 28 SO6948
Evesham H & W 28 SP0344
Evington Leics 39 SK6203
Ewden Village S York 49 SK2796
Ewell Surrey 23 TQ2262
Ewell Minnis Kent 15 TR2643
Ewelme Oxon 21 SU6491
Ewen Gloucs 20 SU0097
Ewenny M Glam 18 SS9077
Ewerby Lincs 50 TF1247
Ewesley Nthumb 68 NZ0591
Ewhurst Surrey 12 TQ0940
Ewhurst E Susx 14 TQ7924
Ewhurst Green Surrey 12 TQ0939
Ewloe Clwyd 46 SJ3066
Eworthy Devon 6 SX4495
Ewshot Hants 22 SU8149
Ewyas Harold H & W 27 SO3828
Exbourne Devon 6 SS6002
Exbury Hants 10 SU4200
Exebridge Somset 7 SS9324
Exelby N York 61 SE2987
Exeter Devon 5 SX9292
Exford Somset 7 SS8538
Exfordsgreen Shrops 36 SJ4505
Exhall Warwks 28 SP1055
Exhall Warwks 39 SP3485
Exlade Street Oxon 21 SU6581
Exminster Devon 5 SX9487
Exmouth Devon 5 SY0081
Exning Cambs 32 TL6265
Exted Kent 15 TR1744
Exton Leics 40 SK9211
Exton Somset 7 SS9233
Exton Hants 11 SU6120
Exton Devon 5 SX9886
Exwick Devon 5 SX9093
Eyam Derbys 48 SK2176
Eydon Nhants 29 SP5449
Eye H & W 27 SO4964
Eye Cambs 41 TF2202
Eye Suffk 33 TM1473
Eyemouth Border 77 NT9464
Eyeworth Beds 31 TL2545
Eyhorne Street Kent 14 TQ8354
Eyke Suffk 33 TM3151
Eynesbury Beds 31 TL1859
Eynsford Kent 23 TQ5465
Eynsham Oxon 29 SP4309
Eype Dorset 8 SY4491
Eyre Highld 90 NG4153
Eythorne Kent 15 TR2849
Eyton Shrops 36 SJ3714
Eyton Shrops 36 SJ4422
Eyton Shrops 36 SO3787
Eyton H & W 27 SO4761
Eyton on Severn Shrops 37 SJ5806
Eyton upon the Weald Moor Shrops 37 SJ6515

F

Faccombe Hants 21 SU3857
Faceby N York 62 NZ4903
Fachwen Powys 36 SJ0316
Faddiley Ches 47 SJ5852
Fadmoor N York 62 SE6789
Faerdre W Glam 18 SN6901
Failand Avon 19 ST5171
Failford Strath 73 NS4626
Failsworth Gt Man 48 SD8901
Fair Oak Hants 10 SU4918
Fair Oak Green Hants 22 SU6660
Fairbourne Gwynd 35 SH6113
Fairburn N York 55 SE4727
Fairfield Derbys 48 SK0673
Fairfield H & W 38 SO9475
Fairford Gloucs 20 SP1501
Fairgirth D & G 66 NX8756
Fairhaven Lancs 53 SD3227
Fairlie Strath 73 NS2054
Fairlight E Susx 14 TQ8511
Fairmile Devon 7 SY0897
Fairmile Surrey 22 TQ1161
Fairnilee Border 76 NT4532
Fairoak Staffs 37 SJ7632
Fairseat Kent 14 TQ6261
Fairstead Essex 24 TL7616
Fairwarp E Susx 13 TQ4626
Fairwater S Glam 18 ST1477
Fairy Cross Devon 6 SS4024
Fakenham Norfk 42 TF9229
Fakenham Magna Suffk 32 TL9176
Fala Loth 76 NT4460
Fala Dam Loth 76 NT4361
Faldingworth Lincs 50 TF0684
Faldouet Jersey 101 JS0000
Falfield Gloucs 20 ST6893
Falkenham Suffk 33 TM2939
Falkirk Cent 82 NS8880
Falkland Fife 83 NO2507
Fallin Cent 82 NS8391
Falloden Nthumb 77 NU1922
Fallowfield Nthumb 68 NY9268
Fallowfield Gt Man 47 SJ8593
Falls of Blarghour Strath 80 NM9913
Falmer E Susx 12 TQ3509
Falmouth Cnwll 2 SW8032
Falnash Border 67 NT3905
Falstone Nthumb 68 NY7287
Fanagmore Highld 98 NC1749
Fancott Beds 30 TL0127
Fanellan Highld 92 NH4942
Fangdale Beck N York 62 SE5694
Fangfoss Humb 56 SE7653
Fanmore Strath 78 NM4144
Fannich Lodge Highld 92 NH2266
Fans Border 76 NT6140
Far Bletchley Bucks 30 SP8533
Far Cotton Nhants 30 SP7559
Far End Cumb 58 SD3098
Far Green Gloucs 20 SO7700
Far Moor Gt Man 46 SD5204
Far Oakridge Gloucs 20 SO9203
Far Sawrey Cumb 59 SD3795
Far Thorpe Lincs 51 TF2674
Farcet Cambs 41 TL2094
Fareham Hants 11 SU5606
Farewell Staffs 38 SK0811
Faringdon Oxon 21 SU2895
Farkhill Tays 82 NO0435
Farlam Cumb 67 NY5558
Farleigh Avon 19 ST5069
Farleigh Surrey 23 TQ3760
Farleigh Hungerford Somset 20 ST8057
Farleigh Wallop Hants 21 SU6247
Farlesthorpe Lincs 51 TF4774
Farleton Cumb 59 SD5380
Farleton Lancs 53 SD5767
Farley Staffs 48 SK0644
Farley Wilts 10 SU2229
Farley Green Suffk 32 TL7353
Farley Green Surrey 12 TQ0545
Farley Hill Berks 22 SU7464
Farleys End Gloucs 28 SO7614
Farlington N York 56 SE6167
Farlow Shrops 37 SO6380
Farmborough Avon 20 ST6660
Farmcote Gloucs 28 SP0628
Farmers Dyfed 17 SN6444
Farmington Gloucs 28 SP1315
Farmoor Oxon 29 SP4506
Farmtown Gramp 94 NJ5051
Farnachty Gramp 94 NJ4261
Farnborough Warwks 29 SP4349
Farnborough Berks 21 SU4381
Farnborough Hants 22 SU8753
Farnborough Gt Lon 23 TQ4464
Farnborough Park Hants 22 SU8755
Farnborough Street Hants 22 SU8756
Farncombe Surrey 12 SU9744
Farndish Beds 30 SP9263
Farndon Ches 46 SJ4154
Farndon Notts 50 SK7651
Farnell Tays 89 NO6255
Farnham N York 55 SE3460
Farnham Dorset 9 ST9515
Farnham Surrey 22 SU8346
Farnham Essex 31 TL4724
Farnham Suffk 33 TM3660

Farnham Common
Frithville

Farnham Common Bucks 22 SU9585
Farnham Royal Bucks 22 SU9583
Farningham Kent 23 TQ5467
Farnley N York 55 SE2148
Farnley W York 55 SE2532
Farnley Tyas W York 55 SE1612
Farnsfield Notts 49 SK6456
Farnworth Gt Man 47 SD7306
Farnworth Ches 46 SJ5187
Farr Highld 99 NC7163
Farr Highld 93 NH6833
Farr Highld 87 NH8203
Farraline Highld 92 NH5621
Farringdon Devon 5 SY0191
Farrington Gurney Avon 19 ST6355
Farthinghoe Nhants 29 SP5339
Farthingstone Nhants 29 SP6154
Fartown W York 55 SE1518
Fartown W York 55 SE2233
Farway Street Devon 8 SY1895
Fasnacloich Strath 86 NN0247
Fasnakyle Highld 92 NH3128
Fassfern Highld 85 NN0278
Fatfield T & W 69 NZ2954
Faulkbourne Essex 24 TL7917
Faulkland Somset 20 ST7354
Fauls Shrops 37 SJ5832
Faversham Kent 15 TR0161
Fawdington N York 55 SE4372
Fawdon Nthumb 77 NU0315
Fawkham Green Kent 14 TQ5865
Fawler Oxon 29 SP3717
Fawley Berks 21 SU3981
Fawley Hants 10 SU4503
Fawley Bucks 22 SU7586
Faxfleet Humb 56 SE8624
Faygate W Susx 12 TQ2134
Fazakerley Mersyd 46 SJ3796
Fazeley Staffs 39 SK2001
Fearby N York 61 SE1981
Fearn Highld 97 NH8378
Fearnan Tays 87 NN7244
Fearnbeg Highld 91 NG7359
Fearnoch Strath 71 NR9279
Featherstone W York 55 SE4221
Featherstone Staffs 38 SJ9305
Feckenham H & W 28 SP0162
Fedderate Gramp 95 NJ8949
Feering Essex 24 TL8720
Feetham N York 61 SD9898
Felbridge Surrey 13 TQ3739
Felbrigg Norfk 43 TG2039
Felcourt Surrey 13 TQ3841
Felday Surrey 12 TQ1144
Felin gwm Isaf Dyfed 17 SN5023
Felin gwm Uchaf Dyfed 17 SN5024
Felindre Dyfed 17 SN5521
Felindre Powys 36 SO1681
Felindre Farchog Dyfed 16 SN1039
Felixkirk N York 62 SE4684
Felixstowe Suffk 25 TM3034
Felixstoweferry Suffk 25 TM3237
Felkirk W York 55 SE3812
Felling T & W 69 NZ2762
Felmersham Beds 30 SP9957
Felmingham Norfk 43 TG2529
Felpham W Susx 12 SZ9499
Felsham Suffk 32 TL9457
Felsted Essex 24 TL6720
Feltham Gt Lon 22 TQ1073
Felthamhill Gt Lon 22 TQ0971
Felthorpe Norfk 43 TG1618
Felton Nthumb 69 NU1800
Felton H & W 27 SO5748
Felton Avon 19 ST5265
Felton Butler Shrops 36 SJ3917
Feltwell Norfk 32 TL7190
Fen Ditton Cambs 31 TL4860
Fen Drayton Cambs 31 TL3368
Fen Street Norfk 42 TL9895
Fence Lancs 54 SD8237
Fence S York 49 SK4485
Fencote N York 61 SE2893
Fencott Oxon 29 SP5716
Fendike Corner Lincs 51 TF4560
Fenham T & W 69 NZ2265
Feniscowles Lancs 54 SD6425
Feniton Devon 8 SY1099
Fenn Green Shrops 37 SO7783
Fenn Street Kent 14 TQ7975
Fenny Bentley Derbys 48 SK1749
Fenny Bridges Devon 8 SY1198
Fenny Compton Warwks 29 SP4152
Fenny Drayton Leics 39 SP3596
Fenstanton Cambs 31 TL3168
Fenstead End Suffk 32 TL8050
Fenton Cumb 67 NY5056
Fenton Staffs 48 SJ8944
Fenton Notts 50 SK7983
Fenton Lincs 50 SK8476
Fenton Lincs 50 SK8751
Fenton Cambs 41 TL3279
Fenton Town Nthumb 77 NT9733
Fenwick Strath 73 NS4643
Fenwick Nthumb 77 NU0640
Fenwick Nthumb 68 NZ0572
Fenwick S York 56 SE5916
Feock Cnwll 2 SW8238
Feolin Ferry Strath 70 NR4469
Feriniquarrie Highld 90 NG1750
Fern Tays 89 NO4861
Ferndale M Glam 18 SS9996
Ferndown Dorset 10 SU0700
Ferness Highld 93 NH9645
Fernham Oxon 21 SU2991
Fernhill Heath H & W 28 SO8759
Fernhurst W Susx 11 SU8928
Fernie Fife 83 NO3115
Ferniegair Strath 74 NS7354
Fernilea Highld 84 NG3732
Fernilee Derbys 48 SK0178
Ferrindonald Highld 85 NG6608
Ferring W Susx 12 TQ0902
Ferry Point Highld 97 NH7385
Ferryden Tays 89 NO7156
Ferryhill Dur 61 NZ2832
Ferryside Dyfed 17 SN3610
Ferrytown Highld 97 NH7387
Fersfield Norfk 32 TM0683
Fersit Highld 86 NN3577
Feshiebridge Highld 87 NH8504
Fetcham Surrey 22 TQ1455
Fetterangus Gramp 95 NJ9850
Fettercairn Gramp 89 NO6573
Fewston N York 55 SE1954
Ffair Rhos Dyfed 35 SN7368
Ffairfach Dyfed 17 SN6321
Ffestiniog Gwynd 45 SH7042
Fforest Dyfed 17 SN5704
Fforest Fach W Glam 17 SS6295
Ffostrasol Dyfed 17 SN3747
Ffrith Clwyd 46 SJ2855
Ffynnongroew Clwyd 46 SJ1382
Fiag Lodge Highld 98 NC4528
Fickleshole Surrey 23 TQ3860
Fiddes Gramp 89 NO8080
Fiddington Gloucs 28 SO9231
Fiddington Somset 19 ST2140
Fiddleford Dorset 9 ST8013
Fiddlers Green Cnwll 2 SW8155
Field Staffs 38 SK0233
Field Broughton Cumb 59 SD3881
Field Dalling Norfk 42 TG0038
Field Head Leics 39 SK4909
Fife Keith Gramp 94 NJ4250
Fifehead Magdalen Dorset 9 ST7821
Fifehead Neville Dorset 9 ST7610
Fifehead St. Quinton Dorset 9 ST7710
Fifield Oxon 29 SP2418
Fifield Berks 22 SU9076
Figheldean Wilts 20 SU1547
Filby Norfk 43 TG4613
Filey N York 63 TA1180
Filgrave Bucks 30 SP8648
Filkins Oxon 29 SP2304
Filleigh Devon 7 SS6627
Filleigh Devon 7 SS7410
Fillingham Lincs 50 SK9485
Fillongley Warwks 39 SP2887
Filton Avon 19 ST6079
Fimber Humb 56 SE8960
Finavon Tays 89 NO4956
Fincham Norfk 42 TF6806
Finchampstead Berks 22 SU7963
Fincharr Strath 79 NM9003
Finchdean Hants 11 SU7312
Finchingfield Essex 24 TL6832
Finchley Gt Lon 23 TQ2690
Findern Derbys 39 SK3030
Findhorn Gramp 93 NJ0364
Findhorn Bridge Highld 93 NH8027
Findo Gask Tays 82 NO0019
Findochty Gramp 94 NJ4667
Findon Gramp 89 NO9397
Findon W Susx 12 TQ1208
Findon Mains Highld 92 NH6060
Findrack House Gramp 89 NJ6004
Finedon Nhants 30 SP9172
Fingal Street Suffk 33 TM2169
Fingask Gramp 95 NJ7827
Fingask Tays 82 NO1619
Fingest Bucks 22 SU7791
Finghall N York 61 SE1889
Fingland D & G 74 NS7517
Finglesham Kent 15 TR3353
Fingringhoe Essex 25 TM0220
Finlarig Cent 81 NN5733
Finmere Oxon 29 SP6332
Finnart Tays 87 NN5157
Finningham Suffk 32 TM0669
Finningley Notts 49 SK6799
Finsbay W Isls 102 NG0786
Finstall H & W 28 SO9770
Finsthwaite Cumb 59 SD3687
Finstock Oxon 29 SP3616
Fintown Ork 103 HY3513
Fintry Gramp 95 NJ7554
Fintry Cent 81 NS6186
Finzean Gramp 89 NO5993
Fionnphort Strath 78 NM3023
Fir Tree Dur 61 NZ1434
Firbank Cumb 60 SD6293
Firbeck S York 49 SK5688
Firby N York 61 SE2686
Firby N York 56 SE7466
Firsby Lincs 51 TF4562
Fishbourne W Susx 11 SU8304
Fishbourne IOW 11 SZ5592
Fishburn Dur 62 NZ3632
Fishcross Cent 82 NS8995
Fisher's Pond Hants 10 SU4820
Fisherford Gramp 95 NJ6735
Fisherrow Loth 75 NT3472
Fisherton Highld 93 NH7451
Fisherton Strath 73 NS2717
Fisherton de la Mere Wilts 20 SU0038
Fishguard Dyfed 16 SM9537
Fishlake S York 56 SE6513
Fishnish Pier Strath 79 NM6542
Fishponds Avon 19 ST6375
Fishtoft Lincs 51 TF3642
Fishtoft Drove Lincs 51 TF3148
Fishwick Border 77 NT9151
Fiskavaig Highld 84 NG3334
Fiskerton Notts 50 SK7351
Fiskerton Lincs 50 TF0471
Fittleton Wilts 20 SU1449
Fittleworth W Susx 12 TQ0019
Fitz Shrops 36 SJ4417
Fitzhead Somset 8 ST1228
Fitzwilliam W York 55 SE4115
Fiunary Highld 79 NM6246
Five Ash Down E Susx 13 TQ4723
Five Ashes E Susx 13 TQ5525
Five Bells Somset 7 ST0642
Five Oak Green Kent 13 TQ6445
Five Oaks Jersey 101 JS0000
Five Oaks W Susx 12 TQ0928
Fivehead Somset 8 ST3522
Fivelanes Cnwll 4 SX2280
Flackwell Heath Bucks 22 SU8989
Fladbury H & W 28 SO9946
Fladdabister Shet 103 HU4332
Flagg Derbys 48 SK1368
Flamborough Humb 57 TA2270
Flamstead Herts 30 TL0714
Flansham W Susx 12 SU9601
Flanshaw W York 55 SE3020
Flasby N York 54 SD9456
Flash Staffs 48 SK0266
Flashader Highld 90 NG3453
Flatt Strath 74 NS6551
Flaunden Herts 22 TL0100
Flawborough Notts 50 SK7842
Flawith N York 55 SE4865
Flax Bourton Avon 19 ST5069
Flaxby N York 55 SE3957
Flaxley Gloucs 28 SO6815
Flaxpool Somset 8 ST1435
Flaxton N York 56 SE6762
Fleckney Leics 39 SP6493
Flecknoe Warwks 29 SP5163
Fledborough Notts 50 SK8072
Fleet Hants 22 SU8053
Fleet Dorset 9 SY6380
Fleet Lincs 41 TF3823
Fleet Hargate Lincs 41 TF3925
Fleetwood Lancs 53 SD3348
Flemingston S Glam 18 ST0169
Flemington Strath 74 NS6559
Flempton Suffk 32 TL8169
Fletchertown Cumb 58 NY2042
Fletching E Susx 13 TQ4223
Flexbury Cnwll 6 SS2107
Flexford Surrey 22 SU9350
Flimby Cumb 58 NY0233
Flimwell E Susx 14 TQ7131
Flint Clwyd 46 SJ2472
Flintham Notts 50 SK7445
Flinton Humb 57 TA2136
Flitcham Norfk 42 TF7326
Flitton Beds 30 TL0535
Flitwick Beds 30 TL0334
Flixborough Humb 56 SE8714
Flixborough Stather Humb 56 SE8614
Flixton N York 63 TA0479
Flixton Suffk 33 TM3186
Flockton W York 55 SE2314
Flockton Green W York 55 SE2515
Flodigarry Highld 90 NG4671
Flookburgh Cumb 59 SD3675
Flordon Norfk 43 TM1897
Flore Nhants 29 SP6460
Flowton Suffk 32 TM0846
Flushing Cnwll 2 SW8034
Fluxton Devon 8 SY0893
Flyford Flavell H & W 28 SO9755
Fobbing Essex 24 TQ7183
Fochabers Gramp 94 NJ3458
Fockerby Humb 56 SE8519
Fodderty Highld 92 NH5159
Foddington Somset 8 ST5729
Foel Powys 35 SH9911
Foffarty Tays 88 NO4145
Foggathorpe Humb 56 SE7537
Fogo Border 76 NT7649
Fogwatt Gramp 94 NJ2356
Foindle Highld 98 NC1948
Folda Tays 88 NO1963
Fole Staffs 48 SK0437
Foleshill W Mids 39 SP3582
Folke Dorset 9 ST6613
Folkestone Kent 15 TR2336
Folkingham Lincs 40 TF0733
Folkington E Susx 13 TQ5603
Folksworth Cambs 40 TL1489
Folkton N York 63 TA0579
Folla Rule Gramp 95 NJ7332
Follifoot N York 55 SE3452
Folly Gate Devon 6 SX5798
Fonthill Bishop Wilts 9 ST9333
Fonthill Gifford Wilts 9 ST9231
Fontmell Magna Dorset 9 ST8616
Fontmell Parva Dorset 9 ST8214
Fontwell W Susx 12 SU9407
Foolow Derbys 48 SK1976
Forbestown Gramp 94 NJ3513
Forcett N York 61 NZ1712
Ford Strath 79 NM8603
Ford Nthumb 77 NT9437
Ford Staffs 48 SK0653
Ford Derbys 49 SK4080
Ford Gloucs 28 SP0829
Ford Bucks 22 SP7709
Ford Devon 6 SS4124
Ford Somset 7 ST0928
Ford Wilts 20 ST8475
Ford W Susx 12 SU9903
Ford Devon 5 SX7940
Ford End Essex 24 TL6716
Ford Street Somset 8 ST1518
Fordcombe Kent 13 TQ5240
Fordell Fife 82 NT1588
Forden Powys 36 SJ2201
Forder Green Devon 5 SX7967
Fordham Norfk 41 TL6199
Fordham Cambs 32 TL6370
Fordham Essex 24 TL9228
Fordingbridge Hants 10 SU1414
Fordon Humb 63 TA0475
Fordoun Gramp 89 NO7475
Fordstreet Essex 24 TL9226
Fordwich Kent 15 TR1859
Fordyce Gramp 94 NJ5563
Forebridge Staffs 38 SJ9322
Foremark Derbys 39 SK3326
Forest Guern 101 GN0000
Forest Becks Lancs 54 SD7851
Forest Gate Gt Lon 23 TQ4085
Forest Green Surrey 12 TQ1241
Forest Hill Oxon 29 SP5807
Forest Hill Gt Lon 23 TQ3672
Forest Lane Head N York 55 SE3356
Forest Lodge Strath 86 NN2742
Forest Mill Cent 82 NS9694
Forest Row E Susx 13 TQ4234
Forestside W Susx 11 SU7612
Forfar Tays 88 NO4550
Forgandenny Tays 82 NO0818
Forge Hammer Gwent 19 ST2895
Forgie Gramp 94 NJ3854
Forgieside Gramp 94 NJ4053
Forgorig Border 76 NT7748
Formby Mersyd 46 SD3006
Forncett End Norfk 43 TM1493
Forncett St. Mary Norfk 43 TM1694
Forncett St. Peter Norfk 43 TM1693
Forneth Tays 88 NO1044
Fornham All Saints Suffk 32 TL8367
Fornham St. Martin Suffk 32 TL8567
Forres Gramp 93 NJ0358
Forsbrook Staffs 48 SJ9641
Forse Highld 100 ND2234
Forse House Highld 100 ND2135
Forsinain Highld 99 NC9148
Forsinard Highld 99 NC8943
Fort Augustus Highld 92 NH3709
Fort George Highld 93 NH7656
Fort Hommet Guern 101 GN0000
Fort William Highld 86 NN1074
Fort le Marchant Guern 101 GN0000
Forter Tays 88 NO1864
Forteviot Tays 82 NO0517
Forth Strath 75 NS9453
Forthampton Gloucs 28 SO8532
Fortingall Tays 87 NN7347
Fortnightly Highld 93 NH9350
Forton Lancs 53 SD4851
Forton Shrops 36 SJ4316
Forton Staffs 37 SJ7521
Forton Somset 8 ST3307
Forton Hants 21 SU4143
Fortrose Highld 93 NH7256
Fortuneswell Dorset 9 SY6873
Forty Hill Gt Lon 23 TQ3398
Fosbury Wilts 21 SU3157
Foscot Oxon 29 SP2421
Fosdyke Lincs 41 TF3133
Foss Tays 87 NN7858
Fossebridge Gloucs 28 SP0711
Foster Street Essex 23 TL4809
Foston N York 56 SE6965
Foston Derbys 39 SK1931
Foston Lincs 50 SK8542
Foston Leics 39 SP6094
Foston on the Wolds Humb 57 TA1055
Fotherby Lincs 51 TF3191
Fotheringhay Nhants 40 TL0593
Fotrie Gramp 94 NJ6645
Foul End Warwks 39 SP2494
Foulden Border 77 NT9256
Foulridge Lancs 54 SD8942
Foulsham Norfk 42 TG0324
Fountainhall Border 76 NT4249
Four Ashes Suffk 32 TM0070
Four Cabots Guern 101 GN0000
Four Crosses Powys 36 SJ2618
Four Elms Kent 13 TQ4648
Four Forks Somset 19 ST2336
Four Gotes Cambs 41 TF4516
Four Lanes Cnwll 2 SW6838
Four Marks Hants 11 SU6735
Four Mile Bridge Gwynd 44 SH2778
Four Oaks W Mids 39 SP2480
Four Roads Dyfed 17 SN4409
Four Throws Kent 14 TQ7729
Fourpenny Highld 97 NH8094
Fourstones Nthumb 68 NY8867
Fovant Wilts 9 SU0028
Foveran Gramp 95 NJ9824
Fowey Cnwll 3 SX1251
Fowlhall Kent 14 TQ6946
Fowlis Tays 83 NO3233
Fowlis Wester Tays 82 NN9224
Fowlmere Cambs 31 TL4245
Fownhope H & W 27 SO5834
Foxbar Strath 73 NS4561
Foxcote Somset 20 ST7155
Foxdale IOM 52 SC2778
Foxearth Essex 32 TL8344
Foxfield Cumb 58 SD2185
Foxhole Cnwll 3 SW9654
Foxholes N York 63 TA0173
Foxley Norfk 42 TG0422
Foxt Staffs 48 SK0348
Foxton N York 62 SE4296
Foxton Leics 40 SP7089
Foxton Cambs 31 TL4148
Foxwood Shrops 37 SO6276
Foy H & W 27 SO5928
Foyers Highld 92 NH4921
Foynesfield Highld 93 NH8953
Fraddon Cnwll 3 SW9158
Fradley Staffs 38 SK1513
Fradswell Staffs 38 SJ9931
Fraisthorpe Humb 57 TA1561
Framfield E Susx 13 TQ4920
Framingham Earl Norfk 43 TG2702
Framingham Pigot Norfk 43 TG2703
Framlingham Suffk 33 TM2863
Frampton Dorset 9 SY6295
Frampton Lincs 41 TF3239
Frampton Cotterell Avon 20 ST6682
Frampton Mansell Gloucs 20 SO9202
Frampton on Severn Gloucs 28 SO7407
Framsden Suffk 33 TM1959
Framwellgate Moor Dur 69 NZ2644
Frances Green Lancs 54 SD6236
Franche H & W 38 SO8278
Frankby Mersyd 46 SJ2486
Frankley H & W 38 SO9980
Frankton Warwks 29 SP4270
Frant E Susx 13 TQ5835
Fraserburgh Gramp 95 NJ9966
Frating Essex 25 TM0722
Frating Green Essex 25 TM0823
Fratton Hants 11 SU6500
Freathy Cnwll 4 SX3952
Freckenham Suffk 32 TL6672
Freckleton Lancs 53 SD4329
Freeby Leics 40 SK8020
Freefolk Hants 21 SU4848
Freeland Oxon 29 SP4112
Freethorpe Norfk 43 TG4005
Freethorpe Common Norfk 43 TG4004
Freiston Lincs 51 TF3743
Fremington N York 61 SE0499
Fremington Devon 6 SS5132
Frenich Tays 87 NN8258
Frensham Surrey 11 SU8441
Freshwater IOW 10 SZ3487
Fressingfield Suffk 33 TM2677
Freston Suffk 25 TM1638
Freswick Highld 100 ND3667
Fretherne Gloucs 28 SO7210
Frettenham Norfk 43 TG2417
Freuchie Fife 83 NO2806
Freystrop Dyfed 16 SM9511
Friday Bridge Cambs 41 TF4604
Friday Street Suffk 33 TM3760
Fridaythorpe Humb 56 SE8759
Friern Barnet Gt Lon 23 TQ2892
Friesland Bay Strath 78 NM1954
Friesthorpe Lincs 50 TF0683
Frieston Lincs 50 SK9347
Frieth Bucks 22 SU7990
Frilford Oxon 21 SU4497
Frilsham Berks 21 SU5473
Frimley Surrey 22 SU8757
Frindsbury Kent 14 TQ7369
Fring Norfk 42 TF7334
Fringford Oxon 29 SP6029
Frinsted Kent 14 TQ8957
Frinton-on-Sea Essex 25 TM2320
Friockheim Tays 89 NO5949
Frisby on the Wreake Leics 40 SK6917
Friskney Lincs 51 TF4655
Friston Suffk 33 TM4160
Friston E Susx 13 TV5598
Fritchley Derbys 49 SK3552
Fritham Hants 10 SU2314
Frithelstock Devon 6 SS4619
Frithelstock Stone Devon 6 SS4518
Frithville Lincs 51 TF3150

Gorstan
Hadley End

Gorstan *Highld* **92** NH3862
Gorstello *Ches* **46** SJ3562
Gorsty Common *H & W* **27** SO4437
Gorsty Hill *Staffs* **38** SK1028
Gorten *Strath* **79** NM7432
Gorthleck *Highld* **92** NH5420
Gorton *Gt Man* **47** SJ8896
Gosbeck *Suffk* **33** TM1555
Gosberton *Lincs* **41** TF2331
Gosfield *Essex* **24** TL7829
Gosforth *Cumb* **58** NY0603
Gosforth *T & W* **69** NZ2368
Gospel End *Staffs* **38** SO8993
Gosport *Hants* **11** SZ6099
Gotham *Notts* **39** SK5330
Gotherington *Gloucs* **28** SO9529
Gotton *Somset* **8** ST2428
Goudhurst *Kent* **14** TQ7237
Goulceby *Lincs* **51** TF2579
Gourdas *Gramp* **95** NJ7741
Gourdie *Tays* **83** NO3532
Gourdon *Gramp* **89** NO8270
Gourock *Strath* **80** NS2477
Govan *Strath* **74** NS5465
Goveton *Devon* **5** SX7546
Gofilon *Gwent* **27** SO2613
Gowdall *Humb* **56** SE6222
Gower *Highld* **92** NH5058
Gowerton *W Glam* **17** SS5896
Gowkhall *Fife* **82** NT0589
Goxhill *Humb* **57** TA1021
Goxhill *Humb* **57** TA1844
Graffham *W Susx* **11** SU9217
Grafham *Cambs* **31** TL1669
Grafham *Surrey* **12** TQ0241
Grafton *N York* **55** SE4163
Grafton *Shrops* **36** SJ4319
Grafton *H & W* **28** SO9837
Grafton *Oxon* **21** SP2600
Grafton Flyford *H & W* **28** SO9655
Grafton Regis *Nhants* **30** SP7546
Grafton Underwood *Nhants* **40** SP9280
Grafty Green *Kent* **14** TQ8748
Graig *Gwynd* **45** SH8071
Graig *Clwyd* **46** SJ0872
Graig-fechan *Clwyd* **46** SJ1454
Grain *Kent* **14** TQ8876
Grainsby *Lincs* **51** TF2799
Grainsby *Lincs* **51** TF2799
Grainthorpe *Lincs* **51** TF3896
Gramisdale *W Isls* **102** NF8155
Grampound *Cnwll* **3** SW9348
Grampound Road *Cnwll* **3** SW9150
Granborough *Bucks* **30** SP7625
Granby *Notts* **40** SK7536
Grand Chemins *Jersey* **101** JS0000
Grandborough *Warwks* **29** SP4966
Grandes Rocques *Guern* **101** GN0000
Grandtully *Tays* **87** NN9153
Grange *Tays* **83** NO2625
Grange *Cumb* **58** NY2517
Grange *Kent* **14** TQ7968
Grange Crossroads *Gramp* **94** NJ4754
Grange Hall *Gramp* **93** NJ0660
Grange Hill *Gt Lon* **23** TQ4492
Grange Lindores *Fife* **83** NO2516
Grange Moor *W York* **55** SE2215
Grange Villa *Dur* **69** NZ2352
Grange-over-Sands *Cumb* **59** SD4077
Grangehall *Strath* **75** NS9642
Grangemill *Derbys* **48** SK2457
Grangemouth *Cent* **82** NS9281
Grangepans *Cent* **82** NT0181
Grangetown *Cleve* **62** NZ5420
Gransmoor *Humb* **57** TA1259
Granston *Dyfed* **16** SM8934
Grantchester *Cambs* **31** TL4355
Grantham *Lincs* **40** SK9135
Granton *Fife* **75** NT2376
Grantown-on-Spey *Highld* **93** NJ0328
Grantshouse *Border* **76** NT8065
Grasby *Lincs* **57** TA0804
Grasmere *Cumb* **59** NY3307
Grassendale *Mersyd* **46** SJ3985
Grassington *N York* **54** SE0063
Grassmoor *Derbys* **49** SK4067
Grassthorpe *Notts* **50** SK7967
Grateley *Hants* **21** SU2741
Graveley *Herts* **31** TL2327
Graveley *Cambs* **31** TL2563
Graveney *Kent* **15** TR0562
Gravesend *Kent* **14** TQ6574
Gravir *W Isls* **102** NB3915
Grayingham *Lincs* **50** SK9396
Grayrigg *Cumb* **59** SD5796
Grays *Essex* **24** TQ6177
Grayshott *Hants* **11** SU8735
Grayswood *Surrey* **11** SU9134
Grazeley *Berks* **22** SU6966
Greasbrough *S York* **49** SK4195
Greasby *Mersyd* **46** SJ2587
Greasley *Notts* **49** SK4846
Great Abington *Cambs* **31** TL5348
Great Addington *Nhants* **30** SP9675
Great Alne *Warwks* **28** SP1259
Great Altcar *Lancs* **46** SD3305
Great Amwell *Herts* **31** TL3712
Great Asby *Cumb* **60** NY6713
Great Ayton *N York* **62** NZ5610
Great Baddow *Essex* **24** TL7304
Great Badminton *Avon* **20** ST8082
Great Bardfield *Essex* **24** TL6730
Great Barford *Beds* **30** TL1351
Great Barrington *Gloucs* **29** SP2113
Great Barrow *Ches* **46** SJ4768
Great Barton *Suffk* **32** TL8967
Great Barugh *N York* **63** SE7479
Great Bavington *Nthumb* **68** NY9880
Great Bedwyn *Wilts* **21** SU2764
Great Bentley *Essex* **25** TM1021
Great Billing *Nhants* **30** SP8162
Great Bircham *Norfk* **42** TF7732
Great Blakenham *Suffk* **33** TM1150
Great Blencow *Cumb* **59** NY4532
Great Bolas *Shrops* **37** SJ6421
Great Bookham *Surrey* **22** TQ1354
Great Bosullow *Cnwll* **2** SW4133
Great Bourton *Oxon* **29** SP4545
Great Bowden *Leics* **40** SP7488
Great Bradley *Suffk* **32** TL6753
Great Braxted *Essex* **24** TL8614
Great Bricett *Suffk* **32** TM0350
Great Brickhill *Bucks* **30** SP9030
Great Bridgeford *Staffs* **38** SJ8827
Great Brington *Nhants* **30** SP6665
Great Bromley *Essex* **25** TM0826
Great Broughton *Cumb* **58** NY0731
Great Broughton *N York* **62** NZ5405
Great Budworth *Ches* **47** SJ6677
Great Burdon *Dur* **62** NZ3116
Great Burstead *Essex* **24** TQ6892
Great Busby *N York* **62** NZ5205
Great Canfield *Essex* **24** TL5918
Great Carlton *Lincs* **51** TF4085
Great Casterton *Leics* **40** TF0008
Great Chart *Kent* **15** TQ9841
Great Chatfield *Wilts* **20** ST8563
Great Chatwell *Staffs* **37** SJ7914
Great Chesterford *Essex* **31** TL5042
Great Cheverell *Wilts* **20** ST9854
Great Chishill *Cambs* **31** TL4238
Great Clacton *Essex* **25** TM1716
Great Cliffe *W York* **55** SE3015
Great Clifton *Cumb* **58** NY0429
Great Coates *Humb* **57** TA2309
Great Comberton *H & W* **28** SO9542
Great Corby *Cumb* **67** NY4754
Great Cornard *Suffk* **32** TL8840
Great Cowden *Humb* **57** TA2342
Great Coxwell *Oxon* **21** SU2693
Great Cransley *Nhants* **30** SP8376
Great Cressingham *Norfk* **42** TF8501
Great Crosthwaite *Cumb* **58** NY2524
Great Cubley *Derbys* **48** SK1638
Great Dalby *Leics* **40** SK7414
Great Doddington *Nhants* **30** SP8864
Great Dunham *Norfk* **42** TF8714
Great Dunmow *Essex* **24** TL6222
Great Durnford *Wilts* **10** SU1338
Great Easton *Leics* **40** SP8492
Great Easton *Essex* **24** TL6025
Great Eccleston *Lancs* **53** SD4240
Great Ellingham *Norfk* **42** TM0196
Great Elm *Somset* **20** ST7449
Great Englebourne *Devon* **5** SX7756
Great Everdon *Nhants* **29** SP5957
Great Eversden *Cambs* **31** TL3653
Great Finborough *Suffk* **32** TM0158
Great Fransham *Norfk* **42** TF8913
Great Gaddesden *Herts* **22** TL0211
Great Gidding *Cambs* **40** TL1183
Great Givendale *Humb* **56** SE8153
Great Glemham *Suffk* **33** TM3361
Great Glen *Leics* **39** SP6597
Great Gonerby *Lincs* **40** SK8938
Great Gransden *Cambs* **31** TL2655
Great Green *Cambs* **31** TL2844
Great Green *Suffk* **32** TL9155
Great Green *Suffk* **32** TL9365
Great Habton *N York* **63** SE7576
Great Hale *Lincs* **50** TF1442
Great Hallingbury *Essex* **31** TL5119
Great Hanwood *Shrops* **36** SJ4409
Great Harrowden *Nhants* **30** SP8770
Great Harwood *Lancs* **54** SD7332
Great Haseley *Oxon* **21** SP6401
Great Hatfield *Humb* **57** TA1842
Great Haywood *Staffs* **38** SJ9922
Great Heck *N York* **56** SE5920
Great Henny *Essex* **24** TL8637
Great Hinton *Wilts* **20** ST9059
Great Hockham *Norfk* **32** TL9592
Great Holland *Essex* **25** TM2019
Great Horkesley *Essex* **25** TL9731
Great Hormead *Herts* **31** TL4029
Great Horton *W York* **55** SE1431
Great Horwood *Bucks* **30** SP7731
Great Houghton *S York* **55** SE4206
Great Houghton *Nhants* **30** SP7958
Great Hucklow *Derbys* **48** SK1777
Great Kelk *Humb* **57** TA1058
Great Kimble *Bucks* **22** SP8205
Great Kingshill *Bucks* **22** SU8797
Great Langdale *Cumb* **58** NY2906
Great Langton *N York* **61** SE2996
Great Leighs *Essex* **24** TL7217
Great Limber *Lincs* **57** TA1308
Great Linford *Bucks* **30** SP8542
Great Livermere *Suffk* **32** TL8871
Great Longstone *Derbys* **48** SK2071
Great Lumley *T & W* **69** NZ2949
Great Malvern *H & W* **28** SO7746
Great Maplestead *Essex* **24** TL8034
Great Marton *Lancs* **53** SD3235
Great Massingham *Norfk* **42** TF7922
Great Milton *Oxon* **21** SP6202
Great Missenden *Bucks* **22** SP8901
Great Mitton *Lancs* **54** SD7138
Great Mongeham *Kent* **15** TR3551
Great Moulton *Norfk* **33** TM1690
Great Musgrave *Cumb* **60** NY7613
Great Ness *Shrops* **36** SJ3919
Great Oak *Gwent* **27** SO3810
Great Oakley *Nhants* **40** SP8785
Great Oakley *Essex* **25** TM1927
Great Offley *Herts* **30** TL1427
Great Ormside *Cumb* **60** NY7017
Great Orton *Cumb* **67** NY3254
Great Ouseburn *N York* **55** SE4461
Great Oxendon *Nhants* **40** SP7383
Great Oxney Green *Essex* **24** TL6606
Great Paxton *Cambs* **31** TL2063
Great Plumpton *Lancs* **53** SD3833
Great Plumstead *Norfk* **43** TG3010
Great Ponton *Lincs* **40** SK9230
Great Preston *W York* **55** SE4029
Great Raveley *Cambs* **41** TL2581
Great Rissington *Gloucs* **29** SP1917
Great Rollright *Oxon* **29** SP3231
Great Ryburgh *Norfk* **42** TF9527
Great Ryle *Nthumb* **68** NU0212
Great Ryton *Shrops* **37** SJ4803
Great Saling *Essex* **24** TL6925
Great Salkeld *Cumb* **59** NY5536
Great Sampford *Essex* **24** TL6435
Great Saughall *Ches* **46** SJ3669
Great Shefford *Berks* **21** SU3875
Great Shelford *Cambs* **31** TL4651
Great Smeaton *N York* **62** NZ3404
Great Snoring *Norfk* **42** TF9434
Great Somerford *Wilts* **20** ST9682
Great Soudley *Shrops* **37** SJ7229
Great Stainton *Dur* **62** NZ3322
Great Stambridge *Essex* **24** TQ8991
Great Staughton *Cambs* **30** TL1264
Great Steeping *Lincs* **51** TF4364
Great Strickland *Cumb* **59** NY5522
Great Stukeley *Cambs* **31** TL2274
Great Sturton *Lincs* **51** TF2176
Great Swinburne *Nthumb* **68** NY9375
Great Tew *Oxon* **29** SP4028
Great Tey *Essex* **24** TL8925
Great Torrington *Devon* **6** SS4919
Great Tosson *Nthumb* **68** NU0200
Great Totham *Essex* **24** TL8611
Great Totham *Essex* **24** TL8713
Great Urswick *Cumb* **58** SD2674
Great Wakering *Essex* **25** TQ9487
Great Waldingfield *Suffk* **32** TL9144
Great Walsingham *Norfk* **42** TF9437
Great Waltham *Essex* **24** TL6913
Great Warley *Essex* **24** TQ5890
Great Washbourne *Gloucs* **28** SO9834
Great Weeke *Devon* **5** SX7187
Great Weldon *Nhants* **40** SP9289
Great Wenham *Suffk* **25** TM0738
Great Whittington *Nthumb* **68** NZ0070
Great Wigborough *Essex* **25** TL9615
Great Wilbraham *Cambs* **31** TL5557
Great Wishford *Wilts* **10** SU0735
Great Witcombe *Gloucs* **28** SO9114
Great Witley *H & W* **28** SO7566
Great Wolford *Warwks* **29** SP2534
Great Wratting *Essex* **32** TL6848
Great Wymondley *Herts* **31** TL2128
Great Wyrley *Staffs* **38** SJ9907
Great Yarmouth *Norfk* **43** TG5207
Great Yeldham *Essex* **24** TL7638
Greatford *Lincs* **40** TF0811
Greatgate *Staffs* **48** SK0539
Greatham *Cleve* **62** NZ4927
Greatham *Hants* **11** SU7730
Greatham *W Susx* **12** TQ0415
Greatstone-on-Sea *Kent* **15** TR0822
Greatworth *Nhants* **29** SP5542
Green End *Warwks* **39** SP2686
Green End *Herts* **31** TL3222
Green End *Herts* **31** TL3333
Green Hammerton *N York* **55** SE4556
Green Heath *Staffs* **38** SJ9913
Green Moor *S York* **49** SK2899
Green Ore *Somset* **19** ST5750
Green Quarter *Cumb* **59** NY4603
Green Street *H & W* **28** SO8749
Green Street *Herts* **31** TL4521
Green Street *Herts* **23** TQ1998
Green Street Green *Kent* **14** TQ5870
Green Tye *Herts* **31** TL4418
Greenburn *Loth* **75** NS9360
Greenfield *Highld* **86** NH2000
Greenfield *Strath* **80** NS2490
Greenfield *Clwyd* **46** SJ1977
Greenfield *Beds* **30** TL0534
Greenford *Gt Lon* **22** TQ1482
Greengairs *Strath* **74** NS7870
Greengates *W York* **55** SE1937
Greenhalgh *Lancs* **53** SD4035
Greenham *Somset* **7** ST0820
Greenhaugh *Nthumb* **68** NY7987
Greenhill *Cent* **82** NS8279
Greenhill *Strath* **75** NS9332
Greenhill *D & G* **67** NY1079
Greenhill *Kent* **15** TR1666
Greenhithe *Kent* **14** TQ5875
Greenholm *Strath* **74** NS5437
Greenhouse *Border* **76** NT5523
Greenhow Hill *N York* **55** SE1164
Greenland *Highld* **100** ND2367
Greenland *S York* **49** SK3988
Greenlaw *Border* **76** NT7146
Greenlea *D & G* **66** NY0375
Greenloaning *Tays* **82** NN8307
Greenmount *Gt Man* **54** SD7714
Greenock *Strath* **80** NS2876
Greenodd *Cumb* **58** SD3182
Greens Norton *Nhants* **30** SP6649
Greenside *T & W* **69** NZ1362
Greenside *W York* **55** SE1716
Greenstead *Essex* **25** TM0125
Greenstead Green *Essex* **24** TL8227
Greensted *Essex* **24** TL5403
Greenway *Somset* **8** ST3124
Greenwich *Gt Lon* **23** TQ3877
Greet *Gloucs* **28** SP0230
Greete *Shrops* **27** SO5770
Greetham *Leics* **40** SK9214
Greetham *Lincs* **51** TF3070
Greetland *W York* **55** SE0821
Greinton *Somset* **19** ST4136
Grenaby *IOM* **52** SC2672
Grendon *Warwks* **39** SP2799
Grendon *Nhants* **30** SP8760
Grendon Underwood *Bucks* **30** SP6820
Grenoside *S York* **49** SK3393
Gresford *Clwyd* **46** SJ3454
Gresham *Norfk* **43** TG1638
Greshornish *Highld* **90** NG3454
Gressenhall *Norfk* **42** TF9615
Gressenhall Green *Norfk* **42** TF9616
Gressingham *Lancs* **53** SD5769
Greta Bridge *Dur* **61** NZ0813
Gretna *D & G* **67** NY3167
Gretna Green *D & G* **67** NY3168
Gretton *Shrops* **37** SO5195
Gretton *Gloucs* **28** SP0030
Gretton *Nhants* **40** SP8994
Grewelthorpe *N York* **61** SE2376
Grey's Green *Oxon* **22** SU7182
Greyrigg *D & G* **66** NY0888
Greysouthern *Cumb* **58** NY0729
Greystoke *Cumb* **59** NY4430
Greystone *Tays* **89** NO5343
Greywell *Hants* **22** SU7151
Griff *Warwks* **39** SP3689
Griffithstown *Gwent* **19** ST2998
Grimeford Village *Lancs* **54** SD6112
Grimesthorpe *S York* **49** SK3689
Grimley *H & W* **28** SO8360
Grimmet *Strath* **73** NS3210
Grimoldby *Lincs* **51** TF3988
Grimpo *Shrops* **36** SJ3526
Grimsargh *Lancs* **54** SD5834
Grimsby *Humb* **57** TA2710
Grimscote *Nhants* **29** SP6553
Grimscott *Cnwll* **6** SS2606
Grimshader *W Isls* **102** NB4025
Grimsthorpe *Lincs* **40** TF0422
Grimston *Leics* **39** SK6821
Grimston *Norfk* **42** TF7222
Grimstone *Dorset* **9** SY6394
Grimstone End *Suffk* **32** TL9368
Grindale *Humb* **57** TA1271
Grindleford *Derbys* **48** SK2477
Grindleton *Lancs* **54** SD7545
Grindley Brook *Shrops* **37** SJ5242
Grindlow *Derbys* **48** SK1877
Grindon *Staffs* **48** SK0854
Gringley on the Hill *Notts* **50** SK7390
Grinsdale *Cumb* **67** NY3758
Grinshill *Shrops* **37** SJ5223
Grinton *N York* **61** SE0498
Grishipoll *Strath* **78** NM1859
Gristhorpe *N York* **63** TA0981
Griston *Norfk* **42** TL9499
Gritley *Ork* **103** HY5504
Grittenham *Wilts* **20** SU0382
Grittleton *Wilts* **20** ST8580
Grizebeck *Cumb* **58** SD2384
Grizedale *Cumb* **59** SD3394
Groby *Leics* **39** SK5207
Groes *Clwyd* **45** SJ0064
Groes-Wen *M Glam* **18** ST1286
Groes-faen *M Glam* **18** ST0680
Groesffordd Marli *Clwyd* **45** SJ0073
Grogport *Strath* **72** NR8144
Gronant *Clwyd* **46** SJ0983
Groom's Hill *H & W* **28** SP0154
Groombridge *E Susx* **13** TQ5337
Grosebay *W Isls* **102** NG1593
Grosmont *N York* **63** NZ8305
Grosmont *Gwent* **27** SO4024
Grossington *Gloucs* **20** SO7302
Groton *Suffk* **32** TL9641
Grouville *Jersey* **101** JS0000
Grove *Notts* **50** SK7479
Grove *Oxon* **21** SU4090
Grove Park *Gt Lon* **23** TQ4072
Grovesend *W Glam* **17** SN5900
Gruids *Highld* **96** NC5603
Gruinard *Highld* **91** NG9489
Gruinart *Strath* **70** NR2966
Grula *Highld* **84** NG3826
Gruline *Strath* **79** NM5440
Grundisburgh *Suffk* **33** TM2251
Gruting *Shet* **103** HU2749
Gualachulain *Highld* **86** NN1145
Guardbridge *Fife* **83** NO4518
Guarlford *H & W* **28** SO8145
Guay *Tays* **88** NN9948
Guestling Green *E Susx* **14** TQ8513
Guestling Thorn *E Susx* **14** TQ8516
Guestwick *Norfk* **42** TG0626
Guide *Lancs* **54** SD7025
Guilden Morden *Cambs* **31** TL2744
Guilden Sutton *Ches* **46** SJ4468
Guildford *Surrey* **12** SU9949
Guildtown *Tays* **82** NO1331
Guilsborough *Nhants* **30** SP6772
Guilsfield *Powys* **36** SJ2211
Guiltreehill *Strath* **73** NS3610
Guineaford *Devon* **6** SS5537
Guisborough *Cleve* **62** NZ6015
Guiseley *W York* **55** SE1942
Guist *Norfk* **42** TG0025
Guiting Power *Gloucs* **28** SP0924
Gullane *Loth* **83** NT4882
Gulval *Cnwll* **2** SW4831
Gulworthy *Devon* **4** SX4572
Gumfreston *Dyfed* **16** SN1001
Gumley *Leics* **39** SP6889
Gun Hill *E Susx* **13** TQ5614
Gunby *Lincs* **40** SK9121
Gunby *Lincs* **51** TF4666
Gundleton *Hants* **11** SU6133
Gunn *Devon* **7** SS6333
Gunnerside *N York* **61** SD9598
Gunnerton *Nthumb* **68** NY9074
Gunness *Humb* **56** SE8411
Gunnislake *Devon* **4** SX4371
Gunnista *Shet* **103** HU5043
Gunthorpe *Notts* **49** SK6844
Gunthorpe *Norfk* **42** TG0134
Gurnard *IOW* **10** SZ4795
Gurney Slade *Somset* **19** ST6249
Gurnos *W Glam* **26** SN7709
Gussage All Saints *Dorset* **9** SU0010
Gussage St. Michael *Dorset* **9** ST9811
Guston *Kent* **15** TR3244
Gutcher *Shet* **103** HU5499
Guthrie *Tays* **89** NO5650
Guyhirn *Cambs* **41** TF4003
Guyzance *Nthumb* **69** NU2103
Gwaenysgor *Clwyd* **46** SJ0781
Gwalchmai *Gwynd* **44** SH3876
Gwaun-Cae-Gurwen *W Glam* **26** SN6911
Gweek *Cnwll* **2** SW7026
Gwenddwr *Powys* **26** SO0643
Gwennap *Cnwll* **2** SW7340
Gwernaffield *Clwyd* **46** SJ2065
Gwernesney *Gwent* **19** SO4101
Gwernogle *Dyfed* **17** SN5333
Gwernymynydd *Clwyd* **46** SJ2162
Gwespyr *Clwyd* **46** SJ1183
Gwinear *Cnwll* **2** SW5937
Gwithian *Cnwll* **2** SW5841
Gwyddelwern *Clwyd* **46** SJ0746
Gwyddgrug *Dyfed* **17** SN4635
Gwytherin *Clwyd* **45** SH8761

H

Habberley *Shrops* **36** SJ3903
Habberley *H & W* **37** SO8177
Habergham *Lancs* **54** SD8033
Habertoft *Lincs* **51** TF5069
Habrough *Humb* **57** TA1413
Hacconby *Lincs* **40** TF1025
Haceby *Lincs* **40** TF0236
Hacheston *Suffk* **33** TM3059
Hackenthorpe *S York* **49** SK4183
Hackford *Norfk* **42** TG0502
Hackforth *N York* **61** SE2492
Hackland *Ork* **103** HY3920
Hackleton *Nhants* **30** SP8055
Hacklinge *Kent* **15** TR3454
Hackness *N York* **63** SE9790
Hackney *Gt Lon* **23** TQ3484
Hackthorn *Lincs* **50** SK9982
Hackthorpe *Cumb* **59** NY5423
Hadden *Border* **76** NT7836
Haddenham *Bucks* **22** SP7308
Haddenham *Cambs* **31** TL4675
Haddington *Loth* **76** NT5173
Haddington *Lincs* **50** SK9162
Haddiscoe *Norfk* **43** TM4497
Haddo *Gramp* **95** NJ8337
Haddon *Cambs* **40** TL1392
Hadham Ford *Herts* **31** TL4321
Hadleigh *Suffk* **32** TM0242
Hadleigh *Essex* **24** TQ8187
Hadley *H & W* **28** SO8564
Hadley End *Staffs* **38** SK1320

Hadley Wood
Heath Green

Hadley Wood *Gt Lon* 23 TQ2698
Hadlow *Kent* 13 TQ6350
Hadlow Down *E Susx* 13 TQ5324
Hadnall *Shrops* 37 SJ5220
Hadstock *Essex* 31 TL5644
Hadzor *H & W* 28 SO9162
Hafodunos *Clwyd* 45 SH8666
Haggerston *Nthumb* 77 NU0443
Haggs *Cent* 81 NS7879
Hagley *H & W* 27 SO5641
Hagley *H & W* 38 SO9180
Hagworthingham *Lincs* 51 TF3469
Hail Weston *Cambs* 31 TL1662
Haile *Cumb* 58 NY0308
Hailsham *E Susx* 13 TQ5909
Hainault *Gt Lon* 23 TQ4591
Hainford *Norfk* 43 TG2218
Hainton *Lincs* 50 TF1884
Haisthorpe *Humb* 57 TA1264
Hakin *Dyfed* 16 SM8905
Halam *Notts* 49 SK6754
Halbeath *Fife* 82 NT1288
Halberton *Devon* 7 ST0112
Halcro *Highld* 100 ND2360
Hale *Cumb* 59 SD5078
Hale *Ches* 46 SJ4782
Hale *Gt Man* 47 SJ7786
Hale *Hants* 10 SU1818
Hale *Surrey* 22 SU8448
Hale Green *E Susx* 13 TQ5514
Hale Street *Kent* 14 TQ6749
Hales *Staffs* 37 SJ7134
Hales *Norfk* 43 TM3797
Hales Place *Kent* 15 TR1459
Halesowen *W Mids* 38 SO9683
Halesworth *Suffk* 33 TM3877
Halford *Shrops* 36 SO4383
Halford *Warwks* 29 SP2645
Halford *Devon* 5 SX8174
Halfpenny Green *Staffs* 38 SO8291
Halfway House *Shrops* 36 SJ3411
Halfway Houses *Kent* 14 TQ9372
Halifax *W York* 55 SE0925
Halistra *Highld* 90 NG2459
Halket *Strath* 73 NS4252
Halkirk *Highld* 100 ND1359
Halkyn *Clwyd* 46 SJ2171
Hall *Strath* 73 NS4154
Hall *Strath* 73 NS4154
Hall Dunnerdale *Cumb* 58 SD2195
Hall Green *W Mids* 38 SP1181
Hall's Green *Herts* 31 TL2728
Halland *E Susx* 13 TQ4916
Hallaton *Leics* 40 SP7896
Hallatrow *Avon* 19 ST6357
Hallbankgate *Cumb* 67 NY5859
Hallen *Avon* 19 ST5580
Hallgarth *Dur* 69 NZ3243
Hallin *Highld* 90 NG2558
Halling *Kent* 14 TQ7063
Hallington *Nthumb* 68 NY9875
Hallington *Lincs* 51 TF3085
Halliwell *Gt Man* 54 SD6910
Halloughton *Notts* 49 SK6951
Hallow *H & W* 28 SO8258
Hallrule *Border* 67 NT5914
Hallsands *Devon* 5 SX8138
Hallyne *Border* 75 NT1940
Halnaker *W Susx* 11 SU9007
Halsall *Lancs* 53 SD3710
Halse *Nhants* 29 SP5640
Halse *Somset* 8 ST1428
Halsetown *Cnwll* 2 SW5038
Halsham *Humb* 57 TA2727
Halstead *Leics* 40 SK7505
Halstead *Essex* 24 TL8130
Halstead *Kent* 23 TQ4861
Halstock *Dorset* 8 ST5308
Halsway *Somset* 18 ST1337
Haltham *Lincs* 51 TF2463
Halton *Nthumb* 68 NY9967
Halton *Lancs* 53 SD5064
Halton *W York* 55 SE3533
Halton *Clwyd* 36 SJ3039
Halton *Bucks* 22 SP8710
Halton East *N York* 55 SE0454
Halton Gill *N York* 60 SD8776
Halton Holegate *Lincs* 51 TF4165
Halton Lea Gate *Nthumb* 68 NY6458
Halton Shields *Nthumb* 68 NZ0168
Halton West *N York* 54 SD8454
Haltwhistle *Nthumb* 68 NY7064
Halvergate *Norfk* 43 TG4106
Halwell *Devon* 5 SX7753
Halwill *Devon* 6 SX4299
Halwill Junction *Devon* 6 SS4400
Ham *Devon* 8 ST2301
Ham *Somset* 8 ST2825
Ham *Gloucs* 20 ST6898
Ham *Wilts* 21 SU3262
Ham *Gt Lon* 23 TQ1772
Ham *Kent* 15 TR3254
Ham Green *H & W* 28 SP0163
Ham Street *Somset* 8 ST5534
Hamble *Hants* 10 SU4806
Hambleden *Bucks* 22 SU7886
Hambledon *Hants* 11 SU6414
Hambledon *Surrey* 12 SU9638
Hambleton *Lancs* 53 SD3742
Hambleton *N York* 56 SE5530
Hambridge *Somset* 8 ST3921
Hambrook *W Susx* 11 SU7806
Hamels *Herts* 31 TL3724
Hameringham *Lincs* 51 TF3167
Hamerton *Cambs* 40 TL1379
Hamilton *Strath* 74 NS7255
Hamlet *Dorset* 9 ST5908
Hammersmith *Gt Lon* 23 TQ2378
Hammerwich *Staffs* 38 SK0707
Hammoon *Dorset* 9 ST8114
Hamnavoe *Shet* 103 HU3735
Hamnavoe *Shet* 103 HU4971
Hampden Park *E Susx* 13 TQ6002
Hampden Row *Bucks* 22 SP8501
Hamperden End *Essex* 24 TL5730
Hampnett *Gloucs* 28 SP0915
Hampole *S York* 55 SE5010
Hampreston *Dorset* 10 SZ0598
Hampsfield *Cumb* 59 SD4080
Hampstead *Gt Lon* 23 TQ2685
Hampstead Norrey's *Berks* 21 SU5276
Hampsthwaite *N York* 55 SE2559
Hampton *Shrops* 37 SO7486
Hampton *H & W* 28 SP0243
Hampton *Wilts* 21 SU1892
Hampton *Gt Lon* 22 TQ1369
Hampton *Kent* 15 TR1568
Hampton Bishop *H & W* 27 SO5637
Hampton Heath *Ches* 46 SJ5049
Hampton Lovett *H & W* 28 SO8865
Hampton Lucy *Warwks* 29 SP2557
Hampton Poyle *Oxon* 29 SP5015
Hampton Wick *Gt Lon* 23 TQ1769
Hampton in Arden *W Mids* 39 SP2080
Hampton in Arden *W Mids* 39 SP2080
Hampton on the Hill *Warwks* 29 SP2564
Hamptworth *Wilts* 10 SU2419
Hamsey *E Susx* 13 TQ4012
Hamstall Ridware *Staffs* 38 SK1019
Hamstead Marshall *Berks* 21 SU4165
Hamsterley *Dur* 69 NZ1156
Hamsterley *Dur* 61 NZ1231
Hamstreet *Kent* 15 TR0033
Hamworthy *Dorset* 9 SY9991
Hanbury *Staffs* 38 SK1727
Hanbury *H & W* 28 SO9664
Hanchurch *Staffs* 38 SJ8441
Hand and Pen *Devon* 7 SY0495
Handbridge *Ches* 46 SJ4065
Handcross *W Susx* 12 TQ2629
Handforth *Ches* 47 SJ8583
Handley *Ches* 46 SJ4657
Handley *Derbys* 49 SK3761
Handsworth *S York* 49 SK4186
Handsworth *W Mids* 38 SP0489
Hanging Langford *Wilts* 20 SU0337
Hangleton *E Susx* 12 TQ2607
Hanham *Avon* 19 ST6472
Hankelow *Ches* 47 SJ6645
Hankerton *Wilts* 20 ST9790
Hanley *Staffs* 47 SJ8847
Hanley Castle *H & W* 28 SO8442
Hanley Child *H & W* 27 SO6565
Hanley Swan *H & W* 28 SO8142
Hanley William *H & W* 28 SO6766
Hanlith *N York* 54 SD8961
Hanmer *Clwyd* 36 SJ4539
Hannaford *Devon* 6 SS6029
Hannington *Nhants* 30 SP8170
Hannington *Wilts* 21 SU1793
Hannington *Hants* 21 SU5355
Hannington Wick *Wilts* 21 SU1795
Hanslope *Bucks* 30 SP8046
Hanthorpe *Lincs* 40 TF0823
Hanwell *Oxon* 29 SP4343
Hanwell *Gt Lon* 22 TQ1579
Hanworth *Norfk* 43 TG1935
Hanworth *Gt Lon* 22 TQ1271
Happendon *Strath* 74 NS8533
Happisburgh *Norfk* 43 TG3831
Happisburgh Common *Norfk* 43 TG3728
Hapsford *Ches* 46 SJ4774
Hapton *Lancs* 54 SD7931
Hapton *Norfk* 43 TM1796
Harberton *Devon* 5 SX7758
Harbertonford *Devon* 5 SX7856
Harbledown *Kent* 15 TR1357
Harborne *W Mids* 38 SP0284
Harborough Magna *Warwks* 39 SP4778
Harbottle *Nthumb* 68 NT9304
Harbourneford *Devon* 5 SX7162
Harbury *Warwks* 29 SP3759
Harby *Leics* 40 SK7431
Harby *Notts* 50 SK8770
Harcombe *Devon* 5 SX8881
Harcombe *Devon* 8 SY1590
Harcombe Bottom *Devon* 8 SY3395
Harden *W York* 55 SE0838
Hardgate *Gramp* 89 NJ7901
Hardgate *Strath* 74 NS5072
Hardgate *D & G* 66 NX8167
Hardham *W Susx* 12 TQ0317
Hardingham *Norfk* 42 TG0403
Hardingstone *Nhants* 30 SP7657
Hardington *Somset* 20 ST7452
Hardington Mandeville *Somset* 8 ST5111
Hardington Marsh *Somset* 8 ST5009
Hardington Moor *Somset* 8 ST5112
Hardisworthy *Devon* 6 SS2320
Hardley *Hants* 10 SU4205
Hardley Street *Norfk* 43 TG3701
Hardraw *N York* 60 SD8691
Hardstoft *Derbys* 49 SK4363
Hardway *Somset* 9 ST7234
Hardway *Hants* 11 SU6001
Hardwick *Oxon* 29 SP3806
Hardwick *Oxon* 29 SP5729
Hardwick *Bucks* 30 SP8019
Hardwick *Nhants* 30 SP8469
Hardwick *Cambs* 31 TL3758
Hardwick *Norfk* 33 TM2289
Hardwicke *Gloucs* 28 SO7912
Hardwicke *Gloucs* 28 SO9027
Hardy's Green *Essex* 25 TL9320
Hare Croft *W York* 55 SE0835
Hare Green *Essex* 25 TM1025
Hare Hatch *Berks* 22 SU8077
Hare Street *Herts* 31 TL3929
Hare Street *Essex* 23 TL4209
Hare Street *Essex* 23 TL5300
Hareby *Lincs* 51 TF3365
Harefield *Gt Lon* 22 TQ0590
Harehill *Derbys* 38 SK1735
Harehills *W York* 55 SE3135
Harelaw *Border* 76 NT5323
Harescombe *Gloucs* 28 SO8310
Haresfield *Gloucs* 28 SO8010
Harestock *Hants* 10 SU4631
Harewood *W York* 55 SE3245
Harewood End *H & W* 27 SO5227
Harford *Devon* 5 SX6359
Hargrave *Ches* 46 SJ4862
Hargrave *Nhants* 30 TL0370
Hargrave Green *Suffk* 32 TL7759
Harkstead *Suffk* 25 TM1834
Harlaston *Staffs* 39 SK2110
Harlaxton *Lincs* 40 SK8832
Harlech *Gwynd* 44 SH5831
Harlescott *Shrops* 37 SJ4916
Harlesden *Gt Lon* 23 TQ2183
Harlesthorpe *Derbys* 49 SK4976
Harleston *Devon* 5 SX7945
Harleston *Suffk* 32 TM0160
Harleston *Norfk* 33 TM2483
Harlestone *Nhants* 30 SP7064
Harley *S York* 49 SK3698
Harleyholm *Strath* 75 NS9238
Harlington *S York* 49 SE4802
Harlington *Beds* 30 TL0330
Harlington *Gt Lon* 22 TQ0877
Harlosh *Highld* 84 NG2841
Harlow *Essex* 23 TL4611
Harlow Hill *Nthumb* 68 NZ0768
Harlthorpe *Humb* 56 SE7337
Harlton *Cambs* 31 TL3852
Harlyn Bay *Cnwll* 3 SW8775
Harman's Cross *Dorset* 9 SY9880
Harmby *N York* 61 SE1289
Harmer Green *Herts* 31 TL2515
Harmer Hill *Shrops* 37 SJ4822
Harmston *Lincs* 50 SK9662
Harnage *Shrops* 37 SJ5604
Harnhill *Gloucs* 20 SP0600
Harold Hill *Gt Lon* 23 TQ5392
Harold Wood *Gt Lon* 24 TQ5590
Haroldston West *Dyfed* 16 SM8615
Haroldston West *Dyfed* 16 SM8615
Haroldswick *Shet* 103 HP6312
Harome *N York* 62 SE6481
Harpenden *Herts* 30 TL1314
Harpford *Devon* 8 SY0990
Harpham *Humb* 57 TA0861
Harpley *H & W* 28 SO6861
Harpley *Norfk* 42 TF7825
Harpole *Nhants* 30 SP6961
Harpsdale *Highld* 100 ND1355
Harpsden *Oxon* 22 SU7680
Harpswell *Lincs* 50 SK9389
Harpurhey *Gt Man* 47 SD8501
Harraby *Cumb* 67 NY4154
Harracott *Devon* 6 SS5527
Harrapool *Highld* 85 NG6523
Harrietfield *Tays* 82 NN9829
Harrietsham *Kent* 14 TQ8652
Harringay *Gt Lon* 23 TQ3188
Harrington *Nhants* 40 SP7780
Harrington *Lincs* 51 TF3671
Harringworth *Nhants* 40 SP9197
Harrogate *N York* 55 SE3054
Harrold *Beds* 30 SP9457
Harrow *Gt Lon* 22 TQ1588
Harrow Green *Suffk* 32 TL8654
Harrow Weald *Gt Lon* 22 TQ1591
Harrow on the Hill *Gt Lon* 22 TQ1587
Harrowbarrow *Cnwll* 4 SX4070
Harston *Leics* 40 SK8331
Harston *Cambs* 31 TL4250
Harswell *Humb* 56 SE8240
Hart *Cleve* 62 NZ4734
Hartburn *Nthumb* 68 NZ0885
Hartest *Suffk* 32 TL8352
Hartfield *E Susx* 13 TQ4735
Hartford *Ches* 47 SJ6372
Hartford *Cambs* 31 TL2572
Hartford End *Essex* 24 TL6817
Hartfordbridge *Hants* 22 SU7757
Hartforth *N York* 61 NZ1606
Harthill *Loth* 74 NS9064
Harthill *Ches* 46 SJ4955
Harthill *S York* 49 SK4980
Hartington *Derbys* 48 SK1260
Hartland *Devon* 6 SS2524
Hartland Quay *Devon* 6 SS2224
Hartlebury *H & W* 38 SO8471
Hartlepool *Cleve* 62 NZ5032
Hartley *Cumb* 60 NY7808
Hartley *Kent* 14 TQ6066
Hartley *Kent* 14 TQ7634
Hartley Wespall *Hants* 22 SU6958
Hartley Wintney *Hants* 22 SU7656
Hartlip *Kent* 14 TQ8464
Harton *T & W* 69 NZ3765
Harton *N York* 56 SE7061
Hartpury *Gloucs* 28 SO7924
Hartshead *W York* 55 SE1822
Hartshill *Staffs* 47 SJ8546
Hartshill *Warwks* 39 SP3194
Hartshorne *Derbys* 39 SK3221
Hartside *Nthumb* 77 NT9716
Hartwell *Nhants* 30 SP7850
Hartwith *N York* 55 SE2161
Hartwood *Strath* 74 NS8459
Hartwoodmyres *Border* 76 NT4324
Harvel *Kent* 14 TQ6563
Harvington *H & W* 38 SO8775
Harvington *H & W* 28 SP0549
Harwell *Notts* 49 SK6891
Harwell *Oxon* 21 SU4989
Harwich *Essex* 25 TM2531
Harwood Dale *N York* 63 SE9695
Harworth *Notts* 49 SK6191
Hasbury *W Mids* 38 SO9582
Hascombe *Surrey* 12 TQ0039
Haselbeach *Nhants* 30 SP7177
Haselbury Plucknett *Somset* 8 ST4710
Haseley *Warwks* 29 SP2367
Haselor *Warwks* 28 SP1257
Hasfield *Gloucs* 28 SO8227
Haskayne *Lancs* 46 SD3508
Hasketon *Suffk* 33 TM2450
Haslemere *Surrey* 11 SU9032
Haslingden *Lancs* 54 SD7823
Haslingfield *Cambs* 31 TL4052
Haslington *Ches* 47 SJ7355
Hassendean *Border* 76 NT5420
Hassingham *Norfk* 43 TG3605
Hassocks *W Susx* 12 TQ3015
Hassop *Derbys* 48 SK2272
Hastingleigh *Kent* 15 TR0945
Hastings *E Susx* 14 TQ8209
Hastingwood *Essex* 23 TL4807
Hastoe *Herts* 22 SP9209
Haswell *Dur* 69 NZ3743
Haswell Plough *Dur* 62 NZ3742
Hatch Beauchamp *Somset* 8 ST3020
Hatch End *Herts* 22 TQ1390
Hatchmere *Ches* 47 SJ5571
Hatcliffe *Humb* 51 TA2100
Hatfield *S York* 56 SE6609
Hatfield *H & W* 27 SO5959
Hatfield *Herts* 23 TL2308
Hatfield Broad Oak *Essex* 24 TL5416
Hatfield Heath *Essex* 31 TL5215
Hatfield Peverel *Essex* 24 TL7911
Hatfield Woodhouse *S York* 56 SE6708
Hatford *Oxon* 21 SU3395
Hatherden *Hants* 21 SU3450
Hatherleigh *Devon* 6 SS5404
Hathern *Leics* 39 SK5022
Hatherop *Gloucs* 28 SP1505
Hathersage *Derbys* 48 SK2381
Hathersage Booths *Derbys* 48 SK2480
Hatherton *Ches* 47 SJ6847
Hatherton *Staffs* 38 SJ9510
Hatley St. George *Cambs* 31 TL2751
Hatt *Cnwll* 4 SX4062
Hatton *Gramp* 95 NK0537
Hatton *Tays* 89 NO4642
Hatton *Ches* 47 SJ5982
Hatton *Derbys* 39 SK2130
Hatton *Shrops* 37 SO4790
Hatton *Warwks* 29 SP2367
Hatton *Lincs* 50 TF1776
Hatton *Gt Lon* 22 TQ0975
Hatton of Fintray *Gramp* 95 NJ8316
Haugh *Strath* 74 NS4925
Haugh of Glass *Gramp* 94 NJ4238
Haugh of Urr *D & G* 66 NX8066
Haugham *Lincs* 51 TF3381
Haughhead Inn *Strath* 81 NS6079
Haughley *Suffk* 32 TM0262
Haughley Green *Suffk* 32 TM0264
Haughton *Shrops* 36 SJ3726
Haughton *Shrops* 37 SJ7408
Haughton *Staffs* 38 SJ8620
Haughton Moss *Ches* 47 SJ5756
Haughton le Skerne *Dur* 62 NZ3116
Haultwick *Herts* 31 TL3323
Haunton *Staffs* 39 SK2310
Hautes Croix *Jersey* 101 JS0000
Hauxley *Nthumb* 69 NU2703
Hauxton *Cambs* 31 TL4452
Havant *Hants* 11 SU7106
Havenstreet *IOW* 11 SZ5690
Haverfordwest *Dyfed* 16 SM9515
Haverhill *Suffk* 32 TL6745
Haverigg *Cumb* 58 SD1578
Havering-atte-Bower *Essex* 23 TQ5193
Haversham *Bucks* 30 SP8242
Haverthwaite *Cumb* 59 SD3483
Havyat *Avon* 19 ST4761
Hawarden *Clwyd* 46 SJ3165
Hawbush Green *Essex* 24 TL7820
Hawe's Green *Norfk* 43 TM2399
Hawen *Dyfed* 17 SN3446
Hawes *N York* 60 SD8789
Hawford *H & W* 28 SO8460
Hawick *Border* 67 NT5014
Hawkchurch *Devon* 8 ST3400
Hawkedon *Suffk* 32 TL7953
Hawkeridge *Wilts* 20 ST8653
Hawkesbury *Avon* 20 ST7686
Hawkesbury Upton *Avon* 20 ST7786
Hawkhurst *Kent* 14 TQ7530
Hawkinge *Kent* 15 TR2139
Hawkley *Hants* 11 SU7429
Hawkridge *Devon* 7 SS8630
Hawkshead *Cumb* 59 SD3598
Hawkshead Hill *Cumb* 59 SD3398
Hawksland *Strath* 74 NS8439
Hawkspur Green *Essex* 24 TL6532
Hawkstone *Shrops* 37 SJ5830
Hawkswick *N York* 54 SD9570
Hawksworth *W York* 55 SE1641
Hawksworth *Notts* 50 SK7543
Hawkwell *Essex* 24 TQ8591
Hawley *Hants* 22 SU8657
Hawling *Gloucs* 28 SP0622
Hawnby *N York* 62 SE5489
Haworth *W York* 55 SE0337
Hawstead *Suffk* 32 TL8559
Hawthorn *Dur* 69 NZ4145
Hawthorn Hill *Lincs* 51 TF2155
Hawton *Notts* 50 SK7851
Haxby *N York* 56 SE6058
Haxey *Humb* 50 SK7799
Hay Green *Norfk* 41 TF5418
Hay Street *Herts* 31 TL3926
Hay-on-Wye *Powys* 27 SO2342
Haydock *Mersyd* 47 SJ5697
Haydon *Dorset* 9 ST6715
Haydon Bridge *Nthumb* 68 NY8464
Haydon Wick *Wilts* 20 SU1387
Hayes *Gt Lon* 22 TQ0980
Hayes *Gt Lon* 23 TQ4066
Hayes End *Gt Lon* 22 TQ0882
Hayfield *Strath* 80 NN0723
Hayfield *Derbys* 48 SK0386
Hayhillock *Tays* 89 NO5242
Hayle *Cnwll* 2 SW5537
Hayley Green *W Mids* 38 SO9582
Hayne *Devon* 7 SS9515
Hayne *Devon* 5 SX7685
Haynes *Beds* 30 TL0740
Haynes West End *Beds* 30 TL0640
Hayscastle *Dyfed* 16 SM8925
Hayscastle Cross *Dyfed* 16 SM9125
Hayton *Cumb* 58 NY1041
Hayton *Cumb* 67 NY5157
Hayton *Humb* 56 SE8245
Hayton *Notts* 49 SK7284
Haytor Vale *Devon* 5 SX7777
Haytown *Devon* 6 SS3814
Haywards Heath *W Susx* 12 TQ3324
Haywood *S York* 56 SE5812
Hazel Grove *Gt Man* 48 SJ9287
Hazelbank *Strath* 74 NS8345
Hazelbury Bryan *Dorset* 9 ST7408
Hazeleigh *Essex* 24 TL8203
Hazelton Walls *Fife* 83 NO3322
Hazelwood *Derbys* 49 SK3245
Hazlemere *Bucks* 22 SU8895
Hazleton *Gloucs* 28 SP0718
Heacham *Norfk* 42 TF6737
Headbourne Worthy *Hants* 10 SU4832
Headcorn *Kent* 14 TQ8344
Headingley *W York* 55 SE2836
Headington *Oxon* 29 SP5207
Headlam *Dur* 61 NZ1818
Headlesscross *Strath* 75 NS9158
Headley *Hants* 21 SU5162
Headley *Hants* 11 SU8236
Headley *Surrey* 23 TQ2054
Headon *Notts* 50 SK7476
Heads *Strath* 74 NS7247
Heads Nook *Cumb* 67 NY5054
Heage *Derbys* 49 SK3750
Healaugh *N York* 61 SE0199
Healaugh *N York* 55 SE5047
Heale *Somset* 8 ST2420
Heale *Somset* 8 ST3825
Healey *N York* 61 SE1780
Healeyfield *Dur* 68 NZ0648
Healing *Humb* 57 TA2110
Heamoor *Cnwll* 2 SW4631
Heanor *Derbys* 49 SK4346
Heanton Punchardon *Devon* 6 SS5035
Heapham *Lincs* 50 SK8788
Heasley Mill *Devon* 7 SS7332
Heast *Highld* 85 NG6417
Heath *W York* 55 SE3520
Heath *Derbys* 49 SK4567
Heath End *Surrey* 22 SU8549
Heath Green *H & W* 38 SP0771

Heath Hill

Hollacombe

Heath Hill *Shrops* 37 SJ7613
Heath Town *W Mids* 38 SO9399
Heath and Reach *Beds* 30 SP9228
Heathcote *Derbys* 48 SK1460
Heather *Leics* 39 SK3910
Heathfield *Somset* 8 ST1626
Heathfield *E Susx* 13 TQ5821
Heathton *Shrops* 37 SO8192
Heatley *Staffs* 38 SK0626
Heaton *T & W* 69 NZ2666
Heaton *W York* 55 SE1335
Heaton *Staffs* 48 SJ9562
Heaton's Bridge *Lancs* 53 SD4011
Heaverham *Kent* 14 TQ5758
Heaverham *Kent* 14 TQ5758
Heavitree *Devon* 5 SX9492
Hebburn *T & W* 69 NZ3164
Hebden *N York* 55 SE0263
Hebden Bridge *W York* 54 SD9927
Hebing End *Herts* 31 TL3122
Hebron *Nthumb* 69 NZ1989
Hebron *Dyfed* 17 SN1827
Heckfield *Hants* 22 SU7160
Heckfield Green *Suffk* 33 TM1875
Heckfordbridge *Essex* 25 TL9421
Heckington *Lincs* 50 TF1444
Heckmondwike *W York* 55 SE1824
Heddington *Wilts* 20 ST9966
Heddon-on-the-Wall *Nthumb* 69 NZ1366
Hedenham *Norfk* 43 TM3193
Hedge End *Hants* 10 SU4912
Hedgerley *Bucks* 22 SU9687
Hedging *Somset* 8 ST3029
Hedley on the Hill *Nthumb* 68 NZ0759
Hednesford *Staffs* 38 SJ9912
Hedon *Humb* 57 TA1928
Hedsor *Bucks* 22 SU9086
Heglibister *Shet* 103 HU3851
Heighington *Dur* 61 NZ2422
Heighington *Lincs* 50 TF0269
Heightington *H & W* 37 SO7671
Heiton *Border* 76 NT7130
Hele *Devon* 6 SS5347
Hele *Devon* 7 SS9902
Hele *Somset* 8 ST1824
Hele *Somset* 8 ST1824
Helensburgh *Strath* 80 NS2982
Helenton *Strath* 73 NS3830
Helford *Cnwll* 2 SW7526
Helford Passage *Cnwll* 2 SW7626
Helhoughton *Norfk* 42 TF8626
Helions Bumpstead *Essex* 32 TL6541
Helland *Cnwll* 3 SX0771
Hellescott *Cnwll* 4 SX2888
Hellesdon *Norfk* 43 TG2010
Hellidon *Nhants* 29 SP5158
Hellifield *N York* 54 SD8556
Hellingly *E Susx* 13 TQ5812
Helmdon *Nhants* 29 SP5943
Helme *W York* 55 SE0912
Helmingham *Suffk* 33 TM1857
Helmsdale *Highld* 97 ND0315
Helmshore *Lancs* 54 SD7821
Helmsley *N York* 62 SE6183
Helperby *N York* 55 SE4469
Helperthorpe *N York* 56 SE9570
Helpringham *Lincs* 50 TF1440
Helpston *Cambs* 40 TF1205
Helsby *Ches* 46 SJ4975
Helston *Cnwll* 2 SW6527
Helstone *Cnwll* 3 SX0881
Helton *Cumb* 59 NY5021
Hemblington *Norfk* 43 TG3411
Hemel Hempstead *Herts* 22 TL0507
Hemerdon *Devon* 4 SX5657
Hemingbrough *N York* 56 SE6730
Hemingby *Lincs* 51 TF2374
Hemingford Abbots *Cambs* 31 TL2871
Hemingford Grey *Cambs* 31 TL2970
Hemingstone *Suffk* 33 TM1454
Hemington *Somset* 20 ST7253
Hemington *Nhants* 40 TL0985
Hemley *Suffk* 33 TM2842
Hempnall *Norfk* 43 TM2494
Hempnall Green *Norfk* 43 TM2493
Hempriggs *Gramp* 93 NJ1063
Hempstead *Norfk* 43 TG1037
Hempstead *Norfk* 43 TG4028
Hempstead *Essex* 24 TL6338
Hempton *Oxon* 29 SP4431
Hempton *Norfk* 42 TF9129
Hemsby *Norfk* 43 TG4917
Hemswell *Lincs* 50 SK9290
Hemsworth *W York* 55 SE4213
Hemyock *Devon* 8 ST1313
Hendersyde Park *Border* 76 NT7435
Hendon *Gt Lon* 23 TQ2389
Hendy *Dyfed* 17 SN5803
Henfield *W Susx* 12 TQ2115
Hengoed *Powys* 27 SO2253
Hengoed *M Glam* 18 ST1494
Hengrave *Suffk* 32 TL8268
Henham *Essex* 24 TL5428
Henhurst *Kent* 14 TQ6669
Heniarth *Powys* 36 SJ1208
Henlade *Somset* 8 ST2623
Henley *Somset* 8 ST4232
Henley *Dorset* 9 ST6904
Henley *W Susx* 11 SU8925
Henley *Suffk* 33 TM1551
Henley's Down *E Susx* 14 TQ7312
Henley-in-Arden *Warwks* 28 SP1566
Henley-on-Thames *Oxon* 22 SU7682
Henllan *Clwyd* 45 SJ0268
Henllan *Dyfed* 17 SN3540
Henllys *Gwent* 19 ST2691
Henlow *Beds* 31 TL1738
Hennock *Devon* 5 SX8381
Henny Street *Essex* 24 TL8738
Henry's Moat (Castell Hendre) *Dyfed* 16 SN0427
Henryd *Gwynd* 45 SH7774
Hensall *N York* 56 SE5923
Henshaw *Nthumb* 68 NY7664
Hensingham *Cumb* 58 NX9816
Henstead *Suffk* 33 TM4885
Hensting *Hants* 10 SU4922
Henstridge *Somset* 9 ST7219
Henstridge Ash *Somset* 9 ST7220
Henton *Oxon* 22 SP7602
Henton *Somset* 19 ST4945
Henwick *H & W* 28 SO8355
Henwood *Cnwll* 4 SX2673
Heol-y-Cyw *M Glam* 18 SS9484
Hepscott *Nthumb* 69 NZ2284
Heptonstall *W York* 54 SD9828
Hepworth *W York* 55 SE1606
Hepworth *Suffk* 32 TL9874
Herbrandston *Dyfed* 16 SM8707
Hereford *H & W* 27 SO5139
Hereson *Kent* 15 TR3865
Heribusta *Highld* 90 NG3970
Heriot *Loth* 76 NT3953
Hermiston *Loth* 75 NT1870
Hermitage *Border* 67 NY5095
Hermitage *Dorset* 9 ST6506
Hermitage *Berks* 21 SU5072
Hermon *Gwynd* 44 SH3968
Hermon *Dyfed* 17 SN2031
Herne *Kent* 15 TR1865
Herne Bay *Kent* 15 TR1768
Herne Pound *Kent* 14 TQ6654
Herner *Devon* 6 SS5826
Hernhill *Kent* 15 TR0660
Herodsfoot *Cnwll* 4 SX2160
Heronden *Kent* 15 TR2954
Heronsford *Strath* 64 NX1283
Herriard *Hants* 22 SU6646
Herringfleet *Suffk* 43 TM4797
Herringswell *Suffk* 32 TL7270
Herringthorpe *S York* 49 SK4492
Herrington *T & W* 69 NZ3453
Hersden *Kent* 15 TR2062
Hersham *Surrey* 22 TQ1164
Herstmonceux *E Susx* 13 TQ6410
Herston *Ork* 103 ND4191
Hertford *Herts* 31 TL3212
Hertford Heath *Herts* 23 TL3510
Hesketh Lane *Lancs* 54 SD6141
Hesleden *Dur* 62 NZ4438
Heslington *N York* 56 SE6250
Hessay *N York* 55 SE5253
Hessenford *Cnwll* 4 SX3057
Hessett *Suffk* 32 TL9361
Hessle *W York* 56 TA0326
Hessle *Humb* 56 TA0326
Heston *Gt Lon* 22 TQ1277
Hestwall *Ork* 103 HY2618
Heswall *Mersyd* 46 SJ2681
Hethe *Oxon* 29 SP5929
Hethersett *Norfk* 43 TG1404
Hethersgill *Cumb* 67 NY4767
Hethpool *Nthumb* 77 NT8928
Hett *Dur* 61 NZ2836
Hetton *N York* 54 SD9658
Hetton-le-Hole *T & W* 69 NZ3547
Heugh *Nthumb* 68 NZ0873
Heugh Head *Border* 77 NT8762
Heugh-Head *Gramp* 94 NJ3811
Heveningham *Suffk* 33 TM3372
Hever *Kent* 13 TQ4745
Heversham *Cumb* 59 SD4983
Hevingham *Norfk* 43 TG1921
Hewas Water *Cnwll* 3 SW9649
Hewelsfield *Gloucs* 19 SO5602
Hewish *Avon* 19 ST4064
Hewish *Somset* 8 ST4208
Hewood *Dorset* 8 ST3502
Hewood *Dorset* 8 ST3502
Hexham *Nthumb* 68 NY9364
Hextable *Kent* 23 TQ5170
Hexthorpe *S York* 49 SE5602
Hexton *Herts* 30 TL1030
Hexworthy *Cnwll* 4 SX3581
Hexworthy *Devon* 5 SX6572
Heybridge *Essex* 24 TL8508
Heybridge *Essex* 24 TQ6398
Heybrook Bay *Devon* 4 SX4949
Heydon *Norfk* 43 TG1127
Heydon *Cambs* 31 TL4339
Heydour *Lincs* 40 TF0039
Heylipoll *Strath* 78 NL9743
Heylor *Shet* 103 HU2980
Heysham *Lancs* 53 SD4160
Heyshott *W Susx* 11 SU8917
Heytesbury *Wilts* 20 ST9242
Heythrop *Oxon* 29 SP3527
Heywood *Gt Man* 54 SD8510
Heywood *Wilts* 20 ST8753
Hibaldstow *Humb* 50 SE9702
Hickleton *S York* 55 SE4805
Hickling *Notts* 40 SK6928
Hickling *Norfk* 43 TG4124
Hickling Green *Norfk* 43 TG4123
Hickstead *W Susx* 12 TQ2620
Hidcote Bartrim *Gloucs* 29 SP1742
Hidcote Boyce *Gloucs* 29 SP1742
High Ackworth *W York* 55 SE4417
High Ardwell *D & G* 64 NX0745
High Auldgirth *D & G* 66 NX9187
High Bankhill *Cumb* 59 NY5542
High Beach *Essex* 23 TQ4198
High Bentham *N York* 54 SD6669
High Bickington *Devon* 6 SS6020
High Biggins *Cumb* 59 SD6078
High Blantyre *Strath* 74 NS6756
High Bonnybridge *Cent* 82 NS8379
High Bray *Devon* 7 SS6934
High Brooms *Kent* 13 TQ5941
High Catton *Humb* 56 SE7153
High Coniscliffe *Dur* 61 NZ2215
High Crosby *Cumb* 67 NY4559
High Cross *Strath* 73 NS4046
High Cross *Warwks* 29 SP2067
High Cross *Hants* 11 SU7126
High Cross *Herts* 31 TL3618
High Drummore *D & G* 64 NX1235
High Easter *Essex* 24 TL6214
High Ellington *N York* 61 SE2083
High Ercall *Shrops* 37 SJ5917
High Etherley *Dur* 61 NZ1728
High Garrett *Essex* 24 TL7727
High Grantley *N York* 55 SE2369
High Green *H & W* 28 SO8745
High Green *Norfk* 43 TG1305
High Green *Norfk* 33 TM1689
High Halden *Kent* 14 TQ8937
High Halstow *Kent* 14 TQ7875
High Ham *Somset* 8 ST4231
High Harrogate *N York* 55 SE3155
High Hartlington *Nthumb* 68 NZ0288
High Hatton *Shrops* 37 SJ6124
High Hawsker *N York* 63 NZ9207
High Hesket *Cumb* 67 NY4744
High Hoyland *S York* 55 SE2710
High Hurstwood *E Susx* 13 TQ4926
High Hutton *N York* 56 SE7568
High Ireby *Cumb* 58 NY2237
High Kilburn *N York* 62 SE5179
High Lands *Dur* 61 NZ1226
High Lane *Gt Man* 48 SJ9585
High Lane *H & W* 28 SO6760
High Lanes *Cnwll* 2 SW5637
High Laver *Essex* 23 TL5208
High Legh *Ches* 47 SJ7084
High Leven *Cleve* 62 NZ4512
High Lorton *Cumb* 58 NY1625
High Marnham *Notts* 50 SK8070
High Melton *S York* 49 SE5001
High Mickley *Nthumb* 68 NZ0761
High Newport *T & W* 69 NZ3754
High Newton *Cumb* 59 SD4082
High Newton by-the-Sea *Nthumb* 77 NU2325
High Nibthwaite *Cumb* 58 SD2989
High Offley *Staffs* 37 SJ7826
High Ongar *Essex* 24 TL5603
High Onn *Staffs* 38 SJ8216
High Park Corner *Essex* 25 TM0320
High Pennyvenie *Strath* 73 NS4907
High Roding *Essex* 24 TL6017
High Salvington *W Susx* 12 TQ1206
High Spen *T & W* 69 NZ1359
High Street *Cnwll* 3 SW9653
High Street *Suffk* 33 TM4355
High Street *Kent* 15 TR0862
High Toynton *Lincs* 51 TF2869
High Trewhitt *Nthumb* 68 NU0105
High Urpeth *Dur* 69 NZ2354
High Valleyfield *Fife* 82 NT0086
High Westwood *Dur* 69 NZ1155
High Wray *Cumb* 59 SD3799
High Wych *Herts* 31 TL4614
High Wycombe *Bucks* 22 SU8693
Higham *Lancs* 54 SD8136
Higham *S York* 55 SE3107
Higham *Derbys* 49 SK3859
Higham *Suffk* 32 TL7465
Higham *Suffk* 25 TM0335
Higham *Kent* 13 TQ6048
Higham *Kent* 14 TQ7171
Higham Dykes *Nthumb* 69 NZ1375
Higham Ferrers *Nhants* 30 SP9668
Higham Gobion *Beds* 30 TL1032
Higham Hill *Gt Lon* 23 TQ3590
Higham on the Hill *Leics* 39 SP3895
Highampton *Devon* 6 SS4804
Highams Park *Gt Lon* 23 TQ3891
Highbridge *Somset* 19 ST3247
Highbrook *W Susx* 12 TQ3630
Highburton *W York* 55 SE1813
Highbury *Somset* 20 ST6949
Highbury *Gt Lon* 23 TQ3185
Highclere *Hants* 21 SU4359
Highcliffe *Dorset* 10 SZ2193
Highclifflane *Derbys* 49 SK2947
Higher Ansty *Dorset* 9 ST7604
Higher Bartle *Lancs* 53 SD5033
Higher Bockhampton *Dorset* 9 SY7292
Higher Brixham *Devon* 5 SX9155
Higher Chillington *Somset* 8 ST3810
Higher Combe *Somset* 7 SS9030
Higher Gabwell *Devon* 5 SX9169
Higher Irlam *Gt Man* 47 SJ7295
Higher Kinnerton *Clwyd* 46 SJ3261
Higher Melcombe *Dorset* 9 ST7402
Higher Muddiford *Devon* 6 SS5638
Higher Penwortham *Lancs* 53 SD5128
Higher Town *IOS* 2 SV9215
Higher Town *Cnwll* 2 SW8044
Higher Town *Cnwll* 3 SX0061
Higher Walton *Lancs* 53 SD5727
Higher Walton *Ches* 47 SJ5985
Higher Wambrook *Somset* 8 ST2908
Higher Waterston *Dorset* 9 SY7295
Higher Wheelton *Lancs* 54 SD6022
Higher Whitley *Ches* 47 SJ6180
Higher Wraxhall *Dorset* 8 ST5601
Higher Wych *Ches* 46 SJ4943
Highfield *Strath* 73 NS3150
Highfield *T & W* 69 NZ1458
Highgate *Gt Lon* 23 TQ2887
Highlane *S York* 49 SK4081
Highleadon *Gloucs* 28 SO7623
Highleigh *W Susx* 11 SZ8498
Highley *Shrops* 37 SO7483
Highmoor *Oxon* 22 SU7084
Highmoor Cross *Oxon* 22 SU7084
Highnam *Gloucs* 28 SO7817
Highnam Green *Gloucs* 28 SO7920
Highsted *Kent* 14 TQ9061
Highstreet Green *Surrey* 12 SU9835
Highstreet Green *Essex* 24 TL7634
Hightae *D & G* 67 NY0978
Hightown Green *Suffk* 32 TL9756
Highweek *Devon* 5 SX8472
Highwood Hill *Gt Lon* 23 TQ2193
Highworth *Wilts* 21 SU2092
Hilden Park *Kent* 13 TQ5747
Hildenborough *Kent* 13 TQ5648
Hildersham *Cambs* 31 TL5448
Hilderstone *Staffs* 38 SJ9534
Hilderthorpe *Humb* 57 TA1766
Hilfield *Dorset* 9 ST6305
Hilgay *Norfk* 41 TL6298
Hill *Warwks* 29 SP4566
Hill *Avon* 19 ST6495
Hill Brow *Hants* 11 SU7926
Hill Chorlton *Staffs* 37 SJ7939
Hill Common *Somset* 8 ST1426
Hill Dyke *Lincs* 51 TF3447
Hill End *Fife* 82 NT0395
Hill End *Gloucs* 28 SO9037
Hill Green *Kent* 14 TQ8362
Hill Head *Hants* 11 SU5402
Hill Ridware *Staffs* 38 SK0817
Hill Side *W York* 55 SE1717
Hill Top *W York* 55 SE3315
Hill of Beath *Fife* 82 NT1590
Hill of Fearn *Highld* 97 NH8377
Hillam *N York* 55 SE5028
Hillbutts *Dorset* 9 ST9901
Hillcott *Wilts* 20 SU1158
Hillend *Strath* 74 NS8267
Hillend *Fife* 82 NT1483
Hillend *Loth* 75 NT2566
Hillesden *Bucks* 30 SP6828
Hillesley *Avon* 20 ST7689
Hillfarrance *Somset* 8 ST1624
Hillfoot *Strath* 74 NS5472
Hillhead *Strath* 75 NS9840
Hillhead of Cocklaw *Gramp* 95 NK0844
Hillhead of Durno *Gramp* 95 NJ7128
Hilliclay *Highld* 100 ND1764
Hillingdon *Gt Lon* 22 TQ0782
Hillington *Strath* 74 NS5164
Hillington *Norfk* 42 TF7225
Hillmorton *Warwks* 39 SP5373
Hillowtan *D & G* 66 NX7763
Hills Town *Derbys* 49 SK4869
Hillside *T & W* 89 NO6960
Hillside *Gramp* 89 NO9197
Hillstreet *Hants* 10 SU3416
Hillswick *Shet* 103 HU2877
Hilltown *Devon* 4 SX5380
Hillwell *Shet* 103 HU3714
Hilmarton *Wilts* 20 SU0175
Hilperton *Wilts* 20 ST8759
Hilsea *Hants* 11 SU6503
Hilston *Humb* 57 TA2833
Hilton *Border* 77 NT8750
Hilton *Cumb* 60 NY7320
Hilton *Dur* 61 NZ1622
Hilton *Cleve* 62 NZ4611
Hilton *Derbys* 39 SK2430
Hilton *Shrops* 37 SO7795
Hilton *Dorset* 9 ST7802
Hilton *Cambs* 31 TL2966
Hilton of Cadboll *Highld* 97 NH8776
Himbleton *H & W* 28 SO9458
Himley *Staffs* 38 SO8891
Hincaster *Cumb* 59 SD5084
Hinckley *Leics* 39 SP4294
Hinderclay *Suffk* 32 TM0276
Hinderwell *N York* 63 NZ7916
Hindhead *Surrey* 11 SU8835
Hindley *Gt Man* 47 SD6104
Hindlip *H & W* 28 SO8858
Hindolveston *Norfk* 42 TG0329
Hindon *Wilts* 9 ST9132
Hindringham *Norfk* 42 TF9836
Hingham *Norfk* 42 TG0202
Hinnington *Shrops* 37 SJ7404
Hinstock *Shrops* 37 SJ6925
Hintlesham *Suffk* 32 TM0843
Hinton *Shrops* 36 SJ4008
Hinton *H & W* 27 SO3338
Hinton *Avon* 20 ST7376
Hinton Ampner *Hants* 11 SU6027
Hinton Blewett *Somset* 19 ST5956
Hinton Charterhouse *Avon* 20 ST7758
Hinton Martell *Dorset* 9 SU0106
Hinton Parva *Wilts* 21 SU2383
Hinton St. George *Somset* 8 ST4212
Hinton St. Mary *Dorset* 9 ST7816
Hinton Waldrist *Oxon* 21 SU3799
Hinton on the Green *H & W* 28 SP0240
Hinton-in-the-Hedges *Nhants* 29 SP5636
Hints *Staffs* 38 SK1502
Hinwick *Beds* 30 SP9361
Hinxhill *Kent* 15 TR0442
Hinxton *Cambs* 31 TL4945
Hinxworth *Herts* 31 TL2340
Hipperholme *W York* 55 SE1225
Hipswell *N York* 61 SE1898
Hirn *Gramp* 89 NJ7200
Hirnant *Powys* 36 SJ0422
Hirst *Nthumb* 69 NZ2787
Hirst Courtney *N York* 56 SE6124
Hirwaun *M Glam* 26 SN9505
Hiscott *Devon* 6 SS5426
Histon *Cambs* 31 TL4463
Hitcham *Suffk* 32 TL9851
Hitcham Causeway *Suffk* 32 TL9852
Hitcham Street *Suffk* 32 TL9851
Hitchin *Herts* 31 TL1829
Hither Green *Gt Lon* 23 TQ3874
Hittisleigh *Devon* 7 SX7395
Hive *Humb* 56 SE8230
Hixon *Staffs* 38 SK0025
Hoaden *Kent* 15 TR2759
Hoar Cross *Staffs* 38 SK1323
Hoarwithy *H & W* 27 SO5429
Hoath *Kent* 15 TR2064
Hobarris *Shrops* 36 SO3178
Hobkirk *Border* 67 NT5811
Hobson *Dur* 69 NZ1756
Hoby *Leics* 39 SK6617
Hockering *Norfk* 42 TG0713
Hockerton *Notts* 49 SK7156
Hockley *Essex* 24 TQ8392
Hockley Heath *W Mids* 38 SP1572
Hockliffe *Beds* 30 SP9726
Hockwold cum Wilton *Norfk* 32 TL7388
Hockworthy *Devon* 7 ST0319
Hoddesdon *Herts* 23 TL3708
Hoddlesden *Lancs* 54 SD7122
Hoddom Cross *D & G* 67 NY1873
Hoddom Mains *D & G* 67 NY1572
Hodgeston *Dyfed* 16 SS0399
Hodnet *Shrops* 37 SJ6128
Hodsall Street *Kent* 14 TQ6263
Hodsock *Notts* 49 SK6185
Hodson *Wilts* 21 SU1780
Hodthorpe *Derbys* 49 SK5376
Hoe *Norfk* 42 TF9916
Hogben's Hill *Kent* 15 TR0356
Hoggeston *Bucks* 30 SP8024
Hoghton *Lancs* 54 SD6125
Hognaston *Derbys* 48 SK2350
Hogrill's End *Warwks* 39 SP2292
Hogsthorpe *Lincs* 51 TF5372
Holbeach *Lincs* 41 TF3624
Holbeach Drove *Lincs* 41 TF3212
Holbeach Hurn *Lincs* 41 TF3926
Holbeach St. Johns *Lincs* 41 TF3518
Holbeach St. Mark's *Lincs* 41 TF3731
Holbeach St. Matthew *Lincs* 41 TF4132
Holbeck *Notts* 49 SK5473
Holberrow Green *H & W* 28 SP0259
Holbeton *Devon* 5 SX6150
Holborn *Gt Lon* 23 TQ3181
Holbrook *Derbys* 49 SK3644
Holbrook *Suffk* 25 TM1636
Holbrook Moor *Derbys* 49 SK3645
Holbury *Hants* 10 SU4303
Holcombe *Somset* 20 ST6749
Holcombe *Devon* 5 SX9574
Holcombe Rogus *Devon* 7 ST0518
Holcot *Nhants* 30 SP7969
Holden *Lancs* 54 SD7749
Holden *Lancs* 54 SD8833
Holdenby *Nhants* 30 SP6967
Holder's Green *Essex* 24 TL6328
Holdgate *Shrops* 37 SO5689
Holdingham *Lincs* 50 TF0547
Holditch *Dorset* 8 ST3402
Hole *Devon* 6 SS4206
Holford *Somset* 19 ST1541
Holgate *N York* 56 SE5851
Holker *Cumb* 59 SD3676
Holkham *Norfk* 42 TF8943
Holkham *Norfk* 42 TF8943
Hollacombe *Devon* 6 SS3702

Holland Fen Ingham

Holland Fen *Lincs* 51 TF2349
Holland-on-Sea *Essex* 25 TM1916
Hollandstoun *Ork* 103 HY7553
Hollesley *Suffk* 33 TM3544
Hollicombe *Devon* 5 SX8962
Hollingbourne *Kent* 14 TQ8455
Hollingdon *Bucks* 30 SP8727
Hollington *Staffs* 48 SK0538
Hollington *Derbys* 48 SK2239
Hollingworth *Gt Man* 48 SK0096
Hollins Green *Ches* 47 SJ6990
Hollinsclough *Staffs* 48 SK0666
Hollocombe *Devon* 7 SS6311
Holloway *Derbys* 49 SK3256
Holloway *Gt Lon* 23 TQ3086
Hollowell *Nhants* 30 SP6971
Hollowmoor Heath *Ches* 46 SJ4868
Holly Green *H & W* 28 SO8641
Hollybush *Strath* 73 NS3915
Hollybush *Gwent* 19 SO1603
Hollybush *H & W* 28 SO7536
Hollym *Humb* 57 TA3425
Holmbridge *W York* 55 SE1206
Holmbury St. Mary *Surrey* 12 TQ1143
Holmbush *Cnwll* 3 SX0352
Holmcroft *Staffs* 38 SJ9024
Holme *Cumb* 59 SD5278
Holme *W York* 55 SE1105
Holme *N York* 62 SE3582
Holme *Notts* 50 SK8059
Holme *Cambs* 40 TL1987
Holme Chapel *Lancs* 54 SD8728
Holme Green *N York* 56 SE5541
Holme Hale *Norfk* 42 TF8807
Holme Lacy *H & W* 27 SO5535
Holme Marsh *H & W* 27 SO3454
Holme Pierrepont *Notts* 49 SK6238
Holme St. Cuthbert *Cumb* 67 NY1047
Holme next the Sea *Norfk* 42 TF7043
Holme on the Wolds *Humb* 56 SE9646
Holme upon Spalding Moor *Humb* 56 SE8038
Holmer *H & W* 27 SO5042
Holmer Green *Bucks* 22 SU9097
Holmes Chapel *Ches* 47 SJ7667
Holmesfield *Derbys* 49 SK3277
Holmeswood *Lancs* 53 SD4316
Holmethorpe *Surrey* 12 TQ2851
Holmewood *Derbys* 49 SK4365
Holmfirth *W York* 55 SE1408
Holmhead *Strath* 74 NS5620
Holmpton *Humb* 57 TA3623
Holmrook *Cumb* 58 SD0799
Holmwood *Surrey* 12 TQ1647
Holne *Devon* 5 SX7069
Holnest *Dorset* 9 ST6510
Holnicote *Somset* 7 SS9146
Holsworthy *Devon* 6 SS3403
Holsworthy Beacon *Devon* 6 SS3608
Holt *Clwyd* 46 SJ4053
Holt *H & W* 28 SO8362
Holt *Wilts* 20 ST8661
Holt *Dorset* 9 SU0303
Holt *Norfk* 42 TG0838
Holt End *H & W* 28 SP0769
Holt Heath *H & W* 28 SO8163
Holtby *N York* 56 SE6754
Holton *Oxon* 29 SP6006
Holton *Somset* 9 ST6826
Holton *Suffk* 33 TM4077
Holton St. Mary *Suffk* 25 TM0536
Holton cum Beckering *Lincs* 50 TF1181
Holton le Clay *Lincs* 51 TA2802
Holton le Moor *Lincs* 50 TF0897
Holwell *Leics* 40 SK7323
Holwell *Oxon* 29 SP2309
Holwell *Dorset* 9 ST6911
Holwell *Herts* 31 TL1633
Holwick *Dur* 60 NY9126
Holy Island *Nthumb* 77 NU1241
Holybourne *Hants* 11 SU7340
Holyhead *Gwynd* 44 SH2482
Holylee *Border* 76 NT3937
Holymoorside *Derbys* 49 SK3369
Holyport *Berks* 22 SU8977
Holystone *Nthumb* 68 NT9502
Holytown *Strath* 74 NS7660
Holywell *Clwyd* 46 SJ1875
Holywell *Dorset* 9 ST5904
Holywell *Cnwll* 2 SW7659
Holywell *Cambs* 31 TL3370
Holywell Green *W York* 55 SE0819
Holywell Lake *Somset* 8 ST1020
Holywell Row *Suffk* 32 TL7177
Holywood *D & G* 66 NX9480
Homer *Shrops* 37 SJ6101
Homer Green *Mersyd* 46 SD3402
Homersfield *Suffk* 33 TM2885
Homington *Wilts* 10 SU1226
Honey Tye *Suffk* 25 TL9535
Honeybourne *H & W* 28 SP1144
Honeychurch *Devon* 7 SS6303
Honeystreet *Wilts* 20 SU1061
Honiley *Warwks* 39 SP2372
Honing *Norfk* 43 TG3227
Honingham *Norfk* 43 TG1011
Honington *Lincs* 50 SK9443
Honington *Warwks* 29 SP2642
Honington *Suffk* 32 TL9174
Honiton *Devon* 8 ST1600
Honley *W York* 55 SE1311
Hoo *Kent* 14 TQ7872
Hoo End *Herts* 31 TL1820
Hoo Green *Ches* 47 SJ7182
Hooe *Devon* 4 SX5052
Hooe *E Susx* 14 TQ6809
Hooe Common *E Susx* 14 TQ6910
Hoohill *Lancs* 53 SD3237
Hook *Humb* 56 SE7625
Hook *Dyfed* 16 SM9711
Hook *Wilts* 20 SU0784
Hook *Hants* 22 SU7254
Hook *Surrey* 23 TQ1864
Hook *Kent* 14 TQ6170
Hook Green *Kent* 13 TQ6535
Hook Norton *Oxon* 29 SP3533
Hooke *Dorset* 8 ST5300
Hookway *Devon* 7 SX8598
Hooton Levitt *S York* 49 SK5291
Hooton Pagnell *S York* 55 SE4807
Hooton Roberts *S York* 49 SK4897
Hope *Clwyd* 46 SJ3058
Hope *Staffs* 48 SK1254
Hope *Derbys* 48 SK1783
Hope *Shrops* 37 SO5974
Hope *Devon* 5 SX6740
Hope Bowdler *Shrops* 37 SO4792
Hope End Green *Essex* 24 TL5720
Hope Mansell *H & W* 27 SO6219
Hope under Dinmore *H & W* 27 SO5052
Hopehouse *Border* 75 NT2916
Hopeman *Gramp* 93 NJ1469
Hopesay *Shrops* 36 SO3983
Hopperton *N York* 55 SE4256
Hopstone *Shrops* 37 SO7894
Hopton *Staffs* 38 SJ9426
Hopton *Derbys* 49 SK2653
Hopton *Suffk* 32 TL9979
Hopton Cangeford *Shrops* 37 SO5480
Hopton Castle *Shrops* 36 SO3678
Hopton Wafers *Shrops* 37 SO6376
Hopton on Sea *Norfk* 43 TM5299
Hoptonheath *Shrops* 36 SO3877
Hopwas *Staffs* 38 SK1804
Hopwas *Staffs* 38 SK1804
Hopwood *H & W* 38 SP0375
Horam *E Susx* 13 TQ5717
Horbling *Lincs* 40 TF1135
Horbury *W York* 55 SE2918
Hordle *Hants* 10 SZ2795
Hordley *Shrops* 36 SJ3831
Horfield *Avon* 19 ST5976
Horham *Suffk* 33 TM2072
Horkesley Heath *Essex* 25 TL9829
Horkstow *Humb* 56 SE9817
Horley *Oxon* 29 SP4144
Horley *Surrey* 12 TQ2842
Hornblotton Green *Somset* 9 ST5833
Hornby *N York* 62 NZ3605
Hornby *Lancs* 54 SD5868
Hornby *N York* 61 SE2293
Horncastle *Lincs* 51 TF2669
Hornchurch *Gt Lon* 23 TQ5387
Horncliffe *Nthumb* 77 NT9249
Horndean *Border* 77 NT9049
Horndean *Hants* 11 SU7013
Horndon *Devon* 4 SX5280
Horndon on the Hill *Essex* 24 TQ6683
Horne *Surrey* 12 TQ3344
Horne *Surrey* 12 TQ3344
Horner *Somset* 7 SS9045
Horning *Norfk* 43 TG3417
Horninghold *Leics* 40 SP8097
Horninglow *Staffs* 39 SK2425
Horningsea *Cambs* 31 TL4962
Horningsham *Wilts* 20 ST8141
Horningtoft *Norfk* 42 TF9323
Horns Cross *Devon* 6 SS3823
Hornsea *Humb* 57 TA1947
Hornsey *Gt Lon* 23 TQ3089
Hornton *Oxon* 29 SP3945
Horra *Shet* 103 HU4693
Horrabridge *Devon* 4 SX5169
Horridge *Devon* 5 SX7674
Horringer *Suffk* 32 TL8261
Horrocksford *Lancs* 54 SD7543
Horsebridge *Shrops* 36 SJ3606
Horsebridge *Hants* 10 SU3430
Horsebridge *Devon* 4 SX4075
Horsebridge *E Susx* 13 TQ5811
Horseheath *Cambs* 31 TL6147
Horsehouse *N York* 61 SE0480
Horsell *Surrey* 22 SU9959
Horseman's Green *Clwyd* 36 SJ4441
Horsenden *Bucks* 22 SP7902
Horseshoes *Wilts* 20 ST9159
Horsey *Somset* 19 ST3239
Horsey *Norfk* 43 TG4622
Horsford *Norfk* 43 TG1916
Horsforth *W York* 55 SE2338
Horsham *H & W* 28 SO7358
Horsham *W Susx* 12 TQ1731
Horsham St. Faith *Norfk* 43 TG2115
Horsington *Somset* 9 ST7023
Horsington *Lincs* 50 TF1968
Horsley *Nthumb* 68 NY8496
Horsley *Nthumb* 68 NZ0965
Horsley *Derbys* 49 SK3744
Horsley *Gloucs* 20 ST8497
Horsley Woodhouse *Derbys* 49 SK3944
Horsleycross Street *Essex* 25 TM1228
Horsleyhill *Border* 76 NT5319
Horsmonden *Kent* 14 TQ7040
Horspath *Oxon* 29 SP5705
Horstead *Norfk* 43 TG2619
Horsted Keynes *W Susx* 13 TQ3828
Horton *Lancs* 54 SD8550
Horton *Shrops* 37 SJ6814
Horton *Staffs* 48 SJ9457
Horton *Nhants* 30 SP8154
Horton *Bucks* 30 SP9219
Horton *W Glam* 17 SS4785
Horton *Somset* 8 ST3214
Horton *Avon* 20 ST7584
Horton *Dorset* 9 SU0307
Horton *Wilts* 20 SU0463
Horton *Berks* 22 TQ0175
Horton Green *Ches* 46 SJ4549
Horton Kirby *Kent* 14 TQ5668
Horton in Ribblesdale *N York* 54 SD8071
Horton-cum-Studley *Oxon* 29 SP5912
Horwich *Gt Man* 54 SD6311
Horwood *Devon* 6 SS5027
Hoscote *Border* 67 NT3911
Hose *Leics* 40 SK7329
Hosh *Tays* 82 NN8523
Hoswick *Shet* 103 HU4123
Hotham *Humb* 56 SE8934
Hothfield *Kent* 15 TQ9644
Hoton *Leics* 39 SK5722
Hott *Nthumb* 68 NY7785
Houdston *Strath* 64 NX2097
Hough *Ches* 47 SJ7151
Hough Green *Ches* 46 SJ4886
Hough-on-the-Hill *Lincs* 50 SK9246
Hougham *Lincs* 50 SK8844
Houghton *Dyfed* 16 SM9807
Houghton *Hants* 10 SU3432
Houghton *Cambs* 31 TL2872
Houghton *W Susx* 12 TQ0111
Houghton Conquest *Beds* 30 TL0441
Houghton Green *E Susx* 14 TQ9222
Houghton Regis *Beds* 30 TL0123
Houghton St. Giles *Norfk* 42 TF9235
Houghton le Spring *T & W* 69 NZ3449
Houghton on the Hill *Leics* 39 SK6703
Hound Green *Hants* 22 SU7359
Houndslow *Border* 76 NT6347
Houndwood *Border* 77 NT8463
Hounslow *Gt Lon* 22 TQ1375
Hounslow Green *Essex* 24 TL6518
Househill *Highld* 93 NH8855
Houses Hill *W York* 55 SE1916
Housieside *Gramp* 95 NJ8926
Houston *Strath* 73 NS4066
Houstry *Highld* 100 ND1534
Houton *Ork* 103 HY3104
Hove *E Susx* 12 TQ2804
Hoveringham *Notts* 49 SK6946
Hoveton *Norfk* 43 TG3018
Hovingham *N York* 62 SE6675
How *Cumb* 67 NY5056
How Caple *H & W* 27 SO6030
Howden *Humb* 56 SE7428
Howden-le-Wear *Dur* 61 NZ1633
Howe *Highld* 100 ND3061
Howe *N York* 62 SE3580
Howe *Norfk* 43 TM2799
Howe Green *Essex* 24 TL7403
Howe Street *Essex* 24 TL6914
Howe Street *Essex* 24 TL6934
Howe of Teuchar *Gramp* 95 NJ7946
Howegreen *Essex* 24 TL8301
Howell *Lincs* 50 TF1346
Howes *D & G* 67 NY1866
Howey *Powys* 26 SO0558
Howgate *Loth* 75 NT2457
Howick *Nthumb* 77 NU2417
Howle *Dur* 61 NZ0926
Howle *Shrops* 37 SJ6923
Howle Hill *H & W* 27 SO6020
Howlett End *Essex* 24 TL5834
Howley *Somset* 8 ST2609
Howmore *W Isls* 102 NF7536
Hownam *Border* 76 NT7719
Howsham *N York* 56 SE7362
Howsham *Humb* 57 TA0404
Howtel *Nthumb* 77 NT8934
Howwood *Strath* 73 NS3960
Hoxne *Suffk* 33 TM1777
Hoylake *Mersyd* 46 SJ2189
Hoyland Nether *S York* 49 SE3700
Hoyland Swaine *S York* 55 SE2604
Huby *N York* 55 SE2747
Huby *N York* 56 SE5665
Hucclecote *Gloucs* 28 SO8717
Hucking *Kent* 14 TQ8458
Hucknall *Notts* 49 SK5349
Huddersfield *W York* 55 SE1416
Huddington *H & W* 28 SO9457
Hudswell *N York* 61 NZ1400
Huggate *Humb* 56 SE8855
Hugh Town *IOS* 2 SV9010
Hughenden Valley *Bucks* 22 SU8697
Hughley *Shrops* 37 SO5698
Huish *Devon* 6 SS5311
Huish *Wilts* 20 SU1463
Huish Champflower *Somset* 7 ST0529
Huish Episcopi *Somset* 8 ST4326
Hulcott *Bucks* 30 SP8516
Hulland *Derbys* 48 SK2446
Hulland Ward *Derbys* 48 SK2546
Hullavington *Wilts* 20 ST8981
Hullbridge *Essex* 24 TQ8095
Hulme *Gt Man* 47 SJ8396
Hulme *Staffs* 48 SJ9345
Hulme End *Staffs* 48 SK1059
Hulme Walfield *Ches* 47 SJ8465
Hulver Street *Suffk* 33 TM4686
Hulverstone *IOW* 10 SZ3984
Humberston *Humb* 57 TA3105
Humberstone *Leics* 39 SK6305
Humbie *Loth* 76 NT4662
Humbleton *Humb* 57 TA2234
Humby *Lincs* 40 TF0032
Hume *Border* 76 NT7041
Humshaugh *Nthumb* 68 NY9171
Huna *Highld* 100 ND3573
Huncote *Leics* 39 SP5197
Hundalee *Border* 76 NT6418
Hunderthwaite *Dur* 61 NY9821
Hundleby *Lincs* 51 TF3966
Hundleton *Dyfed* 16 SM9600
Hundon *Suffk* 32 TL7348
Hundred End *Lancs* 53 SD4122
Hungarton *Leics* 40 SK6907
Hungerford *Somset* 7 ST0440
Hungerford *Berks* 21 SU3368
Hungerford Newtown *Berks* 21 SU3571
Hungerstone *H & W* 27 SO4435
Hunmanby *N York* 63 TA0977
Hunningham *Warwks* 29 SP3767
Hunsdon *Herts* 31 TL4114
Hunsingore *N York* 55 SE4253
Hunslet *W York* 55 SE3130
Hunsonby *Cumb* 59 NY5835
Hunstanton *Norfk* 42 TF6740
Hunstanworth *Dur* 68 NY9448
Hunston *W Susx* 11 SU8601
Hunston *Suffk* 32 TL9768
Hunstrete *Avon* 19 ST6462
Hunsworth *W York* 55 SE1827
Hunters Quay *Strath* 80 NS1879
Hunterston *Ches* 47 SJ6946
Huntham *Somset* 8 ST3426
Hunthill Lodge *Tays* 89 NO4771
Huntingdon *H & W* 27 SO2553
Huntingdon *Cambs* 31 TL2471
Huntingfield *Suffk* 33 TM3374
Huntington *Loth* 76 NT4874
Huntington *N York* 56 SE6156
Huntington *Staffs* 38 SJ9712
Huntingtower *Tays* 82 NO0724
Huntley *Gloucs* 28 SO7219
Huntly *Gramp* 94 NJ5339
Hunton *N York* 61 SE1892
Hunton *Hants* 21 SU4840
Hunton *Kent* 14 TQ7149
Huntscott *Somset* 7 SS9144
Huntsham *Devon* 7 ST0020
Huntshaw *Devon* 6 SS5023
Huntspill *Somset* 19 ST3145
Huntstile *Somset* 8 ST2633
Huntworth *Somset* 8 ST3134
Hunwick *Dur* 61 NZ1832
Hunworth *Norfk* 42 TG0635
Hurdcott *Wilts* 10 SU1733
Hurdsfield *Ches* 48 SJ9274
Hurley *Warwks* 39 SP2495
Hurley *Berks* 22 SU8283
Hurley Common *Warwks* 39 SP2496
Hurlford *Strath* 73 NS4536
Hurn *Dorset* 10 SZ1296
Hursley *Hants* 10 SU4225
Hurst *Berks* 22 SU7973
Hurst Green *Lancs* 54 SD6838
Hurst Green *Surrey* 13 TQ3951
Hurst Green *E Susx* 14 TQ7327
Hurstbourne Priors *Hants* 21 SU4346
Hurstbourne Tarrant *Hants* 21 SU3853
Hurstley *H & W* 27 SO3548
Hurstpierpoint *W Susx* 12 TQ2716
Hurstwood *Lancs* 54 SD8831
Hurtiso *Ork* 103 HY5001
Hurworth-on-Tees *Dur* 61 NZ3009
Husbands Bosworth *Leics* 39 SP6484
Husborne Crawley *Beds* 30 SP9635
Husthwaite *N York* 62 SE5175
Huthwaite *Notts* 49 SK4659
Huttoft *Lincs* 51 TF5176
Hutton *Border* 77 NT9053
Hutton *Lancs* 53 SD4926
Hutton *Avon* 19 ST3558
Hutton *Humb* 56 TA0253
Hutton *Essex* 24 TQ6395
Hutton Bonville *N York* 62 NZ3300
Hutton Buscel *N York* 63 SE9784
Hutton Conyers *N York* 62 SE3273
Hutton Cranswick *Humb* 56 TA0252
Hutton End *Cumb* 59 NY4538
Hutton Henry *Dur* 62 NZ4236
Hutton Lowcross *Cleve* 62 NZ5914
Hutton Magna *Dur* 61 NZ1212
Hutton Roof *Cumb* 59 NY3734
Hutton Roof *Cumb* 59 SD5677
Hutton Rudby *N York* 62 NZ4606
Hutton Sessay *N York* 62 SE4776
Hutton Wandesley *N York* 55 SE5050
Hutton-le-Hole *N York* 62 SE7090
Huxham *Devon* 7 SX9497
Huxley *Ches* 46 SJ5061
Huyton *Mersyd* 46 SJ4490
Hycemoor *Cumb* 58 SD0989
Hyde *Gt Man* 48 SJ9494
Hyde Heath *Bucks* 22 SP9300
Hyde Lea *Staffs* 38 SJ9120
Hynish *Strath* 78 NL9839
Hyssington *Powys* 36 SO3194
Hythe *Hants* 10 SU4207
Hythe *Kent* 15 TR1634
Hythe End *Berks* 22 TQ0172

I

Ibberton *Dorset* 9 ST7807
Ible *Derbys* 48 SK2457
Ibsley *Hants* 10 SU1509
Ibstock *Leics* 39 SK4009
Ibstone *Bucks* 22 SU7593
Ibthorpe *Hants* 21 SU3753
Iburndale *N York* 63 NZ8707
Ibworth *Hants* 21 SU5654
Ickburgh *Norfk* 42 TL8195
Ickenham *Gt Lon* 22 TQ0786
Ickford *Bucks* 29 SP6407
Ickham *Kent* 15 TR2258
Ickleford *Herts* 31 TL1831
Icklesham *E Susx* 14 TQ8716
Ickleton *Cambs* 31 TL4943
Icklingham *Suffk* 32 TL7772
Ickornshaw *N York* 54 SD9642
Ickwell Green *Beds* 30 TL1545
Icomb *Gloucs* 29 SP2122
Idbury *Oxon* 29 SP2319
Iddesleigh *Devon* 6 SS5708
Ide *Devon* 5 SX8990
Ide Hill *Kent* 13 TQ4851
Ideford *Devon* 5 SX8977
Iden *E Susx* 14 TQ9123
Iden Green *Kent* 14 TQ7437
Iden Green *Kent* 14 TQ8031
Idle *W York* 55 SE1737
Idless *Cnwll* 2 SW8147
Idlicote *Warwks* 29 SP2844
Idmiston *Wilts* 10 SU1937
Idridgehay *Derbys* 49 SK2849
Idrigill *Highld* 90 NG3863
Idstone *Oxon* 21 SU2584
Idvies *Tays* 89 NO5347
Iffley *Oxon* 21 SP5203
Ifield *W Susx* 12 TQ2537
Iford *Dorset* 10 SZ1393
Iford *E Susx* 13 TQ4007
Ifton *Gwent* 19 ST4688
Ightham *Kent* 14 TQ5956
Ightfield *Shrops* 37 SJ5938
Iken *Suffk* 33 TM4155
Ilam *Staffs* 48 SK1350
Ilchester *Somset* 8 ST5222
Ilderton *Nthumb* 77 NU0121
Ilford *Somset* 8 ST3617
Ilford *Gt Lon* 23 TQ4486
Ilfracombe *Devon* 6 SS5247
Ilkeston *Derbys* 49 SK4641
Ilketshall St. Andrew *Suffk* 33 TM3887
Ilketshall St. Margaret *Suffk* 33 TM3485
Ilkley *W York* 55 SE1147
Illand *Cnwll* 4 SX2878
Illey *W Mids* 38 SO9881
Illogan *Cnwll* 2 SW6743
Illston on the Hill *Leics* 40 SP7099
Ilmer *Bucks* 22 SP7605
Ilmington *Warwks* 29 SP2143
Ilminster *Somset* 8 ST3614
Ilsington *Devon* 5 SX7875
Ilston *W Glam* 17 SS5590
Ilton *N York* 61 SE1978
Ilton *Somset* 8 ST3517
Imachar *Strath* 72 NR8640
Immingham *Humb* 57 TA1814
Immingham Dock *Humb* 57 TA1916
Ince *Ches* 46 SJ4576
Ince Blundell *Mersyd* 46 SD3203
Ince-in-Makerfield *Gt Man* 47 SD5904
Inchbae Lodge *Highld* 92 NH4069
Inchbare *Tays* 89 NO6065
Inchberry *Gramp* 94 NJ3055
Inchinnan *Strath* 73 NS4868
Inchlaggan *Highld* 86 NH1701
Inchmagranachan *Tays* 88 NN9944
Inchmichael *Tays* 83 NO2425
Inchnacardoch Hotel *Highld* 92 NH3810
Inchnadamph *Highld* 96 NC2521
Inchture *Tays* 83 NO2728
Inchvuilt *Highld* 92 NH2438
Inchyra *Tays* 82 NO1820
Indian Queens *Cnwll* 3 SW9159
Ingatestone *Essex* 24 TQ6499
Ingbirchworth *S York* 55 SE2205
Ingestre *Staffs* 38 SJ9724
Ingham *Lincs* 50 SK9483
Ingham *Norfk* 43 TG3926

Ingham King's Lynn

Ingham *Suffk* 32 TL8570
Ingham Corner *Norfk* 43 TG3927
Ingleby *Derbys* 39 SK3426
Ingleby Arncliffe *N York* 62 NZ4400
Ingleby Barwick *Cleve* 62 NZ4513
Ingleby Greenhow *N York* 62 NZ5706
Ingleigh Green *Devon* 6 SS6007
Inglesbatch *Avon* 20 ST7061
Inglesham *Wilts* 21 SU2098
Ingleston *D & G* 65 NX6048
Ingleston *D & G* 66 NX9865
Ingleton *Dur* 61 NZ1720
Ingleton *N York* 54 SD6972
Inglewhite *Lancs* 53 SD5439
Ingliston *Tays* 88 NO4248
Ingoe *Nthumb* 68 NZ0374
Ingoldisthorpe *Norfk* 42 TF6832
Ingoldmells *Lincs* 51 TF5668
Ingoldsby *Lincs* 40 TF0129
Ingon *Warwks* 29 SP2157
Ingram *Nthumb* 77 NU0115
Ingrow *W York* 55 SE0539
Ingst *Avon* 19 ST5887
Ingthorpe *Leics* 40 SK9908
Ingworth *Norfk* 43 TG1929
Inkberrow *H & W* 28 SP0157
Inkhorn *Gramp* 95 NJ9239
Inkpen *Berks* 21 SU3664
Inkstack *Highld* 100 ND2570
Innellan *Strath* 73 NS1570
Innerleithen *Border* 75 NT3336
Innerleven *Fife* 83 NO3700
Innermessan *D & G* 64 NX0862
Innerwick *Loth* 76 NT7273
Innesmill *Gramp* 94 NJ2863
Insch *Gramp* 94 NJ6228
Insh *Highld* 87 NH8101
Inskip *Lancs* 53 SD4637
Instow *Devon* 6 SS4730
Intake *S York* 49 SK3884
Inver *Highld* 97 NH8682
Inver *Tays* 88 NO0142
Inver *Gramp* 88 NO2293
Inver-boyndie *Gramp* 94 NJ6664
Inverailort *Highld* 85 NM7681
Inveralligin *Highld* 91 NG8457
Inverallochy *Gramp* 95 NK0365
Inveran *Highld* 96 NH5797
Inveraray *Strath* 80 NN0908
Inverarish *Highld* 84 NG5535
Inverarity *Tays* 88 NO4544
Inverarnan *Cent* 80 NN3118
Inveravon *Cent* 82 NS9579
Inverawe *Strath* 80 NN0231
Inverbervie *Gramp* 89 NO8272
Inverbroom *Highld* 96 NH1883
Inverchaolain *Strath* 80 NS0975
Invercreran House Hotel *Strath* 86 NN0146
Inverdruie *Highld* 93 NH8911
Inveresk *Loth* 75 NT3471
Inveresragan *Strath* 80 NM9835
Inverey *Gramp* 88 NO0889
Inverfarigaig *Highld* 92 NH5123
Inverfolia *Strath* 86 NM9544
Invergarry *Highld* 86 NH3001
Invergeldie *Tays* 81 NN7327
Invergloy *Highld* 86 NN2288
Invergordon *Highld* 93 NH7068
Invergowrie *Tays* 83 NO3430
Inverguseran *Highld* 85 NG7407
Inverhadden *Tays* 87 NN6757
Inverherive Hotel *Cent* 80 NN3626
Inverie *Highld* 85 NG7600
Inverinan *Strath* 80 NM9917
Inverinate *Highld* 85 NG9221
Inverkeilor *Tays* 89 NO6649
Inverkeithing *Fife* 82 NT1383
Inverkeithny *Gramp* 94 NJ6247
Inverkip *Strath* 80 NS2072
Inverkirkaig *Highld* 98 NC0719
Inverlael *Highld* 96 NH1885
Inverlair *Highld* 86 NN3479
Inverliever Lodge *Strath* 79 NM8905
Inverlochlarig *Cent* 81 NN4318
Inverlochy *Strath* 80 NN1927
Invermarkie *Gramp* 94 NJ4239
Invermoriston *Highld* 92 NH4216
Inverneg *Strath* 80 NS3497
Inverness *Highld* 93 NH6645
Invernoaden *Strath* 80 NS1297
Inveroran Hotel *Strath* 86 NN2741
Inverquharity *Tays* 88 NO4057
Inverquhomery *Gramp* 95 NK0146
Inverroy *Highld* 86 NN2581
Inversanda *Highld* 86 NM9459
Invershiel *Highld* 85 NG9319
Invershin *Highld* 96 NH5796
Invershore *Highld* 100 ND2435
Inversnaid Hotel *Cent* 80 NN3308
Inverugie *Gramp* 95 NK0948
Inveruglas *Strath* 80 NN3109
Inveruglass *Highld* 87 NH8000
Inverurie *Gramp* 95 NJ7721
Inwardleigh *Devon* 6 SX5699
Inworth *Essex* 24 TL8717
Iping *W Susx* 11 SU8522
Ipplepen *Devon* 5 SX8366
Ipsden *Oxon* 21 SU6285
Ipstones *Staffs* 48 SK0149
Ipswich *Suffk* 33 TM1644
Irby *Mersyd* 46 SJ2584
Irby in the Marsh *Lincs* 51 TF4663
Irby upon Humber *Humb* 57 TA1904
Irchester *Nhants* 30 SP9265
Ireby *Cumb* 58 NY2338
Ireby *Lancs* 60 SD6575
Ireland *Beds* 30 TL1341
Ireleth *Cumb* 58 SD2277
Ireshopeburn *Dur* 60 NY8638
Ireton Wood *Derbys* 49 SK2847
Irlam *Gt Man* 47 SJ7294
Irnham *Lincs* 40 TF0226
Iron Acton *Avon* 20 ST6783
Ironbridge *Shrops* 37 SJ6703
Ironmacannie *D & G* 65 NX6675
Ironville *Derbys* 49 SK4351
Irstead *Norfk* 43 TG3620
Irthington *Cumb* 67 NY4961
Irthlingborough *Nhants* 30 SP9470
Irton *N York* 63 TA0184
Irvine *Strath* 73 NS3238
Isbister *Shet* 103 HU3790
Isfield *E Susx* 13 TQ4417
Isham *Nhants* 30 SP8873
Isington *Hants* 11 SU7842
Isle Abbotts *Somset* 8 ST3520
Isle Brewers *Somset* 8 ST3621
Isle of Whithorn *D & G* 65 NX4736
Isleham *Cambs* 32 TL6474
Isleornsay *Highld* 85 NG7012
Islesteps *D & G* 66 NX9672
Islet Village *Guern* 101 GN0000
Isley Walton *Leics* 39 SK4224
Islington *Gt Lon* 23 TQ3184
Islip *Oxon* 29 SP5214
Islip *Nhants* 40 SP9879
Islivig *W Isls* 102 NB0029
Isombridge *Shrops* 37 SJ6113
Itchen Abbas *Hants* 11 SU5333
Itchen Stoke *Hants* 11 SU5532
Itchingfield *W Susx* 12 TQ1328
Itteringham *Norfk* 43 TG1430
Itton *Gwent* 19 ST4995
Itton *Devon* 7 SX6899
Ivegill *Cumb* 67 NY4143
Iver *Bucks* 22 TQ0381
Iver Heath *Bucks* 22 TQ0283
Iveston *Dur* 69 NZ1350
Ivinghoe *Bucks* 30 SP9416
Ivinghoe Aston *Bucks* 30 SP9517
Ivington *H & W* 27 SO4756
Ivington Green *H & W* 27 SO4656
Ivy Hatch *Kent* 14 TQ5854
Ivybridge *Devon* 5 SX6356
Ivychurch *Kent* 15 TR0327
Iwade *Kent* 14 TQ9067
Iwerne Courtney or Shroton *Dorset* 9 ST8512
Iwerne Minster *Dorset* 9 ST8614
Ixworth *Suffk* 32 TL9370
Ixworth Thorpe *Suffk* 32 TL9173

J

Jack-in-the-Green *Devon* 7 SY0195
Jackton *Strath* 74 NS5952
Jacobstow *Cnwll* 6 SX1995
Jacobstowe *Devon* 6 SS5801
Jameston *Dyfed* 16 SS0598
Jamestown *Highld* 92 NH4756
Jamestown *Strath* 80 NS3981
Janets-town *Highld* 100 ND3551
Janetstown *Highld* 100 ND1932
Jardine Hall *D & G* 67 NY1088
Jarrow *T & W* 69 NZ3364
Jasper's Green *Essex* 24 TL7226
Jawcraig *Cent* 74 NS8475
Jaywick *Essex* 25 TM1413
Jedburgh *Border* 76 NT6420
Jeffreston *Dyfed* 16 SN0906
Jemimaville *Highld* 93 NH7165
Jerbourg *Guern* 101 GN0000
Jesmond *T & W* 69 NZ2566
Jevington *E Susx* 13 TQ5601
Jockey End *Herts* 30 TL0413
John O'Groats *Highld* 100 ND3872
Johnby *Cumb* 59 NY4332
Johnshaven *Gramp* 89 NO7967
Johnston *Dyfed* 16 SM9310
Johnstone *Strath* 73 NS4263
Johnstonebridge *D & G* 67 NY1092
Joppa *Strath* 73 NS4119
Joppa *Dyfed* 34 SN5666
Jordanston *Dyfed* 16 SM9132
Juniper Green *Loth* 75 NT1968
Jurby *IOM* 52 SC3598

K

Kaber *Cumb* 60 NY7911
Kalnakill *Highld* 91 NG6955
Kames *Strath* 71 NR9771
Kames *Strath* 74 NS6926
Kea *Cnwll* 2 SW8142
Keal Cotes *Lincs* 51 TF3660
Kearsley *Gt Man* 47 SD7504
Kearsney *Kent* 15 TR2844
Kearstwick *Cumb* 59 SD6079
Kedington *Suffk* 32 TL7046
Kedleston *Derbys* 49 SK3040
Keelby *Lincs* 57 TA1610
Keele *Staffs* 47 SJ8045
Keelham *W York* 55 SE0732
Keeston *Dyfed* 16 SM9019
Keevil *Wilts* 20 ST9258
Kegworth *Leics* 39 SK4826
Kehelland *Cnwll* 2 SW6241
Keig *Gramp* 94 NJ6119
Keighley *W York* 55 SE0541
Keillour *Tays* 82 NN9725
Keiloch *Gramp* 88 NO1891
Keils *Strath* 70 NR5268
Keinton Mandeville *Somset* 8 ST5430
Keir Mill *D & G* 66 NX8593
Keisley *Cumb* 60 NY7124
Keiss *Highld* 100 ND3461
Keith *Gramp* 94 NJ4250
Keithick *Tays* 82 NO2038
Keithock *Tays* 89 NO6063
Keithtown *Gramp* 92 NH5256
Kelbrook *Lancs* 54 SD9044
Kelburn *Strath* 73 NS2156
Kelby *Lincs* 50 TF0041
Keld *N York* 60 NY8900
Kelfield *N York* 56 SE5938
Kelham *Notts* 50 SK7755
Kelhead *D & G* 67 NY1469
Kellamergh *Lancs* 53 SD4029
Kellas *Gramp* 94 NJ1654
Kellas *Tays* 83 NO4535
Kellaton *Devon* 5 SX8039
Kelling *Norfk* 43 TG0942
Kellington *N York* 56 SE5524
Kelloe *Dur* 62 NZ3436
Kelly *Devon* 4 SX3981
Kelmarsh *Nhants* 40 SP7379
Kelmscot *Oxon* 21 SU2499
Kelsale *Suffk* 33 TM3865
Kelsall *Ches* 46 SJ5268
Kelshall *Herts* 31 TL3336
Kelsick *Cumb* 67 NY1950
Kelso *Border* 76 NT7234
Kelstedge *Derbys* 49 SK3363
Kelstern *Lincs* 51 TF2489
Kelston *Avon* 20 ST7067
Keltneyburn *Tays* 87 NN7749
Kelton *D & G* 66 NX9970
Kelty *Fife* 82 NT1494
Kelvedon *Essex* 24 TL8619
Kelvedon Hatch *Essex* 24 TQ5698
Kelynack *Cnwll* 2 SW3729
Kemback *Fife* 83 NO4115
Kemberton *Shrops* 37 SJ7204
Kemble *Wilts* 20 ST9897
Kemerton *H & W* 28 SO9536
Kemeys Commander *Gwent* 27 SO3404
Kemnay *Gramp* 95 NJ7316
Kemp Town *E Susx* 12 TQ3303
Kempley *Gloucs* 28 SO6629
Kempley Green *Gloucs* 28 SO6728
Kempsey *H & W* 28 SO8549
Kempsford *Gloucs* 20 SU1696
Kempshott *Hants* 21 SU6050
Kempston *Beds* 30 TL0347
Kempton *Shrops* 36 SO3682
Kemsing *Kent* 23 TQ5558
Kenardington *Kent* 15 TQ9732
Kenchester *H & W* 27 SO4342
Kencot *Oxon* 29 SP2504
Kendal *Cumb* 59 SD5192
Kenilworth *Warwks* 39 SP2871
Kenley *Shrops* 37 SJ5500
Kenley *Gt Lon* 23 TQ3260
Kenmore *Highld* 91 NG7557
Kenmore *Tays* 87 NN7745
Kenn *Avon* 19 ST4268
Kenn *Devon* 5 SX9285
Kennacraig *Strath* 71 NR8262
Kennerleigh *Devon* 7 SS8107
Kennessee Green *Mersyd* 46 SD3801
Kennet *Cent* 82 NS9291
Kennet *Cent* 82 NS9291
Kennethmont *Gramp* 94 NJ5428
Kennett *Cambs* 32 TL7068
Kennford *Devon* 5 SX9186
Kenninghall *Norfk* 32 TM0386
Kennington *Oxon* 21 SP5201
Kennington *Kent* 15 TR0245
Kennoway *Fife* 83 NO3502
Kenny *Somset* 8 ST3117
Kennyhill *Suffk* 32 TL6679
Kennythorpe *N York* 56 SE7865
Kenovay *Strath* 78 NL9946
Kensaleyre *Highld* 90 NG4151
Kensington *Gt Lon* 23 TQ2579
Kensworth *Beds* 30 TL0319
Kensworth Common *Beds* 30 TL0317
Kent's Green *Gloucs* 28 SO7423
Kent's Oak *Hants* 10 SU3224
Kentallen *Highld* 86 NN0057
Kentchurch *H & W* 27 SO4125
Kentford *Suffk* 32 TL7066
Kentisbeare *Devon* 7 ST0608
Kentisbury *Devon* 6 SS6243
Kentish Town *Gt Lon* 23 TQ2884
Kentmere *Cumb* 59 NY4504
Kenton *T & W* 69 NZ2267
Kenton *Devon* 5 SX9583
Kenton *Suffk* 33 TM1965
Kenton *Gt Lon* 23 TQ1788
Kentra *Highld* 79 NM6569
Kenwyn *Cnwll* 2 SW8145
Keoldale *Highld* 98 NC3866
Keppoch *Highld* 85 NG8924
Kepwick *N York* 62 SE4690
Keresley *W Mids* 39 SP3282
Kerris *Cnwll* 2 SW4427
Kerry *Powys* 36 SO1490
Kerrycroy *Strath* 73 NS1061
Kersall *Notts* 49 SK7162
Kersbrook *Devon* 5 SY0683
Kersey *Suffk* 32 TM0044
Kershader *W Isls* 102 NB3320
Kershopefoot *D & G* 67 NY4782
Kerswell *Devon* 7 ST0806
Kerswell Green *H & W* 28 SO8646
Kesgrave *Suffk* 33 TM2245
Kessingland *Suffk* 33 TM5286
Kestle *Cnwll* 3 SW9845
Kestle Mill *Cnwll* 3 SW8459
Keston *Gt Lon* 23 TQ4164
Keswick *Cumb* 58 NY2623
Keswick *Norfk* 43 TG2004
Ketsby *Lincs* 51 TF3676
Kettering *Nhants* 30 SP8678
Ketteringham *Norfk* 43 TG1603
Kettins *Tays* 83 NO2338
Kettlebaston *Suffk* 32 TL9650
Kettlebridge *Fife* 83 NO3007
Kettleburgh *Suffk* 33 TM2660
Kettleholm *D & G* 67 NY1577
Kettleshulme *Ches* 48 SJ9879
Kettlesing *N York* 55 SE2256
Kettlesing Bottom *N York* 55 SE2357
Kettlestoft *Ork* 103 HY6538
Kettlestone *Norfk* 42 TF9631
Kettlethorpe *Lincs* 50 SK8475
Kettlewell *N York* 54 SD9672
Ketton *Leics* 40 SK9704
Kew *Gt Lon* 23 TQ1876
Kexby *N York* 56 SE7050
Kexby *Lincs* 50 SK8785
Key Green *Ches* 48 SJ8963
Key Street *Kent* 14 TQ8764
Keyham *Leics* 39 SK6706
Keyhaven *Hants* 10 SZ3091
Keyingham *Humb* 57 TA2425
Keymer *W Susx* 12 TQ3115
Keynsham *Avon* 19 ST6568
Keysoe Row *Beds* 30 TL0861
Keyston *Cambs* 30 TL0475
Keyworth *Notts* 39 SK6130
Kibbleworth *T & W* 69 NZ2456
Kibworth Beauchamp *Leics* 39 SP6893
Kibworth Harcourt *Leics* 39 SP6894
Kidbrooke *Gt Lon* 23 TQ4176
Kidderminster *H & W* 38 SO8376
Kidlington *Oxon* 29 SP4913
Kidmore End *Oxon* 22 SU6979
Kidsdale *D & G* 64 NX4336
Kidsgrove *Staffs* 47 SJ8454
Kidwelly *Dyfed* 17 SN4006
Kiel Crofts *Strath* 79 NM9039
Kielder *Nthumb* 68 NY6293
Kiells *Strath* 70 NR4168
Kilbeg *Highld* 85 NG6506
Kilberry *Strath* 71 NR7164
Kilbirnie *Strath* 73 NS3154
Kilbride *W Isls* 102 NF7514
Kilbride *Strath* 79 NM8525
Kilbride *Strath* 71 NR7279
Kilbride *Strath* 72 NS0367
Kilburn *N York* 62 SE5179
Kilburn *Derbys* 49 SK3845
Kilburn *Gt Lon* 23 TQ2483
Kilby *Leics* 39 SP6295
Kilchamaig *Strath* 71 NR8060
Kilchattan *Strath* 70 NR3795
Kilchattan *Strath* 73 NS1054
Kilchenzie *Strath* 72 NR6724
Kilcheran *Strath* 79 NM8239
Kilchiaran *Strath* 70 NR2060
Kilchoan *Highld* 79 NM4863
Kilchrenan *Strath* 80 NN0322
Kilconquhar *Fife* 83 NO4802
Kilcot *Gloucs* 28 SO6925
Kilcoy *Highld* 92 NH5751
Kilcreggan *Strath* 80 NS2480
Kildale *N York* 62 NZ6009
Kildalloig *Strath* 72 NR7518
Kildary *Highld* 97 NH7674
Kildavanan *Strath* 72 NS0266
Kildonan *Highld* 97 NC9120
Kildonan *Strath* 72 NS0321
Kildonan Lodge *Highld* 97 NC9022
Kildonnan *Highld* 84 NM4885
Kildrochet House *D & G* 64 NX0856
Kildrummy *Gramp* 94 NJ4617
Kildwick *N York* 54 SE0046
Kilehoman *Strath* 70 NR2163
Kilfinan *Strath* 71 NR9378
Kilfinnan *Highld* 86 NN2795
Kilgetty *Dyfed* 16 SN1207
Kilgrammie *Strath* 73 NS2502
Kilgwrrwg Common *Gwent* 19 ST4797
Kilham *Humb* 57 TA0664
Kilkenneth *Strath* 78 NL9444
Kilkerran *Strath* 73 NS3003
Kilkhampton *Cnwll* 6 SS2511
Killamarsh *Derbys* 49 SK4581
Killay *W Glam* 17 SS6092
Killay *W Glam* 17 SS6092
Killearn *Cent* 81 NS5286
Killen *Highld* 93 NH6758
Killerby *Dur* 61 NZ1919
Killerton *Devon* 7 SS9700
Killichonan *Tays* 87 NN5458
Killiechronan *Strath* 79 NM5441
Killiecrankie *Tays* 87 NN9162
Killilan *Highld* 85 NG9430
Killin *Cent* 81 NN5733
Killinghall *N York* 55 SE2858
Killington *Cumb* 59 SD6188
Killingworth *T & W* 69 NZ2770
Killochyett *Border* 76 NT4545
Killundine *Highld* 79 NM5949
Kilmacolm *Strath* 73 NS3567
Kilmahog *Cent* 81 NN6108
Kilmahumaig *Strath* 71 NR7893
Kilmaluag *Highld* 90 NG4374
Kilmany *Fife* 83 NO3821
Kilmarie *Highld* 84 NG5517
Kilmarnock *Strath* 73 NS4237
Kilmartin *Strath* 71 NR8398
Kilmaurs *Strath* 73 NS4141
Kilmelford *Strath* 79 NM8512
Kilmeny *Strath* 70 NR3965
Kilmersdon *Somset* 20 ST6952
Kilmeston *Hants* 11 SU5825
Kilmichael *Strath* 71 NR8593
Kilmichael of Inverlussa *Strath* 71 NR7786
Kilmington *Wilts* 20 ST7736
Kilmington *Devon* 8 SY2797
Kilmington Common *Wilts* 9 ST7735
Kilmington Street *Wilts* 9 ST7835
Kilmory *Strath* 79 NM8825
Kilmorack *Highld* 92 NH4944
Kilmore *Highld* 85 NG6507
Kilmory *Highld* 79 NM5270
Kilmory *Strath* 71 NR7074
Kilmuir *Highld* 90 NG2547
Kilmuir *Highld* 90 NG3770
Kilmuir *Highld* 93 NH6749
Kilmuir *Highld* 97 NH7573
Kilmun *Strath* 80 NS1781
Kiln Green *Berks* 22 SU8178
Kiln Pit Hill *Nthumb* 68 NZ0355
Kilnave *Strath* 70 NR2871
Kilncadzow *Strath* 74 NS8848
Kilndown *Kent* 14 TQ7035
Kilninver *Strath* 79 NM8221
Kilnsea *Humb* 57 TA4115
Kilnsey *N York* 54 SD9767
Kilnwick *Humb* 56 SE9949
Kiloran *Strath* 70 NR3996
Kilpeck *H & W* 27 SO4430
Kilpin *Humb* 56 SE7726
Kilsby *Nhants* 39 SP5671
Kilspindie *Tays* 82 NO2125
Kilstay *D & G* 64 NX1238
Kilsyth *Strath* 81 NS7178
Kiltarlity *Highld* 92 NH5041
Kilton *Cleve* 62 NZ7018
Kilton Thorpe *Cleve* 62 NZ6917
Kilvaxter *Highld* 90 NG3869
Kilve *Somset* 18 ST1442
Kilvington *Notts* 50 SK8042
Kilwinning *Strath* 73 NS3043
Kimberley *Notts* 49 SK4944
Kimberley *Norfk* 42 TG0603
Kimberworth *S York* 49 SK4093
Kimblesworth *Dur* 69 NZ2547
Kimbolton *H & W* 27 SO5261
Kimbolton *Cambs* 30 TL1067
Kimcote *Leics* 39 SP5886
Kimmeridge *Dorset* 9 SY9179
Kimpton *Hants* 21 SU2746
Kimpton *Herts* 31 TL1718
Kinbrace *Highld* 99 NC8631
Kinbuck *Cent* 81 NN7905
Kincaple *Fife* 83 NO4618
Kincardine *Highld* 97 NH6089
Kincardine *Fife* 82 NS9387
Kincardine O'Neil *Tays* 89 NO5999
Kinclaven *Tays* 82 NO1538
Kincorth *Gramp* 89 NJ9403
Kincorth House *Gramp* 93 NJ0161
Kincraig *Highld* 87 NH8305
Kincraigie *Tays* 88 NN9849
Kindallachan *Tays* 88 NN9949
Kinerarach *Strath* 71 NR6553
Kineton *Gloucs* 28 SP0926
Kineton *Warwks* 29 SP3350
Kinfauns *Tays* 82 NO1622
Kinfig *M Glam* 18 SS8081
King's Bromley *Staffs* 38 SK1216
King's Cliffe *Nhants* 40 TL0097
King's Coughton *Warwks* 28 SP0859
King's Heath *W Mids* 38 SP0781
King's Lynn *Norfk* 41 TF6120

King's Mills
Land-hallow

King's Mills Guern 101 GN0000
King's Norton Leics 39 SK6800
King's Norton W Mids 38 SP0579
King's Nympton Devon 7 SS6819
King's Pyon H & W 27 SO4450
King's Somborne Hants 10 SU3531
King's Stag Dorset 9 ST7210
King's Stanley Gloucs 20 SO8103
King's Sutton Oxon 29 SP4936
King's Walden Herts 31 TL1623
Kingarth Strath 73 NS0956
Kingcausie Gramp 89 NO8699
Kingcoed Gwent 27 SO4305
Kingerby Lincs 50 TF0592
Kingford Devon 6 SS2806
Kingford Devon 6 SS2806
Kingham Oxon 29 SP2624
Kingholm Quay D & G 66 NX9773
Kinglassie Loth 82 NT2298
Kingoldrum Tays 88 NO3355
Kingoodie Tays 83 NO3329
Kings Caple H & W 27 SO5528
Kings House Hotel Highld 86 NN2654
Kings Langley Herts 22 TL0702
Kings Meaburn Cumb 60 NY6221
Kings Muir Border 75 NT2539
Kings Newnham Warwks 39 SP4577
Kings Ripton Cambs 31 TL2676
Kings Weston Avon 19 ST5477
Kings Worthy Hants 10 SU4932
Kingsand Cnwll 4 SX4350
Kingsbarns Fife 83 NO5912
Kingsbridge Somset 7 SS9837
Kingsbridge Devon 5 SX7344
Kingsburgh Highld 90 NG3955
Kingsbury Warwks 39 SP2196
Kingsbury Gt Lon 23 TQ1988
Kingsbury Episcopi Somset 8 ST4321
Kingsclere Hants 21 SU5258
Kingscote Gloucs 20 ST8196
Kingscott Devon 6 SS5318
Kingscross Strath 72 NS0428
Kingsdon Somset 8 ST5126
Kingsdown Wilts 20 SU1688
Kingsdown Kent 15 TR3748
Kingseat Fife 82 NT1290
Kingsey Bucks 22 SP7406
Kingsfold W Susx 12 TQ1636
Kingsford Strath 73 NS4447
Kingsgate Kent 15 TR3970
Kingshall Street Suffk 32 TL9161
Kingsheanton Devon 6 SS5537
Kingshouse Hotel Cent 81 NN5620
Kingskerswell Devon 5 SX8767
Kingskettle Fife 83 NO3008
Kingsland H & W 27 SO4461
Kingsley Ches 47 SJ5574
Kingsley Staffs 48 SK0146
Kingsley Hants 11 SU7838
Kingsley Green W Susx 11 SU8930
Kingsley Park Nhants 30 SP7762
Kingsmuir Tays 89 NO4849
Kingsmuir Fife 83 NO5308
Kingsnorth Kent 15 TR0039
Kingsteignton Devon 5 SX8773
Kingsthorne H & W 27 SO4931
Kingsthorpe Nhants 30 SP7563
Kingston Gramp 94 NJ3365
Kingston Loth 83 NT5482
Kingston Dorset 9 ST7509
Kingston Cnwll 4 SX3675
Kingston Devon 5 SX6347
Kingston Dorset 9 SY9579
Kingston IOW 10 SZ4781
Kingston Cambs 31 TL3455
Kingston Kent 15 TR1950
Kingston Bagpuize Oxon 21 SU4098
Kingston Blount Oxon 22 SU7399
Kingston Deverill Wilts 20 ST8437
Kingston Lisle Oxon 21 SU3287
Kingston Russell Dorset 8 SY5791
Kingston Seymour Avon 19 ST4066
Kingston St. Mary Somset 8 ST2229
Kingston by Sea W Susx 12 TQ2305
Kingston near Lewes E Susx 13 TQ3908
Kingston on Soar Notts 39 SK5027
Kingston upon Hull Humb 57 TA0829
Kingston upon Thames Gt Lon 12 TQ1869
Kingstone Staffs 38 SK0629
Kingstone H & W 27 SO4235
Kingstone Somset 8 ST3713
Kingswear Devon 5 SX8851
Kingswear Devon 5 SX8851
Kingswells Gramp 89 NJ8606
Kingswinford W Mids 38 SO8888
Kingswood Warwks 38 SP1871
Kingswood Bucks 30 SP6919
Kingswood Somset 18 ST1037
Kingswood Avon 19 ST6473
Kingswood Gloucs 20 ST7491
Kingswood Surrey 23 TQ2455
Kingswood Common Staffs 38 SJ8302
Kingthorpe Lincs 50 TF1275
Kington H & W 27 SO2956
Kington H & W 28 SO9956
Kington Avon 19 ST6290
Kington Langley Wilts 20 ST9276
Kington Magna Dorset 9 ST7622
Kington St. Michael Wilts 20 ST9077
Kingussie Highld 87 NH7500
Kingweston Somset 8 ST5230
Kinharrachie Gramp 95 NJ9231
Kinharvie D & G 66 NX9266
Kinkell Bridge Tays 82 NN9316
Kinknockie Gramp 95 NK0041
Kinleith Loth 75 NT1866
Kinlet Shrops 37 SO7180
Kinloch Highld 98 NC3434
Kinloch Highld 99 NC5552
Kinloch Highld 84 NM4099
Kinloch Tays 88 NO1444
Kinloch Tays 88 NO2644
Kinloch Hourn Highld 85 NG9506
Kinloch Rannoch Tays 87 NN6658
Kinlochard Cent 81 NN4502
Kinlochbervie Highld 98 NC2256
Kinlocheil Highld 85 NM9779
Kinlochewe Highld 91 NH0261
Kinlochleven Highld 86 NN1861
Kinlochmoidart Highld 85 NM7172
Kinlochnanuagh Highld 85 NM7384
Kinlochspelve Strath 79 NM6526
Kinloss Gramp 93 NJ0661
Kinmel Bay Clwyd 45 SH9880
Kinmount House D & G 67 NY1368
Kinmuck Gramp 95 NJ8119
Kinmundy Gramp 95 NJ8817
Kinnadie Gramp 95 NJ9743
Kinnahaird Highld 92 NH4755
Kinnaird Tays 88 NN9559
Kinnaird Tays 83 NO2428
Kinnaird Castle Tays 89 NO6357
Kinneddar Gramp 94 NJ2269
Kinneff Gramp 89 NO8574
Kinnelhead D & G 66 NT0201
Kinnell Tays 89 NO6150
Kinnell Tays 89 NO6150
Kinnerley Shrops 36 SJ3320
Kinnersley H & W 27 SO3449
Kinnersley H & W 28 SO8743
Kinnerton Powys 27 SO2463
Kinnesswood Tays 82 NO1702
Kinninvie Dur 61 NZ0521
Kinnordy Tays 88 NO3655
Kinoulton Notts 39 SK6730
Kinross Tays 82 NO1102
Kinrossie Tays 82 NO1832
Kinsham H & W 27 SO3665
Kinsham H & W 28 SO9335
Kinsley W York 55 SE4114
Kinson Dorset 10 SZ0796
Kintbury Berks 21 SU3866
Kintillo Tays 82 NO1317
Kinton Shrops 36 SJ3719
Kinton H & W 36 SO4174
Kintore Gramp 95 NJ7916
Kintour Strath 70 NR4551
Kintra Strath 78 NM3125
Kintraw Strath 79 NM8204
Kinveachy Highld 93 NH9018
Kinver Staffs 38 SO8483
Kippax W York 55 SE4130
Kippen Cent 81 NS6494
Kippford or Scaur D & G 66 NX8354
Kipping's Cross Kent 13 TQ6440
Kirbister Ork 103 HY3607
Kirby Bedon Norfk 43 TG2705
Kirby Bellars Leics 40 SK7117
Kirby Cane Norfk 43 TM3794
Kirby Cross Essex 25 TM2120
Kirby Fields Leics 39 SK5203
Kirby Grindalythe N York 56 SE9067
Kirby Hill N York 61 NZ1406
Kirby Hill N York 55 SE3968
Kirby Knowle N York 62 SE4687
Kirby Misperton N York 63 SE7779
Kirby Muxloe Leics 39 SK5104
Kirby Row Norfk 33 TM3792
Kirby Sigston N York 62 SE4194
Kirby Underdale Humb 56 SE8058
Kirby Wiske N York 62 SE3784
Kirby le Soken Essex 25 TM2121
Kirby-in-Furness Cumb 58 SD2282
Kirconnel D & G 66 NX9868
Kirdford W Susx 12 TQ0126
Kirk Highld 100 ND2859
Kirk Bramwith S York 56 SE6211
Kirk Deighton N York 55 SE3950
Kirk Ella Humb 56 TA0129
Kirk Hallam Derbys 49 SK4540
Kirk Hammerton N York 55 SE4655
Kirk Ireton Derbys 49 SK2650
Kirk Langley Derbys 49 SK2838
Kirk Merrington Dur 61 NZ2631
Kirk Sandall S York 56 SE6108
Kirk Smeaton N York 55 SE5216
Kirk Yetholm Border 77 NT8228
Kirk of Shotts Strath 74 NS8462
Kirkabister Shet 103 HU4938
Kirkandrews D & G 65 NX6048
Kirkandrews upon Eden Cumb 67 NY3558
Kirkbampton Cumb 67 NY3056
Kirkbean D & G 66 NX9759
Kirkbride Cumb 67 NY2256
Kirkbuddo Tays 89 NO5043
Kirkburn Border 75 NT2938
Kirkburn Humb 56 SE9855
Kirkburton W York 55 SE1912
Kirkby N York 62 NZ5305
Kirkby Mersyd 46 SJ4099
Kirkby Lincs 50 TF0592
Kirkby Fleetham N York 61 SE2894
Kirkby Green Lincs 50 TF0857
Kirkby Lonsdale Cumb 59 SD6178
Kirkby Malham N York 54 SD8960
Kirkby Mallory Leics 39 SK4500
Kirkby Malzeard N York 61 SE2374
Kirkby Overblow N York 55 SE3249
Kirkby Stephen Cumb 60 NY7708
Kirkby Thore Cumb 60 NY6325
Kirkby Underwood Lincs 40 TF0727
Kirkby Wharf N York 55 SE5041
Kirkby in Ashfield Notts 49 SK4856
Kirkby la Thorpe Lincs 50 TF0946
Kirkby on Bain Lincs 51 TF2462
Kirkbymoorside N York 62 SE6986
Kirkcaldy Fife 83 NT2892
Kirkcaldy Fife 83 NT2892
Kirkcambeck Cumb 67 NY5368
Kirkchrist D & G 65 NX6751
Kirkcolm D & G 64 NX0268
Kirkconnel D & G 66 NS7311
Kirkconnell D & G 65 NX6760
Kirkcowan D & G 64 NX3260
Kirkcudbright D & G 65 NX6850
Kirkdale Mersyd 46 SJ3493
Kirkfieldbank Strath 74 NS8643
Kirkgunzeon D & G 66 NX8666
Kirkham Lancs 53 SD4232
Kirkham N York 56 SE7365
Kirkhamgate W York 55 SE2922
Kirkharle Nthumb 68 NZ0182
Kirkhaugh Nthumb 68 NY6949
Kirkheaton Nthumb 68 NZ0177
Kirkheaton W York 55 SE1818
Kirkhill Highld 92 NH5545
Kirkhope Strath 66 NS9606
Kirkhope Border 76 NT3723
Kirkibost Highld 84 NG5518
Kirkinch Tays 88 NO3044
Kirkinner D & G 64 NX4251
Kirkintilloch Strath 74 NS6573
Kirkland D & G 66 NS7213
Kirkland D & G 64 NX4356
Kirkland D & G 66 NX8190
Kirkland D & G 66 NY0389
Kirkland Cumb 58 NY0718
Kirkleatham Cleve 62 NZ5921
Kirklevington Cleve 62 NZ4309
Kirkley Suffk 33 TM5391
Kirkleyditch Ches 47 SJ8778
Kirklington N York 62 SE3181
Kirklington Notts 49 SK6757
Kirklinton Cumb 67 NY4367
Kirkliston Loth 75 NT1274
Kirkmabreck D & G 65 NX4856
Kirkmaiden D & G 64 NX1236
Kirkmichael Tays 88 NO0759
Kirkmichael Strath 73 NS3408
Kirkmichael IOM 52 SC3190
Kirkmuirhill Strath 74 NS7842
Kirknewton Fife 75 NT1166
Kirknewton Nthumb 77 NT9130
Kirkney Gramp 94 NJ5132
Kirkoswald Strath 73 NS2407
Kirkoswald Cumb 59 NY5541
Kirkpatrick D & G 66 NX9090
Kirkpatrick Durham D & G 66 NX7870
Kirkpatrick-Fleming D & G 67 NY2770
Kirksanton Cumb 58 SD1380
Kirkstall W York 55 SE2635
Kirkstead Lincs 50 TF1762
Kirkstile Gramp 94 NJ5235
Kirkstile D & G 67 NY3690
Kirkstyle Highld 100 ND3472
Kirkthorpe W York 55 SE3621
Kirkton Highld 85 NG8227
Kirkton Highld 85 NG9141
Kirkton Gramp 94 NJ6425
Kirkton Gramp 95 NJ8243
Kirkton Tays 88 NN9618
Kirkton Fife 83 NO3625
Kirkton Border 67 NT5413
Kirkton D & G 66 NX9781
Kirkton Manor Border 75 NT2238
Kirkton of Airlie Tays 88 NO3151
Kirkton of Auchterhouse Tays 83 NO3438
Kirkton of Collace Tays 82 NO1931
Kirkton of Craig Tays 89 NO6956
Kirkton of Logie Buchan Gramp 95 NJ9829
Kirkton of Monikie Tays 83 NO5138
Kirkton of Skene Gramp 95 NJ8007
Kirkton of Tealing Tays 83 NO4038
Kirkton of Strathmartine Tays 83 NO3735
Kirktown Gramp 95 NJ9965
Kirktown Gramp 95 NK0852
Kirktown of Alvah Gramp 95 NJ6760
Kirktown of Bourtie Gramp 95 NJ8025
Kirktown of Fetteresso Gramp 89 NO8486
Kirktown of Mortlach Gramp 94 NJ3138
Kirktown of Slains Gramp 95 NK0329
Kirkwall Ork 103 HY4411
Kirkwhelpington Nthumb 68 NY9984
Kirmington Humb 57 TA1011
Kirmond le Mire Lincs 50 TF1892
Kirn Strath 80 NS1878
Kirn Strath 80 NS1878
Kirstead Green Norfk 43 TM2997
Kirtlebridge D & G 67 NY2372
Kirtling Cambs 32 TL6857
Kirtling Green Suffk 32 TL6855
Kirtlington Oxon 29 SP4919
Kirtomy Highld 99 NC7463
Kirton Gramp 94 NJ6113
Kirkton Strath 73 NS1655
Kirton Notts 49 SK6969
Kirton Lincs 41 TF3038
Kirton Suffk 33 TM2740
Kirton in Lindsey Lincs 50 SK9398
Kirkton of Barevan Highld 93 NH8347
Kirkton of Durris Gramp 89 NO7796
Kirkton of Glenbuchat Gramp 94 NJ3715
Kirkton of Glenisla Tays 88 NO2160
Kirkton of Menmuir Tays 89 NO5364
Kirkton of Rayne Gramp 95 NJ6930
Kirkton of Strathmartine Tays 83 NO3735
Kirtonhill Strath 80 NS3875
Kirwaugh D & G 64 NX4054
Kislingbury Nhants 30 SP6959
Kittisford Somset 7 ST0822
Kittybrewster Gramp 95 NJ9207
Kivernoll H & W 27 SO4632
Knaith Lincs 50 SK8284
Knap Corner Dorset 9 ST8023
Knaphill Surrey 22 SU9658
Knaplock Somset 7 SS8633
Knapp Somset 8 ST3025
Knapton N York 56 SE5652
Knapton N York 63 SE8876
Knapton Norfk 43 TG3034
Knapwell Cambs 31 TL3362
Knaresborough N York 55 SE3557
Knarsdale Nthumb 68 NY6754
Knaven Gramp 95 NJ8943
Knayton N York 62 SE4387
Knebworth Herts 31 TL2520
Knedlington Humb 56 SE7327
Kneesall Notts 49 SK7064
Kneesworth Cambs 31 TL3444
Kneeton Notts 49 SK7146
Knelston W Glam 17 SS4688
Knenhall Staffs 48 SJ9237
Knightcote Warwks 29 SP4054
Knightley Staffs 37 SJ8125
Knighton Staffs 37 SJ7240
Knighton Staffs 37 SJ7527
Knighton Leics 39 SK6001
Knighton Powys 36 SO2872
Knighton Somset 19 ST1944
Knighton Dorset 9 ST6111
Knighton on Teme H & W 27 SO6369
Knightwick H & W 28 SO7356
Knill H & W 27 SO2960
Knill H & W 27 SO2960
Knipton Leics 40 SK8231
Kniveton Derbys 48 SK2050
Knock W Isls 102 NB4931
Knock Highld 85 NG6709
Knock Gramp 94 NJ5452
Knock Cumb 60 NY6727
Knock Castle Strath 73 NS1963
Knockally Highld 100 ND1429
Knockan Highld 96 NC2110
Knockandhu Gramp 94 NJ2023
Knockando Gramp 94 NJ1941
Knockbain Highld 92 NH5543
Knockbain Highld 92 NH6256
Knockbrex D & G 65 NX5849
Knockdee Highld 100 ND1760
Knockdown Wilts 20 ST8388
Knockeen Strath 64 NX3195
Knockenkelly Strath 72 NS0427
Knockentiber Strath 73 NS4039
Knockespock House Gramp 94 NJ5423
Knockholt Kent 23 TQ4658
Knockholt Pound Kent 23 TQ4859
Knockin Shrops 36 SJ3322
Knockinlaw Strath 73 NS4239
Knocknain D & G 64 NW9764
Knocksheen D & G 65 NX5882
Knockvennie Smithy D & G 65 NX7571
Knodishall Suffk 33 TM4262
Knole Somset 8 ST4825
Knolls Green Ches 47 SJ8079
Knolton Clwyd 36 SJ3739
Knook Wilts 20 ST9341
Knossington Leics 40 SK8008
Knott End-on-Sea Lancs 53 SD3548
Knotting Beds 30 TL0063
Knotting Green Beds 30 TL0062
Knottingley W York 55 SE5023
Knowbury Shrops 37 SO5775
Knowe D & G 64 NX3171
Knowehead D & G 65 NX6090
Knoweside Strath 73 NS2512
Knowl Hill Berks 22 SU8279
Knowle Shrops 37 SO5973
Knowle W Mids 38 SP1876
Knowle Devon 6 SS4938
Knowle Devon 7 SS7801
Knowle Somset 7 SS9643
Knowle Devon 7 ST0007
Knowle Avon 19 ST6070
Knowle Devon 5 SY0582
Knowle Devon 5 SY0582
Knowle Green Lancs 54 SD6338
Knowle St. Giles Somset 8 ST3411
Knowlton Kent 15 TR2853
Knowsley Mersyd 46 SJ4395
Knowstone Devon 7 SS8323
Knox Bridge Kent 14 TQ7840
Knucklas Powys 36 SO2574
Knuston Nhants 30 SP9266
Knutsford Ches 47 SJ7578
Krumlin W York 55 SE0518
Kuggar Cnwll 2 SW7216
Kyle of Lochalsh Highld 85 NG7627
Kyleakin Highld 85 NG7526
Kylerhea Highld 85 NG7820
Kylesku Highld 98 NC2233
Kylesmorar Highld 85 NM8093
Kylestrome Highld 98 NC2234
Kynnersley Shrops 37 SJ6716
Kyrewood H & W 27 SO5967

L

L'Ancresse Guern 101 GN0000
L'Eree Guern 101 GN0000
L'Etacq Jersey 101 JS0000
La Beilleuse Guern 101 GN0000
La Fontenelle Guern 101 GN0000
La Fosse Guern 101 GN0000
La Greve Guern 101 GN0000
La Greve de Lecq Jersey 101 JS0000
La Hougue Bie Jersey 101 JS0000
La Houguette Guern 101 GN0000
La Passee Guern 101 GN0000
La Pulente Jersey 101 JS0000
La Rocque Jersey 101 JS0000
La Rousaillerie Guern 101 GN0000
La Villette Guern 101 GN0000
Laceby Humb 57 TA2106
Lacey Green Bucks 22 SP8200
Lach Dennis Ches 47 SJ7071
Lackford Suffk 32 TL7970
Lackford Green Suffk 32 TL7970
Lacock Wilts 20 ST9168
Ladbroke Warwks 29 SP4158
Laddingford Kent 14 TQ6948
Ladock Cnwll 3 SW8950
Ladock Cnwll 3 SW8950
Lady Hall Cumb 58 SD1986
Ladybank Fife 83 NO3009
Ladygill Strath 75 NS9428
Ladykirk Border 77 NT8847
Ladykirk Ho Border 77 NT8845
Ladywood H & W 28 SO8661
Ladywood W Mids 38 SP0586
Lag D & G 66 NX8786
Lagavulin Strath 70 NR4045
Lagg Strath 72 NR9521
Laggan Highld 86 NN2997
Laggan Highld 87 NN6194
Laggan Strath 64 NX0982
Laid Highld 98 NC4159
Laide Highld 91 NG9091
Laig Highld 84 NM4687
Laigh Church Strath 73 NS4647
Laigh Fenwick Strath 73 NS4542
Laigh Glenmuir Strath 74 NS6120
Laighstonehall Strath 74 NS7054
Laindon Essex 24 TQ6889
Lairg Highld 96 NC5806
Laisterdyke W York 55 SE1932
Lake Wilts 10 SU1339
Lake Dorset 9 SY9990
Lakenheath Suffk 32 TL7182
Lakesend Norfk 41 TL5196
Laleston M Glam 18 SS8779
Lamarsh Essex 24 TL8835
Lamas Norfk 43 TG2423
Lambden Border 76 NT7443
Lamberhurst Kent 14 TQ6736
Lamberhurst Down Kent 14 TQ6735
Lamberton Border 77 NT9658
Lambfair Green Suffk 32 TL7153
Lambley Nthumb 68 NY6759
Lambley Notts 49 SK6345
Lambourn Berks 21 SU3278
Lambourne End Essex 23 TQ4794
Lambs Green W Susx 12 TQ2136
Lamerton Devon 4 SX4577
Lamerton Devon 4 SX4577
Lamesley T & W 69 NZ2557
Lamington Strath 75 NS9731
Lamlash Strath 72 NS0231
Lamonby Cumb 59 NY4036
Lamorna Cnwll 2 SW4424
Lamorran Cnwll 3 SW8741
Lampeter Dyfed 17 SN5747
Lampeter Velfrey Dyfed 17 SN1514
Lamphey Dyfed 16 SN0100
Lamplugh Cumb 58 NY0820
Lamplugh Cumb 58 NY0820
Lamport Nhants 30 SP7574
Lamyatt Somset 19 ST6536
Lanark Strath 74 NS8843
Lancaster Lancs 53 SD4761
Lanchester Dur 69 NZ1647
Lancing W Susx 12 TQ1804
Land-hallow Highld 100 ND1833

Landbeach Little Bradley

Landbeach *Cambs* 31 TL4765
Landcross *Devon* 6 SS4523
Landerberry *Gramp* 89 NJ7404
Landewednack *Cnwll* 2 SW7012
Landford *Wilts* 10 SU2519
Landimore *W Glam* 17 SS4692
Landkey *Devon* 6 SS603
Landkey *Devon* 6 SS603
Landkey Town *Devon* 6 SS5931
Landore *W Glam* 18 SS6695
Landrake *Cnwll* 4 SX3760
Landscove *Devon* 5 SX7766
Landulph *Cnwll* 4 SX4361
Lane *Cnwll* 2 SW8260
Lane End *Cumb* 58 SD1093
Lane End *Wilts* 20 ST8145
Lane End *Bucks* 22 SU8091
Lane Ends *Derbys* 39 SK2334
Lane Head *Dur* 61 NZ1211
Laneast *Cnwll* 4 SX2283
Laneham *Notts* 50 SK8076
Lanehead *Dur* 60 NY8441
Langaller *Somset* 8 ST2626
Langar *Notts* 40 SK7234
Langbank *Strath* 80 NS3873
Langbar *N York* 55 SE0951
Langcliffe *N York* 54 SD8264
Langdale End *N York* 63 SE9391
Langdown *Hants* 10 SU4206
Langdyke *Fife* 83 NO3304
Langenhoe *Essex* 25 TM0018
Langford *Notts* 50 SK8258
Langford *Oxon* 21 SP2402
Langford *Devon* 7 ST0203
Langford *Beds* 31 TL1841
Langford *Essex* 24 TL8309
Langford Budville *Somset* 8 ST1122
Langford End *Beds* 31 TL1753
Langham *Leics* 40 SK8411
Langham *Norfk* 42 TG0141
Langham *Suffk* 32 TL9769
Langham *Essex* 25 TM0333
Langho *Lancs* 54 SD7034
Langholm *D & G* 67 NY3684
Langley *Nthumb* 68 NY8261
Langley *Warwks* 29 SP1965
Langley *Somset* 7 ST0828
Langley *Hants* 10 SU4401
Langley *W Susx* 11 SU8029
Langley *Herts* 31 TL2122
Langley *Essex* 31 TL4334
Langley *Berks* 22 TQ0178
Langley *Kent* 14 TQ8052
Langley Burrell *Wilts* 20 ST9375
Langley Green *Essex* 24 TL8722
Langley Marsh *Somset* 7 ST0729
Langley Street *Norfk* 43 TG3601
Langleybury *Herts* 22 TL0700
Langney *E Susx* 13 TQ6302
Langold *Notts* 49 SK5886
Langore *Cnwll* 4 SX2986
Langport *Somset* 8 ST4226
Langrick *Lincs* 51 TF2648
Langridge *Avon* 20 ST7469
Langrigg *Cumb* 67 NY1645
Langrish *Hants* 11 SU7023
Langsett *S York* 48 SE2100
Langshaw *Border* 76 NT5139
Langside *Tays* 81 NN7913
Langstone *Gwent* 19 ST3789
Langstone *Hants* 11 SU7204
Langthorne *N York* 61 SE2491
Langthorpe *N York* 55 SE3867
Langthwaite *N York* 61 NZ0001
Langtoft *Humb* 56 TA0066
Langtoft *Lincs* 40 TF1212
Langton *Dur* 61 NZ1619
Langton *N York* 56 SE7966
Langton *Lincs* 51 TF2368
Langton *Lincs* 51 TF3970
Langton Green *Kent* 13 TQ5439
Langton Herring *Dorset* 9 SY6182
Langton by Wragby *Lincs* 50 TF1476
Langtree *Devon* 6 SS4515
Langwathby *Cumb* 59 NY5733
Langwell House *Highld* 100 ND1122
Langworth *Lincs* 50 TF0676
Lanivet *Cnwll* 3 SX0464
Lank *Cnwll* 3 SX0875
Lanlivery *Cnwll* 3 SX0759
Lanner *Cnwll* 2 SW7139
Lanreath *Cnwll* 3 SX1857
Lansallos *Cnwll* 3 SX1751
Lanteglos *Cnwll* 3 SX0882
Lanteglos Highway *Cnwll* 3 SX1453
Lantilio-Crossenny *Gwent* 27 SO3914
Lanton *Border* 76 NT6221
Lanton *Nthumb* 77 NT9231
Lapford *Devon* 7 SS7308
Laphroaig *Strath* 70 NR3845
Lapley *Staffs* 38 SJ8712
Lapworth *Warwks* 38 SP1671
Larachbeg *Highld* 79 NM6948
Larbert *Cent* 82 NS8582
Largie *Gramp* 94 NJ6131
Largiemore *Strath* 71 NR9486
Largoward *Fife* 83 NO4607
Largs *Strath* 73 NS2059
Largybeg *Strath* 72 NS0423
Largymore *Strath* 72 NS0424
Larkfield *Strath* 80 NS2475
Larkfield *Kent* 14 TQ7058
Larkhall *Strath* 74 NS7651
Larkhill *Wilts* 20 SU1244
Larling *Norfk* 32 TL9889
Lartington *Dur* 61 NZ0117
Lasham *Hants* 11 SU6742
Lask Edge *Staffs* 48 SJ9156
Lassodie *Fife* 82 NT1292
Lasswade *Loth* 75 NT3065
Lastingham *N York* 63 SE7290
Latchingdon and Snoreham *Essex* 24 TL8800
Latchley *Cnwll* 4 SX4173
Latebrook *Staffs* 47 SJ8453
Lathbury *Bucks* 30 SP8744
Latheron *Highld* 100 ND2033
Latheronwheel *Highld* 100 ND1832
Lathones *Fife* 83 NO4708
Latimer *Bucks* 22 TQ0199
Latteridge *Avon* 20 ST6684
Lattiford *Somset* 9 ST6926
Latton *Wilts* 20 SU0995
Lauder *Border* 76 NT5347
Laugharne *Dyfed* 17 SN3010
Laughterton *Lincs* 50 SK8375
Laughton *Lincs* 50 SK8497
Laughton *Leics* 39 SP6688
Laughton *Lincs* 40 TF0731
Laughton *E Susx* 13 TQ4913
Laughton-en-le-Morthen *S York* 49 SK5187
Launcells *Cnwll* 6 SS2405
Launceston *Cnwll* 4 SX3384
Launton *Oxon* 29 SP6022
Laurencekirk *Gramp* 89 NO7171
Laurieston *Cent* 82 NS9179
Laurieston *D & G* 65 NX6864
Lavendon *Bucks* 30 SP9153
Lavenham *Suffk* 32 TL9149
Lavernock *S Glam* 19 ST1868
Laversdale *Cumb* 67 NY4762
Laverstock *Wilts* 10 SU1630
Laverstoke *Hants* 21 SU4948
Laverton *N York* 61 SE2273
Laverton *Gloucs* 28 SP0735
Laverton *Somset* 20 ST7753
Lavister *Clwyd* 46 SJ3758
Law *Strath* 74 NS8252
Law Hill *Strath* 74 NS8251
Lawers *Tays* 81 NN6739
Lawford *Somset* 18 ST1336
Lawford *Essex* 25 TM0831
Lawgrove *Tays* 82 NO0926
Lawhitton *Cnwll* 4 SX3582
Lawkland *N York* 54 SD7766
Lawrenny *Dyfed* 16 SN0106
Lawshall *Suffk* 32 TL8654
Laxay *W Isls* 102 NB3321
Laxdale *W Isls* 102 NB4234
Laxey *IOM* 52 SC4384
Laxfield *Suffk* 33 TM2972
Laxford Bridge *Highld* 98 NC2346
Laxo *Shet* 103 HU4463
Laxton *Humb* 56 SE7925
Laxton *Notts* 49 SK7267
Laxton *Nhants* 40 SP9596
Laycock *W York* 55 SE0341
Layer Breton *Essex* 25 TL9417
Layer Marney *Essex* 24 TL9217
Layer-de-la-Haye *Essex* 25 TL9620
Layham *Suffk* 32 TM0240
Laymore *Dorset* 8 ST3804
Laysters Pole *H & W* 27 SO5563
Laytham *Humb* 56 SE7439
Laythes *Cumb* 67 NY2455
Lazonby *Cumb* 59 NY5439
Le Bigard *Guern* 101 GN0000
Le Bourg *Guern* 101 GN0000
Le Bourg *Jersey* 101 JS0000
Le Gron *Guern* 101 GN0000
Le Haquais *Jersey* 101 JS0000
Le Hocq *Jersey* 101 JS0000
Le Villocq *Guern* 101 GN0000
Lea *Derbys* 49 SK3257
Lea *Lincs* 50 SK8286
Lea *Shrops* 36 SO3589
Lea *H & W* 27 SO6521
Lea *Wilts* 20 ST9586
Lea *Wilts* 20 ST9586
Lea Marston *Warwks* 39 SP2093
Leachkin *Highld* 92 NH6344
Leadburn *Loth* 75 NT2355
Leaden Roding *Essex* 24 TL5913
Leadenham *Lincs* 50 SK9452
Leadgate *Dur* 69 NZ1251
Leadhills *Strath* 74 NS8815
Leafield *Oxon* 29 SP3115
Leagrave *Beds* 30 TL0523
Leake Common Side *Lincs* 51 TF3952
Lealholm *N York* 63 NZ7607
Lealt *Highld* 90 NG5060
Leamington Hastings *Warwks* 29 SP4467
Leasgill *Cumb* 59 SD4983
Leasingham *Lincs* 50 TF0548
Leasingthorne *Dur* 61 NZ2530
Leatherhead *Surrey* 23 TQ1656
Leathley *N York* 55 SE2347
Leaths *D & G* 66 NX7862
Leaton *Shrops* 36 SJ4618
Leaveland *Kent* 15 TR0053
Leavenheath *Suffk* 25 TL9537
Leavening *N York* 56 SE7863
Leaves Green *Gt Lon* 23 TQ4161
Lebberston *N York* 63 TA0782
Lechampstead Thicket *Berks* 21 SU4276
Lechlade *Wilts* 21 SU2199
Leck *Lancs* 60 SD6476
Leckbuie *Tays* 81 NN7040
Leckford *Hants* 10 SU3737
Leck Gruinart *Strath* 70 NR2768
Leckhampstead *Bucks* 30 SP7237
Leckhampstead *Berks* 21 SU4375
Leckhampton *Gloucs* 28 SO9419
Leckmelm *Highld* 96 NH1689
Leconfield *Humb* 56 TA0143
Ledaig *Strath* 79 NM9037
Ledburn *Bucks* 30 SP9021
Ledbury *H & W* 28 SO7137
Ledgemoor *H & W* 27 SO4150
Ledmore Junction *Highld* 96 NC2412
Ledsham *W York* 55 SE4529
Ledston *W York* 55 SE4328
Ledwell *Oxon* 29 SP4128
Lee *Devon* 6 SS4846
Lee *Gt Lon* 23 TQ3875
Lee Brockhurst *Shrops* 37 SJ5427
Lee Chapel *Essex* 24 TQ6987
Lee Clump *Bucks* 22 SP9004
Leeds *W York* 55 SE2932
Lee Mill *Devon* 5 SX5955
Lee-on-the-Solent *Hants* 11 SU5600
Leebotwood *Shrops* 37 SO4798
Leece *Cumb* 53 SD2469
Leeds *Kent* 14 TQ8253
Leedstown *Cnwll* 2 SW6034
Leek *Staffs* 48 SJ9856
Leek Wootton *Warwks* 29 SP2868
Leeming *N York* 61 SE2989
Leeming Bar *N York* 61 SE2889
Lees *Gt Man* 54 SD9504
Lees *Derbys* 49 SK2637
Lees Green *Derbys* 49 SK2637
Leesthorpe *Leics* 40 SK7813
Leetown *Tays* 82 NO2121
Leftwich *Ches* 47 SJ6672
Legbourne *Lincs* 51 TF3784
Legerwood *Border* 76 NT5843
Legsby *Lincs* 50 TF1385
Leicester *Leics* 39 SK5804
Leicester Forest East *Leics* 39 SK5202
Leigh *Mersyd* 47 SJ6599
Leigh *H & W* 28 SO7853
Leigh *Gloucs* 28 SO8626
Leigh *Dorset* 9 ST6108
Leigh *Wilts* 20 SU0692
Leigh *Surrey* 12 TQ2246
Leigh *Kent* 13 TQ5446
Leigh Beck *Essex* 24 TQ8183
Leigh Delamere *Wilts* 20 ST8879
Leigh Green *Kent* 14 TQ9033
Leigh Knoweglass *Strath* 74 NS6350
Leigh Sinton *H & W* 28 SO7750
Leigh Woods *Avon* 19 ST5672
Leigh upon Mendip *Somset* 20 ST6947
Leigh-on-Sea *Essex* 24 TQ8286
Leighterton *Gloucs* 20 ST8290
Leighton *Powys* 36 SJ2306
Leighton *Shrops* 37 SJ6105
Leighton Bromswold *Cambs* 30 TL1175
Leighton Buzzard *Beds* 30 SP9225
Leinthall Earls *H & W* 27 SO4467
Leinthall Starkes *H & W* 27 SO4369
Leintwardine *H & W* 36 SO4074
Leire *Leics* 39 SP5290
Leiston *Suffk* 33 TM4462
Leitfie *Tays* 88 NO2545
Leith *Loth* 75 NT2776
Leitholm *Border* 76 NT7944
Lelant *Cnwll* 2 SW5437
Lelley *Humb* 57 TA2032
Lem Hill *H & W* 37 SO7275
Lempitlaw *Border* 76 NT7832
Lemreway *W Isls* 102 NB3711
Lemsford *Herts* 31 TL2212
Lenchwick *H & W* 28 SP0347
Lendalfoot *Strath* 64 NX1390
Lendrick *Cent* 81 NN5506
Lendrum Terrace *Gramp* 95 NK1141
Lenham *Kent* 14 TQ8952
Lenham Heath *Kent* 14 TQ9149
Lenie *Highld* 92 NH5126
Lennel *Border* 77 NT8540
Lennox Plunton *D & G* 65 NX6051
Lennoxlove *Loth* 76 NT5172
Lennoxtown *Strath* 74 NS6277
Lenton *Lincs* 40 TF0230
Lenzie *Strath* 74 NS6572
Leochel-Cushnie *Gramp* 94 NJ5210
Leominster *H & W* 27 SO4959
Leonard Stanley *Gloucs* 20 SO8003
Leoville *Jersey* 101 JS0000
Lephin *Highld* 90 NG1749
Leppington *N York* 56 SE7661
Lepton *W York* 55 SE2015
Lerags *Strath* 79 NM8324
Lerryn *Cnwll* 3 SX1457
Lerwick *Shet* 103 HU4741
Les Arquets *Guern* 101 GN0000
Les Hubits *Guern* 101 GN0000
Les Lohiers *Guern* 101 GN0000
Les Murchez *Guern* 101 GN0000
Les Nicolles *Guern* 101 GN0000
Les Quartiers *Guern* 101 GN0000
Les Quennevais *Jersey* 101 JS0000
Les Sages *Guern* 101 GN0000
Les Villets *Guern* 101 GN0000
Lesbury *Nthumb* 69 NU2311
Leslie *Gramp* 94 NJ5924
Leslie *Fife* 83 NO2501
Lesmahagow *Strath* 74 NS8139
Lesnewth *Cnwll* 4 SX1390
Lessingham *Norfk* 43 TG3928
Lessonhall *Cumb* 67 NY2250
Leswalt *D & G* 64 NX0163
Letchmore Heath *Herts* 22 TQ1597
Letchworth *Herts* 31 TL2232
Letcombe Bassett *Oxon* 21 SU3784
Letcombe Regis *Oxon* 21 SU3886
Letham *Fife* 83 NO3014
Letham *Tays* 89 NO5348
Letham *Border* 68 NT6709
Letham Grange *Tays* 89 NO6345
Lethenty *Gramp* 94 NJ5820
Lethenty *Gramp* 95 NJ8140
Letheringham *Suffk* 33 TM2757
Letheringsett *Norfk* 42 TG0638
Letterfinlay Lodge Hotel *Highld* 86 NN2491
Letterfearn *Highld* 85 NG8823
Lettermorar *Highld* 85 NM7389
Letters *Highld* 96 NH1687
Lettershaw *Strath* 74 NS8920
Letterston *Dyfed* 16 SM9429
Lettoch *Highld* 93 NJ0219
Lettoch *Highld* 93 NJ1032
Letton *H & W* 27 SO3346
Letty Green *Herts* 23 TL2810
Letwell *S York* 49 SK5686
Leuchars *Fife* 83 NO4521
Leurbost *W Isls* 102 NB3725
Levedale *Staffs* 38 SJ8916
Level's Green *Essex* 31 TL4724
Leven *Fife* 83 NO3800
Leven *Humb* 57 TA1045
Levencorroch *Strath* 72 NS0021
Levens *Cumb* 59 SD4886
Levens *Cumb* 59 SD4886
Levens Green *Herts* 31 TL3522
Levenshulme *Gt Man* 47 SJ8794
Levenwick *Shet* 103 HU4021
Leverburgh *W Isls* 102 NG0186
Leverington *Cambs* 41 TF4411
Leverstock Green *Herts* 22 TL0806
Leverton *Lincs* 51 TF4047
Levington *Suffk* 33 TM2339
Levisham *N York* 63 SE8390
Lew *Oxon* 29 SP3206
Lewannick *Cnwll* 4 SX2780
Lewdown *Devon* 4 SX4586
Lewes *E Susx* 13 TQ4110
Leweston *Dyfed* 16 SM9322
Lewisham *Gt Lon* 23 TQ3774
Lewiston *Highld* 92 NH5129
Lewknor *Oxon* 22 SU7197
Lewson Street *Kent* 15 TQ9661
Lewtrenchard *Devon* 4 SX4586
Lexworthy *Somset* 8 ST2535
Leybourne *Kent* 14 TQ6858
Leyburn *N York* 61 SE1190
Leygreen *Herts* 31 TL1624
Leyland *Lancs* 53 SD5422
Leylodge *Gramp* 95 NJ7613
Leys *Gramp* 95 NK0052
Leys *Tays* 83 NO2537
Leys of Cossans *Tays* 88 NO3849
Leysdown-on-Sea *Kent* 15 TR0370
Leysmill *Tays* 89 NO6047
Leyton *Gt Lon* 23 TQ3786
Leytonstone *Gt Lon* 23 TQ3987
Lezant *Cnwll* 4 SX3479
Lezayre *IOM* 52 SC4294
Lhanbryde *Gramp* 94 NJ2761
Libanus *Powys* 26 SN9925
Libberton *Strath* 75 NS9943
Liberton *Loth* 75 NT2769
Lichfield *Staffs* 38 SK1109
Lickey *H & W* 38 SO9975
Lickey End *H & W* 38 SO9772
Lickfold *W Susx* 11 SU9226
Liddesdale *Highld* 79 NM7759
Liddington *Wilts* 21 SU2081
Lidgate *Suffk* 32 TL7258
Lidlington *Beds* 30 SP9939
Liff *Tays* 83 NO3332
Lifford *W Mids* 38 SP0580
Lifton *Devon* 4 SX3885
Liftondown *Devon* 4 SX3685
Lighthorne *Warwks* 29 SP3355
Lightwater *Surrey* 22 SU9362
Lilbourne *Nhants* 39 SP5676
Lilleshall *Shrops* 37 SJ7315
Lilley *Herts* 30 TL1126
Lilliesleaf *Border* 76 NT5325
Lillingstone Dayrell *Bucks* 30 SP7039
Lillingstone Lovell *Bucks* 30 SP7140
Lillington *Dorset* 9 ST6212
Lilstock *Somset* 19 ST1645
Limbury *Beds* 30 TL0724
Lime Street *H & W* 28 SO8130
Limekilnburn *Strath* 74 NS7050
Limekilns *Fife* 82 NT0883
Limerigg *Cent* 74 NS8571
Limerstone *IOW* 10 SZ4482
Limington *Somset* 8 ST5422
Limmerhaugh *Strath* 74 NS6127
Limpenhoe *Norfk* 43 TG3903
Limpley Stoke *Wilts* 20 ST7860
Limpsfield *Surrey* 13 TQ4053
Limpsfield Chart *Surrey* 13 TQ4251
Linby *Notts* 49 SK5351
Linchmere *W Susx* 11 SU8630
Lincluden *D & G* 66 NX9677
Lincoln *Lincs* 50 SK9771
Lincomb *H & W* 28 SO8268
Lindal in Furness *Cumb* 58 SD2475
Lindale *Cumb* 59 SD4180
Lindean *Border* 76 NT4931
Lindfield *W Susx* 12 TQ3425
Lindford *Hants* 11 SU8036
Lindley *W York* 55 SE1217
Lindley Green *N York* 55 SE2248
Lindores *Fife* 83 NO2616
Lindridge *H & W* 28 SO6769
Lindsell *Essex* 24 TL6427
Lindsey *Suffk* 32 TL9745
Lindsey Tye *Suffk* 32 TL9845
Lingdale *Cleve* 62 NZ6716
Lingen *H & W* 27 SO3667
Lingwood *Norfk* 43 TG3508
Linicro *Highld* 90 NG3966
Linkend *H & W* 28 SO8231
Linkenholt *Hants* 21 SU3657
Linkinhorne *Cnwll* 4 SX3173
Linktown *Fife* 83 NT2790
Linkwood *Gramp* 94 NJ2361
Linley *Shrops* 36 SO3592
Linley Green *H & W* 28 SO6953
Linleygreen *Shrops* 37 SO6898
Linlithgow *Loth* 75 NS9977
Linsidemore *Highld* 96 NH5499
Linslade *Beds* 30 SP9125
Linstead Parva *Suffk* 33 TM3377
Linstock *Cumb* 67 NY4258
Linthurst *H & W* 38 SO9972
Linthwaite *W York* 55 SE1014
Lintlaw *Border* 77 NT8258
Lintlaw *Border* 77 NT8258
Lintmill *Gramp* 94 NJ5165
Linton *Border* 76 NT7726
Linton *N York* 54 SD9962
Linton *W York* 55 SE3946
Linton *Derbys* 39 SK2716
Linton *H & W* 28 SO6625
Linton *Cambs* 31 TL5646
Linton *Kent* 14 TQ7550
Linton Hill *Gloucs* 28 SO6624
Linton-on-Ouse *N York* 55 SE4860
Lintrathen *Tays* 88 NO2854
Linwood *Strath* 73 NS4464
Linwood *Lincs* 50 TF1186
Lionel *W Isls* 102 NB5263
Liphook *Hants* 11 SU8431
Liscard *Mersyd* 46 SJ2991
Liscombe *Devon* 7 SS8732
Liskeard *Cnwll* 4 SX2564
Liss *Hants* 11 SU7727
Lissett *Humb* 57 TA1458
Lissington *Lincs* 50 TF1083
Lisvane *S Glam* 19 ST1883
Litcham *Norfk* 42 TF8817
Litchborough *Nhants* 29 SP6354
Litchfield *Hants* 21 SU4653
Litherland *Mersyd* 46 SJ3397
Litlington *Cambs* 31 TL3142
Litlington *E Susx* 13 TQ5201
Little Abington *Cambs* 31 TL5349
Little Addington *Nhants* 30 SP9673
Little Airies *D & G* 64 NX4248
Little Alne *Warwks* 28 SP1461
Little Amwell *Herts* 23 TL3511
Little Asby *Cumb* 60 NY6909
Little Aston *Staffs* 38 SK0900
Little Ayton *N York* 62 NZ5610
Little Baddow *Essex* 24 TL7707
Little Badminton *Avon* 20 ST8084
Little Bampton *Cumb* 67 NY2755
Little Bardfield *Essex* 24 TL6531
Little Barford *Beds* 31 TL1756
Little Barningham *Norfk* 43 TG1333
Little Barrington *Gloucs* 29 SP2012
Little Barrow *Ches* 46 SJ4769
Little Bavington *Nthumb* 68 NY9878
Little Bedwyn *Wilts* 21 SU2866
Little Bentley *Essex* 25 TM1125
Little Berkhamsted *Herts* 23 TL2907
Little Billing *Nhants* 30 SP8061
Little Billington *Beds* 30 SP9322
Little Birch *H & W* 27 SO5130
Little Blakenham *Suffk* 33 TM1048
Little Blencow *Cumb* 59 NY4532
Little Bognor *W Susx* 12 TQ0020
Little Bolehill *Derbys* 49 SK2954
Little Bookham *Surrey* 22 TQ1254
Little Bourton *Oxon* 29 SP4544
Little Bradley *Suffk* 32 TL6852

Llay Lynton

Llay *Clwyd* 46 SJ3355
Llechryd *Dyfed* 17 SN2143
Lledrod *Dyfed* 35 SN6470
Llithfaen *Gwynd* 44 SH3542
Llowes *Powys* 27 SO1941
Llwydcoed *M Glam* 26 SN9904
Llwydiarth *Powys* 36 SJ0315
Llwyncelyn *Dyfed* 34 SN4459
Llwyndafydd *Dyfed* 34 SN3755
Llwyngwril *Gwynd* 34 SH5909
Llwynmawr *Clwyd* 36 SJ2237
Llwynypia *M Glam* 18 SS9993
Llynclys *Shrops* 36 SJ2824
Llynfaes *Gwynd* 44 SH4178
Llys-y-fran *Dyfed* 16 SN0424
Llysfaen *Clwyd* 45 SH8977
Llyswen *Powys* 26 SO1337
Llysworney *S Glam* 18 SS9673
Llywel *Powys* 26 SN8630
Loan *Cent* 75 NS9675
Loanhead *Loth* 75 NT2865
Loaningfoot *D & G* 66 NX9655
Loans *Strath* 73 NS3431
Lobhillcross *Devon* 4 SX4686
Loch Katrine Pier *Cent* 81 NN4907
Loch Loyal Lodge *Highld* 99 NC6146
Loch Maree Hotel *Highld* 91 NG9170
Lochailort *Highld* 85 NM7682
Lochans *D & G* 64 NX0656
Locharbriggs *D & G* 66 NX9980
Lochavich *Strath* 80 NM9415
Lochawe *Strath* 80 NN1227
Lochboisdale *W Isls* 102 NF7919
Lochbuie *Strath* 79 NM6025
Lochcarron *Highld* 85 NG8939
Lochdon *Strath* 79 NM7233
Lochead *Strath* 71 NR7778
Lochearnhead *Cent* 81 NN5823
Lochee *Tays* 83 NO3731
Lochee *Tays* 83 NO3731
Locheilside Station *Highld* 85 NM9978
Lochend *Highld* 92 NH5937
Locheport *W Isls* 102 NF8563
Lochfoot *D & G* 66 NX8973
Lochgair *Strath* 71 NR9290
Lochgelly *Fife* 82 NT1893
Lochgilphead *Strath* 71 NR8688
Lochgoilhead *Strath* 80 NN2001
Lochieheads *Fife* 83 NO2513
Lochill *Gramp* 94 NJ2964
Lochindorb Lodge *Highld* 93 NH9635
Lochinver *Highld* 98 NC0922
Lochluichart *Highld* 92 NH3363
Lochmaben *D & G* 66 NY0882
Lochmaddy *W Isls* 102 NF9169
Lochore *Fife* 82 NT1796
Lochranza *Strath* 72 NR9350
Lochside *Highld* 93 NH8152
Lochside *Gramp* 89 NO7364
Lochton *Strath* 64 NX2579
Lochty *Fife* 83 NO5208
Lochty *Tays* 89 NO5362
Lochuisge *Highld* 79 NM7955
Lochwinnoch *Strath* 73 NS3559
Lochwood *Strath* 74 NS6966
Lochwood *D & G* 66 NY0896
Lockengate *Cnwll* 3 SX0361
Lockerbie *D & G* 67 NY1381
Lockeridge *Wilts* 20 SU1467
Lockerley *Hants* 10 SU3025
Locking *Avon* 19 ST3659
Lockington *Humb* 56 SE9947
Lockleywood *Shrops* 37 SJ6928
Locksbottom *Gt Lon* 23 TQ4265
Lockton *N York* 63 SE8490
Loddington *Leics* 40 SK7902
Loddington *Nhants* 30 SP8178
Loddiswell *Devon* 5 SX7248
Loddon *Norfk* 43 TM3698
Lode *Cambs* 31 TL5362
Lode Heath *W Mids* 38 SP1580
Loders *Dorset* 8 SY4994
Lodsworth *W Susx* 11 SU9223
Lofhouse Gate *W York* 55 SE3324
Lofthouse *N York* 61 SE1073
Lofthouse *W York* 55 SE3325
Loftus *Cleve* 63 NZ7218
Logan *Strath* 74 NS5820
Loganlea *Loth* 75 NS9762
Loggerheads *Staffs* 37 SJ7336
Logie *Gramp* 93 NJ0150
Logie *Fife* 83 NO4020
Logie *Tays* 89 NO6963
Logie Coldstone *Gramp* 88 NJ4304
Logie Pert *Tays* 89 NO6664
Logierait *Tays* 88 NN9752
Login *Dyfed* 17 SN1623
Lolworth *Cambs* 31 TL3664
Lonbain *Highld* 91 NG6852
Londesborough *Humb* 56 SE8645
London *Gt Lon* 23 TQ2879
London Apprentice *Cnwll* 3 SX0049
London Colney *Herts* 23 TL1803
Londonderry *N York* 61 SE3087
Londonthorpe *Lincs* 40 SK9537
Londubh *Highld* 91 NG8680
Long Ashton *Avon* 19 ST5570
Long Bank *H & W* 37 SO7674
Long Bennington *Lincs* 50 SK8344
Long Bredy *Dorset* 8 SY5690
Long Buckby *Nhants* 29 SP6367
Long Clawson *Leics* 40 SK7227
Long Compton *Staffs* 38 SJ8522
Long Compton *Warwks* 29 SP2832
Long Crendon *Bucks* 22 SP6908
Long Crichel *Dorset* 9 ST9710
Long Ditton *Surrey* 23 TQ1766
Long Duckmanton *Derbys* 49 SK4471
Long Eaton *Derbys* 39 SK4833
Long Green *Ches* 46 SJ4770
Long Green *H & W* 28 SO8433
Long Itchington *Warwks* 29 SP4165
Long Lawford *Warwks* 39 SP4776
Long Load *Somset* 8 ST4623
Long Marston *N York* 55 SE5051
Long Marston *Warwks* 28 SP1548
Long Marston *Herts* 30 SP8915
Long Marton *Cumb* 60 NY6624
Long Melford *Suffk* 32 TL8645
Long Newnton *Gloucs* 20 ST9192
Long Newton *Loth* 76 NT5164
Long Preston *N York* 54 SD8358
Long Riston *Humb* 57 TA1242
Long Stratton *Norfk* 33 TM1992
Long Street *Bucks* 30 SP7947
Long Sutton *Somset* 8 ST4725
Long Sutton *Hants* 22 SU7347
Long Sutton *Lincs* 41 TF4322
Long Thurlow *Suffk* 32 TM0068
Long Waste *Shrops* 37 SJ6115
Long Whatton *Leics* 39 SK4723
Long Wittenham *Oxon* 21 SU5493
Longbenton *T & W* 69 NZ2668
Longborough *Gloucs* 29 SP1729
Longbridge *W Mids* 38 SP0177
Longbridge Deverill *Wilts* 20 ST8640
Longburton *Dorset* 9 ST6412
Longcliffe *Derbys* 48 SK2255
Longcombe *Devon* 5 SX8359
Longcot *Oxon* 21 SU2790
Longden *Shrops* 36 SJ4406
Longdon *Staffs* 38 SK0714
Longdon *H & W* 28 SO8336
Longdon Green *Staffs* 38 SK0813
Longdon upon Tern *Shrops* 37 SJ6115
Longdown *Devon* 5 SX8691
Longdowns *Cnwll* 2 SW7434
Longfield *Kent* 14 TQ6069
Longford *Shrops* 37 SJ6434
Longford *Shrops* 37 SJ7218
Longford *Derbys* 48 SK2137
Longford *Gloucs* 28 SO8320
Longforgan *Tays* 83 NO2929
Longformacus *Border* 76 NT6957
Longframlington *Nthumb* 69 NU1300
Longham *Dorset* 10 SZ0698
Longham *Norfk* 42 TF9416
Longhill *Gramp* 95 NJ9953
Longhirst *Nthumb* 69 NZ2289
Longhope *Gloucs* 28 SO6918
Longhorsley *Nthumb* 69 NZ1494
Longhoughton *Nthumb* 77 NU2415
Longlane *Derbys* 48 SK2437
Longlevens *Gloucs* 28 SO8519
Longleys *Tays* 88 NO2643
Longmanhill *Gramp* 95 NJ7362
Longmoor Camp *Hants* 11 SU7931
Longmorn *Gramp* 94 NJ2358
Longnewton *Border* 76 NT5827
Longney *Gloucs* 28 SO7612
Longniddry *Loth* 76 NT4476
Longnor *Shrops* 37 SJ4800
Longnor *Staffs* 48 SK0864
Longparish *Hants* 21 SU4345
Longridge *Loth* 75 NS9462
Longridge *Lancs* 54 SD6037
Longriggend *Strath* 74 NS8270
Longrock *Cnwll* 2 SW5031
Longsdon *Staffs* 48 SJ9654
Longside *Gramp* 95 NK0347
Longstanton *Cambs* 31 TL3966
Longstock *Hants* 10 SU3537
Longstowe *Cambs* 31 TL3054
Longstreet *Wilts* 20 SU1451
Longthorpe *Cambs* 40 TL1698
Longthwaite *Cumb* 59 NY4323
Longton *Lancs* 53 SD4825
Longton *Staffs* 48 SJ9143
Longtown *Cumb* 67 NY3768
Longtown *H & W* 27 SO3229
Longueville *Jersey* 101 JS0000
Longville in the Dale *Shrops* 37 SO5393
Longwick *Bucks* 22 SP7905
Longwitton *Nthumb* 68 NZ0788
Longwood *D & G* 65 NX7060
Longworth *Oxon* 21 SU3899
Longyester *Loth* 76 NT5465
Lonmay *Gramp* 95 NK0159
Lonmore *Highld* 90 NG2646
Looe *Cnwll* 4 SX2553
Loose *Kent* 14 TQ7552
Loosley Row *Bucks* 22 SP8100
Lootcherbrae *Gramp* 94 NJ6053
Lopen *Somset* 8 ST4214
Loppington *Shrops* 36 SJ4629
Lornty *Tays* 88 NO1746
Loscoe *Derbys* 49 SK4247
Lossiemouth *Gramp* 94 NJ2370
Lostock Gralam *Ches* 47 SJ6974
Lostock Green *Ches* 47 SJ6973
Lostwithiel *Cnwll* 3 SX1059
Lothbeg *Highld* 97 NC9410
Lothersdale *N York* 54 SD9545
Lothmore *Highld* 97 NC9611
Loughborough *Leics* 39 SK5319
Loughor *W Glam* 17 SS5698
Loughton *Shrops* 37 SO6182
Loughton *Bucks* 30 SP8337
Loughton *Essex* 23 TQ4296
Lound *Notts* 49 SK6986
Lound *Lincs* 40 TF0618
Lound *Suffk* 43 TM5099
Lound *Suffk* 43 TM5099
Lount *Leics* 39 SK3819
Louth *Lincs* 51 TF3287
Love Clough *Lancs* 54 SD8127
Lovedean *Hants* 11 SU6812
Lover *Wilts* 10 SU2120
Loversall *S York* 49 SK5798
Loves Green *Essex* 24 TL6404
Loveston *Dyfed* 16 SN0808
Lovington *Somset* 9 ST5930
Low Ackworth *W York* 55 SE4517
Low Barbeth *D & G* 64 NX0166
Low Biggins *Cumb* 59 SD6077
Low Borrowbridge *Cumb* 59 NY6101
Low Bradfield *S York* 49 SK2691
Low Bradley *N York* 54 SE0048
Low Burnham *Humb* 50 SE7802
Low Catton *Humb* 56 SE7053
Low Crosby *Cumb* 67 NY4459
Low Dinsdale *Dur* 62 NZ3411
Low Eggborough *N York* 56 SE5623
Low Ellington *N York* 61 SE1983
Low Gartachorrans *Cent* 81 NS4685
Low Grantley *N York* 55 SE2370
Low Ham *Somset* 8 ST4329
Low Harrogate *N York* 55 SE2955
Low Hesket *Cumb* 67 NY4646
Low Hill *H & W* 38 SO8473
Low Hutton *N York* 56 SE7667
Low Lorton *Cumb* 58 NY1525
Low Marnham *Notts* 50 SK8069
Low Mill *N York* 62 SE6795
Low Moorsley *T & W* 69 NZ3446
Low Mowthorpe *N York* 56 SE8966
Low Row *Cumb* 67 NY5863
Low Row *N York* 61 SD9797
Low Salchrie *D & G* 64 NX0365
Low Santon *Humb* 56 SE9412
Low Skeog *D & G* 65 NX4540
Low Tharston *Norfk* 43 TM1895
Low Worsall *N York* 62 NZ3909
Low Wray *Cumb* 59 NY3701
Lowdham *Notts* 49 SK6646
Lower Aisholt *Somset* 8 ST2035
Lower Ansty *Dorset* 9 ST7603
Lower Apperley *Gloucs* 28 SO8527
Lower Arncott *Oxon* 29 SP6019
Lower Ashton *Devon* 5 SX8484
Lower Assendon *Oxon* 22 SU7484
Lower Bartle *Lancs* 53 SD4933
Lower Beeding *W Susx* 12 TQ2127
Lower Benefield *Nhants* 40 SP9988
Lower Bentham *N York* 54 SD6469
Lower Bentley *H & W* 28 SO9865
Lower Boddington *Nhants* 29 SP4852
Lower Bourne *Surrey* 22 SU8444
Lower Brailes *Warwks* 29 SP3139
Lower Breakish *Highld* 85 NG6723
Lower Broadheath *H & W* 28 SO8157
Lower Bullingham *H & W* 27 SO5138
Lower Burgate *Hants* 10 SU1515
Lower Caldecote *Beds* 31 TL1746
Lower Cam *Gloucs* 20 SO7400
Lower Catesby *Nhants* 29 SP5159
Lower Chapel *Powys* 26 SO0235
Lower Chicksgrove *Wilts* 9 ST9729
Lower Chute *Wilts* 21 SU3153
Lower Clapton *Gt Lon* 23 TQ3485
Lower Clent *H & W* 38 SO9279
Lower Cumberworth *W York* 55 SE2209
Lower Dean *Beds* 30 TL0569
Lower Diabaig *Highld* 91 NG7960
Lower Dicker *E Susx* 13 TQ5511
Lower Down *Shrops* 36 SO3484
Lower Dunsforth *N York* 55 SE4464
Lower Egleton *H & W* 27 SO6245
Lower End *Bucks* 30 SP9238
Lower Eythorne *Kent* 15 TR2849
Lower Failand *Avon* 19 ST5173
Lower Farringdon *Hants* 11 SU7035
Lower Feltham *Gt Lon* 22 TQ0971
Lower Fittleworth *W Susx* 12 TQ0118
Lower Froyle *Hants* 22 SU7544
Lower Gabwell *Devon* 5 SX9169
Lower Gledfield *Highld* 96 NH5890
Lower Godney *Somset* 19 ST4742
Lower Gravenhurst *Beds* 30 TL1035
Lower Green *Norfk* 42 TF9837
Lower Green *Kent* 13 TQ5640
Lower Green *Kent* 13 TQ6341
Lower Halliford *Surrey* 22 TQ0866
Lower Halstow *Kent* 14 TQ8567
Lower Hamworthy *Dorset* 9 SY9990
Lower Hardres *Kent* 15 TR1553
Lower Hartwell *Bucks* 30 SP7912
Lower Hergest *H & W* 27 SO2755
Lower Heyford *Oxon* 29 SP4824
Lower Irlam *Gt Man* 47 SJ7193
Lower Killeyan *Strath* 70 NR2742
Lower Kinnerton *Ches* 46 SJ3462
Lower Langford *Avon* 19 ST4560
Lower Largo *Fife* 83 NO4102
Lower Leigh *Staffs* 38 SK0135
Lower Loxhore *Devon* 6 SS6137
Lower Lydbrook *Gloucs* 27 SO5916
Lower Lye *H & W* 27 SO4066
Lower Machen *Gwent* 19 ST2288
Lower Middleton Cheney *Nhants* 29 SP5041
Lower Moor *W Mids* 28 SO9747
Lower Morton *Avon* 19 ST6491
Lower Nazeing *Essex* 23 TL3906
Lower Penarth *S Glam* 19 ST1869
Lower Penn *Staffs* 38 SO8796
Lower Peover *Ches* 47 SJ7474
Lower Pond Street *Essex* 31 TL4537
Lower Quinton *Warwks* 29 SP1847
Lower Raydon *Suffk* 25 TM0338
Lower Roadwater *Somset* 7 ST0339
Lower Seagry *Wilts* 20 ST9580
Lower Shelton *Beds* 30 SP9942
Lower Shiplake *Oxon* 22 SU7679
Lower Shuckburgh *Warwks* 29 SP4862
Lower Shurlach *Ches* 47 SJ6772
Lower Slaughter *Gloucs* 28 SP1622
Lower Standen *Kent* 15 TR2340
Lower Stanton St. Quintin *Wilts* 20 ST9180
Lower Stoke *Kent* 14 TQ8375
Lower Stone *Gloucs* 20 ST6794
Lower Stow Bedon *Norfk* 42 TL9694
Lower Street *Dorset* 9 SY8399
Lower Street *Norfk* 43 TG2635
Lower Street *Suffk* 33 TM1052
Lower Sundon *Beds* 30 TL0526
Lower Swanwick *Hants* 10 SU4909
Lower Swell *Gloucs* 29 SP1725
Lower Tean *Staffs* 48 SK0138
Lower Town *Dyfed* 16 SM9637
Lower Town *Devon* 5 SX7172
Lower Tysoe *Warwks* 29 SP3445
Lower Upcott *Devon* 5 SX8880
Lower Upham *Hants* 11 SU5219
Lower Vexford *Somset* 8 ST1135
Lower Weare *Somset* 19 ST4053
Lower Westmancote *H & W* 28 SO9337
Lower Whatley *Somset* 20 ST7447
Lower Whitley *Ches* 47 SJ6179
Lower Wield *Hants* 21 SU6340
Lower Willingdon *E Susx* 13 TQ5803
Lower Winchendon *Bucks* 30 SP7312
Lower Woodford *Wilts* 10 SU1235
Lower Wraxhall *Dorset* 8 ST5700
Lowesby *Leics* 40 SK7207
Lowestoft *Suffk* 43 TM5493
Loweswater *Cumb* 58 NY1421
Lowfield Heath *W Susx* 12 TQ2739
Lowick *Nthumb* 77 NU0139
Lowick *Nhants* 40 SP9881
Lowick Green *Cumb* 58 SD2985
Lowsonford *Warwks* 29 SP1868
Lowther *Cumb* 59 NY5323
Lowtherton *D & G* 67 NY2466
Lowthorpe *Humb* 57 TA0860
Lowton *Somset* 8 ST1918
Loxbeare *Devon* 7 SS9116
Loxhill *Surrey* 12 TQ0038
Loxhore *Devon* 6 SS6138
Loxhore Cott *Devon* 6 SS6138
Loxley *Warwks* 29 SP2553
Loxton *Avon* 19 ST3755
Loxwood *W Susx* 12 TQ0331
Lubcroy *Highld* 96 NC3501
Lubenham *Nhants* 40 SP7087
Lucas Green *Surrey* 22 SU9460
Luccombe *Somset* 7 SS9243
Luccombe Village *IOW* 11 SZ5879
Lucker *Nthumb* 77 NU1530
Luckett *Cnwll* 4 SX3873
Lucking Street *Essex* 24 TL8134
Luckington *Wilts* 20 ST8383
Lucklawhill *Fife* 83 NO4221
Luckwell Bridge *Somset* 7 SS9038
Lucton *H & W* 27 SO4364
Ludborough *Lincs* 51 TF2995
Ludbrook *Devon* 5 SX6654
Ludbrook *Devon* 5 SX6654
Ludbrook *Devon* 5 SX6654
Ludchurch *Dyfed* 16 SN1411
Luddenden *W York* 55 SE0426
Luddenden Foot *W York* 55 SE0325
Luddesdown *Kent* 14 TQ6666
Luddington *Humb* 56 SE8316
Luddington *Warwks* 28 SP1652
Luddington in the Brook *Nhants* 40 TL1083
Ludford *Shrops* 37 SO5174
Ludford *Lincs* 50 TF1989
Ludgershall *Bucks* 29 SP6517
Ludgershall *Wilts* 21 SU2650
Ludgvan *Cnwll* 2 SW5033
Ludham *Norfk* 43 TG3818
Ludlow *Shrops* 37 SO5175
Ludney *Somset* 8 ST3812
Ludwell *Wilts* 9 ST9122
Ludworth *Dur* 62 NZ3641
Luffincott *Devon* 6 SX3394
Luffness *Loth* 83 NT4780
Lugar *Strath* 74 NS5921
Luggate Burn *Loth* 76 NT5974
Luggiebank *Strath* 74 NS7672
Lugton *Strath* 73 NS4152
Lugwardine *H & W* 27 SO5540
Luib *Highld* 84 NG5627
Lulham *H & W* 27 SO4141
Lullington *Derbys* 39 SK2412
Lullington *Somset* 20 ST7851
Lulsgate Bottom *Avon* 19 ST5165
Lulsley *H & W* 28 SO7455
Lumb *Lancs* 54 SD8324
Lumb *W York* 55 SE0221
Lumby *N York* 55 SE4830
Lumloch *Strath* 74 NS6370
Lumphanan *Gramp* 89 NJ5804
Lumphinnans *Fife* 82 NT1792
Lumsden *Gramp* 94 NJ4722
Lunan *Tays* 89 NO6851
Lunanhead *Tays* 89 NO4752
Luncarty *Tays* 82 NO0929
Lund *N York* 56 SE6532
Lund *Humb* 56 SE9647
Lundford Magna *Lincs* 50 TF1989
Lundie *Cent* 81 NN7304
Lundie *Tays* 83 NO2836
Lundin Links *Fife* 83 NO4002
Lunna *Shet* 103 HU4869
Lunsford *Kent* 14 TQ6959
Lunsford's Cross *E Susx* 14 TQ7210
Lunt *Mersyd* 46 SD3402
Luppitt *Devon* 8 ST1606
Lupridge *Devon* 5 SX7153
Lupset *W York* 55 SE3119
Lupton *Cumb* 59 SD5581
Lurgashall *W Susx* 11 SU9326
Lurley *Devon* 7 SS9215
Luscombe *Devon* 5 SX7957
Luss *Strath* 80 NS3692
Luss *Strath* 80 NS3699
Lusta *Highld* 90 NG2656
Lustleigh *Devon* 5 SX7881
Luston *H & W* 27 SO4863
Luthermuir *Gramp* 89 NO6568
Luthrie *Fife* 83 NO3319
Luton *Devon* 7 ST0802
Luton *Devon* 5 SX9076
Luton *Beds* 30 TL0921
Luton *Kent* 14 TQ7766
Lutterworth *Leics* 39 SP5484
Lutton *Devon* 5 SX5959
Lutton *Lincs* 41 TF4325
Lutton *Nhants* 40 TL1187
Luxborough *Somset* 7 SS9738
Luxulyan *Cnwll* 3 SX0558
Lybster *Highld* 100 ND2435
Lydbury North *Shrops* 36 SO3486
Lydd *Kent* 15 TR0420
Lydden *Kent* 15 TR2645
Lydden *Kent* 15 TR3567
Lyddington *Leics* 40 SP8797
Lyde Green *Hants* 22 SU7057
Lydeard St. Lawrence *Somset* 8 ST1332
Lydford *Devon* 4 SX5185
Lydford on Fosse *Somset* 8 ST5630
Lydgate *W York* 54 SD9225
Lydham *Shrops* 36 SO3391
Lydiard Millicent *Wilts* 20 SU0986
Lydiard Tregoze *Wilts* 20 SU1085
Lydiate *Mersyd* 46 SD3604
Lydiate Ash *H & W* 38 SO9775
Lydlinch *Dorset* 9 ST7413
Lydney *Gloucs* 19 SO6303
Lydstep *Dyfed* 16 SS0898
Lye *W Mids* 38 SO9284
Lye Green *Warwks* 29 SP1965
Lye Green *E Susx* 13 TQ5134
Lye's Green *Wilts* 20 ST8146
Lyford *Oxon* 21 SU3994
Lymbridge Green *Kent* 15 TR1244
Lyme *Border* 75 NT2041
Lyme Regis *Dorset* 8 SY3492
Lyminge *Kent* 15 TR1641
Lymington *Hants* 10 SZ3295
Lyminster *W Susx* 12 TQ0204
Lymm *Ches* 47 SJ6887
Lympne *Kent* 15 TR1135
Lympsham *Somset* 19 ST3354
Lympstone *Devon* 5 SX9984
Lynch Green *Norfk* 43 TG1505
Lynchat *Highld* 87 NH7801
Lyndhurst *Hants* 10 SU3008
Lyndon *Leics* 40 SK9004
Lyne *Surrey* 22 TQ0166
Lyne Hill *Staffs* 38 SJ9212
Lyne of Skene *Gramp* 95 NJ7610
Lyneal *Shrops* 36 SJ4433
Lynegar *Highld* 100 ND2257
Lyneham *Oxon* 29 SP2720
Lyneham *Wilts* 20 SU0278
Lyness *Ork* 103 ND3094
Lyng *Somset* 8 ST3329
Lyng *Norfk* 42 TG0617
Lynmouth *Devon* 18 SS7249
Lynn of Shenval *Gramp* 94 NJ2129
Lynsted *Kent* 14 TQ9460
Lynton *Devon* 18 SS7249

Lyon's Gate Mickley Green

Lyon's Gate *Dorset* **9** ST6505
Lyonshall *H & W* **27** SO3355
Lytchett Matravers *Dorset* **9** SY9495
Lytchett Minster *Dorset* **9** SY9693
Lytham *Lancs* **53** SD3627
Lytham St. Anne's *Lancs* **53** SD3427
Lyth *Highld* **100** ND2762
Lythe *N York* **63** NZ8413
Lythmore *Highld* **100** ND0566

M

Mabe Burnthouse *Cnwll* **2** SW7634
Mabie *D & G* **66** NX9570
Mablethorpe *Lincs* **51** TF5085
Macclesfield *Ches* **48** SJ9173
Macclesfield Forest *Ches* **48** SJ9772
Macduff *Gramp* **95** NJ7064
Macharioch *Strath* **72** NR7309
Machen *M Glam* **19** ST2189
Machire *Strath* **70** NR2164
Machrie Farm *Strath* **72** NR9033
Machrihanish *Strath* **72** NR6320
Machrins *Strath* **70** NR3693
Machynlleth *Powys* **35** SH7400
Machynys *Dyfed* **17** SS5198
Mackworth *Derbys* **49** SK3137
Macmerry *Loth* **76** NT4372
Maddaford *Devon* **6** SX5494
Madderty *Tays* **82** NN9522
Maddiston *Cent* **75** NS9476
Madeley *Staffs* **47** SJ7744
Madingley *Cambs* **31** TL3960
Madley *H & W* **27** SO4238
Madresfield *H & W* **28** SO8047
Madron *Cnwll* **2** SW4531
Maen-y-groes *Dyfed* **34** SN3858
Maenclochog *Dyfed* **16** SN0827
Maendy *S Glam* **18** ST0076
Maentwrog *Gwynd* **45** SH6640
Maer *Staffs* **37** SJ7938
Maerdy *M Glam* **18** SS9798
Maesbrook *Shrops* **36** SJ3021
Maesbury Marsh *Shrops* **36** SJ3125
Maesllyn *Dyfed* **17** SN3644
Maesteg *M Glam* **18** SS8590
Maesteg *M Glam* **18** SS8590
Maesybont *Dyfed* **17** SN5616
Maesycwmmer *M Glam* **19** ST1594
Magdalen Laver *Essex* **23** TL5108
Maggieknockater *Gramp* **94** NJ3145
Maggots End *Essex* **31** TL4827
Magham Down *E Susx* **13** TQ6011
Maghull *Mersyd* **46** SD3703
Magor *Gwent* **19** ST4286
Maiden Bradley *Wilts* **20** ST8038
Maiden Head *Avon* **19** ST5666
Maiden Newton *Dorset* **9** SY5997
Maiden Wells *Dyfed* **16** SR9799
Maidencombe *Devon* **5** SX9268
Maidenhay *Devon* **8** SY2795
Maidenhead *Berks* **22** SU8980
Maidens *Strath* **73** NS2107
Maidenwell *Lincs* **51** TF3179
Maidford *Nhants* **29** SP6052
Maids Moreton *Bucks* **30** SP7035
Maidstone *Kent* **14** TQ7555
Maidwell *Nhants* **30** SP7476
Mains of Bainakettle *Gramp* **89** NO6274
Mains of Balhall *Tays* **89** NO5163
Mains of Cairnborrow *Gramp* **94** NJ4640
Mains of Dalvey *Highld* **93** NJ1132
Mains of Haulkerton *Gramp* **89** NO7172
Mains of Throsk *Cent* **82** NS8690
Mainsforth *Dur* **62** NZ3131
Mainsriddle *D & G* **66** NX9456
Mainstone *Shrops* **36** SO2787
Maisemore *Gloucs* **28** SO8121
Makeney *Derbys* **49** SK3544
Malborough *Devon* **5** SX7139
Malden *Surrey* **23** TQ2166
Maldon *Essex* **24** TL8506
Malham *N York* **54** SD9063
Mallaig *Highld* **85** NM6796
Mallaigvaig *Highld* **85** NM6897
Malleny Mills *Loth* **75** NT1665
Malltraeth *Gwynd* **44** SH4068
Mallwyd *Gwynd* **35** SH8612
Malmesbury *Wilts* **20** ST9387
Malmsmead *Somset* **18** SS7947
Malpas *Ches* **46** SJ4847
Malpas *Gwent* **19** ST3090
Malpas *Cnwll* **3** SW8442
Maltby *Cleve* **62** NZ4613
Maltby *S York* **49** SK5392
Maltby le Marsh *Lincs* **51** TF4681
Malting Green *Essex* **25** TL9720
Maltman's Hill *Kent* **14** TQ9043
Malton *N York* **56** SE7871
Malvern Link *H & W* **28** SO7947
Malvern Wells *H & W* **28** SO7742
Malzie *D & G* **64** NX3754
Mamble *H & W* **37** SO6871
Mamhilad *Gwent* **19** SO3003
Manaccan *Cnwll* **2** SW7624
Manafon *Powys* **36** SJ1102
Manaton *Devon* **5** SX7581
Manby *Lincs* **51** TF3986
Mancetter *Warwks* **39** SP3296
Manchester *Gt Man* **47** SJ8497
Mancot *Clwyd* **46** SJ3167
Mandally *Highld* **86** NH2900
Manea *Cambs* **41** TL4789
Maney *W Mids* **38** SP1195
Manfield *N York* **61** NZ2113
Mangotsfield *Avon* **20** ST6676
Mangrove Green *Herts* **30** TL1224
Manish *W Isls* **102** NG1089
Manley *Ches* **46** SJ5071
Manmoel *Gwent* **19** SO1803
Mannel *Strath* **78** NL9840
Manning's Heath *W Susx* **12** TQ2028
Manningford Bohune *Wilts* **20** SU1357
Manningford Bruce *Wilts* **20** SU1358
Manningham *W York* **55** SE1435
Mannington *Dorset* **10** SU0605
Manningtree *Essex* **25** TM1031
Mannofield *Gramp* **89** NJ9104
Manor Park *Gt Lon* **23** TQ4285
Manorbier *Dyfed* **16** SS0697
Manorbier Newton *Dyfed* **16** SN0400
Manorhill *Border* **76** NT6632
Manorowen *Dyfed* **16** SM9336
Mansell Gamage *H & W* **27** SO3944
Mansell Lacy *H & W* **27** SO4245
Mansfield *Strath* **66** NS6214
Mansfield *Notts* **49** SK5361
Mansfield Woodhouse *Notts* **49** SK5363
Manston *W York* **55** SE3634
Manston *Dorset* **9** ST8115
Manswood *Dorset* **9** ST9708
Manthorpe *Lincs* **40** TF0715
Manton *Humb* **50** SE9302
Manton *Leics* **40** SK8704
Manuden *Essex* **31** TL4926
Maolachy *Strath* **79** NM8913
Maperton *Somset* **9** ST6726
Maperton *Somset* **9** ST6726
Maplebeck *Notts* **49** SK7060
Mapledurham *Oxon* **22** SU6776
Mapledurwell *Hants* **22** SU6851
Maplehurst *W Susx* **12** TQ1824
Maplescombe *Kent* **14** TQ5664
Mapleton *Derbys* **48** SK1647
Mapperley *Derbys* **49** SK4342
Mapperley Park *Notts* **49** SK5842
Mapperton *Dorset* **8** SY5099
Mappleborough Green *Warwks* **28** SP0866
Mappleton *Humb* **57** TA2243
Mappowder *Dorset* **9** ST7306
Marazanvose *Cnwll* **2** SW7950
Marazion *Cnwll* **2** SW5130
Marbury *Ches* **47** SJ5645
March *Strath* **66** NS9914
March *Cambs* **41** TL4196
Marcham *Oxon* **21** SU4596
Marchamley *Shrops* **37** SJ5929
Marchington *Staffs* **38** SK1330
Marchwiel *Clwyd* **46** SJ3547
Marchwood *Hants* **10** SU3810
Marcross *S Glam* **18** SS9269
Marden *H & W* **27** SO5146
Marden *Wilts* **20** SU0857
Marden *Kent* **14** TQ7444
Marden Thorn *Kent* **14** TQ7642
Mardleybury *Herts* **31** TL2618
Mardy *Gwent* **27** SO3015
Mare Green *Somset* **8** ST3326
Mareham le Fen *Lincs* **51** TF2761
Mareham on the Hill *Lincs* **51** TF2867
Marehill *W Susx* **12** TQ0618
Maresfield *E Susx* **13** TQ4624
Marfleet *Humb* **57** TA1429
Marford *Clwyd* **46** SJ3556
Margam *W Glam* **18** SS7887
Margaret Marsh *Dorset* **9** ST8218
Margaretting *Essex* **24** TL6701
Margaretting Tye *Essex* **24** TL6800
Margate *Kent* **15** TR3571
Margnaheglish *Strath* **72** NS0332
Margrie *D & G* **65** NX5950
Margrove Park *Cleve* **62** NZ6515
Marham *Norfk* **42** TF7009
Marhamchurch *Cnwll* **6** SS2203
Marholm *Cambs* **40** TF1401
Mariansleigh *Devon* **7** SS7422
Marine Town *Kent* **14** TQ9274
Marionburgh *Gramp* **89** NJ7006
Marishader *Highld* **90** NG4963
Maristow *Devon* **4** SX4764
Marjoriebanks *D & G* **66** NY0883
Mark *D & G* **64** NX1157
Mark *Somset* **19** ST3847
Mark Cross *E Susx* **13** TQ5010
Mark Cross *E Susx* **13** TQ5831
Markbeech *Kent* **13** TQ4742
Markby *Lincs* **51** TF4878
Market Bosworth *Leics* **39** SK4002
Market Deeping *Lincs* **40** TF1310
Market Drayton *Shrops* **37** SJ6734
Market Harborough *Leics* **40** SP7387
Market Lavington *Wilts* **20** SU0154
Market Overton *Leics* **40** SK8816
Market Rasen *Lincs* **50** TF1089
Market Stainton *Lincs* **51** TF2279
Market Street *Norfk* **43** TG2921
Market Weighton *Humb* **56** SE8741
Market Weston *Suffk* **32** TL9877
Markfield *Leics* **39** SK4809
Markham *Gwent* **19** SO1601
Markham Moor *Notts* **49** SK7173
Markinch *Fife* **83** NO2901
Markington *N York* **55** SE2865
Marks Tey *Essex* **24** TL9023
Marksbury *Avon* **20** ST6662
Markshall *Essex* **24** TL8425
Markyate *Herts* **30** TL0616
Marlborough *Wilts* **21** SU1868
Marlcliff *Warwks* **28** SP0950
Marldon *Devon* **5** SX8663
Marlesford *Suffk* **33** TM3258
Marlingford *Norfk* **43** TG1309
Marloes *Dyfed* **16** SM7908
Marlow *Bucks* **22** SU8486
Marlpit Hill *Kent* **13** TQ4347
Marnhull *Dorset* **9** ST7818
Marnoch *Gramp* **94** NJ5950
Marple *Gt Man* **48** SJ9588
Marr *S York* **55** SE5105
Marrick *N York* **61** SE0798
Marsden *T & W* **69** NZ3964
Marsden *W York* **55** SE0411
Marsh Baldon *Oxon* **21** SU5699
Marsh Gibbon *Bucks* **29** SP6422
Marsh Green *Devon* **5** SY0493
Marsh Green *Kent* **13** TQ4344
Marsh Lane *Derbys* **49** SK4079
Marsh Street *Somset* **7** SS9944
Marshalswick *Herts* **23** TL1608
Marsham *Norfk* **43** TG1923
Marshborough *Kent* **15** TR3057
Marshbrook *Shrops* **36** SO4489
Marshchapel *Lincs* **51** TF3599
Marshfield *Gwent* **19** ST2582
Marshfield *Avon* **20** ST7873
Marshgate *Cnwll* **4** SX1592
Marshwood *Dorset* **8** SY3899
Marske *N York* **61** NZ1000
Marske-by-the-Sea *Cleve* **62** NZ6322
Marston *Staffs* **38** SJ9227
Marston *Lincs* **50** SK8943
Marston *H & W* **27** SO3557
Marston *Oxon* **29** SP5208
Marston *Wilts* **20** ST9656
Marston Green *W Mids* **38** SP1785
Marston Magna *Somset* **9** ST5922
Marston Meysey *Wilts* **20** SU1297
Marston Montgomery *Derbys* **48** SK1337
Marston Moretaine *Beds* **30** SP9941
Marston St. Lawrence *Nhants* **29** SP5341
Marston Stannet *H & W* **27** SO5655
Marston Trussell *Nhants* **40** SP6985
Marston on Dove *Derbys* **39** SK2329
Marstow *H & W* **27** SO5518
Marsworth *Bucks* **30** SP9114
Marten *Wilts* **21** SU2860
Marthall *Ches* **47** SJ7975
Martham *Norfk* **43** TG4518
Martin *Hants* **10** SU0619
Martin *Lincs* **50** TF1259
Martin *Lincs* **51** TF2466
Martin *Kent* **15** TR3447
Martin *Kent* **15** TR3447
Martin Hussingtree *H & W* **28** SO8860
Martinhoe *Devon* **18** SS6648
Martinstown *Dorset* **9** SY6489
Martlesham *Suffk* **33** TM2547
Martletwy *Dyfed* **16** SN0310
Martley *H & W* **28** SO7555
Martock *Somset* **8** ST4619
Marton *Cleve* **62** NZ5115
Marton *N York* **55** SE4162
Marton *N York* **63** SE7383
Marton *Shrops* **36** SJ2802
Marton *Ches* **47** SJ8568
Marton *Lincs* **50** SK8381
Marton *Warwks* **29** SP4068
Marton *Humb* **57** TA1739
Marton-le-Moor *N York* **55** SE3770
Martyr Worthy *Hants* **11** SU5132
Martyr's Green *Surrey* **22** TQ0857
Marwick *Ork* **103** HY2324
Marwood *Devon* **6** SS5437
Mary Tavy *Devon* **4** SX5079
Marybank *Highld* **92** NH4853
Maryburgh *Highld* **92** NH5456
Maryculter *Gramp* **89** NO8599
Maryhill *Gramp* **95** NJ8245
Maryhill *Strath* **74** NS5669
Marykirk *Gramp* **89** NO6865
Marylebone *Gt Man* **47** SD5807
Marypark *Gramp* **94** NJ1938
Maryport *D & G* **64** NX1434
Maryport *Cumb* **58** NY0336
Marystow *Devon* **4** SX4382
Maryton *Tays* **89** NO6856
Marywell *Tays* **89** NO5895
Marywell *Tays* **89** NO6544
Marywell *Gramp* **89** NO9399
Masham *N York* **61** SE2280
Masongill *N York* **60** SD6675
Mastin Moor *Derbys* **49** SK4575
Matching *Essex* **23** TL5212
Matching Green *Essex* **23** TL5311
Matching Tye *Essex* **23** TL5111
Matfen *Nthumb* **68** NZ0371
Matfield *Kent* **13** TQ6541
Mathern *Gwent* **19** ST5290
Mathon *H & W* **28** SO7346
Mathry *Dyfed* **16** SM8832
Matlaske *Norfk* **43** TG1534
Matlock *Derbys* **49** SK3059
Matlock Bank *Derbys* **49** SK3060
Matson *Gloucs* **28** SO8515
Mattersey *Notts* **49** SK6889
Mattingley *Hants* **22** SU7357
Mattishall *Norfk* **42** TG0511
Mattishall Burgh *Norfk* **42** TG0512
Mauchline *Strath* **74** NS4927
Maud *Gramp* **95** NJ9148
Maufant *Jersey* **101** JS0000
Maugersbury *Gloucs* **29** SP2025
Maughold *IOM* **52** SC4991
Mauld *Highld* **92** NH4038
Maulden *Beds* **30** TL0538
Maulds Meaburn *Cumb* **60** NY6216
Maunby *N York* **62** SE3586
Maund Bryan *H & W* **27** SO5650
Maundown *Somset* **7** ST0628
Mautby *Norfk* **43** TG4812
Mavesyn Ridware *Staffs* **38** SK0816
Mavis Enderby *Lincs* **51** TF3666
Mawbray *Cumb* **66** NY0846
Mawdesley *Lancs* **53** SD4914
Mawdlam *M Glam* **18** SS8081
Mawgan *Cnwll* **2** SW7025
Mawgan Porth *Cnwll* **3** SW8567
Mawla *Cnwll* **2** SW7045
Mawnan *Cnwll* **2** SW7827
Mawnan Smith *Cnwll* **2** SW7728
Maxey *Cambs* **40** TF1208
Maxstoke *Warwks* **39** SP2386
Maxted Street *Kent* **15** TR1244
Maxton *Border* **76** NT6130
Maxton *Kent* **15** TR3041
Maxwell Town *D & G* **66** NX9676
Maxwellheugh *Border* **76** NT7333
Maxworthy *Cnwll* **4** SX2593
May Bank *Staffs* **47** SJ8547
Maybole *Strath* **73** NS2909
Maybury *Surrey* **22** TQ0159
Mayfield *Loth* **75** NT3565
Mayfield *Staffs* **48** SK1446
Mayfield *E Susx* **13** TQ5826
Mayford *Surrey* **22** SU9956
Maynard's Green *E Susx* **13** TQ5818
Maypole Green *Suffk* **32** TL9159
Maypole Green *Norfk* **43** TM4195
Meadgate *Avon* **20** ST6758
Meadle *Bucks* **22** SP8005
Meadwell *Devon* **4** SX4081
Mealrigg *Cumb* **67** NY1345
Meamskirk *Strath* **74** NS5455
Meanwood *W York* **55** SE2837
Meare *Somset* **19** ST4541
Meare *Somset* **19** ST4541
Meare Green *Somset* **8** ST2922
Mears Ashby *Nhants* **30** SP8366
Measham *Leics* **39** SK3311
Meathop *Cumb* **59** SD4380
Meavy *Devon* **4** SX5467
Medbourne *Leics* **40** SP8093
Medmenham *Berks* **22** SU8084
Medomsley *Dur* **69** NZ1154
Medstead *Hants* **11** SU6537
Meer End *W Mids* **39** SP2474
Meerbrook *Staffs* **48** SJ9860
Meesden *Herts* **31** TL4332
Meeth *Devon* **6** SS5408
Meeting House Hill *Norfk* **43** TG3028
Meidrim *Dyfed* **17** SN2920
Meifod *Powys* **36** SJ1513
Meigle *Tays* **88** NO2844
Meikle Carco *D & G* **66** NS7813
Meikle Earnock *Strath* **74** NS7053
Meikle Kilmory *Strath* **72** NS0560
Meikle Obney *Tays* **82** NO0337
Meikle Wartle *Gramp* **95** NJ7230
Meikleour *Tays* **82** NO1539
Meinciau *Dyfed* **17** SN4610
Meir *Staffs* **48** SJ9342
Melbourn *Cambs* **31** TL3844
Melbourne *Humb* **56** SE7543
Melbourne *Derbys* **39** SK3825
Melbury Abbas *Dorset* **9** ST8820
Melbury Bubb *Dorset* **9** ST5906
Melbury Osmond *Dorset* **8** ST5707
Melchbourne *Beds* **30** TL0265
Melcombe Bingham *Dorset* **9** ST7602
Meldon *Nthumb* **69** NZ1183
Meldon *Devon* **4** SX5692
Meldreth *Cambs* **31** TL3746
Meldrum *Cent* **81** NS7299
Melfort *Strath* **79** NM8313
Melgund Castle *Tays* **89** NO5455
Meliden *Clwyd* **45** SJ0680
Melin-y-wig *Clwyd* **45** SJ0448
Melkinthorpe *Cumb* **59** NY5525
Melkridge *Nthumb* **68** NY7364
Melksham *Wilts* **20** ST9063
Melldalloch *Strath* **71** NR9374
Melling *Mersyd* **46** SD3800
Melling *Lancs* **54** SD5970
Mellis *Suffk* **33** TM0974
Mellon Charles *Highld* **91** NG8491
Mellon Udrigle *Highld* **91** NG8996
Mellor *Lancs* **54** SD6530
Mellor *Gt Man* **48** SJ9888
Mellor Brook *Lancs* **54** SD6431
Mells *Somset* **20** ST7248
Melmerby *Cumb* **59** NY6137
Melmerby *N York* **61** SE0785
Melmerby *N York* **62** SE3376
Melness *Highld* **99** NC5861
Melplash *Dorset* **8** SY4898
Melrose *Border* **76** NT5434
Melsetter *Ork* **103** ND2689
Melsonby *N York* **61** NZ1908
Meltham *S York* **55** SE1010
Melton *Humb* **56** SE9726
Melton *Suffk* **33** TM2850
Melton Constable *Norfk* **42** TG0432
Melton Mowbray *Leics* **40** SK7518
Melton Ross *Humb* **57** TA0610
Melvaig *Highld* **91** NG7486
Melverley *Shrops* **36** SJ3316
Melvich *Highld* **99** NC8764
Membury *Devon* **8** ST2803
Memsie *Gramp* **95** NJ9762
Menai Bridge *Gwynd* **44** SH5571
Mendham *Suffk* **33** TM2782
Mendlesham *Suffk* **33** TM1065
Mendlesham Green *Suffk* **33** TM0963
Menheniot *Cnwll* **4** SX2863
Mennock *D & G* **66** NS8107
Menston *W York* **55** SE1643
Menstrie *Cent* **82** NS8597
Mentmore *Bucks* **30** SP9019
Meoble *Highld* **85** NM7987
Meole Brace *Shrops* **37** SJ4810
Meonstoke *Hants* **11** SU6119
Meopham *Kent* **14** TQ6466
Mepal *Cambs* **41** TL4481
Meppershall *Beds* **30** TL1336
Mere *Ches* **47** SJ7281
Mere *Wilts* **9** ST8132
Mere *Wilts* **9** ST8132
Mere Brow *Lancs* **53** SD4218
Mereclough *Lancs* **54** SD8730
Mereworth *Kent* **13** TQ6553
Meriden *W Mids* **39** SP2482
Merkadale *Highld* **84** NG3931
Merrion *Dyfed* **16** SR9397
Merriott *Somset* **8** ST4412
Merrow *Surrey* **12** TQ0250
Merry Hill *Herts* **22** TQ1394
Merryhill *W Mids* **38** SO8897
Merrymeet *Cnwll* **4** SX2766
Mersham *Kent* **15** TR0540
Merston *W Susx* **11** SU8902
Merstone *IOW* **11** SZ5285
Merther *Cnwll* **3** SW8644
Merthyr Cynog *Powys* **26** SN9837
Merthyr Mawr *M Glam* **18** SS8877
Merthyr Tydfil *M Glam* **26** SO0406
Merthyr Vale *M Glam* **18** ST0799
Merton *Oxon* **29** SP5717
Merton *Devon* **6** SS5212
Merton *Norfk* **42** TL9098
Merton *Gt Lon* **23** TQ2570
Meshaw *Devon* **7** SS7619
Meshaw *Devon* **7** SS7619
Messing *Essex* **24** TL8918
Messingham *Humb* **56** SE8904
Metfield *Suffk* **33** TM2980
Metherell *Cnwll* **4** SX4069
Metheringham *Lincs* **50** TF0661
Methil *Fife* **83** NT3799
Methley *W York* **55** SE3926
Methlick *Gramp* **95** NJ8537
Methven *Tays* **82** NO0225
Methwold *Norfk* **42** TL7394
Methwold Hythe *Norfk* **42** TL7194
Mettingham *Suffk* **33** TM3689
Metton *Norfk* **43** TG2037
Mevagissey *Cnwll* **3** SX0144
Mexborough *S York* **49** SE4700
Mey *Highld* **100** ND2872
Meylteyrn *Gwynd* **44** SH2332
Meysey Hampton *Gloucs* **20** SP1100
Miavaig *W Isls* **102** NB0834
Michaelchurch *H & W* **27** SO5225
Michaelchurch Escley *H & W* **27** SO3134
Michaelston-le-Pit *S Glam* **19** ST1572
Michaelstone-y-Fedw *Gwent* **19** ST2484
Michaelstow *Cnwll* **3** SX0778
Micheldever *Hants* **11** SU5139
Micheldever Station *Hants* **21** SU5143
Michelmersh *Hants* **10** SU3426
Mickfield *Suffk* **33** TM1361
Mickle Trafford *Ches* **46** SJ4469
Micklebring *S York* **49** SK5194
Mickleby *N York* **63** NZ8012
Micklefield *W York* **55** SE4432
Mickleham *Surrey* **12** TQ1653
Mickleover *Derbys* **39** SK3033
Mickleton *Dur* **61** NY9623
Mickleton *Gloucs* **28** SP1643
Mickletown *W York* **55** SE4027
Mickley *N York* **61** SE2576
Mickley *N York* **61** SE2576
Mickley Green *Suffk* **32** TL8457

Mucklestone

Newton Mountain

Mucklestone *Staffs* 37 SJ7237
Muckton *Lincs* 51 TF3781
Mucomir *Highld* 86 NN1884
Muddiford *Devon* 6 SS5638
Muddles Green *E Susx* 13 TQ5413
Mudeford *Dorset* 10 SZ1892
Mudford *Somset* 8 ST5719
Mudford Sock *Somset* 8 ST5519
Mudgock *Cent* 74 NS5577
Mugeary *Highld* 84 NG4439
Mugginton *Derbys* 49 SK2842
Muggleswick *Dur* 68 NZ0449
Muir of Fowlis *Gramp* 94 NJ5612
Muir of Miltonduff *Gramp* 94 NJ1859
Muir of Ord *Highld* 92 NH5250
Muir of Thorn *Tays* 82 NO0637
Muirden *Gramp* 95 NJ7054
Muirdrum *Tays* 83 NO5637
Muiresk *Gramp* 95 NJ6948
Muirhead *Fife* 83 NO2805
Muirhead *Tays* 83 NO3434
Muirhead *Strath* 74 NS6869
Muirhouselaw *Border* 76 NT6328
Muirhouses *Cent* 82 NT0180
Muirkirk *Strath* 74 NS6927
Muirmill *Cent* 81 NS7283
Muirshearlich *Highld* 86 NN1380
Muirtack *Gramp* 95 NJ9937
Muirton Mains *Highld* 92 NH4553
Muirton of Ardblair *Tays* 88 NO1643
Muirtown *Tays* 82 NN9211
Muker *N York* 60 SD9097
Mulbarton *Norfk* 43 TG1901
Mulben *Gramp* 94 NJ3550
Mulindry *Strath* 70 NR3659
Mullion *Cnwll* 2 SW6719
Mumby *Lincs* 51 TF5174
Muncher's Green *Herts* 31 TL3126
Munderfield Row *H & W* 27 SO6451
Munderfield Stocks *H & W* 27 SO6550
Mundesley *Norfk* 43 TG3136
Mundford *Norfk* 42 TL8093
Mundford *Norfk* 42 TL8093
Mundham *Norfk* 43 TM3397
Mundon Hill *Essex* 24 TL8602
Mungrisdale *Cumb* 59 NY3630
Munlochy *Highld* 92 NH6453
Munnoch *Strath* 73 NS2548
Munsley *H & W* 28 SO6640
Munslow *Shrops* 37 SO5287
Munslow Aston *Shrops* 37 SO5186
Murchington *Devon* 5 SX6888
Murcott *Oxon* 29 SP5815
Murkle *Highld* 100 ND1668
Murlaggan *Highld* 85 NN0192
Murroes *Tays* 83 NO4635
Murrow *Cambs* 41 TF3707
Mursley *Bucks* 30 SP8128
Murthill *Tays* 89 NO4657
Murthly *Tays* 82 NO1038
Murton *Nthumb* 77 NT9748
Murton *Cumb* 60 NY7221
Murton *Dur* 69 NZ3847
Murton *N York* 56 SE6452
Musbury *Devon* 8 SY2794
Musselburgh *Loth* 75 NT3472
Muston *Leics* 40 SK8237
Muston *N York* 63 TA0979
Mustow Green *H & W* 38 SO8774
Muswell Hill *Gt Lon* 23 TQ2889
Mutehill *D & G* 65 NX6848
Mutford *Suffk* 33 TM4888
Muthill *Tays* 82 NN8717
Mybster *Highld* 100 ND1652
Myddfai *Dyfed* 26 SN7730
Myddle *Shrops* 36 SJ4623
Mydroilyn *Dyfed* 34 SN4555
Mylor *Cnwll* 2 SW8135
Mylor Bridge *Cnwll* 2 SW8036
Mynachlog ddu *Dyfed* 16 SN1430
Myndtown *Shrops* 36 SO3989
Mynydd-bach *W Glam* 18 SS6597
Mynydd-bach *Gwent* 19 ST4894
Myrebird *Gramp* 89 NO7398
Myredykes *Border* 67 NY5998
Mytchett *Surrey* 22 SU8855
Mytholm *W York* 54 SD9827
Mytholmroyd *W York* 54 SE0126
Myton-on-Swale *N York* 55 SE4366

N

Naast *Highld* 91 NG8283
Naburn *N York* 56 SE5945
Nackington *Kent* 15 TR1554
Nacton *Suffk* 33 TM2240
Nafferton *Humb* 57 TA0559
Nag's Head *Gloucs* 20 ST8898
Nailsbourne *Somset* 8 ST2128
Nailsea *Avon* 19 ST4770
Nailsea *Avon* 19 ST4770
Nailstone *Leics* 39 SK4106
Nailsworth *Gloucs* 20 ST8499
Nairn *Highld* 93 NH8856
Nannerch *Clwyd* 46 SJ1669
Nanpantan *Leics* 39 SK5017
Nanpean *Cnwll* 3 SW9556
Nanstallon *Cnwll* 3 SX0367
Nant Peris *Gwynd* 44 SH6058
Nant-y-moel *M Glam* 18 SS9392
Nanternis *Dyfed* 34 SN3756
Nantgaredig *Dyfed* 17 SN4921
Nantglyn *Clwyd* 45 SJ0061
Nantmel *Powys* 26 SO0366
Nantmor *Gwynd* 44 SH6046
Nantwich *Ches* 47 SJ6552
Naphill *Bucks* 22 SU8496
Napleton *H & W* 28 SO8648
Napton on the Hill *Warwks* 29 SP4661
Narberth *Dyfed* 16 SN1015
Narborough *Leics* 39 SP5497
Narborough *Norfk* 42 TF7412
Nasareth *Gwynd* 44 SH4749
Naseby *Nhants* 30 SP6978
Nash *Shrops* 37 SO6071
Nash *Bucks* 30 SP7833
Nash *Gwent* 19 ST3483
Nash's Green *Hants* 22 SU6745
Nassington *Nhants* 40 TL0696
Nasty *Herts* 31 TL3524
Nateby *Cumb* 60 NY7706
Nateby *Lancs* 53 SD4644
Natland *Cumb* 59 SD5289
Naughton *Suffk* 32 TM0249
Naunton *H & W* 28 SO8645
Naunton *H & W* 28 SO8739
Naunton *Gloucs* 28 SP1123
Naunton Beauchamp *H & W* 28 SO9652
Navenby *Lincs* 50 SK9858
Navestock *Essex* 23 TQ5397
Navestock Side *Essex* 24 TQ5697
Navidale House Hotel *Highld* 97 ND0316
Navity *Highld* 93 NH7864
Nawton *N York* 62 SE6584
Nayland *Suffk* 25 TL9734
Nazeing *Essex* 23 TL4106
Neap *Shet* 103 HU5058
Near Cotton *Staffs* 48 SK0646
Near Sawry *Cumb* 59 SD3795
Neasden *Gt Lon* 23 TQ2185
Neasham *Dur* 62 NZ3210
Neath *W Glam* 18 SS7597
Neatham *Hants* 11 SU7440
Neatishead *Norfk* 43 TG3420
Nebo *Gwynd* 44 SH4850
Nebo *Gwynd* 45 SH8355
Nebo *Dyfed* 34 SN5465
Necton *Norfk* 42 TF8709
Nedd *Highld* 98 NC1331
Nedging *Suffk* 32 TL9948
Nedging Tye *Suffk* 32 TM0149
Needham *Norfk* 33 TM2281
Needham Market *Suffk* 32 TM0855
Needingworth *Cambs* 31 TL3472
Neen Savage *Shrops* 37 SO6777
Neen Sollars *Shrops* 37 SO6672
Neenton *Shrops* 37 SO6387
Nefyn *Gwynd* 44 SH3040
Neilston *Strath* 73 NS4857
Nelson *Lancs* 54 SD8638
Nelson *M Glam* 18 ST1195
Nemphlar *Strath* 74 NS8544
Nempnett Thrubwell *Avon* 19 ST5260
Nenthead *Cumb* 68 NY7743
Nenthorn *Border* 76 NT6837
Nercwys *Clwyd* 46 SJ2360
Nereabolls *Strath* 70 NR2255
Nerston *Strath* 74 NS6456
Nesbit *Nthumb* 77 NT9833
Nesfield *N York* 55 SE0949
Nesscliffe *Shrops* 36 SJ3819
Neston *Ches* 46 SJ2977
Neston *Wilts* 20 ST8668
Netchwood *Shrops* 37 SO6291
Nether Alderley *Ches* 47 SJ8476
Nether Blainslie *Border* 76 NT5443
Nether Broughton *Notts* 40 SK6925
Nether Burrow *Lancs* 59 SD6174
Nether Cassock *D & G* 67 NT2303
Nether Cerne *Dorset* 9 SY6798
Nether Compton *Dorset* 9 ST5917
Nether Crimond *Gramp* 95 NJ8222
Nether Dallachy *Gramp* 94 NJ3563
Nether Exe *Devon* 7 SS9300
Nether Fingland *Strath* 66 NS9310
Nether Handwick *Tays* 88 NO3641
Nether Haugh *S York* 49 SK4196
Nether Headon *Notts* 50 SK7477
Nether Heage *Derbys* 49 SK3650
Nether Heyford *Nhants* 30 SP6658
Nether Howcleugh *Strath* 66 NT0312
Nether Kellet *Lancs* 53 SD5068
Nether Kinmundy *Gramp* 95 NK0543
Nether Moor *Derbys* 49 SK3866
Nether Newton *Cumb* 59 SD4082
Nether Padley *Derbys* 48 SK2478
Nether Poppleton *N York* 56 SE5654
Nether Silton *N York* 62 SE4592
Nether Stowey *Somset* 19 ST1939
Nether Wallop *Hants* 10 SU3036
Nether Wasdale *Cumb* 58 NY1204
Nether Wellwood *Strath* 74 NS6526
Nether Westcote *Oxon* 29 SP2220
Nether Whitacre *Warwks* 39 SP2392
Nether Whitecleuch *Strath* 74 NS8319
Netheravon *Wilts* 20 SU1448
Netherbrae *Gramp* 95 NJ7959
Netherburn *Strath* 74 NS7947
Netherbury *Dorset* 8 SY4799
Netherby *N York* 55 SE3346
Nethercleuch *D & G* 67 NY1186
Netherend *Gloucs* 19 SO5900
Netherfield *E Susx* 14 TQ7019
Netherfield Road *E Susx* 14 TQ7417
Netherhampton *Wilts* 10 SU1029
Netherhay *Dorset* 8 ST4105
Netherlaw *D & G* 65 NX7444
Netherley *Gramp* 89 NO8493
Nethermill *D & G* 66 NY0487
Nethermuir *Gramp* 95 NJ9044
Netherplace *Strath* 74 NS5255
Netherseal *Derbys* 39 SK2812
Netherthong *W York* 55 SE1309
Netherton *Tays* 88 NO1452
Netherton *Tays* 89 NO5457
Netherton *Cent* 81 NS5579
Netherton *Strath* 74 NS7854
Netherton *Nthumb* 68 NT9807
Netherton *W York* 55 SE2816
Netherton *Shrops* 37 SO7382
Netherton *W Mids* 38 SO9488
Netherton *Devon* 5 SX8971
Netherton *Devon* 5 SX8971
Nethertown *Highld* 100 ND3578
Nethertown *Cumb* 58 NX9907
Nethertown *Staffs* 38 SK1017
Netherwitton *Nthumb* 68 NZ0990
Nethy Bridge *Highld* 93 NJ0020
Netley *Hants* 10 SU4508
Netley Marsh *Hants* 10 SU3313
Nettlebed *Oxon* 22 SU6986
Nettlebridge *Somset* 19 ST6448
Nettlecombe *Dorset* 8 SY5195
Nettleden *Herts* 22 TL0110
Nettleham *Lincs* 50 TF0075
Nettlestead *Kent* 14 TQ6852
Nettlestead Green *Kent* 14 TQ6850
Nettlestone *IOW* 11 SZ6290
Nettlesworth *Dur* 69 NZ2547
Nettleton *Wilts* 20 ST8278
Nettleton *Lincs* 50 TA1100
Netton *Wilts* 10 SU1336
Nevern *Dyfed* 16 SN0840
Nevill Holt *Leics* 40 SP8193
New Abbey *D & G* 66 NX9666
New Aberdour *Gramp* 95 NJ8863
New Addington *Gt Lon* 23 TQ3763
New Alresford *Hants* 11 SU5832
New Alyth *Tays* 88 NO2447
New Ash Green *Kent* 14 TQ6065
New Balderton *Notts* 50 SK8152
New Barn *Kent* 14 TQ6169
New Barnet *Gt Lon* 23 TQ2695
New Bewick *Nthumb* 77 NU0620
New Bilton *Warwks* 39 SP4875
New Bolingbroke *Lincs* 51 TF3057
New Boultham *Lincs* 50 SK9670
New Bradwell *Bucks* 30 SP8341
New Brampton *Derbys* 49 SK3771
New Brancepeth *Dur* 61 NZ2241
New Brighton *Mersyd* 46 SJ3093
New Buckenham *Norfk* 32 TM0890
New Byth *Gramp* 95 NJ8254
New Costessey *Norfk* 43 TG1810
New Crofton *W York* 55 SE3817
New Cross *Somset* 8 ST4119
New Cross *Gt Lon* 23 TQ3676
New Cumnock *Strath* 66 NS6213
New Deer *Gramp* 95 NJ8847
New Denham *Bucks* 22 TQ0484
New Denham *Bucks* 22 TQ0485
New Duston *Nhants* 30 SP7162
New Earswick *N York* 56 SE6155
New Edlington *S York* 49 SK5398
New Elgin *Gramp* 94 NJ2261
New Ellerby *Humb* 57 TA1639
New Eltham *Gt Lon* 23 TQ4472
New End *H & W* 28 SP0560
New Fletton *Cambs* 40 TL1997
New Galloway *D & G* 65 NX6377
New Gilston *Fife* 83 NO4208
New Grimsby *IOS* 2 SV8815
New Holkham *Norfk* 42 TF8839
New Holland *Humb* 57 TA0823
New Houghton *Derbys* 49 SK4965
New Houghton *Norfk* 42 TF7927
New Hutton *Cumb* 59 SD5691
New Inn *Dyfed* 17 SN4736
New Inn *Gwent* 19 ST3099
New Invention *Shrops* 36 SO2976
New Kelso *Highld* 91 NG9442
New Lanark *Strath* 74 NS8842
New Langholm *D & G* 67 NY3684
New Leake *Lincs* 51 TF4057
New Leeds *Gramp* 95 NJ9954
New Luce *D & G* 64 NX1764
New Malden *Gt Lon* 23 TQ2168
New Marston *Oxon* 29 SP5407
New Mill *Gramp* 89 NO7883
New Mill *W York* 55 SE1609
New Mill *Cnwll* 2 SW4534
New Mills *Powys* 36 SJ0901
New Mills *Derbys* 48 SK0085
New Mills *Cnwll* 3 SW8952
New Milton *Hants* 10 SZ2495
New Mistley *Essex* 25 TM1131
New Moat *Dyfed* 16 SN0625
New Ollerton *Notts* 49 SK6667
New Pitsligo *Gramp* 95 NJ8855
New Prestwick *Strath* 73 NS3424
New Quay *Dyfed* 34 SN3959
New Rackheath *Norfk* 43 TG2812
New Radnor *Powys* 27 SO2161
New Ridley *Nthumb* 68 NZ0559
New Romney *Kent* 15 TR0624
New Rossington *Notts* 49 SK6198
New Scone *Tays* 82 NO1326
New Sharlston *W York* 55 SE3819
New Silksworth *T & W* 69 NZ3853
New Somerby *Lincs* 40 SK9235
New Stevenston *Strath* 74 NS7659
New Town *Loth* 76 NT4470
New Town *Somset* 8 ST2712
New Town *Dorset* 9 ST8318
New Town *Dorset* 9 ST9515
New Town *Dorset* 9 ST9918
New Town *Beds* 31 TL1945
New Town *E Susx* 13 TQ4720
New Tredegar *M Glam* 18 SO1403
New Trows *Strath* 74 NS8038
New Walsoken *Cambs* 41 TF4609
New Waltham *Humb* 57 TA2804
New Wimpole *Cambs* 31 TL3549
New Winton *Loth* 76 NT4271
New York *Lincs* 51 TF2455
New Zealand *Derbys* 39 SK3336
Newall *W York* 55 SE1946
Newark *D & G* 66 NS7808
Newark-on-Trent *Notts* 50 SK7953
Newarthill *Strath* 74 NS7859
Newbattle *Loth* 75 NT3365
Newbie *D & G* 67 NY1764
Newbiggin *Cumb* 59 NY4729
Newbiggin *Cumb* 67 NY5549
Newbiggin *Cumb* 60 NY6228
Newbiggin *Dur* 60 NY9127
Newbiggin *N York* 61 SE0086
Newbiggin-by-the-Sea *Nthumb* 69 NZ3087
Newbiggin-on-Lune *Cumb* 60 NY7005
Newbigging *Tays* 88 NO2841
Newbigging *Tays* 83 NO4237
Newbigging *Strath* 75 NT0145
Newbold *Derbys* 49 SK3672
Newbold Pacey *Warwks* 29 SP2957
Newbold Verdon *Leics* 39 SK4403
Newbold on Stour *Warwks* 29 SP2446
Newborough *Gwynd* 44 SH4265
Newborough *Staffs* 38 SK1325
Newborough *Cambs* 41 TF2005
Newbourn *Suffk* 33 TM2743
Newbridge *Loth* 75 NT1272
Newbridge *D & G* 66 NX9479
Newbridge *Gwent* 19 ST2097
Newbridge *Hants* 10 SU2915
Newbridge *Cnwll* 2 SW4231
Newbridge *Cnwll* 2 SW4231
Newbridge *IOW* 10 SZ4187
Newbridge Green *H & W* 28 SO8439
Newbridge on Wye *Powys* 26 SO0158
Newbrough *Nthumb* 68 NY8767
Newbuildings *Devon* 7 SS7903
Newburgh *Gramp* 95 NJ9659
Newburgh *Gramp* 95 NJ9925
Newburgh *Fife* 83 NO2318
Newburgh *Lancs* 53 SD4810
Newburgh Priory *N York* 62 SE5476
Newburn *T & W* 69 NZ1665
Newbury *Somset* 20 ST6949
Newbury *Berks* 21 SU4766
Newby *Cumb* 59 NY5921
Newby *N York* 62 NZ5012
Newby *N York* 54 SD7269
Newby *Lancs* 54 SD8146
Newby Bridge *Cumb* 59 SD3686
Newby East *Cumb* 67 NY4758
Newby West *Cumb* 67 NY3753
Newby Wiske *N York* 62 SE3687
Newcastle *Shrops* 36 SO2582
Newcastle *Gwent* 27 SO4417
Newcastle Emlyn *Dyfed* 17 SN3040
Newcastle upon Tyne *T & W* 69 NZ2464
Newcastle-under-Lyme *Staffs* 47 SJ8445
Newcastleton *D & G* 67 NY4887
Newchapel *Dyfed* 17 SN2239
Newchapel *Surrey* 12 TQ3641
Newchurch *Staffs* 38 SK1423
Newchurch *Powys* 27 SO2150
Newchurch *Gwent* 19 ST4597
Newchurch *IOW* 11 SZ5685
Newchurch *Kent* 15 TR0531
Newcraighall *Loth* 75 NT3272
Newdigate *Surrey* 12 TQ1942
Newell Green *Berks* 22 SU8770
Newenden *Kent* 14 TQ8327
Newent *Gloucs* 28 SO7225
Newfield *Highld* 97 NH7877
Newfield *Dur* 61 NZ2033
Newgale *Dyfed* 16 SM8522
Newgate Street *Herts* 23 TL3005
Newhall *Ches* 47 SJ6145
Newhaven *E Susx* 13 TQ4401
Newholm *N York* 63 NZ8610
Newhouse *Strath* 74 NS7961
Newick *E Susx* 13 TQ4121
Newington *Oxon* 21 SU6096
Newington *Kent* 14 TQ8564
Newington *Kent* 15 TR1837
Newland *N York* 56 SE6824
Newland *Gloucs* 27 SO5509
Newland *H & W* 28 SO7948
Newland *Somset* 7 SS8238
Newland *Humb* 57 TA0631
Newlandrig *Loth* 76 NT3762
Newlands *Border* 67 NY5094
Newlands *Nthumb* 68 NZ0855
Newlands of Dundurcas *Gramp* 94 NJ2951
Newlyn *Cnwll* 2 SW4628
Newmachar *Gramp* 95 NJ8919
Newmains *Strath* 74 NS8256
Newman's Green *Suffk* 32 TL8843
Newmarket *Cumb* 59 NY3438
Newmarket *Suffk* 32 TL6463
Newmill *Gramp* 94 NJ4352
Newmill *Border* 67 NT4510
Newmill of Inshewan *Tays* 88 NO4260
Newmillerdam *W York* 55 SE3215
Newmills *Fife* 82 NT0186
Newmills *Loth* 75 NT1667
Newmills *Gwent* 27 SO5107
Newmiln *Tays* 82 NO1230
Newmilns *Strath* 74 NS5337
Newney Green *Essex* 24 TL6507
Newnham *H & W* 27 SO6469
Newnham *Gloucs* 28 SO6911
Newnham *Hants* 22 SU7053
Newnham *Herts* 31 TL2437
Newnham *Kent* 14 TQ9557
Newport *Highld* 100 ND1324
Newport *Humb* 56 SE8530
Newport *Shrops* 37 SJ7419
Newport *Dyfed* 16 SN0539
Newport *Devon* 6 SS5632
Newport *Gwent* 19 ST3188
Newport *Gloucs* 20 ST7097
Newport *IOW* 10 SZ5089
Newport *Essex* 31 TL5234
Newport Pagnell *Bucks* 30 SP8743
Newport-on-Tay *Fife* 83 NO4228
Newquay *Cnwll* 2 SW8161
Newseat *Gramp* 95 NJ7032
Newsham *N York* 61 NZ1010
Newsham *N York* 61 NZ1010
Newsham *Nthumb* 69 NZ3080
Newsham *Lancs* 53 SD5136
Newsham *N York* 62 SE3784
Newsholme *Humb* 56 SE7129
Newstead *Border* 76 NT5634
Newstead *Nthumb* 77 NU1527
Newstead *Notts* 49 SK5152
Newtack *Gramp* 94 NJ4446
Newthorpe *N York* 55 SE4632
Newton *Highld* 92 NH5850
Newton *Highld* 93 NH7448
Newton *Highld* 93 NH7866
Newton *Gramp* 94 NJ1663
Newton *Gramp* 94 NJ3362
Newton *Strath* 80 NS0498
Newton *Strath* 74 NS6760
Newton *Strath* 75 NS9331
Newton *Loth* 75 NT0977
Newton *Border* 76 NT6020
Newton *D & G* 67 NY1195
Newton *Nthumb* 68 NZ0364
Newton *Cumb* 53 SD2271
Newton *Lancs* 53 SD4430
Newton *Lancs* 59 SD5974
Newton *Lancs* 54 SD6950
Newton *Ches* 46 SJ4167
Newton *Ches* 46 SJ5059
Newton *Staffs* 38 SK0325
Newton *Derbys* 49 SK4459
Newton *Notts* 49 SK6841
Newton *H & W* 27 SO3432
Newton *H & W* 27 SO5153
Newton *Warwks* 39 SP5378
Newton *Nhants* 40 SP8883
Newton *M Glam* 18 SS8377
Newton *Somset* 18 ST1038
Newton *Lincs* 40 TF0436
Newton *Cambs* 41 TF4314
Newton *Norfk* 42 TF8315
Newton *Beds* 31 TL2344
Newton *Cambs* 31 TL4349
Newton *Suffk* 32 TL9240
Newton Abbot *Devon* 5 SX8571
Newton Arlosh *Cumb* 67 NY2055
Newton Aycliffe *Dur* 61 NZ2724
Newton Bewley *Cleve* 62 NZ4626
Newton Blossomville *Bucks* 30 SP9251
Newton Bromswold *Beds* 30 SP9966
Newton Burgoland *Leics* 39 SK3708
Newton Ferrers *Cnwll* 4 SX3466
Newton Ferrers *Devon* 4 SX5548
Newton Ferry *W Isls* 102 NF8978
Newton Flotman *Norfk* 43 TM2198
Newton Harcourt *Leics* 39 SP6497
Newton Heath *Gt Man* 47 SD8700
Newton Kyme *N York* 55 SE4644
Newton Longville *Bucks* 30 SP8431
Newton Mearns *Strath* 74 NS5355
Newton Morrel *N York* 61 NZ2309
Newton Mountain *Dyfed* 16 SM9808

Newton Poppleford
Old Windsor

Newton Poppleford *Devon* 8 SY0889
Newton Purcell *Oxon* 29 SP6230
Newton Regis *Warwks* 39 SK2707
Newton Reigny *Cumb* 59 NY4731
Newton Row *Highld* 100 ND3449
Newton Solney *Derbys* 39 SK2825
Newton St. Cyres *Devon* 7 SX8898
Newton St. Faith *Norfk* 43 TG2217
Newton St. Loe *Avon* 20 ST7064
Newton St. Petrock *Devon* 6 SS4112
Newton Stacey *Hants* 21 SU4140
Newton Stewart *D & G* 64 NX4065
Newton Toney *Wilts* 21 SU2140
Newton Tracey *Devon* 6 SS5226
Newton Valence *Hants* 11 SU7232
Newton by Toft *Lincs* 50 TF0487
Newton of Balcanquhal *Tays* 82 NO1610
Newton on Ouse *N York* 55 SE5159
Newton on Trent *Lincs* 50 SK8373
Newton under Roseberry *Cleve* 62 NZ5713
Newton upon Derwent *Humb* 56 SE7149
Newton-le-Willows *N York* 61 SE2189
Newton-le-Willows *Mersyd* 47 SJ5995
Newton-on-the-Moor *Nthumb* 69 NU1705
Newtonairds *D & G* 66 NX8880
Newtongarry Croft *Gramp* 94 NJ5735
Newtongrange *Loth* 75 NT3364
Newtonhill *Gramp* 89 NO9193
Newtonloan *Loth* 75 NT3362
Newtonmill *Tays* 89 NO6064
Newtonmore *Highld* 87 NN7098
Newtown *Highld* 86 NH3504
Newtown *D & G* 66 NS7710
Newtown *Nthumb* 68 NU0300
Newtown *Cumb* 67 NY1048
Newtown *Cumb* 67 NY5062
Newtown *Gt Man* 47 SD5604
Newtown *Shrops* 36 SJ4222
Newtown *Shrops* 37 SJ4731
Newtown *Ches* 47 SJ6247
Newtown *Ches* 48 SJ9060
Newtown *Powys* 36 SO1091
Newtown *H & W* 27 SO5333
Newtown *H & W* 27 SO6145
Newtown *Gloucs* 20 SO6702
Newtown *H & W* 28 SO7037
Newtown *H & W* 28 SO8755
Newtown *H & W* 28 SO8755
Newtown *Devon* 7 SS7625
Newtown *Wilts* 9 ST9129
Newtown *Hants* 11 SU6013
Newtown *Dorset* 9 SZ0393
Newtown *IOW* 10 SZ4290
Newtown Linford *Leics* 39 SK5209
Newtown St. Boswells *Border* 76 NT5732
Newtown of Beltrees *Strath* 73 NS3758
Newtyle *Tays* 88 NO2941
Newyork *Strath* 80 NM9611
Neyland *Dyfed* 16 SM9605
Nicholashayne *Devon* 8 ST1016
Nicholaston *W Glam* 17 SS5288
Nidd *N York* 55 SE3060
Nigg *Highld* 93 NH8071
Nigg *Gramp* 89 NJ9402
Nightcott *Devon* 7 SS8925
Nine Elms *Wilts* 20 SU1085
Ninebanks *Nthumb* 68 NY7853
Nineveh *H & W* 27 SO6265
Ninfield *E Susx* 14 TQ7012
Ningwood *IOW* 10 SZ3989
Nisbet *Border* 76 NT6725
Nisbet Hill *Border* 76 NT7950
Niton *IOW* 10 SZ5076
Nitshill *Strath* 74 NS5260
No Man's Heath *Ches* 46 SJ5148
No Man's Heath *Warwks* 39 SK2808
Nocton *Lincs* 50 TF0564
Noke *Oxon* 29 SP5413
Nolton *Dyfed* 16 SM8618
Nolton Haven *Dyfed* 16 SM8618
Nomansland *Devon* 7 SS8313
Nomansland *Wilts* 10 SU2517
Noneley *Shrops* 37 SJ4828
Nonington *Kent* 15 TR2552
Nook *Cumb* 59 SD5481
Norbiton Common *Gt Lon* 23 TQ2067
Norbury *Ches* 47 SJ5547
Norbury *Staffs* 37 SJ7823
Norbury *Derbys* 48 SK1241
Norbury *Shrops* 36 SO3692
Norbury *Gt Lon* 23 TQ3069
Norchard *H & W* 28 SO8568
Nordelph *Norfk* 41 TF5501
Nordley *Shrops* 37 SO6996
Norham *Nthumb* 77 NT9047
Norland Town *W York* 55 SE0622
Norley *Ches* 47 SJ5772
Norleywood *Hants* 10 SZ3597
Norman's Green *Devon* 7 ST0503
Normanby *Cleve* 62 NZ5418
Normanby *N York* 63 SE7381
Normanby *Humb* 56 SE8816
Normanby *Lincs* 50 SK9988
Normanby le Wold *Lincs* 50 TF1295
Normandy *Surrey* 22 SU9351
Normanton *W York* 55 SE3822
Normanton *Derbys* 39 SK3433
Normanton *Notts* 49 SK7054
Normanton *Leics* 50 SK8140
Normanton *Lincs* 50 SK9446
Normanton le Heath *Leics* 39 SK3712
Normanton on Soar *Notts* 39 SK5122
Normanton on Trent *Notts* 50 SK7868
Normanton on the Wolds *Notts* 39 SK6232
Norney *Surrey* 12 SU9444
North Anston *S York* 49 SK5184
North Aston *Oxon* 29 SP4828
North Baddesley *Hants* 10 SU3920
North Ballachulish *Highld* 86 NN0560
North Barrow *Somset* 9 ST6129
North Barsham *Norfk* 42 TF9135
North Benfleet *Essex* 24 TQ7588
North Bersted *W Susx* 11 SU9201
North Berwick *Loth* 83 NT5485
North Boarhunt *Hants* 11 SU6010
North Bovey *Devon* 5 SX7484
North Bradley *Wilts* 20 ST8555
North Brentor *Devon* 4 SX4881
North Brewham *Somset* 20 ST7236
North Buckland *Devon* 6 SS4840
North Burlingham *Norfk* 43 TG3609
North Cadbury *Somset* 9 ST6327
North Carlton *Notts* 49 SK5984
North Carlton *Lincs* 50 SK9477
North Cave *Humb* 56 SE8932
North Cerney *Gloucs* 28 SP0107
North Charford *Hants* 10 SU1919
North Charlton *Nthumb* 77 NU1622
North Cheam *Gt Lon* 23 TQ2365
North Cheriton *Somset* 9 ST6925
North Chideock *Dorset* 8 SY4294
North Cliffe *Humb* 56 SE8736
North Clifton *Notts* 50 SK8272
North Cockerington *Lincs* 51 TF3790
North Collingham *Notts* 50 SK8362
North Common *E Susx* 13 TQ3921
North Connel *Strath* 79 NM9034
North Cornelly *M Glam* 18 SS8181
North Corry *Highld* 79 NM8353
North Cotes *Lincs* 51 TA3400
North Cove *Suffk* 33 TM4689
North Cowton *N York* 61 NZ2803
North Crawley *Bucks* 30 SP9244
North Creake *Norfk* 42 TF8538
North Curry *Somset* 8 ST3125
North Dalton *Humb* 56 SE9351
North Deighton *N York* 55 SE3951
North Duffield *N York* 56 SE6837
North Elham *Kent* 15 TR1844
North Elmham *Norfk* 42 TF9820
North Elmsall *W York* 55 SE4712
North End *Nhants* 30 SP9668
North End *Hants* 10 SU1016
North End *Hants* 11 SU6502
North End *W Susx* 12 SU9703
North End *Essex* 24 TL6618
North Erradale *Highld* 91 NG7480
North Evington *Leics* 39 SK6204
North Fambridge *Essex* 24 TQ8597
North Feorline *Strath* 72 NR9029
North Ferriby *Humb* 56 SE9826
North Frodingham *Humb* 57 TA1053
North Gorley *Hants* 10 SU1611
North Green *Suffk* 33 TM3162
North Grimston *N York* 56 SE8467
North Hayling *Hants* 11 SU7303
North Hill *Cnwll* 4 SX2776
North Hillingdon *Gt Lon* 22 TQ0784
North Hinksey *Oxon* 29 SP4905
North Huish *Devon* 5 SX7156
North Hykeham *Lincs* 50 SK9465
North Kelsey *Humb* 50 TA0401
North Kessock *Highld* 93 NH6548
North Killingholme *Humb* 57 TA1417
North Kilvington *N York* 62 SE4285
North Kilworth *Leics* 39 SP6183
North Kyme *Lincs* 50 TF1552
North Lee *Bucks* 22 SP8308
North Lee *Bucks* 22 SP8308
North Leigh *Oxon* 29 SP3813
North with Habblesthorpe *Notts* 50 SK7882
North Lopham *Norfk* 32 TM0382
North Luffenham *Leics* 40 SK9303
North Marden *W Susx* 11 SU8016
North Marston *Bucks* 30 SP7722
North Middleton *Loth* 75 NT3559
North Milmain *D & G* 64 NX0852
North Molton *Devon* 7 SS7329
North Moreton *Oxon* 21 SU5689
North Mundham *W Susx* 11 SU8702
North Muskham *Notts* 50 SK7958
North Newbald *Humb* 56 SE9136
North Newington *Oxon* 29 SP4240
North Newnton *Wilts* 20 SU1257
North Newton *Somset* 8 ST3031
North Nibley *Gloucs* 20 ST7495
North Ormsby *Lincs* 51 TF2893
North Otterington *N York* 62 SE3689
North Owersby *Lincs* 50 TF0594
North Perrott *Somset* 8 ST4709
North Petherton *Somset* 8 ST2833
North Petherwin *Cnwll* 4 SX2789
North Pickenham *Norfk* 42 TF8606
North Piddle *H & W* 28 SO9654
North Pool *Devon* 5 SX7741
North Poorton *Dorset* 8 SY5298
North Quarme *Somset* 7 SS9236
North Queensferry *Fife* 82 NT1380
North Radworthy *Devon* 7 SS7534
North Rauceby *Lincs* 50 TF0246
North Reston *Lincs* 51 TF3883
North Rigton *N York* 55 SE2749
North Rode *Ches* 47 SJ8866
North Runcton *Norfk* 42 TF6416
North Scarle *Lincs* 50 SK8466
North Shian *Strath* 79 NM9143
North Shields *T & W* 69 NZ3568
North Shoebury *Essex* 24 TQ9286
North Shore *Lancs* 53 SD3037
North Side *Cambs* 41 TL2799
North Skirlaugh *Humb* 57 TA1439
North Somercotes *Lincs* 51 TF4296
North Stainley *N York* 61 SE2876
North Stifford *Essex* 24 TQ6080
North Stoke *Avon* 20 ST7069
North Stoke *Oxon* 21 SU6186
North Stoke *W Susx* 12 TQ0110
North Street *Berks* 21 SU6371
North Street *Kent* 15 TR0157
North Sunderland *Nthumb* 77 NU2131
North Tamerton *Cnwll* 6 SX3197
North Tawton *Devon* 7 SS6601
North Third *Cent* 81 NS7589
North Tidworth *Wilts* 21 SU2349
North Town *Devon* 6 SS5109
North Town *Somset* 19 ST5642
North Town *Berks* 22 SU8882
North Tuddenham *Norfk* 42 TG0314
North Walsham *Norfk* 43 TG2830
North Waltham *Hants* 21 SU5646
North Warnborough *Hants* 22 SU7351
North Weald Basset *Essex* 23 TL4904
North Wheatley *Notts* 50 SK7585
North Widcombe *Somset* 19 ST5758
North Willingham *Lincs* 50 TF1688
North Wingfield *Derbys* 49 SK4065
North Witham *Lincs* 40 SK9221
North Wootton *Somset* 19 ST5641
North Wootton *Dorset* 9 ST6514
North Wootton *Norfk* 42 TF6424
North Wraxall *Wilts* 20 ST8175
Northall *Bucks* 30 SP9520
Northallerton *N York* 62 SE3694
Northam *Devon* 6 SS4529
Northam *Hants* 10 SU4312
Northampton *H & W* 28 SO8365
Northampton *Nhants* 30 SP7560
Northaw *Herts* 23 TL2702
Northay *Somset* 8 ST2811
Northborough *Cambs* 40 TF1507
Northbourne *Kent* 15 TR3352
Northbrook *Hants* 11 SU5139
Northchapel *W Susx* 12 SU9529
Northchurch *Herts* 22 SP9708
Northcott *Devon* 4 SX3392
Northcourt *Oxon* 21 SU4998
Northdown *Kent* 15 TR3770
Northend *Warwks* 29 SP3952
Northenden *Gt Man* 47 SJ8289
Northfield *Gramp* 95 NJ9008
Northfield *Gramp* 95 NJ9008
Northfield *W Mids* 38 SP0279
Northfield *Humb* 56 TA0326
Northfields *Lincs* 40 TF0208
Northfleet *Essex* 14 TQ6374
Northiam *E Susx* 14 TQ8324
Northill *Beds* 30 TL1446
Northington *Hants* 11 SU5637
Northlands *Lincs* 51 TF3453
Northleach *Gloucs* 28 SP1114
Northleigh *Devon* 6 SS6034
Northleigh *Devon* 8 SY1995
Northlew *Devon* 6 SX5099
Northmoor *Oxon* 21 SP4202
Northmuir *Tays* 88 NO3854
Northney *Hants* 11 SU7303
Northolt *Gt Lon* 22 TQ1384
Northop *Clwyd* 46 SJ2468
Northop Hall *Clwyd* 46 SJ2667
Northorpe *Lincs* 50 SK8997
Northorpe *Lincs* 41 TF2036
Northowram *W York* 55 SE1126
Northport *Dorset* 9 SY9288
Northrepps *Norfk* 43 TG2439
Northway *Somset* 8 ST1329
Northwich *Ches* 47 SJ6673
Northwick *H & W* 28 SO8458
Northwold *Norfk* 42 TL7597
Northwood *Shrops* 36 SJ4633
Northwood *IOW* 10 SZ4992
Northwood *Gt Lon* 22 TQ0990
Northwood End *Beds* 30 TL0941
Northwood Green *Gloucs* 28 SO7216
Norton *Cleve* 62 NZ4421
Norton *S York* 56 SE5415
Norton *N York* 56 SE7971
Norton *Shrops* 37 SJ7200
Norton *Notts* 49 SK5771
Norton *Powys* 27 SO3067
Norton *Gloucs* 28 SO8524
Norton *H & W* 28 SO8751
Norton *H & W* 28 SP0447
Norton *Nhants* 29 SP5963
Norton *Wilts* 20 ST8884
Norton *W Susx* 11 SU9206
Norton *Suffk* 32 TL9565
Norton *E Susx* 13 TQ4701
Norton Bavant *Wilts* 20 ST9043
Norton Bridge *Staffs* 38 SJ8630
Norton Bridge *Staffs* 38 SJ8630
Norton Canes *Staffs* 38 SK0107
Norton Canon *H & W* 27 SO3847
Norton Disney *Lincs* 50 SK8859
Norton Fitzwarren *Somset* 8 ST1925
Norton Green *IOW* 10 SZ3488
Norton Hawkfield *Avon* 19 ST5964
Norton Heath *Essex* 24 TL6004
Norton Lindsey *Warwks* 29 SP2263
Norton Little Green *Suffk* 32 TL9766
Norton Malreward *Avon* 19 ST6064
Norton St. Philip *Somset* 20 ST7755
Norton Subcourse *Norfk* 43 TM4198
Norton Wood *H & W* 27 SO3648
Norton in Hales *Shrops* 37 SJ7038
Norton sub Hamdon *Somset* 8 ST4615
Norton-Juxta-Twycross *Leics* 39 SK3207
Norton-le-Clay *N York* 55 SE4071
Norwell *Notts* 50 SK7761
Norwell Woodhouse *Notts* 50 SK7362
Norwich *Norfk* 43 TG2308
Norwick *Shet* 103 HP6414
Norwood *Cent* 82 NS8793
Norwood Green *Gt Lon* 22 TQ1378
Norwood Hill *Surrey* 12 TQ2343
Noseley *Leics* 40 SP7398
Noss Mayo *Devon* 4 SX5447
Nosterfield *N York* 61 SE2780
Nostie *Highld* 85 NG8527
Notgrove *Gloucs* 28 SP1020
Nottage *M Glam* 18 SS8177
Notter *Cnwll* 4 SX3960
Nottingham *Notts* 49 SK5739
Notton *W York* 55 SE3413
Notton *Wilts* 20 ST9169
Noutard's Green *H & W* 28 SO8066
Nox *Shrops* 36 SJ4110
Nuffield *Oxon* 22 SU6687
Nun Monkton *N York* 55 SE5057
Nuneaton *Warwks* 39 SP3691
Nuneham Courtenay *Oxon* 21 SU5599
Nunhead *Gt Lon* 23 TQ3475
Nunkeeling *Humb* 57 TA1449
Nunnerie *Strath* 66 NS9612
Nunney *Somset* 20 ST7345
Nunnington *N York* 62 SE6679
Nunsthorpe *Humb* 57 TA2607
Nunsthorpe *Humb* 57 TA2607
Nunthorpe *N York* 56 SE6050
Nunthorpe Village *Cleve* 62 NZ5413
Nunton *Wilts* 10 SU1526
Nunwick *N York* 62 SE3274
Nupend *Gloucs* 28 SO7806
Nursling *Hants* 10 SU3716
Nutbourne *W Susx* 11 SU7705
Nutbourne *W Susx* 12 TQ0718
Nutfield *Surrey* 12 TQ3050
Nuthall *Notts* 49 SK5243
Nuthampstead *Herts* 31 TL4034
Nuthurst *W Susx* 12 TQ1925
Nutley *E Susx* 13 TQ4427
Nybster *Highld* 100 ND3663
Nyetimber *W Susx* 11 SZ8998
Nyewood *W Susx* 11 SU8021
Nymet Rowland *Devon* 7 SS7108
Nymet Tracey *Devon* 7 SS7200
Nympsfield *Gloucs* 20 SO8000
Nyton *W Susx* 11 SU9305

O

Oad Street *Kent* 14 TQ8762
Oadby *Leics* 39 SK6200
Oak Cross *Devon* 6 SX5399
Oakamoor *Staffs* 48 SK0444
Oakbank *Loth* 75 NT0766
Oakdale *Gwent* 19 ST1898
Oake *Somset* 8 ST1525
Oaken *Staffs* 38 SJ8602
Oakenclough *Lancs* 53 SD5447
Oakengates *Shrops* 37 SJ7010
Oakenshaw *Dur* 61 NZ1937
Oakenshaw *W York* 55 SE1727
Oaker Side *Derbys* 49 SK2760
Oakford *Dyfed* 34 SN4558
Oakford *Devon* 7 SS9121
Oakfordbridge *Devon* 7 SS9122
Oakham *Leics* 40 SK8608
Oakhanger *Hants* 11 SU7635
Oakhill *Somset* 19 ST6347
Oakington *Cambs* 31 TL4164
Oakle Street *Gloucs* 28 SO7517
Oakley *Bucks* 29 SP6412
Oakley *Hants* 21 SU5650
Oakley *Beds* 30 TL0153
Oakley *Suffk* 33 TM1677
Oakridge *Gloucs* 20 SO9103
Oaksey *Wilts* 20 ST9993
Oakthorpe *Leics* 39 SK3212
Oakthorpe *Leics* 39 SK3212
Oakwoodhill *Surrey* 12 TQ1337
Oakworth *W York* 55 SE0338
Oare *Somset* 18 SS7947
Oare *Wilts* 20 SU1563
Oare *Kent* 15 TR0063
Oasby *Lincs* 40 TF0039
Oath *Somset* 8 ST3827
Oathlaw *Tays* 89 NO4756
Oatlands Park *Surrey* 22 TQ0865
Oban *Strath* 79 NM8629
Obley *Shrops* 36 SO3377
Obney *Tays* 82 NO0237
Oborne *Dorset* 9 ST6518
Occlestone Green *Ches* 47 SJ6962
Occold *Suffk* 33 TM1570
Ochiltree *Strath* 74 NS5021
Ockbrook *Derbys* 39 SK4235
Ockham *Surrey* 22 TQ0756
Ockle *Highld* 79 NM5570
Ockley *Surrey* 12 TQ1440
Ocle Pychard *H & W* 27 SO5945
Odcombe *Somset* 8 ST5015
Odd Down *Avon* 20 ST7462
Oddingley *H & W* 28 SO9159
Oddington *Gloucs* 29 SP2225
Oddington *Oxon* 29 SP5515
Odell *Beds* 30 SP9657
Odiham *Hants* 22 SU7451
Odsal *W York* 55 SE1529
Odsey *Herts* 31 TL2938
Odstock *Wilts* 10 SU1426
Odstone *Leics* 39 SK3907
Offchurch *Warwks* 29 SP3565
Offenham *H & W* 28 SP0546
Offham *W Susx* 12 TQ0208
Offham *E Susx* 13 TQ4012
Offham *Kent* 14 TQ6557
Offord Cluny *Cambs* 31 TL2267
Offord Darcy *Cambs* 31 TL2266
Offton *Suffk* 32 TM0649
Offwell *Devon* 8 SY1999
Ogbourne Maizey *Wilts* 21 SU1871
Ogbourne St. Andrew *Wilts* 21 SU1872
Ogbourne St. George *Wilts* 21 SU2074
Ogle *Nthumb* 69 NZ1378
Oglet *Mersyd* 46 SJ4481
Ogmore *M Glam* 18 SS8876
Ogmore Vale *M Glam* 18 SS9390
Ogmore Vale *M Glam* 18 SS9390
Ogmore-by-Sea *M Glam* 18 SS8675
Okeford Fitzpaine *Dorset* 9 ST8010
Okehampton *Devon* 6 SX5995
Old *Nhants* 30 SP7872
Old Aberdeen *Gramp* 95 NJ9407
Old Alresford *Hants* 11 SU5834
Old Auchenbrack *D & G* 65 NX7597
Old Basford *Notts* 49 SK5543
Old Basing *Hants* 22 SU6652
Old Bewick *Nthumb* 77 NU0621
Old Bolingbroke *Lincs* 51 TF3565
Old Bramhope *W York* 55 SE2343
Old Brampton *Derbys* 49 SK3371
Old Bridge of Urr *D & G* 66 NX7767
Old Buckenham *Norfk* 32 TM0691
Old Burghclere *Hants* 21 SU4657
Old Byland *N York* 62 SE5585
Old Church Stoke *Powys* 36 SO2894
Old Clee *Humb* 57 TA2808
Old Cleeve *Somset* 7 ST0441
Old Dailly *Strath* 64 NX2299
Old Dalby *Leics* 39 SK6723
Old Deer *Gramp* 95 NJ9747
Old Edington *S York* 49 SK5397
Old Ellerby *Humb* 57 TA1637
Old Felixstowe *Suffk* 25 TM3135
Old Fletton *Cambs* 40 TL1997
Old Forge *H & W* 27 SO5518
Old Grimsby *IOS* 2 SV8915
Old Hall Green *Herts* 31 TL3722
Old Harlow *Essex* 23 TL4711
Old Hunstanton *Norfk* 42 TF6842
Old Hutton *Cumb* 59 SD5688
Old Kea *Cnwll* 3 SW8441
Old Kilpatrick *Strath* 81 NS4672
Old Knebworth *Herts* 31 TL2320
Old Langho *Lancs* 54 SD7035
Old Leake *Lincs* 51 TF4050
Old Malton *N York* 56 SE7972
Old Micklefield *W York* 55 SE4433
Old Milverton *Warwks* 29 SP2967
Old Newton *Suffk* 32 TM0562
Old Radnor *Powys* 27 SO2558
Old Rattray *Gramp* 95 NK0857
Old Rayne *Gramp* 95 NJ6728
Old Romney *Kent* 15 TR0325
Old Romney *Kent* 15 TR0325
Old Scone *Tays* 82 NO1126
Old Shoreham *W Susx* 12 TQ2006
Old Shoremore *Highld* 98 NC2058
Old Sodbury *Avon* 20 ST7581
Old Somerby *Lincs* 40 SK9633
Old Stratford *Nhants* 30 SP7741
Old Sunnford *W Mids* 38 SO9083
Old Thirsk *N York* 62 SE4382
Old Town *Cumb* 59 SD5982
Old Town *IOS* 2 SV9110
Old Town *E Susx* 13 TV5999
Old Town *E Sisx* 13 TV5999
Old Trafford *Gt Man* 47 SJ8196
Old Warden *Beds* 30 TL1343
Old Weston *Cambs* 30 TL0977
Old Wick *Highld* 100 ND3649
Old Windsor *Berks* 22 SU9874

Old Wives Lees
Pentre

Old Wives Lees Kent **15** TR0754
Old Woking Surrey **22** TQ0157
Oldany Highld **98** NC0932
Oldberrow Warwks **28** SP1265
Oldbury Shrops **37** SO7192
Oldbury W Mids **38** SO9888
Oldbury Warwks **39** SP3194
Oldbury on the Hill Gloucs **20** ST8188
Oldbury-on-Severn Avon **19** ST6092
Oldcastle Gwent **27** SO3224
Oldcotes Notts **49** SK5888
Oldfield H & W **28** SO8464
Oldford Somset **20** ST7850
Oldhall Green Suffk **32** TL8956
Oldham Gt Man **54** SD9204
Oldhamstocks Loth **76** NT7470
Oldhurst Cambs **31** TL3077
Oldland Avon **20** ST6771
Oldmeldrum Gramp **95** NJ8127
Oldmill Cnwll **4** SX3673
Oldmixon Avon **19** ST3358
Oldstead N York **62** SE5379
Oldwall Cumb **67** NY4761
Oldwalls W Glam **17** SS4891
Oldwhat Gramp **95** NJ8651
Olive Green Staffs **38** SK1118
Oliver Border **75** NT0924
Oliver's Battery Hants **10** SU4527
Ollaberry Shet **103** HU3680
Ollach Highld **84** NG5137
Ollerton Shrops **37** SJ6425
Ollerton Ches **47** SJ7776
Ollerton Notts **49** SK6567
Olney Bucks **30** SP8951
Olrig House Highld **100** ND1866
Olton W Mids **38** SP1382
Olveston Avon **19** ST6086
Ombersley H & W **28** SO8463
Ompton Notts **49** SK6865
Onchan IOM **52** SC3978
Onecote Staffs **48** SK0455
Onibury Shrops **36** SO4579
Onich Highld **86** NN0261
Onllwyn W Glam **26** SN8410
Onneley Staffs **37** SJ7542
Onslow Village Surrey **12** SU9849
Onston Ches **47** SJ5873
Opinan Highld **91** NG7472
Orbliston Gramp **94** NJ3057
Orbliston Gramp **94** NJ3057
Orbost Highld **90** NG2543
Orby Lincs **51** TF4967
Orchard Portman Somset **8** ST2421
Orcheston Wilts **20** SU0545
Orcop H & W **27** SO4726
Orcop Hill H & W **27** SO4727
Ord Highld **84** NG6113
Ord Gramp **94** NJ6258
Ordhead Gramp **94** NJ6610
Ordie Gramp **88** NJ4501
Ordiequish Gramp **94** NJ3357
Ordley Nthumb **68** NY9459
Ordsall Notts **49** SK7079
Ore E Susx **14** TQ8311
Orford Ches **47** SJ6190
Orford Suffk **33** TM4250
Organford Dorset **9** SY9392
Orlestone Kent **15** TR0034
Orleton H & W **27** SO4967
Orleton H & W **28** SO7067
Orlingbury Nhants **30** SP8572
Ormesby Cleve **62** NZ5317
Ormesby St. Margaret Norfk **43** TG4914
Ormesby St. Michael Norfk **43** TG4714
Ormiscaig Highld **91** NG8590
Ormiston Loth **76** NT4169
Ormsaigmore Highld **79** NM4763
Ormsary Strath **71** NR7472
Ormskirk Lancs **46** SD4108
Oronsay Strath **70** NR3588
Orphir Ork **103** HY3404
Orpington Gt Lon **23** TQ4666
Orrell Gt Man **46** SD5303
Orrell Mersyd **46** SJ3496
Orroland D & G **65** NX7746
Orsett Essex **24** TQ6482
Orslow Staffs **37** SJ8015
Orston Notts **50** SK7740
Orton Cumb **60** NY6208
Orton Staffs **38** SO8795
Orton Nhants **40** SP8079
Orton Longueville Cambs **40** TL1796
Orton Waterville Cambs **40** TL1595
Orton-on-the-Hill Leics **39** SK3003
Orwell Cambs **31** TL3650
Osbaldeston Lancs **54** SD6431
Osbaldwick N York **56** SE6251
Osbaston Shrops **36** SJ3222
Osbaston Leics **39** SK4204
Osbournby Lincs **40** TF0638
Oscroft Ches **46** SJ5067
Osgathorpe Leics **39** SK4319
Osgodby N York **56** SE6433
Osgodby N York **63** TA0584
Osgodby Lincs **50** TF0792
Oskaig Highld **84** NG5438
Oskamull Strath **79** NM4540
Osmanthorpe W York **55** SE3333
Osmaston Derbys **48** SK1943
Osmington Dorset **9** SY7283
Osmington Mills Dorset **9** SY7381
Osmotherley N York **62** SE4596
Osney Oxon **29** SP4906
Ospringe Kent **15** TR0060
Ossett W York **55** SE2720
Ossington Notts **50** SK7564
Oswaldkirk N York **62** SE6278
Oswaldtwistle Lancs **54** SD7327
Oswestry Shrops **36** SJ2929
Otford Kent **23** TQ5359
Otham Kent **14** TQ7953
Othery Somset **8** ST3831
Otley W York **55** SE2045
Otley Suffk **33** TM2055
Otter Ferry Strath **71** NR9384
Otterbourne Hants **10** SU4522
Otterburn Nthumb **68** NY8893
Otterburn N York **54** SD8857
Otterham Cnwll **4** SX1690
Otterhampton Somset **19** ST2443
Ottershaw Surrey **22** TQ0263
Otterswick Shet **103** HU5285
Otterton Devon **5** SY0684
Ottery Devon **4** SX4475
Ottery St. Mary Devon **8** SY1095
Ottinge Kent **15** TR1642
Ottringham Humb **57** TA2624
Oughterside Cumb **58** NY1140
Oughtibridge S York **49** SK3093
Oughtrington Ches **47** SJ6987
Oulston N York **62** SE5474
Oulton Cumb **67** NY2450
Oulton Staffs **38** SJ9035
Oulton Norfk **43** TG1328
Oulton Suffk **43** TM5294
Oulton Broad Suffk **33** TM5192
Oulton Broad Suffk **33** TM5192
Oulton Street Norfk **43** TG1527
Oundle Nhants **40** TL0388
Ounsdale Staffs **38** SO8693
Ousby Cumb **59** NY6134
Ousden Suffk **32** TL7459
Ousefleet Humb **56** SE8323
Ouston Dur **69** NZ2554
Outgate Cumb **59** SD3599
Outhgill Cumb **60** NY7801
Outhill Warwks **28** SP1066
Outlane W York **55** SE0817
Outwell Norfk **41** TF5103
Outwood Surrey **12** TQ3145
Outwoods Staffs **37** SJ7817
Ouzlewell Green W York **55** SE3326
Over Cambs **31** TL3770
Over Compton Dorset **9** ST5816
Over Green Warwks **38** SP1694
Over Haddon Derbys **48** SK2066
Over Kellet Lancs **53** SD5169
Over Kiddington Oxon **29** SP4021
Over Norton Oxon **29** SP3128
Over Silton N York **62** SE4493
Over Stenton Fife **83** NT2799
Over Stowey Somset **19** ST1838
Over Stratton Somset **8** ST4315
Over Wallop Hants **10** SU2838
Over Whitacre Warwks **39** SP2590
Over Worton Oxon **29** SP4329
Overbury H & W **28** SO9537
Overleigh Somset **8** ST4835
Overpool Ches **46** SJ3877
Overscaig Hotel Highld **96** NC4123
Overseal Derbys **39** SK2915
Oversland Kent **15** TR0557
Overstone Nhants **30** SP7966
Overstrand Norfk **43** TG2440
Overthorpe Nhants **29** SP4840
Overton Gramp **95** NJ8714
Overton Lancs **53** SD4358
Overton W York **55** SE2516
Overton N York **56** SE5555
Overton Clwyd **36** SJ3741
Overton Shrops **37** SO5072
Overton W Glam **17** SS4685
Overton Hants **21** SU5149
Overtown Strath **74** NS8053
Overtown Lancs **60** SD6275
Overy Staithe Norfk **42** TF8444
Oving Bucks **30** SP7821
Oving W Susx **11** SU9004
Ovingdean E Susx **12** TQ3503
Ovingham Nthumb **68** NZ0863
Ovington Nthumb **68** NZ0663
Ovington Dur **61** NZ1314
Ovington Hants **11** SU5631
Ovington Norfk **42** TF9202
Ovington Essex **32** TL7642
Ower Hants **10** SU3215
Owermoigne Dorset **9** SY7685
Owlerton S York **49** SK3389
Owlsmoor Berks **22** SU8462
Owlswick Bucks **22** SP7806
Owmby Lincs **57** TA0704
Owmby Lincs **50** TF0087
Owslebury Hants **11** SU5123
Owston S York **56** SE5511
Owston Leics **40** SK7707
Owston Ferry Humb **50** SE8000
Owstwick Humb **57** TA2732
Owthorne Humb **57** TA3328
Owthorpe Notts **39** SK6733
Oxborough Norfk **42** TF7401
Oxbridge Dorset **8** SY4797
Oxcombe Lincs **51** TF3177
Oxen End Essex **24** TL6629
Oxen Park Cumb **58** SD3187
Oxenhope W York **55** SE0335
Oxenpill Somset **19** ST4441
Oxenton Gloucs **28** SO9531
Oxenwood Wilts **21** SU3058
Oxford Oxon **29** SP5106
Oxhey Herts **22** TQ1295
Oxhill Warwks **29** SP3146
Oxley W Mids **38** SJ9001
Oxley Green Essex **24** TL9014
Oxley's Green E Susx **14** TQ6921
Oxlode Cambs **41** TL4886
Oxnam Border **76** NT6918
Oxnead Norfk **43** TG2224
Oxshott Surrey **22** TQ1460
Oxspring S York **49** SE2601
Oxted Surrey **13** TQ3852
Oxton Border **76** NT4953
Oxton N York **55** SE5043
Oxton Notts **49** SK6351
Oxwich W Glam **17** SS4986
Oxwich Green W Glam **17** SS4985
Oykel Bridge Highld **96** NC3801
Oyne Gramp **95** NJ6725
Oystermouth W Glam **17** SS6187

P

Packington Leics **39** SK3614
Padanaram Tays **88** NO4251
Padbury Bucks **30** SP7230
Paddington Gt Lon **23** TQ2681
Paddlesworth Kent **14** TQ6862
Paddlesworth Kent **15** TR1939
Paddock Wood Kent **14** TQ6744
Padiham Lancs **54** SD7933
Padside N York **55** SE1659
Padstow Cnwll **3** SW9175
Padworth Berks **21** SU6166
Pagham W Susx **11** SZ8897
Paglesham Essex **24** TQ9293
Paignton Devon **5** SX8860
Pailton Warwks **39** SP4781
Painscastle Powys **27** SO1646
Painshawfield Nthumb **68** NZ0560
Painsthorpe Humb **56** SE8158
Painswick Gloucs **28** SO8609
Painter's Forstal Kent **15** TQ9958
Paisley Strath **73** NS4864
Pakefield Suffk **33** TM5390
Pakenham Suffk **32** TL9267
Paley Street Berks **22** SU8776
Palgrave Suffk **33** TM1178
Pallington Dorset **9** SY7891
Palmerston Strath **74** NS5019
Palnackie D & G **66** NX8157
Palnure D & G **65** NX4563
Palterton Derbys **49** SK4768
Pamber End Hants **21** SU6158
Pamber Green Hants **21** SU6159
Pamber Heath Hants **21** SU6162
Pamington Gloucs **28** SO9433
Pamphill Dorset **9** ST9900
Pampisford Cambs **31** TL4948
Panbride Tays **83** NO5635
Pancrasweek Devon **6** SS2905
Pandy Gwent **27** SO3322
Pandy Tudur Clwyd **45** SH8564
Panfield Essex **24** TL7325
Panfield Essex **24** TL7325
Pangbourne Berks **21** SU6376
Pangdean W Susx **12** TQ2911
Pannal N York **55** SE3051
Pannal Ash N York **55** SE2953
Pannanich Wells Hotel Gramp **88** NO4097
Pant Shrops **36** SJ2722
Pant-glas Gwynd **44** SH4747
Pant-y-dwr Powys **35** SN9874
Pant-y-mwyn Clwyd **46** SJ1964
Pantasaph Clwyd **46** SJ1675
Pantglas Powys **35** SN7797
Panton Lincs **50** TF1778
Panxworth Norfk **43** TG3513
Papcastle Cumb **58** NY1031
Papigoe Highld **100** ND3851
Papple Loth **76** NT5972
Papplewick Notts **49** SK5451
Papworth Everard Cambs **31** TL2862
Papworth St. Agnes Cambs **31** TL2664
Par Cnwll **3** SX0753
Parbold Lancs **53** SD4911
Parbrook Somset **19** ST5736
Parc Gwynd **45** SH8834
Parc Seymour Gwent **19** ST4091
Pardshaw Cumb **58** NY0924
Parham Suffk **33** TM3060
Park Gramp **89** NO7898
Park D & G **66** NX9091
Park Nthumb **68** NY6861
Park Corner Oxon **22** SU6988
Park Gate W York **55** SE1841
Park Gate Hants **11** SU5108
Park Royal Gt Lon **23** TQ1982
Parkend Gloucs **27** SO6108
Parkers Green Kent **13** TQ6148
Parkgate D & G **66** NY0288
Parkgate Surrey **12** TQ2043
Parkhall Strath **81** NS4871
Parkham Devon **6** SS3921
Parkhill House Gramp **95** NJ8914
Parkmill W Glam **17** SS5489
Parkside Dur **69** NZ4248
Parkstone Dorset **9** SZ0391
Parndon Essex **23** TL4308
Parr Bridge Gt Man **47** SD7001
Parracombe Devon **7** SS6745
Parson Drove Cambs **41** TF3708
Parson's Heath Essex **25** TM0226
Partick Strath **74** NS5467
Partington Gt Man **47** SJ7191
Partney Lincs **51** TF4068
Parton D & G **65** NX6970
Parton Cumb **58** NX9820
Partridge Green W Susx **12** TQ1919
Parwich Derbys **48** SK1854
Passenham Nhants **30** SP7839
Passfield Hants **11** SU8234
Paston Norfk **43** TG3234
Patcham E Susx **12** TQ3008
Patching W Susx **12** TQ0806
Patchway Avon **19** ST6082
Pateley Bridge N York **55** SE1565
Path of Condie Tays **82** NO0711
Pathhead Gramp **89** NO7263
Pathhead Strath **66** NS6114
Pathhead Fife **83** NT2992
Pathhead Loth **76** NT3964
Patna Strath **73** NS4110
Patney Wilts **20** SU0758
Patrick IOM **52** SC2482
Patrick Brompton N York **61** SE2190
Patricroft Gt Man **47** SJ7597
Patrington Humb **57** TA3122
Patrixbourne Kent **15** TR1855
Patterdale Cumb **59** NY3915
Pattingham Staffs **38** SO8299
Pattishall Nhants **30** SP6754
Pattiswick Green Essex **24** TL8124
Paul Cnwll **2** SW4627
Paul's Dene Wilts **10** SU1432
Paulerspury Bucks **30** SP7145
Paull Humb **57** TA1626
Paulton Avon **19** ST6556
Pauperhaugh Nthumb **68** NZ1099
Pavenham Beds **30** SP9955
Pawlett Somset **19** ST2942
Paxford Gloucs **29** SP1837
Paxton Border **77** NT9353
Payhembury Devon **7** ST0901
Paythorne Lancs **54** SD8251
Peacehaven E Susx **13** TQ4101
Peak Forest Derbys **48** SK1179
Peakirk Cambs **40** TF1606
Pean Kent **15** TR1837
Peanmeanach Highld **85** NM7180
Pearsie Tays **88** NO3659
Pease Pottage W Susx **12** TQ2633
Peasedown St. John Avon **20** ST7057
Peaseland Green Norfk **42** TG0516
Peasemore Berks **21** SU4577
Peasenhall Suffk **33** TM3569
Peaslake Surrey **12** TQ0844
Peasley Cross Mersyd **46** SJ5294
Peasmarsh E Susx **14** TQ8822
Peat Inn Fife **83** NO4509
Peathill Gramp **95** NJ9366
Peatling Magna Leics **39** SP5992
Peatling Parva Leics **39** SP5889
Pebmarsh Essex **24** TL8533
Pebworth H & W **28** SP1347
Pecket Well W York **54** SD9929
Peckforton Ches **46** SJ5356
Peckham Gt Lon **23** TQ3476
Peckleton Leics **39** SK4701
Pedlinge Kent **15** TR1335
Pedmore W Mids **38** SO9182
Pedwell Somset **19** ST4236
Peebles Border **75** NT2540
Peel IOM **52** SC2483
Pegsdon Beds **30** TL1130
Pegswood Nthumb **69** NZ2287
Pegwell Kent **15** TR3664
Peinchorran Highld **84** NG5233
Peinlich Highld **90** NG4158
Pelaw T & W **69** NZ3061
Peldon Essex **25** TL9816
Pelsall W Mids **38** SK0203
Pelton Dur **69** NZ2553
Pelynt Cnwll **4** SX2055
Pemberton Gt Man **47** SD5503
Pemberton Dyfed **17** SN5300
Pembrey Dyfed **17** SN4301
Pembridge H & W **27** SO3958
Pembroke Dyfed **16** SM9801
Pembroke Dock Dyfed **16** SM9603
Pembury Kent **13** TQ6240
Pen Rhiwfawr W Glam **26** SN7410
Pen-bont Rhydybeddau Dyfed **35** SN6783
Pen-ffordd Dyfed **16** SN0722
Pen-twyn Gwent **27** SO5209
Pen-y-bont Clwyd **36** SJ2123
Pen-y-bryn Dyfed **17** SN1742
Pen-y-clawdd Gwent **27** SO4507
Pen-y-coedcae M Glam **18** ST0587
Pen-y-cwn Dyfed **16** SM8523
Pen-y-felin Clwyd **46** SJ1569
Pen-y-graig Gwynd **44** SH2033
Pen-y-stryt Clwyd **46** SJ1952
Penallt Gwent **27** SO5210
Penally Dyfed **16** SS1199
Penalt H & W **27** SO5629
Penarth S Glam **19** ST1871
Penbryn Dyfed **17** SN2951
Pencader Dyfed **17** SN4436
Pencaitland Loth **76** NT4468
Pencarnisiog Gwynd **44** SH3573
Pencarreg Dyfed **17** SN5445
Pencelli Powys **26** SO0925
Penclawdd W Glam **17** SS5495
Pencoed M Glam **18** SS9581
Pencombe H & W **27** SO5952
Pencraig Powys **36** SJ0426
Pencraig H & W **27** SO5620
Pendeen Cnwll **2** SW3834
Penderyn M Glam **26** SN9408
Pendine Dyfed **17** SN2208
Pendlebury Gt Man **47** SD7802
Pendleton Lancs **54** SD7539
Pendock H & W **28** SO7832
Pendoggett Cnwll **3** SX0279
Pendomer Somset **8** ST5210
Pendoylan S Glam **18** ST0576
Penegoes Powys **35** SH7600
Pengam Gwent **19** ST1597
Pengam S Glam **19** ST2177
Penge Gt Lon **23** TQ3570
Pengelly Cnwll **3** SX0783
Pengrugla Cnwll **3** SW9947
Penhallow Cnwll **2** SW7651
Penhalvean Cnwll **2** SW7038
Penhill Wilts **20** SU1588
Penhow Gwent **19** ST4290
Penifiler Highld **84** NG4841
Peninver Strath **72** NR7524
Penistone S York **55** SE2403
Penkill Strath **64** NX2398
Penkridge Staffs **38** SJ9213
Penlean Cnwll **6** SX2098
Penley Clwyd **36** SJ4040
Penllyn S Glam **18** SS9775
Penmachno Gwynd **45** SH7950
Penmaen W Glam **17** SS5288
Penmaen Gwent **19** ST1897
Penmaenmawr Gwynd **45** SH7276
Penmaenpool Gwynd **35** SH6918
Penmark S Glam **18** ST0568
Penmorfa Gwynd **44** SH5540
Penmynydd Gwynd **44** SH5074
Penn Bucks **22** SU9193
Penn Street Bucks **22** SU9295
Pennal Gwynd **35** SH6900
Pennan Gramp **95** NJ8465
Pennant Powys **35** SN8897
Pennard W Glam **17** SS5688
Pennerley Shrops **36** SO3599
Pennington Cumb **58** SD2677
Pennorth Powys **26** SO1125
Penny Bridge Cumb **58** SD3083
Penny Hill Lincs **41** TF3526
Pennycross Strath **79** NM5025
Pennyghael Strath **79** NM5125
Pennyglen Strath **73** NS2710
Pennymoor Devon **7** SS8611
Penparc Dyfed **17** SN2047
Penperlleni Gwent **27** SO3204
Penpoll Cnwll **3** SX1454
Penponds Cnwll **2** SW6339
Penpont D & G **66** NX8494
Pen-rhiw Dyfed **17** SN2440
Penrhiwceiber M Glam **18** ST0597
Penrhiwllan Dyfed **17** SN3641
Penrhiwpal Dyfed **17** SN3445
Penrhos Gwynd **44** SH3433
Penrhos Gwent **27** SO4111
Penrhyn Bay Gwynd **45** SH8281
Penrhyncoch Dyfed **35** SN6384
Penrhyndeudraeth Gwynd **45** SH6139
Penrice W Glam **17** SS4987
Penrioch Strath **72** NR8744
Penrith Cumb **59** NY5130
Penrose Cnwll **3** SW8770
Penruddock Cumb **59** NY4227
Penryn Cnwll **2** SW7834
Pensarn Clwyd **45** SH9578
Pensax H & W **28** SO7269
Penselwood Somset **9** ST7531
Pensford Avon **19** ST6263
Pensham H & W **28** SO9444
Penshurst Kent **13** TQ5243
Pensilva Cnwll **4** SX2970
Pentewan Cnwll **3** SX0147
Pentir Gwynd **44** SH5766
Pentire Cnwll **2** SW7961
Pentlow Essex **32** TL8146
Pentney Norfk **42** TF7214
Penton Grafton Hants **21** SU3247
Penton Mewsey Hants **21** SU3247
Pentraeth Gwynd **44** SH5278
Pentre Shrops **36** SJ3617

Preston Wynne Rishangles

Preston Wynne *H & W* 27 SO5546
Preston on Stour *Warwks* 29 SP2049
Preston on Wye *H & W* 27 SO3842
Preston on the Hill *Ches* 47 SJ5780
Preston upon the Weald Moors *Shrops* 37 SJ6815
Preston-under-Scar *N York* 61 SE0691
Prestonpans *Loth* 76 NT3874
Prestwich *Gt Man* 47 SD8104
Prestwick *Strath* 73 NS3525
Prestwood *Bucks* 22 SP8700
Prickwillow *Cambs* 41 TL5982
Priddy *Somset* 19 ST5250
Priest Hutton *Lancs* 59 SD5273
Priestweston *Shrops* 36 SO2997
Primrosehill *Border* 76 NT7857
Primsidemill *Border* 76 NT8126
Princes Risborough *Bucks* 22 SP8003
Princethorpe *Warwks* 29 SP4070
Princetown *Devon* 5 SX5873
Priors Hardwick *Warwks* 29 SP4756
Priors Marston *Warwks* 29 SP4957
Priors Norton *Gloucs* 28 SO8624
Priston *Avon* 20 ST6960
Prittlewell *Essex* 24 TQ8687
Privett *Hants* 11 SU6727
Probus *Cnwll* 3 SW8947
Prospect *Cumb* 58 NY1140
Prospidnick *Cnwll* 2 SW6431
Protstonhill *Gramp* 95 NJ8163
Prudhoe *Nthumb* 68 NZ0962
Ptarmigan Lodge *Cent* 80 NN3500
Publow *Avon* 19 ST6264
Puckeridge *Herts* 31 TL3823
Puckington *Somset* 8 ST3718
Pucklechurch *Avon* 20 ST6976
Puddington *Ches* 46 SJ3273
Puddington *Devon* 7 SS8310
Puddletown *Dorset* 9 SY7594
Pudsey *W York* 55 SE2232
Pulborough *W Susx* 12 TQ0418
Pulford *Ches* 46 SJ3758
Pulham *Dorset* 9 ST7008
Pulham Market *Norfk* 33 TM1986
Pulham St. Mary *Norfk* 33 TM2085
Pulloxhill *Beds* 30 TL0634
Pumpherston *Loth* 75 NT0669
Pumsaint *Dyfed* 26 SN6540
Pumsaint *Dyfed* 26 SN6540
Puncheston *Dyfed* 16 SN0129
Puncknowle *Dorset* 8 SY5388
Punnett's Town *E Susx* 13 TQ6220
Purbrook *Hants* 11 SU6707
Purfleet *Essex* 24 TQ5578
Puriton *Somset* 19 ST3241
Purleigh *Essex* 24 TL8402
Purley *Berks* 22 SU6675
Purley *Gt Lon* 23 TQ3161
Purse Caundle *Dorset* 9 ST6917
Purtington *Somset* 8 ST3908
Purton *Gloucs* 28 SO6904
Purton *Gloucs* 28 SO6705
Purton *Wilts* 20 SU0987
Purton Stoke *Wilts* 20 SU0990
Pury End *Nhants* 30 SP7145
Pusey *Oxon* 21 SU3596
Putley *H & W* 27 SO6337
Putley Green *H & W* 27 SO6437
Putloe *Gloucs* 28 SO7709
Putney *Gt Lon* 23 TQ2374
Putron Village *Guern* 101 GN0000
Puttenham *Surrey* 22 SU9247
Puxley *Nhants* 30 SP7542
Puxton *Avon* 19 ST4063
Pwll *Dyfed* 17 SN4801
Pwll Trap *Dyfed* 17 SN2616
Pwll-du *Gwent* 27 SO2411
Pwll-y-glaw *W Glam* 18 SS7993
Pwllgloyw *Powys* 26 SO0333
Pwllheli *Gwynd* 44 SH3735
Pwllmeyric *Gwent* 19 ST5292
Pye Bridge *Derbys* 49 SK4452
Pye Corner *Herts* 31 TL4412
Pyecombe *W Susx* 12 TQ2813
Pyle *M Glam* 18 SS8282
Pyleigh *Somset* 8 ST1330
Pylle *Somset* 19 ST6038
Pymore *Dorset* 8 SY4694
Pymore *Cambs* 41 TL4986
Pyrford *Surrey* 22 TQ0358
Pyrton *Oxon* 22 SU6896
Pytchley *Nhants* 30 SP8574
Pyworthy *Devon* 6 SS3102

Q

Quabbs *Shrops* 36 SO2180
Quadring *Lincs* 41 TF2233
Quainton *Bucks* 30 SP7420
Quarley *Hants* 21 SU2743
Quarley *Hants* 21 SU2743
Quarndon *Derbys* 49 SK3340
Quarrier's Homes *Strath* 73 NS3666
Quarrington *Lincs* 50 TF0544
Quarrington Hill *Dur* 62 NZ3337
Quarry Bank *W Mids* 38 SO9386
Quarrywood *Gramp* 94 NJ1763
Quarter *Strath* 74 NS7251
Quatford *Shrops* 37 SO7391
Quatt *Shrops* 37 SO7588
Quebec *Dur* 69 NZ1743
Quedgeley *Gloucs* 28 SO8014
Queen Adelaide *Cambs* 41 TL5681
Queen Camel *Somset* 9 ST5924
Queen Charlton *Avon* 19 ST6367
Queen Oak *Dorset* 9 ST7831
Queen Street *Kent* 14 TQ6845
Queen's Bower *IOW* 11 SZ5684
Queenborough *Kent* 14 TQ9172
Queenhill *H & W* 28 SO8537
Queensbury *W York* 55 SE1030
Queensferry *Clwyd* 46 SJ3168
Queenzieburn *Strath* 74 NS6977
Quendon *Essex* 31 TL5130
Queniborough *Leics* 39 SK6412
Quenington *Gloucs* 28 SP1404
Quethiock *Cnwll* 4 SX3164
Quidenham *Norfk* 32 TM0287
Quidhampton *Wilts* 10 SU1030
Quinish House *Strath* 78 NM4154
Quinton *Nhants* 30 SP7754
Quintrell Downs *Cnwll* 3 SW8460
Quither *Devon* 4 SX4481
Quixwood *Border* 76 NT7863
Quoditch *Devon* 6 SX4097
Quorndon *Leics* 39 SK5616
Quothquan *Strath* 75 NS9939
Quoyburray *Ork* 103 HY5005
Quoyloo *Ork* 103 HY2420

R

Rableyheath *Herts* 31 TL2319
Rachan Mill *Border* 75 NT1134
Rachub *Gwynd* 45 SH6267
Rackenford *Devon* 7 SS8518
Rackham *W Susx* 12 TQ0413
Rackheath *Norfk* 43 TG2814
Rackwick *Ork* 103 ND2099
Radbourne *Derbys* 39 SK2836
Radcliffe *Nthumb* 69 NU2602
Radcliffe *Gt Man* 47 SD7806
Radcliffe on Trent *Notts* 49 SK6439
Radclive *Bucks* 30 SP6734
Radernie *Fife* 83 NO4609
Radford Semele *Warwks* 29 SP3464
Radlett *Herts* 23 TL1600
Radley *Oxon* 21 SU5398
Radley Green *Essex* 24 TL6205
Radnage *Bucks* 22 SU7897
Radstock *Avon* 20 ST6854
Radstone *Nhants* 29 SP5840
Radway *Warwks* 29 SP3648
Radwell *Beds* 30 TL0057
Radwell *Herts* 31 TL2335
Radwinter *Essex* 24 TL6037
Radyr *S Glam* 18 ST1280
Raecleugh *D & G* 66 NT0311
Rafford *Gramp* 93 NJ0556
Ragdale *Leics* 39 SK6619
Raglan *Gwent* 27 SO4107
Ragnall *Notts* 50 SK8073
Raigbeg *Highld* 93 NH8128
Rainbow Hill *H & W* 28 SO8555
Rainford *Gt Man* 46 SD4700
Rainham *Gt Lon* 23 TQ5282
Rainham *Kent* 14 TQ8165
Rainhill *Mersyd* 46 SJ4991
Rainhill Stoops *Mersyd* 46 SJ5090
Rainow *Ches* 48 SJ9475
Rainton *N York* 62 SE3675
Rainworth *Notts* 49 SK5858
Raisthorpe *N York* 56 SE8561
Rait *Tays* 82 NO2226
Raithby *Lincs* 51 TF3084
Raithby *Lincs* 51 TF3766
Rake *W Susx* 11 SU8027
Ralia *Highld* 87 NN7097
Ramasaig *Highld* 90 NG1644
Rame *Cnwll* 2 SW7233
Rame *Cnwll* 4 SX4249
Rampisham *Dorset* 8 ST5602
Rampside *Cumb* 53 SD2366
Rampton *Notts* 50 SK8078
Rampton *Cambs* 31 TL4267
Ramridge End *Beds* 30 TL1023
Ramsbottom *Gt Man* 54 SD7916
Ramsbury *Wilts* 21 SU2771
Ramscraigs *Highld* 100 ND1427
Ramsdean *Hants* 11 SU7022
Ramsdell *Hants* 21 SU5857
Ramsden *Oxon* 29 SP3515
Ramsden Bellhouse *Essex* 24 TQ7194
Ramsey *IOM* 52 SC4594
Ramsey *Cambs* 41 TL2885
Ramsey *Essex* 25 TM2130
Ramsey Forty Foot *Cambs* 41 TL3087
Ramsey Heights *Cambs* 41 TL2484
Ramsey Island *Essex* 25 TL9405
Ramsey Mereside *Cambs* 41 TL2889
Ramsey St. Mary's *Cambs* 41 TL2587
Ramsgate *Kent* 15 TR3865
Ramsgill *N York* 55 SE1170
Ramshope *Nthumb* 68 NT7304
Ramshorn *Staffs* 48 SK0845
Ramsnest Common *Surrey* 12 SU9432
Ranby *Notts* 49 SK6580
Ranby *Lincs* 51 TF2278
Rand *Lincs* 50 TF1078
Randwick *Gloucs* 28 SO8306
Ranfurly *Strath* 73 NS3865
Rangemore *Staffs* 38 SK1822
Rangeworthy *Avon* 20 ST6986
Rankinston *Strath* 73 NS4513
Rann *Lancs* 54 SD7124
Rannoch Station *Tays* 86 NN4257
Ranochan *Highld* 85 NM8282
Ranscombe *Somset* 7 SS9443
Ranskill *Notts* 49 SK6587
Ranton *Staffs* 38 SJ8524
Ranton Green *Staffs* 38 SJ8423
Ranworth *Norfk* 43 TG3514
Raploch *Cent* 81 NS7894
Rapness *Ork* 103 HY5141
Rapps *Somset* 8 ST3316
Rascarrel *D & G* 66 NX7948
Rashfield *Strath* 80 NS1483
Rashwood *H & W* 28 SO9165
Raskelf *N York* 55 SE4971
Ratagan *Highld* 85 NG9119
Ratby *Leics* 39 SK5105
Ratcliffe Culey *Leics* 39 SP3299
Ratcliffe on Soar *Notts* 39 SK4928
Ratcliffe on the Wreake *Leics* 39 SK6314
Rathen *Gramp* 95 NJ9960
Rathillet *Fife* 83 NO3620
Rathmell *N York* 54 SD8059
Ratho *Loth* 75 NT1370
Rathven *Gramp* 94 NJ4465
Ratley *Warwks* 29 SP3847
Ratling *Kent* 15 TR2453
Ratlinghope *Shrops* 36 SO4096
Rattar *Highld* 100 ND2673
Rattery *Devon* 5 SX7461
Rattlesden *Suffk* 32 TL9758
Ratton Village *E Susx* 13 TQ5901
Rattray *Tays* 88 NO1845
Raunds *Nhants* 30 SP9972
Raven Meols *Mersyd* 46 SD2905
Ravenfield *S York* 49 SK4895
Ravenglass *Cumb* 58 SD0896
Raveningham *Norfk* 43 TM3996
Ravenscliffe *Staffs* 47 SJ8452
Ravensden *Beds* 30 TL0754
Ravenshead *Notts* 49 SK5654
Ravensthorpe *W York* 55 SE2220
Ravensthorpe *Nhants* 30 SP6670
Ravenstone *Leics* 39 SK4013
Ravenstone *Bucks* 30 SP8451
Ravenstonedale *Cumb* 60 NY7203
Ravenstruther *Strath* 75 NS9245
Ravensworth *N York* 61 NZ1308
Rawcliffe *N York* 56 SE5854
Rawcliffe *Humb* 56 SE6822
Rawling Street *Kent* 14 TQ9059
Rawmarsh *S York* 49 SK4396
Rawreth *Essex* 24 TQ7893
Rawridge *Devon* 8 ST2006
Rawtenstall *Lancs* 54 SD8123
Raydon *Suffk* 25 TM0438
Rayleigh *Essex* 24 TQ8090
Rayne *Essex* 24 TL7222
Raynes Park *Gt Lon* 23 TQ2368
Reach *Cambs* 31 TL5666
Read *Lancs* 54 SD7634
Reading *Berks* 22 SU7173
Reading Street *Kent* 14 TQ9230
Reading Street *Kent* 15 TR3869
Reagill *Cumb* 59 NY6017
Rearquhar *Highld* 97 NH7492
Rearsby *Leics* 39 SK6514
Reaster *Highld* 100 ND2565
Reay *Highld* 99 NC9664
Reay *Highld* 99 NC9664
Reculver *Kent* 15 TR2269
Red Ball *Devon* 7 ST0917
Red Hill *Warwks* 28 SP1356
Red Hill *Dorset* 10 SZ0995
Red Roses *Dyfed* 17 SN2011
Red Row *T & W* 69 NZ2599
Red Wharf Bay *Gwynd* 44 SH5281
Redberth *Dyfed* 16 SN0804
Redbourn *Herts* 30 TL1012
Redbourne *Lincs* 50 SK9799
Redbrook *Clwyd* 37 SJ5041
Redbrook *Gloucs* 27 SO5309
Redbrook Street *Kent* 14 TQ9336
Redburn *Highld* 93 NH9447
Redcar *Cleve* 62 NZ6024
Redcastle *Highld* 92 NH5849
Redcastle *D & G* 66 NX8165
Redding *Cent* 82 NS9278
Reddingmuirhead *Cent* 75 NS9177
Redditch *H & W* 28 SP0467
Rede *Suffk* 32 TL8055
Redenhall *Norfk* 33 TM2684
Redesmouth *Nthumb* 68 NY8682
Redford *Tays* 89 NO5644
Redford *Gramp* 89 NO7570
Redford *W Susx* 11 SU8626
Redfordgreen *Border* 76 NT3616
Redgorton *Tays* 82 NO0828
Redgrave *Suffk* 32 TM0477
Redhill *Gramp* 89 NJ7704
Redhill *Avon* 19 ST4962
Redhill *Herts* 31 TL3033
Redhill *Surrey* 12 TQ2750
Redisham *Suffk* 33 TM4084
Redland *Ork* 103 HY3724
Redland *Avon* 19 ST5775
Redlingfield *Suffk* 33 TM1870
Redlingfield Green *Suffk* 33 TM1871
Redlynch *Somset* 9 ST7033
Redlynch *Wilts* 10 SU2021
Redmarley *H & W* 28 SO7666
Redmarley D'Abitot *Gloucs* 28 SO7531
Redmarshall *Cleve* 62 NZ3821
Redmile *Leics* 40 SK7935
Redmire *N York* 61 SE0491
Redmyre *Gramp* 89 NO7575
Rednal *Shrops* 36 SJ3628
Redpath *Border* 76 NT5835
Redruth *Cnwll* 2 SW6942
Redstone *Tays* 82 NO1834
Redwick *Gwent* 19 ST4184
Redwick *Avon* 19 ST5486
Redworth *Dur* 61 NZ2423
Reed *Herts* 31 TL3636
Reedham *Norfk* 43 TG4201
Reedness *Humb* 56 SE7923
Reepham *Lincs* 50 TF0473
Reepham *Norfk* 43 TG1022
Reeth *N York* 61 SE0399
Reeves Green *W Mids* 39 SP2677
Reiff *Highld* 98 NB9614
Reigate *Surrey* 12 TQ2550
Reighton *N York* 63 TA1375
Reisque *Gramp* 95 NJ8819
Reiss *Highld* 100 ND3354
Relubbus *Cnwll* 2 SW5631
Relugas *Gramp* 93 NH9948
Remenham *Berks* 22 SU7684
Remenham Hill *Berks* 22 SU7882
Remony *Tays* 87 NN7644
Rempstone *Notts* 39 SK5724
Rendcomb *Gloucs* 28 SP0209
Rendham *Suffk* 33 TM3464
Renfrew *Strath* 74 NS5067
Renhold *Beds* 30 TL0852
Renishaw *Derbys* 49 SK4577
Rennington *Nthumb* 77 NU2118
Renswick *Cumb* 67 NY5943
Renton *Strath* 80 NS3877
Repps *Norfk* 43 TG4217
Repton *Derbys* 39 SK3026
Resaurie *Highld* 93 NH7045
Rescassa *Cnwll* 3 SW9842
Resipole *Highld* 79 NM7264
Reskadinnick *Cnwll* 2 SW6341
Resolis *Highld* 93 NH6765
Resolven *W Glam* 18 SN8302
Rest and be Thankful *Strath* 80 NN2307
Reston *Border* 77 NT8862
Reswallie *Tays* 89 NO5051
Retford *Notts* 49 SK7081
Rettendon *Essex* 24 TQ7698
Revesby *Lincs* 51 TF2961
Rew Street *IOW* 10 SZ4794
Rewe *Devon* 7 SX9499
Reydon *Suffk* 33 TM4977
Reymerston *Norfk* 42 TG0206
Reynalton *Dyfed* 16 SN0908
Reynoldston *W Glam* 17 SS4889
Rezare *Cnwll* 4 SX3677
Rhandirmwyn *Dyfed* 26 SN7843
Rhayader *Powys* 35 SN9768
Rheindown *Highld* 92 NH5147
Rhes-y-cae *Clwyd* 46 SJ1871
Rhewl *Clwyd* 46 SJ1060
Rhewl *Clwyd* 46 SJ1744
Rhicarn *Highld* 98 NC0825
Rhiconich *Highld* 98 NC2552
Rhicullen *Highld* 93 NH6971
Rhigos *M Glam* 26 SN9205
Rhireavach *Highld* 91 NH0295
Rhives *Highld* 97 NC8200
Rhiwbina *S Glam* 19 ST1682
Rhiwderyn *Gwent* 19 ST2687
Rhiwlas *Gwynd* 44 SH5765
Rhoden Green *Kent* 14 TQ6845
Rhodes Minnis *Kent* 15 TR1542
Rhodiad-y-brenin *Dyfed* 16 SM7627
Rhonehouse or Kelton Hill *D & G* 65 NX7459
Rhoose *S Glam* 18 ST0666
Rhos *Dyfed* 17 SN3835
Rhos *W Glam* 18 SN7302
Rhos-hill *Dyfed* 17 SN1940
Rhos-on-Sea *Clwyd* 45 SH8480
Rhos-y-gwaliau *Gwynd* 45 SH9434
Rhoscolyn *Gwynd* 44 SH2267
Rhoscrowther *Dyfed* 16 SM9002
Rhosesmor *Clwyd* 46 SJ2168
Rhosgoch *Powys* 27 SO1847
Rhoshirwaun *Gwynd* 44 SH2029
Rhosllanerchrugog *Clwyd* 46 SJ2946
Rhosmeirch *Gwynd* 44 SH4677
Rhosneigr *Gwynd* 44 SH3173
Rhossili *W Glam* 17 SS4187
Rhostryfan *Gwynd* 44 SH4957
Rhostyllen *Clwyd* 46 SJ3148
Rhosybol *Gwynd* 44 SH4288
Rhosymedre *Clwyd* 36 SJ2842
Rhu *Strath* 80 NS2684
Rhuallt *Clwyd* 46 SJ0775
Rhubodach *Strath* 80 NS0273
Rhuddlan *Clwyd* 45 SJ0278
Rhunahaorine *Strath* 72 NR7048
Rhyd *Gwynd* 45 SH6341
Rhyd-Ddu *Gwynd* 44 SH5652
Rhyd-uchaf *Gwynd* 45 SH9037
Rhyd-y pennau *Dyfed* 35 SN6385
Rhyd-y-clafdy *Gwynd* 44 SH3234
Rhyd-y-foel *Clwyd* 45 SH9176
Rhyd-y-groes *Gwynd* 44 SH5867
Rhydargaeau *Dyfed* 17 SN4326
Rhydcymerau *Dyfed* 17 SN5738
Rhydlewis *Dyfed* 17 SN3447
Rhydowen *Dyfed* 17 SN4445
Rhydyfro *W Glam* 26 SN7105
Rhyl *Clwyd* 45 SJ0081
Rhymney *M Glam* 26 SO1107
Rhynd *Tays* 82 NO1520
Rhynie *Highld* 97 NH8479
Rhynie *Gramp* 94 NJ4927
Ribbesford *H & W* 37 SO7874
Ribbleton *Lancs* 53 SD5631
Ribchester *Lancs* 54 SD6535
Riby *Lincs* 57 TA1807
Riccall *N York* 56 SE6237
Riccarton *Strath* 73 NS4236
Riccarton *Border* 67 NY5494
Richards Castle *H & W* 27 SO4969
Richmond *N York* 61 NZ1701
Richmond *S York* 49 SK4085
Richmond Fort *Guern* 101 GN0000
Richmond upon Thames *Gt Lon* 23 TQ1774
Rickerscote *Staffs* 38 SJ9220
Rickford *Avon* 19 ST4859
Rickham *Devon* 5 SX7537
Rickinghall Inferior *Suffk* 32 TM0475
Rickinghall Superior *Suffk* 32 TM0375
Rickling *Essex* 31 TL4931
Rickling Green *Essex* 31 TL5129
Rickmansworth *Herts* 22 TQ0694
Riddell *Border* 76 NT5124
Riddlecombe *Devon* 6 SS6113
Riddlesden *W York* 55 SE0742
Ridge *Wilts* 9 ST9531
Ridge *Dorset* 9 SY9386
Ridge *Herts* 23 TL2100
Ridge Lane *Warwks* 39 SP2994
Ridgehill *Avon* 19 ST5462
Ridgeway *Derbys* 49 SK4081
Ridgewell *Essex* 32 TL7340
Ridgewood *E Susx* 13 TQ4719
Ridgmont *Beds* 30 SP9736
Riding Mill *Nthumb* 68 NZ0161
Ridlington *Leics* 40 SK8402
Ridlington *Norfk* 43 TG3430
Ridsdale *Nthumb* 68 NY9084
Rievaulx *N York* 62 SE5785
Rigg *D & G* 67 NY2966
Riggend *Strath* 74 NS7670
Righoul *Highld* 93 NH8851
Rigsby *Lincs* 51 TF4375
Rigside *Strath* 74 NS8735
Riley Green *Lancs* 54 SD6225
Rilla Mill *Cnwll* 4 SX2973
Rillington *N York* 63 SE8574
Rimington *Lancs* 54 SD8045
Rimpton *Somset* 9 ST6121
Rimswell *Humb* 57 TA3128
Rinaston *Dyfed* 16 SM9825
Rindleford *Shrops* 37 SO7395
Ringford *D & G* 65 NX6957
Ringland *Norfk* 43 TG1313
Ringmer *E Susx* 13 TQ4412
Ringmore *Devon* 5 SX6546
Ringmore *Devon* 5 SX9272
Ringorm *Gramp* 94 NJ2644
Ringsfield *Suffk* 33 TM4088
Ringsfield Corner *Suffk* 33 TM4087
Ringshall *Bucks* 30 SP9814
Ringshall *Suffk* 32 TM0452
Ringshall Stocks *Suffk* 32 TM0551
Ringstead *Nhants* 30 SP9875
Ringstead *Norfk* 42 TF7040
Ringwood *Hants* 10 SU1505
Ringwould *Kent* 15 TR3548
Ripe *E Susx* 13 TQ5110
Ripley *N York* 55 SE2860
Ripley *Derbys* 49 SK3950
Ripley *Hants* 10 SZ1698
Ripley *Surrey* 22 TQ0556
Riplington *Hants* 11 SU6623
Ripon *N York* 55 SE3171
Rippingale *Lincs* 40 TF0927
Ripple *H & W* 28 SO8737
Ripple *Kent* 15 TR3550
Ripponden *W York* 55 SE0319
Risabus *Strath* 70 NR3143
Risbury *H & W* 27 SO5455
Risby *Suffk* 32 TL8066
Risca *Gwent* 19 ST2391
Rise *Humb* 57 TA1542
Risegate *Lincs* 41 TF2129
Riseley *Berks* 22 SU7263
Riseley *Beds* 30 TL0462
Rishangles *Suffk* 33 TM1668

Rishton Sawston

Rishton *Lancs* 54 SD7230
Rishworth *W York* 55 SE0318
Risley *Derbys* 39 SK4535
Risplith *N York* 55 SE2468
River *W Susx* 11 SU9323
River *Kent* 15 TR2943
Riverford *Highld* 92 NH5454
Riverhead *Kent* 23 TQ5156
Rivington *Lancs* 54 SD6214
Road Weedon *Nhants* 29 SP6359
Roade *Nhants* 30 SP7651
Roadmeetings *Strath* 74 NS8649
Roadside *Highld* 100 ND1560
Roadside *Strath* 74 NS5717
Roadside of Catterline *Gramp* 89 NO8579
Roadside of Kinneff *Gramp* 89 NO8477
Roadwater *Somset* 7 ST0338
Roag *Highld* 90 NG2744
Roan of Craigoch *Strath* 73 NS2904
Roast Green *Essex* 31 TL4632
Roath *S Glam* 19 ST1977
Roberton *Strath* 75 NS9428
Roberton *Border* 67 NT4214
Robertsbridge *E Susx* 14 TQ7423
Roberttown *W York* 55 SE1922
Robeston Wathen *Dyfed* 16 SN0815
Robgill Tower *D & G* 67 NY2471
Robin Hood's Bay *N York* 63 NZ9505
Roborough *Devon* 6 SS5717
Roby *Mersyd* 46 SJ4390
Rocester *Staffs* 48 SK1039
Roch *Dyfed* 16 SM8821
Rochdale *Gt Man* 54 SD8913
Roche *Cnwll* 3 SW9860
Rochester *Nthumb* 68 NY8298
Rochester *Kent* 14 TQ7468
Rochford *H & W* 27 SO6268
Rochford *Essex* 24 TQ8790
Rochville *Strath* 80 NS2390
Rock *Nthumb* 77 NU2020
Rock *H & W* 37 SO7371
Rock *Cnwll* 3 SW9375
Rock Ferry *Mersyd* 46 SJ3386
Rockbeare *Devon* 7 SY0194
Rockbourne *Hants* 10 SU1118
Rockcliffe *D & G* 66 NX8454
Rockcliffe *Cumb* 67 NY3561
Rockfield *Highld* 97 NH9282
Rockfield *Gwent* 27 SO4814
Rockford *Devon* 18 SS7547
Rockhampton *Gloucs* 19 ST6593
Rockhill *Shrops* 36 SO2978
Rockingham *Nhants* 40 SP8691
Rockland All Saints *Norfk* 42 TL9996
Rockland St. Mary *Norfk* 43 TG3104
Rockland St. Peter *Norfk* 42 TL9897
Rockley *Notts* 49 SK7174
Rockley *Wilts* 20 SU1571
Rockwell End *Bucks* 22 SU7988
Rookwith *N York* 61 SE2086
Rodborough *Gloucs* 28 SO8404
Rodborough *Wilts* 20 SU1485
Rodbourne *Wilts* 20 ST9383
Rodden *Dorset* 9 SY6184
Rode *Somset* 20 ST8053
Rode Heath *Ches* 47 SJ8056
Rodel *W Isls* 102 NG0483
Roden *Shrops* 37 SJ5716
Rodhuish *Somset* 7 ST0139
Rodington *Shrops* 37 SJ5814
Rodington Heath *Shrops* 37 SJ5814
Rodley *Gloucs* 28 SO7411
Rodmarton *Gloucs* 20 ST9498
Rodmell *E Susx* 13 TQ4106
Rodmersham *Kent* 14 TQ9261
Rodmersham Green *Kent* 14 TQ9161
Rodney Stoke *Somset* 19 ST4849
Rodono Hotel *Border* 75 NT2321
Rodsley *Derbys* 48 SK2040
Roe Green *Herts* 23 TL2107
Roe Green *Herts* 31 TL3133
Roecliffe *N York* 55 SE3765
Roehampton *Gt Lon* 23 TQ2273
Roewen *Gwynd* 45 SH7671
Roffey *W Susx* 12 TQ1932
Rogart *Highld* 97 NC7304
Rogate *W Susx* 11 SU8023
Rogerstone *Gwent* 19 ST2787
Rogiet *Gwent* 19 ST4587
Roke *Oxon* 21 SU6293
Roker *T & W* 69 NZ4058
Rollesby *Norfk* 43 TG4416
Rolleston *Staffs* 39 SK2327
Rolleston *Leics* 40 SK7300
Rolston *Humb* 57 TA2144
Rolston *Humb* 57 TA2144
Rolvenden *Kent* 14 TQ8431
Rolvenden Layne *Kent* 14 TQ8530
Romaldkirk *Dur* 61 NY9922
Romanby *N York* 62 SE3693
Romanno Bridge *Border* 75 NT1647
Romansleigh *Devon* 7 SS7220
Romesdal *Highld* 90 NG4053
Romford *Dorset* 10 SU0709
Romford *Gt Lon* 23 TQ5188
Romiley *Gt Man* 48 SJ9490
Romsey *Hants* 10 SU3521
Romsley *Shrops* 37 SO7883
Romsley *H & W* 38 SO9680
Ronachan *Strath* 71 NR7454
Rookhope *Dur* 61 NY9342
Rookley *IOW* 10 SZ5084
Rooks Bridge *Somset* 19 ST3652
Rooks Nest *Somset* 7 ST0933
Roos *Humb* 57 TA2830
Roothams Green *Beds* 30 TL0957
Ropley *Hants* 11 SU6431
Ropley Dean *Hants* 11 SU6232
Ropsley *Lincs* 40 SK9933
Rora *Gramp* 95 NK0650
Rorrington *Shrops* 36 SJ3000
Rosarie *Gramp* 94 NJ3850
Rose *Cnwll* 2 SW7754
Rose Ash *Devon* 7 SS7921
Rose Green *W Susx* 11 SZ9099
Rose Green *Essex* 24 TL9028
Rose Green *Suffk* 25 TL9337
Rose Green *Suffk* 32 TL9744
Rose Hill *Lancs* 54 SD8231
Rose Lands *E Susx* 13 TQ6200
Rosebank *Strath* 74 NS8049
Rosebush *Dyfed* 16 SN0729
Rosedale Abbey *N York* 63 SE7296
Rosehall *Highld* 96 NC4701
Rosehearty *Gramp* 95 NJ9267
Roseisle *Gramp* 93 NJ1466
Rosemarket *Dyfed* 16 SM9508
Rosemarkie *Highld* 93 NH7357
Rosemary Lane *Devon* 8 ST1514
Rosemount *Tays* 88 NO1843
Rosenannon *Cnwll* 3 SW9566
Rosewell *Loth* 75 NT2862
Roseworth *Cleve* 62 NZ4221
Rosgill *Cumb* 59 NY5316
Rosgill *Cumb* 59 NY5316
Roshven *Highld* 85 NM7078
Roskhill *Highld* 90 NG2744
Rosley *Cumb* 67 NY3245
Roslin *Loth* 75 NT2763
Rosliston *Derbys* 39 SK2416
Rosneath *Strath* 80 NS2583
Ross *D & G* 65 NX6444
Ross-on-Wye *H & W* 27 SO5923
Rossett *Clwyd* 46 SJ3657
Rossett Green *N York* 55 SE2952
Rossington *Notts* 49 SK6298
Rosskeen *Highld* 93 NH6869
Rossland *Strath* 73 NS4370
Roster *Highld* 100 ND2639
Rostherne *Ches* 47 SJ7483
Rosthwaite *Cumb* 58 NY2514
Roston *Derbys* 48 SK1340
Rosyth *Loth* 82 NT1082
Rothbury *Nthumb* 68 NU0501
Rothienorman *Gramp* 95 NJ7235
Rotherby *Leics* 39 SK6716
Rotherfield *E Susx* 13 TQ5529
Rotherfield Greys *Oxon* 22 SU7282
Rotherfield Peppard *Oxon* 22 SU7182
Rotherham *S York* 49 SK4392
Rothersthorpe *Nhants* 30 SP7156
Rotherwick *Hants* 22 SU7156
Rothes *Gramp* 94 NJ2749
Rothesay *Strath* 73 NS0864
Rothiebrisbane *Gramp* 95 NJ7437
Rothiemay *Gramp* 94 NJ5548
Rothley *Leics* 39 SK5812
Rothmaise *Gramp* 95 NJ6832
Rothwell *W York* 55 SE3428
Rothwell *Nhants* 40 SP8181
Rothwell *Lincs* 50 TF1499
Rottal Lodge *Tays* 88 NO3769
Rottingdean *E Susx* 12 TQ3602
Rottington *Cumb* 58 NX9613
Roucan *D & G* 66 NY0277
Rough Common *Kent* 15 TR1259
Rougham *Norfk* 42 TF8320
Rougham Green *Suffk* 32 TL9061
Roughton *Shrops* 37 SO7594
Roughton *Lincs* 51 TF2464
Roughton *Norfk* 43 TG2136
Roundbush Green *Essex* 24 TL5814
Roundham *Somset* 8 ST4209
Roundhay *W York* 55 SE3337
Roundway *Wilts* 20 SU0163
Roundyhill *Tays* 88 NO3750
Rous Lench *H & W* 28 SP0153
Rousdon *Devon* 8 SY2991
Rousham *Oxon* 29 SP4724
Routenburn *Strath* 73 NS1961
Routh *Humb* 57 TA0942
Row *Cumb* 59 SD4589
Row *Cnwll* 3 SX0976
Row Green *Essex* 24 TL7420
Rowanburn *D & G* 67 NY4177
Rowardennan Hotel *Cent* 80 NS3698
Rowarth *Derbys* 48 SK0189
Rowberrow *Somset* 19 ST4558
Rowde *Wilts* 20 ST9762
Rowfoot *Nthumb* 68 NY6860
Rowington *Warwks* 29 SP2069
Rowland *Derbys* 48 SK2172
Rowland's Castle *Hants* 11 SU7310
Rowland's Gill *T & W* 69 NZ1658
Rowledge *Surrey* 11 SU8243
Rowley *Dur* 68 NZ0848
Rowley *Humb* 56 SE9732
Rowley Green *W Mids* 39 SP3483
Rowley Regis *W Mids* 38 SO9787
Rowlstone *H & W* 27 SO3727
Rowner *Hants* 11 SU5801
Rowney Green *H & W* 38 SP0471
Rownhams *Hants* 10 SU3817
Rowsham *Bucks* 30 SP8417
Rowsley *Derbys* 48 SK2565
Rowston *Lincs* 50 TF0856
Rowton *Ches* 46 SJ4564
Rowton *Shrops* 37 SJ6119
Roxburgh *Border* 76 NT6930
Roxby *Humb* 56 SE9116
Roxton *Beds* 30 TL1554
Roxwell *Essex* 24 TL6408
Roy Bridge *Highld* 86 NN2681
Royal Leamington Spa *Warwks* 29 SP3265
Royal Tunbridge Wells *Kent* 13 TQ5839
Roydon *Norfk* 42 TF7023
Roydon *Essex* 23 TL4010
Roydon *Norfk* 33 TM1080
Roydon Hamlet *Essex* 23 TL4107
Royston *S York* 55 SE3611
Royston *Herts* 31 TL3540
Royton *Gt Man* 54 SD9107
Rozel *Jersey* 101 JS0000
Ruabon *Clwyd* 46 SJ3043
Ruaig *Strath* 78 NM0747
Ruan Lanihorne *Cnwll* 3 SW8942
Ruan Major *Cnwll* 2 SW7016
Ruan Minor *Cnwll* 2 SW7115
Ruardean *Gloucs* 27 SO6217
Ruardean Hill *Gloucs* 27 SO6317
Ruardean Woodside *Gloucs* 27 SO6216
Rubery *H & W* 38 SO9977
Ruckinge *Kent* 15 TR0233
Ruckley *Shrops* 37 SJ5300
Rudby *N York* 62 NZ4706
Rudchester *Nthumb* 69 NZ1167
Ruddington *Notts* 39 SK5732
Rudge *Somset* 20 ST8251
Rudgeway *Avon* 19 ST6386
Rudgwick *W Susx* 12 TQ0834
Rudley Green *Essex* 24 TL8303
Rudry *M Glam* 19 ST2086
Rudston *Humb* 57 TA0967
Rudyard *Staffs* 48 SJ9557
Ruecastle *Border* 76 NT6120
Rufford *Lancs* 53 SD4615
Rufforth *N York* 55 SE5251
Rugby *Warwks* 39 SP5075
Rugeley *Staffs* 38 SK0418
Ruishton *Somset* 8 ST2625
Ruislip *Gt Lon* 22 TQ0987
Ruletown Head *Border* 68 NT6113
Rumbach *Gramp* 94 NJ3852
Rumbling Bridge *Tays* 82 NT0199
Rumburgh *Suffk* 33 TM3481
Rumford *Cent* 75 NS9377
Rumford *Cnwll* 3 SW8970
Rumney *S Glam* 19 ST2178
Runcorn *Ches* 46 SJ5182
Runcton *W Susx* 11 SU8802
Runcton Holme *Norfk* 41 TF6109
Runfold *Surrey* 22 SU8647
Runhall *Norfk* 42 TG0507
Runham *Norfk* 43 TG4610
Runnington *Somset* 8 ST1221
Runswick *N York* 63 NZ8016
Runtaleave *Tays* 88 NO2867
Runwell *Essex* 24 TQ7594
Runwell *Essex* 24 TQ7594
Ruscombe *Berks* 22 SU7976
Rush Green *Essex* 25 TM1515
Rush Green *Gt Lon* 23 TQ5187
Rushall *H & W* 27 SO6435
Rushall *Wilts* 20 SU1255
Rushall *Norfk* 33 TM1982
Rushbrooke *Suffk* 32 TL8961
Rushbury *Shrops* 37 SO5191
Rushden *Nhants* 30 SP9566
Rushden *Herts* 31 TL3031
Rushford *Norfk* 32 TL9281
Rushlake Green *E Susx* 13 TQ6218
Rushmere *Suffk* 33 TM4986
Rushmoor *Surrey* 11 SU8740
Rushock *H & W* 27 SO3058
Rushock *H & W* 38 SO8871
Rusholme *Gt Man* 47 SJ8594
Rushton *Ches* 47 SJ5863
Rushton *Nhants* 40 SP8482
Rushton Spencer *Staffs* 48 SJ9362
Rushwick *H & W* 28 SO8254
Rushyford *Dur* 61 NZ2828
Ruskie *Cent* 81 NN6200
Ruskington *Lincs* 50 TF0851
Rusland *Cumb* 59 SD3488
Rusper *W Susx* 12 TQ2037
Ruspidge *Gloucs* 28 SO6611
Russ Hill *Surrey* 12 TQ2240
Russell's Water *Oxon* 22 SU7089
Rusthall *Kent* 13 TQ5639
Rustington *W Susx* 12 TQ0402
Ruston *N York* 63 SE9583
Ruston Parva *Humb* 57 TA0661
Ruswarp *N York* 63 NZ8809
Rutherford *Border* 76 NT6430
Rutherglen *Strath* 74 NS6161
Ruthernbridge *Cnwll* 3 SX0166
Ruthin *Clwyd* 46 SJ1258
Ruthrieston *Gramp* 89 NJ9204
Ruthven *Highld* 93 NH8132
Ruthven *Gramp* 94 NJ5046
Ruthven *Highld* 87 NN7699
Ruthven *Tays* 88 NO2848
Ruthven House *Tays* 88 NO3047
Ruthvoes *Cnwll* 3 SW9260
Ruthwell *D & G* 67 NY0967
Ruyton-XI-Towns *Shrops* 36 SJ3922
Ryal *Nthumb* 68 NZ0174
Ryall *H & W* 28 SO8640
Ryall *Dorset* 8 SY4095
Ryarsh *Kent* 14 TQ6660
Rydal *Cumb* 59 NY3606
Ryde *IOW* 11 SZ5992
Rye *E Susx* 14 TQ9220
Rye Foreign *E Susx* 14 TQ8922
Rye Street *H & W* 28 SO7835
Ryhall *Leics* 40 TF0310
Ryhope *T & W* 69 NZ4152
Ryland *Lincs* 50 TF0179
Rylands *Notts* 39 SK5335
Rylstone *N York* 54 SD9658
Ryme Intrinseca *Dorset* 9 ST5810
Ryther *N York* 56 SE5539
Ryton *T & W* 69 NZ1564
Ryton *Shrops* 37 SJ7602
Ryton-on-Dunsmore *Warwks* 39 SP3874

S

Sabden *Lancs* 54 SD7837
Sacombe *Herts* 31 TL3319
Sacombe Green *Herts* 31 TL3419
Sacriston *T & W* 69 NZ2447
Sadberge *Dur* 62 NZ3416
Saddell *Strath* 72 NR7832
Saddington *Leics* 39 SP6691
Saddle Bow *Norfk* 41 TF6015
Saddlescombe *W Susx* 12 TQ2711
Saffron Walden *Essex* 24 TL5438
Sageston *Dyfed* 16 SN0503
Saham Hills *Norfk* 42 TF9003
Saham Toney *Norfk* 42 TF8901
Saighton *Ches* 46 SJ4462
Saintbury *Gloucs* 28 SP1139
Salachail *Strath* 86 NN0551
Salcombe *Devon* 5 SX7439
Salcombe Regis *Devon* 8 SY1588
Salcott *Essex* 25 TL9413
Sale *Gt Man* 47 SJ7991
Sale Green *H & W* 28 SO9358
Saleby *Lincs* 51 TF4578
Salehurst *E Susx* 14 TQ7524
Salem *Gwynd* 44 SH5456
Salem *Dyfed* 35 SN6684
Salen *Strath* 79 NM5743
Salen *Highld* 79 NM6864
Salford *Gt Man* 47 SJ8197
Salford *Oxon* 29 SP2828
Salford *Beds* 30 SP9339
Salford Priors *Warwks* 28 SP0751
Salfords *Surrey* 12 TQ2846
Salhouse *Norfk* 43 TG3114
Saline *Fife* 82 NT0292
Salisbury *Wilts* 10 SU1429
Salkeld Dykes *Cumb* 59 NY5437
Sall *Norfk* 43 TG1024
Sallachy *Highld* 96 NC5408
Salmonby *Lincs* 51 TF3273
Salmond's Muir *Tays* 83 NO5837
Salperton *Gloucs* 28 SP0720
Salsburgh *Strath* 74 NS8262
Salt *Staffs* 38 SJ9527
Saltaire *W York* 55 SE1438
Saltash *Cnwll* 4 SX4258
Saltburn *Highld* 93 NH7270
Saltburn-by-the-Sea *Cleve* 62 NZ6621
Saltby *Leics* 40 SK8526
Saltcoats *Strath* 73 NS2441
Saltdean *E Susx* 13 TQ3802
Salterbeck *Cumb* 58 NX9926
Salterforth *Lancs* 54 SD8845
Salterton *Wilts* 10 SU1236
Saltfleet *Lincs* 51 TF4593
Saltfleetby All Saints *Lincs* 51 TF4590
Saltfleetby St. Clements *Lincs* 51 TF4691
Saltfleetby St. Peter *Lincs* 51 TF4489
Saltford *Avon* 20 ST6867
Salthouse *Norfk* 42 TG0743
Saltmarshe *Humb* 56 SE7824
Saltney *Ches* 46 SJ3865
Salton *N York* 63 SE7179
Saltrens *Devon* 6 SS4522
Saltwood *Kent* 15 TR1535
Salvington *W Susx* 12 TQ1205
Salwarpe *H & W* 28 SO8762
Salwayash *Dorset* 8 SY4596
Sambourne *Warwks* 28 SP0662
Sambrook *Shrops* 37 SJ7124
Samlesbury *Lancs* 54 SD5930
Sampford Arundel *Somset* 8 ST1118
Sampford Brett *Somset* 7 ST0741
Sampford Courtenay *Devon* 7 SS6301
Sampford Moor *Somset* 8 ST1118
Sampford Peverell *Devon* 7 ST0314
Sampford Spiney *Devon* 4 SX5372
Samsonlane *Ork* 103 HY6526
Samuelston *Loth* 76 NT4870
Sanaigmore *Strath* 70 NR2370
Sancreed *Cnwll* 2 SW4129
Sancton *Humb* 56 SE8939
Sand Hills *W York* 55 SE3739
Sand Hole *Humb* 56 SE8137
Sand Hutton *N York* 56 SE6958
Sandaig *Highld* 85 NG7102
Sandal Magna *W York* 55 SE3417
Sandavore *Highld* 84 NM4785
Sandbach *Ches* 47 SJ7560
Sandbank *Strath* 80 NS1680
Sandbanks *Dorset* 10 SZ0487
Sandend *Gramp* 94 NJ5566
Sanderstead *Gt Lon* 23 TQ3461
Sandford *Strath* 74 NS7143
Sandford *Cumb* 60 NY7316
Sandford *Devon* 7 SS8202
Sandford *Avon* 19 ST4259
Sandford *Hants* 10 SU1601
Sandford *IOW* 11 SZ5381
Sandford Orcas *Dorset* 9 ST6220
Sandford St. Martin *Oxon* 29 SP4226
Sandford-on-Thames *Oxon* 21 SP5301
Sandgate *Kent* 15 TR2035
Sandhaven *Gramp* 95 NJ9667
Sandhead *D & G* 64 NX0949
Sandhills *Surrey* 11 SU9337
Sandhoe *Nthumb* 68 NY9666
Sandhole *Strath* 80 NS0098
Sandholme *Humb* 56 SE8230
Sandhurst *Gloucs* 28 SO8223
Sandhurst *Berks* 22 SU8361
Sandhurst *Kent* 14 TQ8028
Sandhutton *N York* 62 SE3881
Sandilands *Lincs* 51 TF5280
Sandleheath *Hants* 10 SU1215
Sandley *Dorset* 9 ST7724
Sandness *Shet* 103 HU1957
Sandon *Staffs* 38 SJ9429
Sandon *Herts* 31 TL3234
Sandon *Essex* 24 TL7404
Sandon Bank *Staffs* 38 SJ9428
Sandown *IOW* 11 SZ5984
Sandplace *Cnwll* 4 SX2557
Sandridge *Herts* 23 TL1710
Sandringham *Norfk* 42 TF6928
Sandsend *N York* 63 NZ8612
Sandside House *Highld* 99 NC9565
Sandtoft *Humb* 56 SE7408
Sandwich *Kent* 15 TR3358
Sandwick *Shet* 103 HU4323
Sandwith *Cumb* 58 NX9614
Sandy *Beds* 31 TL1649
Sandy Lane *Wilts* 20 ST9668
Sandy Park *Devon* 5 SX7189
Sandyford *D & G* 67 NY2093
Sandygate *IOM* 52 SC3797
Sandygate *Devon* 5 SX8674
Sandyhills *D & G* 66 NX8855
Sandylands *Lancs* 53 SD4263
Sandystones *Border* 76 NT5926
Sangobeg *Highld* 98 NC4266
Sangomore *Highld* 98 NC4067
Sankyn's Green *H & W* 28 SO7965
Sanna Bay *Highld* 79 NM4469
Santon Bridge *Cumb* 58 NY1101
Santon Downham *Suffk* 32 TL8187
Sapcote *Leics* 39 SP4893
Sapey Common *H & W* 28 SO7064
Sapiston *Suffk* 32 TL9175
Sapperton *Gloucs* 20 SO9403
Sapperton *Lincs* 40 TF0133
Saracen's Head *Lincs* 41 TF3427
Sarclet *Highld* 100 ND3443
Sarisbury *Hants* 10 SU5008
Sarn *Gwynd* 44 SH2432
Sarn *Powys* 35 SN9597
Sarn *Powys* 36 SO2090
Sarnau *Powys* 36 SJ2315
Sarnau *Dyfed* 17 SN3150
Sarnesfield *H & W* 27 SO3750
Saron *Gwynd* 44 SH5365
Saron *Dyfed* 17 SN6012
Sarratt *Herts* 22 TQ0499
Sarre *Kent* 15 TR2565
Sarsden *Oxon* 29 SP2822
Satley *Dur* 69 NZ1143
Satterleigh *Devon* 7 SS6622
Satterthwaite *Cumb* 59 SD3392
Sauchen *Gramp* 95 NJ7011
Saucher *Tays* 82 NO1933
Sauchieburn *Gramp* 89 NO6669
Saul *Gloucs* 28 SO7409
Saundby *Notts* 50 SK7888
Saundby *Notts* 50 SK7888
Saundersfoot *Dyfed* 16 SN1304
Saunderton *Bucks* 22 SP7901
Saunton *Devon* 6 SS4637
Sausthorpe *Lincs* 51 TF3868
Savile Town *W York* 55 SE2420
Sawbridge *Warwks* 29 SP5065
Sawbridgeworth *Herts* 31 TL4814
Sawdon *N York* 63 SE9485
Sawley *Lancs* 54 SD7746
Sawley *N York* 55 SE2467
Sawston *Cambs* 31 TL4849

Simons Burrow St. Blazey

Simons Burrow *Devon* **8** ST1416
Simonsbath *Somset* **7** SS7739
Simonstone *Lancs* **54** SD7734
Simpson *Bucks* **30** SP8836
Simpson Cross *Dyfed* **16** SM8919
Sinclair's Hill *Border* **76** NT8150
Sinclairston *Strath* **73** NS4716
Sinderby *N York* **62** SE3482
Sinderland Green *Gt Man* **47** SJ7389
Sindlesham *Berks* **22** SU7769
Singleton *Lancs* **53** SD3838
Singleton *W Susx* **11** SU8713
Singlewell *Kent* **14** TQ6570
Sinnarhard *Gramp* **94** NJ4713
Sinnington *N York* **63** SE7485
Sinton *H & W* **28** SO8160
Sinton Green *H & W* **28** SO8160
Sissinghurst *Kent* **14** TQ7937
Siston *Avon* **20** ST6875
Sithney *Cnwll* **2** SW6328
Sittingbourne *Kent* **14** TQ9063
Six Ashes *Staffs* **37** SO7988
Six Mile Bottom *Cambs* **31** TL5756
Six Rues *Jersey* **101** JS0000
Sixhills *Lincs* **50** TF1787
Sixpenny Handley *Dorset* **9** ST9917
Skaill *Ork* **103** HY5806
Skaith *D & G* **64** NX3766
Skares *Strath* **74** NS5317
Skateraw *Loth* **76** NT7375
Skeabost *Highld* **90** NG4148
Skeeby *N York* **61** NZ1902
Skeffington *Leics* **40** SK7402
Skeffling *Humb* **57** TA3719
Skegby *Notts* **49** SK4961
Skegby *Notts* **50** SK7869
Skegness *Lincs* **51** TF5663
Skelbo *Highld* **97** NH7895
Skelbo Street *Highld* **97** NH7994
Skelbrooke *S York* **55** SE5012
Skeldyke *Lincs* **41** TF3337
Skellingthorpe *Lincs* **50** SK9272
Skelmanthorpe *W York* **55** SE2310
Skelmersdale *Lancs* **46** SD4606
Skelmorlie *Strath* **73** NS1967
Skelpick *Highld* **99** NC7256
Skelston *D & G* **66** NX8285
Skelton *Cumb* **59** NY4335
Skelton *Cleve* **62** NZ6618
Skelton *N York* **55** SE3668
Skelton *N York* **56** SE5756
Skelton *Humb* **56** SE7625
Skelwith Bridge *Cumb* **59** NY3403
Skendleby *Lincs* **51** TF4369
Skene House *Gramp* **95** NJ7610
Skenfrith *Gwent* **27** SO4520
Skerne *Humb* **57** TA0455
Skerray *Highld* **99** NC6563
Skerricha *Highld* **98** NC2350
Skerton *Lancs* **53** SD4763
Sketchley *Leics* **39** SP4292
Sketty *W Glam* **17** SS6292
Skewsby *N York* **56** SE6270
Skiall *Highld* **100** ND0267
Skidby *Humb* **56** TA0133
Skigersta *W Isls* **102** NB5461
Skilgate *Somset* **7** SS9827
Skillington *Lincs* **40** SK8925
Skinburness *Cumb* **67** NY1256
Skinflats *Cent* **82** NS9082
Skinidin *Highld* **90** NG2247
Skipness *Strath* **71** NR9057
Skipsea *Humb* **57** TA1654
Skipton *N York* **54** SD9851
Skipton-on-Swale *N York* **62** SE3679
Skipwith *N York* **56** SE6638
Skirling *Border* **75** NT0739
Skirmett *Bucks* **22** SU7790
Skirpenbeck *Humb* **56** SE7456
Skirwith *Cumb* **59** NY6132
Skirza *Highld* **100** ND3868
Skulamus *Highld* **85** NG6622
Skullomie *Highld* **99** NC6161
Skye Green *Essex* **24** TL8722
Skye of Curr *Highld* **93** NH9924
Slack *W York* **54** SD9728
Slackadale *Gramp* **95** NJ7454
Slacks of Cairnbanno *Gramp* **95** NJ8445
Slad *Gloucs* **28** SO8707
Slade *Devon* **6** SS5046
Slade *Somset* **7** SS8327
Slade Green *Kent* **23** TQ5276
Slade Hooton *S York* **49** SK5288
Slaggan *Highld* **91** NG8494
Slaggyford *Nthumb* **68** NY6752
Slagnaw *D & G* **65** NX7458
Slagnaw *D & G* **65** NX7458
Slaidburn *Lancs* **54** SD7152
Slaithwaite *W York* **55** SE0813
Slaley *Nthumb* **68** NY9657
Slamannan *Cent* **74** NS8572
Slapton *Nhants* **29** SP6446
Slapton *Bucks* **30** SP9320
Slapton *Devon* **5** SX8245
Slaugham *W Susx* **12** TQ2528
Slaughterford *Wilts* **20** ST8473
Slawston *Leics* **40** SP7894
Sleaford *Hants* **11** SU8038
Sleaford *Lincs* **50** TF0645
Sleagill *Cumb* **59** NY5919
Sleapford *Shrops* **37** SJ6315
Sleasdairidh *Highld* **97** NH6496
Sledmere *Humb* **56** SE9364
Sleightholme *Dur* **61** NY9510
Sleights *N York* **63** NZ8607
Slickly *Highld* **100** ND2966
Sliddery *Strath* **72** NR9323
Sligachan *Highld* **84** NG4829
Sligrachan *Strath* **80** NS1791
Slimbridge *Gloucs* **20** SO7303
Slindon *Staffs* **38** SJ8232
Slindon *W Susx* **12** SU9608
Slinfold *W Susx* **12** TQ1131
Slingsby *N York* **62** SE6974
Slip End *Beds* **30** TL0718
Slip End *Herts* **31** TL2837
Slipton *Nhants* **40** SP9579
Slitting Mill *Staffs* **38** SK0217
Slockavullin *Strath* **71** NR8297
Slogarie *D & G* **65** NX6568
Sloncombe *Devon* **5** SX7386
Sloothby *Lincs* **51** TF4970
Slough *Berks* **22** SU9879
Slough Green *Somset* **8** ST2719
Slumbay *Highld* **85** NG8938
Slyne *Lancs* **53** SD4765
Smailholm *Border* **76** NT6436
Small Dole *W Susx* **12** TQ2112
Small Heath *W Mids* **38** SP1085
Small Hythe *Kent* **14** TQ8930
Smallburgh *Norfk* **43** TG3324
Smalley *Derbys* **49** SK4044
Smallfield *Surrey* **12** TQ3143
Smallridge *Devon* **8** ST3001
Smallworth *Norfk* **32** TM0080
Smannell *Hants* **21** SU3749
Smarden *Kent* **14** TQ8742
Smarden Bell *Kent* **14** TQ8742
Smart's Hill *Kent* **13** TQ5242
Smearisary *Highld* **85** NM6476
Smeatharpe *Devon* **8** ST1910
Smeeth *Kent* **15** TR0739
Smeeton Westerby *Leics* **39** SP6892
Smerral *Highld* **100** ND1733
Smestow *Staffs* **38** SO8591
Smethwick *W Mids* **38** SP0287
Smisby *Derbys* **39** SK3418
Smith's Green *Essex* **32** TL6640
Smithfield *Cumb* **67** NY4465
Smithstown *Highld* **91** NG7977
Smithton *Highld* **93** NH7145
Smoo *Highld* **98** NC4167
Smythe's Green *Essex* **24** TL9218
Snade *D & G* **66** NX8485
Snaigow House *Tays* **88** NO0843
Snailwell *Cambs* **32** TL6467
Snainton *N York* **63** SE9282
Snaith *Humb* **56** SE6422
Snape *N York* **61** SE2684
Snape *Suffk* **33** TM3959
Snape Street *Suffk* **33** TM3958
Snarestone *Leics* **39** SK3409
Snarford *Lincs* **50** TF0482
Snargate *Kent* **15** TQ9928
Snave *Kent* **15** TR0129
Sneaton *N York* **63** NZ8907
Snelland *Lincs* **50** TF0780
Snelston *Derbys* **48** SK1543
Snetterton *Norfk* **32** TL9991
Snettisham *Norfk* **42** TF6834
Snig's End *Gloucs* **28** SO7828
Sniperhill *Kent* **14** TQ9163
Snitter *Nthumb* **68** NU0203
Snitterby *Lincs* **50** SK9894
Snitterfield *Warwks* **29** SP2159
Snitton *Shrops* **37** SO5575
Snodland *Kent* **14** TQ7061
Snow End *Herts* **31** TL4032
Snowshill *Gloucs* **28** SP0933
Soake *Hants* **11** SU6611
Soberton *Hants* **11** SU6116
Soberton Heath *Hants* **11** SU6014
Sockburn *Nthumb* **62** NZ3406
Soham *Cambs* **31** TL5973
Soldridge *Hants* **11** SU6535
Sole Street *Kent* **15** TR0949
Solihull *W Mids* **38** SP1679
Solitote *Highld* **90** NG4274
Sollas *W Isls* **102** NF8074
Sollers Dilwyn *H & W* **27** SO4255
Sollers Hope *H & W* **27** SO6132
Solva *Dyfed* **16** SM8024
Solwaybank *D & G* **67** NY3077
Somerby *Leics* **40** SK7710
Somerby *Lincs* **57** TA0606
Somercotes *Derbys* **49** SK4253
Somerford Keynes *Gloucs* **20** SU0195
Somerley *W Susx* **11** SZ8198
Somerleyton *Suffk* **43** TM4897
Somersal Herbert *Derbys* **38** SK1335
Somersby *Lincs* **51** TF3472
Somersham *Cambs* **31** TL3678
Somersham *Suffk* **32** TM0848
Somerton *Oxon* **29** SP4928
Somerton *Somset* **8** ST4928
Somerton *Suffk* **32** TL8153
Sompting *W Susx* **12** TQ1505
Sonning *Berks* **22** SU7575
Sonning Common *Oxon* **22** SU7180
Sonning Eye *Oxon* **22** SU7476
Sopley *Hants* **10** SZ1596
Sopworth *Wilts* **20** ST8286
Sorbie *D & G* **64** NX4346
Sordale *Highld* **100** ND1462
Sorisdale *Strath* **78** NM2763
Sorn *Strath* **74** NS5526
Sortat *Highld* **100** ND2863
Sosgill *Cumb* **58** NY1024
Sotby *Lincs* **51** TF2078
Sots Hole *Lincs* **50** TF1264
Sotterly *Suffk* **33** TM4484
Sotwell *Oxon* **21** SU5890
Soughton *Clwyd* **46** SJ2466
Soulbury *Bucks* **30** SP8826
Soulby *Cumb* **60** NY7411
Souldern *Oxon* **29** SP5231
Souldrop *Beds* **30** SP9861
Sound Muir *Gramp* **94** NJ3652
Soundwell *Avon* **19** ST6575
Sourton *Devon* **4** SX5390
Soutergate *Cumb* **58** SD2281
South Acre *Norfk* **42** TF8114
South Alkham *Kent* **15** TR2441
South Allington *Devon* **5** SX7938
South Alloa *Cent* **82** NS8791
South Ambersham *W Susx* **11** SU9120
South Anston *S York* **49** SK5183
South Ashford *Kent* **15** TR0041
South Baddesley *Hants* **10** SZ3596
South Bank *N York* **56** SE5950
South Barrow *Somset* **9** ST6028
South Beddington *Gt Lon* **23** TQ2863
South Benfleet *Essex* **24** TQ7787
South Bersted *W Susx* **11** SU9300
South Bramwith *S York* **56** SE6211
South Brent *Devon* **5** SX6960
South Brewham *Somset* **20** ST7236
South Broomhill *Nthumb* **69** NZ2499
South Burlingham *Norfk* **43** TG3807
South Cadbury *Somset* **9** ST6325
South Cairn *D & G* **64** NW9769
South Carlton *Notts* **49** SK5883
South Carlton *Lincs* **50** SK9476
South Cave *Humb* **56** SE9230
South Cerney *Gloucs* **20** SU0497
South Charlton *Nthumb* **77** NU1620
South Cheriton *Somset* **9** ST6924
South Church *Dur* **61** NZ2128
South Cliffe *Humb* **56** SE8735
South Clifton *Notts* **50** SK8270
South Collingham *Notts* **50** SK8261
South Cornelly *M Glam* **18** SS8280
South Cove *Suffk* **33** TM4981
South Creake *Norfk* **42** TF8536
South Croxton *Leics* **39** SK6810
South Dalton *Humb* **56** SE9645
South Duffield *N York* **56** SE6833
South Elkington *Lincs* **51** TF2988
South Elmsall *W York* **55** SE4711
South Erradale *Highld* **91** NG7471
South Fambridge *Essex* **24** TQ8694
South Fawley *Berks* **21** SU3880
South Feorline *Strath* **72** NR9028
South Ferriby *Humb* **56** SE9820
South Field *Humb* **56** TA0225
South Gorley *Hants* **10** SU1610
South Gosworth *T & W* **69** NZ2467
South Green *Norfk* **42** TG0510
South Green *Essex* **24** TQ6893
South Green *Kent* **14** TQ8560
South Hanningfield *Essex* **24** TQ7497
South Harting *W Susx* **11** SU7819
South Hayling *Hants* **11** SZ7299
South Heath *Bucks* **22** SP9101
South Hetton *Cleve* **69** NZ3845
South Hiendley *W York* **55** SE3912
South Hill *Cnwll* **4** SX3272
South Hinksey *Oxon* **29** SP5104
South Holmwood *Surrey* **12** TQ1744
South Hornchurch *Gt Lon* **23** TQ5183
South Huish *Devon* **5** SX6941
South Hykeham *Lincs* **50** SK9364
South Hylton *T & W* **69** NZ3556
South Kelsey *Lincs* **50** TF0498
South Kessock *Highld* **93** NH6547
South Killingholme *Humb* **57** TA1416
South Kilvington *N York* **62** SE4284
South Kilworth *Nhants* **39** SP6081
South Kirkby *W York* **55** SE4410
South Kyme *Lincs* **50** TF1749
South Lambeth *Gt Lon* **23** TQ3077
South Lawn *Oxon* **29** SP2814
South Leigh *Oxon* **29** SP3909
South Leverton *Notts* **50** SK7881
South Lopham *Norfk* **32** TM0481
South Luffenham *Leics* **40** SK9301
South Mains *D & G* **66** NS7807
South Malling *E Susx* **13** TQ4210
South Marston *Wilts* **21** SU1987
South Milford *N York* **55** SE4931
South Milton *Devon* **5** SX7042
South Mimms *Herts* **23** TL2201
South Molton *Devon* **7** SS7125
South Moor *Dur* **69** NZ1951
South Moreton *Oxon* **21** SU5688
South Mundham *W Susx* **11** SU8700
South Newbald *Humb* **56** SE9035
South Newington *Oxon* **29** SP4033
South Newton *Wilts* **10** SU0834
South Normanton *Derbys* **49** SK4456
South Norwood *Gt Lon* **23** TQ3368
South Ockendon *Essex* **24** TQ5983
South Ormsby *Lincs* **51** TF3675
South Otterington *N York* **62** SE3787
South Owersby *Lincs* **50** TF0693
South Park *Surrey* **12** TQ2448
South Perrott *Dorset* **8** ST4706
South Petherton *Somset* **8** ST4316
South Petherwin *Cnwll* **4** SX3181
South Pickenham *Norfk* **42** TF8504
South Pill *Cnwll* **4** SX4259
South Pool *Devon* **5** SX7740
South Poorton *Dorset* **8** SY5297
South Queensferry *Loth* **82** NT1378
South Radworthy *Devon* **7** SS7432
South Rauceby *Lincs* **50** TF0245
South Raynham *Norfk* **42** TF8723
South Reston *Lincs* **51** TF4083
South Runcton *Norfk* **41** TF6308
South Scarle *Notts* **50** SK8463
South Shian *Strath* **79** NM9042
South Shields *T & W* **69** NZ3666
South Shore *Lancs* **53** SD3033
South Skirlaugh *Humb* **57** TA1438
South Stainley *N York* **55** SE3063
South Stoke *Avon* **20** ST7461
South Stoke *Oxon* **21** SU5983
South Stoke *W Susx* **12** TQ0209
South Street *E Susx* **13** TQ3918
South Street *Kent* **15** TR0557
South Street *Kent* **15** TR1265
South Tarbrax *Strath* **75** NT0353
South Tawton *Devon* **7** SX6594
South Thoresby *Lincs* **51** TF4076
South Tidworth *Hants* **21** SU2347
South Walsham *Norfk* **43** TG3613
South Warnborough *Hants* **22** SU7247
South Weald *Essex* **24** TQ5694
South Weston *Oxon* **22** SU7098
South Wheatley *Cnwll* **4** SX2492
South Widcombe *Somset* **19** ST5856
South Wigston *Leics* **39** SP5897
South Willesborough *Kent* **15** TR0240
South Willingham *Lincs* **50** TF1983
South Wingate *Dur* **62** NZ4134
South Wingfield *Derbys* **49** SK3755
South Witham *Lincs* **40** SK9219
South Woodham Ferrers *Essex* **24** TQ8097
South Wootton *Norfk* **42** TF6422
South Wraxall *Wilts* **20** ST8364
South Zeal *Devon* **5** SX6593
Southall *Gt Lon* **22** TQ1279
Southam *Gloucs* **28** SO9725
Southam *Warwks* **29** SP4161
Southampton *Hants* **10** SU4112
Southborough *Gt Lon* **23** TQ4267
Southborough *Kent* **13** TQ5842
Southbourne *W Susx* **11** SU7705
Southbourne *Dorset* **10** SZ1491
Southburgh *Norfk* **42** TG0005
Southburn *Humb* **56** SE9854
Southchurch *Essex* **24** TQ9086
Southcott *Cnwll* **6** SX1995
Southcott *Devon* **6** SX5495
Southcott *Devon* **5** SX7580
Southcourt *Bucks* **30** SP8112
Southease *E Susx* **13** TQ4205
Southend *Strath* **72** NR6908
Southend-on-Sea *Essex* **24** TQ8885
Southerndown *M Glam* **18** SS8873
Southerness *D & G* **66** NX9754
Southery *Norfk* **41** TL6194
Southfield *Cent* **74** NS8472
Southfleet *Kent* **14** TQ6171
Southgate *W Glam* **17** SS5587
Southgate *Gt Lon* **23** TQ2994
Southill *Beds* **30** TL1542
Southington *Hants* **21** SU5049
Southleigh *Devon* **8** SY2093
Southminster *Essex* **25** TQ9599
Southmoor *Oxon* **21** SU3998
Southmuir *Tays* **88** NO3852
Southoe *Cambs* **31** TL1864
Southolt *Suffk* **33** TM1968
Southorpe *Cambs* **40** TF0803
Southover *Dorset* **9** SY6294
Southowram *W York* **55** SE1123
Southport *Mersyd* **53** SD3317
Southrepps *Norfk* **43** TG2536
Southrey *Lincs* **50** TF1366
Southrop *Gloucs* **21** SP1903
Southrope *Hants* **22** SU6644
Southsea *Hants* **11** SZ6599
Southside *Dur* **61** NZ1026
Southside *Dur* **61** NZ1026
Southtown *Norfk* **43** TG5106
Southwaite *Cumb* **67** NY4445
Southwark *Gt Lon* **23** TQ3279
Southwater *W Susx* **12** TQ1526
Southwell *Notts* **49** SK6953
Southwick *T & W* **69** NZ3758
Southwick *Wilts* **20** ST8355
Southwick *Hants* **11** SU6208
Southwick *Nhants* **40** TL0292
Southwick *W Susx* **12** TQ2405
Southwold *Suffk* **33** TM5076
Sowerby *N York* **62** SE4380
Sowerby Bridge *W York* **55** SE0523
Sowood *W York* **55** SE0818
Sowton *Devon* **4** SX5065
Sowton *Devon* **5** SX9792
Soyland Town *W York* **55** SE0320
Spain's End *Essex* **24** TL6637
Spalding *Lincs* **41** TF2422
Spaldington *Humb* **56** SE7633
Spaldwick *Cambs* **30** TL1372
Spalford *Notts* **50** SK8369
Sparham *Norfk* **42** TG0719
Spark Bridge *Cumb* **58** SD3084
Sparkford *Somset* **9** ST6025
Sparkhill *W Mids* **38** SP1083
Sparkwell *Devon* **5** SX5857
Sparrowpit *Derbys* **48** SK0880
Sparrows Green *E Susx* **13** TQ6332
Sparsholt *Oxon* **21** SU3487
Sparsholt *Hants* **10** SU4331
Spaunton *N York* **63** SE7289
Spaxton *Somset* **19** ST2237
Spean Bridge *Highld* **86** NN2281
Spearywell *Hants* **10** SU3127
Speen *Berks* **21** SU4567
Speen *Bucks* **22** SU8499
Speeton *N York* **63** TA1574
Speke *Mersyd* **46** SJ4383
Speldhurst *Kent* **13** TQ5541
Spellbrook *Herts* **31** TL4817
Spen Green *Ches* **47** SJ8160
Spencers Wood *Berks* **22** SU7166
Spennithorne *N York* **61** SE1388
Spennymoor *Dur* **61** NZ2533
Spetchley *H & W* **28** SO8953
Spettisbury *Dorset* **9** ST9102
Spexhall *Suffk* **33** TM3780
Spey Bay *Gramp* **94** NJ3565
Speybridge *Highld* **93** NJ0326
Speyview *Gramp* **94** NJ2541
Spilsby *Lincs* **51** TF4066
Spinkhill *Derbys* **49** SK4578
Spinningdale *Highld* **97** NH6789
Spital *Berks* **22** SU9675
Spital Hill *Notts* **49** SK6193
Spittal *Highld* **100** ND1654
Spittal *Loth* **76** NT4677
Spittal *Nthumb* **77** NU0051
Spittal *Dyfed* **16** SM9723
Spittal of Glenmuick *Gramp* **88** NO3085
Spittal of Glenshee *Tays* **88** NO1070
Spittal-on-Rule *Border* **76** NT5819
Spittalfield *Tays* **82** NO1040
Spixworth *Norfk* **43** TG2415
Splatt *Devon* **6** SS6005
Splayne's Green *E Susx* **13** TQ4224
Splottlands *S Glam* **19** ST2077
Spofforth *N York* **55** SE3651
Spooner Row *Norfk* **43** TM0997
Sporle *Norfk* **42** TF8411
Spott *Loth* **76** NT6775
Spottiswoode *Border* **76** NT6049
Spratton *Nhants* **30** SP7169
Spreakley *Surrey* **11** SU8341
Spreyton *Devon* **7** SX6996
Spriddlestone *Devon* **4** SX5351
Spridlington *Lincs* **50** TF0084
Springburn *Strath* **74** NS6068
Springfield *Fife* **83** NO3411
Springfield *D & G* **67** NY3268
Springfield *Essex* **24** TL7208
Springholm *D & G* **66** NX8070
Springkell *D & G* **67** NY2575
Springside *Strath* **73** NS3738
Springthorpe *Lincs* **50** SK8789
Springwell *T & W* **69** NZ2858
Sproatley *Humb* **57** TA1934
Sproston Green *Ches* **47** SJ7366
Sprotbrough *S York* **49** SE5301
Sproughton *Suffk* **33** TM1244
Sprouston *Border* **76** NT7535
Sprowston *Norfk* **43** TG2512
Sproxton *N York* **62** SE6181
Sproxton *Leics* **40** SK8524
Spurstow *Ches* **47** SJ5657
Spyway *Dorset* **8** SY5293
Squirrel's Heath *Gt Lon* **23** TQ5389
St. Abbs *Border* **77** NT9167
St. Agnes *Loth* **76** NT6763
St. Agnes *Cnwll* **2** SW7150
St. Albans *Herts* **22** TL1407
St. Allen *Cnwll* **2** SW8250
St. Andrew *Guern* **101** GN0000
St. Andrew's Major *S Glam* **18** ST1371
St. Andrews *Fife* **83** NO5116
St. Andrews Well *Dorset* **8** SY4793
St. Ann's *D & G* **66** NY0793
St. Ann's Chapel *Devon* **5** SX6647
St. Anne's *Lancs* **53** SD3228
St. Anthony *Cnwll* **2** SW7825
St. Anthony's Hill *E Susx* **13** TQ6201
St. Arvans *Gwent* **19** ST5296
St. Asaph *Clwyd* **45** SJ0374
St. Athan *S Glam* **18** ST0167
St. Aubin *Jersey* **101** JS0000
St. Austell *Cnwll* **3** SX0152
St. Bees *Cumb* **58** NX9711
St. Blazey *Cnwll* **3** SX0654

St. Boswells
Stoke St. Michael

St. Boswells *Border* 76 NT5930
St. Brelade *Jersey* 101 JS0000
St. Brelades Bay *Jersey* 101 JS0000
St. Breock *Cnwll* 3 SW9771
St. Breward *Cnwll* 3 SX0977
St. Briavels *Gloucs* 27 SO5604
St. Bride's Major *M Glam* 18 SS8974
St. Brides Wentlooge *Gwent* 19 ST2982
St. Brides super-Ely *S Glam* 18 ST0977
St. Budeaux *Devon* 4 SX4558
St. Buryan *Cnwll* 2 SW4025
St. Catherines *Strath* 80 NN1207
St. Chloe *Gloucs* 20 SO8401
St. Clears *Dyfed* 17 SN2816
St. Cleer *Cnwll* 4 SX2468
St. Clement *Jersey* 101 JS0000
St. Clement *Cnwll* 3 SW8543
St. Clether *Cnwll* 4 SX2084
St. Colmac *Strath* 72 NS0467
St. Columb Major *Cnwll* 3 SW9163
St. Columb Minor *Cnwll* 3 SW8362
St. Columb Road *Cnwll* 3 SW9159
St. Combs *Gramp* 95 NK0563
St. Cross South Elmham *Suffk* 33 TM2984
St. Cyrus *Gramp* 89 NO7464
St. David's *Tays* 82 NN9420
St. Davids *Dyfed* 16 SM7525
St. Day *Cnwll* 2 SW7242
St. Decumans *Somset* 7 ST0642
St. Dennis *Cnwll* 3 SW9557
St. Dogmaels *Dyfed* 17 SN1645
St. Donats *S Glam* 18 SS9368
St. Endellion *Cnwll* 3 SW9978
St. Enoder *Cnwll* 3 SW8956
St. Erme *Cnwll* 3 SW8449
St. Erney *Cnwll* 4 SX3559
St. Erth *Cnwll* 2 SW5535
St. Erth Praze *Cnwll* 2 SW5735
St. Ervan *Cnwll* 3 SW8970
St. Ewe *Cnwll* 3 SW9746
St. Fagans *S Glam* 18 ST1277
St. Fergus *Gramp* 95 NK0952
St. Fillans *Tays* 81 NN6924
St. Florence *Dyfed* 16 SN0801
St. Gennys *Cnwll* 6 SX1497
St. George *Clwyd* 45 SH9775
St. George's *S Glam* 18 ST1076
St. George's *S Glam* 18 ST1076
St. Georges *Avon* 19 ST3762
St. Germans *Cnwll* 4 SX3657
St Giles in the Wood *Devon* 6 SS5319
St. Giles-on-the-Heath *Cnwll* 4 SX3690
St. Harmon *Powys* 35 SN9872
St. Helen Auckland *Dur* 61 NZ1826
St. Helena *Norfk* 43 TG1816
St. Helens *IOW* 11 SZ6289
St Helens *Mersyd* 46 SJ5195
St. Helier *Jersey* 101 JS0000
St. Helier *Gt Lon* 23 TQ2567
St. Hilary *S Glam* 18 ST0173
St. Hilary *Cnwll* 2 SW5431
St. Ibbs *Herts* 31 TL1926
St. Illtyd *Gwent* 19 SO2202
St. Ishmaels *Dyfed* 16 SM8307
St. Issey *Cnwll* 3 SW9271
St. Ive *Cnwll* 4 SX3167
St. Ives *Cnwll* 2 SW5140
St. Ives *Cambs* 31 TL3171
St. Jame's End *Nhants* 30 SP7460
St. James South Elmham *Suffk* 33 TM3281
St. John *Jersey* 101 JS0000
St. John *Cnwll* 4 SX4053
St. John's *IOM* 52 SC2781
St. John's Chapel *Dur* 60 NY8837
St. John's Chapel *Devon* 6 SS5329
St. John's Fen End *Norfk* 41 TF5312
St. John's Kirk *Strath* 75 NS9836
St. John's Town of Dalry *D & G* 65 NX6281
St. John's Wood *Gt Lon* 23 TQ2683
St. Johns *H & W* 28 SO8454
St. Johns *Surrey* 22 SU9857
St. Johns *Kent* 23 TQ5356
St. Jude's *IOM* 52 SC3996
St. Just *Cnwll* 2 SW3731
St. Just *Cnwll* 3 SW8435
St. Katherines *Gramp* 95 NJ7834
St. Keverne *Cnwll* 2 SW7921
St. Kew *Cnwll* 3 SX0276
St. Kew Highway *Cnwll* 3 SX0375
St. Keyne *Cnwll* 4 SX2461
St. Laurence *Kent* 15 TR3665
St. Lawrence *Jersey* 101 JS0000
St. Lawrence *IOW* 11 SZ5376
St. Lawrence *Essex* 25 TL9604
St. Lawrence *Essex* 25 TL9604
St. Leonards *Bucks* 22 SP9007
St. Leonards *E Susx* 14 TQ8009
St. Leonards Street *Kent* 14 TQ6756
St. Levan *Cnwll* 2 SW3822
St. Lythans *S Glam* 18 ST1072
St. Mabyn *Cnwll* 3 SX0473
St. Margaret South Elmham *Suffk* 33 TM3183
St. Margaret's at Cliffe *Kent* 15 TR3544
St. Margarets *H & W* 27 SO3533
St. Margarets *Herts* 23 TL3811
St. Margarets Hope *Ork* 103 ND4493
St. Marks *IOM* 52 SC2974
St. Martin *Guern* 101 GN0000
St. Martin *Jersey* 101 JS0000
St. Martin *Cnwll* 4 SX2555
St. Martin's *Tays* 82 NO1530
St. Martins *Shrops* 36 SJ3236
St. Mary *Jersey* 101 JS0000
St. Mary Bourne *Hants* 21 SU4250
St. Mary Church *S Glam* 18 ST0071
St. Mary Cray *Gt Lon* 23 TQ4768
St. Mary in the Marsh *Kent* 15 TR0627
St. Mary's *Ork* 103 HY4701
St. Mary's Bay *Kent* 15 TR0827
St. Mary's Hoo *Kent* 14 TQ8076
St. Marychurch *Devon* 5 SX9166
St. Marylebone *Gt Lon* 23 TQ2782
St. Maughans Green *Gwent* 27 SO4717
St. Mawes *Cnwll* 3 SW8433
St. Mawgan *Cnwll* 3 SW8765
St. Mellion *Cnwll* 4 SX3965
St. Mellons *S Glam* 19 ST2281
St. Merryn *Cnwll* 3 SW8874
St. Mewan *Cnwll* 3 SW9951
St. Michael Caerhays *Cnwll* 3 SW9642
St. Michael Church *Somset* 8 ST3030
St. Michael Penkevil *Cnwll* 3 SW8541
St. Michael South Elmham *Suffk* 33 TM3483
St. Michael's on Wyre *Lancs* 53 SD4641
St. Michaels *H & W* 27 SO5865
St. Michaels *Kent* 14 TQ8835
St. Minver *Cnwll* 3 SW9677
St. Minver *Cnwll* 3 SW9677
St. Monans *Fife* 83 NO5201
St. Neot *Cnwll* 3 SX1868
St. Neots *Cambs* 31 TL1860
St. Neots *Cambs* 31 TL1860
St. Newlyn East *Cnwll* 2 SW8256
St. Nicholas *Dyfed* 16 SM9035
St. Nicholas *S Glam* 18 ST0974
St. Nicholas at Wade *Kent* 15 TR2666
St. Ninians *Cent* 81 NS7991
St. Olaves *Norfk* 43 TM4599
St. Osyth *Essex* 25 TM1215
St. Ouen *Jersey* 101 JS0000
St. Owens Cross *H & W* 27 SO5324
St. Paul's Walden *Herts* 31 TL1922
St. Pauls Cray *Gt Lon* 23 TQ4768
St. Peter *Jersey* 101 JS0000
St. Peter Port *Guern* 101 GN0000
St. Peter's *Guern* 101 GN0000
St. Peter's *Kent* 15 TR3868
St. Pinnock *Cnwll* 4 SX2063
St. Quivox *Strath* 73 NS3723
St. Sampson *Guern* 101 GN0000
St. Saviour *Guern* 101 GN0000
St. Saviour *Jersey* 101 JS0000
St. Stephen *Cnwll* 3 SW9453
St. Stephens *Cnwll* 4 SX3285
St. Stephens *Cnwll* 4 SX4158
St. Stephen's Coombe *Cnwll* 3 SW9451
St. Teath *Cnwll* 3 SX0680
St. Teath *Cnwll* 3 SX0680
St. Tudy *Cnwll* 3 SX0676
St. Twynnells *Dyfed* 16 SR9597
St. Veep *Cnwll* 3 SX1455
St. Vigeans *Tays* 89 NO6443
St. Wenn *Cnwll* 3 SW9664
St. Weonards *H & W* 27 SO4924
Stableford *Shrops* 37 SO7598
Stacey Bank *Derbys* 49 SK2890
Stackhouse *N York* 54 SD8165
Stackpole *Dyfed* 16 SR9896
Staddiscombe *Devon* 4 SX5151
Stadhampton *Oxon* 21 SU6098
Staffield *Cumb* 59 NY5442
Staffin *Highld* 90 NG4967
Stafford *Staffs* 38 SJ9223
Stagsden *Beds* 30 SP9848
Stainburn *Cumb* 58 NY0129
Stainburn *N York* 55 SE2548
Stainby *Lincs* 40 SK9022
Staincross *S York* 55 SE3210
Staindrop *Dur* 61 NZ1220
Staindrop *Dur* 61 NZ1220
Staines *Surrey* 22 TQ0371
Stainforth *N York* 54 SD8267
Stainforth *S York* 56 SE6411
Staining *Lancs* 53 SD3436
Stainland *W York* 55 SE0719
Stainsacre *N York* 63 NZ9108
Stainton *Cumb* 59 NY4828
Stainton *Dur* 61 NZ0718
Stainton *Cleve* 62 NZ4714
Stainton *Cumb* 59 SD5285
Stainton *S York* 49 SK5593
Stainton by Langworth *Lincs* 50 TF0677
Stainton le Vale *Lincs* 50 TF1794
Stainton with Adgarley *Cumb* 53 SD2472
Staintondale *N York* 63 SE9998
Stair *Strath* 73 NS4423
Stair Haven *D & G* 64 NX2153
Staithes *N York* 63 NZ7818
Stakeford *Nthumb* 69 NZ2685
Stakes *Hants* 11 SU6808
Stalbridge *Dorset* 9 ST7317
Stalbridge Weston *Dorset* 9 ST7116
Stalham *Norfk* 43 TG3725
Stalisfield Green *Kent* 14 TQ9552
Stallen *Dorset* 9 ST6016
Stallingborough *Humb* 57 TA1911
Stalmine *Lancs* 53 SD3745
Stalybridge *Gt Man* 48 SJ9698
Stambourne *Essex* 24 TL7238
Stambourne Green *Essex* 24 TL6938
Stamford *Nthumb* 77 NU2219
Stamford *Lincs* 40 TF0307
Stamford Bridge *Humb* 56 SE7155
Stamford Bridge *Ches* 46 SJ4667
Stamford Hill *Gt Lon* 23 TQ3387
Stamfordham *Nthumb* 68 NZ0771
Stamton Lees *Derbys* 48 SK2562
Stanbridge *Beds* 30 SP9624
Stanbury *W York* 54 SE0137
Stand *Strath* 74 NS7668
Standburn *Cent* 75 NS9274
Standeford *Staffs* 38 SJ9107
Standen *Kent* 14 TQ8540
Standerwick *Somset* 20 ST8150
Standford *Hants* 11 SU8134
Standingstone *Cumb* 58 NY0533
Standish *Gt Man* 53 SD5610
Standish *Gt Man* 53 SD5610
Standlake *Oxon* 21 SP3903
Standon *Staffs* 37 SJ8135
Standon *Hants* 10 SU4226
Standon *Herts* 31 TL3922
Stane *Strath* 74 NS8859
Stanfield *Norfk* 42 TF9320
Stanford *Beds* 31 TL1640
Stanford *Kent* 15 TR1238
Stanford Bishop *H & W* 28 SO6851
Stanford Bridge *H & W* 28 SO7265
Stanford Dingley *Berks* 21 SU5771
Stanford in the Vale *Oxon* 21 SU3493
Stanford le Hope *Essex* 24 TQ6882
Stanford on Avon *Nhants* 39 SP5978
Stanford on Soar *Notts* 39 SK5421
Stanford on Teme *H & W* 28 SO7065
Stanfree *Derbys* 49 SK4773
Stanghow *Cleve* 62 NZ6715
Stanground *Cambs* 41 TL2097
Stanhoe *Norfk* 42 TF8036
Stanhope *Border* 75 NT1229
Stanhope *Dur* 61 NY9939
Stanion *Nhants* 40 SP9186
Stanley *Tays* 82 NO1033
Stanley *Dur* 69 NZ1953
Stanley *Staffs* 48 SJ9352
Stanley *Derbys* 49 SK4140
Stanley Crook *Dur* 61 NZ1637
Stanley Pontlarge *Gloucs* 28 SP0030
Stanmer *E Susx* 12 TQ3309
Stanmore *Hants* 10 SU4628
Stanmore *Gt Lon* 23 TQ1692
Stannersburn *Nthumb* 68 NY7286
Stannington *Nthumb* 69 NZ2179
Stannington *S York* 49 SK2987
Stansbatch *H & W* 27 SO3461
Stansfield *Suffk* 32 TL7852
Stanstead *Suffk* 32 TL8449
Stanstead Abbots *Herts* 23 TL3811
Stanstead Street *Suffk* 32 TL8448
Stansted *Kent* 14 TQ6062
Stansted Mountfitchet *Essex* 31 TL5125
Stanton *Nthumb* 69 NZ1390
Stanton *Staffs* 48 SK1245
Stanton *Gloucs* 28 SP0634
Stanton *Suffk* 32 TL9673
Stanton Drew *Avon* 19 ST5963
Stanton Drew *Avon* 19 ST5963
Stanton Fitzwarren *Wilts* 21 SU1790
Stanton Harcourt *Oxon* 29 SP4105
Stanton Lacy *Shrops* 37 SO4978
Stanton Long *Shrops* 37 SO5791
Stanton Prior *Avon* 20 ST6762
Stanton St. Bernard *Wilts* 20 SU0961
Stanton St. John *Oxon* 29 SP5709
Stanton St. Quintin *Wilts* 20 ST9079
Stanton Street *Suffk* 32 TL9566
Stanton Wick *Avon* 19 ST6162
Stanton by Bridge *Derbys* 39 SK3726
Stanton by Dale *Derbys* 49 SK4637
Stanton in Peak *Derbys* 48 SK2364
Stanton on the Wolds *Notts* 39 SK6330
Stanton under Bardon *Leics* 39 SK4610
Stanton upon Hine Heath *Shrops* 37 SJ5624
Stanway *Gloucs* 28 SP0632
Stanway *Essex* 25 TL9424
Stanwell *Surrey* 22 TQ0574
Stanwick *Nhants* 30 SP9771
Stanwix *Cumb* 67 NY4057
Stape *N York* 63 SE7994
Stapeley *Ches* 47 SJ6749
Stapenhill *Staffs* 39 SK2521
Staple *Somset* 18 ST1141
Staple *Kent* 15 TR2756
Staple Cross *Devon* 7 ST0320
Staple Cross *E Susx* 14 TQ7822
Staple Fitzpaine *Somset* 8 ST2618
Staplefield *W Susx* 12 TQ2728
Stapleford *Notts* 49 SK4837
Stapleford *Leics* 40 SK8018
Stapleford *Lincs* 50 SK8857
Stapleford *Wilts* 10 SU0737
Stapleford *Herts* 31 TL3117
Stapleford *Cambs* 31 TL4751
Stapleford Abbotts *Essex* 23 TQ5194
Staplegrove *Somset* 8 ST2126
Staplehay *Somset* 8 ST2121
Staplehurst *Kent* 14 TQ7843
Staplestreet *Kent* 15 TR0660
Stapleton *N York* 61 NZ2612
Stapleton *Shrops* 37 SJ4704
Stapleton *H & W* 27 SO3265
Stapleton *Leics* 39 SP4398
Stapleton *Somset* 8 ST4621
Stapleton *Somset* 8 ST4621
Stapley *Somset* 8 ST1913
Staploe *Beds* 30 TL1560
Staplow *H & W* 28 SO6941
Star *Fife* 83 NO3103
Star *Dyfed* 17 SN2434
Star *Somset* 19 ST4358
Starbeck *N York* 55 SE3255
Starbotton *N York* 61 SD9574
Starcross *Devon* 5 SX9781
Stareton *Warwks* 39 SP3371
Starlings Green,*Essex* 31 TL4631
Starston *Norfk* 33 TM2384
Startforth *Dur* 61 NZ0415
Startley *Wilts* 20 ST9482
Statenborough *Kent* 15 TR3155
Stathe *Somset* 8 ST3728
Stathern *Leics* 40 SK7731
Staughton Green *Cambs* 30 TL1365
Staughton Highway *Cambs* 30 TL1364
Staunton *Gloucs* 27 SO5512
Staunton *Gloucs* 28 SO7829
Staunton Green *H & W* 27 SO3661
Staunton on Arrow *H & W* 27 SO3660
Staunton on Wye *H & W* 27 SO3644
Staveley *Cumb* 59 SD3786
Staveley *Cumb* 59 SD4698
Staveley *N York* 55 SE3662
Staveley *Derbys* 49 SK4374
Staverton *Gloucs* 28 SO8923
Staverton *Nhants* 29 SP5361
Staverton *Wilts* 20 ST8560
Staverton *Devon* 5 SX7964
Stawell *Somset* 19 ST3738
Stawley *Somset* 7 ST0622
Staxigoe *Highld* 100 ND3852
Staxton *N York* 63 TA0179
Staynall *Lancs* 53 SD3643
Stean *N York* 61 SE0973
Steane *Nhants* 29 SP5538
Stearsby *N York* 56 SE6171
Steart *Somset* 19 ST2745
Stebbing *Essex* 24 TL6624
Stebbing Green *Essex* 24 TL6823
Stebbing Park *Essex* 24 TL6524
Stedham *W Susx* 11 SU8622
Steel *Nthumb* 68 NY9458
Steele Road *Border* 67 NY5293
Steen's Bridge *H & W* 27 SO5357
Steen's Bridge *H & W* 27 SO5357
Steep *Hants* 11 SU7425
Steep Lane *W York* 55 SE0223
Steeple *Dorset* 9 SY9080
Steeple *Essex* 25 TL9303
Steeple Ashton *Wilts* 20 ST9056
Steeple Aston *Oxon* 29 SP4725
Steeple Barton *Oxon* 29 SP4424
Steeple Bumpstead *Essex* 32 TL6841
Steeple Claydon *Bucks* 30 SP7026
Steeple Gidding *Cambs* 40 TL1381
Steeple Langford *Wilts* 20 SU0337
Steeple Morden *Cambs* 31 TL2842
Steeton *W York* 55 SE0344
Stein *Highld* 90 NG2656
Stelling Minnis *Kent* 15 TR1447
Stembridge *Somset* 8 ST4220
Stenalees *Cnwll* 3 SX0156
Stenhouse *D & G* 66 NX8093
Stenhousemuir *Cent* 82 NS8783
Stenscholl *Highld* 90 NG4767
Stenton *Loth* 76 NT6274
Stepaside *Dyfed* 16 SN1407
Stepney *Gt Lon* 23 TQ3681
Steppingley *Beds* 30 TL0035
Stepps *Strath* 74 NS6568
Sternfield *Suffk* 33 TM3861
Stert *Wilts* 20 SU0259
Stetchworth *Cambs* 32 TL6459
Stevenage *Herts* 31 TL2325
Stevenston *Strath* 73 NS2742
Steventon *Oxon* 21 SU4691
Steventon *Hants* 21 SU5447
Steventon End *Essex* 31 TL5942
Stevington *Beds* 30 SP9853
Stewartby *Beds* 30 TL0142
Stewarton *Strath* 72 NR6919
Stewarton *Strath* 73 NS4245
Stewkley *Bucks* 30 SP8526
Stewley *Somset* 8 ST3118
Steyning *W Susx* 12 TQ1711
Steynton *Dyfed* 16 SM9107
Stibb *Cnwll* 6 SS2210
Stibb Cross *Devon* 6 SS4314
Stibb Green *Wilts* 21 SU2262
Stibbard *Norfk* 42 TF9828
Stibbington *Cambs* 40 TL0898
Stichill *Border* 76 NT7138
Stichill *Border* 76 T7138
Sticker *Cnwll* 3 SW9750
Stickford *Lincs* 51 TF3560
Sticklepath *Devon* 7 SX6494
Stickling Green *Essex* 31 TL4732
Stickney *Lincs* 51 TF3457
Stiffkey *Norfk* 42 TF9742
Stile Bridge *Kent* 14 TQ7547
Stilligarry *W Isls* 102 NF7638
Stillingfleet *N York* 56 SE5940
Stillington *Cleve* 62 NZ3723
Stillington *N York* 56 SE5867
Stilton *Cambs* 40 TL1689
Stinchcombe *Gloucs* 20 ST7298
Stinsford *Dorset* 9 SY7091
Stirling *Gramp* 95 NK1242
Stirling *Cent* 81 NS7993
Stirtloe *Cambs* 31 TL1966
Stirton *N York* 54 SD9752
Stisted *Essex* 24 TL8024
Stithians *Cnwll* 2 SW7336
Stivichall *W Mids* 39 SP3376
Stixwould *Lincs* 50 TF1765
Stoak *Ches* 46 SJ4273
Stobo *Border* 75 NT1837
Stoborough *Dorset* 9 SY9286
Stoborough Green *Dorset* 9 SY9285
Stobs Castle *Border* 67 NT5008
Stobswood *Nthumb* 69 NZ2195
Stock *Avon* 19 ST4561
Stock *Essex* 24 TQ6998
Stock Green *H & W* 28 SO9859
Stock Wood *H & W* 28 SP0058
Stockbridge *Hants* 10 SU3535
Stockbriggs *Strath* 74 NS7936
Stockbury *Kent* 14 TQ8461
Stockcross *Berks* 21 SU4368
Stockerston *Leics* 40 SP8397
Stocking *H & W* 27 SO6230
Stocking Pelham *Herts* 31 TL4529
Stockingford *Warwks* 39 SP3391
Stockland *Devon* 8 ST2404
Stockland Bristol *Somset* 19 ST2443
Stockleigh English *Devon* 7 SS8506
Stockleigh Pomeroy *Devon* 7 SS8703
Stockley *Wilts* 20 ST9967
Stocklinch *Somset* 8 ST3817
Stockport *Gt Man* 48 SJ8990
Stockport *Gt Man* 48 SJ8990
Stocksbridge *S York* 49 SK2698
Stocksfield *Nthumb* 68 NZ0561
Stockton *Shrops* 37 SJ7716
Stockton *H & W* 27 SO5261
Stockton *Shrops* 37 SO7299
Stockton *Warwks* 29 SP4363
Stockton *Wilts* 20 ST9838
Stockton *Norfk* 43 TM3894
Stockton Heath *Ches* 47 SJ6185
Stockton on Teme *H & W* 28 SO7167
Stockton on the Forest *N York* 56 SE6556
Stockton-on-Tees *Cleve* 62 NZ4419
Stockwood *Dorset* 9 ST5906
Stockwood *Avon* 19 ST6368
Stodmarsh *Kent* 15 TR2260
Stody *Norfk* 42 TG0535
Stoer *Highld* 98 NC0328
Stoford *Somset* 8 ST5613
Stoford *Wilts* 10 SU0835
Stogumber *Somset* 7 ST0937
Stogursey *Somset* 19 ST2042
Stoke *W Mids* 39 SP3778
Stoke *Devon* 6 SS2324
Stoke *Hants* 21 SU4051
Stoke *Hants* 11 SU7202
Stoke *Kent* 14 TQ8274
Stoke Abbott *Dorset* 8 ST4500
Stoke Albany *Nhants* 40 SP8088
Stoke Ash *Suffk* 33 TM1170
Stoke Bardolph *Notts* 49 SK6441
Stoke Bliss *H & W* 27 SO6563
Stoke Bruerne *Nhants* 30 SP7449
Stoke Canon *Devon* 7 SX9398
Stoke Charity *Hants* 10 SU4839
Stoke Climsland *Cnwll* 4 SX3674
Stoke Cross *H & W* 27 SO6250
Stoke D'Abernon *Surrey* 22 TQ1258
Stoke Doyle *Nhants* 40 TL0286
Stoke Dry *Leics* 40 SP8596
Stoke Farthing *Wilts* 10 SU0525
Stoke Ferry *Norfk* 42 TF7000
Stoke Fleming *Devon* 5 SX8648
Stoke Gabriel *Devon* 5 SX8557
Stoke Gifford *Avon* 19 ST6279
Stoke Golding *Leics* 39 SP3997
Stoke Goldington *Bucks* 30 SP8348
Stoke Hammond *Bucks* 30 SP8829
Stoke Hammond *Bucks* 30 SP8829
Stoke Holy Cross *Norfk* 43 TG2301
Stoke Lacy *H & W* 27 SO6249
Stoke Lyne *Oxon* 29 SP5628
Stoke Mandeville *Bucks* 22 SP8310
Stoke Newington *Gt Lon* 23 TQ3386
Stoke Orchard *Gloucs* 28 SO9128
Stoke Poges *Bucks* 22 SU9783
Stoke Prior *H & W* 27 SO5256
Stoke Prior *H & W* 28 SO9467
Stoke Rivers *Devon* 7 SS6335
Stoke Rochford *Lincs* 40 SK9127
Stoke Row *Oxon* 22 SU6884
Stoke Row *Oxon* 22 SU6884
Stoke St. Gregory *Somset* 8 ST3427
Stoke St. Mary *Somset* 8 ST2622
Stoke St. Michael *Somset* 20 ST6646

Stoke St. Milborough Tandridge

Stoke St. Milborough Shrops 37 SO5682
Stoke Talmage Oxon 22 SU6799
Stoke Trister Somset 9 ST7428
Stoke Wake Dorset 9 ST7606
Stoke by Clare Suffk 32 TL7443
Stoke sub Hamdon Somset 8 ST4717
Stoke upon Tern Shrops 37 SJ6328
Stoke-by-Nayland Suffk 25 TL9836
Stoke-on-Trent Staffs 47 SJ8747
Stoke-upon-Trent Staffs 47 SJ8745
Stokeford Dorset 9 SY8687
Stokeham Notts 50 SK7876
Stokeinteignhead Devon 5 SX9170
Stokenchurch Bucks 22 SU7696
Stokenham Devon 5 SX8042
Stokesay Shrops 36 SO4381
Stokesby Norfk 43 TG4310
Stokesley N York 62 NZ5208
Stolford Somset 7 ST0332
Stolford Somset 19 ST2345
Ston Easton Somset 19 ST6253
Stondon Massey Essex 24 TL5800
Stone Staffs 38 SJ9034
Stone S York 49 SK5589
Stone H & W 38 SO8675
Stone Bucks 30 SP7812
Stone Gloucs 20 ST6895
Stone Kent 14 TQ9427
Stone Allerton Somset 19 ST3951
Stone Cross Kent 15 TR3257
Stone Street Suffk 32 TL9639
Stone Street Suffk 33 TM3882
Stone Street Kent 14 TQ5754
Stonebridge Avon 19 ST3859
Stonebury Herts 31 TL3828
Stonechrubie Highld 96 NC2419
Stonecrouch Kent 14 TQ7033
Stoneferry Humb 57 TA1031
Stonefield Castle Hotel Strath 71 NR8671
Stonegate E Susx 14 TQ6628
Stonegrave N York 62 SE6577
Stonehall H & W 28 SO8848
Stonehaven Gramp 89 NO8786
Stonehouse Strath 74 NS7546
Stonehouse D & G 66 NX8268
Stonehouse Ches 46 SJ5070
Stonehouse Gloucs 28 SO8005
Stonehouse Gloucs 28 SO8005
Stonehouse Devon 4 SX4654
Stoneleigh Warwks 39 SP3372
Stones Green Essex 25 TM1626
Stonesby Leics 40 SK8224
Stonesfield Oxon 29 SP3917
Stonewells Gramp 94 NJ2865
Stoney Middleton Derbys 48 SK2375
Stoney Stanton Leics 39 SP4994
Stoney Stoke Somset 9 ST7032
Stoney Stratton Somset 19 ST6539
Stoney Stretton Shrops 36 SJ3809
Stoneybridge W Isls 102 NF7532
Stoneyburn Loth 75 NS9862
Stoneygate Leics 39 SK6002
Stoneykirk D & G 64 NX0853
Stoneywood Gramp 95 NJ8811
Stoneywood Cent 81 NS7982
Stonham Aspal Suffk 33 TM1359
Stonnall Staffs 38 SK0603
Stonor Oxon 22 SU7388
Stonton Wyville Leics 40 SP7395
Stony Houghton Derbys 49 SK4966
Stony Stratford Bucks 30 SP7840
Stoodleigh Devon 7 SS6532
Stopham W Susx 12 TQ0219
Stopsley Beds 30 TL1023
Stormy Corner Lancs 46 SD4707
Stornoway W Isls 102 NB4232
Storrington W Susx 12 TQ0814
Storwood Humb 56 SE7144
Stotfold Beds 31 TL2136
Stottesdon Shrops 37 SO6782
Stoughton Leics 39 SK6402
Stoughton W Susx 11 SU8011
Stoughton Surrey 12 SU9851
Stoul Highld 85 NM7594
Stoulton H & W 28 SO9049
Stour Provost Dorset 9 ST7921
Stour Row Dorset 9 ST8221
Stourbridge W Mids 38 SO8983
Stourpaine Dorset 9 ST8609
Stourport-on-Severn H & W 37 SO8171
Stourton Staffs 38 SO8684
Stourton Warwks 29 SP2936
Stourton Wilts 9 ST7734
Stourton Caundle Dorset 9 ST7115
Stove Shet 103 HU4224
Stove Shet 103 HU4224
Stoven Suffk 33 TM4481
Stow Border 76 NT4544
Stow Lincs 50 SK8882
Stow Bardolph Norfk 41 TF6206
Stow Bedon Norfk 42 TL9596
Stow Longa Cambs 30 TL1070
Stow Maries Essex 24 TQ8399
Stow cum Quy Cambs 31 TL5260
Stow-on-the-Wold Gloucs 29 SP1925
Stowbridge Norfk 41 TF6007
Stowe Shrops 36 SO3173
Stowe by Chartley Staffs 38 SK0026
Stowell Somset 9 ST6822
Stowey Somset 19 ST5959
Stowford Devon 7 SS6541
Stowford Devon 4 SX4387
Stowlangtoft Suffk 32 TL9568
Stowmarket Suffk 32 TM0458
Stowting Kent 15 TR1242
Stowting Common Kent 15 TR1243
Stowupland Suffk 32 TM0760
Straanruie Highld 93 NH9916
Strachan Gramp 89 NO6692
Strachur Strath 80 NN0901
Stradbroke Suffk 33 TM2373
Stradishall Suffk 32 TL7552
Stradsett Norfk 42 TF6605
Straiton Strath 73 NS3804
Straiton Loth 75 NT2766
Straloch Gramp 95 NJ8620
Straloch Tays 88 NO0463
Stramshall Staffs 38 SK0735
Strang IOM 52 SC3578
Strangford H & W 27 SO5827
Stranraer D & G 64 NX0560
Stratfield Mortimer Berks 22 SU6664
Stratfield Saye Hants 22 SU6861
Stratfield Turgis Hants 22 SU6959
Stratford Gt Lon 23 TQ3884
Stratford St. Andrew Suffk 33 TM3560
Stratford St. Mary Suffk 25 TM0434
Stratford Tony Wilts 10 SU0926
Stratford-upon-Avon Warwks 29 SP2055
Strath Highld 100 ND2652
Strath Highld 91 NG7978
Strathan Highld 98 NC0821
Strathan Highld 99 NC5764
Strathan Highld 99 NC5764
Strathan Highld 85 NM9791
Strathaven Strath 74 NS7044
Strathblane Cent 81 NS5679
Strathcarron Sta Highld 91 NG9442
Strathcoil Strath 79 NM6830
Strathdon Gramp 94 NJ3512
Strathkanaird Highld 96 NC1501
Strathkinness Fife 83 NO4516
Strathmashie House Tays 87 NN5891
Strathmiglo Fife 82 NO2109
Strathpeffer Highld 92 NH4858
Strathwhillan Strath 72 NS0235
Strathy Highld 99 NC8464
Strathy Inn Highld 99 NC8365
Strathyre Cent 81 NN5617
Stratton Gloucs 20 SP0103
Stratton Cnwll 6 SS2306
Stratton Dorset 9 SY6593
Stratton Audley Oxon 29 SP6025
Stratton St. Margaret Wilts 21 SU1786
Stratton St. Michael Norfk 43 TM2093
Stratton Strawless Norfk 43 TG2220
Stratton-on-the-Fosse Somset 20 ST6650
Stravithie Fife 83 NO5313
Stream Somset 7 ST0639
Streat E Susx 12 TQ3515
Streatham Gt Lon 23 TQ3071
Streatley Berks 21 SU5980
Streatley Beds 30 TL0728
Street Somset 19 ST4836
Street Devon 8 SY1888
Street Ashton Warwks 39 SP4582
Street Dinas Shrops 36 SJ3338
Street End W Susx 11 SZ8599
Street End Kent 15 TR1453
Street Gate T & W 69 NZ2159
Street on the Fosse Somset 19 ST6239
Streethay Staffs 38 SK1410
Streetlam N York 61 SE3098
Strelitz Tays 82 NO1836
Strelley Notts 49 SK5141
Strensall N York 56 SE6360
Strete Devon 5 SX8446
Stretford Gt Man 47 SJ7994
Strethall Essex 31 TL4839
Stretham Cambs 31 TL5174
Stretham Cambs 31 TL5174
Strettington W Susx 11 SU8907
Stretton Ches 47 SJ6282
Stretton Staffs 38 SJ8811
Stretton Staffs 39 SK2526
Stretton Derbys 49 SK3961
Stretton Leics 40 SK9415
Stretton Grandison H & W 27 SO6344
Stretton Sugwas H & W 27 SO4642
Stretton Westwood Shrops 37 SO5998
Stretton on Fosse Warwks 29 SP2238
Stretton under Fosse Warwks 39 SP4581
Stretton-on-Dunsmore Warwks 39 SP4072
Strichen Gramp 95 NJ9455
Stringston Somset 19 ST1742
Strixton Nhants 30 SP9061
Stroat Gloucs 19 ST5797
Stromeferry Highld 85 NG8634
Stromness Ork 103 HY2508
Stronachlachar Cent 80 NN4010
Stronafian Strath 80 NS0281
Strone Highld 86 NN1481
Strone Strath 80 NS1980
Stronenaba Highld 86 NN2084
Stronmilchan Strath 80 NN1528
Strontian Highld 79 NM8161
Strood Kent 14 TQ7269
Stroud Gloucs 28 SO8505
Stroud Hants 11 SU7223
Stroud Green Gloucs 28 SO8007
Stroud Green Essex 24 TQ8590
Stroxton Lincs 40 SK9030
Struan Highld 84 NG3438
Struan Tays 87 NN8065
Strumpshaw Norfk 43 TG3407
Strutherhill Strath 74 NS7649
Struthers Fife 83 NO3709
Struy Highld 92 NH4040
Stuartfield Gramp 95 NJ9745
Stubbington Hants 11 SU5503
Stubbins Gt Man 54 SD7918
Stubton Lincs 50 SK8748
Stuckton Hants 10 SU1613
Studham Beds 30 TL0215
Studholme Cumb 67 NY2556
Studland Dorset 9 SZ0382
Studland Dorset 9 SZ0382
Studley Warwks 28 SP0764
Studley Wilts 20 ST9671
Studley Wilts 20 ST9671
Studley Roger N York 55 SE2970
Studley Royal N York 55 SE2770
Stuntney Cambs 31 TL5578
Sturmer Essex 32 TL6943
Sturminster Common Dorset 9 ST7812
Sturminster Marshall Dorset 9 ST9500
Sturminster Newton Dorset 9 ST7814
Sturry Kent 15 TR1760
Sturton Humb 56 SE9604
Sturton by Stow Lincs 50 SK8980
Sturton le Steeple Notts 50 SK7883
Stuston Suffk 33 TM1377
Stutton N York 55 SE4841
Stutton Suffk 25 TM1534
Styal Ches 47 SJ8383
Stynie Gramp 94 NJ3360
Styrrup Notts 49 SK6090
Succoth Strath 80 NN2905
Suckley H & W 28 SO7251
Sudborough Nhants 40 SP9682
Sudbourne Suffk 33 TM4153
Sudbrook Lincs 50 SK9744
Sudbrook Gwent 19 ST5087
Sudbrooke Lincs 50 TF0376
Sudbury Derbys 38 SK1631
Sudbury Suffk 32 TL8741
Sudbury Gt Lon 23 TQ1685
Suddie Highld 93 NH6554
Suddington H & W 28 SO8463
Suffield N York 63 SE9890
Suffield Norfk 43 TG2232
Sugnall Staffs 37 SJ7931
Sugwas Pool H & W 27 SO4541
Suisnish Highld 84 NG5816
Sulby IOM 52 SC3894
Sulgrave Nhants 29 SP5544
Sulham Berks 21 SU6474
Sulhamstead Berks 21 SU6368
Sulhamstead Abbots Berks 21 SU6467
Sullom Shet 103 HU3573
Sullom Voe Shet 103 HU4075
Sully S Glam 19 ST1568
Sully S Glam 19 ST1568
Summerbridge N York 55 SE2062
Summercourt Cnwll 3 SW8856
Summerfield Norfk 42 TF7538
Summerhouse Dur 61 NZ2019
Summersdale W Susx 11 SU8606
Summersdale W Susx 11 SU8606
Summerseat Gt Man 54 SD7914
Summertown Oxon 29 SP5009
Sunbury Surrey 22 TQ1168
Sundaywell D & G 66 NX8284
Sunderland Strath 70 NR2464
Sunderland Cumb 58 NY1735
Sunderland T & W 69 NZ3957
Sunderland Lancs 53 SD4255
Sunderland Bridge Dur 61 NZ2637
Sundhope Border 75 NT3325
Sundridge Kent 23 TQ4855
Sunningdale Surrey 22 SU9567
Sunninghill Surrey 22 SU9367
Sunningwell Oxon 21 SP4900
Sunniside Dur 61 NZ1438
Sunnyhill Derbys 39 SK3432
Sunnyhurst Lancs 54 SD6722
Sunnylaw Cent 81 NS7998
Sunnymead Oxon 29 SP5009
Sunwick Border 77 NT9052
Surbiton Gt Lon 23 TQ1867
Surfleet Lincs 41 TF2528
Surlingham Norfk 43 TG3106
Surrex Essex 24 TL8722
Sustead Norfk 43 TG1837
Susworth Lincs 50 SE8302
Sutcombe Devon 6 SS3411
Sutcombemill Devon 6 SS3411
Sutterby Lincs 51 TF3872
Sutterton Lincs 41 TF2835
Sutton N York 55 SE4925
Sutton Staffs 37 SJ7622
Sutton Notts 49 SK6784
Sutton Notts 40 SK7637
Sutton Shrops 37 SO7386
Sutton W Susx 12 SU9715
Sutton Devon 5 SX7042
Sutton Norfk 43 TG3823
Sutton Cambs 40 TL0998
Sutton Beds 31 TL2247
Sutton Cambs 41 TL4479
Sutton Suffk 33 TM3046
Sutton Gt Lon 23 TQ2564
Sutton Kent 15 TR3349
Sutton E Susx 13 TV4999
Sutton Bassett Nhants 40 SP7790
Sutton Benger Wilts 20 ST9478
Sutton Bingham Somset 8 ST5410
Sutton Bingham Somset 8 ST5410
Sutton Bonington Notts 39 SK5024
Sutton Bridge Lincs 41 TF4721
Sutton Cheney Leics 39 SK4100
Sutton Coldfield W Mids 38 SP1295
Sutton Courtenay Oxon 21 SU5094
Sutton Grange N York 61 SE2873
Sutton Green Surrey 22 TQ0054
Sutton Howgrave N York 62 SE3179
Sutton Maddock Shrops 37 SJ7201
Sutton Mallet Somset 19 ST3736
Sutton Mandeville Wilts 9 ST9828
Sutton Montis Somset 9 ST6224
Sutton Scotney Hants 10 SU4639
Sutton St. Edmund Lincs 41 TF3613
Sutton St. James Lincs 41 TF3918
Sutton St. Nicholas H & W 27 SO5245
Sutton Valence Kent 14 TQ8149
Sutton Veny Wilts 20 ST9041
Sutton Waldron Dorset 9 ST8615
Sutton Weaver Ches 47 SJ5479
Sutton Wick Avon 19 ST5759
Sutton Wick Oxon 21 SU4894
Sutton at Hone Kent 23 TQ5569
Sutton in Ashfield Notts 49 SK4958
Sutton le Marsh Lincs 51 TF5280
Sutton on Sea Lincs 51 TF5281
Sutton on Trent Notts 50 SK7965
Sutton on the Hill Derbys 39 SK2333
Sutton upon Derwent Humb 56 SE7047
Sutton-in-Craven N York 54 SE0043
Sutton-on-Hull Humb 57 TA1232
Sutton-on-the-Forest N York 56 SE5864
Sutton-under-Brailes Warwks 29 SP3037
Sutton-under-Whitestonecliffe N York 62 SE4882
Swaby Lincs 51 TF3877
Swadlincote Derbys 39 SK2919
Swaffham Norfk 42 TF8108
Swaffham Bulbeck Cambs 31 TL5562
Swaffham Prior Cambs 31 TL5764
Swafield Norfk 43 TG2832
Swainby N York 62 NZ4701
Swainsthorpe Norfk 43 TG2101
Swainswick Avon 20 ST7668
Swalcliffe Oxon 29 SP3737
Swalecliffe Kent 15 TR1367
Swalecliffe Kent 15 TR1367
Swallow Lincs 57 TA1703
Swallow Beck Lincs 50 SK9467
Swallowcliffe Wilts 9 ST9627
Swallowfield Berks 22 SU7264
Swan Green Ches 47 SJ7373
Swanage Dorset 9 SZ0378
Swanbourne Bucks 30 SP8026
Swanland Humb 56 SE9928
Swanley Kent 23 TQ5168
Swanley Village Kent 23 TQ5369
Swanmore Hants 11 SU5716
Swannington Leics 39 SK4116
Swannington Norfk 43 TG1319
Swanpool Garden Suberb Lincs 50 SK9569
Swanscombe Kent 14 TQ6074
Swansea W Glam 18 SS6592
Swanton Abbot Norfk 43 TG2625
Swanton Morley Norfk 42 TG0117
Swanton Novers Norfk 42 TG0231
Swanwick Derbys 49 SK4053
Swanwick Hants 11 SU5109
Swarby Lincs 50 TF0440
Swardeston Norfk 43 TG2002
Swarkestone Derbys 39 SK3728
Swarland Nthumb 69 NU1602
Swarraton Hants 11 SU5636
Swarthmoor Cumb 58 SD2777
Swaton Lincs 40 TF1337
Swavesey Cambs 31 TL3668
Sway Hants 10 SZ2798
Swayfield Lincs 40 SK9922
Swaythling Hants 10 SU4416
Sweetham Devon 7 SX8899
Sweethaws E Susx 13 TQ5028
Sweets Cnwll 6 SX1595
Sweetshouse Cnwll 3 SX0861
Swefling Suffk 33 TM3463
Swepstone Leics 39 SK3610
Swerford Oxon 29 SP3731
Swettenham Ches 47 SJ8067
Swiftsden E Susx 14 TQ7328
Swilland Suffk 33 TM1852
Swillington W York 55 SE3830
Swimbridge Devon 6 SS6230
Swimbridge Newland Devon 6 SS6030
Swinbrook Oxon 29 SP2812
Swincliffe N York 55 SE2458
Swincliffe N York 55 SE2458
Swinderby Lincs 50 SK8663
Swindon Staffs 38 SO8690
Swindon Gloucs 28 SO9325
Swindon Wilts 20 SU1484
Swine Humb 57 TA1335
Swinefleet Humb 56 SE7621
Swineshead Lincs 51 TF2340
Swineshead Beds 30 TL0565
Swiney Highld 100 ND2335
Swinford Leics 39 SP5679
Swingfield Minnis Kent 15 TR2142
Swingfield Street Kent 15 TR2343
Swingleton Green Suffk 32 TL9647
Swinhill Strath 74 NS7748
Swinhoe Nthumb 77 NU2128
Swinithwaite N York 61 SE0489
Swinscoe Staffs 48 SK1247
Swinside Cumb 58 NY2421
Swinstead Lincs 40 TF0122
Swinton Border 77 NT8347
Swinton Gt Man 47 SD7701
Swinton N York 61 SE2179
Swinton N York 63 SE7573
Swinton S York 49 SK4599
Swithland Leics 39 SK5512
Swordale Highld 92 NH5765
Swordland Highld 85 NM7891
Swordly Highld 99 NC7463
Swynnerton Staffs 38 SJ8535
Swyre Dorset 8 SY5288
Sychtyn Powys 35 SH9907
Syde Gloucs 28 SO9511
Sydenham Oxon 22 SP7301
Sydenham Gt Lon 23 TQ3671
Sydenham Damerel Devon 4 SX4176
Syderstone Norfk 42 TF8332
Sydling St. Nicholas Dorset 9 SY6399
Sydmonton Hants 21 SU4857
Syerston Notts 50 SK7447
Sykehouse S York 56 SE6316
Symbister Shet 103 HU5462
Symington Strath 73 NS3831
Symington Strath 75 NS9935
Symonds Yat H & W 27 SO5515
Symondsbury Dorset 8 SY4493
Synton Border 76 NT4822
Syre Highld 99 NC6943
Syre Highld 99 NC6943
Syreford Gloucs 28 SP0220
Syresham Nhants 29 SP6241
Syston Leics 39 SK6211
Syston Lincs 50 SK9240
Sytchampton H & W 28 SO8466
Sywell Nhants 30 SP8267

T

Tackley Oxon 29 SP4719
Tacolneston Norfk 43 TM1495
Tadcaster N York 55 SE4843
Taddington Derbys 48 SK1371
Taddington Gloucs 28 SP0831
Tadley Hants 21 SU6061
Tadlow Cambs 31 TL2847
Tadmarton Oxon 29 SP3937
Tadworth Surrey 23 TQ2257
Taff's Well M Glam 18 ST1283
Taibach W Glam 18 SS7788
Tain Highld 100 ND2266
Tain Highld 97 NH7781
Takeley Essex 24 TL5621
Takeley Street Essex 24 TL5421
Tal-y-Bont Gwynd 45 SH7668
Tal-y-bont Gwynd 34 SH5921
Tal-y-bont Gwynd 44 SH6070
Tal-y-cafn Gwynd 45 SH7871
Tal-y-coed Gwent 27 SO4115
Tal-y-garn M Glam 18 ST0379
Talachddu Powys 26 SO0833
Talaton Devon 7 SY0699
Talbenny Dyfed 16 SM8411
Talerddig Powys 35 SH9300
Talgarreg Dyfed 17 SN4251
Talgarth Powys 27 SO1533
Taliesin Dyfed 35 SN6591
Talisker Highld 84 NG3230
Talkin Cumb 67 NY5557
Talla Linnfoots Border 75 NT1320
Talladale Highld 91 NG9170
Tallaminnock Strath 64 NX4098
Tallarn Green Clwyd 46 SJ4444
Tallentire Cumb 58 NY1035
Talley Dyfed 17 SN6332
Tallington Lincs 40 TF0908
Talmine Highld 99 NC5863
Talog Dyfed 17 SN3325
Talsarn Dyfed 34 SN5456
Talsarnau Gwynd 45 SH6135
Talskiddy Cnwll 3 SW9165
Talwrn Gwynd 44 SH4877
Talybont Dyfed 35 SN6589
Talybont-on-Usk Powys 26 SO1122
Talysarn Gwynd 44 SH4952
Tamerton Foliot Devon 4 SX4761
Tamworth Staffs 39 SK2003
Tan Office Green Suffk 32 TL7858
Tan-y-groes Dyfed 17 SN2849
Tandlemuir Strath 73 NS3361
Tandridge Surrey 13 TQ3750

Titsey
Ullesthorpe

Titsey Surrey 23 TQ4054
Tittensor Staffs 38 SJ8738
Tittleshall Norfk 42 TF8921
Titton H & W 28 SO8370
Tiverton Ches 47 SJ5560
Tiverton Devon 7 SS9512
Tivetshall St. Margaret Norfk 33 TM1787
Tivetshall St. Mary Norfk 33 TM1686
Tivington Somset 7 SS9345
Tixall Staffs 38 SJ9722
Tixover Leics 40 SK9700
Toab Shet 103 HU3811
Toadmoor Derbys 49 SK3451
Tobermory Strath 79 NM5055
Toberonochy Strath 79 NM7408
Tocher Gramp 95 NJ6932
Tochieneal Gramp 94 NJ5165
Tockenham Wilts 20 SU0379
Tockington Avon 19 ST6086
Tockwith N York 55 SE4652
Todber Dorset 9 ST7919
Todburn Nthumb 69 NZ1295
Toddington Gloucs 28 SP0333
Toddington Beds 30 TL0128
Todds Green Herts 31 TL2226
Todenham Gloucs 29 SP2335
Todhills Tays 83 NO4239
Todhills Cumb 67 NY3762
Todmorden W York 54 SD9324
Todwick S York 49 SK4984
Toft Shet 103 HU4376
Toft Lincs 40 TF0717
Toft Cambs 31 TL3656
Toft Hill Dur 61 NZ1528
Toft Monks Norfk 43 TM4294
Toft next Newton Lincs 50 TF0388
Toftrees Norfk 42 TF8927
Tofts Highld 100 ND3668
Togston Nthumb 69 NU2402
Tokavaig Highld 84 NG6011
Tokers Green Oxon 22 SU7077
Toll Bar S York 56 SE5507
Tolland Somset 8 ST1032
Tollard Royal Wilts 9 ST9417
Toller Fratrum Dorset 8 SY5797
Toller Porcorum Dorset 8 SY5698
Toller Whelme Dorset 8 ST5101
Tollerton N York 55 SE5164
Tollerton N York 55 SE5164
Tollerton Notts 39 SK6134
Tollesbury Essex 25 TL9510
Tolleshunt D'Arcy Essex 24 TL9211
Tolleshunt Knights Essex 24 TL9114
Tolleshunt Major Essex 24 TL9011
Tolpuddle Dorset 9 SY7994
Tolsta W Isls 102 NB5347
Tolworth Gt Lon 23 TQ1966
Tomaknock Tays 82 NN8721
Tomatin Highld 93 NH8028
Tomchrasky Highld 92 NH2512
Tomdoun Highld 86 NH1500
Tomich Highld 97 NC6005
Tomich Highld 92 NH3027
Tomich Highld 92 NH5348
Tomich Highld 93 NH6971
Tomintoul Gramp 94 NJ1619
Tomintoul Gramp 88 NO1490
Tomnacross Highld 92 NH5141
Tomnavoulin Gramp 94 NJ2126
Tonbridge Kent 13 TQ5846
Tondu M Glam 18 SS8984
Tonedale Somset 8 ST1321
Tong W York 55 SE2230
Tong Shrops 37 SJ7907
Tong Kent 14 TQ9556
Tong Norton Shrops 37 SJ7908
Tong Street W York 55 SE1930
Tonge Leics 39 SK4223
Tongham Surrey 22 SU8848
Tongland D & G 65 NX6954
Tongue Highld 99 NC5957
Tongwynlais S Glam 18 ST1382
Tonna W Glam 18 SS7798
Tonwell Herts 31 TL3316
Tonypandy M Glam 18 SS9991
Tonyrefail M Glam 18 ST0188
Toot Baldon Oxon 21 SP5600
Toot Hill Essex 23 TL5102
Toothill Wilts 20 SU1183
Tooting Gt Lon 23 TQ2771
Tooting Bec Gt Lon 23 TQ2872
Topcliffe N York 62 SE3976
Topcroft Norfk 43 TM2693
Topcroft Street Norfk 33 TM2691
Toppesfield Essex 24 TL7437
Toprow Norfk 43 TM1698
Toprow Norfk 43 TM1698
Topsham Devon 5 SX9688
Torbeg Strath 72 NR8929
Torboll Highld 97 NH7599
Torbreck Highld 92 NH6441
Torbryan Devon 5 SX8266
Torcastle Highld 86 NN1378
Torcross Devon 5 SX8241
Tore Highld 92 NH6052
Torksey Lincs 50 SK8378
Tormarton Avon 20 ST7678
Tormitchell Strath 64 NX2394
Tormore Strath 72 NR8932
Tornagrain Highld 93 NH7650
Tornaveen Gramp 89 NJ6106
Torness Highld 92 NH5826
Torness Strath 79 NM6532
Toronto Nthumb 61 NZ1930
Torosay Castle Strath 79 NM7335
Torpenhow Cumb 58 NY2039
Torphichen Loth 75 NS9672
Torphins Gramp 89 NJ6202
Torpoint Cnwll 4 SX4355
Torquay Devon 5 SX9164
Torquhan Border 76 NT4448
Torran Highld 90 NG5949
Torrance Strath 74 NS6173
Torranyard Strath 73 NS3544
Torridon Highld 91 NG9055
Torridon House Highld 91 NG8657
Torrin Highld 84 NG5721
Torrisdale Highld 99 NC6761
Torrisdale Square Strath 72 NR7936
Torrish Highld 97 NC9718
Torrisholme Lancs 53 SD4563
Torrobull Highld 97 NC5904
Torry Gramp 89 NJ9405
Torryburn Fife 82 NT0286
Torrylin Strath 72 NR9521
Tortan H & W 38 SO8472
Torteval Guern 101 GN0000
Torthorwald D & G 66 NY0378
Tortington W Susx 12 TQ0004
Tortworth Avon 20 ST7093
Torvaig Highld 90 NG4944
Torver Cumb 58 SD2894
Torwood Cent 82 NS8385
Torwoodlee Border 76 NT4738
Torworth Notts 49 SK6586
Torworth Notts 49 SK6586
Toscaig Highld 85 NG7138
Toseland Cambs 31 TL2462
Tosside Lancs 54 SD7656
Tostock Suffk 32 TL9563
Totaig Highld 90 NG2050
Tote Highld 90 NG4149
Tote Hill W Susx 11 SU8624
Totland IOW 10 SZ3287
Totley S York 49 SK3079
Totnes Devon 5 SX8060
Totronald Strath 78 NM1656
Totscore Highld 90 NG3866
Tottenham Gt Lon 23 TQ3390
Tottenhill Norfk 42 TF6411
Totteridge Gt Lon 23 TQ2494
Totternhoe Beds 30 SP9821
Tottington Gt Man 54 SD7712
Totton Hants 10 SU3613
Toulton Somset 8 ST1931
Toulvaddie Highld 97 NH8880
Toux Gramp 94 NJ5459
Tovil Kent 14 TQ7554
Tow Law Dur 61 NZ1138
Toward Strath 73 NS1368
Toward Quay Strath 73 NS1167
Towcester Nhants 30 SP6948
Towednack Cnwll 2 SW4838
Towersey Oxon 22 SP7305
Towie Gramp 94 NJ4312
Town End Cambs 41 TL4195
Town Littleworth E Susx 13 TQ4117
Town Street Suffk 32 TL7785
Town Yetholm Border 76 NT8128
Townhead D & G 66 NY0088
Townhead S York 48 SE1602
Townhead of Greenlaw D & G 65 NX7464
Townhill Loth 82 NT1089
Towns End Hants 21 SU5659
Townshend Cnwll 2 SW5932
Towthorpe N York 56 SE6258
Towton N York 55 SE4839
Toxteth Mersyd 46 SJ3588
Toy's Hill Kent 13 TQ4651
Toynton All Saints Lincs 51 TF3963
Trabboch Strath 73 NS4421
Trabbochburn Strath 73 NS4621
Tradespark Highld 93 NH8656
Trafford Park Gt Man 47 SJ7896
Trallong Powys 26 SN9629
Tranent Loth 76 NT4072
Tranmere Mersyd 46 SJ3187
Trantelbeg Highld 99 NC8952
Trantlemore Highld 99 NC8953
Trap Dyfed 26 SN6518
Traquair Border 75 NT3334
Traveller's Rest Devon 6 SS6127
Trawden Lancs 54 SD9138
Trawsfynydd Gwynd 45 SH7035
Tre-groes Dyfed 17 SN4044
Trealaw M Glam 18 ST0092
Treales Lancs 53 SD4332
Trearddur Bay Gwynd 44 SH2579
Treaslane Highld 90 NG3953
Trebarwith Cnwll 4 SX0586
Trebetherick Cnwll 3 SW9378
Trebullett Cnwll 4 SX3278
Treburley Cnwll 4 SX3577
Trecastle Powys 26 SN8829
Trecwn Dyfed 16 SM9632
Trecynon M Glam 18 SN9903
Tredaule Cnwll 4 SX2381
Tredegar Gwent 26 SO1408
Tredington Gloucs 28 SO9029
Tredington Warwks 29 SP2543
Tredunhock Gwent 19 ST3794
Treen Cnwll 2 SW3923
Treeton S York 49 SK4387
Trefacca Powys 26 SO1431
Trefasser Dyfed 16 SM8938
Trefeglwys Powys 35 SN9690
Treffgarne Dyfed 16 SM9523
Treffgarne Owen Dyfed 16 SM8625
Trefilan Dyfed 34 SN5456
Trefnant Clwyd 45 SJ0570
Trefonen Shrops 36 SJ2526
Trefforest M Glam 18 ST0888
Trefrew Cnwll 4 SX1084
Trefriw Gwynd 45 SH7863
Tregadillett Cnwll 4 SX2983
Tregare Gwent 27 SO4110
Tregaron Dyfed 26 SN6759
Tregarth Gwynd 44 SH6067
Tregeare Cnwll 4 SX2486
Tregeiriog Clwyd 36 SJ1733
Tregele Gwynd 44 SH3592
Tregidden Cnwll 2 SW7523
Treglemais Dyfed 16 SM8229
Tregole Cnwll 6 SX1998
Tregonce Cnwll 3 SW9373
Tregonetha Cnwll 3 SW9563
Tregony Cnwll 3 SW9244
Tregoyd Powys 27 SO1937
Tregynon Powys 36 SO0998
Trehafod M Glam 18 ST0490
Trehan Cnwll 4 SX4058
Treharris M Glam 18 ST0996
Treherbert M Glam 18 SS9498
Trekenner Cnwll 4 SX3478
Treknow Cnwll 4 SX0586
Trelawnyd Clwyd 46 SJ0979
Trelech Dyfed 17 SN2830
Treleddyd-fawr Dyfed 16 SM7528
Trelewis M Glam 18 ST1096
Trelights Cnwll 3 SW9979
Trelill Cnwll 3 SX0478
Trelleck Gwent 27 SO5005
Trelogan Clwyd 46 SJ1180
Trelow Cnwll 3 SW9269
Tremadog Gwynd 44 SH5640
Tremail Cnwll 4 SX1686
Tremain Dyfed 17 SN2348
Tremaine Cnwll 4 SX2389
Tremar Cnwll 4 SX2568
Trematon Cnwll 4 SX3959
Tremeirchion Clwyd 46 SJ0873
Trenance Cnwll 3 SW8568
Trenance Cnwll 3 SW9270
Trencreek Cnwll 6 SX1896
Trenear Cnwll 2 SW6731
Treneglos Cnwll 4 SX2088
Trent Dorset 9 ST5918
Trentishoe Devon 18 SS6448
Treoes S Glam 18 SS9478
Treorchy M Glam 18 SS9597
Trequite Cnwll 3 SX0377
Trerhyngyll S Glam 18 ST0077
Trerulefoot Cnwll 4 SX3358
Tresaith Dyfed 17 SN2751
Trescowe Cnwll 2 SW5731
Tresean Cnwll 2 SW7858
Tresham Avon 20 ST7991
Tresillian Cnwll 3 SW8646
Treskinnick Cross Cnwll 6 SX2098
Tresmeer Cnwll 4 SX2387
Tresparrett Cnwll 4 SX1491
Tressait Tays 87 NN8160
Tresta Shet 103 HU3650
Tresta Shet 103 HU6090
Treswell Notts 50 SK7879
Trethevey Cnwll 4 SX0789
Trethewey Cnwll 2 SW3823
Trethurgy Cnwll 3 SX0355
Tretire H & W 27 SO5123
Tretower Powys 27 SO1821
Treuddyn Clwyd 46 SJ2557
Trevague Cnwll 4 SX2379
Trevalga Cnwll 4 SX0890
Trevalyn Clwyd 46 SJ3856
Trevanson Cnwll 3 SW9773
Trevarrian Cnwll 3 SW8566
Treveal Cnwll 2 SW7858
Treveighan Cnwll 3 SX0779
Trevellas Downs Cnwll 2 SW7452
Trevelmond Cnwll 4 SX2063
Treverva Cnwll 2 SW7531
Trevescan Cnwll 2 SW3524
Trevine Dyfed 16 SM8432
Treviscoe Cnwll 3 SW9455
Trevone Cnwll 3 SW8975
Trevor Gwynd 44 SH3746
Trevor Clwyd 36 SJ2742
Trewalder Cnwll 3 SX0782
Trewarlett Cnwll 4 SX3380
Trewarmett Cnwll 4 SX0686
Treween Cnwll 4 SX2182
Trewen Cnwll 3 SX0577
Trewint Cnwll 4 SX2180
Trewithian Cnwll 3 SW8737
Trewoon Cnwll 3 SW9952
Treyford W Susx 11 SU8218
Triangle W York 55 SE0422
Trimdon Dur 62 NZ3634
Trimdon Colliery Dur 62 NZ3735
Trimdon Grange Dur 62 NZ3635
Trimingham Norfk 43 TG2838
Trimley Suffk 25 TM2737
Trimley Heath Suffk 25 TM2738
Trimsaran Dyfed 17 SN4504
Trimstone Devon 6 SS5043
Trinafour Tays 87 NN7264
Tring Herts 22 SP9211
Trinity Jersey 101 JS0000
Trinity Tays 89 NO6061
Trinity Gask Tays 82 NN9718
Triscombe Somset 7 SS9237
Triscombe Somset 8 ST1535
Trislaig Highld 86 NN0874
Trispen Cnwll 3 SW8450
Tritlington Nthumb 69 NZ2092
Trochry Tays 82 NN9740
Troedrhiwfuwch M Glam 26 SO1204
Troedyraur Dyfed 17 SN3245
Troedyrhiw M Glam 18 SO0702
Trois Bois Jersey 101 JS0000
Troon Strath 73 NS3230
Troon Cnwll 2 SW6638
Troquhain D & G 65 NX6879
Trossachs Hotel Cent 81 NN5107
Troston Suffk 32 TL8972
Trots Hill H & W 28 SO8855
Trottiscliffe Kent 14 TQ6460
Trotton W Susx 11 SU8322
Troughend Nthumb 68 NY8692
Troutbeck Cumb 59 NY4002
Troutbeck Bridge Cumb 59 NY4000
Troway Derbys 49 SK3879
Trowbridge Wilts 20 ST8558
Trowse Newton Norfk 43 TG2406
Trudoxhill Somset 20 ST7443
Trull Somset 8 ST2122
Trumpan Highld 90 NG2261
Trumpet H & W 27 SO6539
Trumpington Cambs 31 TL4454
Trunch Norfk 43 TG2834
Truro Cnwll 2 SW8244
Trusham Devon 5 SX8582
Trusley Derbys 39 SK2535
Trysull Staffs 38 SO8594
Tubney Oxon 21 SU4399
Tuckenhay Devon 5 SX8156
Tuckhill Shrops 37 SO7888
Tuckingmill Wilts 9 ST9329
Tuckingmill Cnwll 2 SW6540
Tuckton Dorset 10 SZ1492
Tuddenham Suffk 32 TL7371
Tuddenham Suffk 33 TM1948
Tudeley Kent 13 TQ6245
Tudhoe Dur 61 NZ2535
Tudweiloig Gwynd 44 SH2436
Tuffley Gloucs 28 SO8314
Tufton Dyfed 16 SN0428
Tufton Hants 21 SU4546
Tugby Leics 40 SK7601
Tugford Shrops 37 SO5587
Tughall Nthumb 77 NU2126
Tullibody Cent 82 NS8595
Tullich Highld 92 NH6328
Tullich Highld 97 NH8576
Tullich Strath 80 NN0815
Tulliemet Tays 88 NO0052
Tulloch Gramp 95 NJ8031
Tulloch Cent 81 NN5120
Tulloch Station Highld 86 NN3580
Tullochgorm Strath 71 NR9695
Tullybeagles Lodge Tays 82 NO0136
Tullynessie Gramp 94 NJ5519
Tumble Dyfed 17 SN5411
Tumby Lincs 51 TF2359
Tumby Woodside Lincs 51 TF2757
Tummel Bridge Tays 87 NN7659
Tunstall T & W 69 NZ3953
Tunstall Lancs 59 SD6073
Tunstall N York 61 SE2196
Tunstall Staffs 37 SJ7727
Tunstall Staffs 47 SJ8651
Tunstall Humb 57 TA3031
Tunstall Norfk 43 TG4107
Tunstall Suffk 33 TM3655
Tunstall Kent 14 TQ8961
Tunstead Derbys 48 SK1074
Tunstead Norfk 43 TG3022
Tunstead Milton Derbys 48 SK0180
Tunworth Hants 22 SU6748
Tur Langton Leics 40 SP7194
Turgis Green Hants 22 SU6959
Turkdean Gloucs 28 SP1017
Turleigh Wilts 20 ST8060
Turnastone H & W 27 SO3536
Turnberry Strath 73 NS2005
Turnditch Derbys 49 SK2946
Turner's Hill W Susx 12 TQ3435
Turners Puddle Dorset 9 SY8393
Turnworth Dorset 9 ST8207
Turriff Gramp 95 NJ7250
Turton Bottoms Gt Man 54 SD7315
Turvey Beds 30 SP9452
Turville Bucks 22 SU7691
Turweston Bucks 29 SP6037
Tushielaw Inn Border 75 NT3017
Tushingham cum Grindley Ches 46 SJ5246
Tutbury Staffs 39 SK2128
Tutshill Gloucs 19 ST5494
Tuttington Norfk 43 TG2227
Tuxford Notts 50 SK7471
Twatt Shet 103 HU3253
Twatt Ork 103 HY2724
Twechar Strath 74 NS6975
Tweedmouth Nthumb 77 NT9952
Tweedsmuir Border 75 NT1024
Twelve Oaks E Susx 14 TQ6820
Twelveheads Cnwll 2 SW7542
Twemlow Green Ches 47 SJ7868
Twenty Lincs 40 TF1520
Twerton Avon 20 ST7264
Twickenham Gt Lon 23 TQ1673
Twigworth Gloucs 28 SO8422
Twineham W Susx 12 TQ2519
Twinstead Essex 24 TL8636
Twitchen Devon 7 SS7930
Two Dales Derbys 49 SK2763
Twycross Leics 39 SK3304
Twyford Derbys 39 SK3228
Twyford Leics 40 SK7210
Twyford Bucks 30 SP6626
Twyford Hants 10 SU4824
Twyford Berks 22 SU7976
Twyford Norfk 42 TG0123
Twynholm D & G 65 NX6654
Twyning Gloucs 28 SO8936
Twyning Green Gloucs 28 SO9036
Twynllanan Dyfed 26 SN7524
Twywell Nhants 30 SP9578
Ty'n-dwr Clwyd 36 SJ2341
Ty'n-y-groes Gwynd 45 SH7771
Ty-croes Dyfed 17 SN6010
Ty-nant Clwyd 45 SH9944
Tyberton H & W 27 SO3839
Tycrwyn Powys 36 SJ1018
Tydd Gote Lincs 41 TF4518
Tydd St. Giles Cambs 41 TF4216
Tydd St. Mary Lincs 41 TF4418
Tye Green Essex 24 TL5424
Tye Green Essex 24 TL5935
Tyldesley Gt Man 47 SD6802
Tyler Hill Kent 15 TR1461
Tylorstown M Glam 18 ST0095
Tyn-y-nant M Glam 18 ST0685
Tyndrum Cent 80 NN3230
Tynemouth T & W 69 NZ3669
Tyninghame Loth 83 NT6179
Tynron D & G 66 NX8093
Tynygraig Dyfed 35 SN6969
Tyringham Bucks 30 SP8547
Tythegston M Glam 18 SS8578
Tytherington Ches 48 SJ9175
Tytherington Avon 20 ST6688
Tytherington Wilts 20 ST9141
Tytherleigh Devon 8 ST3103
Tywardreath Cnwll 3 SX0854

U

Ubbeston Green Suffk 33 TM3271
Ubley Avon 19 ST5258
Uckerby N York 61 NZ2402
Uckfield E Susx 13 TQ4721
Uckinghall H & W 28 SO8637
Uckington Shrops 37 SJ5709
Uckington Gloucs 28 SO9124
Uddingston Strath 74 NS6960
Uddington Strath 74 NS8633
Udimore E Susx 14 TQ8719
Udny Green Gramp 95 NJ8726
Uffculme Devon 7 ST0612
Uffington Oxon 21 SU3089
Ufford Cambs 40 TF0903
Ufford Suffk 33 TM2952
Ufton Warwks 29 SP3762
Ufton Nervet Berks 21 SU6367
Ugadale Strath 72 NR7828
Ugborough Devon 5 SX6755
Uggeshall Suffk 33 TM4480
Ugglebarnby N York 63 NZ8707
Ughill Derbys 48 SK2590
Ugley Essex 31 TL5228
Ugley Green Essex 31 TL5227
Ugthorpe N York 63 NZ7911
Uig W Isls 102 NB0533
Uig Highld 90 NG1952
Uig Highld 90 NG3963
Uig Strath 78 NM1654
Uigshader Highld 90 NG4346
Uisken Strath 78 NM3919
Ulbster Highld 100 ND3241
Ulcat Row Cumb 59 NY4022
Ulceby Humb 57 TA1014
Ulceby Lincs 51 TF4272
Ulceby Skitter Humb 57 TA1215
Ulcombe Kent 14 TQ8448
Uldale Cumb 58 NY2437
Uley Gloucs 20 ST7898
Ulgham Nthumb 69 NZ2392
Ullapool Highld 96 NH1294
Ullenhall Warwks 28 SP1267
Ulleskelf N York 55 SE5239
Ullesthorpe Leics 39 SP5087

Ulley

Waterloo

Ulley *S York* 49 SK4687
Ullingswick *H & W* 27 SO5949
Ullinish *Highld* 84 NG3237
Ullock *Cumb* 58 NY0724
Ulpha *Cumb* 58 SD1993
Ulrome *Humb* 57 TA1656
Ulsta *Shet* 103 HU4680
Ulverston *Cumb* 58 SD2878
Ulwell *Dorset* 9 SZ0280
Umachan *Highld* 90 NG6050
Umberleigh *Devon* 6 SS6023
Unapool *Highld* 98 NC2333
Under Burnmouth *D & G* 67 NY4783
Under River *Kent* 13 TQ5552
Underbarrow *Cumb* 59 SD4692
Undercliffe *W York* 55 SE1834
Underdale *Shrops* 37 SJ5013
Underwood *Notts* 49 SK4750
Undy *Gwent* 19 ST4386
Union Mills *IOM* 52 SC3577
Unstone *Derbys* 49 SK3777
Up Cerne *Dorset* 9 ST6502
Up Exe *Devon* 7 SS9402
Up Holland *Lancs* 46 SD5205
Up Marden *W Susx* 11 SU7913
Up Mudford *Somset* 8 ST5718
Up Nately *Hants* 22 SU6951
Up Somborne *Hants* 10 SU3932
Up Sydling *Dorset* 9 ST6201
Upavon *Wilts* 20 SU1354
Upchurch *Kent* 14 TQ8467
Upcott *Devon* 7 SS7529
Upcott *Somset* 7 SS9025
Upgate *Norfk* 43 TG1318
Uphall *Loth* 75 NT0671
Uphall *Dorset* 8 ST5502
Upham *Devon* 7 SS8808
Upham *Hants* 11 SU5320
Uphampton *H & W* 27 SO3963
Uphampton *H & W* 28 SO8364
Uphill *Avon* 19 ST3158
Uplawmoor *Strath* 73 NS4355
Upleadon *Gloucs* 28 SO7527
Upleatham *Cleve* 62 NZ6319
Uploders *Dorset* 8 SY5093
Uplowman *Devon* 7 ST0115
Uplyme *Devon* 8 SY3293
Upminster *Gt Lon* 24 TQ5686
Upottery *Devon* 8 ST2007
Upottery *Devon* 8 ST2007
Upper Affcot *Shrops* 36 SO4486
Upper Ardchronie *Highld* 97 NH6188
Upper Arley *H & W* 37 SO7680
Upper Basildon *Berks* 21 SU5976
Upper Beeding *W Susx* 12 TQ1910
Upper Benefield *Nhants* 40 SP9789
Upper Bentley *H & W* 28 SO9966
Upper Bighouse *Highld* 99 NC8856
Upper Boddington *Nhants* 29 SP4852
Upper Brailes *Warwks* 29 SP3039
Upper Breakish *Highld* 85 NG6823
Upper Broadheath *H & W* 28 SO8056
Upper Broughton *Notts* 39 SK6826
Upper Bucklebury *Berks* 21 SU5468
Upper Burgate *Hants* 10 SU1516
Upper Cairn *D & G* 66 NS6912
Upper Caldecote *Beds* 31 TL1645
Upper Catesby *Nhants* 29 SP5259
Upper Chapel *Powys* 26 SO0040
Upper Chicksgrove *Wilts* 9 ST9529
Upper Chute *Wilts* 21 SU2953
Upper Clapton *Gt Lon* 23 TQ3487
Upper Clatford *Hants* 21 SU3543
Upper Coberley *Gloucs* 28 SO9816
Upper Cound *Shrops* 37 SJ5505
Upper Cumberworth *W York* 55 SE2008
Upper Dallachy *Gramp* 94 NJ3662
Upper Deal *Kent* 15 TR3651
Upper Dean *Beds* 30 TL0467
Upper Denby *W York* 55 SE2207
Upper Dicker *E Susx* 13 TQ5509
Upper Dovercourt *Essex* 25 TM2330
Upper Drumbane *Cent* 81 NN6606
Upper Dunsforth *N York* 55 SE4463
Upper Eashing *Surrey* 12 SU9543
Upper Egleton *H & W* 27 SO6344
Upper Elkstone *Staffs* 48 SK0558
Upper Ellastone *Staffs* 48 SK1043
Upper Elmers End *Gt Lon* 23 TQ3667
Upper Ethrie *Highld* 93 NH7662
Upper Farringdon *Hants* 11 SU7135
Upper Framilode *Gloucs* 28 SO7510
Upper Froyle *Hants* 11 SU7543
Upper Godney *Somset* 19 ST4842
Upper Gravenhurst *Beds* 30 TL1136
Upper Green *Berks* 21 SU3763
Upper Green *Essex* 24 TL5935
Upper Hale *Surrey* 22 SU8349
Upper Halliford *Surrey* 22 TQ0968
Upper Hambleton *Leics* 40 SK9007
Upper Harbledown *Kent* 15 TR1158
Upper Hartfield *E Susx* 13 TQ4634
Upper Hatherley *Gloucs* 28 SO9220
Upper Heaton *W York* 55 SE1719
Upper Helmsley *N York* 56 SE6956
Upper Hergest *H & W* 27 SO2654
Upper Heyford *Oxon* 29 SP4925
Upper Heyford *Nhants* 30 SP6659
Upper Hill *H & W* 27 SO4753
Upper Hopton *W York* 55 SE1918
Upper Hulme *Staffs* 48 SK0160
Upper Inglesham *Wilts* 21 SU2096
Upper Keith *Loth* 76 NT4562
Upper Killay *W Glam* 17 SS5892
Upper Kinchrackine *Strath* 80 NN1627
Upper Lambourn *Berks* 21 SU3080
Upper Landywood *Staffs* 38 SJ9805
Upper Langford *Avon* 19 ST4659
Upper Langwith *Derbys* 49 SK5169
Upper Largo *Fife* 83 NO4203
Upper Leigh *Staffs* 38 SK0136
Upper Lochton *Gramp* 89 NO6997
Upper Longdon *Staffs* 38 SK0614
Upper Lybster *Highld* 100 ND2537
Upper Lydbrook *Gloucs* 27 SO6015
Upper Lye *H & W* 27 SO3965
Upper Milton *H & W* 37 SO8172
Upper Minety *Wilts* 20 SU0091
Upper Moor *H & W* 28 SO9747
Upper Mulben *Gramp* 94 NJ3551
Upper Nesbet *Border* 76 NT6727
Upper Netchwood *Shrops* 37 SO6092
Upper Nobut *Staffs* 38 SK0335
Upper Norwood *W Susx* 11 SU9317
Upper Ollach *Highld* 84 NG5136
Upper Pond Street *Essex* 31 TL4636
Upper Poppleton *N York* 56 SE5553
Upper Quinton *Warwks* 29 SP1846
Upper Ratley *Hants* 10 SU3223
Upper Rochford *H & W* 27 SO6367
Upper Ruscoe *D & G* 65 NX5661
Upper Sapey *H & W* 28 SO6863
Upper Seagry *Wilts* 20 ST9480
Upper Shelton *Beds* 30 SP9843
Upper Sheringham *Norfk* 43 TG1441
Upper Slaughter *Gloucs* 28 SP1523
Upper Soudley *Gloucs* 27 SO6510
Upper Standen *Kent* 15 TR2139
Upper Stepford *D & G* 66 NX8681
Upper Stoke *Norfk* 43 TG2502
Upper Stondon *Beds* 30 TL1435
Upper Stowe *Nhants* 29 SP6456
Upper Street *Hants* 10 SU1518
Upper Street *Norfk* 43 TG3217
Upper Street *Norfk* 43 TG3616
Upper Street *Suffk* 32 TL7851
Upper Street *Suffk* 33 TM1050
Upper Sundon *Beds* 30 TL0428
Upper Swell *Gloucs* 29 SP1726
Upper Tasburgh *Norfk* 43 TM2095
Upper Tean *Staffs* 48 SK0139
Upper Town *Derbys* 48 SK2361
Upper Town *H & W* 27 SO5848
Upper Town *Avon* 19 ST5265
Upper Town *Suffk* 32 TL9267
Upper Tysoe *Warwks* 29 SP3343
Upper Victoria *Tays* 83 NO5336
Upper Wardington *Oxon* 29 SP4945
Upper Weedon *Nhants* 29 SP6258
Upper Wellingham *E Susx* 13 TQ4313
Upper Weybread *Suffk* 33 TM2379
Upper Wield *Hants* 11 SU6238
Upper Winchendon *Bucks* 30 SP7414
Upper Woodford *Wilts* 10 SU1237
Upper Wraxall *Wilts* 20 ST8074
Upperby *Cumb* 67 NY4153
Upperglen *Highld* 90 NG3151
Uppermill *Gt Man* 54 SD9905
Upperthong *W York* 55 SE1208
Upperton *W Susx* 12 SU9522
Uppertown *Highld* 100 ND3576
Uppingham *Leics* 40 SP8699
Uppington *Shrops* 37 SJ5909
Upsall *N York* 62 SE4586
Upsettlington *Border* 77 NT8846
Upshire *Essex* 23 TL4101
Upshire *Essex* 23 TL4101
Upstreet *Kent* 15 TR2263
Upton *W York* 55 SE4713
Upton *Mersyd* 46 SJ2788
Upton *Ches* 46 SJ4069
Upton *Notts* 50 SK7354
Upton *Notts* 50 SK7476
Upton *Lincs* 50 SK8686
Upton *Leics* 39 SP3699
Upton *Bucks* 22 SP7711
Upton *Somset* 7 SS9928
Upton *Devon* 7 ST0902
Upton *Somset* 8 ST4526
Upton *Hants* 21 SU3555
Upton *Hants* 10 SU3716
Upton *Oxon* 21 SU5187
Upton *Berks* 22 SU9779
Upton *Cnwll* 4 SX2772
Upton *Devon* 5 SX7043
Upton *Dorset* 9 SY7483
Upton *Dorset* 9 SY9893
Upton *Cambs* 40 TF1000
Upton *Norfk* 43 TG3912
Upton *Cambs* 31 TL1778
Upton Cheyney *Avon* 20 ST6970
Upton Cressett *Shrops* 37 SO6592
Upton Crews *H & W* 27 SO6527
Upton Cross *Cnwll* 4 SX2872
Upton Grey *Hants* 22 SU6948
Upton Hellions *Devon* 7 SS8403
Upton Lovell *Wilts* 20 ST9440
Upton Magna *Shrops* 37 SJ5512
Upton Noble *Somset* 20 ST7139
Upton Pyne *Devon* 7 SX9198
Upton Scudamore *Wilts* 20 ST8647
Upton Snodsbury *H & W* 28 SO9454
Upton St. Leonards *Gloucs* 28 SO8615
Upton Warren *H & W* 28 SO9267
Upton upon Severn *H & W* 28 SO8540
Upwaltham *W Susx* 12 SU9413
Upwell *Norfk* 41 TF4902
Upwick Green *Herts* 31 TL4524
Upwood *Cambs* 41 TL2582
Urchfont *Wilts* 20 SU0357
Urmston *Gt Man* 47 SJ7694
Urquhart *Gramp* 94 NJ2862
Urra *N York* 62 NZ5601
Urray *Highld* 92 NH5052
Ushaw Moor *Dur* 61 NZ2242
Usk *Gwent* 19 SO3700
Usselby *Lincs* 50 TF0993
Usworth *T & W* 69 NZ3057
Utley *W York* 55 SE0542
Uton *Devon* 7 SX8298
Utterby *Lincs* 51 TF3093
Uttoxeter *Staffs* 38 SK0933
Uxbridge *Gt Lon* 22 TQ0584
Uyeasound *Shet* 103 HP5901
Uzmaston *Dyfed* 16 SM9714

V

Vale *Guern* 101 GN0000
Valley End *Surrey* 22 SU9564
Valtos *W Isls* 102 NB0936
Valtos *Highld* 90 NG5163
Vange *Essex* 24 TQ7186
Vatsetter *Shet* 103 HU5389
Vatten *Highld* 90 NG2843
Vaynor *M Glam* 26 SO0410
Velindre *Powys* 27 SO1836
Venn Ottery *Devon* 8 SY0891
Venngreen *Devon* 6 SS3711
Ventnor *IOW* 11 SZ5677
Venton *Devon* 5 SX5956
Vernham Dean *Hants* 21 SU3356
Vernham Street *Hants* 21 SU3457
Verwood *Dorset* 10 SU0809
Veryan *Cnwll* 3 SW9139
Vickerstown *Cumb* 53 SD1868
Victoria *Cnwll* 3 SW9861
Vidlin *Shet* 103 HU4765
Viewfield *Gramp* 94 NJ2864
Viewpark *Strath* 74 NS7061
Vigo *Kent* 14 TQ6361
Ville la Bas *Jersey* 101 JS0000
Villiaze *Guern* 101 GN0000
Vine's Cross *E Susx* 13 TQ5917
Virginia Water *Surrey* 22 TQ0067
Virginstow *Devon* 4 SX3792
Vobster *Somset* 20 ST7048
Voe *Shet* 103 HU4062
Vowchurch *H & W* 27 SO3636

W

Wackerfield *Dur* 61 NZ1522
Wacton *Norfk* 33 TM1791
Wadborough *H & W* 28 SO9047
Waddesdon *Bucks* 30 SP7416
Waddeton *Devon* 5 SX8756
Waddingham *Lincs* 50 SK9896
Waddington *Lancs* 54 SD7343
Waddington *Lancs* 54 SD7343
Waddington *Lincs* 50 SK9764
Waddon *Dorset* 9 SY6285
Wadebridge *Cnwll* 3 SW9972
Wadeford *Somset* 8 ST3110
Wadenhoe *Nhants* 40 TL0183
Wadesmill *Herts* 31 TL3617
Wadhurst *E Susx* 13 TQ6431
Wadshelf *Derbys* 49 SK3170
Wadworth *S York* 49 SK5696
Wainfleet All Saints *Lincs* 51 TF4959
Wainhouse Corner *Cnwll* 6 SX1895
Wainscott *Kent* 14 TQ7470
Wainstalls *W York* 55 SE0428
Waitby *Cumb* 60 NY7508
Waithe *Lincs* 51 TA2800
Wakefield *W York* 55 SE3320
Wakerley *Nhants* 40 SP9599
Wakes Colne *Essex* 24 TL8928
Walberswick *Suffk* 33 TM4974
Walberton *W Susx* 12 SU9705
Walbutt *D & G* 65 NX7468
Walcombe *Somset* 19 ST5546
Walcot *Shrops* 37 SJ5912
Walcot *Wilts* 20 SU1684
Walcot *Lincs* 40 TF0635
Walcot *Lincs* 50 TF1356
Walcot Green *Norfk* 33 TM1280
Walcote *Leics* 39 SP5683
Walcott *Norfk* 43 TG3532
Walden Stubbs *N York* 56 SE5516
Walderslade *Kent* 14 TQ7663
Walderton *W Susx* 11 SU7910
Walditch *Dorset* 8 SY4892
Waldridge *Dur* 69 NZ2549
Waldringfield *Suffk* 33 TM2845
Waldron *E Susx* 13 TQ5419
Wales *S York* 49 SK4882
Wales *Somset* 9 ST5824
Walesby *Notts* 49 SK6870
Walesby *Lincs* 50 TF1392
Walford *H & W* 36 SO3872
Walford *H & W* 27 SO5820
Walford Heath *Shrops* 36 SJ4419
Walgherton *Ches* 47 SJ6948
Walgrave *Nhants* 30 SP8071
Walk Mill *Lancs* 54 SD8729
Walkden *Gt Man* 47 SD7302
Walker *T & W* 69 NZ2864
Walker's Green *H & W* 27 SO5247
Walkerburn *Border* 76 NT3637
Walkeringham *Notts* 50 SK7792
Walkerith *Notts* 50 SK7892
Walkern *Herts* 31 TL2826
Walkerton *Fife* 83 NO2301
Walkhampton *Devon* 4 SX5369
Walkington *Humb* 56 SE9936
Walkley *S York* 49 SK3388
Walkwood *H & W* 28 SP0364
Wall *Border* 76 NT4622
Wall *Nthumb* 68 NY9168
Wall *Staffs* 38 SK1006
Wallacetown *Strath* 73 NS2703
Wallacetown *Strath* 73 NS3422
Wallands Park *E Susx* 13 TQ4010
Wallasey *Mersyd* 46 SJ2992
Wallfield *Fife* 82 NO1909
Wallingford *Oxon* 21 SU6089
Wallington *Hants* 11 SU5806
Wallington *Herts* 31 TL2933
Wallington *Gt Lon* 23 TQ2864
Wallisdown *Dorset* 10 SZ0694
Walls *Shet* 103 HU2449
Wallsend *T & W* 69 NZ2966
Wallyford *Loth* 76 NT3671
Walmer *Kent* 15 TR3750
Walmer Bridge *Lancs* 53 SD4724
Walpole *Suffk* 33 TM3674
Walpole Cross Keys *Norfk* 41 TF5119
Walpole Highway *Norfk* 41 TF5114
Walpole St. Andrew *Norfk* 41 TF5017
Walpole St. Peter *Norfk* 41 TF5016
Walsall *W Mids* 38 SP0198
Walsden *W York* 54 SD9321
Walsham le Willows *Suffk* 32 TM0071
Walshaw *W York* 54 SD9731
Walshford *N York* 55 SE4153
Walsoken *Norfk* 41 TF4710
Walston *Strath* 75 NT0545
Walsworth *Herts* 31 TL1930
Waltham *Humb* 57 TA2603
Waltham *Kent* 15 TR1048
Waltham Abbey *Essex* 23 TL3800
Waltham Chase *Hants* 11 SU5614
Waltham Cross *Herts* 23 TL3600
Waltham St. Lawrence *Berks* 22 SU8276
Waltham on the Wolds *Leics* 40 SK8024
Walthamstow *Gt Lon* 23 TQ3689
Walton *Cumb* 67 NY5264
Walton *W York* 55 SE3516
Walton *W York* 55 SE4447
Walton *Shrops* 37 SJ5818
Walton *Derbys* 49 SK3568
Walton *Powys* 27 SO2559
Walton *Leics* 39 SP5987
Walton *Bucks* 30 SP8936
Walton *Somset* 19 ST4636
Walton *W Susx* 11 SU8104
Walton *Suffk* 25 TM2935
Walton Cardiff *Gloucs* 28 SO9032
Walton East *Dyfed* 16 SN0223
Walton Elm *Dorset* 9 ST7717
Walton Lower Street *Suffk* 25 TM2834
Walton Park *Avon* 19 ST4172
Walton West *Dyfed* 16 SM8612
Walton on the Hill *Surrey* 23 TQ2255
Walton on the Naze *Essex* 25 TM2522
Walton on the Wolds *Leics* 39 SK5919
Walton-in-Gordano *Avon* 19 ST4273
Walton-on-Thames *Surrey* 22 TQ1066
Walton-on-Trent *Derbys* 39 SK2118
Walton-on-the-Hill *Staffs* 38 SJ9520
Walworth *Dur* 61 NZ2318
Walwyn's Castle *Dyfed* 16 SM8711
Wambrook *Somset* 8 ST2907
Wamphray *D & G* 67 NY1295
Wanborough *Wilts* 21 SU2082
Wanborough *Surrey* 22 SU9348
Wandel *Strath* 75 NS9427
Wangford *Suffk* 33 TM4679
Wanlip *Leics* 39 SK5910
Wanlockhead *D & G* 66 NS8712
Wannock *E Susx* 13 TQ5703
Wansford *Humb* 57 TA0656
Wansford *Cambs* 40 TL0799
Wanshurst Green *Kent* 14 TQ7645
Wanstead *Gt Lon* 23 TQ4088
Wanstrow *Somset* 20 ST7141
Wanswell *Gloucs* 20 SO6801
Wantage *Oxon* 21 SU3988
Wapley *Avon* 20 ST7179
Wappenbury *Warwks* 29 SP3769
Wappenham *Nhants* 29 SP6245
Warbister *Ork* 103 HY3932
Warbleton *E Susx* 13 TQ6018
Warborough *Oxon* 21 SU5993
Warboys *Cambs* 41 TL3080
Warbreck *Lancs* 53 SD3238
Warbstow *Cnwll* 4 SX2090
Warburton *Gt Man* 47 SJ7089
Warcop *Cumb* 60 NY7415
Warden *Nthumb* 68 NY9166
Wardington *Oxon* 29 SP4846
Wardle *Gt Man* 54 SD9116
Wardle *Ches* 47 SJ6156
Wardley *Leics* 40 SK8300
Wardlow *Derbys* 48 SK1874
Wardy Hill *Cambs* 41 TL4782
Ware *Herts* 31 TL3514
Wareham *Dorset* 9 SY9287
Warehorne *Kent* 15 TQ9832
Warenford *Nthumb* 77 NU1328
Wareside *Herts* 31 TL3915
Waresley *Cambs* 31 TL2554
Warfield *Berks* 22 SU8872
Warfleet *Devon* 5 SX8750
Wargrave *Berks* 22 SU7978
Warham All Saints *Norfk* 42 TF9541
Warham St. Mary *Norfk* 42 TF9441
Wark *Nthumb* 77 NT8238
Wark *Nthumb* 68 NY8577
Warkleigh *Devon* 7 SS6422
Warkton *Nhants* 40 SP8979
Warkworth *Nthumb* 69 NU2406
Warkworth *Nhants* 29 SP4840
Warlaby *N York* 62 SE3491
Warleggan *Cnwll* 3 SX1569
Warley Town *W York* 55 SE0524
Warlingham *Surrey* 23 TQ3658
Warmanbie *D & G* 67 NY1969
Warmfield *W York* 55 SE3720
Warmingham *Ches* 47 SJ7061
Warmington *Warwks* 29 SP4147
Warmington *Nhants* 40 TL0790
Warminster *Wilts* 20 ST8745
Warmley *Avon* 20 ST6673
Warmsworth *S York* 49 SE5400
Warmwell *Dorset* 9 SY7585
Warnford *Hants* 11 SU6223
Warnham *W Susx* 12 TQ1533
Warningcamp *W Susx* 12 TQ0307
Warninglid *W Susx* 12 TQ2426
Warren *Ches* 47 SJ8870
Warren *Dyfed* 16 SR9397
Warren Row *Berks* 22 SU8180
Warren Street *Kent* 14 TQ9252
Warrenhill *Strath* 75 NS9438
Warrington *Ches* 47 SJ6088
Warrington *Bucks* 30 SP8953
Warriston *Loth* 75 NT2575
Warsash *Hants* 10 SU4906
Warslow *Staffs* 48 SK0858
Warsop *Notts* 49 SK5667
Warter *Humb* 56 SE8750
Warthermaske *N York* 61 SE2078
Warthill *N York* 56 SE6755
Wartling *E Susx* 13 TQ6509
Wartnaby *Leics* 40 SK7123
Warton *Lancs* 53 SD4128
Warton *Lancs* 53 SD4972
Warton *Warwks* 39 SK2803
Warwick *Cumb* 67 NY4656
Warwick *Warwks* 29 SP2865
Wasdale Head *Cumb* 58 NY1808
Washaway *Cnwll* 3 SX0369
Washbourne *Devon* 5 SX7954
Washbrook *Suffk* 33 TM1142
Washfield *Devon* 7 SS9315
Washfold *N York* 61 NZ0502
Washford *Somset* 7 ST0541
Washford Pyne *Devon* 7 SS8111
Washingborough *Lincs* 50 TF0170
Washington *T & W* 69 NZ3155
Washington *W Susx* 12 TQ1112
Wasperton *Warwks* 29 SP2658
Wass *N York* 62 SE5579
Watchet *Somset* 7 ST0743
Watchfield *Oxon* 21 SU2490
Watchgate *Cumb* 59 SD5299
Water *Devon* 5 SX7580
Water Eaton *Oxon* 29 SP5112
Water End *Humb* 56 SE7938
Water End *Herts* 22 TL0310
Water End *Essex* 31 TL5840
Water Newton *Cambs* 40 TL1097
Water Orton *Warwks* 38 SP1790
Water Stratford *Bucks* 29 SP6534
Waterbeach *W Susx* 11 SU8908
Waterbeach *Cambs* 31 TL4965
Waterbeck *D & G* 67 NY2477
Watercombe *Dorset* 9 SY7585
Waterfall *Staffs* 48 SK0851
Waterfoot *Strath* 74 NS5655
Waterford *Herts* 31 TL3114
Watergate *Cnwll* 3 SX1181
Waterhead *Strath* 73 NS5411
Waterheads *Border* 75 NT2451
Waterhouses *Staffs* 48 SK0850
Wateringbury *Kent* 14 TQ6853
Waterloo *Highld* 85 NG6623
Waterloo *Tays* 82 NO0537

Waterloo

Wetherden

Waterloo Strath 74 NS8154
Waterloo Mersyd 46 SJ3298
Waterloo Dyfed 16 SM9803
Waterlooville Hants 11 SU6809
Watermillock Cumb 59 NY4422
Waterperry Oxon 29 SP6206
Waterrow Somset 7 ST0525
Waters Upton Shrops 37 SJ6319
Watersfield W Susx 12 TQ0115
Waterside Strath 73 NS4308
Waterside Strath 73 NS4843
Waterside Strath 74 NS6773
Waterside Lancs 54 SD7123
Waterstock Oxon 29 SP6305
Waterston Dyfed 16 SM9305
Watford Nhants 29 SP6069
Watford Herts 22 TQ1196
Wath N York 55 SE1467
Wath N York 62 SE3277
Wath upon Dearne S York 49 SE4300
Watlington Oxon 22 SU6894
Watlington Norfk 41 TF6111
Watten Highld 100 ND2454
Wattisfield Suffk 32 TM0074
Wattisham Suffk 32 TM0151
Watton Dorset 8 SY4591
Watton Humb 56 TA0150
Watton Norfk 42 TF9100
Watton-at-Stone Herts 31 TL3019
Wattsville Gwent 19 ST2091
Wauldby Humb 56 SE9629
Waulkmill Gramp 89 NO6492
Waunarlwydd W Glam 17 SS6095
Waunfawr Gwynd 44 SH5259
Waunfawr Dyfed 34 SN6081
Wavendon Bucks 30 SP9137
Waverbridge Cumb 67 NY2249
Waverton Cumb 67 NY2247
Waverton Ches 46 SJ4663
Wawne Humb 57 TA0936
Waxham Norfk 43 TG4426
Way Village Devon 7 SS8810
Wayford Somset 8 ST4006
Waytown Dorset 8 SY4797
Weacombe Somset 18 ST1140
Weald Oxon 21 SP3002
Wealdstone Gt Lon 22 TQ1589
Wear Head Dur 60 NY8539
Weardley W York 55 SE2944
Weardley W York 55 SE2944
Weare Somset 19 ST4152
Weare Giffard Devon 6 SS4721
Wearne Somset 8 ST4228
Weasenham All Saints Norfk 42 TF8421
Weasenham St. Peter Norfk 42 TF8522
Weasle Gt Man 47 SJ8098
Weaverham Ches 47 SJ6174
Weaverthorpe N York 56 SE9670
Webheath H & W 28 SP0266
Wedderlairs Gramp 95 NJ8532
Weddington Warwks 39 SP3693
Wedhampton Wilts 20 SU0557
Wedmore Somset 19 ST4347
Wednesbury W Mids 38 SO9895
Wednesfield W Mids 38 SJ9400
Weedon Bucks 30 SP8118
Weedon Lois Nhants 29 SP6046
Weeford Staffs 38 SK1403
Week Somset 7 SS9133
Week St. Mary Cnwll 6 SX2397
Weeke Hants 10 SU4630
Weekley Nhants 40 SP8881
Weel Humb 57 TA0639
Weeley Essex 25 TM1422
Weeley Heath Essex 25 TM1520
Weem Tays 87 NN8449
Weethley Hamlet Warwks 28 SP0555
Weeting Norfk 32 TL7788
Weeton Lancs 53 SD3834
Weeton W York 55 SE2847
Weeton Humb 57 TA3520
Weetwood W York 55 SE2737
Weir Lancs 54 SD8625
Weir Quay Devon 4 SX4365
Welborne Norfk 42 TG0610
Welbourn Lincs 50 SK9654
Welburn N York 56 SE7267
Welbury N York 62 NZ3902
Welby Lincs 40 SK9738
Welches Dam Cambs 41 TL4686
Welcombe Devon 6 SS2318
Welford Nhants 39 SP6480
Welford Berks 21 SU4073
Welford-on-Avon Warwks 28 SP1452
Welham Notts 49 SK7281
Welham Leics 40 SP7692
Welham Green Herts 23 TL2305
Well N York 61 SE2681
Well N York 61 SE2681
Well Hants 22 SU7646
Well Lincs 51 TF4473
Well Head Herts 31 TL1727
Welland H & W 28 SO7940
Wellbank Tays 83 NO4737
Wellbury Herts 30 TL1329
Wellesbourne Warwks 29 SP2855
Welling Gt Lon 23 TQ4675
Wellingborough Nhants 30 SP8967
Wellingham Norfk 42 TF8722
Wellingore Lincs 50 SK9856
Wellington Cumb 58 NY0704
Wellington Shrops 37 SJ6511
Wellington H & W 27 SO4948
Wellington Somset 8 ST1320
Wellington Heath H & W 28 SO7140
Wellow Notts 49 SK6766
Wellow Avon 20 ST7458
Wellow IOW 10 SZ3888
Wells Somset 19 ST5445
Wells-Next-The-Sea Norfk 42 TF9143
Wellstye Green Essex 24 TL6318
Welltree Tays 82 NN9622
Wellwood Fife 82 NT0988
Welney Norfk 41 TL5293
Welsh Frankton Shrops 36 SJ3533
Welsh Newton H & W 27 SO5017
Welsh St. Donats S Glam 18 ST0276
Welshampton Shrops 36 SJ4335
Welshpool Powys 36 SJ2207
Welton Cumb 67 NY3544
Welton Humb 56 SE9627
Welton Nhants 29 SP5865
Welton Lincs 50 TF0179
Welton le Marsh Lincs 51 TF4768
Welton le Wold Lincs 51 TF2787
Welwick Humb 57 TA3421
Welwyn Herts 31 TL2316
Welwyn Garden City Herts 31 TL2312
Wem Shrops 37 SJ5128
Wembdon Somset 19 ST2837
Wembley Gt Lon 23 TQ1885
Wembury Devon 4 SX5248
Wembworthy Devon 7 SS6609
Wemyss Bay Strath 73 NS1969
Wendens Ambo Essex 31 TL5136
Wendlebury Oxon 29 SP5619
Wendlebury Oxon 29 SP5619
Wendling Norfk 42 TF9312
Wendover Bucks 22 SP8607
Wendron Cnwll 2 SW6731
Wendy Cambs 31 TL3247
Wenhaston Suffk 33 TM4275
Wennington Lancs 54 SD6170
Wennington Cambs 41 TL2379
Wensley N York 61 SE0989
Wensley Derbys 49 SK2661
Wentbridge W York 55 SE4817
Wentnor Shrops 36 SO3892
Wentworth S York 49 SK3898
Wentworth Cambs 31 TL4878
Wenvoe S Glam 18 ST1272
Weobley H & W 27 SO4051
Weobley Marsh H & W 27 SO4151
Wepham W Susx 12 TQ0408
Wereham Norfk 42 TF6801
Werrington Cnwll 4 SX3287
Werrington Cambs 40 TF1603
Wervin Ches 46 SJ4271
Wesham Lancs 53 SD4133
Wessington Derbys 49 SK3757
West Acre Norfk 42 TF7815
West Alvington Devon 5 SX7243
West Anstey Devon 7 SS8527
West Appleton N York 61 SE2294
West Ashby Lincs 51 TF2672
West Ashling W Susx 11 SU8107
West Ashton Wilts 20 ST8755
West Auckland Dur 61 NZ1826
West Ayton N York 63 SE9884
West Bagborough Somset 8 ST1733
West Bank Ches 46 SJ5183
West Barkwith Lincs 50 TF1580
West Barnby N York 63 NZ8212
West Barns Loth 83 NT6578
West Barsham Norfk 42 TF9033
West Bay Dorset 8 SY4690
West Beckham Norfk 43 TG1439
West Bedfont Surrey 22 TQ0674
West Bergholt Essex 25 TL9527
West Bexington Dorset 8 SY5386
West Bilney Norfk 42 TF7115
West Blatchington E Susx 12 TQ2707
West Boldon T & W 69 NZ3561
West Bourton Dorset 9 ST7629
West Bowling W York 55 SE1630
West Brabourne Kent 15 TR0842
West Bradenham Norfk 42 TF9108
West Bradford Lancs 54 SD7444
West Bradley Somset 19 ST5536
West Bretton W York 55 SE2813
West Bridgford Notts 39 SK5836
West Bromwich W Mids 38 SP0091
West Buccleigh Hotel Border 67 NT3214
West Buckland Devon 7 SS6531
West Burnside Gramp 89 NO7070
West Burton N York 61 SE0186
West Butterwick Humb 56 SE8305
West Cairngaan D & G 64 NX1231
West Caister Norfk 43 TG5011
West Calder Loth 75 NT0163
West Camel Somset 8 ST5724
West Chaldon Dorset 9 SY7782
West Challow Oxon 21 SU3688
West Charleton Devon 5 SX7542
West Chelborough Dorset 8 ST5405
West Chevington Nthumb 69 NZ2297
West Chiltington W Susx 12 TQ0818
West Chinnock Somset 8 ST4613
West Cliffe Kent 15 TR3444
West Coker Somset 8 ST5113
West Compton Somset 19 ST5942
West Compton Dorset 8 SY5694
West Cottingwith N York 56 SE6942
West Cowick Humb 56 SE6421
West Craigneuk Strath 74 NS7765
West Cross W Glam 17 SS6189
West Curthwaite Cumb 67 NY3249
West Dean Wilts 10 SU2526
West Dean W Susx 11 SU8612
West Deeping Lincs 40 TF1008
West Derby Mersyd 46 SJ3993
West Dereham Norfk 42 TF6500
West Down Devon 6 SS5142
West Drayton Notts 49 SK7074
West Drayton Gt Lon 22 TQ0579
West Dunnet Highld 100 ND2171
West Ella Humb 56 TA0029
West End Beds 30 SP9853
West End Avon 19 ST4569
West End Wilts 9 ST9824
West End Wilts 9 ST9824
West End Hants 10 SU4614
West End Berks 22 SU8275
West End Surrey 22 SU9461
West End Norfk 43 TG5011
West End Herts 23 TL2608
West End Herts 23 TL3306
West End Surrey 22 TQ1263
West End Green Hants 22 SU6661
West Farleigh Kent 14 TQ7152
West Farndon Nhants 29 SP5251
West Felton Shrops 36 SJ3425
West Firle E Susx 13 TQ4707
West Grafton Wilts 21 SU2460
West Green Hants 22 SU7456
West Grimstead Wilts 10 SU2026
West Grinstead W Susx 12 TQ1720
West Haddlesey N York 56 SE5626
West Haddon Nhants 39 SP6371
West Hagbourne Oxon 21 SU5187
West Hagley H & W 38 SO9080
West Hallam Derbys 49 SK4341
West Halton Humb 56 SE9020
West Ham Gt Lon 23 TQ3983
West Handley Derbys 49 SK3977
West Hanney Oxon 21 SU4092
West Hanningfield Essex 24 TQ7399
West Harnham Wilts 10 SU1329
West Harptree Avon 19 ST5556
West Harting W Susx 11 SU7820
West Hatch Somset 8 ST2821
West Hatch Wilts 9 ST9227
West Heath W Mids 38 SP0277
West Helmsdale Highld 97 ND0115
West Hendred Oxon 21 SU4488
West Heslerton N York 63 SE9176
West Hewish Avon 19 ST3963
West Hill Devon 7 SY0794
West Hoathly W Susx 12 TQ3632
West Holme Dorset 9 SY8885
West Horrington Somset 19 ST5747
West Horsley Surrey 12 TQ0752
West Hougham Kent 15 TR2640
West Howe Dorset 10 SZ0595
West Huntspill Somset 19 ST3044
West Hythe Kent 15 TR1234
West Ilsley Berks 21 SU4782
West Itchenor W Susx 11 SU7901
West Kennet Wilts 20 SU1168
West Kilbride Strath 73 NS2048
West Kingsdown Kent 14 TQ5763
West Kington Wilts 20 ST8077
West Kirby Mersyd 46 SJ2186
West Knapton N York 63 SE8775
West Knighton Dorset 9 SY7387
West Knoyle Wilts 9 ST8632
West Lambrook Somset 8 ST4118
West Langdon Kent 15 TR3247
West Laroch Highld 86 NN0758
West Lavington Wilts 20 SU0052
West Lavington W Susx 11 SU8920
West Layton N York 61 NZ1410
West Leake Notts 39 SK5226
West Leigh Devon 7 SS6805
West Leigh Somset 8 ST1230
West Leigh Devon 5 SX7557
West Lexham Norfk 42 TF8417
West Lilling N York 56 SE6465
West Linton Border 75 NT1551
West Littleton Avon 20 ST7675
West Lockinge Oxon 21 SU4187
West Lulworth Dorset 9 SY8280
West Lutton N York 56 SE9369
West Lydford Somset 8 ST5631
West Lyng Somset 8 ST3128
West Lynn Norfk 41 TF6120
West Malling Kent 14 TQ6757
West Malvern H & W 28 SO7646
West Marden W Susx 11 SU7713
West Markham Notts 49 SK7272
West Marsh Humb 57 TA2509
West Marton N York 54 SD8950
West Melbury Dorset 9 ST8720
West Meon Hants 11 SU6423
West Mersea Essex 25 TM0112
West Milton Dorset 8 SY5096
West Minster Kent 14 TQ9073
West Monkton Somset 8 ST2628
West Moors Dorset 10 SU0802
West Morden Dorset 9 SY9095
West Mudford Somset 8 ST5620
West Ness N York 62 SE6879
West Newton Somset 8 ST2829
West Newton Humb 57 TA2037
West Newton Norfk 42 TF6928
West Norwood Gt Lon 23 TQ3171
West Ogwell Devon 5 SX8270
West Orchard Dorset 9 ST8216
West Overton Wilts 20 SU1267
West Parley Dorset 10 SZ0896
West Peckham Kent 13 TQ6452
West Pelton Dur 69 NZ2353
West Pennard Somset 19 ST5438
West Pentire Cnwll 2 SW7760
West Perry Cambs 30 TL1466
West Preston W Susx 12 TQ0602
West Pulham Dorset 9 ST7008
West Putford Devon 6 SS3616
West Quantoxhead Somset 18 ST1141
West Raddon Devon 7 SS8902
West Rainton T & W 69 NZ3246
West Rasen Lincs 50 TF0689
West Raynham Norfk 42 TF8725
West Rounton N York 62 NZ4103
West Row Suffk 32 TL6775
West Rudham Norfk 42 TF8127
West Runton Norfk 43 TG1842
West Saltoun Loth 76 NT4667
West Sandford Devon 7 SS8102
West Sandwick Shet 103 HU4588
West Scrafton N York 61 SE0783
West Stafford Dorset 9 SY7289
West Stoke W Susx 11 SU8208
West Stour Dorset 9 ST7822
West Stourmouth Kent 15 TR2562
West Stow Suffk 32 TL8171
West Stowell Wilts 20 SU1361
West Street Suffk 32 TL9871
West Tanfield N York 61 SE2678
West Taphouse Cnwll 3 SX1463
West Tarbert Strath 71 NR8467
West Tarring W Susx 12 TQ1103
West Thorney W Susx 11 SU7602
West Thorpe Notts 39 SK6225
West Thurrock Essex 24 TQ5877
West Tilbury Essex 24 TQ6678
West Tisted Hants 11 SU6529
West Torrington Lincs 50 TF1381
West Town Avon 19 ST4868
West Town Hants 11 SZ7199
West Town Hants 11 SZ7199
West Tytherley Hants 10 SU2729
West Tytherton Wilts 20 ST9474
West Walton Norfk 41 TF4613
West Walton Highway Norfk 41 TF4913
West Wellow Hants 10 SU2819
West Wembury Devon 4 SX5249
West Wemyss Fife 83 NT3294
West Wick Avon 19 ST3761
West Wickham Cambs 31 TL6149
West Wickham Gt Lon 23 TQ3766
West Williamston Dyfed 16 SN0305
West Winch Norfk 41 TF6316
West Winterslow Wilts 10 SU2331
West Wittering W Susx 11 SZ7898
West Witton N York 61 SE0588
West Woodburn Nthumb 68 NY8987
West Woodhay Berks 21 SU3963
West Worldham Hants 11 SU7436
West Worthing W Susx 12 TQ1302
West Wratting Essex 31 TL6052
West Youlstone Cnwll 6 SS2615
Westbere Kent 15 TR1961
Westborough Lincs 50 SK8544
Westbourne W Susx 11 SU7507
Westbrook Berks 21 SU4272
Westbrook Kent 15 TR3470
Westbury Shrops 36 SJ3509
Westbury Bucks 29 SP6235
Westbury Wilts 20 ST8751
Westbury Leigh Wilts 20 ST8649
Westbury on Severn Gloucs 28 SO7114
Westbury-on-Trym Avon 19 ST5777
Westbury-sub-Mendip Somset 19 ST5049
Westby Lancs 53 SD3831
Westcliff-on-Sea Essex 24 TQ8685
Westcombe Somset 20 ST6739
Westcote Gloucs 29 SP2120
Westcott Bucks 30 SP7116
Westcott Devon 7 ST0204
Westcott Surrey 12 TQ1448
Westcott Barton Oxon 29 SP4325
Westcourt Wilts 21 SU2261
Westdean E Susx 13 TV5299
Westdowns Cnwll 3 SX0582
Wester Drumashie Highld 92 NH6032
Wester Essenside Border 76 NT4320
Wester Ochiltree Loth 75 NT0374
Wester Pitkierie Fife 83 NO5505
Westerdale Highld 100 ND1251
Westerdale N York 62 NZ6605
Westerfield Suffk 33 TM1747
Westergate W Susx 11 SU9305
Westerham Kent 23 TQ4454
Westerhope T & W 69 NZ1966
Westerland Devon 5 SX8662
Westerleigh Avon 20 ST6979
Westerton Tays 89 NO6754
Westfield Loth 75 NS9472
Westfield D & G 58 NX9926
Westfield Avon 20 ST6753
Westfield Norfk 42 TF9909
Westfield E Susx 14 TQ8115
Westfields of Rattray Tays 88 NO1746
Westgate Dur 60 NY9038
Westgate Humb 56 SE7707
Westgate Norfk 42 TF9740
Westgate on Sea Kent 15 TR3270
Westhall Gramp 95 NJ6726
Westhall Suffk 33 TM4280
Westham Somset 19 ST4046
Westham Dorset 9 SY6679
Westham E Susx 13 TQ6404
Westhampnett W Susx 11 SU8806
Westhay Somset 19 ST4342
Westhide H & W 27 SO5843
Westhill Gramp 95 NJ8307
Westhope H & W 27 SO4651
Westhope Shrops 37 SO4786
Westhorpe Lincs 41 TF2231
Westhorpe Suffk 32 TM0468
Westhoughton Gt Man 47 SD6506
Westhouse N York 60 SD6773
Westhouses Derbys 49 SK4157
Westhumble Surrey 12 TQ1651
Westlake Devon 5 SX6253
Westleigh Devon 6 SS4728
Westleigh Devon 7 ST0617
Westleton Suffk 33 TM4369
Westley Suffk 32 TL8264
Westley Waterless Cambs 31 TL6156
Westlington Bucks 22 SP7610
Westlinton Cumb 67 NY3964
Westmarsh Kent 15 TR2761
Westmeston E Susx 12 TQ3313
Westmill Herts 31 TL3627
Westmuir Tays 88 NO3652
Westnewton Cumb 67 NY1344
Westoe T & W 69 NZ3765
Weston W York 55 SE1747
Weston Shrops 36 SJ2927
Weston Shrops 37 SJ5629
Weston Ches 47 SJ7352
Weston Staffs 38 SJ9726
Weston Notts 50 SK7767
Weston Nhants 29 SP5846
Weston Devon 8 ST1400
Weston Avon 20 ST7366
Weston Berks 21 SU3973
Weston Hants 11 SU7221
Weston Devon 8 SY1688
Weston Lincs 41 TF2924
Weston Herts 31 TL2530
Weston Beggard H & W 27 SO5841
Weston Colley Hants 10 SU5039
Weston Colville Cambs 31 TL6153
Weston Corbett Hants 22 SU6846
Weston Coyney Staffs 48 SJ9343
Weston Favell Nhants 30 SP7962
Weston Green Cambs 32 TL6252
Weston Heath Shrops 37 SJ7713
Weston Jones Staffs 37 SJ7624
Weston Longville Norfk 43 TG1115
Weston Lullingfields Shrops 36 SJ4224
Weston Patrick Hants 22 SU6946
Weston Rhyn Shrops 36 SJ2835
Weston Subedge Gloucs 28 SP1241
Weston Turville Bucks 22 SP8510
Weston Underwood Derbys 49 SK2942
Weston Underwood Bucks 30 SP8650
Weston by Welland Nhants 40 SP7791
Weston under Penyard H & W 27 SO6322
Weston under Wetherley Warwks 29 SP3669
Weston-Super-Mare Avon 19 ST3260
Weston-in-Gordano Avon 19 ST4474
Weston-on-Trent Derbys 39 SK4027
Weston-on-the-Green Oxon 29 SP5318
Weston-under-Lizard Staffs 37 SJ8010
Westonbirt Gloucs 20 ST8589
Westoning Beds 30 TL0332
Westonzoyland Somset 8 ST3534
Westow N York 56 SE7565
Westport Strath 72 NR6526
Westport Somset 8 ST3820
Westquarter Cent 82 NS9178
Westridge Green Berks 21 SU5679
Westrigg Loth 74 NS9067
Westrop Wilts 21 SU2093
Westruther Border 76 NT6349
Westry Cambs 41 TL4098
Westward Cumb 67 NY2744
Westward Ho Devon 6 SS4329
Westwell Oxon 29 SP2209
Westwell Kent 15 TQ9947
Westwell Leacon Kent 15 TQ9647
Westwick Cambs 31 TL4265
Westwood Wilts 20 ST8059
Westwood Devon 7 SY0199
Westwood Kent 15 TR3667
Westwoodside Humb 50 SE7400
Wetheral Cumb 67 NY4654
Wetherby W York 55 SE4048
Wetherden Suffk 32 TM0062

Phone before you go

NATIONAL ROADWORKS AND WEATHER

AA ROADWATCH

National Motorways	0836-401-110
1. South-east England	see below
2. West Country	0836-401-111
3. Wales	0836-401-112
4. Midlands	0836-401-113
5. East Anglia	0836-401-114
6. North-west England	0836-401-115
7. North-east England	0836-401-116
8. Scotland	0836-401-117
9. Northern Ireland	0836-401-118

LONDON AND THE SOUTH-EAST – TRAFFIC, ROADWORKS AND WEATHER

Central London (inside North/South Circulars)		0836-401-122
Motorways/roads between M4 and M1	A	0836-401-123
Motorways/roads between M1 and Dartford Tunnel	B	0836-401-124
Motorways/roads between Dartford Tunnel and M23	C	0836-401-125
Motorways/roads between M23 and M4	D	0836-401-126
M25 London Orbital only		0836-401-127

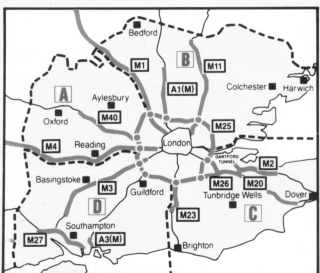

Messages last from 1 up to 7 minutes and are charged at a rate of 25p per minute cheap rate and 38p per minute at all other times. Callers pay only for the time they use. Prices are correct at time of going to press. Prices for mobile calls can vary – see your Service Provider. This service supplements the existing telephone information services for AA members.